MONTANA STATE COLLEGE LIBRARY
BOZEMA

P9-AFR-218

THE LOOM
OF
LANGUAGE

FIG. 1. THE ROSETTA STONE

This inscription, which came to light during Napoleon's campaign in Egypt, made it possible to decipher the ancient picture writing (top third) of the Egyptian priesthood. The Greek translation is at the bottom. The middle part is the equivalent in a later form (*demotic*) of Egyptian writing. The demotic was an ideographic script of which the symbols had lost their pictorial character (see pp. 44–7).

LANCELOT HOGBEN, Editor

THE LOOM
OF
LANGUAGE

By FREDERICK BODMER

NEW YORK
W · W · NORTON & COMPANY · INC ·
PUBLISHERS

Copyright, 1944, by
W. W. NORTON & COMPANY, INC.
70 Fifth Avenue, New York, N. Y.

PRINTED IN THE UNITED STATES OF AMERICA
FOR THE PUBLISHERS BY THE VAIL-BALLOU PRESS

Contents

PART ONE

THE NATURAL HISTORY OF LANGUAGE

PART TWO

OUR HYBRID HERITAGE

PART THREE

THE WORLD LANGUAGE PROBLEM

72072

PART FOUR

LANGUAGE MUSEUM

List of Plates

Editor's Foreword

As NEVER before America is now language conscious and will become more so if she is to make a constructive contribution to the peace commensurate with her role in the war. A book of this scope therefore needs no apology on account of its novelty or break with traditional methods, which are unsuited to the needs of adults taking up the study of language for the first time, or, at most, with little groundwork behind them.

First and foremost *The Loom of Language* is a book which adults can use as a basis for sustained study, and a book from which teachers alert to new techniques of instruction to meet the needs of the ordinary citizen can get helpful suggestions with a direct bearing on their daily task. Its design is based on the conviction that in the past the orientation of studies in many of our schools and universities has not provided a sufficient equipment for the constructive tasks of the society in which we live, that radical changes in the scope and methods of education are a necessary condition of continued social progress, that such educational reforms will not come about unless there is a vigorous popular demand for them.

Years ago, when Dr. Bodmer was my colleague on the staff of the University of Cape Town, we discussed the project in a preliminary way. Shortly before the war we drew up a detailed plan based on joint discussion, chiefly in English country pubs during the course of a motor trip from Aberdeen to London via the Yorkshire moors and Suffolk, back again by way of the Lake district. There I supposed my job as editor of the series finished, at least till I read the page proofs. In reality, collaboration has been closer. During the writing of the book Dr. Bodmer lived in a small croft which I used to rent in the Scottish Highlands while I held down a chair in Aberdeen. I saw him during the week ends continuously. I read the first drafts of each chapter, and was able to suggest how to get round difficulties of ordinary people who are like myself poor linguists. I shall always be grateful for what was a highly educative experience and one which kept me intellectually alive during a period of somewhat discouraging conditions for my own research.

As time passed the task became more and more a co-operative effort in which I acted as a sieve, or, if you like, as a bit of litmus paper. Dr. Bodmer submitted to suggestions for the benefit of readers who find languages as formidable as I do with more readiness than those of us who have a normal modicum of egotism and a less developed social conscience. When the rising cost of paper forced us to curtail the scope to some extent, I took a hand in the job of condensing and rewriting some sections. Consequently I have had the greatest difficulty in preventing Dr. Bodmer from refusing to publish the book without my name as a coauthor on the cover. I have got him to see that limitations which vindicate my editorial qualifications for recognizing the difficulties of ordinary people would make me a laughing stock in the capacity of joint author with presumptive claims to expert knowledge which I do not possess. We have compromised on the understanding that I make clear the extent of my contribution in this foreword. The erudition is the author's. If the reader takes exception to irresponsible or facetious remarks put in to strew a few more flowers on the path of knowledge, it is probably fair to blame the editor.

The merits of the two predecessors of *The Loom of Language* in their later editions are due in no small measure to the co-operation of scores of readers who have sent in suggestions for further clarification or have drawn attention to author's slips or to printer's errors. In a book of this size, produced under exceptionally difficult conditions for publisher, printer and author, blemishes are inevitable in a first edition. The editor and publishers hope that readers will show appreciation of Dr. Bodmer's achievement by contributing constructive criticism for use in later impressions or editions.

Because this book is a successor to *Mathematics for the Million* and *Science for the Citizen*, its motif is social and its bias is practical. It does not touch on the aesthetic aspects of language. What aesthetic merits some people find, and—we may hope—will continue to find, in their home languages have little to do with difficulties which beset the beginner learning a new one or with technical problems of devising ways and means of communication on a planetary scale in an age of potential plenty.

LANCELOT HOGBEN

CHAPTER I

Introduction

WHAT language we habitually speak depends upon a geographical accident. It has nothing to do with the composition of the human sperm or of the human egg. A child grows up to speak or to write the language used at home or at school. If born in a bilingual country it may grow up to use two languages without any formal instruction in either. Many Welsh, Breton, Belgian, and South African children do so. There is nothing to suggest that the chromosomes of the Welsh, Belgians, Bretons, and South Africans have an extra share of genes which bestow the gift of tongues. Experience also shows that adult emigrants to a new country eventually acquire the knack of communicating inoffensively with the natives. So scarcely anyone can have any rational basis for the belief that he or she is congenitally incapable of becoming a linguist. If a language phobia exists, it must be a by-product of formal education or other agencies of social environment.

By the same token it is not difficult to understand why the Scandinavians or Dutch enjoy the reputation of being good linguists. In small speech communities the market for talkies or for specialist textbooks is small, and it is not economically practicable to produce them. Thus the Norwegian boy or girl who hopes to enter a profession grows up with the knowledge that proficiency in English, German, or French is an essential educational tool. In any part of Scandinavia a visit to the motion picture is a language lesson. Translation of the English, German, or French dialogue flashes on the screen as the narrative proceeds. To all the cultural barriers which linguistic isolation imposes on a small speech community we have to add exigencies of external trade and a stronger impulse to travel. In short, members of the smaller European speech communities experience a far greater need to study foreign languages and enjoy greater opportunities for doing so.

Special circumstances combine to encourage a distaste for linguistic studies among those who speak the Anglo-American language. One is that the water frontiers of Britain, and still more those of the United States, isolate most British and American citizens from daily experience of linguistic contacts. Another is that formal education fails to supply a compelling reason for a pursuit which has little connection with the needs of everyday life. Reasons commonly given for learning foreign languages are manifestly insincere, or, to put it more charitably, are out of date. For instance, it is obviously easy to exaggerate the utility of linguistic accomplishments for foreign travel. Only relatively prosperous people can continue to travel after marriage; and tourist facilities for young people of modest means rarely, if ever, take them into situations where nobody understands Anglo-American. There is even less sincerity in the plea for linguistic proficiency as a key to the treasure house of the world's literature. American and British publishers scour the Continent for translation rights of new authors. So the doors of the treasure house are wide open. Indeed, any intelligent adolescent with access to a modern lending library can check up on the teacher who expresses enthusiasm over the pleasures of reading Thomas Mann or Anatole France in the original. People who do so are content to get their knowledge of Scandinavian drama, the Russian novel, or the Icelandic sagas from American or British translations.

In spite of all obstacles, anyone who has been brought up to speak the Anglo-American language enjoys a peculiarly favored position. It is a hybrid. It has a basic stratum of words derived from the same stock as German, Dutch, and the Scandinavian languages. It has assimilated thousands of Latin origin. It has also incorporated an impressive battery of Greek roots. A random sample of one word from each of the first thousand pages of the *Concise Oxford Dictionary* gives the following figures: words of Romance (Latin, French, Italian, Spanish) origin 53.6 per cent, Teutonic (Old English, Scandinavian, Dutch, German) 31.1 per cent, Greek 10.8 per cent. With a little knowledge of the evolution of English itself, of the parallel evolution of the Teutonic languages and of the modern descendants of Latin, as set forth in the second part of this book, the American or the Briton has therefore a key to ten living European languages. No one outside the Anglo-American speech community enjoys this privilege; and no one who knows how to take full advantage of it need despair of getting a good working knowledge of the languages which our nearest neighbors speak.

Though each of us is entitled to a personal distaste, as each of us is entitled to a personal preference, for study of this sort, the usefulness of learning languages is not *merely* a personal affair. Linguistic differences are a perpetual source of international misunderstanding, a well-nigh inexhaustible supply of inflammable material which warmongers can use for their own evil ends. Some knowledge about the languages people speak is therefore one prerequisite of keeping the world's peace. Keeping the world's peace is everybody's proper business; but keeping the world's peace is not the only reason why study of languages concerns all of us as citizens. Linguistic differences lead to a vast leakage of intellectual energy which might be enlisted to make the potential plenty of modern science available to all mankind.

Human beings are unique in two ways. Man is a tool-bearing animal and a talkative animal. In the pursuit of their tool-bearing activities, men and women have learned to co-operate on a planetary scale; but such co-operation is perpetually thwarted by local limitations of their speech habits. What is characteristic of the intellectual achievements of mankind in the age of hydroelectricity, magnesium-aluminum alloys, broadcasting, aviation, synthetic plastics, and chemotherapy is a common possession of all nations which encourage scientific research, but nations have no common idiom through which workers by brain or hand can communicate results of research or collaborate in applying them to human welfare. Modern technology is a supernational culture which ministers to the common needs of human beings, while language limps behind the human endeavor to satisfy needs which all human beings share.

To canalize the interest of intelligent men and women into the constructive task of devising or of adopting an *auxiliary* medium to *supplement* existing national languages is therefore one of the foremost needs of our time. This concerns us all, and it calls for a lively knowledge of the limitations imposed on languages by the laws of their growth. It will therefore be one of the tasks of *The Loom of Language* to trace the history of the languages in which the technical resources of our age have been recorded. It will not be a record of deliberate and intelligent prevision. It is partly a story of confusion resulting from a continuous record of slovenliness and of obstinate complacency toward the mistakes of our grandparents. It is also a

story of ancestor worship, and of makeshifts to conserve the inepti-
tudes of a supposedly heroic past. It affects us more intimately than
the fate of the dinosaurs. It unearths remains not less dramatic than
the jawbone of the ape man of Java. It points the way down dim
paths of prehistory from which we return with imagination fired by
a vista of future possibilities.

This does not mean that *The Loom of Language* is first and foremost a plea for language planning. There are other good enough

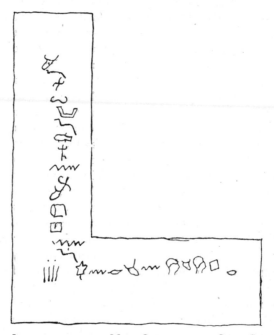

FIG. 2.—INSCRIPTION FROM MINE SHAFT IN THE SINAI PENINSULA

Tracings on a mine shaft in the Sinai Peninsula made by a workman who
signs himself as Number 4 and gives his name as SAHMILAT.

reasons why its readers may need or wish to study existing languages.
Traveling facilities are becoming cheaper and daily less inconvenient
or time-consuming. If the states of Europe are ever united under
common democratic government, with its own air service, many of
us who had never expected to travel far afield may hope to see more
of the world before we die. Inevitably we shall become more interested in the speech habits of our neighbors. Though a knowledge of

foreign languages is not indispensable to an American or an English-man who wishes to travel, it adds to the fun and promotes a more friendly understanding with people one may meet.

The literary arguments for language study are manifestly bogus when based on the claims of fiction or drama for which cheap transla-tions are readily accessible. Nonetheless, some types of literature are accessible only to people who know languages other than their own. A large volume of scientific publications which record new dis-coveries in physics, medicine, chemistry, agriculture, and engineering appear in many different languages. Their contents do not become accessible in books till several years have elapsed. Professional scien-tific workers are therefore handicapped if they have no knowledge of such languages as German, French, or Spanish. What is more im-portant from the standpoint of the wider public which *The Loom of Language* may reach is this: challenging statistics of social welfare from foreign countries may never find their way into the columns of our newspapers. So the only way of getting a thorough firsthand knowledge of foreign affairs is to read yearbooks and periodicals published in other countries.

For these and other reasons many people who have little or no knowledge of foreign languages would like to have more; and many would study them, if they were not discouraged by the very poor results which years of study at school or in college produce. One thing *The Loom of Language* aims at doing is to show that there is no real reason for being discouraged. Though the difficulties of learning languages are real, they are also easy to exaggerate. Generally, the adult has more to show after a three months' course at a commercial institute than an adolescent after three years' study of a foreign lan-guage in a British secondary or American high school. One reason for this is that the adult pupil is clear about why he or she is taking the course. Another is that the teacher is usually clear about why he or she is giving it.

This is not the whole story. To sins of omission we have to add all the positive obstacles which early formal education places in the way of those who have no strong personal inclination for linguistic studies. The greatest impediment, common to most branches of school and university education, is the dead hand of Plato. We have not yet got away from education designed for the sons of gentlemen. Educational Platonism sacrifices realizable proficiency by encouraging the pursuit of unattainable perfection. The child or the immigrant learns a language by blundering his or her way into greater self-confidence. Adults accept the mistakes of children with tolerant good humor, and the genial flow of social intercourse is not interrupted by a barrage of pedantic protests. The common sense of ordinary parents or customs officials recognizes that commonplace communication unhampered by the sting of grammatical guilt must precede real progress in the arts of verbal precision. Most of us could learn languages more easily if we could learn to forgive our own linguistic trespasses.

Where perfectionist pedantry has inserted the sting of grammatical guilt, a sense of social inferiority rubs salt into the wound. According to the standards of educated adults, very few adolescents can speak and write the home language with fluency and grammatical precision before eighteen years of age. To be able to speak more than two new languages without any trace of foreign accent or idiom is a lifework. So linguistic polish is a perquisite of prosperous people whose formal education has been supplemented by the attentions of foreign governesses and by frequent trips abroad. It is the cultural trademark of a leisure class. Indeed no type of knowledge has more ostentation value.

No one who wants to speak a foreign language like a native can rely upon this book or on any other. Its aim is to lighten the burden of learning for the home student who is less ambitious. One of the useful results of recent attempts to devise languages for world citizenship has been to show how educational practice, dictated by antisocial theories which gratify the itch for leisure-class ostentation, exaggerates the difficulties arising from the intrinsic characteristics of language. The intrinsic difficulties depend on the large amount of effort expended before tangible results of self-expression or comprehension bring their own reward. Self-assurance depends on reducing this period of unrequited effort to a minimum. Pioneers of international communication such as C. K. Ogden, the inventor of Basic English, have made a special study of this, because the success of their work depends on the ease with which a language for world-wide use can be learned. Whether their own proposals prosper or fail, they have revolutionized the problem of learning existing languages.

Tricks discovered in the task of devising a simple, direct, and easily acquired language for world citizenship have not yet found their way into most grammar books, and the reader who starts to learn a foreign language can get all the fun of tackling a new problem by applying them. To understand the essential peculiarities or similarities of languages most closely related to one another does not demand a special study of each. If you compare the following equivalents of a request which occurs in the Lord's Prayer, you can see this for yourself:

Gib uns heute unser täglich Brot	(German)
Geef ons heden ons dagelijksch brood	(Dutch)
Giv os i Dag vort daglige Brød	(Danish)
Giv oss i dag vårt dagliga bröd	(Swedish)
Gef oss i dag vort daglegt brauð	(Icelandic)

Now compare these with the following translations of the same petition in Latin and its daughter languages:

Da nobis hodie panem nostrum quotidianum	(Latin)
Donne-nous aujourd'hui notre pain quotidien	(French)
Danos hoy nuestro pan cotidiano	(Spanish)
Dacci oggi il nostro pane cotidiano	(Italian)
O pão nosso de cada dia dai-nos hoje	(Portuguese)

By the time you have read through the first five, you will probably have realized without recourse to a dictionary that they correspond to the English sentence: *Give us this day our daily bread*. That the next five mean the same might also be obvious to a Frenchman, though it may not be obvious to us if we do not already know French, or a language like French. If we are told that all ten sentences mean the same thing, it is not difficult to see that German, Dutch, Swedish, Danish, and Icelandic share with English common features which English does not share with the other five languages, and that French, Italian, Spanish, and Portuguese share with Latin common features which they do not share with the Germanic group.

It is a common belief that learning two languages calls for twice as much effort as learning one. This may be roughly true, if the two languages are not more alike than French and German, and if the beginner's aim is to speak either like a native. If they belong to the same family, and if the beginner has a more modest end in view, it is not true. Many people will find that the effort spent on building up a small, workmanlike vocabulary and getting a grasp of essential grammatical peculiarities of four closely related languages is not much greater than the effort spent on getting an equivalent knowledge of one alone. The reason for this is obvious if we approach learning languages as a problem of applied biology. The ease with which we remember things depends on being able to associate one thing with another. In many branches of knowledge, a little learning is a *difficult* thing.

As an isolated act it is difficult, because extremely tedious, to memorize the peculiarities of each individual bone of a rabbit. When we realize that bones are the alphabet of the written record of evolution in the sedimentary rocks, the study of their peculiarities is full of interest. Biologists with experience of elementary teaching know that it is far more satisfying—and therefore more easy—to learn the essential peculiarities of the bones of representative types from *all* the various classes of vertebrates than to memorize in great detail the skeleton of a single isolated specimen. So it may well be that many people with a knowledge of Anglo-American would benefit by trying to learn German along with Dutch, which is a halfway house between German and *Mayflower* English. Every grammatical rule then becomes a fresh layer of rock from which to chisel vestiges of creation. Each word is a bone labeled with a question mark.

This suggestion may not appeal to everyone or suit every type of home student. Still, most people who find it difficult to learn a foreign language can relieve themselves of some of their difficulties, if they start with a little knowledge of how languages have evolved. Part of the task which *The Loom of Language* has undertaken is to bring the dead bones to life with this elixir. Some people may say that the difficulties are too great, because we start with so little raw material for comparison. They will say that it is possible to give the general reader an intelligible account of organic evolution, only because any intelligent person who first meets a textbook definition of such words as *fish, amphibian, reptile, bird, mammal*, can already give several examples of each class. Indeed, most of us can subdivide some of them, as when we speak of dogs and cats as carnivores, mice and rabbits as rodents, or sheep and cattle as ruminants. Most of us could also give some outstanding anatomical peculiarities which serve to distinguish species placed in a particular group, as when we define ruminants as beasts which chew the cud and divide the hoof.

Admittedly, there is no such common basis of universal knowledge about language species and their anatomical peculiarities. Most Britons and most Americans speak or read only one language. At best, very few well-educated people can read more than three. Those we usually learn are not recognizably of a kind; and there are no public language museums with attractive and instructive exhibits. All the same, it is not impossible for an intelligent person who has had no training in foreign languages to get some insight into the way in which languages

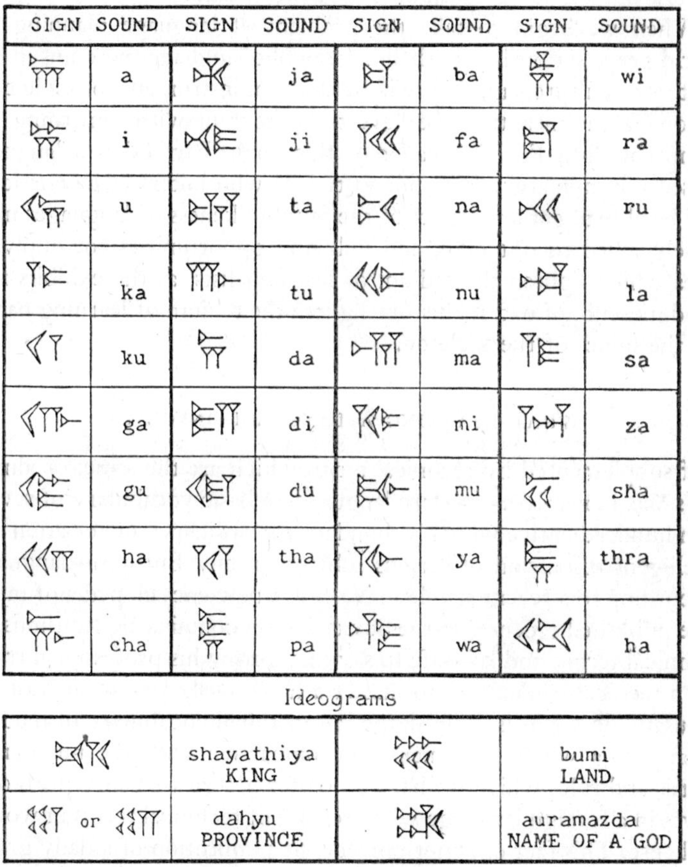

SIGN	SOUND	SIGN	SOUND	SIGN	SOUND	SIGN	SOUND
⟅	a	⟅	ja	⟅	ba	⟅	wi
⟅	i	⟅	ji	⟅	fa	⟅	ra
⟅	u	⟅	ta	⟅	na	⟅	ru
⟅	ka	⟅	tu	⟅	nu	⟅	la
⟅	ku	⟅	da	⟅	ma	⟅	sa
⟅	ga	⟅	di	⟅	mi	⟅	za
⟅	gu	⟅	du	⟅	mu	⟅	sha
⟅	ha	⟅	tha	⟅	ya	⟅	thra
⟅	cha	⟅	pa	⟅	wa	⟅	ha

Ideograms			
⟅	shayathiya KING	⟅	bumi LAND
⟅ or ⟅	dahyu PROVINCE	⟅	auramazda NAME OF A GOD

Fig. 3.—Old Persian Cuneiform Syllabary

Cuneiform is the name for a type of syllable writing which owes its distinctive characteristics to the impress of a wedge-shaped tool on soft clay. Related syllabaries of the same type were widely distributed over the Middle East about 2000 B.C. Elamites, Babylonians, Syrians and Hittites all had cuneiform scripts.

evolve. There are no straight lines in biological evolution, and there are no straight lines in the evolution of languages. We can recognize similar processes in the growth of all languages. We can see characteristics which predominate in languages so far apart as Chinese, Hungarian, and Greek competing for mastery in the growth of Anglo-American from the English of Alfred the Great.

When we begin to take the problem of language planning for world peace seriously, we shall have public language museums in our centers of culture, and they will be essential instruments of civic education. In the meantime we have to be content with something less comprehensive. For the reader of this book, Part IV is a language museum in miniature. The home student who loiters in its corridors will be able to get a prospect of the family likeness of languages most closely allied to our own, and will find opportunities for applying rules which lighten the tedium of learning lists, as the exhibits in a good museum of natural history lighten the tedium of learning names for the bones of the skeleton.

WHAT LEARNING A LANGUAGE INVOLVES

If supplemented by technical terms which are the same, or almost the same, in nearly all modern languages, a basic vocabulary of seventeen hundred native words is abundant for ordinary conversation and intelligent discussion of serious subjects in any European language. According to a recent article in *Nature*, a new encyclopedia of medicine published recently in the Soviet Union contains eighty thousand technical terms, and it is safe to say that during his professional training a medical student has to master a new vocabulary of at least ten thousand new words. Indeed, the international vocabulary of modern science as a whole is immense in comparison with the number of words and rules which we have to master before we can express ourselves in a foreign language with free use of technical terms in worldwide use. This fact does not prevent the publication of a daily growing volume of good popular books which explain for the benefit of any reader with average intelligence basic principles and interesting facts dealt with in natural sciences. With the help of the exhibits in our own language museum (Part IV) there is no reason why interesting facts about the way in which languages grow, the way in which people use them, the diseases from which they suffer, and the way in which other social habits and human relationships shape them, should not be accessible to us. There is no reason why we should not use knowledge of this sort to lighten the drudgery of assimilating disconnected information by sheer effort of memory and tedious repetition.

Helpful tricks which emerge from a comparative study of language as a basis for promoting a common language of world citizenship will turn up in the following chapters, and will be set forth collectively at a later stage. In the meantime, anyone appalled by the amount of drudgery which learning a language supposedly entails can get some encouragement from two sources. One is that no expenditure on tuition can supply the stimulus you can get from spontaneous intercourse with a correspondent, if the latter is interested in what you have to say, and has something interesting to contribute to a discussion. The other is that unavoidable memory work is much less than most of us suppose; and it need not be dull, if we fortify our efforts by scientific curiosity about the relative defects and merits of the language we are studying, about its relation to other languages which people speak, and about the social agencies which have affected its growth or about circumstances which have molded its character in the course of history.

In short, we can stiffen self-confidence by recognizing at the outset that the difficulties of learning a language, though real, are far less than most of us usually suppose. One great obstacle to language learning is that usual methods of instruction take no account of the fact that learning any language involves at least three kinds of skill as different as arithmetic, algebra and geometry. One is learning to *read* easily. One is learning to *express oneself* in speech or in writing. The third is being able to *follow the course of ordinary conversation* among people who use a language habitually. This distinction helps to resolve some of the greatest difficulties which confront beginners. Whether it is best to concentrate on one to the exclusion of others in the initial stages of learning depends partly on the temperament of the beginner, partly on how the foreign one resembles the home language, and partly on the social circumstances which control opportunities for study or use. We can best see what these circumstances are if we first get clear about the separate problems which arise in reading, in self-expression, and in oral recognition, about the several uses to which we can put our knowledge of a language, and about the various opportunities for getting practice in using it.

Most educated people find that oral recognition of ordinary conversation is the last stage in mastering a language, and does not come unless they have spent at least a few weeks or months in a country where it is habitually spoken. It then comes quickly to anyone who can read and write it. The reason why it demands a skill quite different from the skill of learning to read quickly or to write and to speak correctly is that no one pronounces distinctly the separate words of a sentence as one writes it, and as a beginner or a child speaks it. In speaking, people fuse one word with another, and blur syllables which form an essential part of the *visual* picture of the individual word. What we recognize is not a succession of separate units, but a composite pattern of which the character is partly determined by emphasis and rhythm.

This difficulty does not arise in reading or writing a foreign language. When we are learning to read or to write a language, we concentrate on the individual words as separate visual symbols, and when we are learning to speak, we concentrate our attention on the sound values and stresses of each syllable. So it is possible to detect the meaning or to pronounce flawlessly the individual words of *I am kind of fond of you, baby* without recognizing it when it impinges on the ear as *ymkynnafonavyubaybee.* Of course, the extent of the difficulties which the beginner has to face depends partly on personal make-up, and partly on that of the language. Some people with histrionic gifts pick up word patterns quickly, and may therefore benefit more than others from gramophone records, which are an invaluable help for getting good pronunciation. Some languages are more *staccato* than others. Individual words as spoken are more clear-cut. People who speak them habitually do not slough off syllables. Stress is evenly distributed. In this sense, German is more staccato than English, and English far more so than French. From knowledge of the written language, it is a small step for the student of German to follow a conversation or a broadcast. From a good reading knowledge of French to an understanding of what a French taxi driver says when he is quarreling with the policeman is a much longer road.

Formal instruction is at best a very laborious way of surmounting these difficulties. The element of curiosity which plays such a large part in molding everyday speech is stifled by the certainty that the teacher is not saying anything particularly interesting, or, if interesting, anything which he or she could not explain with less trouble in a language we already understand. The same remark also applies to formal instruction in writing, to exercises in translation, or to conversational instruction. The teacher then plays the role of *critic* in a situation which proffers no vital *problem* for solution. Though this is not true of radio, which gives us opportunities for getting a new slant on foreign affairs, the time we can devote to a foreign broadcast is generally short. Radio does not impose on us the sheer necessity of proficiency, as do the disadvantages of failing to reserve a seat in a railway car, or the need to replace a broken collar button. Worst of all, it will not repeat itself for the benefit of the listener.

Since the need for oral recognition does not arise in an acute form unless we are living in a foreign country, these difficulties are not as discouraging as they seem. If occasion arises, anyone who can read and write or speak can quickly learn to understand a language when he or she hears it spoken *incessantly*. So the best advice for most of us is to concentrate on reading, writing, and speaking, with what help we can get from listening in, till we go abroad. Opportunities for conversation with children are often reassuring, when we first do so. In large English and American cities there are colonies of foreigners, many of them tradespeople, who do not mind if we add to our purchases a bit of talk, however defective in grammar and pronunciation.

From a practical point of view, it is more important to be clear about the difference between what is involved in learning to read, and what is involved in learning to speak or to write a language. When engaged in ordinary conversation or letter writing the vocabulary of most people, even highly educated people, is very small in comparison with the vocabulary of a newspaper or of a novel. In his professional capacity the journalist himself, or the novelist herself, uses many more words than suffice for the needs of everyday life, and the vocabulary of one author differs very much from that of another. If only for these reasons, the vocabulary which suffices for fluent self-expression is *much* smaller than the vocabulary needed for indiscriminate reading. There are many other reasons why this is so. One is the fact that ordinary speech rings the changes on a large assortment of common *synonyms* and common expressions which are for practical purposes interchangeable. Such equivocations are innumerable. In everyday life, few of us pay much attention to the different shades of meaning in such expressions as: *he would like to, he wants to, he prefers to, he desires to, he wishes to, he would rather.*

Another important distinction is connected with the use of *idiom,* i.e., expressions of which the meaning cannot be inferred from the usual significance of the individual words and a knowledge of the grammatical rules for arranging them. *How do you do?* is an obvious example of idiomatic speech; but everyday speech is saturated with idioms which are not obvious as such. In English, the fact that *a cat is in the room* can also be expressed by saying *there is a cat in the room.* We could not infer this from the *customary* meaning of the word *there* and the other words in the sentence, as given in a pocket dictionary.

From the standpoint of a person learning a foreign language, there is a big difference between the two forms of statement. We can translate the first word for word into Dutch, German, Swedish, or Danish. The expression *there is* must be translated by idiomatic combinations which do not literally, i.e., in the usual sense of the separate words, mean the same in any two of them. In French we have to translate *there is* by *il y a*, which literally means *it there has*. In the same context, the German would write *es ist*, literally *it is*, equivalent to the Danish *det er*. The Swede would say *det finns*, i.e., *it is found.* We could not use the German *es ist*, as we could still use the Danish *det er*, if we had to translate *there are no snakes in Iceland*. The English idiom *there is* would make way for *es gibt*, or literally *it gives.*

To read a language with ease we therefore need to have a *relatively* big battery of synonyms and idioms with which we can dispense in speaking or writing. To some extent, similar remarks apply to *grammatical* conventions. In modern English it is never obligatory to use what is called the *genitive case form* of the words *father* or *day*, as in *my father's hat*, or *his day's wages*. When speaking or writing English we are at liberty to say, *the hat of my father*, or *his wages for the day*. So we do not need to know the grammatical rule which tells us how to form the singular genitive *father's*, or the plural genitive *fathers'*. A foreigner (i.e., one who does not speak the Anglo-American language) does not need to know that it is our custom to apply the rule only to names of animate objects, astronomical or calendrical terms and measures.

To this extent, it looks as if self-expression is much easier to master than a good reading knowledge of a language. In other ways it is more difficult. On the debit side of our account we have to reckon with two other features of the art of learning. One is that our knowledge of the words we use in expressing ourselves is not prompted by the situation, as our recognition of words on a printed page is helped by the context. Though the number of words and expressions we need is *fewer*, we need to know them so *thoroughly*, that we can recall them without prompting. Another circumstance makes reading more easy than writing or speaking. Most languages carry a load of grammatical conventions which have no more value than the *coccyx* (vestigial tail) of the human skeleton. The rule that we add -*s* to the stem of the English verb, if preceded by *he*, *she*, or *it*, as when we say *he needs*, is a convention of usage. We make no distinction between the form of the verb when we say *I need, you need, we need, they need*. Though we should correct a child (or a foreigner), we should know what he or she meant by saying: *the train leave* at 11:15. So it contributes nothing to our facility in getting at the meaning of a sentence. From this point of view, proficient oral self-expression makes less demand than writing. Many grammatical conventions such as the apostrophe in *fathers'* have no *phonetic value*. That is to say, we do not recognize them as sounds. This is specially true of French.

What *The Loom of Language* has to say about *phonetics*, i.e., principles of pronunciation, and the practical hints it gives, will be of little use to anyone who hopes to speak a foreign language intelligibly, unless supplemented by other sources of instruction. We can surmount the particular difficulties of oral expression painlessly with the use of gramophone (p. 256) records, if we have the money to buy them. Whether speaking or writing is easier when the gramophone is available, depends chiefly on the individual. People who are good mimics will make more progress in speaking with the same expenditure of effort. Individuals of the visual or motor types, i.e., those who learn best by eye or touch, will get on better at writing. For many of us the choice is limited by whether we can find a willing correspondent or an accessible acquaintance through business connections, or through some such organization as the educational department of the International Ladies' Garment Workers in New York. No teacher can supply the stimulus that comes from communication which is spontaneously gratifying, because novel, to both parties.

We may sum up the essential differences between the skill required for wide reading and the skill required for proficient self-expression in this way. To express ourselves correctly we need to have a *ready* knowledge of a *relatively small* number of words—fifteen hundred or two thousand at most—and a *precise knowledge* of the *essential* grammatical conventions of straightforward statement. To read widely without a dictionary, we need a *nodding acquaintance* with a relatively *large* vocabulary (fifteen thousand words may be given as a rough estimate), and a general familiarity with a *wide range* of grammatical conventions, which we can recognize at sight, if meaningful.

We can waste an immense amount of time, if we are not clear at the outset about what this distinction implies, or if we proceed on the assumption that learning how to read is the same job as learning to express ourselves.

THE BASIC VOCABULARY

When we are reading a thriller or a historical novel, we continually meet unfamiliar words for articles of clothing and inaccessible items of a menu list. We also meet forbidding technical terms for architectural features, nautical expressions, hayseed dialects, and military slang. The fact that we should hesitate to attempt a precise definition of them does not bother us. We do not keep a dictionary at the bedside, and rarely ask a friend the meaning of a word which we have not met before. If we do meet a word for the first time, we often notice it several times during the course of the ensuing week. Sooner or later the context in which we meet it will reveal its meaning. In this way, the vocabulary of our home language continually grows without deliberate effort. In the same way we can acquire a good reading knowledge of a foreign language when we have mastered a few essentials. It is discouraging and wasteful to torture the meaning of every word of a foreign novel page by page, and so destroy the enjoyment which the narrative supplies. To get to this stage with the minimum of effort involves realizing clearly what the bare minimum of essential knowledge is.

Analogous remarks apply to self-expression. When we realize what is the essential minimum for one or the other, we can decide on what we have to *memorize deliberately*, and what we can leave to look after itself. For self-expression or for reading, the essentials are of two kinds, a minimum vocabulary of individual words, and a minimum of grammatical rules, i.e., rules about how words change and how to arrange them in a sentence. Till recently, language textbooks paid little attention to the problem of how to build up this minimum vocabulary. More modern ones have faced it and tackled it by basing selection on words which are used most *frequently*.

There are several objections to the method of extracting from the contents of a dictionary the thousand or so words which occur most often in printed matter. One is that many of the commonest words are synonyms. So while it is true that we can express ourselves clearly with a little circumlocution if we know about fifteen hundred words of any language (i.e., about five months' work at the rate of only ten new words a day), we might have to learn the fifteen thousand most common words before we had at our disposal all the fifteen hundred words we actually need. At best, word frequency is a good recipe for the first step toward *reading*, as opposed to writing or to speaking. Even so, it is not a very satisfactory one, because the relative frequency of words varies so much in accordance with the kind of material we intend to read. Words such as *hares* and *hawthorn*, *byre* and *bilberry*, *plow* and *pigsty*, are the verbal stuffing of Nobel Prize novels. They rarely intrude into business correspondence, or even into the news columns.

The statistical method used in compiling word lists given in the most modern textbooks for teaching foreign languages evades the essence of our problem. If we want to get a speaking or writing equipment with the minimum of effort, fuss, and bother, we need to know how to pick the assortment of words *which suffice to convey the meaning of any plain statement*. Anyone who has purchased one of the inexpensive little books * on Basic English will find that C. K. Ogden has solved this problem for us. The essential list of only 850 words goes on a single sheet. Mr. Ogden did not choose these words by first asking the irrelevant question: which words occur most often in Nobel Prize novels or in presidential orations? The question he set himself was: *What other words do we need in order to define something when we do not already know the right word for it?*

For example, we can define a plow as the *machine* we *make* use of to *get* the ground ready for the seed. For ordinary circumstances this will make sufficiently clear what we are talking or writing about. If not, we can elaborate our definition by using other general words like *machine*, or verbs like *make* and *get*, which serve for all sorts of definitions. In Basic English there are only sixteen of these *verbs* to learn. If we use only words in the 850-word list, it may take us a little longer than otherwise to explain what we mean; but the result is still correct, simple, and lucid English. Indeed, the fact that we have to examine the precise meaning of words which do not occur in the list compels us to be more precise than we might otherwise be.

It is possible to go so far with so few words in good English because a large number of words which belong to the *verb* class are not essential. We do not need *burn, finish, err*, because we can *make* a fire of, *make* an end of, *make* a mistake about. We do not need to *fly* in an

* Especially *Basic English: A General Introduction* and *Brighter Basic*.

airplane, *drive* in a cab, *cycle* on a bicycle, *travel* in a train, *ride* on a horse, or *walk*. It is enough to say that we *go* on foot, on a horse, or in a vehicle. For straightforward, intelligible and correct statement in other European languages, we have to add between three hundred and six hundred words of the verb class to our list of essential words. This thrifty use of verbs is a peculiar characteristic of English and of the Celtic group among European languages. Where a Swede uses a different verb, when a child *goes* in a train, and when a train *goes*, or when an aviator *goes* up, and when he *goes* across the road, one English word suffices. If we also make allowance for the usefulness of having single ordinary names for common objects not included in the Basic Word List, a vocabulary of less than two thousand words is sufficient for fluent self-expression in any European tongue. This is less than a tenth of the vocabulary which we meet when reading novels indiscriminately. So reading is a very laborious way of getting the thorough knowledge of the relatively few words we need when speaking or writing.

One of the reasons why Basic is so thrifty in its use of verbs is that we can do much in English by combining some verbs with another class of words called *directives*. We do so when we substitute go *in* for *enter*, go *up* for *ascend*, go *on* for *continue*, go *by* for *pass*, go *through* for *traverse*, go *off* for *leave*, and go *away* for *depart*. In modern European languages, these words recur constantly. There is a relatively small number of them. Unlike nouns (name words), such as *train* or *automobile*, which are sometimes the same and often similar in different languages, they are difficult to guess. The same remarks apply to link words such as *and, but, when, because, or;* and to a large class of words called adverbs, such as *often, again, perhaps, soon, here, forward*. These three groups of words together make up the class which grammarians call *particles*. Since they are essential words for clear statement, and are not the sort of words of which we can guess the meaning, it is interesting to know how many of them there are, and how frequently they occur.

Comparison of two passages printed below illustrates a type of experiment which the reader can repeat with other materials, if or when able to recognize words put in this class. The first (*a*) is from the *Dream of John Ball*, by William Morris. The second (*b*) is from *Elementary Mathematical Astronomy*, by Barlow and Bryan. So the sources represent widely different types of expression and characteristics of our language. In describing the arrival of one of Wycliffe's poor preachers, Morris tries to follow the essentially Teutonic idiom of the people for whom Wycliffe translated the Bible. The textbook specimen uses many words which are entirely foreign to the English of Wycliffe's Bible, or to the later version dedicated to James I. They come, directly or indirectly, from Latin or Greek sources, chiefly from the former. In each passage, words which cannot be traced back to the blending of Teutonic dialects in English before the Norman Conquest, are in italics.

a) BUT WHEN John Ball FIRST *mounted* the steps OF the *cross*, a lad AT someone's bidding had run OFF TO stop the ringers, AND SO *PRESENTLY* the *voice* OF the bells fell dead, leaving ON men's minds that *sense* OF *blankness* OR EVEN *disappointment* which is ALWAYS *caused* BY the sudden stopping OF a *sound* one has got *used* TO AND found *pleasant*. BUT a great *expectation* had fallen BY NOW ON all that throng, AND NO word was spoken EVEN IN a whisper, AND all hearts AND eyes were *fixed* UPON the dark *figure* standing straight UP NOW BY the tall white shaft OF the *cross*, his hands stretched OUT BEFORE him, one *palm* laid UPON the other. AND FOR me AS (I) made ready TO hearken, (I) felt a *joy* IN my soul that I had NEVER YET felt.

b) AS the *result* OF *observations extending* OVER a *large number* OF *lunar* months, it is found that the moon does NOT *describe EXACTLY* the same *ellipse* OVER AND OVER AGAIN, AND that THEREFORE the laws *stated* are ONLY *approximate*. EVEN IN a *single* month the *departure* FROM *simple elliptic motion* is QUITE *appreciable*, OWING *CHIEFLY* TO the *disturbance* called the *Variation*. The *disturbance* known AS the *Evection causes* the *eccentricity* TO *change APPRECIABLY* FROM month TO month. FURTHER, the *motions described cause* the roughly *elliptical orbit* TO *change* its *position*. The *complete investigation* OF these *changes* belongs TO the *domain* OF *gravitational astronomy*. It will be *necessary* HERE TO *enumerate* the *chief perturbations* ON *account* OF the *important part* they play IN *determining* the *circumstances* OF *eclipses*.

In these selections words belonging to the class called *particles* are in capital letters. If you count the various classes of words, you can tabulate your results as follows:

	Dream of John Ball	Mathematical Astronomy
Words of Latin or Greek origin..	11 per cent	30 per cent
Particles	31 per cent	27 per cent

Though the sources of the figures are so different in content, and though they use such a different stock in trade of words, they contain almost exactly the same number of *particles*, i.e., 29 ± 2 per cent, or nearly a third of the total. A similar estimate would not be far out for languages spoken by our nearest European neighbors. Since more than a quarter of the words we meet on the printed page are particles, it is interesting to ask how many *essential*, and how many *common*, particles we need or meet. For two reasons it is impossible to cite absolute figures. One is that people who speak some languages make distinctions which others do not recognize. Thus a Swede or a Frenchman has to use different words for the English *before* according as it signifies *at an earlier time than*, or *in front of*. Apart from this, some common particles are synonymous in a particular context, as when we substitute *as* or *since* for the more explicit link word *because*. With due allowance to these considerations, we may put the number of *essential* particles at less than one hundred, and the total number which we *commonly* meet in speech or reading at less than two hundred.

This leads us to a very simple recipe for getting ahead quickly with the task of building up a word list which will suffice for self-expression. It also shows us how to reduce by more than 25 per cent the tedium of continual reference to a dictionary when we first begin to read. Our first concern, and it is usually the last thing grammar books help us to do, should be what a foreigner has to do when he starts to learn Basic English. We should begin our study of a modern European language by committing to memory the *essential particles;* and a very small class of exceedingly common words, such as *I, him, who,* called *pronouns* (pp. 83–90). At the same time we should familiarize ourselves with the less essential particles so that we recognize them when we meet them. That is to say, we should begin by learning the FOREIGN EQUIVALENTS for the eighty or so most ESSENTIAL ones, and, since it is always easier to recognize a foreign word we have previously met than to recall it, the ENGLISH EQUIVALENT for about a hundred and fifty other most COMMON foreign synonyms of this class. How we should choose our basic particles and pronouns, how it is best to set about memorizing them, and what we should then do, will turn up later.

ESSENTIAL GRAMMAR

First we have to decide what to do about grammar, and this means that we must be clear about what is meant by the *grammar* of a language. Having a list of words of which we know the usual meaning does not get us very far unless we have knowledge of another kind. We cannot rely on the best dictionary to help us out of all our difficulties.

To begin with, most dictionaries leave out many words which we can construct according to more or less general rules from those included in them. A Spaniard who wants to learn English will not find the words *father's, fathers,* or *fathers'.* In their place, the dictionary would give the single word *father.* An ordinary dictionary does not tell you another thing which you need to know. It does not tell you how to arrange words, or the circumstances in which you choose between certain words which are closely related. If a German tried to learn English with a dictionary, he might compose the following sentence: *probably will the girl to the shop come if it knows that its sweetheart there be will.* A German does not arrange words in a sentence as we do, and his choice of words equivalent to *he, she,* and *it* does not depend upon anatomy, as in our own language. So we should have some difficulty in recognizing this assertion as his own way of stating: *the girl will probably come to the shop if she knows that her sweetheart will be there.*

There are three kinds of rules which we need to guide us when learning a language, whether to read, to write, to speak, or to listen intelligently. We need rules for forming word derivatives,* rules for the arrangement of words, and rules about which of several related words we have to use in a particular situation. Closely allied European languages differ very much with respect to the relative importance of such rules, the difficulties which they put in the way of a beginner, and how far they are essential to a reading, writing, or speaking knowledge. Bible English has very simple and very rigid

---

* Here and elsewhere *derivative* means any word derived from some dictionary item according to rules given in grammar books. So defined, its use in this book is the *editor's* suggestion, to which the author assents with some misgiving, because philologists employ it in a more restricted sense. The justification for the meaning it has in *The Loom* is the absence of any other explicit word for all it signifies.

rules about arranging words, and these rules, which are nearly the same as those of Scandinavian languages, are totally different from the less simple but rigid rules of German or Dutch. Word order does not count for so much in the study of Latin and Greek *authors*. Latin and Greek writing abounds with derivatives comparable to *loves* or *loved*, from *love*, or *father's* from *father* in English. The connection between words of a statement depends less on arrangement than on the idiomatic (p. 195) use of derivatives. Thus it is impossible to read these languages without an immense number of rules about derivative words.

If we aim at learning a language with as little effort as possible, rules of one kind or another may be more or less important from another point of view. In English we use the derivative *speaks* after *he*, *she*, or *it*, instead of *speak* after *I*, *you*, *we*, or *they*. Since we pronounce the final *-s*, it is important for a foreigner, who wishes to conform to our customs, to know how to use this rule in speaking as well as in writing. When we use *he*, *she*, or *it*, we do not add an *-s* to *spoke*. So the *-s* is not really essential to the meaning of a statement, and a foreigner would still be able to understand a written sentence if he did not know the rule. French has more complicated rules about these endings. Their usefulness depends on whether we are talking, writing or reading. If a Frenchman wants to write *I speak*, *you speak*, *we speak*, *they speak*, he uses different endings for each. The French equivalents of what is called the "present tense" (p. 90) of *speak*, are:

je parl*e*	I speak	nous parl*ons*	we speak
tu parl*es*	you speak	vous parl*ez*	you speak
il parle	he speaks	ils parl*ent*	they speak

None of these endings adds anything to the meaning of a statement. They are just there as vestiges from the time when Romans did not use words such as *I*, *we*, *they*, in front of a verb, but indicated them by the ending. As such they are not relevant to a reading knowledge of French. Four of the six, italicized because they are vestiges in another sense, are not *audibly* distinct. They have no real existence in the spoken language. Thus some rules about derivative words are important only for writing, some for writing and speaking, others for reading as well. That many rules about correct writing deal with vestiges which have ceased to have any function in the living language does not mean that writing demands a knowledge of *more*

FIG. 4. CUNEIFORM TABLET RECORDING BABYLONIAN LEGEND OF THE DELUGE

grammar than reading. It signifies that it calls for more knowledge of a *particular type*. Complicated rules for the use of many French derivatives are not essential for self-expression because we can dispense with them as we dispense with the English derivative *day's*. For reading we need a *nodding* acquaintance with many rules which we are not compelled to use when writing or speaking.

The difficulties of learning the essential minimum of rules which are helpful from any point of view have been multiplied a thousand-fold by a practice which has its roots in the Latin scholarship of the

FIG. 5.—BILINGUAL SEAL OF KING ARNUWANDAS II, A HITTITE KING

The Hittite language was probably Aryan. The seal shows cuneiform syllabic signs round the margin and pictograms in the center. (See also Fig. 9.)

humanists, and in the teaching of Greek in schools of the Reformation. As explained in Chapter III, Latin and Greek form large classes of derivative words of two main types called *conjugations* (p. 95) and *declensions* (p. 104). The rules embodied in these conjugations and declensions tell you much you need to know in order to translate classical authors with the help of a dictionary. Grammarians who had spent their lives in learning them, and using them, carried over the same trick into the teaching of languages of a different type. They ransacked the literature of living languages to find examples of similarities which they could also arrange in systems of declensions and conjugations, and they did so without regard to whether we really need to know them, or if so, in what circumstances. The words which do not form such derivatives, that is to say, the *particles* which play such a large part in modern speech, were pushed into the background except in so far as they affected the endings (see p. 258) of words placed next to them. Any special class of derivatives characteristic of a particular language was neglected (see p. 269). The effect of this was to burden the memory with an immense store of unnecessary luggage without furnishing rules which make the task of learning easier.*

When sensible people began to see the absurdity of this system, still preserved in many grammar books, there was a swing of the pendulum from the perfectionist to the nudist (or DIRECT) method of teaching a language by conversation and pictures, without any rules. The alleged justification for this is that children first learn to speak without any rules, and acquire grammar rules governing the home language, if at all, when they are word perfect. This argument is based on several misconceptions. A child's experience is slight. Its vocabulary is proportionately small. Its idiom is necessarily more stereotyped, and its need for grammar is limited by its ability to communicate complicated statements about a large variety of things and their relations to one another. Apart from this, the child is in continuous contact with persons who can use the home language according to approved standards, and has no other means of communicating intelligibly with them. So neither the conditions of nor the motives for learning are those of an older person making *intermittent* efforts to acquire a language which is neither heard nor used during the greater part of the day.

Since *The Loom of Language* is not a children's book, there is no need to dwell on the ludicrous excesses of educational theorists who advocated the direct method † and fooled some teachers into taking

---

* For the benefit of the reader who already knows some French, the following quotation from Dimnet (*French Grammar Made Clear*) emphasizes lack of common sense in textbooks still used in the schools:

"Are the four conjugations equally important? Most grammars very unwisely lead the student to imagine that it is so. In reality there are (according to Hatzfeld and Darmester's well-known *Dictionary*) only 20 verbs in -OIR, some 80 in -RE, 300 in -IR, and all the other verbs (about 4,000) end in -ER. Whenever the French invent or adopt a new verb, they conjugate it like *aimer* (in a few cases like *finir*) and for this reason the two conjugations in -ER or -IR are called 'living,' while the less important conjugations in -OIR and -RE are termed 'dead.' The conjugation in -ER is the easiest of the four, and has only two irregular verbs in daily use."

To this we may add that there are only four common verbs which behave like *recevoir*, the type specimen of the so-called *third* conjugation of the "regular" verbs in the schoolbooks. The -re verbs of the *fourth* conjugation of "regular" verbs include four distinct types and a miscellaneous collection of others.

† The silliness of the direct method when tried out on adults was pointed out by Henry Sweet in 1899:

"The fundamental objection, then, to the natural method is that it puts the adult into the position of an infant, which he is no longer capable of utilizing, and, at the same time, does

it up. The most apparent reason for its vogue is that it exempts the teacher from having any intelligent understanding of the language which he or she is teaching. Common experience shows that adult immigrants left to pick up the language of their adopted country by ear alone rarely learn to speak or to write correctly; and adults who wish to learn the language of another country rarely have the leisure to waste on time-consuming instruction of the type given in urban schools where insipid pictures of rural scenes mollify the tedium of repetitive conversation.

Because the kind of grammar you most need depends partly on how you intend to use a language, it is impossible to give a general recipe for writing a compact and useful grammar book. The learner who wishes to get as far as possible with as little inconvenience generally has to pick and choose from books which contain more than enough. To do this intelligently is easier if we start with a general idea of how languages differ. The relative importance of rules of grammar depends, among other things, on whether the language one is learning more or less closely resembles one's own or another already mastered, and if so, in what way.

If we aim at learning to write a *modern* language, the formal grammar of conjugations and declensions explained in Chapters III and IV usually boils down to a comparatively small number of rules, far fewer than those given in most primers. On the other hand, few except the more advanced textbooks have much to say about other equally important rules. One class of such rules already mentioned depends on the fact that each language or group of closely related languages has its own *characteristic* types of *derivative* words. Thus *reader* and *builder*, *childhood* and *widowhood*, *reshape*, *rebuild*, *restate* and *fellowship*, *kingship*, illustrate four ways of building new words in English and in other Teutonic languages. Such rules may be as useful as the rules for forming such derivatives as *father's*.

If two languages are closely related as are Swedish and English, or Spanish and Italian, it is also helpful to know rules which tell us how the spelling or pronunciation of a word in one of them differs from the spelling or pronunciation of a corresponding word in another. For example, the SH in the English *ship* becomes SK in the Swedish *skep*, which means the same thing. Similarly the Swedish for *to shine* is *att skinna*. The vowel symbol JU in Swedish generally becomes I

---

not allow him to make use of his own special advantages. These advantages are, as we have seen, the power of analysis and generalization—in short, the power of using a grammar and a dictionary."

in corresponding English words. Thus *att sjunga*, with the ending *-a* common to all Swedish verbs, preceded by *att* (to) means *to sing*. In English, all verbs which change as *sing* to *sang* and *sung* are old Teutonic words. So we expect to find them in Swedish, which is also a Teutonic language, and can guess correctly that the Swedish equivalent of *to sink* would be *att sjunka*.

It is essential to know one thing about the use of words before we can begin to make a basic word list. Correspondence between the use of words in different languages is never perfect. It is more or less complete according to the grammatical class to which words are assigned. Thus numerals and name words or *nouns* such as *father*, *bird*, or *ship*, offer little difficulty when we consult a dictionary. The greatest trouble arises with particles, especially *directives*, i.e., such words as *in*, *on*, *to*, *at*. There is never absolute correspondence between such words in any two languages, even when they are very closely related as are Swedish and Danish. The English word *in* usually corresponds to the Swedish *i*, and the English *on* to Swedish *på*, but the British expression, *in the street*, is translated by *på gatan*. A Swede might get into difficulties if he gave his English hostess a word-for-word translation of *en kvinna jag träffade* (a lady I met) *på gatan*.

The dictionary usually gives several synonyms for each foreign equivalent of any directive, and leaves us to find out for ourselves when to use one or the other. To tell us how to do is one of the most important tasks of practical grammar. Thus it is quite useless to have a list of basic particles unless we know the *distinctive* use of each. If we are clear about this, we can recognize them when we are using a particle of our own language in an *idiomatic* sense. If we do not know the correct idiomatic equivalent in another language, we can paraphrase the expression in which it occurs without using it (see p. 130).

When making our word list for another language, we have also to be wary about one of the defects of English overcome by the small number of verbs in Ogden's Basic. Idiomatic English, as usually spoken and written, has a large number of very common verbs which we should not include in the English column of our word lists. *Try*, which is one of them, means in different contexts the same as (*a*) *attempt*, (*b*) *endeavor*, (*c*) *test*, (*d*) *judge*. Another very common English verb, *ask*, can mean: (*a*) *question*, (*b*) *request*, (*c*) *invite*. So an English-Swedish or English-French dictionary will not give one equivalent for *ask* or one for *try*. If you look up these words you may find for the first four and for the second three foreign substitutes which are *not* true synonyms. The moral of this is: do not include such words as *ask* or *try* in the English column of an essential word list. In place of them put each of the more explicit words given above.

A foreign language may have a fixed word order like our own, or a fixed word order which is quite different. If the order of words is very different from what we are accustomed to, rules of word order are among the most important rules of its grammar; and it is impossible to get confidence in reading, in speaking, or in writing till we have got used to them. In the initial stages of learning an unfamiliar pattern of this sort makes the task of reading much more difficult than it would otherwise be. That is why German and Dutch, though closely related to English, offer greater difficulties to an Englishman or an American than French. A trick which helps to fix rules of this kind is to make a habit of twisting an English sentence into the Germanic word order without translating it. The results are often funny, and that makes it easier to learn them. In German word order, the last few words would be: *and that makes it easier them to learn*.

In the chapters which follow we shall first look at the way languages differ from and resemble one another. This will help us to get clearer about the best way to begin learning any particular one. We shall then be in a position to judge whether it is best to concentrate on speaking, writing, or reading in the early stages, and to decide what course to pursue in writing or speaking in order to fix the minimum vocabulary and grammatical rules we have to use. In so doing we shall also recognize defects which we ought not to perpetuate, and merits which we should incorporate, in a language of world citizenship.

HOW TO READ THIS BOOK

Among other things, *The Loom of Language* aims at giving the reader who wishes to learn the languages spoken by our nearest European neighbors a working knowledge of the indispensable elements of grammar, with a basic vocabulary for self-expression. Much of the material relevant to the subject matter of the two chapters (VII and IX) primarily devoted to this is in tabular form. The tables illustrate aspects of the natural history of language discussed elsewhere. To get the best out of it as a self-educator, the wisest plan is to read it through quickly. After getting a bird's-eye view, the reader can then settle down to detailed study with pen, paper, and a book marker for reference backwards or forwards to tables printed in some other context, as indicated by the cross references throughout the succeeding chapters. Pen (or pencil) and paper are essential help. We are most apt to forget what we take in by ear, least likely to forget what we learn by *touch*. No one who has learned to swim or cycle forgets the trick of doing so.

The languages which we shall study in greatest detail to illustrate the way in which languages grow belong to the *Teutonic* and *Romance* groups, placed in the great *Indo-European* family. The latter also contains the *Slavonic* group to which Russian belongs, the *Celtic*, in which *Welsh* and *Erse* are placed, and the *Indo-Iranian* group, which includes *Persian* and numerous languages of India. The Teutonic group is made up of German, Dutch, and the Scandinavian dialects. The Romance languages, such as French, Portuguese, Spanish, and Italian, are all descendants of Latin. English is essentially a Teutonic language which has assimilated an enormous number of words of Latin origin. So Teutonic or Romance languages have most in common with English. Fortunately for us they include all the languages spoken by the nearest neighbors (other than Amerindian) of English-speaking peoples on the continents of Europe and America.

The reader, who has not yet realized how languages, like different species of animals or plants, differ from and resemble one another, will find it helpful to *browse* among the exhibits set out as tables throughout *The Loom*. Above all, the home student will find it helpful to loiter in the corridors of the home museum which makes up the fourth part of the book. On its shelves there is ample material for getting clear insight into the characteristics which French, Spanish, and Italian share with their Latin parent, as also of features common to the Teutonic family. One shelf of exhibits shows Greek words which are the bricks of an international vocabulary of technical terms in the age of hydroelectricity and synthetic plastics. The diversion which the reader of *The Loom* can get from noticing differences and detecting essential word similarities in adjacent columns in the light of laws of language growth set forth elsewhere (Chapters V and VI) will help to fix items of an essential vocabulary with a minimum of tedium and effort.

One of the difficulties which besets the home student who starts to learn a new language is the large number of grammatical terms used in most textbooks. The object of the four chapters that follow is to show how languages grow, and the reader who does not know many grammatical terms will discover the use of important ones. The reader who already knows the sort of grammar taught in schools and colleges may make the discovery that grammar is not intrinsically dull, and may learn something about the principles which must motivate a rational judgment about language planning for a world at peace.

The popular myth that it is more difficult for an adult than for a child to learn languages has been disproved by experimental research carried out by modern educationists. Much of the effort put into early education is defeated by the limitations of the child's experience and interests. The ease with which we remember things depends largely on the ease with which we can link them up to things we know already. Since the adult's experience of life and the adult's vocabulary are necessarily more varied than those of the child, the mental equipment of the adult provides a far broader basis of association for fresh facts. Thus an intelligent grown-up person approaches the study of a new language with knowledge of social customs and of history, with a world picture of change and growth gained by general reading or study, and with a stock of foreign words, foreign idioms or derivatives of borrowed roots gleaned from daily reading about *international* affairs (cf. *canard, démarche, Quai d'Orsay, Wilhelmstrasse, blitz-krieg*), advertisements of proprietary products (*glaxo, aspirin, cutex, innoxa, ovaltine*), or technical innovations (*cyanamide, carbide, hydrogenation, radiotherapy, calories, vitamins, selenium*). Children learn their own language and a foreign one *pari passu*. The adult can capitalize the knowledge of his or her own language as a basis for learning a new one related to it. Above all, an adult can visualize a distant goal more easily than a child.

One of the difficulties with which a child has to contend is the haphazard way in which we pick up the home language. Children acquire a vocabulary with little deliberate elucidation from parents or from brothers and sisters, and they do so in a restricted environment which exempts them from dangers of misunderstanding in a larger, less intimate one. Before school age our language diet is nobody's business. So the power of definition and substitution, so essential to rapid progress in a foreign language, comes late in life, if at all. Indeed most of us never realize the inherent irrationalities and obscurities of natural language until we begin to grapple with a foreign one. The discovery may then come as a shock, discouraging further effort.

Many difficulties which beset the beginner are due to the fact that few of us are alert to tricks of expression *peculiar to our own language*. In fact we need to know something about the language we habitually speak before we can learn another one with the minimum of effort. The object of Chapter IV of *The Loom* is to give first aid to the home student who is not as yet language conscious in this sense. The reader who intends to use it as a preliminary to the study of a new language will find helpful hints in it to repay what has been an exploit of endurance for the publisher and typesetter. The reader who is on the lookout for a bright book for the bedside will do well to give it the go-by or drink an old-fashioned before getting down to it.

PART ONE

THE NATURAL HISTORY
OF LANGUAGE

CHAPTER II

The Story of the Alphabet

LANGUAGE implies more than learning to signal like a firefly or to talk like a parrot. It means more than the unique combination which we call human *speech*. It also includes how man can communicate across continents and down the ages through the impersonal and permanent record which we call *writing*. One difference between speech and writing is important to anyone who is trying to learn a foreign language, especially if it is closely related to a language already familiar.

The spoken language of a speech community is continually changing. Where uniformity exists, local dialects crop up. In less than a thousand years what was a local dialect may become the official speech of a nation which cannot communicate with its neighbors without the help of interpreter or translator. Writing does not respond quickly to this process. It may not respond at all. The written word is more conservative than speech. It perpetuates similarities which are no longer recognizable when people speak, and where two languages have split apart in comparatively recent times, it is often easy to guess the meaning of written words in one of them, if we know the meaning of corresponding words in the other. Indeed we can go far beyond guesswork, if we know something about the history of sound correspondence (Chapter V, p. 179). To make the best of our knowledge we should also know something about the evolution of writing itself.

The reader will meet illustrations of this again and again in subsequent chapters (especially Chapter VI), and will be able to make good use of rules given in them while wandering about the corridors of the miniature language museum of Part IV. One example must suffice for the present. The German word for *water* is *Wasser*, which looks like its English equivalent on paper. As uttered, it does not. The German letter W stands now for our sound *v*, as the German V in *Vater* (father) stands for our *f* sound. The reason for this is that the pronunciation of the sound represented by W in older German dialects (including Old English) has changed since what is now called German became a written language. Before German became a written language another change of pronunciation was taking place in the region of southern and middle Germany. Spelling incorporated this change of the *t*-sound to a hiss represented by *ss*, as also various other changes (p. 226) which took place about the same time.

Thus the home student of living languages can reduce the difficulties of learning by getting to know:

a) How similarities of spelling which do not correspond to similarities of pronunciation may conserve identity of words in related languages that have drifted far apart.

b) How to recognize borrowed words by spelling conventions characteristic of the language from which they came.

c) How different ways of spelling equivalent words, once identical, reflect changes of pronunciation which involve nearly all words at a certain stage in the divergence of two languages with a common ancestry.

Broadly speaking, we may distinguish between two different kinds of writing. One includes *picture* writing and *logographic* writing, the others *sound* or phonetic writing. We can divide the latter into *syllable* writing and *alphabet* writing. Picture writing and logographic writing have no direct connection with sounds we make. That is to say, people can communicate by picture writing or logographic writing without being able to understand one another when they talk. This is not true of Old Persian *cuneiform* (Fig. 3), of the writing of ancient Cyprus (Figs. 13 and 14), or of modern Japanese *Kana* (Figs. 42 and 43). Such writing is made up of symbols which stand for the *sounds* we make when we separate words into *syllables*. They do not stand for separate objects or directions, as do the symbols of picture or logographic writing. Individually, they have no significance when isolated from the context in which they occur. The same is true of alphabet writing, which is a simplified form of syllable writing. The dissection of the words has gone much further, and the number of elementary symbols is less. So it is easier to master.

This fact about the alphabet is of great social importance. In communities which now use alphabets, ability to learn to write and to read what is written is generally accepted as the test of normal intelligence. We regard people who cannot be taught to do so as mentally defective. This is another way of saying that the alphabet has made the record of human knowledge accessible to mankind as a whole. The use of picture or logographic scripts, like early syllable

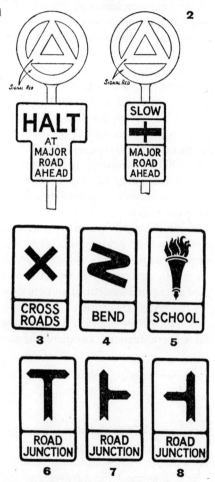

FIG. 6.—BRITISH TRAFFIC SIGNS

Nos. 3, 4, 6, 7, 8 are simple pictograms. No. 5 is an ideogram (logogram). No. 1 contains an ideogram with alphabetic writing. No. 2 shows a pictogram, ideogram, and phonograms (alphabetic).

writing, has always been the prerogative of a privileged caste of priests or scholars. The invention of the alphabet made it possible to democratize reading, as the invention of the number o made it possible to democratize the art of calculation. Unlike * the invention of zero, this liberating innovation has only happened once in the history of mankind. Available evidence seems to show that all the alphabets of the world are traceable to one source.

They came into use about three thousand years ago; but the inherent possibilities of an invention which we now recognize as one of the outstanding cultural achievements of mankind incubated slowly during the course of successive millennia. The first peoples who used alphabetic writing did so for short inscriptions in which individual letters might be written upside down or reversed sideways, with little consideration for the reader (Fig. 38). Even when a secular literature spread through the Greek and Roman world, the written language remained a highly artificial product remote from daily speech. Greek writing was never adapted to *rapid* reading, because Greek scribes never *consistently* separated words. The practice of doing so did not become universal among Roman writers. It became a general custom about the tenth century of our own era. When printing began, craftsmen took pride in the ready recognition of the written word, and punctuation marks, which individual writers had used sporadically without agreement, came into their own. Typographers first adopted an agreed system of punctuation, attributed to Aldus Manutius, in the sixteenth century. In the ancient world the reader had to be his own *palaeographer*. To appreciate the gap between modern and ancient reading, compare the sentences printed below:

KINGCHARLESWALKEDANDTALKEDHALFANHOURAFTERHISHEADWASCUTOFF.

King Charles walked and talked. Half an hour after his head was cut off.

To do justice to the story of the alphabet we must start by examining the meaning of a few technical terms. *Word* is itself a technical term. It is not easy to define what we mean by a separate word in all circumstances. So let us imagine what a traveler would do if he came to live with an illiterate tribe in the interior of Borneo. By pointing at things around he might soon learn which sounds stand for *picturable* objects. By comparing similar things he might also learn to recognize sounds signifying qualities such as *red*, *rough*, or *round*. By watching people together he could also detect sounds which are signals of action like *James! Here! Come! Hurry!* All this would not

* *Mathematics for the Million*, pp. 65, 286, 332.

make a complete inventory of the elements of a continuous conversation. If the language contained words corresponding to *and*, *during*, *meanwhile*, *for*, or *according*, he would take a long while to decide how to use them, because they never stand by themselves. For the same reason it would also be difficult to decide whether to regard them as separate words.

The difficulty of arriving at a definition of what we call separate words is also complicated by the fact that languages are not static. Elements of speech once recognized as distinct entities become fused, as when we condense *I am* to *I'm*, or *do not* to *don't*. So long as you write *I am* in the form *I'm*, you signify that it is to be regarded as two separate words glued together. When you write it in the form *Im*, as Bernard Shaw writes it, you signify that we do not break it up when we say it. Thus we can distinguish between words of three kinds. Some are the smallest elements of speech of which ordinary people can recognize the meaning. Some, separated by careful study, are products of grammatical comparison of situations in which they recur. People of a preliterate community would not recognize them as separate elements of speech. We recognize others as separate, merely because of the usual conventions of writing. The missionary or trader who first commits the speech of a nonliterate people to script has to use his own judgment about what are separate words, and his judgment is necessarily influenced by his own language.

For the present, we had better content ourselves with the statement that *words are what are listed in dictionaries*. According to the conventions of most English dictionaries, *godfather*, *father*, and *god* are different words, and *apples* is a derivative (footnote, p. 21) of the word *apple*. We shall see later why dictionaries do in fact list some noises as words, and omit other equally common noises, i.e., *derivatives* in the sense defined on page 21. Since dictionaries are our usual source of accessible necessary information, when we set out to learn a language we shall put up with their vagaries for the time being.

When highbrows want a word for all pronounceable constituents of a printed page, each with a distinct meaning or usage of its own, they may speak of them as *vocables*. Vocables include words listed in dictionaries, and derivatives which are not. We do not necessarily pronounce two vocables in a different way. Thus several vocables correspond to the spelling and pronunciation of *bay*, as in dogs that *bay at the moon*, a wreath of *bay leaves*, or the *Bay of Biscay*. Such vocables which have the same sound, but do not mean the same thing, are called *homophones*. We do not speak of them as homophones if derived from the same word which once had a more restricted meaning. Thus *boy*, meaning immature male of the human species, and *boy*, meaning juvenile male employee, are not homophones in the strict sense of the term, as are *sun* and *son*.

To discuss scripts intelligibly we need to have some labels for parts of words. When we separate a word with a succession of vowels into the bricks which come apart most easily as units of pronunciation, we call each brick a *syllable*. A syllable usually contains a vowel. Thus *manager* is a trisyllabic word made up of the syllables *ma-*, *-na-*, *-ger*, or, if you prefer it otherwise: *man-*, *-ag-*, and *-er*. Syllables need have no recognizable meaning when they stand by themselves. It is an accident that the syllables *man* and *age* in the word *manage* have a meaning when they stand by themselves. It has nothing to do with the past history of the word, of which the first syllable is connected with the Latin *manus* for *hand*, hence *manual*. If we break up *manliness* into *man-*, *-li-*, and *-ness*, the fact that *man* has a meaning is not an accident. It is the foundation-brick of the word, which was originally built up as follows:

man   + ly   = manly
manly + ness = manliness

Such syllables which have a meaning relevant to the meaning of the whole word are called *roots*, though root words are not necessarily *single* syllables. The part *-ly*, common to many English vocables, comes from the Old English word (*lic*) for *like*. Originally it stuck to names as compounds signifying qualities, i.e., *manly* is *manlike*. Later the process extended to many other words (e.g. *normal—normally*) long after *-ly* had lost identity as a separate element of speech. We do not call syllables of this sort *roots*. We call them *prefixes* or *suffixes* according as they occur like *un-* in *unmanly*, at the beginning, or like *-ly*, at the end. Suffixes or prefixes may be made up of more than one syllable either because they came from words of more than one syllable (e.g. *anti-*), or because the process of adding an *affix* (prefix or suffix) has happened more than once. Thus *manliness* has a bisyllabic suffix.

The suffix *-ly* in *unmanly* reminds us that the line between an affix and a root is not a clear-cut one. Affixes are the product of growth. In this process of growth three things occur. We call one of

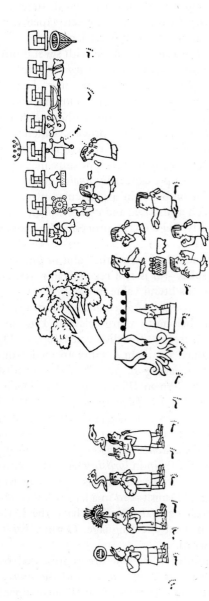

FIG. 7.—PICTOGRAPHIC WRITING OF AZTEC CIVILIZATION IN MEXICO

them *agglutination,** or gluing of native words together. A second is
analogical extension. The third, which is self-explanatory, is *borrowing* words like *pre* or *anti* from another language.

   The same native word may combine with several others to form a
class of compound words like *churchyard* or *brickyard,* in which
the two roots contribute to the whole meaning. At a later stage, the
original meaning of one root may begin to lose its sharp outline. People may then attach it to other roots without recalling its precise
meaning when it stands alone. This process, which is the beginning
of *analogical extension,* goes on after the original meaning of an affix
has ceased to be dimly recognizable. The affix may tack itself on to
roots merely because people expect by *analogy* that words of a particular sort must end or begin in a particular way. The large class
of English words such as *durable* and *commendable,* or *frightful* and
soulful, are in an early stage of the process. The suffix *-able* has not
yet lost its individuality as a separate vocable, though it has a less
clear-cut meaning than it had, when the habit of gluing it on to other
words began. The suffix *-ful* is still recognizable as a contraction of
full, which preserves its literal value in *handful.*

   Such words as *friendship* or *horsemanship* illustrate a further stage
of the process. They belong to a large class of Teutonic words such
as the German *Wissenschaft,* Swedish *vetenskap,* or Danish *Videnskab,* which have glued on them a suffix formed from a common
Teutonic root word meaning *shape.* Thus the Swedish *vetenskap,*
Danish *Videnskab,* or German *Wissenschaft,* for which we now use
the Latin *science,* is really *wit-shape.* In such words a suffix signifying
shape or *form* in a more or less metaphorical sense of the word has
tacked itself on to roots to confer a more abstract meaning. The
-head in *godhead* and *maidenhead* has no more connection with the
anatomical term than the *-ship* in *lordship* has to do with ocean transport. Like the *-hood* in *widowhood,* it is equivalent to the German
-heit, Swedish *-het,* and Danish *-hed* in a large class of abstract words
for which the English equivalents often have the Latin suffix *-ity.*
In the oldest known Teutonic language, Gothic, *haiduz* (*manner*)
was still a separate word.

   The ultimate bricks of a vocable are represented by the *vowel*
symbols (in English script *a, e, i, o, u*) and the *consonants* which
correspond to the remaining letters of our Roman alphabet. In com-

---

* *Agglutination* has also a more restricted meaning (p. 80) which is not
important in this context.

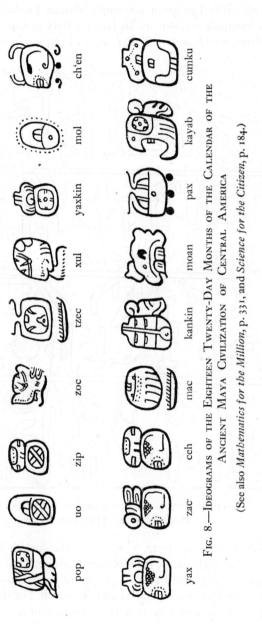

FIG. 8.—IDEOGRAMS OF THE EIGHTEEN TWENTY-DAY MONTHS OF THE CALENDAR OF THE ANCIENT MAYA CIVILIZATION OF CENTRAL AMERICA

(See also *Mathematics for the Million*, p. 331, and *Science for the Citizen*, p. 184.)

parison with other European languages, spoken English is astonish-
ingly rich in simple consonants. In fact we have at least twenty-two
simple consonants (*b, d, f, g, h, k, l, m, n* of *sin*, *n* of *sing*, *p, r, s, sh*,

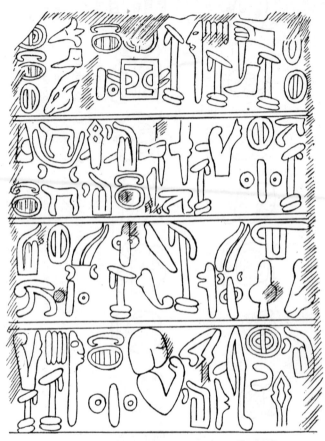

FIG. 9.—ANCIENT PICTURE WRITING OF THE HITTITES FROM AN
INSCRIPTION AT HAMA IN SYRIA

t, th of *thin*, *th* of *then*, *v, w, y, z, zh*) in the spoken language for
which only seventeen simple symbols are available. Two of them (Q,
C) are supernumerary and two (J, X) stand for compound sounds.
English dialects have at least twelve simple vowels. For these we have
five symbols supplemented by *w* after (as in *saw*), or *y* before any one
of them (as in *yet*). A complete Anglo-American alphabet with a

symbol for each simple vowel and consonant would demand between forty and fifty symbols to accommodate the range found in all the dialects taken together.

PICTURE WRITING AND SYLLABLE WRITING

In so far as the difficulties of modern spelling arise from the fact that we have too few symbols, the difficulties of the earliest peoples were opposite to ours. The earliest scripts consisted of separate symbols for individual vocables, and were therefore excessively cumbersome. These word symbols, of which the earliest Egyptian and Chinese writing is made up, were of two kinds: *pictograms* and *logograms*. A pictogram is a more or less simplified picture of an object which can be so represented. A logogram may be: (*a*) a pictorial symbol substituted for something which we cannot easily represent by a picture; (*b*) any sign used to indicate an attribute of a group (*red, age, movement, noise, wet*), or a direction for action, such as *Halt! Major Road Ahead!* or *Go Slow!*

British traffic signs (Fig. 6) for motorists illustrate all such symbols. A thick line for the main road with a thinner one crossing it is a pictogram for a crossroad. The conventionalized picture of the torch of learning is a pictorial logogram which stands for *school*. The triangle and circle which stands for *Stop!* has no obvious association with any other picturable object. Like the number 4, it is a pure logogram. We still use some logograms in printed books. Besides numbers, we have signs such as &, £, and $. The signs ♂, ♀, and ☿ in books on astronomy stand for *Mars, Venus*, and *Mercury*. In books on biology they stand for *male, female*, and *hermaphrodite*. The plural forms are ♂ ♂ (males), etc. Similarly the Chinese use the sign 木 for *tree*, and write 木木 for *forest*. Such signs as ♂, ♀, ☿ mean the same to astronomers and biologists all over the world, whether they do or do not *speak* the same language.

The expression *picture writing*, in contradistinction to *logographic* writing, is a little misleading. Anything which we can properly call writing, in contradistinction to cave painting, sculpture, or other ways of recording events visibly, must be made up of something more than conventional drawings of picturable objects. When we speak of picture writing as the most primitive level of script (Figs. 5 and 7–10), we mean a more or less explicit record or instruction set forth in symbols, most of which are either pictograms or logograms of the *School Ahead* type. If it is not possible to represent elements of speech by simple pictures, it may be possible to suggest them represented by the picture of an object which we associate with them. Thus we hopefully associate (Fig. 6) the torch of learning with a building used for scholastic purposes. The Chinese sign for *not* is 不, originally a line drawn over the top of a plant. This suggests that something got in the way of its growth—obstruction, *not* progress, *not* getting bigger, just *not*.

When we speak of logographic writing, we mean writing in which symbols for picturable objects, general characteristics, or directions for action have lost their explicit pictorial meaning. We can no longer guess what they do mean unless we have some key. This does not mean that all logograms start by being pictures of definite objects. At least one class of logograms (or *ideograms*, as some people call them) is as old as the art of writing. It seems clear that the chief practical advantages of the art of writing at a primitive level of human culture are twofold. One is to put on record necessary information which we should otherwise forget. The other is to convey directions or information to a distance when the carrier might forget them or betray them. The former is almost certainly the older of the two. The priestly caste, as the custodian of a calendar based on centuries of precise observation, appear on the scene at the dawn of Egyptian civilization. Men began to keep accurate records of the seasons as soon as there was settled agriculture; and it is unlikely that the need for written messages arose before man began to establish settled grain-growing communities. As man progressed from a primitive hunting or food-gathering stage to herdmanship and skilled agriculture, the need for counting his flocks and keeping track of seasonal pursuits forced him to prime his memory by cutting notches on sticks or making knots in cords.

We may thus take it for granted that one class of logograms, the number symbols, are as old as and possibly much older than any other elements of the most ancient forms of writing. The most ancient number symbols are pictorial in the sense that the first four Roman numerals (I, II, III, IIII) are just notches on the tally stick. Comparison of the relics of the temple civilizations of Central America, Mesopotamia, and Egypt, indicates that the impulse to record social events was mixed up with the primary function of the priests as calendar makers at a time when the person of the priest-king was the focus of an elaborate astronomical magic and calendar ritual. Thus picture writing was necessarily the secret lore of a priestly caste and, as such, a jealously guarded secret. Since picture writing is too cumbersome to convey more than the memory can easily retain, its further elaboration to serve the needs of communication at a distance may have been due to the advantages of secrecy. Whether this is or is not true,

FIG. 10.—DISCUS OF PHAESTOS SHOWING AS YET UNDECIPHERED
PICTOGRAPHIC WRITING OF THE ANCIENT CRETAN CIVILIZATION

the fact that writing was originally a closely guarded secret had important consequences for its subsequent evolution.

The ancient calendar priesthoods had a vested interest in keeping knowledge from the common people. The impulse to preserve secrecy possibly encouraged the gradual degradation of conventional pictures into logograms, which, like the elements of modern Chinese writing, have lost their power to suggest what they stand for. In Chinese scripts we have examples of logographic writing still largely the

Internat. symbol	Hebrew	Greek	Slavonic	Irish	Latin	German black letter
b	ב *beth*	Ββ *beta*	Бб	b	B	ℬ b
d	ד *daleth*	Δδ *delta*	Дд	δ	D	𝔇 δ
f		Φφ *phi*	Фф	F	F	𝔉 f
g	ג *gimel*	Γγ *gamma*	Гг	ᵹ	G	𝔊 g
h	ה *he*	··	— —	h	H	ℌ h
k	כ *kaf*	Κκ *kappa*	Кк	c	C	𝔎 t
l	ל *lamed*	Λλ *lambda*	Лл	ll	L	ℒ l
m	מ *mem*	Μμ *mu*	Мм	m	M	𝔐 m
n	נ *nun*	Νν *nu*	Нн	Nn	N	𝔑 n
p	פ *pe*	Ππ *pi*	Пп	p	P	𝔓 p
s	ס *samek*	Σσς *sigma*	Сс	Sr	S	𝔖 ſs
t	ת *tau*	Ττ *tau*	Тт	c	T	𝔗 t
v	ו *vau*	Ϝ *digamma*	Вв	— —	— —	𝔙 v
w		— —	— —	— —	(V)	— —
z	ז *zayin*	Ζζ *zeta*	Зз	— —	Z	— —
j	*yod*	— —	— —	— —	— —	— —
r or ɹ	ר *resh*	Ρρ *rho*	Рр	Rp	R	ℜ r
ʃ	ש *shin*	— —	Шш	— —	— —	Sch, ſch
ŋ		— —	— —	— —	— —	— —
ʒ		— —	Жж	— —	— —	— —
θ		Θθ *theta*	— —	— —	— —	— —
ð		— —	— —	— —	— —	— —
dʒ	....	— —	Чч	— —	— —	— —
tʃ		— —	— —	— —	— —	— —
ps		Ψψ *psi*	— —	— —	— —	— —
kh	ח *cheth*	Χχ *chi*	Хх	— —	— —	Ch, ch
ʃdʒ		— —	Щщ	— —	— —	— —
ks		Ξξ *xi*	— —	— —	X	𝔛 x
ts	צ *tsadek*	— —	Цц	— —	— —	ℨ ʒ
kw	ק *quof*	— —	— —	— —	QV	— —

FIG. 11.—CONSONANT SYMBOLS OF SOME CONTEMPORARY ALPHABETS

Pronunciation changes in the course of centuries. So it is somewhat arbitrary to give fixed values to Greek symbols which have retained roughly the same shape for twenty-five hundred years. It seems clear that φ originally stood for an aspirated *p* rendered as *PH* in Latin transcription. The symbol for *p* (π) replaces φ in the first syllable of the *reduplicated* past tense form of verbs which begin with the latter (cf. λυω = *I loose* and λελυκα = *I have loosed* with monopoly of a scholar caste. Scripts of this class share one important characteristic with picture writing. The individual symbols have *no necessary connection with the sounds associated with them.* This is not difficult to understand if you recall one class of logograms which still survive on the printed page. The Englishman associates with the ideogram 4 the noise which we write as *four* with our imperfect alphabet, or *fɔ:* in modern phonetic script (p. 70). The Frenchman writes it *quatre,* standing for the sound *katr.* The Englishman and the Frenchman both recognize its meaning, though they associate it with different sounds, and a Frenchman could learn to interpret the English traffic signs from a French book without knowing a word of English. In the same way, people from different parts of China can read the same books without being able to utter any mutually intelligible words.

Eventually the priestly scripts of Egypt incorporated a third class of signs as *phonograms.* The learned people began to make puns. That is to say, they sometimes used their picture symbols to build up words of syllables which had the sound associated with them. With a code of such pictograms we can combine 🐝 for *bee* with 🍃 for *leaf* to suggest the word *belief* by putting a frame round them thus:

This is just what the Egyptians *sometimes* did. The constituents of this compound symbol have now no connection with the meaning of the word. We can know the meaning of the word only if we know what it sounds like when spoken.

A trick of this sort may be a stage in the development of one kind of phonetic script called *syllable writing.* The characteristic of syllable writing is that each symbol, like the letters of our alphabet, stands for a sound which has no necessary meaning by itself. Syllable writing in this sense did not evolve directly out of Egyptian picture scripts. Whether the first step toward phonetic combinations of this

---

φραζω = *I declare* and πεφρακα = *I have declared*). This *ph* sound drifted toward *f* which takes its place in many Latin words of common Aryan ancestry, e.g. φερω = *fero* (I carry) and φρατηρ = *frater* (clansman, brother). With the *f* value it had in late Roman times, in technical terms from Greek roots and in modern Greek, it went into the Slavonic alphabet. By then the sound corresponding to β had drifted toward our *v*, its value in modern Greek. The symbol ϝ occurs only in early Greek, probably with a value equivalent to *w*, though evidently akin to the Hebrew *vau* and Latin *F*.

kind was part of the priestly game of preserving script as a secret code, whether the highbrow pastime of making puns and puzzles encouraged it, we do not know. Either because they lacked a sufficient social motive for simplifying their script, or because the intrinsic difficulties were too great, the Egyptian priests never took the decisive step to a consistent system of phonetic writing.

There is no reason to suppose that peoples who have taken this step have done so because they are particularly intelligent or enterprising. Many useful innovations are the reward of ignorance. When illiterate people, ignorant of its language, come into contact with a community equipped with script, they may point at the signs and listen to the sounds the more cultured foreigner makes when he utters them in his own language. In this way they learn the signs as symbols of sounds without any separate meaning. Imagine what might have happened if the English had used public notices in picture writing during the wars of Edward III. Let us also suppose that the French had been wholly illiterate at the time. When a Frenchman pointed to the pictogram ⅄, the informative Englishman would utter the sound *cock*, corresponding to the French *coq*. When he pointed at the logogram ♛, he would get the response *lord*, sufficiently near to the French vocable *lourde*, which means *heavy*. Without knowing precisely what significance an Englishman attached to the symbols, the Frenchman might make up the combination ⅄ ♛ standing for *coquelourde* (meaning a *pasqueflower*) in the belief that he was learning the new English trick of writing things down.

Needless to say, this is a parable. We must not take it too literally. We know next to nothing about what the *living* languages of *dead* civilizations were like; but one thing is certain. Transition from a cumbersome script of logograms, or from a muddle of pictograms, logograms, and phonographic puns, to the relative simplicity of syllable writing, demands an effort which no privileged class of scholar-priests has ever been able to make. It has happened when illiterate people with no traditional prejudices about the correct way of doing things have come into contact with an already literate culture. Whether they can succeed in doing so depends on a *lock and key* relation between the structure of the living languages involved in the contact between a literate and nonliterate culture. They can succeed if, and only if, it is easy to break up most words they use into bricks with roughly the same sounds as *whole* words in the language equipped with the parent logographic script.

Our most precise information about this lock and key relationship is based on adaptation of Chinese script by the Japanese. In order to understand it the first thing to be clear about is the range of possible combinations of elementary sounds. In round numbers, a language such as ours requires twenty distinct consonants and twenty vowels including diphthongs. This means that if our language were made up entirely of monosyllabic words of the same *open* type as *me*, or exclusively of the same open type as *at*, we could have a vocabulary of 20 × 20, or four hundred words, without using any compound consonants such as *st*, *tr*, or *kw*. To a large extent Chinese vernaculars

VOWELS—								
Slavonic _	Aa Әə	Ee Ии	Ii	Oo Уy	Юю	Яя	Ыы
Greek __	A α¹	Eε² Hη³	Ii⁴	Oo⁵ Ωω⁶	Uu⁷		
Roman _ _	A	E	I	O	V		
Irish ___	a	e	ɟ	o	u		
German _	2l a	Œe	Ʒi	O	Uu		

¹alpha ²epsilon ³eta ⁴iota ⁵omicron ⁶omega ⁷upsilon

Hebrew symbols with no equivalents in our alphabets . . . .   א aleph   ע ayin   ט teth
throat sounds

FIG. 12.—VOWEL SYMBOLS OF SOME CONTEMPORARY ALPHABETS

(p. 430) consist of open syllables like *my* and *so*. The Chinese have to do everything with about four hundred and twenty basic words.

The small size of its vocabulary is not a necessary consequence of the fact that Chinese is monosyllabic. If a language consisted exclusively of monosyllabic words belonging to the *closed* type such as *bed*, more common in English, we could make roughly 20 × 20 × 20, or eight thousand words, without using *double* consonants. A language such as English can therefore be immensely rich in monosyllables without being exclusively made up of them. Chinese is able to express so much with about four hundred and twenty monosyllables, partly because it makes combinations like the undergraduate slang *god-box* for *church*, partly because it is extremely rich in homophones like our words *flea-flee* or *right-write*, and partly because it is able to distinguish some homophones by nuances of *tone* such as we make when we say "yes" as a symbol of deliberate assent, interrogation, suspense or excitement, ironical agreement or boredom. The number of homophones in the Chinese language is enormous, and this is inevitable because of the small number of available vocables. A Chinese dictionary lists no less than ninety-eight different meanings for the sound group, represented by CHI. Of these ninety-eight, no less

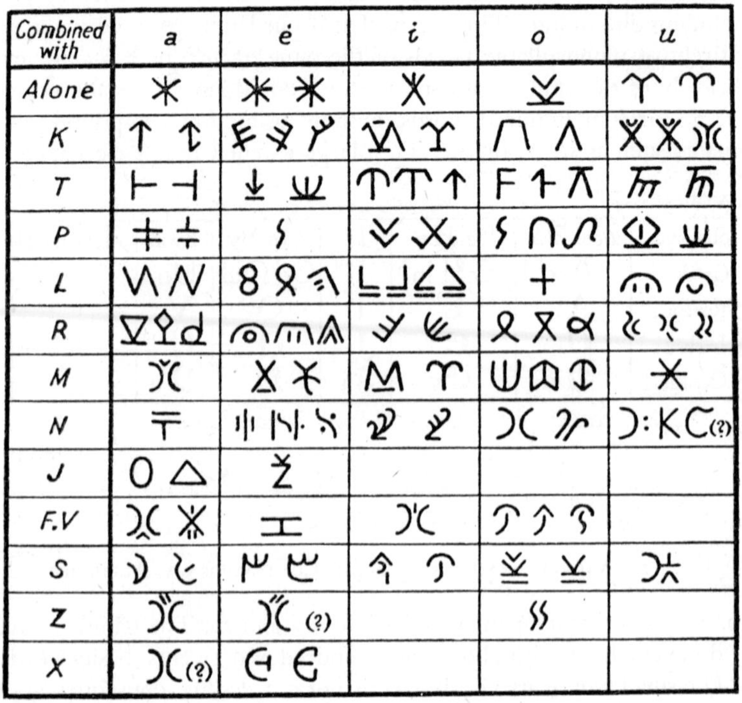

Combined with	a	é	i	o	u
Alone	✳	✳ ✳	✕	⩔	⋏ ⋏
K	↑ ↿	⨏⩔⫏	⩕ ⋏	⋂ ⋀	✕ ✕ ⟆
T	⊢ ⊣	⊻ ⼚	⊤⊤↑	⨍ � ⅄	⼌ ⼌
P	╪ ╪	⼂	⩔ ⤬	⼂ ⋂ ⼂	⧂ ⼌
L	⋁ ⋀	8 ⅄ ⟑	⌶⌶⟍⟍	+	⌒ ⌒
R	⩔⼛d	⊙⼔⋀	⤏ ⼚	⼛ ✕ ⼂	⟪ ⟩ ⟫
M	⼚	✕ ✕	M ⋏	⋃⼚⼁	✳
N	⊤	‖ ⼂·⼓	⼚ ⼚	⟩⟨ ⼫	⟩⁚KC(?)
J	0 △	⼚			
F.V	⟩⟨ ✕	⥊	⟩⟨	⋏ ⼓ ⼓	
S	⼚ ⼋	⼛ ⼛	⼓ ⋏	⩔ ⩔	⼌
Z	⟩⟨	⟩⟨ (?)		⫻	
X	⟩⟨(?)	⊖ ⊖			

FIG. 13.—THE ANCIENT CYPRIOTIC SYLLABARY

Showing the five vowel signs in the top row and the symbols for open syllables made by combining any or all of them with the consonant sound represented by the letter in the left-hand vertical column. Thus the symbols of the second row run: *ka, ke, ki, ko, ku.*

than forty-eight have the same rising tone corresponding roughly to our questioning "ye-es?"

The Chinese way of representing a *grove* or *forest* by combining the picture symbols for *tree* illustrates one device by which a comparatively rich equipment of written words is built up by pairing a relatively small battery—i.e., 214 in all—of elementary logograms called *radicals* (see Fig. 40). Mere juxtaposition of the picture symbol for each of them may represent a quality or an activity common to two objects. Thus the logogram for the word MING, which can mean *bright*, is made up of the character for the moon next to the character for the sun. Originally the characters were recognizable picture symbols, and the composite sign would then have been something like this: ⊙ ☽. In the course of centuries the basic picture symbols have become more and more conventionalized, partly owing to changes in the use of writing instruments (style, brush, wood blocks), or of materials (bone, ink, paper).

A second sort of compound characters (Fig. 41) is a halfhearted step toward sound writing, based on the time-honored device of punning. One member of the pair suggests the meaning of the character in a general way. The other stands for a homophone, that is to say a word which has (or originally had) the same sound as the word represented by the pair taken together. A fictitious example, based on two English words which have familiar homophones, illustrates this trick. Suppose we represent the words *sun* and *buoy* respectively by the picture symbols ⊙ and ♗, as biologists use the character ♂ for *male*. What the Chinese do by this method would then be equivalent to using the combination ♂ ⊙ for our word *son* (which has the same sound as *sun*) or ♂ ♗ for *boy*. It is not certain how this practice arose. One possibility is that it developed in response to the way in which a word widens its meaning by the process called *metaphorical extension*. What this means is illustrated by our word *boy*, which originally meant a sexually immature male of the human species, and may also mean a son or a juvenile employee.

All this has led to the accumulation of an immense number of complex signs. There are between four and seven thousand relatively common ones. Anyone who wants to be an accomplished scholar of Chinese must learn them. Among the four thousand used most commonly, about three-quarters consist of a homophone element and a *classifier* analogous to the symbol for *male* in the hypothetical model cited above. Owing to changes of pronunciation in the course of centuries, the homophone part, which was once a sort of *phonogram*, or sound symbol, may have lost its significance as such. It no longer then gives a clue to the spoken word. Today, Chinese script is almost purely logographic. People who have the time to master it associate the characters with the vocables they themselves utter. These vocables are now very different in different parts of China, and have changed beyond recognition since the script came into use many centuries back. So educated Chinese who cannot converse in the same tongue can read the same notices in shops, or the same writings of moralists and poets who lived more than a thousand years ago.

The remarkable thing about Chinese script is not so much that it is cumbersome according to our standards, as that it is possible to reproduce the content of the living language in this way. This is so because the living language is not like that of any European people except the British (p. 111). The Chinese word is invariable, like our "verb" *must*. It does not form a cluster of derivatives like *lusts, lusted, lusting, lusty*. What we call the grammar of an Indo-European language is largely about the form and choice of such derivatives, and it would be utterly impossible to learn a logographic script with enough characters to accommodate all of them. A large proportion of the affixes of such derivatives are useless, e.g. the *-s* in *lusts* (see p. 84). So presumably they would have no place in a logographic script. A large proportion of our affixes do the same job, as illustrated by pater*nity*, father*hood*, reproduc*tion*, guardian*ship*. The same character would therefore serve for a single cluster. Hence a logographic script in which Frenchmen or Germans could communicate with their fellow citizens would be a code based on conventions quite different from the grammar of the spoken language.

The Japanese, who got their script from China, speak a language which is totally different from Chinese dialects. They use symbols (Figs. 42 and 43) for syllables, i.e., for the *sounds* of affixes which go to make up their words, and not merely for objects, directions, qualities, and other categories of meaning represented by separate vocables. The sounds corresponding to these symbols are more complex than those represented by our own letters, with four of which (*a, e, m, t*) we can make up thirteen monosyllables (*am, at, ate, eat, mate, meat, me, met, tame, tea, team*). So syllable writing calls for a larger battery of symbols than an alphabet, reformed or otherwise. Nonetheless, it is much easier to learn a syllable script than a logographic script in which the words have individual signs. The surprising thing about Japanese script is the small number of characters which make up its syllabary.

We have examined the essential characteristics of the Chinese key. Let us now examine the Japanese lock, that is to say, the word pattern into which symbols corresponding to Chinese root words had to fit. We can do this best, if we compare Japanese with English. If all English words were made up like *father*, we could equip it with a syllable script from the logographic or picture scripts of any language with a sufficiently rich collection of open monosyllables like *fa:* (far) and ðə (the). This would take at most about four hundred signs. The same would be true if all English words were built to the same design as *adage* (*ad* + *age*) in which two open syllables with a final consonant combine. The problem is immensely more complicated if a language contains a high proportion of words like *handsome* or *mandrill*. If there are twenty consonants and twenty vowels all pronounceable closed monosyllables then exceed eight thousand. This means that the word pattern of the language which borrows its script decides whether the language itself can assimilate a syllabary which is not too cumbersome for use.

Japanese, like Finnish and Hungarian, has its place in a class called *agglutinating* languages. We shall learn more about their characteristics in later chapters. Here it is enough to say that *agglutinating* languages are languages of which root words can attach to themselves a relatively small range of affixed syllables (pp. 190–194). The significance of the affixes is easy to recognize, and the affixes themselves are relatively few and *regular*. Thus words derived from the same roots grow by addition of a limited number of *fixed* syllables like the -*ing* which we add to *love*, *have*, *go*, *bind* and *think*, in *loving*, *having*, *going*, *binding*, and *thinking*. They do not admit of the great variety among corresponding derivatives of another class such as *loved*, *had*, *gone*, *bound*, *thought*. This, of course, means that the word pattern of an agglutinating language is necessarily more simple than that of such languages as our own.

The sound pattern of Japanese words is much simpler and more regular than that of English for another and more significant reason. Affixes of Japanese words are all simple vowels or open monosyllables consisting like *pea* of a simple consonant followed by a simple vowel. The only exception to this rule is that some syllables, like some *Chinese* words, end in *n*. Thus the familar place names YO-KO-HA-MA or FU-JI-YA-MA are typical of the language as a whole. We can split up all Japanese words in this way, and the number of possible syllables is limited by the narrow range of clear-cut consonants and vowels— fifteen of the former and five of the latter. This accounts for the possible existence of seventy-five syllables, to which we must add five vowels standing alone, like the last syllable in TO-KI-O, and the terminal *n*, making a complete battery of eighty-one (Fig. 44).

Thus the Japanese are able to represent all their words by combining the signs for a small number of Chinese (see Figs. 42 and 43) vocables. Though their writing is based on syllables, the Japanese use a script which *need* not contain many more signs than the letters of an alphabet reformed to represent all English simple consonants and vowels by individual symbols.* At first, the Japanese used their *kana* or syllable signs exclusively, and still do so, for telegrams or in schoolbooks for the young. Otherwise (p. 443) they have gone back to the old school tradition. In books printed today they generally use Chinese characters for root words, with Kana signs for the affixes.

We do not certainly know whether the people who first made up Japanese syllable writing were scholars. Like the Oriental traders who revolutionized our number system by using a dot for the modern zero sign to signify the empty column of the counting frame, they may well have been practical men who earned a livelihood in the countinghouse, or as pilots on ships. Scholars naturally favor the view that they were men of learning directly skilled in the use of Chinese. Undoubtedly such men existed in Japan, when it adapted Chinese symbols to its own use somewhere about A.D. 750; but if it was a scholar who first hit on the trick, it is quite possible that he learned it from the mistakes of his pupils. From what we do know we may be certain of this. Those who introduced Japanese *kana* were men who had no sacrosanct national tradition of writing in this way, and therefore brought to their task the unsophisticated attitude of the Island Greeks who absorbed the practical advantages of Egyptian or Semitic learning without assimilating all the superstitions of their teachers. In the ancient world and in medieval times, mankind had not got used to rapid change. Great innovations were possible only when circumstances conspired to force people to face new problems without the handicap of old habits. The Japanese had to take this step because their language was polysyllabic and comparatively rich in derivative words. They were able to take it because the affixes

* "In Amharic (an Ethiopian language) which is printed syllabically there are 33 consonantal sounds, each of which may combine with any of the 7 vowels. Hence to print a page of an Amharic book, 7 × 33, or 231 different types are required: instead of the 40 types which would suffice on an alphabet method. In Japanese this difficulty is less formidable than in many other languages, owing to the simplicity of the phonetic system which possesses only 5 vowel sounds and 15 consonantal sounds. There are, therefore, only 75 possible syllabic combinations of a consonant followed by a vowel. Several of these potential combinations do not occur in the language, and hence it is possible with somewhat less than 50 distinct syllabic signs to write down any Japanese word."— Taylor: *The Alphabet*, vol. i, p. 35.

Fig. 14. Stone Inscription from Paphos (Eighth Century b.c.)

of their derivative words were few, and because the sound values of individual syllables correspond to those of Chinese words.

When the Chinese is up against a situation comparable to that of the Japanese at the time when they first got their syllabic scripts, he treats his own characters in the same way. For foreign names the Chinese use their characters purely as sound syllables, as we might write 3.40 to suggest the sound *three for tea*. This emphasizes how favorable combinations of unusual circumstances influence the possibility of rapid advance or retardation in the cultural evolution of different communities. It is one of the many reasons why we should be suspicious when people attribute one or the other to national and racial genius or defect. The simplicity of the Chinese language made it easy for the Chinese to develop a more consistent and workable system of picture writing than any other nation at an early stage in its history. Since then it has been a cultural millstone round their necks.

If the Russians, the Germans, or any other Aryan-speaking people had come into contact with Chinese script while they were still barbarians, they could not have used the Chinese symbols to make up a satisfactory battery of affixes for two reasons. One reason for this is that the total number of affixes in derivative words of an Indo-European language is far greater than the number of Japanese affixes. A second is that Chinese has no sounds corresponding to the large class of closed monosyllables which occur as affixes, such as the *-ness* in *manliness*. A third is that words of the Aryan languages are rich in consonant clusters. So a European people would have reaped little advantage by using Chinese characters as symbols of sound instead of as symbols of meaning. That transition from logographic script to sound writing depends on the lock as well as on the key is easy to test. Make a table of English monosyllabic words of the *open* type and use it to build up English, French, or German polysyllables with the aid of a dictionary. You will then discover this. The possibility of achieving a more simple method of writing for such languages as English, French, or German involved another unique combination of circumstances.

THE COMING OF THE ALPHABET

In the ancient Mediterranean world, syllable scripts were in use among Semitic peoples, Cypriots, and Persians. They got the bricks, as the Japanese got their syllabaries from the Chinese, from their neighbors of Mesopotamia and Egypt, where forms of picture writing first appeared. None of these syllabaries has survived. All have made way for the alphabet.

The dissection of a word into syllables—especially the words of an agglutinating language—is not a very difficult achievement. The

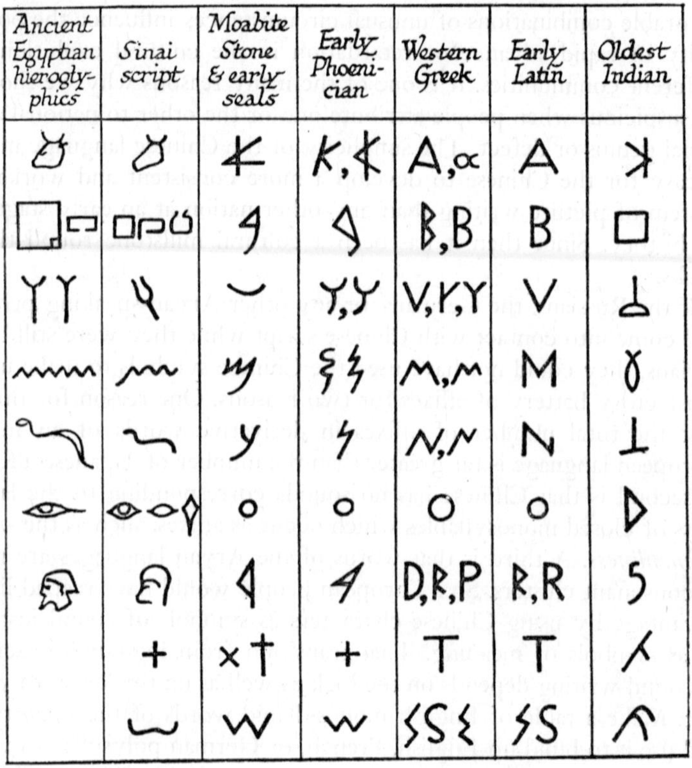

Ancient Egyptian hieroglyphics	Sinai script	Moabite Stone & early seals	Early Phoenician	Western Greek	Early Latin	Oldest Indian
			K,𝔎	A,α	A	
				β,B	B	
			Υ,Υ	V,Γ,Υ	V	
				Μ,Μ	M	
				Ν,Ν	N	
		o	o	O	O	
				D,R,P	R,R	
+	×†	+	T	T	
	W	w	ϟSϟ	ϟS	

FIG. 15.—SOME SIGNS FROM EARLY ALPHABETS

splitting of the syllable into consonants and vowels was a much more difficult step to take. The fact that all true alphabets have an unmistakable family likeness if we trace them back far enough forces us to believe that mankind has once only taken this step (Fig. 15). We know roughly when this happened, who were responsible, and in what circumstances it took place. Through inscriptions in the mines of the Sinai Peninsula (Fig. 2) about 1500 B.C., and in other places

between this date and about 1000 B.C., archaeologists can trace the
transformation of a battery of about twenty Egyptian pictograms
into the symbols of the early Semitic alphabet. This early Semitic
alphabet was not an ABC. It was a BCD. It was made up of consonants only.

One peculiarity of the Semitic languages gives us a clue to the
unique circumstances which made possible this immense simplification. Semitic *root* words nearly always have the form which such
proper names as *Jacob, Rachel, David, Moloch, Balak,* or *Balaam*
recall. They are made up of three consonants separated by two intervening vowels, and the three consonants in a particular order are
characteristic of a particular root. This means that if *cordite* (kɔ:dait)
were a Hebrew word, all possible combinations which we can make
by putting different vowels between *k* and *d* or *d* and *t* would have
something to do with the explosive denoted by the usual spelling.
This unique regularity of word pattern led the old rabbinical scholars
to speak of the consonants as the body and the vowel as the soul of
the word. In so far as we can recognize bodies without theological
assistance the metaphor is appropriate. Consonants are in fact the
most tangible part of the *written* word. A comparison of the next
two lines in which the same sentence is written, first without consonants, and then without vowels, is instructive from this point of
view:

..e.e a.e .u.. .o.e ea.y .o .ea

Then turn the page upside down and read this:

p··ɹ ·ɹ ·s·· ·ɹ·ɯ ɥɔ·ɯ ·ɹ· ·s·ɥʇ

If you carry out experiments of this kind you will discover two
things. One is that it is easy to read a passage without vowels in
English if there is something to show where the vowels should be,
as in the above. The other is that it is much less easy to do so if
there is nothing to show *where the vowels ought to come.* Thus it
would be difficult to interpret:

ths r mch mr s t rd

Owing to the buildup of Semitic root words, we have no need of
dots to give us this information. Once we know the consonants, we
hold the key to their meaning. Any syllabary based on twenty-odd
open monosyllables with a different consonant would therefore meet

all the needs of a script capable of representing the typical root words of a Semitic language. The Semitic trading peoples of the Mediterranean took twenty-two syllable signs from Egyptian priestly writing, as the Japanese took over the Chinese monosyllabic logograms. They used them to represent the sounds for which they stood, instead of to represent what the sounds stood for in the parent language. Because they did not need to bother about the vowels, they used twenty-one of the Egyptian symbols to represent the consonant

Phoenician	Old		Classical	
	Greek	Latin	Greek	Latin
◁	△	▷	△	D
ㄱ	7Г	⟨C	Γ	G
ㄴ	⼃Λ	⼌L	Λ	L
ㄱ	7Γ	ΓP	Π	P
⼂	⼂P	R	P	R
⩗	⥾	⟨	Σ	S

FIG. 16.—EARLY AND LATER FORM OF SOME GREEK AND LATIN LETTERS
The reader should compare these with the writing in Figs. 35–38.

sounds of the root, without paying attention to the vowel originally attached.

Thus the alphabet began as an alphabet of consonants (Fig. 15). Such an alphabet, or B-C-D, was only workable in the hands of the Semitic peoples. If we had no English vowel symbols, the succession of consonants represented by *mlch* could stand for *milch* (in *milch cow*), or for the Bible name *Moloch*. Similarly *vst* could stand for *vest* or *visit*, and *pts* could stand for *pities* or *Patsy*. This was the dilemma of the Aryan-speaking colonizers and traders of Island Greece who came into contact with the syllable writing of Cyprus (Figs. 13 and 14) and the consonant writing of the Phoenicians. They used a language which was extremely rich in consonant combinations.

The Greek word for *man* is ανθρωπος, from which we get *philanthropy* and *anthropology*. If you write the consonants only in phonetic script (p. 70), this is nθrps. There is nothing in the word pattern of the Greek language to exclude all the possible arrangements which we can make by filling up each of the blanks indicated below with each of a dozen simple or compound vowel sounds:

. n . θ . r . p . s

The number of pronounceable arrangements of twelve different vowel sounds in combination with this range of consonants is about three million. It would be surprising if some of them were not true vocables. So it is easy to see that the same succession of consonants might stand for several different Greek words. It is equally easy to see why the syllable script of Cyprus (Figs. 13 and 14) was an unsatisfactory way of dealing with the same difficulty.

To adapt the Phoenician alphabet to their own use, the Greeks had to introduce vowels, which were probably monosyllables, like our own words *a* or *I*, taken from syllabaries of other peoples, such as the Cypriots, with whom they came in contact. This step was momentous. The primitive Semitic alphabets which had no vowels were good enough for simple inscriptions or for Holy Writ to be read again and again. They could not convey the grammatical niceties which result from internal vowel change of the sort illustrated by *sing-sang-sung*. Since Semitic languages abound in tricks of this sort, the ancient Semitic scripts were not well adapted to produce the rich secular literature which germinated in the Greek world.

The Greek alphabet (Figs. 11 and 12) had seven vowel symbols, namely, α ε η ι υ ω ο. The Italian peoples who got their alphabet from the Greeks also spoke dialects poor in vowels, and they discarded two of the Greek signs, i.e., η and ω. Divergence of the form of the symbols which make up the classical Greek and Latin alphabets came about owing to a variety of circumstances. The first people to use alphabetic writing did not write at length and were not fussy about whether they wrote from right to left or from top to bottom. Quite ephemeral reasons would influence the choice, as for example the advantage of inscribing a short epitaph vertically on a pole or horizontally on a flat stone. Thus the orientation of letters underwent local change through the whims of scribes or stonemasons, so that the same symbols were twisted about vertically or laterally, as illustrated in Fig. 16, which shows the divergence of the Greek and Latin symbols for D, L, G, P, R. While the art of writing and reading was still the privilege of the few, the need for speedy recognition was not compelling, and the urge for standardization was weak.

In one or other of the earliest specimens (Figs. 37 and 38) of Island Greek writing of the sixth or seventh centuries B.C., we can find any one of the old Phoenician consonant symbols unchanged. The absence of printing type to standardize the use of letter symbols, the effect of the writing materials on the ease with which they could be written, the limitation of primitive writing to short messages, records, or inscriptions, the small size of the reading public, and the fact that pronunciation changes in the course of several generations and varies among people still able to converse with difficulty in their own dialects, were other circumstances which contributed to the divergence of the alphabets. So there is now no recognizable resemblance between the classical Hebrew and Greek alphabets (Figs. 11 and 12) which came from the same Semitic source. Though Arabic is a Semitic language with a script written like Hebrew from right to left, the symbols of the Arabic consonants have no obvious resemblance to those of Hebrew. In the five different Arabic scripts, only the symbols for L, M, and S are now recognizable derivatives of their Phoenician ancestors.

Throughout the East, an enormous variety of alphabetic scripts do service for peoples with languages which, like Persian or many of those spoken in India, belong to the great Indo-European family, and like Burmese or Tibetan belong to the same family as Chinese. They are also in use among peoples with other languages, e.g. Manchu, Korean, Turkish, or Javanese. These belong to none of the three great language families which have been the chief custodians of knowledge and literature. Most scholars now believe that all these alphabetic scripts were offshoots of those used by Semitic peddlers who set forth across the great trade routes bridging the gulf between Eastern and Western culture in ancient times. To a Western eye, familiar with the simple lines and curves of the printed page in contradistinction to ordinary writing, they have a superficial resemblance due to the complex curvature of the symbols. It is not likely that any of these *cursive* scripts will overcome the direct appeal of the simpler signs, which printing and typewriting have now standardized in all highly industrialized countries.

Toward the end of the Middle Ages, when the Chinese invention of printing came into Europe, several forms of the Latin alphabet were in use in different countries. The more rectilinear Italian symbols, being better adapted to movable type, eventually superseded the more cursive variants such as the German *Black Letters* (Fig. 11) of the monkish missals. Partly perhaps because the Lutheran Bible was printed in this script, it persisted in Germany, where it has been fostered by nationalism. Before the Nazis took over, one newspaper had begun to follow the practice of scientific textbooks, drama, and modern novels in step with Western civilization. The Brown Shirts brought back the black letters.

Circumstances which have influenced the choice and character of scripts in use may be material on the one hand, and social on the other. Among the material circumstances are the nature of the surface (stone, bone, clay, ivory, wax, parchment, paper), and the nature of the instrument (chisel, style, brush, pen, wood block, or lead type), used for the process of transcription. Among social circumstances of first-rate importance we have to reckon with the range of sounds which a speech community habitually uses at the time when it gets its script, and the range of sounds represented by the parent alphabet. Intelligent planning based on the ease with which it is possible to adapt an alien script to the speech of an illiterate people played little, if any, part in selection before Kemal Ataturk introduced the Roman alphabet in Turkey (Fig. 46). Missionary enterprise has been the single most significant social agency which has influenced choice. This circumstance has left a permanent impress on the study of speech habits.

Conquests, political, religious, or both, have imposed scripts on languages ill adapted for them. This is true of Burmese and Siamese which have Sanskrit and Pali scripts. It is even more true of Arabic script, which Islam has forced upon communities with languages of a phonetic structure quite different from that of the Semitic family, e.g. Berber, Persian, Baluchi, Sindhi, Malay, Turkish, Swahili, etc. The secular impetus which trading gave to the spread of writing among the Mediterranean civilizations of classical antiquity extended to Northern Europe without having a permanent influence upon it. Before they adopted Roman Christianity, and with it the Roman alphabet, some Teutonic peoples were already literate. In various parts of Northern Europe, and especially in Scandinavian countries, there are inscriptions in symbols like those which pre-Christian invaders from the Continent also brought to Britain. This *Runic* script (Figs. 17 and 29) has no straightforward similarity to any other.

Supposedly it is a degenerate form of early Greek writing carried across Europe by migratory Germanic (Goths) and probably also by Celtic tribes, who learned it from trade contacts. It probably reached Scandinavia during the third century A.D. The letters illustrate the influence of the materials used. They are the sort of marks which are easy to chip on wood in the direction of the grain. We can recognize them as such in some of the Runic *clog almanacs* still in existence. The first surviving specimen (Fig. 30) of Runic comes

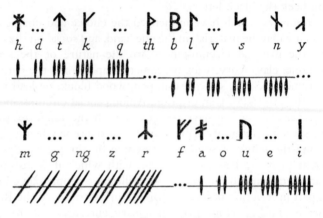

Scandinavian Runic & Ogam Symbols

FIG. 17.—KEY TO RUNIC AND OGAM SCRIPTS

Compare with Runic and Ogam inscriptions of Figs. 18 and 29.

The Runic symbols lie above the Roman equivalents, the Ogam below them.

from Gallehus in Schleswig. It is an inscription on a horn, and is worth quoting to illustrate the modest beginnings of writing for secular use: *ek hlewagastir holtingar horna tawiðo* = I LUIGAST THE HOLTING MADE (*this*) HORN.

There are inscriptions of another type (Figs. 17, 18, and 39) on stone monuments in Scotland, Wales, and Ireland. The script is pre-Christian but probably not older than the beginning of the Roman occupation of Britain. This *Ogam* writing, as it is called, has an alphabet of twenty letters. Each letter is a fixed number of from one to five strokes, with a definite orientation to a base line which was usually the edge of the stone. Five letters (*h, d, t, k, q*) are represented by one to five vertical strokes above the line; five (*b, l, v, s, n*) by one to five vertical strokes below the line; five (*a, o, u, e, i*) by vertical strokes across the line; and five (*m, g, ng, z, r*) by one to five strokes across the line sloping upward from left to right. One surmise is that the number of strokes has something to do with the order of the letters in the Roman alphabet, as the people who made this script received them. What led Celtic peoples to devise this system we do not know. It is clear that the Ogam signs are not degenerate representatives of Roman-Greek symbols, as are the Runic letters. Ogam script is a sort of code substitute for the Latin alphabet analogous to

FIG. 18.—BILINGUAL INSCRIPTION IN LATIN (ROMAN LETTERS) AND CELTIC (OGAM SIGNS) FROM A CHURCH AT TRALLONG IN IRELAND

The Celtic reads from right to left.

the Morse code used in telegraphy. Like the latter, it was probably adopted because it was most suitable for the instruments and for the materials available.

The meaning of such inscriptions long remained a mystery like that of others in dead languages still undeciphered. Among the latter Etruscan and Cretan (Fig. 10) are a sealed book to this day. The story of the Rosetta stone discloses the clues which have made it possible for scholars to decipher (Figs. 1, 5, and 18) lost languages. It is told in the following quotation from Griffith's helpful book, *The Story of Letters and Numbers:*

"There were strange stories and fictions about the learning of the Egyptians, so that for a long time men had a strong desire to get back a clear knowledge of the writings. They had nothing to go on; there were no word books or other helps. Then in 1799, by the best of good chances, a man in the French Army, working under Napoleon, saw an old stone in a wall at Rosetta on one of the branches of the river Nile, with three sorts of writing on it. One was the old Egyptian picture writing, which was the same as the writing on the walls of buildings; the second was another of which men had no knowledge, but the third was in Greek, clear and simple. The reading of this was no trouble to men of letters. From the Greek it was seen that the stone gave an account of a king named PTOLEMAIOS, and of the good things which he had done as a mark of his respect for the religion of Egypt. The last line of the Greek says that 'a copy of the writing is to be made on hard stone in the old writing of the men of religion, and in the writing of the country, and in Greek.' The year this was done was 196 B.C. So it was certain that the two strange writings were in Egyptian, but in different sorts of letters, and that the Greek gave the sense of the Egyptian.

"In the Greek, the name PTOLEMAIOS comes eight or nine times, sometimes by itself, and sometimes with the words LOVED OF PTAH in addition. Part of the top of the stone, where the picture writing comes, is broken off, but fourteen lines are there, and in these are five groups of letters or pictures with a line round them, having two long parallel sides and curved ends with a short upright line at one end. This seems to have been the Egyptian way of 'underlining' important words. Three of the groups are shorter than the other two, but the longer ones are started with the same, or almost the same, letters or pictures. So it seems probable that the outlined words are PTOLEMAIOS and PTOLEMAIOS LOVED OF PTAH. Ptah was one of the higher beings of the religion of Egypt.

"On other stones to the memory of the great dead, groups of letters are to be seen with the line round them, which makes us more certain that such outlined words are the names of kings and queens. One such name on an old stone was KLEOPATRA, the name of a queen who was living in Egypt two hundred years before the Cleopatra of Shakespeare's *Antony and Cleopatra*. . . .

"This much and a little more was the discovery of Dr. Thomas Young, an English man of science, who made, in addition, some attempt at reading the second form of the Egyptian writing on the stone. The reading of the picture writing in full was the work of J. F. Champollion, a Frenchman. He was able to do this as he had a good knowledge of the Coptic language. The Copts were, and still are, Egyptian Christians, and in the old days their language was Egyptian. In time small changes came about, as is natural. Their writing was in Greek, with seven special letters for sounds which are not in Greek. In Coptic churches to this day the books of religion are in Coptic, though only a small number, even of the readers, have knowledge of the language. It went out of common use five hundred years back. With the help of this language, Champollion was able to make out the other signs after the name PTOLM:S, and much more, for the Copts had word books giving Egyptian words in the Coptic writing."

The preceding account does not expose all the relevant circumstances which led to this discovery. The reader will find further details in *Science for the Citizen* (p. 1080). On his expedition to Egypt, Napoleon took with him a staff of savants, including some of the greatest men of science of that time. A discovery which may seem remote from *useful* knowledge, if we overlook the deplorable social consequences of arrogantly dismissing the cultural debt of any favored race or nation to the rest of mankind, was the direct outcome of encouraging research with a practical end in view. We may hope for greater progress in our knowledge of the evolution of languages when there are fewer scholars who cherish their trademark of gentlemanly uselessness, and more real *humanists* who, like Sweet, Jespersen, Ogden, or Sapir, modestly accept their responsibility as citizens, cooperating in the task of making language an instrument for peaceful collaboration between nations. A civilization which produces poison

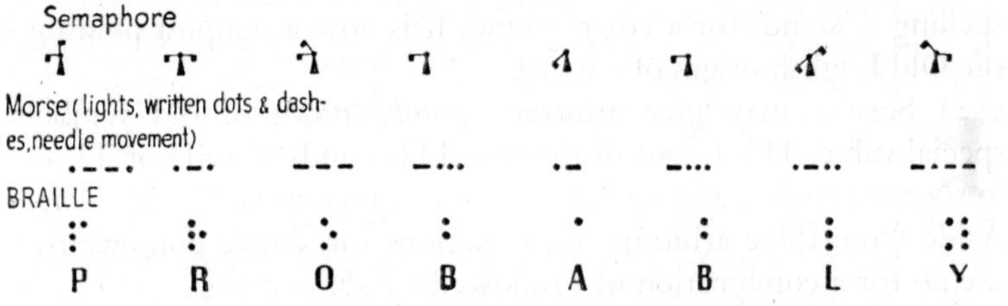

Semaphore

Morse (lights, written dots & dashes, needle movement)

BRAILLE

P R O B A B L Y

FIG. 19.—SEMAPHORE, MORSE AND BRAILLE CODES

(By kind permission of Mr. I. J. Pitman)

gas and thermite has no need for humanists who are merely grammarians. What we now need is the grammarian who is truly a humanist.

RATIONAL SPELLING

The fact that all alphabets come from one source has an important bearing on the imperfection of all existing systems of spelling. Although there are perhaps about a dozen simple consonants and half a dozen vowels approximately equivalent in most varieties of human speech, the range of speech sounds is rarely the same in closely related languages. Thus the Scots trilled *r*, the U in *guid*, and the throaty CH in "it's a braw bricht munelicht nicht the nicht" are absent in other Anglo-American dialects. When a preliterate community with a language of its own adopts the alphabetic symbols of an alien culture it will often happen that there will be no symbols for some of its sounds, or no sounds for some of the symbols available. English spelling illustrates what then happens.

1) Scribes may invent *new* letters. Thus Old English, like modern Icelandic (Fig. 31), had the two symbols þ (*thorn*) and ð (*etha*) for

the two sounds respectively represented by TH in *thin* and *then*. Our letter J is not in the Latin alphabet, which is the basis of Western European scripts. It has acquired different values in different languages. In Teutonic languages (e.g. in Norwegian and in German) it is equivalent to our Y in *Yule* (Scandinavian *Jul*). In French it is the peculiar consonant represented by S or SI in *pleasure, treasure, measure,* or *vision, incision, division.* In English it stands for a compound consonant made by saying *d* softly before the French J. The initial *w* (cf. *wait*) in Teutonic words was represented by *uu* (*oo-oo-ait*). Eventually the two *us* fused to form a single letter. In Welsh spelling *w* stands for a vowel sound. It is now a signpost pointing to the Old English origin of a word.

2) Scribes may give arbitrary *combinations* of old symbols a special value. This is true of the two TH sounds, the SH or TI sound in *short* or *nation,* and the NG in *singer* (as contrasted with *hunger*). Aside from these arbitrary combinations for simple consonants, we use *ch* for a combination of *t* followed by *sh*.

These combinations and their vagaries are valuable signposts for the home student. Neither of the sounds represented by *th* exists in Latin or French, the soft one (ð) exists only in Teutonic languages and the hard one (þ) only in Teutonic languages and in Greek, among languages which chiefly supply the roots of our vocabulary. The SH sound so spelt is Teutonic. The SH sound spelt as TI (e.g. *nation*) is always of French-Latin origin.

For this reason many words carry the hallmark of their origin. There is another way in which the irregularities of English spelling help us to recognize the source of a word. Pronunciation may change in the course of a hundred years, while writing lags behind for centuries. This explains the behavior of our capricious GH, which is usually silent and sometimes like an *f*. It survives from a period when the pronunciation of *light* was more like the Scots *licht*, in which there is a rasping sound represented by χ in phonetic symbols. In such words the earlier English conventional GH stands for a sound which was once common in the Teutonic languages, and is still common in German. When we meet GH, we know that the word in which it occurs is a word * of Teutonic origin; and it is a safe bet that the equivalent German word will correspond closely to the Scots form. Thus the German for light is *Licht*, for brought *brachte*, for eight *acht*, for night *Nacht*, for right *Recht* and for might *Macht*. English

* Notable exceptions are *haughty* (French *haut*) and *delight*.

is not the only language which has changed in this way. At one time the German W, now pronounced like an English V, stood for a softer sound, more like ours. So phonetic spelling would make it more difficult to recognize the meaning of *Wind, Wasser, und Wetter* (wind, water, and weather).

A third way in which spelling gets out of step with speech is connected with how grammar evolves. Like other languages in the same great Indo-European or Aryan family, English was once rich in endings like the *'s* in *father's*. Separate words have now taken over the function of such endings, as when we say *of my father*, instead of *my father's*. Having ceased to have any use, the endings have decayed; and because writing changes more slowly than speech, they have left behind in the written language, relics which have no existence in the spoken. This process of simplification, dealt with in Chapter III, has gone much further in English than in her sister languages. On this account written English is particularly rich in *vowel* endings which are not audible.

This way in which pronunciation changes in the course of time is responsible for spelling anomalies in most European languages. Two English examples illustrate it forcibly. On paper there is a very simple rule which tells us how to form the *plural* (i.e., the derivative we use when we speak of more than one object or person) of the overwhelming majority of modern English nouns. We add *-s*. There is also a simple paper rule which usually tells us how to form the *past* form of most English verbs. We add *-ed*, or *-d* (if the dictionary form ends in *-e*), as when we make the change from *part* to *parted*, or *love* to *loved*. Nowadays we rarely pronounce the final *-ED* unless it follows *d* or *t*. Till comparatively recently it was always audible as a separate syllable. Sometimes we still pronounce it as such in poetic drama. If we are church addicts, we may also do so in religious ritual. All of us do so when we speak of a belov*ed* husband or a learn*ed* wife. In Chaucer's English the plural *-s* was preceded by a vowel, and the combination *-es* was audibly distinct as a separate syllable. When fusion of the final *-s* of the plural, and *-ed* of the past with the preceding consonant of the noun or verb stem took place, *necessary* changes occurred. We pronounce *cats* as *kats* and *cads* as *kadz*. We pronounce *sobbed* as *sobd*, and *helped* as *helpt*. Thus the grammatical rules of English would be a little more complicated, if we spelt all words as we pronounce them. We should have a large new class of plurals in *-z*, and many more past forms of the verb ending, like *slept*, in *-t*.

The reason why these changes had to occur is that certain combinations of consonants are difficult to make, when we speak without effort. When we do speak without effort, we invariably replace them by others according to simple rules. Such rules can shed some light on the stage of evolution a language had reached when master printers, heads of publishing houses, or scholars settled its spelling conventions. One simple rule of this kind is that many consonants which combine easily with *s* or *t* do not combine easily with *z* or *d*, and vice versa. We can arrange them as follows:

With S
or T }   *p f k th* (þ) *ch* (tʃ) *sh* (ʃ) *"voiceless"*

With Z
or D }   *b v g th* (ð) *j* (dʒ) *si* (ʒ) *"voiced"*

This rule is easy to test. Compare, for instance, the way you pronounce *writhed* (ðd) and *thrived* (vd), with the way you pronounce (*without effort*) *pithed* (θt) and *laughed* (ft). In the same way, compare the pronunciation of the final consonants in *crabs* and *traps*, *crabbed* and *trapped*, or notice the difference between the final *-s* in *lives* and *wife's*.

Vowels illustrate sources of irregularity in the spelling conventions of European languages more forcibly than do the consonants, because Italic-Latin which bequeathed its alphabet to the West of Europe had a very narrow range of vowel sounds, for which five symbols suffice. This is one reason why Italian spelling is so much more regular than that of other European languages, except the newest Norwegian reformed *rettskrivning*. Another reason is that Italian pronunciation and grammar have changed little since Dante's time. In English dialects we have generally about twelve simple and about ten compound vowels (diphthongs) for which the five Roman vowel signs are supplemented by a Teutonic W and a Greek Y. The situation is much the same with most other European languages, except Spanish which stands close to Italian. Several devices are in use to deal with shortage of vowel symbols.

1) Introduction of new vowel symbols. Thus modern Norwegian (Fig. 32) has two, the ø of Danish and the å of Swedish. The Russian alphabet, based on the Greek, has eight instead of seven vowel symbols, of which only three correspond precisely to the Greek models.

2) Introduction of accents, such as the dots placed above *ö* or *ä* in

Swedish and German, or those used to distinguish the four French sounds, *e, é, è, ê.*

3) Use of combinations such as *aa* to distinguish the long *a* of *father* from the short *a* of *fat* in *bazaar* is specially characteristic of Dutch spelling. On this account Dutch words look rather long. The same plan (see table of vowels on p. 71) would meet all the needs of a reformed English spelling. As things stand we have only three combinations which we use consistently—*aw* (in *claw*), *ee* (in *meet*), and *oi* or *oy* (in *soil, joy*). The last is a signpost of Norman-French origin.

4) The more characteristically English trick of using a silent *e* after a succeeding consonant to distinguish the preceding vowel, as in *mad-made, Sam-same, pin-pine, win-wine.* A silent *h* may also lengthen the preceding vowel in German, as in our words *ah! eh! oh!*

5) The use of a double consonant to indicate that the foregoing vowel is short. German and the newest Norwegian spelling (1938) relies on this consistently.

From rhymes in poems, we have good reason to believe that English spelling was regular at the time of the Norman Conquest. The present chaos, especially with reference to the vowels, is partly due to the practice of Norman scribes when a large number of French words invaded English during the thirteenth and fourteenth centuries. This coincided more or less with a profound change in the pronunciation of English vowels, and the decay of endings. In other words, the spelling conventions we now use became current coinage at a time when the sound values of English words were in a state of flux. The Norman scribes were responsible for several important changes affecting the consonants as well as the vowels. They introduced J for a new sound which came with the Conquest. The Old English C became K. The symbols þ and ð for two sounds which do not occur in French disappeared in favor of TH and Y. After a time the Y (as in the solecism *ye olde tea shoppe*) acquired a new use, and TH served for both sounds. At a later date the breach between spelling and speech widened through the interference of classical scholars in the light of current and often mistaken views about word origin. Thus *debt* though derived directly from the French word *dette*, sucked in a silent *b* to indicate the common origin of both from the Latin *debitum*. For what regularities do exist we owe far more to the printers than to the scholars. Printing checked individual practices to which scribes—like stenographers—were prone, when the art of writing was still (like stenography) a learned profession.

ENGLISH CONSONANTS IN PHONETIC SCRIPT

1. b	as in bib	13. t	as in ten
2. d	" " did	14. v	" " vet
3. f	" " fed	15. w	" " wet
4. g	" " get	16. z	" " zest
5. h	" " hit	17. j = y	" " yet
6. k	" " kit	18. ʃ = sh	" " shin
7. l	" " lit	19. ʒ = si	" " vision
8. m	" " men	20. θ = th	" " thin
9. n	" " nib	21. ð = th	" " then
10. p	" " pit	22. ŋ = ng	" " sing
11. r	" " red	23. dʒ = j	" " jam
12. s	" " sit	24. tʃ = ch	" " chat

Even when two languages which share the same alphabet enjoy the benefit of a comparatively regular system of spelling as do Norwegian, German, and Spanish, many of the symbols have different values when we pass from one to another. So spelling is never a reliable guide to pronunciation of a foreign language. For this reason linguists have devised a reformed alphabet for use as a key to help us to pronounce words of any language with at least sufficient accuracy to make intelligible communication possible without recourse to personal instruction. In this international alphabet, sixteen of the consonant symbols (see above) have their *characteristic* English values common to European usage in so far as a specific sound usually corresponds to one alone. With these good European symbols are others which do not occur in the Latin alphabet. One of them, *j*, stands for the sound it represents (our initial Y) in Scandinavian languages and in German. Three of the supplementary ones are taken from the Greek, Irish, and Icelandic scripts (Fig. 11). The remainder are inventions.

In our table of English vowels in phonetic script, some of the individual symbols which stand for simple vowel sounds in other European languages occur only in compounds (diphthongs). Other symbols such as those which stand for the French nasal vowels do not occur at all. The majority of the consonant sounds of European languages are approximately alike. For that reason many of the consonant signs of different scripts exhibited on page 46 correspond with one another, and with the equivalent symbols of the international script devised for all nations. So the symbols for the consonants are

ENGLISH VOWELS IN PHONETIC SCRIPT

SIMPLE			DIPHTHONGS		
a = a	as in	h*a*t	ai = ei	as in	*Ei*nstein
a: = aa	" "	baz*aa*r	au = ow	" "	h*ow*
e = e	" "	bed	ei = ai	" "	b*ai*t
i = i	" "	b*i*d	eə = air	" "	p*air*
i: = ee	" "	m*ee*t	iə = ier	" "	p*ier*
ɔ = o	" "	h*o*t	ɔi = oi	" "	b*oi*l
ɔ: = au	" "	*au*ght	ou = oa	" "	m*oa*t
u = oo	" "	f*oo*t	ju = ew	" "	h*e̊w*
u: = ou	" "	b*oo*t			
ʌ = u	" "	c*u*t			
ə = er	" "	work*er*			
ə: = or	" "	w*or*ker			

less difficult to handle, and a few hours practice will suffice for proficiency in using them. With the help of the tables you can translate the following sentence, and thereafter write out others:

frm ðə teiblz əv vauəlz n kɔnsənənts ju ʃd bi eibl tə fɔ:m ə kliərə dʒʌdʒmint əbaut ðə tʃi:f ri:znz fə θʌrə meʒəz if wi wɔnt ə hapi səl(j)u:ʃn əv auə preznt speliŋ difikltiz.

·səiʇlnɔᴉɟɟᴉp ᵷuᴉllǝds ʇuǝsǝɹd ɹno ɟo uoᴉʇnlos ʎddɐɥ ɐ ʇuɐʍ ǝʍ ɟᴉ sǝɹnsɐǝɯ ɥᵷnoɹoɥʇ ɹoɟ suosɐǝɹ ɟǝᴉɥɔ ǝɥʇ ʇnoqɐ ʇuǝɯᵷpnɾ ɹǝɹɐǝlɔ ɐ ɯɹoɟ oʇ ǝlqɐ ǝq plnoɥs noʎ sʇuɐuosuoɔ puɐ slǝʍoʌ ɟo sǝlqɐʇ ǝɥʇ ɯoɹℲ

Because the same symbols may have different values in different languages—Z stands for θ in Spanish, and for *ts* in German—the larger dictionaries use phonetic alphabets in which a symbol represents one sound and one only. For each word listed the phonetic spelling is printed side by side with the ordinary one. Once you have mastered the key to this phonetic spelling you know how to pronounce the foreign word, however fantastic its spelling may be. If your dictionary uses the *International Phonetic Alphabet* you may find at the beginning a list incorporating the two on this and the preceding page. With the help of this key you are able to pronounce the following French words even if you do not know any French:

bête	(bɛːt)		commerce	(kɔmɛrs)
bord	(bɔːr)		fédéré	(federe)
chaine	(ʃɛːn)		plaine	(plɛːn)
clocher	(klɔʃe)		prix	(pri)
		toute	(tut)	

EYE AND GESTURE LANGUAGE IN THE WORLD TODAY

A bird's-eye view of visual language, in contradistinction to that of the ear, would be distorted if it took in nothing but the evolution of signs used in ancient stone inscriptions, manuscripts or modern books, and newspapers. Visual communication may be of two kinds, transient or persistent. The first includes gesture which reinforces daily speech, and the several types of gestural language respectively used for communication between deaf and dumb people, or in military and naval signaling. Signaling may be of two types. Like deaf and dumb gesture language, it may depend on human movements which recall symbols used in alphabetic writing. Signaling by flag displays based on codes is like logographic writing. The signs used by bookies or hotel porters are a logographic gesture script.

Codes used in telegraphy overlap the territories of audible communication, visual communication which is transient, and visual communication for permanent record. Like the Ogam script, it depends on the alphabet; and, since each alphabet symbol is made up of long or short strokes like prolonged or sharp taps, the same system serves equally well for recognition by eye, ear, or tactile sensation. A two-stroke system of this kind is a mechanical necessity dictated by the design of the first telegraphs to take advantage of the fact that a magnetic needle turns right or left in accordance with the direction of an electric current. The inventors of the telegraphic codes lived in a less leisurely age than the Ogam stonemasons, and took full advantage of the possibility of varying the *order* in which it is possible to arrange a limited number of strokes of two different types (Fig. 19). Like Ogam script a telegraphic code is suitable for purely tactile recognition by the blind, who were cut off from access to the written record when parchment, papyrus, or paper took the place of stone, wax, or clay tablets as writing material. In practice, the Braille script, based on different arrangements of raised dots, is more satisfactory, because it takes up less space.

Within the narrower limits of the permanent record different types of scripts may serve different ends. Apart from cryptographic scripts devised for secret inventions and recipes, political messages or military dispatches, we can broadly distinguish two types. In books, periodicals, and correspondence, the convenience of the *reader* is the main desideratum, and ready *visual recognition* is all-important. What is most important about a script for habitual and *personal* use is whether it is adapted to rapid *transcription*. For this reason an increasing proportion of transcription in commerce, law courts, and conference is taken down in scripts which are not based on the alpha-

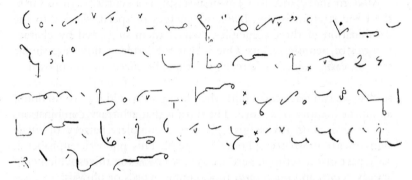

FIG. 20.—FACSIMILE NOTE IN PITMAN'S SHORTHAND BY BERNARD SHAW

Mr. Shaw has told us that much of his writing has been done in trains, and that practically all of it is written in shorthand for subsequent transcription by a secretary typist. The specimen of his shorthand reproduced here reads: "This the way I write. I could of course substitute (here follows an abbreviation) with an apparent gain in brevity, but as a matter of fact it takes longer to contract. Writing shorthand with the maximum of contraction is like cutting telegrams: unless one is in constant practice it takes longer to devise the contractions than to write in full; and I now never think of contracting except by ordinary logograms."

bet, and have been designed for speedy writing. For such purposes ready recognition by anyone except the writer is of secondary usefulness.

Roman writers of the age of Cicero were alive to the inconvenience of alphabetic writing from this point of view, and used various abbreviations for particles and other common elements of speech. A consistent system of shorthand is an English invention. The first attempt was made by Timothy Bright, who dedicated his book called *Characterie, the art of short, swift and secret writing* to Elizabeth in 1588. Timothy Bright's system, which was very difficult to memorize, paved the way for others, notably Willis's *Art of Stenography* (1602). In 1837, when Sir Isaac Pitman perfected what is still a very successful shorthand script "for the diffusion of knowledge among the middle classes of society," about two hundred different sorts of shorthand had been put forward. Shorthand as we know it today is the product of many experiments in which some of the most enlightened linguists of the seventeenth and eighteenth centuries took a hand. It is the fruit of close study of the merits or demerits of different systems of writing and typography in general use.

Modern shorthand, like Japanese script, is a synthesis. In so far as the basic stratum is alphabetic, advantages of speed are due to the combination of three principles, two of them suggested by characteristics of Semitic scripts. One is that the letter symbols are simple strokes, easily joined. We recognize them by *direction* as opposed to *shape*. A second is that the vowels are detached from the consonants, so that we can leave them out, when doing so would lead to no doubt about the identity of a word. The third is that arbitrary combinations of consonants or vowels give place to a complete battery of *single* signs in a consistently phonetic system. This phonetic alphabet is only part of the setup. There are *syllable signs* for affixes which constantly recur, and *logograms* for common words or phrases.

No tracts about the Real Presence, treatises on marginal utility and table turning, or expositions of the Hegelian dialectic and the Aryan virtues are accessible in Morse code or shorthand editions. Still, students of language planning for the Age of Plenty have something to learn from the work of those who have contributed to such inventions and from the efforts of those who have worked to make the written record available to the deaf and blind. Of the two foremost pioneers of language planning in the seventeenth century, one, George Dalgarno, was the inventor of a deaf-and-dumb alphabet; the other, Bishop Wilkins, put forward an early system of phonetic shorthand. One result of early controversies over shorthand systems was a lively interest in the defects of spelling, and hence in the sound-composition of words. An evolutionary attitude toward language was not possible until students of language began to study how the sound of a word changes in the course of a few generations.

To organize prosperity on a world-wide scale, we need to supplement the languages of local speech communities with an international medium of discourse. Whether such a world-wide language will eventually displace all others, we cannot say. What is certain is that such a change will not happen till many centuries have elapsed. In the meantime, the most we can aim at is to make every citizen of the Age of Plenty bilingual, that is to say, equally fluent in a home language, and in the common language of world citizenship, or of some unit larger than the sovereign states of the present day. Hardly less important is another need. Few but experts realize the babel of scripts in the modern world. Many of them are ill suited for their purpose, laborious to learn and space-consuming. Nonexploitive collaboration between East and West requires international adoption of the Roman alphabet, supplemented where necessary by additional symbols. Lenin said this to comrade Agamaly-Ogly, president of the Central Pan-Soviet Committee of National Alphabets: *Romanization, there lies the great revolution of the East.*

Regularization of script on a world-wide scale is alike prerequisite to liquidation of illiteracy in the Orient and worthwhile spelling reform in the West. Spelling reform is long overdue; but it is not a purely national affair, nor merely the task of devising consistent rules based on a priori principles. It must necessarily be a compromise between conflicting claims—recognition of language affinities in the form of the written word, preservation of structural uniformities, such as our plural -*s*, which transgress phonetic proprieties, the disadvantage of an unwieldy battery of signs and the undesirability of setting up an arbitrary norm without due regard to dialect differences.*

FURTHER READING

GRIFFITH	*The Story of Letters and Numbers.*
LLOYD JAMES	*Our Spoken Language.*
JENSEN	*Geschichte der Schrift.*
KARLGREN	*Sound and Symbol in Chinese.*
RIPMAN	*English Phonetics.*
TAYLOR	*The Alphabet.*
THOMPSON	*The ABC of our Alphabet.*

* The *International Institute of Intellectual Co-operation* has published a report (1934), prefaced by Jespersen, on the promotion of the use of the Roman alphabet among peoples with unsuitable scripts or no script at all.

CHAPTER III

Accidence—The Table Manners of Language

MEN built hotels for celestial visitors before they devoted much ingenuity to their own housing problems. The temple observatories of the calendar priests, and the palaces of their supposedly sky-born rulers, are among the earliest and are certainly the most enduring monuments of architecture. In the dawn of civilization, when agriculture had become an established practice, the impulse to leave a record in building and in decoration went hand in hand with the need for a storehouse of nightly observations on the stars and a record of the flocks and crops. So writing of some sort is the signal that civilization has begun. The beginning of writing is also the beginning of our firsthand knowledge of language.

Our fragmentary information about the speech habits of mankind extends over about four thousand of the eighty thousand or more years since true speech began. We know nothing about human speech between the time when the upright ape first used sounds to co-operate in work or defense, and the time when people began to write. It is therefore unwise to draw conclusions about the birth of language from the very short period which furnishes us with facts. We can be certain of one thing. If we had necessary information for tracing the evolution of human speech in relation to human needs and man's changing social environment, we should not approach the task of classifying sounds as the orthodox grammarian does. The recognition of words as units of speech has grown hand in hand with the elaboration of script. In the preliterate millennia of the human story, social needs which prompted men to take statements to pieces would arise only in connection with difficulties of young children, and through contacts with migrant or warring tribes. We can be quite sure that primitive man used gestures liberally to convey his meaning. So a classification of the elements of language appropriate to a primitive level of human communication might plausibly take shape in a fourfold division as follows:*

a) *Substantives*, or individual words used for distinct objects or events which can be indicated by pointing at things, i.e., such as our words *dog* or *thunder*, and at a later stage, for qualities of a group, such as *red* or *noisy*.

b) *Vocatives*, or short signals used to call forth some response, such as our words *where? stop, run, come, pull!* and names of individuals.

c) *Demonstratives*, or gesture substitutes which direct the attention of the listener to a particular point in the situation, i.e., *that, here, behind, in front*.

d) *Incorporatives*, or recitative combinations of sound used in ritual incantations without any recognition of separate elements corresponding to what we should call *words*.

From a biological point of view, it is reasonable to guess that the last antedate anything we can properly call speech, that they take us back to the monkey chorus of sundown when the mosquitoes are about, that they persisted long after the recognition of separate words emerged out of active co-operation in hunting, fishing, or building, and that they were later refined into sequences of meaningful words by a process as adventitious as the insertion of the vocables into such a nursery rhyme sequence as "ena, mena, mina, mo, catch a nigger by his toe. . . ." Perhaps we can recognize the first separate vocables in warning signals of the pack leader. If so, the second class,

* Grammarians have oscillated between two views. According to one, primitive speech was made up of discrete monosyllables like Chinese. Under the influence of Jespersen and his disciples, the pendulum has now swung to the opposite extreme, and primitive speech is supposed to be holophrastic, i.e., without discrete words. This singsong view, like nonsense written at one time about so-called *incorporative* languages (e.g. those of the Mexicans or Greenland Esquimaux), and now disproved by the work of Sapir, is essentially a concoction of the study. It is the product of academic preoccupation with the works of poets or other forms of sacred composition. Practical biologists or psychologists have to give consideration: (a) to how children, travelers, or immigrants learn a language without recourse to interpreters and grammar books, (b) to how human speech differs from the chatter of monkeys or the mimetic exploits of parrots. In contradistinction to such animal noises, human speech is above all an instrument of co-operation in productive *work* or mutual defense, and as such is *partly* made up of discrete signals for *individual* actions and manipulation of *separate* objects. To this extent (see p. 37) the recognition of some sounds as *words* is presumably as old as the first flint instruments. Conversely, other formal elements which we also call *words* are products of grammatical comparison. They do not emerge from the speech matrix before the written record compels closer analysis.   (EDITOR)

or *vocatives,* are the oldest sound elements of co-operation in mutually beneficial activities. What seems almost certain is this: Until writing forced people to examine more closely the significance of the sounds they used, the recognition of words was confined to sounds which they could associate with gesture.

Here we are on speculative ground. It will not be possible to get any further light on the early evolution of speech till anthropologists have made more progress in researches for which Professor Malinowski has made an eloquent plea:*

"The point of view of the philologist who deals only with remnants of dead languages must differ from that of the ethnographer who, deprived of the ossified, fixed data of inscriptions, has to rely on the living reality of spoken language *in fluxu.* The former has to reconstruct the general situation, i.e., the culture of a past people, from the extant statements; the latter can study directly the conditions and situations characteristic of a culture and interpret the statements through them. Now I claim that the ethnographer's perspective is the one relevant and real for the formation of fundamental linguistic conceptions and for the study of the life of languages. . . . For language in its origins has been merely the free, spoken sum total of utterances such as we find now in a savage tongue."

Study of speech in backward communities from this point of view is still in its infancy. Many years must elapse before it influences the tradition of language teaching in our schools and universities. Meanwhile, the infant science of language carries a load of unnecessary intellectual luggage from its parental preoccupation with sacred texts or ancient wisdom. Grammar, as the classification of speech and writing habits, did not begin because human beings were curious about their social equipment. What originally prompted the study of Semitic (p. 426), Hindu (p. 412)—and to a large extent that of European—grammar was the requirements of ritual. Though the impact of biological discovery has now forced European scholars to look at language from an evolutionary point of view, academic tradition has never outgrown the limitations imposed on it by the circumstances of its origin.

Modern European grammar began about the time when the Protestant Reformation was in progress. Scholars were busy producing an open Bible for the common people, or translations of texts by the political apologists of the Greek city state. Those who did so were

* See *The Meaning of Meaning,* by C. K. Ogden and I. A. Richards.

primarily interested in finding tricks of expression corresponding to Greek and Latin models in modern European languages. Usually they had no knowledge of non-European languages, and, if they also knew languages now placed in the Semitic group, gained their knowledge by applying the classical yardstick. It goes without saying that they did not classify ways of using words as they would have done if they had been interested in finding out how English has changed since the time of Alfred the Great. Since then a language, which once had many of the most characteristic features of Latin or Greek, has changed past recognition. It now shares some of the most remarkable peculiarities of Chinese.

What schools used to teach as English grammar was really an introduction to the idiosyncrasies of Latin. It was not concerned with the outstanding characteristics of the English language; and most educationists in America or England now condemn time wasted in the mental confusion resulting from trying to fit the tricks of our own terse idiom into this foreign mold. Without doubt learning grammar is not of much help to a person who wants to write modern English. Nonetheless, the so-called English grammar of thirty years ago had its use. Other European languages which belong to the same great Indo-European family as Bible English and Latin and Greek, have not traveled so far on the road which English has traversed. So knowledge of old-fashioned grammar did make it a little easier to learn *some* peculiarities of French, German, or other languages which are still used. Anyone who starts to learn one of them without some knowledge of grammatical terms meets a large class of unnecessary difficulties. The proper remedy for this is not to go back to grammar of the old-fashioned type, but to get a more general grasp of how English resembles and differs from other languages, what vestiges of speech habits characteristic of its nearest neighbors persist in it, and what advantages or disadvantages result from the way in which it has diverged from them. To do this we shall need to equip ourselves with some technical terms. They are almost indispensable if we want to learn foreign languages.

HOW WORDS GROW

None of us needs to be told that we cannot write a foreign language, or even translate from one with accuracy, by using a dictionary or learning its contents by heart. From a practical point of view, we can define grammar as the rules we need to know *before we can use a dictionary with profit*. So we shall take the dictionary as our foundation stone in this chapter and the next. We have already seen that dictionaries of languages do not contain all vocables we commonly use. They include certain classes of *derivative* * words, and exclude others. Thus an ordinary English dictionary which contains *behave* and *behavior*, does not list *behaved, behaves*, or *behaving*. The part of grammar called *accidence* consists of rules for detecting how to form such derivatives and how they affect the meaning of a dictionary word which shares the same root. Our first task must therefore be to recall (p. 38) how single words can *grow*.

First of all, they can do so by fusing with one another or with *meaningful* affixes:

    a) Because the meaning of the *compound word* (e.g. *brickyard*) so formed is sufficiently suggested by the ordinary meaning of its separate parts in a given context. This is a trick specially characteristic of Teutonic languages, Greek, and Chinese.

    b) Because two native words constantly occur in the same context and get glued together through slipshod pronunciation, as in the shortened forms *dont, wont, cant, shant* for *do not, will not, can not, shall not*, as also *don* (= do on) and *doff* (= do off).

    c) Because an affix (p. 38) *borrowed* from another language is attached to them, as the Latin *ante-* (before) is used in *antenatal clinic*, or the Greek *anti-* (against) in *anti-fascist, anti-comintern*, and *anti*-anything-else-which-we-do-not-like.

It is useful to distinguish fusion due to speech habits, i.e., (*b*) from fusion associated with meaning, i.e., (*a*) and (*c*). The word *agglutination* refers to the former, i.e., to fusion arising from *context and pronunciation without regard to meaning*. Once fusion has begun another process begins to work. The meaning like the form of a word part becomes blurred. People get careless about the meaning of an affix. We expect a word to end (or to begin) in the same way, when we have made a habit of using similar words with the same affix in a similar *context*. This leads to a habit of tacking on the same affix to new words without regard to its original meaning. Having

---

    * It is often impossible to say what is root and what is affix, but many English words can be *derived* by adding affixes like *-s, -ed* or *-ing* to the dictionary form. In what follows the Editor suggests that we should speak of them as derivatives of the latter. As explained in the footnote on page 21, this is not precisely the way in which linguists use the word *derivative*.

made a word *mastodon*, we add the *-s* of *mastodons* because we are used to treating animals in this way.

What grammarians call *analogical extension* includes this process of extending the use of an affix by analogy with pre-existing words built up in the same way. Children and immigrants (see p. 161), as well as native adults, take a hand in the way languages change for better or for worse. For instance, an American or British child who is accustomed to saying *I caught*, when he means that he has made his *catch*, may also say *the eggs haught* for *the eggs hatched;* or, being more accustomed to adding *-ed*, may say *I catched* for *I caught*. This process is immensely important (see p. 197) in building up new words or in changing old ones. We should, therefore, recognize its limitations at the outset. Analogical extension may explain what is responsible for the origin of the *majority* of word derivatives of a particular type. It cannot explain how the habit of building them up *began*.

People who make dictionaries do not leave out all derivatives formed according to simple rules. The reason why some derivatives of the word *bake*, such as *bakehouse, baker*, or *bakery* are in English dictionaries, while *bakes, baking*, or *baked* are not, has nothing to do with whether the rules for adding *-house*, *-er*, or *-ery* are more easy to apply than the rules for adding *-s, -ing*, or *-(e)d*. We can tack the ending *-er*, now common to an enormous class of Danish, German, and English vocables, on the dictionary words *write, fish, sing*, or *teach;* but we can add the suffix *-ed* only to the second (cf. *wrote, fished, sang*, or *taught*). Since the way in which the meaning of a word is affected by both affixes is obvious, the fact that *-er* derivatives are in our dictionaries, and that we do not find the *-ed* derivatives in them, shows that people who compile dictionaries do not decide to leave out a vocable because the meaning of the root or dictionary form and that of its affix are equally clear. The real reason has to do with the original job the grammarians had to undertake. Broadly speaking, it is this: vocables are put in grammar books instead of in dictionaries because they correspond to the class of derivatives most common in Latin or Greek.

Grammarians call such derivatives, or their affixes, *flexions*. Flexion is of two kinds, *internal* (root inflexion) and *external* (affixation). The change from *bind* to *bound*, or *foot* to *feet* illustrates one type of internal flexion, i.e., root vowel change. External flexion, or true flexion, which is more common, is simply change of meaning by affixes, like the -*ed* in *baked*. We do not speak of affixes as flexions when they are recognizable as borrowed elements or relics of separate native words, as in the enormous class of English derivatives with the common affix -*ly* in *happily* or *probably*, corresponding to -*lich* in German, -*lijk* in Dutch, -*lik* in Swedish, -*lig* in Danish or Norwegian. Whether derivatives formed by adding affixes are called flexions depends largely on whether they correspond to derivatives formed from a root with the same meaning in Latin or Greek.

According to the way in which derivatives modify its meaning, or are dictated by the context of, a root, grammarians refer to different classes most characteristic of the sacred Indo-European languages, i.e., Latin, Greek, and Sanskrit, as flexions of *number, tense, person, comparison, voice, case, mood*, and *gender*. We can classify root words of Latin, Greek, and Sanskrit according to which of two or more classes of these derivatives they form. Thus *nouns* and *pronouns* have number and case flexion; *verbs* have tense, person, voice, and mood flexions. Words which do not have such derivatives are called *particles*. The distinction between these classes would be meaningless, if we tried to apply it to Chinese. For reasons which we shall now see, it is almost meaningless when we try to classify English words in the same way.

The number of flexional derivatives in the older languages of the Indo-European family is enormous. In English comparable derivatives are relatively few, and are chiefly confined to flexions of number, time, person, and comparison. Formation of the derivative *houses* (external) or *lice* (internal) from *house* or *louse* illustrates flexion of number. The derivatives *bound* (internal) and *loved* (external) from *bind* and *love* illustrate tense flexion. Person flexion turns up only in the addition of -*s* to a verb, e.g. the change as from *bind* to *binds*. Comparison is the derivation of *happier* and *happiest*, or *wiser* and *wisest*, from *happy* and *wise*. English has a few relics of case (e.g. *he, him, his*), and a trace of mood (p. 108) flexion. Flexion of gender has disappeared altogether, and voice flexion never existed in our own language.

Knowing the names for the flexions does not help us to speak or to write correct English, because few survive, and we learn these few in childhood. What it does help us to do is to learn languages in which the flexional system of the old Indo-European languages has decayed far less than in English or in its Eastern counterpart, modern

Persian. The study of how they have arisen, and of circumstances which have contributed to their decay, also helps us to see characteristics to incorporate in a world medium which is easy to learn without being liable to misunderstanding.

FLEXION OF PERSON

It is best to start with flexions of person and tense, because we have more information about the way in which such flexions have arisen or can arise than we have about the origin of number, case, gender, and comparison. Person flexion is probably the older of the two. Since something of the same sort is cropping up again (p. 85), it is easy to guess how it began. Unlike tense, voice, number, and comparison, flexion of person is absolutely useless in many modern European languages. All that remains of it in our own language is the final *s* of a verb which follows certain words such as *he, she, it,* or the names of *single* things, living beings, groups or qualities, e.g. in such more or less intelligible statements as *he bakes, she types,* or *love conquers all.* The derivative forms bake*s*, type*s*, or conquer*s* are dictated by *context* in accordance with the conventions of our language. The final -*s* adds nothing necessary to the meaning of a statement.

This flexion is our only surviving relic of a much more complicated system in the English of Alfred the Great, and still extant in most European languages. To understand its importance in connection with correct usage in many other languages, we have to distinguish a class of words called *personal pronouns.* Since the number of them is small, this is not difficult. Excluding the *possessive* forms *mine, ours,* etc., the personal pronouns are: *I* or *me, we* or *us, you, he* or *him, she* or *her, it,* and *they* or *them. I* or *me* and *we* or *us* are modestly called pronouns of the *first* person, *you* is the English pronoun of the *second* person, and *he* or *him, she* or *her, it, they* or *them* are pronouns of the *third* person. The pronouns of the first person stand for, or include, the person making a statement. The pronoun of the second person stands for the person or persons whom we address, and the pronouns of the third person stand for the persons or things about whom or about which we make a statement or ask a question.

To make room for all the flexions of person in foreign languages, we have to go a stage further in classifying pronouns. If the statement is about *one* person or thing, the pronoun which stands for it is *singular;* if it is about more than one person or thing, the pronoun is said to be *plural.* Thus *I* and *me* are pronouns of the first person singular; *we* and *us* pronouns of first person plural. *He* and *him, she* and *her,* together with *it,* are pronouns of the third person singular, and *they* or *them* are pronouns of the third person plural. In modern English or, as we ought to say and as we shall say in future when we want to distinguish it from Bible English, in *Anglo-American,* there is only one pronoun of the second person singular or plural. In the Bible English of *Mayflower* days there were two. *Thou* and *thee* were the pronouns of the second person singular, and *ye* was for converse with more than one person. *Thou* is *de rigueur* in churches as the pronoun of address for a threefold deity. Orthodox members of the Society of Friends use *thee* when speaking to one another. When ordinary people still used thou, there was another flexion of person. They said *thou speakest,* in contradistinction to *you speak* or *he speaks.*

Classification of the personal pronouns in this way would be quite pointless if everybody used Anglo-American. We can appreciate its usefulness if we compare Anglo-American and French equivalents on page 22. The simple English rule for the surviving *-s* flexion is this: we use it only when a word such as *speak, love, type, write, bake,* or *conquer* follows *he, she,* or *it,* or the name of any *single* person, quality, group, or thing which can be replaced by *it.* The example on page 22 shows that there are *five* different personal forms of the French *verb,* or class to which such words as *love* belong. In more old-fashioned languages the verb root has all six different derivatives corresponding to the singular and plural forms of all the personal pronouns or to the names they can replace. Thus the corresponding forms of the equivalent Italian verb are:

(io)	do	I give	(noi)	diamo	we give
(tu)	dai	thou givest	(voi)	date	you give
(egli)	dà	he gives	(essi)	danno	they give

The Danish equivalent for all these derivative forms of the Italian root *da-* present in our words *donation* or *dative* is *giver.* This is just the same whether the Danish (or Norwegian)equivalent of *I, we, thou, you, he, she, it,* or *they* stands in front of, or as in a question, immediately after it. Since Danes, who produce good beer and good bacon, have no personal flexions, and since Benjamin Franklin could discuss electricity with only one, it is not obvious that the five of Voltaire's French are really necessary tools. If we do not wish to encourage the accumulation of unnecessary linguistic luggage, it is therefore instructive to know how people collected them. The first step is to go back to the common ancestor of French and Italian. The table on page 86 furnishes a clue.

One thing the table exhibits is this. It was not customary to use the personal pronoun equivalent to *I, he, we,* etc., in the older languages of the Indo-European family. The ending attached to the verb really had a use. *It had to do the job now done by putting the pronoun in front of it.* So the ending in modern descendants of such languages is merely the relic of what once did the job of the pronoun. This leads us to ask how the ending came to do so. A clue to a satisfactory answer is also in the table, which exposes a striking family resemblance among the endings of the older verbs of the Indo-European family. Of the five older representatives, four have the suffix *MI* for the form of the verb which corresponds to the first person singular.* This at once reminds you of the English pronoun *me,* which replaces the first person *I* when it comes after the verb in a plain statement. Our table (p. 87) of corresponding pronouns of several languages placed in the Indo-European group, encourages us to believe that the correspondence between the English pronoun *ME* and the ending *MI* is not a mere accident.

The meaning of this coincidence would be more difficult to understand if it were not due to a process which we can see at work in Anglo-American at the present day. When we speak quickly, we do not say *I am, you are, he is.* We say *I'm, you're, he's;* and Bernard Shaw spells them as the single words *Im, youre, hes.* The fact that the agglutinating, or gluing on of the pronoun, takes place in this order need not bother us, because the habit of invariably putting the pronoun before the verb is a new one. In Bible English we commonly meet with constructions such as *thus spake he.* Even in modern speech we say *sez you.* In certain circumstances this inversion generally occurs in other Teutonic languages as in Bible English. It was once a traffic rule of the Aryan family; and it is still customary in one group of Aryan languages. This group, called the Celtic family, furnishes suggestive evidence for the belief that the personal flexions which do the work of the absent pronoun in

---

* The exception is Latin with the terminal *-O*. The Latin I is *ego,* shortened in Italian to *io,* Spanish *yo.*

THE EVOLUTION OF IMPERSONALITY IN VERBS

A. FOSSIL LANGUAGES *

SANSKRIT	OLD PERSIAN	GREEK	OLD SLAV	LATIN	BIBLICAL ENGLISH
dadami	dadami	didomi	dami	do	I give
dadasi	dadahi	didos	dasi	das	thou givest
dadati	dadaiti	didoti	dasti	dat	he (etc.) giveth
dadmas	dademahi	didomes	damu	damus	we give
datta	dasta	didote	daste	datis	ye give
dadati	dadenti	didonti	dadanti	dant	they give

B. LIVING LANGUAGES

ITALIAN	FRENCH	ICELANDIC	DUTCH	ANGLO-AMERICAN	DANISH
io do	je donne	eg gef	ik geef	I give	jeg giver
tu dai	tu donnes	thu gefur	jij geeft	you give	du giver
egli dà	il donne	hann gefur	hij geeft	he gives	han giver
noi diamo	nous donnons	vjer gefum	wij geven	we give	vi giver
voi date	vous donnez	thjer gefith	jullie geven	you give	de giver
essi danno	ils donnent	their gefa	zij geven	they give	de giver

* The spelling conventions follow Bopp, *Vergleich. Gramm.*, vol. 2, p. 334.

FAMILY RESEMBLANCE OF ARYAN PRONOUNS

		SCOTS GAELIC	RUSSIAN	ITALIAN *	LATIN	EARLY GREEK *	ICELANDIC
I			YA	IO	EGO	EGO	EG *or* JEG
ME	Acc.	MI	MENYA	ME	ME	ME	MIG
	Dat.		MNE		MIHI	MOI	MJER
THOU			TI	TU	TU	TU	THU
THEE	Acc.	TU	TEBYA	TE	TE	TE	THIG
	Dat.		TEBE		TIBI	TOI	THJER
WE			MI		NOS	NO	VJER
US	Acc.	SINN	NAS	NOI			OSS
	Dat.		NAM		NOBIS	NON	

* The Italian forms are the stressed ones (p. 363). The later Greek forms of *tu, te, toi* were *su, se, soi*. The Greek NO, NON are dual forms (p. 97). The corresponding plural forms in Doric Greek were *hemes, heme, hemin*. The first is comparable to the Russian MI and to the first person plural terminal of the Greek, Latin, or Sanskrit verb.

Latin or Greek were originally separate pronouns placed after the verb.

The Celtic languages, which include Welsh, Gaelic, Irish, and Breton, have several peculiarities (p. 421) which distinguish them from all other members of the Indo-European group. In Celtic languages, words which are equivalent to a Latin "verb" may or may not have personal flexions. In Old Irish, *as*, which corresponds to our *is* (spelt in the same way in Erse, i.e., modern Irish) has two forms, one used with the pronoun *placed after it*, and a contracted form corresponding to our *I'm* (= *'tis me who*) in which we can recognize the agglutinated part as we still recognize the *not* in *dont, shant, wont*, or *cant*. The two forms are in the table on page 88.

We must not conclude that the Celtic verb is more primitive than the Sanskrit. Sir George Grierson has shown that modern Indic dialects have sloughed off person flexions and subsequently replaced them by new pronoun suffixes. Since pronouns are the most con-

| | | OLD IRISH | | |
LITHUANIAN	SANSKRIT	Extended Form	Contracted	BIBLE ENGLISH
esmi	asmi	as me	am	I *am*
essi	asi	as tu	at	thou *art*
esti	asti	as é	as *or* is	he *is*

servative words of the Indo-European fund of vocables, the result
may be very much like the preceding inflected form. The English
am and *is* do not come directly from the speech of the early Britons.
Our English IS is one form of a common Aryan root, IS, ES, or
AS, which also turns up in Greek and in Latin, as in Sanskrit and
Lithuanian. In Welsh it is not inflected when spelt ŒS. There must
have been several primitive Aryan root words corresponding to what
grammarians call "parts of the verb *to be*" (in English, *am, is, are,
was, were, be, being, been*). The English or Erse *am* or *im* is an
agglutinative contraction from the ES root, like the German *sind*
(Latin *sunt*). The BE-BA-BO-BU root of *being* and *been* turns up
again in Russian, Welsh, or Gaelic, and in the German and Dutch
ich bin or *ik ben* (I am). The AR-ER root which turns up in *are*,
is the single uninflected form *er* of the Danish or Norwegian
"present tense" given above. We meet it again in the Latin imperfect
(p. 93). What is most characteristic of the Teutonic group is the
WAS-WAR root corresponding to our English *was* and *were*.

The modern forms of the verb *to be* in languages most closely
allied to English are in the table below. Those of languages nearest to
French are on page 176. If we go back to Old English, to Old Norse,
and to the earliest known Teutonic language, which is the Gothic of
the Bible translated by Bishop Ulfilas somewhere about A.D. 350, the
sharp contrast between the forms used in contemporary Teutonic
and Romance languages is blurred. The table on page 90 shows this.

Agglutination of pronouns to other words is a very characteristic
feature of the Celtic languages. In all of them pronouns also form
contracted derivatives by fusion with *directives* (prepositions), i.e.,
such words as *with, in, to, from*. Welsh has two forms of the first
personal pronoun, *mi* and *fi*, recognizable in corresponding personal
flexions of the prepositions, e.g.:

| i (*to* or *into*) | + mi | = | *im* (to me) |
| at (*to* or *toward*) | + fi | = | *ataf* (to me) |

TEUTONIC *BE* VERB

ENGLISH	GOTHIC	OLD ENGLISH	GERMAN	DUTCH	SWEDISH	DANISH
I *am*	im	am *or* beo	ich bin	ik ben	jag ⎱ är	jeg ⎱ er
thou *art*	is	arth " bist	du bist	jij bent	Du ⎰	Du ⎰
he *is*	ist	is " bith	er ist	hij is	han	han
we ⎱	sijum	⎰	wir sind	wij ⎱	vi ⎱	vi ⎱
you ⎰ *are*	sijuth	sint " beoth	ihr seid	jullie ⎰ zijn	Ni ⎰ äro	De ⎰ var
they ⎰	sind	⎱	sie sind	zij ⎰	de ⎰	de ⎰
I *was*	was	weas	ich war	ik ⎱	jag ⎱	jeg ⎱
thou *wert*	wast	waere	du warst	jij ⎰ was	Du ⎰ var	Du ⎰ var
he *was*	was	waes	er war	hij ⎰	han	han
we ⎱	wesum		wir waren	wij ⎱	vi ⎱	vi ⎱
you ⎰ *were*	wesuth	waeron	ihr wart	jullie ⎰ waren	Ni ⎰ voro	De ⎰ var
they ⎰	wesun		sie waren	zij ⎰	de ⎰	de ⎰
TO BE	wisan	wesan *or* beon	zu sein	te zijn	att vara	at vaere
BEING	wisands	wesende *or* beonde	seiend	zijnd	vaerende	varrende
BEEN	wisans	gewesen	gewesen	geweest	varit	vaert
BE	sijais	wes *or* beo	sei	zij	var	vaer
Imper. sing.						

FOSSIL FORMS OF THE PRESENT TENSE OF *TO BE*

	LATIN	GOTHIC	OLD NORSE	OLD ENGLISH	
I am	sum	im	em	am *or*	biom (beo)
thou art	es	is	est	arþ	bist
he is	est	ist	es	is	biþ
we are	sumus	sijum	erom	sint	
you are	estis	sijuþ	eroþ	*or*	bioþ
they are	sunt	sind	ero	aron	

The tenses of the old Aryan *be* verb in its Welsh form (BOD) have two corresponding types of flexion in the first person singular. We recognize them without difficulty in the endings of:

bum = I was   *byddaf* = I shall be

Any doubt about the meaning of this coincidence disappears when we compare them with the corresponding forms of the second person plural. The Welsh for *you* is *chwi* and the Welsh for *they* is *hwynt*. The agglutinative character of the personal flexion is therefore unmistakable in:

danoch, under you   *buoch*, you were   *byddwch*, you will be
danynt, under them   *buont*, they were   *byddant*, they will be

Though the Welsh use their verb *to be* of the written language without a separate pronoun, they usually insert a pronoun *after* it in speech. The necessities of daily intercourse compensate for the suppositious merits of a flexional system when its agglutinative origin is no longer recognizable to anybody except the grammarian. The need is greater when a language is imposed on a conquered people, or adopted by its conquerors. The absent pronoun of written Latin has come back in its daughter dialect, French.

TENSE FLEXION

Tense flexion, illustrated by the derivative forms *loved* or *gave*, may be external or internal. We call the English dictionary form (e.g. *love* or *give*) the *present* in contradistinction to the derivative *past* form. The words *past* and *present* suggest that tense flexion *dates* an occurrence. This would be a true description of what the French future tense (p. 93) endings do. It is not an accurate description of what the choice of our English present tense form does in *she plays the piano*. If we want to date the occurrence as *present*, we do not use the so-called present tense form. We resort to the roundabout expression: *she is playing the piano*. In reality the tense forms of a verb have no single clear-cut function. To a greater or less extent in different European languages two distinct functions blend. One is the *time* distinction between past, present, and future. The other, more prominent in English, especially in Russian and in Celtic languages, is what grammarians call *aspect*. Aspect includes the distinction between what is habitual or is going on (*imperfect*) and what is over and done with (*perfect*). This is the essential difference involved in the choice of tense forms in the following:

> *a*) *the earth moves round the sun*   (imperfect)
> *b*) *he moved the pawn to queen four* (perfect)

The last two examples might suggest that the distinction between the meaning of the simple present and past tense forms of English is straightforward. This is not true. We imply future action when we use the present tense form in: *I sail for Nantucket at noon*. We imply knowledge of the past when we use the present in *he often goes to Paris*. The particle *often* and the expression *at noon* date the action or tell us whether it is a habitual occurrence. In fact we rely, and those who speak other European languages rely more and more, on roundabout expressions to do what tense flexion supposedly does.

Such roundabout expressions are of two kinds. We may simply, as in the last examples, insert some qualifying expression or particle which denotes time (e.g. *formerly, now, soon*), or aspect (e.g. *once, habitually*). Alternatively we may use the construction known as a compound tense by combining a *helper* with the dictionary form of the verb (e.g. *I shall sing*) or with one of two derivatives called the *present* and *past participles*. The *present* participle of English verbs is the *-ing* derivative, as in *I am singing*. The *past* participle is the corresponding form in *I have sung*. We can use both to qualify a noun, e.g. *a singing bird* or an *oft-sung song*. All English verbs (except some helpers) have an *-ing* derivative. Verbs which take the *-ed* or *-t* suffix have one form which we can use to qualify a noun (e.g. *a loved one*) as the simple past tense form (e.g. *she loved him*) or with helpers (e.g. *she had loved him* or *she is loved*). In Anglo-American usage the Chinese trick of relying on particles often overrides the distinction otherwise inherent in the use of the helper verb, as in: (*a*) *I am leaving tomorrow;* (*b*) *I am constantly leaving my hat behind.*

There is therefore nothing surprising about the fact that so few of us notice it when we have no tense flexion to lean on. A student of social statistics finds himself (or herself) at no disadvantage because the verb in the following sentences lacks present and past distinction:

Oats cost x dollars a bushel today
Oats cost y dollars a bushel last fall

Indeed, few people who speak the Anglo-American language realize how often they use such verbs every day of their lives. Below is a list of common verbs which have only three forms: the dictionary verb, its *-ing* derivative and the *-s* derivative of the third person singular present:

bet	cost	hurt	quit	shed	split
burst	cut	let	rid	shut	spread
cast	hit	put	set	slit	thrust

The foreigner who wishes to learn the language of Francis Bacon and Benjamin Franklin has nothing more to learn about them, and the time of young children is not wasted with efforts to memorize such anomalies as:

give	gave	given	sing	sang	sung
live	lived	lived	bring	brought	brought

Fortunately most English verbs are *weak*. That is to say, they have a single past derivative with the suffix *-ed* (or *-t*) added to the dictionary form, as in *placed* or *dreamt*. This corresponds to the German terminal *-te* (*schnarchte* = snored) or *-ete* (*redete* = spoke).

In Gothic, the oldest known Teutonic language, we meet such forms as *sokida* (I sought), and *sokidedum* (we sought). Some philologists believe that this is an agglutination of the same root as German *tun*, and English *do* with the verb root. It is as if we said in English I *seekdid* (= *I did seek*), or in German *ich suchetat*. In some hayseed districts a similar combination (e.g. *he did say* = *he said*) is quite customary. The example below shows the old English past of the verb *andswerian* (to answer) and how it may have come about by contraction with *dyde* (did) if this view is correct:

$$\left.\begin{array}{l} \text{Sing.} \end{array}\right\} \quad \begin{array}{ll} \text{I.} & \text{andswerian} + \text{dyde} \; = andswerede \\ \text{II.} & \text{andswerian} + \text{dydest} = andsweredest \\ \text{III.} & \text{andswerian} + \text{dyde} \; = andswerede \end{array}$$

Plural (all persons) andswerian + dydon = *andsweredon*

The English verb of Harold at the Battle of Hastings had personal flexions of the past as of the present forms. All such personal flexions corresponding to a particular class of time or aspect derivatives make up what is called a single *tense*. In Slavonic, Celtic, and Teutonic languages, as in English, there are two simple tenses, corresponding more or less to our present and past. Some of the ancient Indo-European languages and the modern descendants of Latin have a much more elaborate system of derivatives signifying differences of time or aspect. The following table shows that Latin verbs have six forms of tense flexion, each with its own six flexions of person and number, making up six tenses, respectively called (1) *present*, (2) *past imperfect*, (3) *past perfect*, (4) *pluperfect*, (5) *future*, and (6) *future perfect*. French, Spanish, and Italian have two past

LATIN	FRENCH	ANGLO-AMERICAN
1) amo	j'aime	I love I am loving
2) amabam	j'aimais	I used to love I did love I was loving
3) amavi	j'aimai j'ai aimé	I loved I (have) loved
4) amaveram	j'avais aimé	I had loved
5) amabo	j'aimerai	I shall love
6) amavero	j'aurai aimé	I shall have loved

tenses and one future, making four in all. One of the French past tenses has died out in conversation.

The examples cited show that the French future is not much like the Latin form. The latter ceased to be used in the later days of the Roman Empire. It made way for an idiom analogous to our way of expressing future action when we say: "I have to go to town tomorrow." This is just what St. Augustine does. Writing about the coming of the Kingdom of God, he declares: *petant aut non petant venire habet* (whether they ask or do not ask, it will come). The combination of the infinitive *venire* (to come) with the common Aryan *have* verb (*habere* in Latin) means what the French or the Italian future conveys in a slightly more compact form. Fusion took place in the modern descendants of Latin. You can see this if you compare the flexions of the present tense of the French verb "to have" with the future forms. The present tense of the verb *have* in French is as follows:

PERSON	SINGULAR			PLURAL		
1.	(j')	ai	I have	(nous)	avons	we
2.	(tu)	as	you have	(vous)	avez	you } have
3.	(il)	a	he has	(ils)	ont	they

We can get four out of the six personal forms of the French future tense by simply adding the appropriate forms of the present *have* to the "infinitive" form *aimer* (to love) as follows:

aimer + ai = aimerai	aimer + (av)ons = aimerons
aimer + as = aimeras	aimer + (av)ez = aimerez
aimer + a = aimera	aimer + ont = aimeront

This example, representative of the origin of the future tense and conditional mood forms of the verb in other modern Romance dialects (p. 339), shows that tense flexion, like flexion of person, can originate from a process of contraction like what we see at work in such words as *you're* and *don't*. It is likely that the Latin pluperfect and future perfect endings correspond to personal derivatives of the *are* root of our verb *to be*, because all their endings are identical with corresponding personal forms of tenses of its Latin equivalent tacked on to the same stem, i.e., *amav* in the example cited. To anyone who is English-speaking this is not surprising, because we use our verb *to be* in expressions which signify past and future time, e.g. *I was coming* or *I am going*. Indeed it is not improbable that the BE root turns up in the past imperfect (e.g. *amabam*) and the simple future (e.g. *amabo*).

Tense flexions with the same common meaning may have begun by agglutination of the root to *different* elements which decay to a greater or less extent because of the difficulties of pronouncing them distinctly in a new context. This would explain why languages rich in such derivatives generally have several types of tense formation.

The irregularities of the English strong verb, which has few surviving flexions, sufficiently illustrate the difficulties to which such irregularities give rise when a foreigner tries to learn a language. The forms of the English verb (including the *-ing* derivative) are typically *four* in number (e.g. *say, says, saying, said*), or at most *five*, in strong verbs which have internal flexion (e.g. *give, gives, giving, gave* and *given*). The Latin verb root has over a hundred flexional derivatives.

In English there are many verb families such as *love-shove-prove, drink-sing-swim, think-catch-teach*, of which the first includes more than 95 per cent. Grammarians put Latin verbs in one or other of four different families called *conjugations*, of which the third is a miscellany of irregularities. There are also many exceptional ones that do not follow the rules of any conjugation. So it is not surprising that the flexional system of Latin began to wilt when Roman soldiers tried to converse with natives of Gaul, or that it withered after Germanic tribes invaded Italy, France, and the Iberian Peninsula. Personal endings were blurred, and roundabout ways of expressing the same thing replaced tense derivatives.

Our last table shows that we can express the meaning of six Latin tenses by combining our helpers *be, have, shall*, with the *-ed* (*loved*) or *-en* (*given*) form (*past participle*), with the combination *to* and the dictionary verb, or with the *-ing* form. Since there can be no difference of opinion about whether an *analytical* language, which expresses time, aspect, and personal relations in this way, is more easy to learn than a *synthetic* (i.e., flexional) language, it is important to ask whether Europe lost anything in the process of simplification.

Clearly there is no tragedy in the removal of an overgrowth of mispronunciation that led to flexion of person. Similar remarks apply with equal force to the loss of tense flexion. The fine distinctions of time or aspect which old-fashioned grammarians detect in the tense flexions of a language such as Latin or Greek have very little relation to the way in which a scientific worker records the correspondence of events when he is concerned with the order in which they occur; and few tense distinctions of meaning are clear-cut. It is sheer nonsense to pretend that prevision of modern scientific ideas about process and reality guided the evolution of the seven hundred or more disguises of a single Sanskrit verb root. Tenses took shape in the letterless beginnings of language among clockless people into whose nomadic experience the sundials and clepsydras of the ancient Mediterranean priesthoods had not yet intruded.

Again and again history has pronounced its judgment upon the merits of such flexions in culture contacts through trade, conquest, or the migrations of peoples. International intercourse compels those who speak an inflected language to introduce the words which make the flexions useless. If the flexions persist as mummies in the mausoleum of a nation's literature, a large part of its intellectual energy is devoted to the pursuit of grammatical studies which are merely obstructive, while the gap between popular speech and that of highly educated people prevents the spread of technical knowledge essential to intelligent citizenship.

In nearly (see p. 423) all languages of the Indo-European family personal flexion is confined to the class of words called *verbs;* and tense flexion is exclusively characteristic of them. We can still recognize as verbs some English words which have no tense flexion by the personal ending, -*s*, as in *cuts,* or -*ing,* as in *hurting,* but some helpers (*may, can, shall*) have neither -*s* nor -*ing* forms. The outlines of the verb as a class of English words have now become faint. In *written* Swedish, the verb has one ending common to the first, second, and third person singular and another ending common to the first, second, and third person plural. This process of leveling is still going on in Swedish. Only the singular ending is customarily used in speech or correspondence. There is no trace of personal flexion in Danish and Norwegian.

NUMBER

Owing to accidental uniformities which have accompanied the leveling down of the personal flexion, grammar books sometimes refer to the *number* flexion of the verb. What is more properly called number flexion is characteristic of the class of words called *nouns.* In most modern European languages, number flexion, illustrated by the distinction between *ghost* and *ghosts,* or *man* and *men,* simply tells us whether we are talking of *one* or *more than one* creature, thing, quality, or group. The terms *singular* and *plural* stand for the two forms. The singular form is the dictionary word. Some of the older Indo-European languages, e.g. Sanskrit and early Greek, had *dual* forms, as if we were to write *catwo* for *two cats,* in contradistinction to one *cat* or several *cats.*

In the English spoken at the time of Alfred the Great, the personal pronoun still had dual, as well as singular and plural forms. The dual form persists in Icelandic, which is a surviving fossil language, as the duckbill platypus of Tasmania is a surviving fossil animal. At one time all the Indo-European languages had dual forms of the pronouns. The ensuing table shows the Icelandic and Old English alternatives. At an early date the hard Germanic *g* of English softened to *y*, as in many Swedish words. The pronunciation of *git* and *ge* became *yit* and *ye*. The latter was still the plural pronoun of address in *Mayflower* English.

	ICELANDIC	ANGLO-AMERICAN	OLD ENGLISH
Dual	við	we (two)	wit
Plural	vjer	we (all)	we
Dual	okkur	us (both)	uncit
Plural	oss	us (all)	us
Dual	okkar	ours	uncer
Plural	vor	ours	ure
Dual	þið	you (two)	git
Plural	þjer	you (all)	ge
Dual	ykkur	you (both)	incit
Plural	yður	you (all)	eow
Dual	ykkar	yours	incer
Plural	yðar	yours	eower

Dual forms of the pronoun are widely distributed among earlier representatives of different language families and among living dialects of a few backward communities. So it is not surprising that distinctive dual personal flexions of the verb occur also, e.g. in Sanskrit, early Greek, Gothic. Though we meet them both in the old Aryan languages, dual forms of the noun and of the adjective which goes with it are less widely spread than those of the pronoun. Dual forms of one sort or the other now survive *only* in technically backward or isolated communities. They disappeared in Greek in the fourth century B.C., and no distinctive dual forms are found in the earliest Latin. They have persisted in Lithuanian dialects of the western Aryan group, in the Amharic of Abyssinia within the Semitic family, and in two remote dialects of the Finno-Ugrian (p. 190) clan.

Separate dual and plural forms of the pronoun may go back to a time when many human beings lived in scattered and isolated households made up of *two* adults and of their progeny. At this primitive level of culture the stock in trade of words is small, and a relatively considerable proportion would refer to things which go in pairs, e.g. *horns, eyes, ears, hands, feet, arms, legs, breasts.* If so the distinction may have infected other parts of speech by analogical extension. The fate of the two pronoun classes throws light on the fact that the family likeness of Aryan pronouns and verb flexions of the singular is far less apparent in corresponding plural forms. In the everyday speech of Iceland and of the Faeroes the dual now replaces the plural form of the personal pronoun, and one Bavarian dialect has *enk* (equivalent to our Old English *inc*) for the usual German accusative plural *euch* corresponding to the intimate nominative plural *ihr* (p. 115). This means that what is now called the plural form of a personal pronoun or personal flexion of an Aryan verb may really be what was once a dual form. (cf. Latin plural *nos* (we), Greek dual *noi*, and plural *hemeis*.)

The number flexion *-s* of *houses* is not useless, as is the personal *-s* of *bakes*, nor pretentious like the luxuriant Latin tense distinctions. This does not mean that it is an essential or even universal feature of language. Some English name words, such as *sheep* and *grouse*, and a much larger class of modern Swedish words (including all nouns of the *baker-fisher* class and neuter monosyllables) are like their Chinese or Japanese equivalents. That is to say, they have no separate plural form. The absence of a distinctive plural form is not a serious inconvenience. If a fisherman has occasion to emphasize the fact that he has caught *one* trout, the insertion of the number itself, or of the "indefinite article" *a* before the name of the fish solves the problem in sporting circles, where the number flexion is habitually shot off game. Number flexion does not give rise to great difficulties for anyone who does not already know how to write English. Nearly all English nouns form their plural by adding *-s* or replacing *y* and *o* by *-ies* and *-oes*. As in other Germanic languages, there is a class with the plural flexion in *-en* (e.g. *oxen*), and a class with plurals formed by internal vowel change (*louse, mouse, goose, man*). The grand total of these exceptions is less than a dozen. They do not tax the memory. So we should not gain much by getting rid of number flexion.

COMPARISON, AND ADVERB DERIVATION

The same is true of another very regular and useful, though by no means indispensable, flexion called *comparison*. This is confined to, and in English is the only distinguishing mark of, some members of the class of words called *adjectives*. The English equivalent of a Latin or German adjective had already lost other flexions before the Tudor times. We make the two derivatives, respectively called the *comparative* and *superlative* form of the adjective as listed in the dictionary by adding *-er* (*comparative*), and *-est* (*superlative*), as in *kinder* and *kindest*. There are but few irregularities, e.g. *good— better—best, bad—worse—worst, many* or *much—more—most*. With these three outstanding exceptions, use of such derivatives has ceased to be obligatory in Anglo-American. It is quite possible that they will eventually make way for the roundabout expressions illustrated by *more firm*, or *the most firm*. We do not use a comparative or superlative form of long adjectives which stand for qualities such as *hospitable*. Since grammarians also use the word *adjective* for numbers, pointer words (such as *this, that, each*), and other vocables which do not form flexional derivatives of this class, no clear-cut definition of an adjective is applicable to a rational classification of the Anglo-American vocabulary.

The monosyllables *more* and *most* in the roundabout expressions that are squeezing out flexion of comparison in Anglo-American are equivalent to words which have almost completely superseded it in *all* the modern descendants of Latin. They are examples of a group of particles called *adverbs*, including also such words as *now, soon, very, almost, quite, rather, well, seldom*, and *already*. We use words of this class to limit, emphasize, or otherwise qualify the meaning of a typical adjective such as *happy*. We can also use such words to qualify the meaning of a verb, as in *to live well, to speak ill, to eat enough*, or *almost to avoid*. The class of English words which form flexional derivatives in *-er* and *-est* generally form others by adding *-ly*, as in *happily, firmly, steeply*. We use such derivatives in the same way as adverbial particles. Thus we speak of an individual on whom we can depend as a *really* reliable person.

These adverbial derivatives are troublesome to a foreigner for two reasons. One is that the suffix *-ly* is occasionally (as originally) attached to words which have the characteristics of nouns, e.g. in *manly, godly*, or *sprightly* (originally *spritelike* or *fairylike*). Unlike *happily* or *firmly*, such derivatives can be used in front of a noun, as in Shaw's *manly women* and *womanly men*. Another difficulty for the foreigner is that the adverbial flexion is disappearing. Such expressions as *to suffer long,* or *to run fast,* are good Bible English, and Elizabethan grammarians who gave their benediction to a *goodly* heritage did not put a fence of barbed wire around the adverbial suffix. If we accept the expression *to run fast,* we ought not to resist *come quick,* or to object to the undergraduate headline, *Magdalen man makes good* (i.e., the Prince of Wales has been promoted by the death of his father). No reasonable man wants to suffer *lengthily.* English has never been consistent about this custom. It is at best a convention of context, and the complete decay of the adverbial derivative would be a change for the better. Americans are more sensible about it than the British.

GENDER

At one time the adjective (including the "articles" *a* and *the*) was a highly inflected word. It had flexions dictated by the noun with which it kept company. The only trace of this *agreement* or *concord* in English is the distinction between *this* and *these* or *that* and *those.* We say that *this* "agrees" with *goose* because *goose* is singular, and *these* "agrees" with *men* because the latter word is a plural noun. In the time of Alfred the Great, all English words classed as adjectives had number flexion dictated by the noun in this way. They also had flexions of *case* and *gender.* Gender concord is the diagnostic characteristic which labels the adjective and pronoun when a clear-cut distinction between adjectives and other words is recognizable. Grammarians give the name *gender* to three different characteristics of word behavior. In English, two of them are relatively trivial, and offer no difficulty to anyone who wants to learn the language. The third has disappeared completely.

The first is connected with the fact that male and female animals or occupations may have different names derived from the same stem, as illustrated by *lion-lioness, tiger-tigress, actor-actress,* or *poet-poetess.* Although the English word *distress* has the same ending as *adulteress,* grammarians do not call it a *feminine* noun. So far as English is concerned, the distinction implied by calling *poet* or *lion* MASCULINE and *lioness* or *actress* FEMININE nouns, is not specifically grammatical. It is purely anatomical.

Corresponding to it we have a second distinction connected with the use of the *third* person singular pronoun. When we use the latter to replace an English noun, we have to take sex into account. We say *he* instead of *heir* or *nephew,* and *she* instead of *heiress* or *niece.* When we speak of animals we are not so particular. Even if we know the sex, as when we talk of bulls or cows, we are not bound to choose between the masculine *he* and the feminine *she.* More often we use the neuter form *it,* which always replaces a plant, a part of the body, a dead object, a collection, or an abstraction. To speak Anglo-American correctly, all we need to know about "gender" in this sense is:

a) That the masculine and feminine pronouns are used in accordance with sex differences when referring to human beings.

b) That the so-called neuter form *can* replace any other singular noun.

So defined, gender is still a biological distinction, and as such offers no difficulty to anyone who wants to learn our language. What grammarians mean by gender extends far beyond the simple rules which suffice as a guide to correct Anglo-American usage. We get a clue to its vagaries in poetry and in local dialects, when *she* stands for the *moon* or for a *ship.* This custom takes us back to a feature of English as spoken or written before the Norman Conquest, when there was no universal rule about the proper use of the pronoun. Any general rules which could be given to a foreigner who wished to learn the English of Alfred the Great would have had more to do with the endings of names than with the sex or natural class to which an object belongs. If English had preserved this complication, we might call *distress* feminine because it has the same ending as *actress,* and *tractor* masculine because it has the same ending as *actor.* We should then have to say: "his distr*ess* was so great that he could not speak of *her,*" or "the management has inspected the tract*or* and has decided to buy *him.*"

These fictitious illustrations do not fully convey the flimsy connection between biological realities and the classification of words as masculine, feminine, or neuter when such terms are applied to Latin and Greek or German and French nouns. Most nouns have no ending to recall anything which is recognizably male, like *actor,* or female, like *actress.* Names of common animals of either sex may belong to the so-called masculine and feminine categories in most European languages. Whether it has ovaries or testes, the French frog (*la grenouille*) is feminine. In French or in Spanish, there are no neuter nouns, and the foreigner has to choose between two forms of the pronoun respectively called masculine and feminine. Danish and Swedish have two classes of nouns, respectively called *common* and *neuter*. The Scandinavian child like the Scandinavian or German sheep is neuter. A quotation from Mark Twain (*A Tramp Abroad*) illustrates how much unnecessary and useless luggage this adds to the memory. "I translate this," he says, "from a conversation in one of the German Sunday-school books":

Gretchen: Where is the turnip?
Wilhelm: *She* has gone to the kitchen.
Gretchen: Where is the accomplished and beautiful maiden?
Wilhelm: *It* has gone to the Opera.

Greater feats of memory imposed on the beginner by the gender concord of the *adjective* complicate the effort of learning Aryan languages other than English or modern Persian. Since we have no surviving vestige of this, we have to fall back on a fictitious illustration or rely on examples from another language. First, suppose that we had *six* forms corresponding to the two *this* and *these:* three singular, *thor* (to go with words of the *actor* class), *thess* (to go with words of the *actress* class), *thit* (to go with words like *pit*), and three corresponding plurals *thors, thesses,* and *thits.* This gives you a picture of two out of three sets of disguises in the wardrobe of the Old English adjective. The foreigner who tried to speak Old English correctly had to choose the right gender as well as the right number form of a noun, and many so-called masculine, feminine, or neuter nouns had no label like the *-or* of *actor*, the *-ess* of *actress*, or the *-it* of *pit* to guide the choice. Below is an illustration of the four forms of the French adjective.

	CORRESPONDING PRONOUN		CORRESPONDING PRONOUN
le grand homme	il	le grand mur	il
the great man	*he*	*the big wall*	*it*
la grande femme	elle	la grande table	elle
the great woman	*she*	*the big table*	*it*

Because sex is all that is left of gender in English we must not fall into the trap of assuming that the chaotic system of labeling nouns, pronouns, and adjectives as masculine, feminine, common, or neuter forms in other languages arose because of animistic preoccupation with sex at a more primitive level of culture. This is not likely. A more plausible view will emerge when we have learned something more about the languages of backward peoples such as the Australian aborigines, Trobriand Islanders, or Bantu. Meanwhile, let us be clear about one thing. Although many nouns classified by grammarians as masculine and feminine may share the same suffixes (or prefixes) as *newer* names (e.g. *actor-actress*) for males and females, the *older* sex pairs of the Aryan languages, such as *father-mother, bull-cow, horse-mare, boar-sow, ram-ewe* in English, carry no sex label. Even when they stand for adult human beings, the so-called masculine and feminine forms of the pronoun do not invariably replace nouns of the class which their name suggests. Thus the German word *Weib* (wife) is neuter, i.e., the pronoun which takes its place is the neuter *es*, not the feminine *sie* (she).

Since names for objects carry no gender label such as the *-ess* in *actress* in most Aryan languages, gender flexion is not necessarily a characteristic of the noun as such. It is the trademark of the adjective. When there is no gender flexion, as in English, *comparison* is the only basis for a clear-cut distinction between adjective and noun. Since we can indicate which adjective refers to a particular noun by its position immediately before (English) or after (French) the latter, it goes without saying that gender concord, like number concord, adds to the labor of learning a language without contributing anything to the clarity of a statement. If every adjective has three gender forms (masculine, feminine, and neuter) corresponding to each of three numbers (singular, plural, and dual), we have to choose between nine different ways of spelling or pronouncing it whenever we use it; and if there are no certain rules to help us to decide to what gender-class nouns belong, correct judgment demands memorizing many exceptions.

The pathology of adjectives does not end here. When nouns have case flexion, which we shall come to next, adjectives may have corresponding *case* forms. If there are eight cases, as in Sanskrit, which is fortunately a dead language, *case concord* implies that an adjective root may have as many as seventy-two derivatives. The entire battery is called the *declension* of the adjective. In the old Teutonic languages, including modern Icelandic, one and the same adjective has two declensions, i.e., alternative forms for the same number, gender, and case; and it is necessary to learn when to use one or the other (see p. 266).

CASE

The word *declension* stands for all the flexions of the adjective, noun, or pronoun, as the word *conjugation* stands for all the flexions of a verb. The declension of an adjective, noun, or pronoun includes this third class of flexions which must now be discussed. English pronouns have two or three case forms listed below:

SUBJECT FORM (NOMINATIVE CASE)
I, we, you, he, she, it, they, who, which

POSSESSIVE FORM (GENITIVE OR POSSESSIVE CASE)

my, our, your, ⎫ his, ⎫ her, ⎫ its, theirs, whose
mine, ours, yours, ⎭ ⎭ hers, ⎭

OBJECT FORM (OBLIQUE CASE)
me, us, you, him, her, it, them, whom, which

Of these three case forms one, the genitive, *sometimes* fulfills a use denoted by its alternative name, the *possessive*. The English genitives of the personal pronouns other than *he* and *it* have two forms, one used in front of the possessed (*my, your*, etc.), the other (*mine, yours*, etc.) by itself. Grammarians usually call the first the *possessive adjective*. In English as in modern Scandinavian languages the genitive *-s* flexion is all that remains of four case forms (*singular and plural*) for each noun, as for each pronoun and adjective in Old English, Old Norse, or in modern Icelandic, which does not differ from Old Norse more than Bible English differs from Chaucer's. This genitive flexion of the noun has almost completely disappeared in spoken Dutch and in many German dialects. When we still use it in English, we add it only to names of living things, to some calendrical terms (e.g. *day's*), and to some astronomical (e.g. *sun's*). It is never obligatory, because we can always replace it by putting *of* in front of the noun. The French, Italian, and Spanish noun has completely lost case flexion, and the fact that Frenchmen, Italians, and Spaniards can do without it raises the same kind of question which disappearance of other flexions prompts us to ask. Is it an advantage to be able to say *my father's* in preference to the more roundabout *of my father?*

In the number flexion *-s* of the noun there is a common element of meaning, e.g. *more than one*. This is characteristic of all plural derivatives, whatever the root represents. Though the English genitive often indicates possession, as in *father's* pants, it is stretching the meaning of the word to say that the same is obviously true of *uncle's* death, *man's* duty, *father's* bankruptcy, or the *day's* work. In the older Teutonic languages, the genitive was also prescribed for use after certain directives, of which there are fourteen in Icelandic. A few idiomatic survivals of this exist in modern Scandinavian languages, e.g. in Norwegian, til fots (*on foot*), til sengs (*to bed*), til tops (*to the top*). German has many *adverbial* genitives, e.g. *rechts* (to the right), *links* (to the left), *nachts* (at night). The use of the genitive flexion then depends on the *context* of the word to which it sticks. There was no common thread of clear-cut meaning which governed its use when it was still obligatory in Teutonic dialects. It is a trick of language dictated by custom, for reasons buried in a long-forgotten past.

The same verdict applies with equal justice to the distinction between the *nominative* and *objective* (or *oblique*) case forms of the pronoun. We are none the worse because *it* and *you* each have one form corresponding to such pairs as *he-him, they-them*. The grammar book rules for the use of these two pronoun cases in English, or Dutch or Scandinavian languages are: (*a*) we have to use the nominative (*I, we, he,* etc.) when the pronoun is the subject of the verb; (*b*) we have to use the oblique case when the pronoun is not the subject of a verb. The *subject* is the word which answers the question we make when we put *who* or *what* in front of the verb. Thus *this sentence* is the subject of *this sentence is short,* because it answers the question *what is short?* This and nothing more is the grammarian's subject. The subject of the grammarian is not necessarily the agent, as it is in the sentence, *I wrote this.* It becomes the grammarian's *object* when we recast the same sentence in the *passive* form, *this was written by me.* It is not even true to say that the subject is necessarily the agent when the verb is *active* (p. 109) as in *I wrote this.* The grammarian's subject is not the agent in the sentence *I saw a flash.* Plato would have said so, because Plato believed that the eye emits the light. We, who use cameras, know better. Seeing is a result of what the *flash* does to my retina. It is not what *I* do to (or with) the flash.

So far as they affect our choice of the case forms *I* or *me*, the only features common to such statements are: (*a*) if the answer to the question constructed by putting *who* in front of the verb (e.g. *who wrote?* or *who saw?*) is a personal pronoun, it must have the *nominative* form *I* (*thou*), *he, she, it, we, you,* or *they*; (*b*) if the answer to the question formed by putting *whom* or *what* after the verb (*I wrote* or *saw what?*) is a personal pronoun, it must have the objective form *me* (*thee*), *him, her, it, us, you,* or *them.* It gets you no further to have a word *subject* for (*a*) and another word *object* for (*b*), as if subject and object really had a status independent of what the verb *means*. To say that the subject is the nominative case form means as much and as little as the converse. Neither is really a definition of what we mean by the subject, or what the choice of the nominative involves.

Only the customs of our language lead us to prefer *I* to *me* for A or B in such a statement as *A saw him* or *he saw B*. We have no doubt about its meaning when a child or a foreigner offends the conventions by using *I*, as we already use *it* and *you* for A or for B. Till the great Danish linguist Jespersen drew our attention to the customs of Anglo-American speech, old-fashioned pedagogues objected to *that's me* or *it's him*, because grammarians said that the pronoun after *am* or *is* also stands for the subject itself. They overlooked the fact that the authorized version of the Bible contains the question: "*whom* say ye that I am?" i.e., "I am *whom*, say you?"

In the time of Alfred the Great, English pronouns had four case forms, as Icelandic and German pronouns still have. Corresponding to our single object or oblique case form of the pronoun were two, an *accusative* and a *dative*. Icelandic nouns still have four case forms, as have the adjectives, and there is a *distinct* dative ending of plural German nouns placed in the neuter and masculine gender classes. In Old English, in German, or in Icelandic the choice of the accusative or dative case form depends partly on *which preposition* accompanies the noun or pronoun. When no preposition accompanies a noun or pronoun other than the subject of the verb, it depends on how we answer questions constructed by putting the subject and its verb in front of (*a*) *whom* or *what*, (*b*) *to whom* or *to what*. The *direct object* which answers (*a*) must have the accusative case ending. The *indirect object* which answers (*b*) must have the dative case ending.

A sentence which has a direct and an indirect object is: *the bishop gave the baboon a bun*. *The bun* answers the question: *the bishop gave what?* So it is the direct object. *The baboon* answers the question: *the bishop gave to whom?* It is therefore the indirect object. The example cited means exactly the same if we change the order of the two objects and put *to* in front of *the baboon*. It then reads: *the bishop gave a bun to the baboon*. When two nouns or pronouns follow the English verb, we can always leave out the directive *to* by recourse to this trick, i.e., by placing the word which otherwise follows *to* in front of the direct object. What we can achieve by an economical device of word order applicable in *all* circumstances, languages with the dative flexion express by using the appropriate endings of the noun, pronoun, adjective or article.

Two sentences in English, German, and Icelandic given below illustrate this sort of pronoun pathology:

a) Fate gave *him to her* in her hour of need.
Das Geschick gab *ihn ihr* in der Stunde ihrer Not (German).
Örlogin gáfu *henni hann* á stund hennar thurftar (Icelandic).
b) Fate gave *her to him* in his hour of need.
Das Geschick gab *sie ihm* in der Stunde seiner Not (German).
Orlogin gáfu *honum hana* á stund hans thurftar (Icelandic).

If all nouns had the same dative ending attached to the plural and to the singular forms, this would not be an obvious disadvantage. The trouble with case flexion in Aryan languages, as with all other flexions, is this: even when they convey a common element of meaning (e.g. *plurality*) they are not uniform. In languages which have case flexion, the affixes denoting number and case fuse beyond recognition, and the final result depends on the noun itself. Before we can use the Icelandic dative equivalent of *to the baboon* or *to the bishop*, we have to know which of four different dative singular and two different dative plural case endings to choose. Thus teaching or learning the language involves classifying all the nouns in different *declensions* which exhibit the singular and plural case endings appropriate to each.

Latin and Russian have a fifth case respectively called the *ablative* and *instrumental*, which *may* carry with it the meaning we express by putting *with*, as the dative may express putting *to*, in front of an English noun; but Romans used the ablative and Russians use their instrumental case forms in all sorts of different situations. There is some reason to believe that the directive used to come after, instead of before, the noun, as the verb once came before the pronoun in the beginnings of Indo-European speech—and still does in the Celtic languages. It is therefore tempting to toy with the possibility that case endings began by gluing directives to a noun or pronoun. Several facts about modern European languages lend color to this possibility.

It is a commonplace to say that directives easily attach themselves to pronouns as in Celtic dialects (p. 90), or to the definite article as in German or French. In German we meet the contractions *im = in dem* (to the), *zum = zu dem* (to the), *am = an dem* (at the), in French *du = de le, des = de les* (of the) and *au = à le, aux = à les* (to the). Almost any Italian preposition (p. 361) forms analogous contracted combinations with the article, as any Welsh or Gaelic preposition forms contracted combinations with the personal pronouns. The directive glues on to the *beginning* of the word with which it combines in such pairs; but it turns up at the end in the small stillborn English declension represented by *skyward, earthward, Godward*. One member of the Aryan family actually shows something like a new case system by putting the directives at the end of the word. The old Indic case endings of the *Hindustani* noun (p. 416) have completely disappeared. New independent particles like the case suffixes of the Finno-Ugrian languages (p. 190) now replace them.

Here we are on speculative ground. What is certain is that, once started in one way or another, the habit of tacking on case endings continues by the process of analogical extension. The English genitive ending in *kangaroo's* got there after Captain Cook discovered Australia. If the *-s* ever was part of a separate word, it had lost any trace of its identity as such more than a thousand years before white men had any word for the marsupial.

MOOD AND VOICE

We have now dealt with all the flexions characteristic of words classified as nouns, pronouns, or adjectives, and with the two most characteristic flexions of the verb. The six tense forms of Latin already shown, with the three corresponding persons in the singular and plural, account for only 36 of the 101 forms of the ordinary verb. Besides time, person, and number, Latin verbs have two other kinds of flexion. They are called MOOD and VOICE. There are three moods in Latin. To the ordinary, or *indicative* mood of a plain statement, as already mentioned on page 93, we first have to add four tenses, adding twenty-four other forms which make up a "subjunctive" mood. This is reserved for special situations. The only vestige of such purely conventional flexions in Anglo-American is the use of *were* instead of *was* after *if*, in such expressions as *if I were*, or the use of *be*, in *be it so*, for conventional situations of rather obscure utility.

Flexions of person, tense, and mood do not exhaust all the forms of a Latin verb listed in dictionaries under what is called the *infinitive* (with the ending *-are, -ere*, or *-ire*). We shall come to the use of the infinitive later (p. 259). There is no *distinctive* infinitive form of the English verb. What grammarians call the infinitive of modern European languages is the dictionary form we use when we translate the English verb after *to* (*a book to read*) or after helper verbs other than *have* or *be* (I shall *read*). Latin had several verb derivatives more or less equivalent to our present and past *participles* (see p. 274). Another form of the Latin verb is the *imperative*, in expressions equivalent to *come* here, or *give* me that. Its English equivalent is the same as the dictionary form.

Voice flexion duplicates the flexions already mentioned. It has disappeared in the modern descendants of Latin, and is absent in German and English. It exists in the Scandinavian languages, as illustrated by the following Danish expressions with their roundabout English equivalents:

Active:	vi kaller (*we call*)	vi kallede (*we called*)
Passive:	vi kalles (*we are called*)	vi kalledes (*we were called*)

The Scandinavian passive has come into existence during the last thousand years, and we know its history. Its origin depends upon the use of what are known as *reflexive* pronouns to signify that subject and object are the same in such expressions as *you are killing yourself*. In Anglo-American we do not use the reflexive pronoun when the meaning of the verb and its context indicate that the action is self-inflicted. We can say *I have just washed* without adding *myself*. Such expressions often have a passive meaning, illustrated by the fact that *I shot myself* implies that *I am shot*. The passive inflexion of modern Scandinavian languages originated in this way during Viking times, or even before, from the agglutination of the reflexive pronoun (*sik* or *sig*) with the active form of the verb. Old Norse *finna sik* (German *finden sich;* English *find themselves*) became *finnask*, which corresponds to the modern Swedish *finnas* or Danish *findes* (are found). The Scandinavians therefore got their passive flexion independently by the method which Bopp (p. 182) believed to be the origin of the Greek and Latin passive.

The Scandinavian model is instructive for another reason. It is already falling into disuse. Perhaps this is because it is not easy to recognize when speaking quickly. Whatever reason we do give for it, the simple truth is that passive flexion is a device of doubtful advantage in the written as well as in the spoken language. The passive flexion, which is quite regular in modern Scandinavian languages, is not an essential tool of lucid expression. We can always translate the passive form of a Latin or of a Scandinavian verb in two ways. We can build up the sentence in the more direct or *active* way, or we can use the type of roundabout expression given above. Thus we can either say *I called him* or *he was called by me*. The first is the way of the Frenchman or Spaniard. It is what an Englishman prefers if legal education has not encouraged the habit of such preposterous alien circumlocutions as *it will be seen from an examination of Table X. Table X shows* would be more snappy, and would not devitalize the essentially social relation between author and reader by an affectation of impersonality.

DECAY OF FLEXIONS

Our account of the decay of the flexions in English may lead a reader who has not yet attempted to learn another European language to take a discouraging view of the prospect. Let us therefore be clear about two things before we go further. One is that though Anglo-American has shed more of the characteristic flexions of the older Indo-European languages than their contemporary descendants, all of the latter have traveled along the same road. The other is that many of the flexions which still survive in them have no use in the written, and even less in the spoken, language.

In two ways French has gone further than English. It has more completely thrown overboard noun-*case* and adjective-*comparison* in favor of roundabout or, as we shall henceforth say, *analytical* or *isolating* expressions equivalent to our optional *of*, and *more . . . than* or *the most*. Though French has an elaborate tense system on paper, some of its verb flexions never intrude into conversation, and we can short-circuit others by analytical constructions such as our *I am going to*— The Danish, Norwegian, and the *conversational* Swedish verb has lost personal flexion altogether; and the time flexion of German, like that of the Scandinavian languages, is closely parallel to our own. The personal flexion of French is 60 per cent a convention of writing, with no existence in the spoken language. We might almost say the same about the gender and case flexions of the German adjective, because they do not stick out in quick conversation. The mere fact that proofreaders overlook wrong flexional endings far more often than incorrect spelling of the root itself shows how little they contribute to understanding of the written word.

In Teutonic languages such as Dutch, Norwegian, or German, and in Romance languages such as Spanish or French, many flexions for which English has no equivalent contribute nothing to the meaning of a statement, and therefore little to the ease with which we can learn to read quickly or write without being quite unintelligible. So we can make rapid progress in doing either of these, if we concentrate our attention first on the rules of grammar which tell us something about the meaning of a statement. This is the part of grammar called *syntax*. We are going to look at it in the next chapter.

Syntax is the most important part of grammar. The rules of syntax are the only general rules of a monosyllabic language such as Chinese. Since Chinese monosyllables have no internal flexion, e.g. change from *man* to *men* or *mouse* to *mice*, all Chinese root words are particles. Because rules of syntax are also the most essential rules of English, it is helpful to recognize how English, more particularly Anglo-American, has come to resemble Chinese through decay of the flexional system. Three features of this change emphasize their similarities. The first is that English is very rich in monosyllables. The second is the great importance of certain types of monosyllables. The third is that we can no longer draw a clear-cut line between the parts of speech.* In other words, the vocabulary of English is also becoming a vocabulary of particles.

To say that English is rich in monosyllables in this context does not mean that an Englishman necessarily uses a higher proportion of monosyllables than a Frenchman or a German. It means that in speaking or in writing English, we can rely on monosyllables more than we can when we write or speak French or German. The following passage illustrates how the translators of the authorized version of the English Bible drew on their native stock of monosyllables. It is the first ten verses of the fourth Gospel, and the only words made up of more than one syllable are in italics:

In the *beginning* was the Word, and the Word was with God, and the Word was God. The same was in the *beginning* with God. All things were made by him, and *without* him was not *any* thing made that was made. In him was life, and the life was the light of men. And the light shineth in *darkness* and the *darkness comprehended* it not. There was a men sent from God whose name was John. The same came for a *witness* to bear *witness* of the Light that all men through him might *believe*. He was not that Light but was sent to bear *witness* of that Light. That was the true Light which *lighteth every* man that *cometh into* the world. He was in the world, and the world was made by him, and the world knew him not.

---

* Jagger (*English in the Future*) boldly uses the two Chinese categories in the forthright statement: "English words may be classified into what are known as *full* or *empty* words."

A word count of the corresponding passage in some other European languages (British and Foreign Bible Society editions) gives these figures:

LANGUAGE	NO. OF WORDS	NO. OF MONOSYLLABLES	PERCENTAGE
ENGLISH	139	124	90
ICELANDIC	138	100	73
GERMAN	135	100	74
FRENCH	121	78	64.5
LATIN	92	26	28

A comparison between the figures for French and its highly synthetic parent Latin, or between Bible English and German or Icelandic, which are nearer to the English of the Venerable Bede, shows that this feature of English is not an accident of birth. It is a product of evolution due to the disappearance of affixes. Decay of these affixes has gone with the introduction of roundabout expressions involving the use of particles such as *of, to, more than, most*, or of a special class of verbs some of which (e.g. *will, shall, can, may*) have more or less completely lost any meaning unless associated with another verb. These *helper* verbs have few if any of the trademarks of their class. None of them has the one surviving English flexion *-s* of the third person singular; and their alternative forms (*would, should, could, might*) would be difficult to recognize as such unless we know their history. Three of them (*shall, can, may*) never had the *-ing* derivative characteristic of other English verbs; and one helper, not included among the examples cited, has no single distinctive feature of its class. The helper *must* has no flexion of person or tense, and we cannot say *musting*. Called a verb by courtesy in recognition of its versatile past, it is now a particle.

In other Indo-European languages, including the modern Scandinavian dialects which have lost personal flexion, the uninflected verb stem turns up as a separate word only in the *imperative*. Both the present tense and the infinitive after helper verbs in roundabout expressions equivalent to Latin tenses have their characteristic affixes. One invariant English word does service for the present tense form (except in the third person singular), the imperative and the infinitive of other Indo-European verbs. Many verb roots are identical with

those of nouns; and English nouns of this type are often identical with
the verb form which serves for the present tense, infinitive and imperative of other European languages. In very many situations in
which English verbs occur, there is therefore no distinction between
the form of what we call the verb and the form of what we call a
noun. The following comparison between English and Norwegian
illustrates this:

> a *motor* .... en bil
> I *motor* .... jeg bil*er*
> I shall *motor* .... jeg skal bil*e*

A pedant may object to the choice of so new a word. Bible English
provides many examples of the same thing, for instance *fear, sin, love,
praise, delight, promise, hope, need, water;* and the day's work supplies
many others which have been in use as long as *hammer, nail, screw,
use, dust, fire.* When an electrician says he is going to *ground* a terminal, a bacteriologist says that he will *culture* a microorganism, or a
driver says that he will *park* his taxi, each of them is exploiting one of
the most characteristic idiosyncrasies of Shakespeare's English. He is
doing something which would be quite natural to a Chinese but very
shocking to the Venerable Bede.

We can press the comparison between English and Chinese a stage
further. By dropping gender concord, English forfeited the distinguishing characteristic of the *adjective* about the time of Chaucer.
The only trademark left is that certain words equivalent to Latin,
Greek, or German adjectives still have (*a*) *comparative* and *super*lative
derivatives; (*b*) characteristic endings such as *-ical* or *-al* in *Biblical,
commercial, logical,* or *-ic* in *aesthetic, electric, magnetic.* These
adjectival words are different from words (e.g. *Bible, commerce,
logic, aesthetics, electricity, magnetism*) equivalent to corresponding German or Greek nouns. A distinction of this sort was breaking
down before the Pilgrim Fathers embarked on the *Mayflower.* Bible
English contains examples of adjectives identical both with the dictionary forms of nouns such as *gold, silver, iron, copper, leather,* and
with the dictionary form of verbs such as *clean, dry, warm, free, open,
loose.*

Since *Mayflower* times the number of adjective-nouns, or, as Jespersen calls them in recognition of the fact that they are no longer distinguishable, *substantives,* has increased yearly. Some pedants who
have forgotten their *Bible lessons* in *Sunday school* object to *night*

starvation, iceman, sex appeal, gasoline pump, or *road traffic signal,* without realizing that they follow such impressive leadership as the *Knight Templar, Gladstone bag, Prince Consort,* and our *Lady mother.* These objections usually come from the gentry who call a man a *Red* if he wants *income-tax relief for working-class parents.* What is specially characteristic of Anglo-American is the large and growing group of words which can be verbs, nouns, or adjectives in the sense that we *use them to translate words belonging to each of these three classes in languages which have preserved the trademarks of the parts of speech.* Even in this class, some have the sanction of long usage.

For instance, we speak of *water* lilies or *water* power, and we use the municipal *water* supply to *water* the garden, when there is a shortage of *water.* If we have too little *water,* our local representative can put a *question* at *question* time; and does not *question* our grammar when we *test* his professions of goodwill by making the *water* shortage a *test* case. Even headmistresses who do not think that *sex* is a genteel word can put *love* to the *test* by looking for a *love* match in books they *love.* Such words as *water, question, test,* and *love* in this sequence have a single flexion -*s* which can be tacked on the same dictionary form as a function-less personal affix, or as a signal of the plural number. They may also take the affixes -*ing* and -*ed.* Other words of this class, such as *cut* (a *cut* with the knife, a *cut* finger), or *hurt,* have no -*ed* derivative. From Chinese, which has no flexions at all, it is a small step to a language in which the same root can take on the only three surviving flexions of the Anglo-American verb, or the single surviving flexion of the English noun, and can do service as the flexionless English adjective.

LEARNING A MODERN LANGUAGE

Like the story of *Frankie and Johnnie,* our review of the decay of the flexional system has a moral. It is neither the plan of the textbooks which begin with the declension of the noun on page 1, nor the advice of phoneticians who advocate learning by ear. Though we cannot use a dictionary with profit unless we know something about accidence, we can lighten the tedium of getting a reading knowledge of a language, or of writing it intelligibly, if we concentrate first on learning: (*a*) flexional derivatives least easy to recognize, when we look up the standard form given in a dictionary; (*b*) flexional derivatives which still affect the meaning of a statement.

To the first class belong the personal pronouns. It should be our

TEUTONIC PERSONAL PRONOUNS *

ENGLISH	SWEDISH	DANISH	DUTCH	GERMAN	ENGLISH	SWEDISH	DANISH	DUTCH	GERMAN
I	jag	jeg	ik	ich	he	han		hij	er
me	mig		mij	mich (*acc.*) mir (*dat.*)	him	honom	ham	hem	ihn (*acc.*) ihm (*dat.*)
(thou)	Du		jij	du	she	hon	hun	zij	sie
(thee)	Dig		jou	dich dir	her	henne	hende	haar	ihr
we	vi		wij	wir	it (subject)	den (*comm.*) det (*neut.*)	den	het	es
us	oss	os	ons	uns	it (oblique)	den det	det		es (*acc.*) ihm (*dat.*)
you (subject)	Ni	De	U	Sie	they	de		zij	sie
you (oblique)	Er	Dem		Sie (*acc.*) Ihnen (*dat.*)	them	dem		hen (*acc.*) hun (*dat.*)	sie (*acc.*) ihnen (*dat.*)

* The English *thou*, *thee* correspond to familiar, the English *you* to formal address. Dutch has a familiar form for plural address (*jullie*), and so has German (subject *ihr*, object *euch*). In correspondence Swedes sometimes use *mej* and *dej* for *mig* and *dig*, and the Dutch use *je* for *jij*, *we* for *wij*, and *ze* for *zij*.

first task to memorize them, because we have to use them constantly, and because they often have *case forms* which are not recognizably like the dictionary word. Fortunately they are not numerous. The accompanying tables give their equivalents in the Teutonic languages. Their Romance equivalents are on pages 331, 332, 363, 370, 374. In subsequent chapters *The Loom* will set out the minimum of grammar necessary for the reader who wants to get a reading or writing knowledge of them.

TEUTONIC POSSESSIVES *

ENGLISH	SWEDISH	DANISH	DUTCH	GERMAN
my	*min* (etc.)		*mijn* †	mein (etc.)
(thy)	*Din* (etc.)		*jovw*	dein (etc.)
our	*vår* (etc.)	*vor* (etc.)	*onze* or *ons* (n)	unser (etc.)
your	*Er* (etc.)	Deres	*Uw*	Ihr (etc.)
his	hans		*zijn*	sein (etc.)
her	hennes	hendes	*haar*	ihr (etc.)
its	dess	dens	zijn	sein (etc.)
their	deras	deres	*hun*	ihr (etc.)
	Those italicized have neuter singular and plural forms *mitt-mina* or *mit-mine*, *vårt-våra* or *vort-vore*. The form given is the common singular. *Din* and *Er* behave like *min* and *vår* respectively.		† Like other adjectives take -e in plural.	These have case as well as gender and number forms (p. 293) and are declined like *ein*, e.g. unser, unsere, unser. The form given is the masc. nomin. sing.

* Swedish and Danish have no special *mine, ours*, etc., forms. In Dutch they are replaced (cf. French) by the article and the determinative form, e.g. *het mijne* or *de mijne*. German has a triple set of possessive pronouns. Two of them follow the declension of the weak adjective and are used after the definite article (e.g. *der meinige* or *der meine*); the third behaves like the strong adjective and appears when not preceded by *der, die, das* (e.g. *meiner, meine, meines*).

When you have memorized the pronouns in their appropriate situations, concentrate on the following. First, learn the plural forms of the noun, because the difference between one dollar and several dollars is often important. Then learn to recognize and to recall the helper verbs, such as the equivalents of *shall, will, have,* and *is,* etc., how to use them, and with what forms of other verbs (participles or infinitive) they keep company. Before bothering about the tense forms given in other books you may read, you should make sure that those which other books give you * are necessary in ordinary speech or correspondence. The only useful flexions which have not come up for discussion are those of comparison. These have disappeared in the Romance languages (French, Italian, and Spanish). In all the Teutonic languages they are like our own, and will therefore offer little difficulty. Above all, stick to the following rules:

1) Get a *bird's-eye view* of the grammatical peculiarities of a language before trying to memorize anything.

2) Do not waste time trying to memorize the case endings of the nouns, or any of the flexions of the adjective (other than *comparison*), till you have made a start in reading. They contribute little if anything to the meaning of a statement in most European languages which you are likely to want to learn. It is doubtful whether they ever had a clear-cut use in the spoken language, and any use they once had in the written language is now fulfilled by other rules, which we shall learn in the next chapter.

FURTHER READING

GRAY	*Foundation of Language.*
JAGGER	*Modern English.*
	English for the Future.
PALMER	*An Introduction to Modern Linguistics.*
SCHLAUCH	*The Gift of Tongues* (specially recommended).
SHEFFIELD	*Grammar and Thinking.*

* They sometimes divulge this in a footnote, if not in the text.

CHAPTER IV

Syntax—The Traffic Rules of Language

WHAT grammarians who have studied Latin, Greek, or Sanskrit call the *parts of speech* (i.e., verbs, nouns, adjectives, etc.) depends on the way in which we form derivatives from dictionary words of such languages. It is helpful to know about how grammarians use these terms, if we want to learn another Indo-European language, because the student of Russian, German, Italian, French, or even Swedish has to deal with flexions which have wholly or largely disappeared in modern English. This does not mean that putting words in pigeonholes as *nouns, pronouns, adjectives, verbs,* and *particles* has any necessary connection with what words *mean*, or with the way in which we have to arrange them to make a meaningful statement. In fact, classifying words in this way helps us little in the study of languages which have pursued a different line of evolution.

There is, of course, a rough-and-ready correspondence between some of these terms and certain categories of meaning. It is true, for instance, that names of persons and physical objects are nouns, that physical *qualities* used as epithets, i.e., when associated with names of objects or persons, are generally adjectives, and that most verbs indicate action or reaction, i.e., *processes* or *states*. When we have said this, we are left with several circumstances which blur the outlines of a functional definition of the parts of speech in all languages of the Indo-European group.

One that Bacon calls man's inveterate habit of dwelling upon abstractions, has created a large class of names which have the same flexions as nouns, and stand for *qualities* or *processes* cognate with the meaning of adjective or verb forms. Headline idiom breaks through all the functional fences which schoolbooks put up round the parts of speech. Thus YESTERDAY'S MARRIAGE OF HEIRESS TO LOUNGE LIZARD means exactly the same as the more prosaic statement that *an heiress married a lounge lizard yesterday;* and SUDDEN DEATH OF VICE SQUAD CHIEF is just another way of announcing the sad news that *a vice squad chief died suddenly.*

Such examples show that there is no category of meaning exclusively common to the English verb, to the English noun, or to the English adjective when *formally* distinguishable. This is also true of all languages included in the Indo-European group. Similar remarks apply with equal force to the pronoun. When we recognize as such a word which lacks the characteristic terminals of an adjective, a noun, or a verb in a flexional language like Latin, we depend largely on the context. For instance, the English particles *a* or *the* are signals that the next word is *not* a verb or a pronoun, and the presence of a pronoun usually labels the next word of a plain statement as a verb. A pronoun usually stands for some name word previously mentioned; but in certain contexts personal pronouns may stand for *anything* which has gone before, and *it* has no specific reference to anything at all, when used in what grammarians call impersonal constructions such as *it seems.* Neither the pronoun nor the verb, which we recognize as such by the flexional *-s* in the same context as the third person *it*, here fits into any tidy definition based on the function of words in a sentence, i.e., what they mean. Few of us now postulate a force not of ourselves which makes for raininess, when we say *it rains.*

To some extent we select one of several word forms with the same general meaning in accordance with the process of analogical extension which plays such a large part (p. 198) in the growth of speech. In literate communities grammarians also take a hand in shaping the conventions of language by prescribing certain patterns of expression based on precedents established by authors of repute, or on paradigms from the practice of dead languages which have more ostentation value than vernacular utterance. The most time-honored model of this type is called the *subject-predicate* relation (see p. 105).

Till recently grammar books used to say that every sentence has to have at least two components, a verb and its subject, which must either contain a noun or be a pronoun. Accordingly, it is incorrect to write *rainy day, what?* The only intelligible definition which usually tells us what grammarians would call the subject of a Latin or Greek sentence is that it answers the questions formed by putting *who* or *what* in front of the verb; and this does not get us far when we replace the preceding expression by the "sentence": *is it not a rainy day?*

Who or *what* rains, in this context, is less a matter of grammar than of theological opinion. Buddhists and Christians, atheists and agnostics, would not agree about the correct answer, and a Scots schoolmistress of any persuasion would find it difficult to convince a Chinese that the meaning of the ensuing remarks would be more explicit if we put *it is* in front of the first, and *there is* in front of the second:

First English gentleman (looking at the setting sun): Not so dusty, what?

Second English gentleman: No need to rave about it like a damned poet, old man.

Though it is quite true that the absence of a perceived situation makes it necessary to be more explicit in writing than in speech, there are no sufficient reasons for believing that addition of verbs would improve the proverbial: *one man, one vote; more speed, less haste;* or *much cry, little wool.* Most of us use telegrams only on occasions when it is specially important to be rather thrifty with words. When we have to pay for the use of words, we get down to essentials. Even those who can afford to dine habitually in costumes designed to inhibit excessive cerebration do not spend an extra cent for a verb in: *dinner seven-thirty black tie.* If a sentence is a word sequence with a "verb" and a "subject," any issue of a daily paper shows that a *complete* statement, request, direction, or question, sufficiently explicit for rapid reading, need not be a sentence. The following examples from the headlines are in the lineage of the Chartist plea: *more pigs, less parsons:*

CONTROL THREAT TO EXPORT COTTON TRADE: BUSINESS AS USUAL IN SPITE OF WAR: CITY CHOIR OF SIRENS ALL IN HARMONY NOW: CHINESE APPROVAL FOR U.S. CONGRESS MOTION: VIOLENT DEMAND FOR VICE PURGE IN VALEDICTORY SERMON: WHITES IN CONGO WITHOUT MORAL SENSE: NO NEW OFFER FROM NAZI NAPOLEON: MORE PROSPERITY LESS PETTING PLEA FROM LOCAL PULPIT: SHOP WINDOW SILK UNDIES PROTEST FROM PRELATE: PERUVIAN WOOLS TRANSFER TO WHITEHALL POOL: FREEDOM RADIO FORECAST OF FIRTH OF FORTH RAID: ALIENIST ATTACK ON PENITENTIARY FOR PANSY BOY: PLAIN WORDS TO ANTI-PANTIE PARSON.*

* In his book, *The Study of Language,* Hans Oertel draws attention to the absence of any pretense at a subject-predicate form in advertisements which are also composed with due regard for economical use of words, e.g. FOR SALE A LARGE HOUSE WITH GARDEN ALL MODERN IMPROVEMENTS SANITARY PLUMBING SET TUBS. A significant comment on the dead hand of classical paradigms follows this example:

"Many instances of this kind can be found: they seem to be absent in the literary remains of the classical languages, or at least excessively rare. I do

If we have to translate a language, such as Chinese, with no formal distinction between words we classify as nouns, verbs, pronouns, adjectives, and particles, we have to forget everything we may have learned about the models of European grammar. In English we can keep close to the pattern of Chinese without using any verbs at all. The following specimens of Chinese poetry (adapted from Waley's delightful translations) show that the effect is not unpleasing, and the meaning does not suffer, when we retain the telegraphic or headline idiom of the original:

(*a*)

Wedding party on both river banks.
Coming of hour. No boat.
Heart lust. Hope loss.
No view of desire.

(*b*)

Marriage by parent choice
Afar in Earth corner.
Long journey to strange land,
To King of Wu Sun.
Tent for house, walls of felt.
Raw flesh for food,
For drink milk of the mare.
Always home hunger,
Envy of yellow stork
In flight for old home.

Some of the difficultites of grammar are due to the survival of a pretentious belief that accepted habits of expression among European nations are connected with universal principles of reasoning, and that it is the business of grammatical definitions to disclose them. A complete system of logic which carried on its back the disputes of the medieval schoolmen started off with a grammatical misconception about the simplest form of statement. The schoolmen believed that the simplest form of assertion is one which contains the verb *to be*, and that the verb *to be* in this context has some necessary connection with

not recall a single instance excepting list of names . . . or superscriptions . . . or headings implying dates. . . . Perhaps the reason is that the *nominative endings* (of which the modern languages have largely rid themselves) were too strongly charged with the 'functional' meaning of the subject relation: that therefore they could not well appear outside the sentence without the retinue of a verb."

real existence. They therefore had to have a substance called falsity in a suppositious Realm of *Ideas* to accommodate the existence implied in the statement: *such views are false.*

So the type specimen of argument reduced to its simplest terms, as given in the old textbooks of logic, was: *All men are mortal. Socrates is a man. Therefore Socrates is mortal.* In similar situations the translators of the Authorized Version of the Old Testament conscientiously put such words as *is* or *are* in italics. The Hebrew language has no equivalent for them when used in this way. In Semitic, as in many other languages, e.g. Malay, the connection of a name with its attribute is indicated by position, as when we say: *fine paragraph, this.* Headline idiom also shuns the verb *be* as *copula* linking topic and attribute or as mark of identity, e.g. FIVE CRUISERS IN ACTION, PRESIDENT IN BALTIMORE TONIGHT, NEW TENNIS CHAMPION LEFT-HANDED, OHIO PROFESSOR NOBEL PRIZEMAN.

In a simple statement which calls attention to some characteristic of a thing or person, the function of the verb *to be*, when so used, has nothing to do with real existence; and it has nothing to do with the usual role of a verb in a sentence. We recognize it by purely formal criteria in as much as it takes different forms in accordance with the *pronoun* that precedes it, and with the *time* to which the statement refers. Its real function, which is merely to indicate time, could be equally well expressed, as in Chinese, by the use of a particle such as *once* or *formerly* (past), *now* or *still* (present), *henceforth* or *eventually* (future).

From what has been said it is now clear that there is no universal *syntax*, i.e., rules of grammar which deal with how to choose words and arrange them to make a statement with a definite meaning, in all languages. In this chapter we shall confine ourselves mainly to a more modest theme. Our aim will be to get a bird's-eye view of essential rules which help us to learn those languages spoken by our nearest European neighbors, i.e., languages belonging to the Romance and Teutonic divisions of the Indo-European family. To speak, to write, or to read a language, we need to know many derivative words not commonly listed in dictionaries. We have now seen what they are, and which ones are most important in so far as they contribute to the meaning of a statement or question, an instruction or a request. When we can recognize them, and can use those which are essential, without offense to a native, we still need to know in what circumstances a word in one language is *equivalent* to a word in another, how the meaning of a sequence of words is affected by the way in which we *arrange* them, and what derivatives to use in a particular context. Of these three, the last is the least important, if we merely wish to read fluently or to make ourselves intelligible. The second is the most important both for reading or for self-expression. The third is specially important only if we aim at writing correctly.

Humanitarian sentiment compels the writer to issue a warning at this stage. WHAT FOLLOWS IS NOT BEDSIDE READING. The reader who is giving *The Loom* the once-over for the first time should SCAN THE NEXT TWO SECTIONS without undue attention to the examples. Thereafter we shall resume our narrative painlessly.

. THE ANARCHY OF WORDS

Many of the difficulties of learning a foreign language arise through failure to recognize to what extent and in what circumstances words of one language are strictly *equivalent* to words in another. If we start with a clear grasp of what word correspondence involves, we can greatly reduce the tedious memory work involved in fixing a minimum vocabulary for constant and reliable use.

Whether any word in one language corresponds more or less often to a particular word in another depends largely on the class to which it belongs. Numerals are the most reliable, and names or physical qualities also behave well. If such words have homophones, we have no difficulty in recognizing the fact, and a little common sense prevents us from assuming that we are entitled to transplant a metaphorical usage in foreign soil. So it is unnecessary to point out that we cannot correctly translate such expressions as *a yellow streak*, or *a sugar daddy*, by looking up the corresponding name words or epithets in a small dictionary. People who are not language conscious are liable to mishaps of this sort, though few of us are likely to commit the double crime of the English lady who said to the Paris cabman: *Cochon, le printemps est cassé.**

The most capricious words in a language like our own are particles, especially those classified as *directives* (e.g. *to, with, for*) and the link words or *conjunctions* (e.g. *and, because, though*). The difficulties which arise when using particles are of three kinds. One is that in any language particles are specially liable to idiomatic use. A second is that

---

* *Cochon* (pig) for *cocher* (coachman). The word *printemps* means *spring* (season). *The spring* of a cab is *le ressort.*

the meaning of a single particle in any one language may embrace the more restricted meaning of two or more particles in a second. The third is that when two particles with the same meaning are assigned to different situations, we need to know whether a foreign equivalent given in the dictionary is appropriate to the context, before we can translate them.

Any particle has a *characteristic* meaning in the sense that we can use it in a large class of situations to signify the same kind of relationship. Thus the characteristic meaning of the English word *to* involves direction of movement. We may also use a particle in situations where it does not have its characteristic meaning. In such situations we may not be able to detect any common thread of meaning. Thus the directive significance of *to* does not help us to see why we put it in the expression *with reference to*. It does not tell us why we must insert it in *allow me to do this*, or why we omit it in *let me do this*. Since particles of all languages close to our own have idiomatic uses of this sort, dictionaries usually give us the choice of a large number of foreign equivalents for one and the same particle. We can say that a particle of one language corresponds to a single particle in another language only when we are speaking of its *characteristic* meaning, or its use in some particular context.

FRENCH	GERMAN	SWEDISH	ENGLISH
à pied	zu Fuss	till fots	on foot
à Berlin	nach Berlin	till Berlin	to Berlin
à la côte	an der Küste	vid kysten	at the coast
à mes frais	auf meine Kosten	på min räckning	at my expense
dans la rue	auf der Strasse	på gatan	*in* the street
en hiver	im Winter	om vintern	*in* winter
le soir	am Abend	på kvällen	*in* the evening
de bonne heure	zu rechter Zeit	i god tid	*in* good time

Examples given here illustrate pitfalls into which we can fall when using particles. The first four give the German, Swedish, and English expressions equivalent to four French phrases containing the same particle, *à*. The last four give French, German, and Swedish equivalents for four English expressions all of which begin with *in*. The French *à* of these expressions requires four different German, and three different English or Swedish particles. The English *in* of the other set requires four different French or German, and three different Swedish particles.

Just as the largest party in Parliament need not be a party with a clear majority, the *characteristic* meaning of a particle need not be the meaning common to the majority of situations in which we have to use it. It may happen that we can recognize more than one large class of situations in which a particle has a distinctive significance. For instance, the directive *with* turns up commonly in two senses. It has an *instrumental* use for which we can substitute the roundabout expression *by means of* when we open a can of peas *with* a can opener. It has also an *associative* use for which we can substitute *in the company of*, when we go *with* a friend to the theater. The link word *as* is another particle which we use in two ways, both common and each with a characteristic meaning. We may use it when the word *while* would be more suitable, and we often use it when *because* would be more explicit. It is therefore not a necessary word to put in our basic list. Its absence gives rise to no difficulty if we cultivate the habit of examining the meaning of the words we use, and the range of choice which our own language permits.

Few, but very few, English particles are above suspicion from this point of view. Even *and* is not innocuous. It is not always a conjunction (link word). In the peculiarly English class of constructions in which it connects two verbs, it is an instrumental directive equivalent to *in order to* or simply *to*. Thus *try and do so* is equivalent to *try to do so*. Similarly *go and see* may often signify *go in order to see*. To be alert to the peculiarities of our own language in this way is essential if we intend to learn another one with a minimum of effort and tedium. We can then recognize when a particle has its characteristic meaning. If so, it is rarely difficult to choose the right foreign equivalent from the synonyms listed in a good dictionary which gives examples of their use. Those of us who cannot afford a good dictionary may get a clue by looking up the equivalents for another synonymous, or nearly synonymous particle. We may then find that only one equivalent is common to both sets. We sometimes get another clue by the wise precaution of looking up the English words for each of the foreign equivalents listed. Dealing with the difficulty in this way is laborious, and it is never a real economy to buy a small dictionary.

TEUTONIC PREPOSITIONS

ENGLISH	SWEDISH	DANISH	DUTCH	GERMAN
a) TIME:				
after	efter	efter	na	nach
at	om	om	om	um
before	före	før	voor	vor
during (= in)	under	under	gedurende	während
in (= hence)			in	in
since	sedan	siden	sinds	seit
till	till	til	tot	bis
b) PLACE:				
above (= over)	över	over	boven	über
among	bland	blandt	tusschen	unter; zwischen
around	omkring	omkring	om	um
behind (= after)	bakom	bagved	achter	hinter
below (= under)	under	under	onder	unter
beside (= by)	vid	ved	bij	bei; neben
between	mellan	mellem	tusschen	zwischen
in			in	in
in front of (= before)	framför	foran	voor	vor
on (= supported by)	på	paa	op	auf
opposite	mitt emott	over for	tegenover	gegenüber
outside	utanför	udenfor	buiten	ausserhalb
c) DIRECTION:				
across	över	over	over	über
along	längs	längs	langs	längs

English	Swedish	Danish	Dutch	German
around	omkring	omkring	rondom; om	um . . . herum; von
from	från	fra	van	von
into	i	i		
out of	ut	ud	uit	aus
over (= above)	över	over	over	über
past (= beyond)	förbi	forbi	voorbij	an . . vorbei
through	genom	gennem	door	durch
to	till	til	naar	zu; nach
toward	emot	imod	naar . . . toe	auf . . . zu
under (= below)	under	under	onder	unter
d) ASSOCIATION:				
according to	enligt	efter	volgens	gemäss; nach
against (= in opposition to)	emot	imod	tegen	gegen
about (= concerning)	om	om	over; van	über; von
except	utom	undtagen	behalve	ausgenommen
for (= on behalf of)	för	for	voor	für
for (= in place of)	för	for	voor	für
in spite of	trots	trods	in weerwil van	trotz
instead of	i stället för	i Stedet for	in plaats van	anstatt
of	av	af	van	von
on account of (= because of)	på grund av	paa Grund af	wegens	wegen
with (= in the company of)	med	med	met	mit
without	utan	uden	zonder	ohne
e) INSTRUMENTALITY:				
by	av	af	van; door	von; durch
for (= as a means of)	till	til	voor	für
to (= in order to + infinitive)	för att	for at	om te	um zu
with (= by means of)	med	med	met	mit

ROMANCE PREPOSITIONS

ENGLISH	FRENCH	SPANISH	PORTUGUESE	ITALIAN
a) TIME:				
after	après	después de	depois de	dopo
at	à	antes de	a	
before	avant			prima di
during (= in)	pendant	de aquí a	durante	fra
in (= hence)	dans	desde	daquí a	da
since	depuis			
till	jusqu'à	hasta	até	fino a
b) PLACE:				
above (= over)	au-dessus de	encima de	por cima de	sopra di
among	parmi	entre		fra; tra
around	autour de	alrededor de	em redor de	attorno a
behind (= after)	derrière	detrás de	atrás de	dietro
below (= under)	sous; au-dessous de	debajo de	debaixo de	sotto
beside (= by)	près de; à côté de	cerca de; al lado de	perto de; ao lado de	presso di; accanto a
between		entre		fra; tra
in	dans; en	en	em	in
in front of (= before)	devant	delante de	en frente de	davanti a
on (= supported by)	sur	sobre; en; encima de	sôbre; em	su; sopra
opposite	en face de	en frente de	em frente de	di faccia a
outside	hors de	fuera de	fora de	fuori di
c) DIRECTION:				
across	à travers	a través de		attraverso

English	French	Spanish	Portuguese	Italian
around	autour de	alrededor de	em redor de	attorno a
from		de	de	da
into	dans; en	en	em	in
out of	hors de; de	fuera de; de	fora de; de	fuori di; da
over (= above)	par dessus	por encima de	por cima de	al di sopra di
past (= beyond)	au delà de	más allá de	mais adiante de	al di là di
through	à travers; par	a través de; por	por	attraverso; per
to	à		a	
toward	vers	hacia	para	verso
under (= below)	sous	debajo de	por debaixo de	sotto
d) ASSOCIATION:				
about (= concerning)	de; sur	de; sôbre	de; sôbre	di; sopra
according to	selon; d'après	según	de acôrdo com	secondo
against (= in opposition to)	contre	contra	contra	contro
except	excepté	excepto	excepto	eccetto
for (= on behalf of)	pour	por	por	per
for (= in place of)	pour	por	por	per
in spite of	malgré	a pesar de		a dispetto di
instead of	au lieu de	en lugar de	em lugar de	invece di
of		de	de	di
on account of (= because of)	à cause de	a causa de	por causa de	a causa di
to (indirect object)	à		a	
with (= in the company of)	avec	con	com	con
without	sans	sin	sem	senza
e) INSTRUMENTALITY:				
by	par; de	por	por	da
for (= as a means of)	pour	para	para	per
to (= in order to + infinitive)	pour	para	para	per
with (= by means of)	avec	con	com	con

If we are clear about the characteristic meaning of our particles, we can avoid making mistakes in many situations; but we have still to decide what to do when we find ourselves using a particle idiomatically. The answer we give to this question, perhaps more than to any other which commonly arises in connection with the learning of a language, decides how much time we waste before we get to the stage of expressing ourselves clearly without upsetting anyone. Textbooks attempt to solve our difficulty by printing lists of idiomatic expressions such as *by train*, in which particular particles occur. Cursory study of such lists is useful because it helps us to recognize unfamiliar expressions if we meet them again when reading a book in a foreign language; but the effort of memorizing them for use in speech or writing is colossal. Unless we are content to wait until we have got used to them by meeting them often in books, we have to seek for another solution of our difficulty.

The most effortless solution emerges from Mr. C. K. Ogden's work on the simplification of English for international use. The basic rule is: always try to be as *explicit* as possible. This means that when you are going to use a particle, you must first decide whether you are using it with its *characteristic* meaning. If the answer is *yes*, your word list can supply its correct equivalent. If the answer is *no*, the thing to do is to recast the statement without the use of the idiom in which it occurs. You can best see what this means with the help of an illustration. Let us suppose that we want to say in French or in German: *I take no pleasure in skating*. The word *in* has one characteristic meaning, and only one. In English, we say that A is *in* B, if B surrounds, encloses, or contains A. Since skating does not surround, enclose, or contain pleasure, we have got to ask ourselves whether we can say the same thing in other words.

We can get rid of the offending directive by putting this in the form: *skating does not please me*. This is not quite satisfactory, because the English use of the *-ing* derivative of the verb is peculiar; and it is important to understand its peculiarities, if we want to become proficient in a foreign language. We use the *-ing* derivative of the English verb in three ways for which other European languages require at least two and usually three different words. One which corresponds with the so-called *present participle* in other European languages is its use as an epithet in such expression as an *erring* child. A second is its use as a name for a process in the first of the three following equivalent expressions:

Erring is human: forgiving is divine.
To err is human: to forgive divine.
Error is human: forgiveness divine.

When so used, grammar books call it a *verbal noun*. If it takes an object it is called a *gerund*, as in *the difficulties of learning Dutch*, or *the dangers of eating doughnuts*.* To this use as a name word we have to add the *durative* construction with the verb "to be," as in *I am walking, you were sitting, he will be standing*, etc. In other European languages it is impossible to find a single word which corresponds to any *-ing* derivative in such diverse expressions as *a forgiving father, forgiving our trespasses, I am forgiving you*. So the *-ing* terminal is a danger signal. We therefore recast our sentence in the form: *I do not enjoy myself when I skate*. To handle this correctly we have to remember that the word *do* (p. 151) in such a context is also an English idiom. We omit it in translation.

These examples illustrate one outstanding class of difficulties which constantly arise in learning a foreign language. Many of the obstacles we meet exist *because we are not sufficiently alert to the peculiarities of our own language, and fail to seize the opportunity of exploring different ways of saying the same thing*. The directives listed in the tables on pages 126–129 are the ones which are really essential. We do not need equivalents for roundabout directive constructions such as the one in the phrase: *in case of difficulties*. We do not need it, if we have the essential link word *if*. Anyone who knows the equivalent of *if*, can paraphrase it in several ways, e.g. *if we have difficulties, if there are difficulties*.

Our next difficulty when dealing with particles is that the common thread of meaning characteristic of a particle in one language may embrace that of two particles each with a more restricted use in another language. For instance, we use the English word *before* to indicate priority, whether a series consists of dates such as 54 B.C., A.D. 1066, and A.D. 1832, or objects such as the members of a class of boys standing in single file. We can thus dissect what we mean by *before* into subsidiary categories of meaning such as *before (place)*, i.e., *in front of* and *before (time)*, i.e., *earlier than*, or *antecedent to*.

* The Old English present participle ended in *-ende*, e.g. *abidende*. The *-ing* (*-ung* or *-ing*) terminal originally belonged to nouns, as in *schooling*. Later it tacked itself on to verbs, as in *beginning*. So the same verb might have an abstract noun derivative and an adjectival one or true participle, e.g. *abidung* and *abidende*. Eventually the former absorbed the latter. That is why the modern *-ing* form does the work of a participle and a verb noun (gerund).

TEUTONIC CONJUNCTIONS

ENGLISH	SWEDISH	DANISH	DUTCH	GERMAN
after	efter att	efter at	nadat	nachdem
and	och	og	en	und
as (manner)	som		als	wie
as . . . as	lika . . . som	ligesaa . . . som	zoo . . . als	so . . . wie
because	därför att	fordi	omdat	weil
before	innan	før	voor	bevor; ehe
but	men		maar	aber; sondern
either . . . or	antingen . . . eller	enten . . . eller	of . . . of	entweder . . . oder
how	hur	hvordan	hoe	wie
if	om	hvis	indien	wenn
in order that	för att	for at	opdat	damit
neither . . . nor	varken . . . eller	hverken . . . eller	noch . . . noch	weder . . . noch
or	eller		of	oder
since (temporal)	sedan	siden	sedert	seitdem
so that (result)	så att	saa at	zoodat	so dass
than	än	end	dan	als
that	att	at	dat	dass
although	fastän	skønt	ofschoon; hoewel	obschon; obgleich
till	tills	indtil	tot	bis
when	när	naar	wanneer; als	wenn; als
where	där	hvor	waar	wo
whether	om		of	ob
while (temporal)	medan	medens	terwijl	während

This distinction implied by the context in English is essential in French, because a Frenchman uses different words to signify *before* in such phrases as *before the door* and *before the dawn*. When we are drawing up a basic list of particles we have therefore to look beyond the characteristic meaning of the English word.

One of the merits of our own language is that we leave much to the context. Whether the English conjunction *when* refers to an event which has happened once for all, to an event which happens repeatedly, or to something which is still going on is immaterial if the setup makes the distinction clear. We do not customarily use *whenever* unless we wish to

ROMANCE CONJUNCTIONS

ENGLISH	FRENCH	SPANISH	PORTUGUESE	ITALIAN
after	après que	después que	depois que	dopo che
and	et	y(e)	e	e(ed)
as (manner)	comme	como		come
as . . . as	aussi . . . que	tan . . . como	tanto . . . como	così . . . come
because	parce que	porque		perchè
before	avant que	antes que		prima che
but	mais	pero; mas; sino	porêm; mas	ma
either . . . or	ou . . . ou	o . . . o	ou . . . ou	o . . . o
how	comment	como		come
if	si		se	
in order that	pour que; afin que	a fin de que	a fim de que	perchè; affinchè
neither . . . nor	ni . . . ni		nem . . . nem	nè . . . nè
or	ou	o(u)	ou	o
since (temporal)	depuis que	desde que		dacchè
so that (result)	de sorte que	de modo que		di modo che
than	que			di; che
that	que			che
although	quoi que; bien que	aunque	ainda que	benchè
till	jusqu'à ce que	hasta que	até que	finchè
when	quand	cuando	quando	
where	où	donde	onde	dove
whether	si		se	
while (temporal)	pendant que	mientras que	ao tempo que	mentre che

emphasize the repetition of a process, and we are not forced to use *while* unless we wish to emphasize simultaneity. This is not true of German or of Norwegian. If he is talking about something that is over and done with a German uses *als* where we should use *when*. A Norwegian uses *da*. When a German refers to something which occurs repeatedly he has to use *wenn*. The Norwegian uses *når*. Where it would be equally correct for us to use the word *when* or the word *while*, the German equivalent is *während* and the Norwegian is *unner*.

An example taken from the history of the English language is instructive in this connection. In Anglo-American the particle *here* means either *at this place* or *to this place*, and the particle *there* means either *at that place*, or *to that place*. It is equally correct to say *he stood here*, or *he came here;* and it is equally correct to say *he lived there*, or *he goes there*. In *Mayflower* English, the particles *here* and *there* indicated position alone, i.e., *here* meant *at this place*, and *there* meant *at that place*. When we use them to indicate direction, i.e.,

two white **above** two black
two black **below** two white

one white **in front of** two black
two black **behind** one white

one white **among** eight
seven black **around** one white

each black **beside** one white
one white **between** two black

black triangle **in** white circle
black square **outside** white circle

diagonal **across** square
bottom left **towards** top right

one horizontal **on** two vertical
one vertical **opposite** another

THE DIRECTIVES OF PLACE

FIG. 21.

motion toward a place, our great-great-grandfathers would therefore have used *hither* and *thither*. An equivalent distinction exists in Swedish or German. The Swede says *du är här* (*you are here*) or *du var där* (*you were there*) and *kom hit* (*come here*, i.e., *come hither*), or *gå dit* (*go there*, i.e., *go thither*). Such distinctions are very important in connection with the use of correct foreign equivalents for English directives. For that reason it is helpful to classify the latter according as they do or can signify relations of *time, place, motion, association*, and *instrumentality* (Figs. 21–25).

We have still to clear up one difficulty before our troubles with the particles are over. It will be easier to understand what it is, if we first compare the sentences below:

(*a*) He read *after* dinner.   (*c*) He read *after* he dined.
(*b*) He read *during* dinner.   (*d*) He read *while* he dined.

In the first pair, the word *after* has the same meaning whether used as a directive before a noun or as a link word connecting the statement *he read* with the statement *he dined*. Though it would be just as true to say that *during* has the same meaning as *while* in the second pair, it would not be in keeping with the customs of English to interchange them. Each has its appropriate *context* in English, though the German can use the same word in both situations. So in classifying one as a *directive* and the other as a *conjunction*, the distinction refers only to the *situations* in which it is appropriate to use them. English is *relatively* thrifty in its use of particles, because it has *relatively* few

A train goes **off** whistling
from a station —

into and
through a tunnel,

out of it,
past a
signal, ·

up a slope,

across a bridge
over a river flowing
along the line,

and then goes
under another bridge

down
its track   **to** its
destination

DIRECTIVES
OF MOTION

FIG. 22.

which are restricted in this way. For instance, we can use all the *interrogative* particles (*how, when, where,* and *why*) as link words. We can also use all the directives either as *prepositions* in front of a noun, or as *adverbial* particles standing alone. Some English *adverbial* particles (such as *soon, back, forward, here, very*) never stand in front of a noun, but no English words are pure *prepositions*, i.e., cannot stand alone without a noun. In some languages the distinction between the two classes is much sharper. In German we cannot use the same particle to translate *going below* (*adverb*) and *going below the surface* (*preposition*). We have to be equally careful about foreign equivalents of words which can be directives or conjunctions. In Swedish, we have to use *var* for *where* when we ask WHERE *do you live?*, and *där* for *where* when we say *he died* WHERE *he was born*.

When context demands one of two or more equivalents, a good dictionary therefore prints such abbreviations as: *conj., prep., adv., interr.* In making a basic word list it is a good plan to list the same English word in each of these classes to which it may belong, in case it may require different foreign equivalents. It is also useful to pay attention to the fact that some of our common English adverbial particles are BAD ones in the sense that some of our common conjunctions, e.g. *as*, are bad ones. For instance, we use the English word *quite* to signify *somewhat* (e.g. *quite pleasant*), or *completely* (*quite full*), and *rather* to signify *somewhat* (*rather enjoyable*), or *preferably* (*he would rather*). An *essential* word list for self-expression would include *somewhat, completely*, or *preferably*. It would not give equivalents for *quite* or *rather*.

The most troublesome words for our basic vocabulary of link words are *that, which, what, who, whom, whose*. The English *that* can occur in four situations. One context is common to *that, who*, and *which*. One is peculiar to *that*, and one is peculiar to *who* or *which*. They are as follows:

a) *Relative* use of *that, who, whom, whose, which*, as link words after a *noun* or preposition following a noun, e.g.:

> This is the baboon that the bishop gave a bun to.
> This is the baboon to whom (or which) the bishop gave the bun.

In such sentences, *that* can replace either *which* or *who*, and its derivative *whom*, but if they come after prepositions, the latter go to the end of the clause. The use of *that* with *of* rarely replaces *whose*. So we have to enter in our basic list of link words, "*that* (*rel.*)" and "*whose*" as separate items.

b) *Conjunctive* use of *that* as a link word for which there is no substitute, in such sentences as:

> I do not believe *that* the creation took only six days.

We have therefore to enter as a separate item in our basic list of link words, "*that* (*conj.*)."

c) We cannot replace the English words *whom, whom, which,* and *what* by *that* when they do not refer to a person or thing in the main clause, but introduce a clause expressing a note of interrogation, e.g.:

I do not know *whom* you expect.

We must therefore enter *who-which* in our basic list separately for *interrogative* situations when *that* or *whose* cannot take the place of *which, who,* or *whom.*

d) We also use our words *which* and *that* as pointer words or *demonstratives*. Whether we put in or leave out the word *book* is immaterial

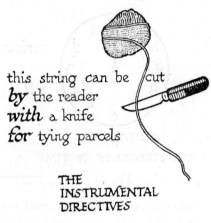

this string can be /cut
by the reader
with a knife
for tying parcels

THE
INSTRUMENTAL
DIRECTIVES

FIG. 23.

to our choice of the pointer word *that* in the sentence: *I have read that book*. In some other languages we have to use one word when the name is present, and a different one when it is left out. This makes it necessary to draw a distinction between a demonstrative adjective and a demonstrative pronoun comparable to our own distinction between the possessive adjective (e.g. *my*) and the possessive pronoun (e.g. *mine*). So in making up a basic list of necessary pointer words, we shall sometimes need to indicate which pointer word stands in front of a noun (*adj.*) and which stands by itself (*pron.*).

Anyone who is familiar with the Anglo-American language alone might yield to the temptation of putting personal pronouns among the class of words which have a high correspondence value. This is not so. Translation of English personal pronouns is complicated by two difficulties. One is the fact that correct choice of pronouns of the third person in most European languages depends on the gender class, as opposed to the sex (p. 101), of the nouns they replace. The other is that many, including most European, languages have special forms of the second person for *intimate* or for polite, i.e., *formal* address. There are thirteen Spanish substitutes for *you*.

In languages such as French, English, or German, there were originally two forms of the pronoun of the second person. One, corresponding to *thou* of *Mayflower* English, for use when addressing

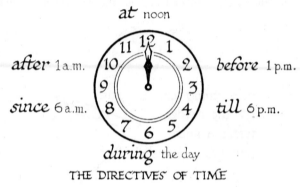

THE DIRECTIVES OF TIME

Fig. 24.

one person; the other, corresponding to *ye*, was for use when addressing more than one. *Thou, thee, ye,* and *you* have now fused in the single Anglo-American word YOU. In most European languages, including Finnish which is not an Aryan language, the *thou* form persists for use among members of the family and intimate acquaintances. What was originally the plural form, cited in our tables as *you*, has persisted in some European languages, e.g. French and Finnish, both as the plural form and as the singular form when the person addressed is not an intimate friend or member of the family circle. This formal use of the plural *you* is comparable to the royal "we."

In some European languages the equivalent of *you* has made way for a pronoun which recalls the oblique idiom of waiters (*will the gentleman take soup?*) For polite address a pronoun of the third person, sometimes *plural*, as in German, or both singular and plural, as in Spanish, has taken over the function of the pronoun of the second person. To use the tables on pages 115, 116, 331, 332, 363, 370, 373 correctly it is important to remember this. The equivalents for *thou* and *you* respectively correspond to (*a*) singular *and* intimate address; (*b*) formal *or* plural address according to *current* usage.

We use one class of English pronouns in two situations for which some languages require different words. The English pronouns *him-*

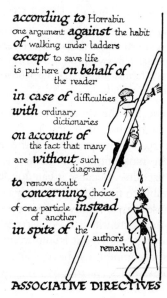

according to Horrabin
one argument **against** the habit
of walking under ladders
except to save life
is put here **on behalf of**
the reader
in case of difficulties
with ordinary
dictionaries
on account of
the fact that many
are **without** such
diagrams
to remove doubt
concerning choice
of one particle **instead**
of another
in spite of the
author's
remarks

ASSOCIATIVE DIRECTIVES

Fig. 25.—Note Our Directive *against* often means the same as *toward*. The one illustrated above is its Characteristic Meaning.

self, *yourselves*, etc., may give *emphasis*, as in *I myself would never do it*, or be *reflexive*, i.e., indicate self-imposed action, as in *she does not give herself the credit*. When an action is commonly reflexive in this sense we nearly always omit it. We assume that washing, shaving, or bathing are personal affairs unless otherwise stated. People who speak other Teutonic languages, or any Romance language, never omit the reflexive pronoun, and some verbs which do not imply a self-imposed action have also appropriated one. Thus the French verb *se repentir*, like its Swedish equivalent *ångra sig* = *to repent, to rue,* always keeps company with a reflexive pronoun. Dictionaries usually print such verbs with the reflexive pronoun, and the two should go together in a word list. Reflexive pronouns of Romance languages and of Teutonic languages other than English are not the same as the emphatic ones. Thus a Frenchman says:

Je le dis moi-même	= I say it myself
Je me lave	= I wash (myself)

In Teutonic and in Romance languages, the reflexive forms of the first and second person are the same as the object (accusative in German) form; and there is a special reflexive pronoun for the third person singular *or* plural which betrays family likeness. The Romance form is *se* or *si,* Scandinavian *sig,* German *sich.*

Many people who realize the vagaries of prepositions and have no need to be told about the use of pronouns for polite and intimate address do not fully realize the anarchy of the verb. The verb (cf. *soak, dig, post*) is the most highly condensed and the most highly abstract element of discourse. Because it can condense so much meaning, it may be impossible to find a foreign equivalent with exactly the same territory. Because it is so highly abstract it is liable to semantic erosion by metaphorical extension. To construct a list of words for self-expression in another language it is important to realize how few of our English verbs in common use have a single clear-cut meaning.

We have met two examples (p. 26); but *ask* and *try* are not exceptional. Sometimes a common thread of meaning is easy to recognize, as when we speak of *beating* (defeating) the Germans and *beating* (chastising) a dog. It is less obvious why we should use the same word when we *admit* visitors and *admit* the possibility of a printer's error in this paragraph. When we make full allowance for metaphorical extension of meaning and for the peculiarly Anglo-American trick (*see below*) of using the same verb intransitively and causatively according to context, we have not disposed of our difficulties. If we *leave* a train we *cease to remain* in it; but when we *leave* a bag in a train the result of our negligence is that the bag *continues to remain* in it. Few ordinary primers accessible to the home student emphasize how much effort we can waste by trying to learn foreign equivalents for the wrong verbs. To get by with the least effort, we must have a lively familiarity with synonyms at our disposal. That is the explanation for the choice of verbs listed in the basic vocabularies at the end of *The Loom* (pp. 521 *et seq.*). Many common English verbs are not there; but the reader will be able to discover the most *explicit synonym* for every one of them; and may well find that it is helpful to hunt them down.

One English verb is tricky for a special reason. Where we use *know* we have the choice of two different verbs in any other Teutonic, or in a Romance, language. In French they are *savoir* and *connaître*, in German *wissen* and *kennen*. The distinction has scarcely any semantic value. Correct use depends on a syntactical custom. *Broadly* speaking the rule is as follows. We have to use *connaître* or *kennen* (Span. *conocer*, Swed. *känna*) when the object is a thing, person, or pronoun equivalent. We have to use *savoir* or *wissen* (Span. *saber*, Swed. *veta*) when the object is a phrase, clause, or pronoun equivalent. Thus the Frenchman says *je le sais* (I know it), if *le* is a statement previously made or some general proposition. If he says *je le connais* the object *le* is a person, book, or other concrete object.

A second difficulty in connection with choice of appropriate equivalents for an English verb is due to the trick mentioned above. Some English verbs such as *design* nearly always precede, and a few such as *sleep* or *come* never take, an *object* (p. 105). It is immaterial whether the object is present, if the English verb can take one. The same verb of other Aryan languages cannot be used in situations where it demands, and in situations where it cannot have, an object. There are still traces of this distinction between the objectless or *intransitive* (neuter) English verb (e.g. *lie*) and the *transitive* (active) verb (e.g. *lay*) which must have an object. Distinctions such as between *lie* and *lay* (= make to lie) are generally established by the context, which tells us whether *cabbages grow* (without our help) or whether we arrange for them to do so, as when we say that *we grow cabbages*. Similarly we say that *something increases* or that *we increase it* (i.e., make it increase). A Frenchman or a German cannot do so. The latter has to use different words, where we use the same verb transitively and intransitively as below:

> The management will *increase* his wages next month.
> Die Leitung wird nächsten Monat seinen Lohn *erhöhen*.
>
> The length of the day will *increase* next month.
> Die Länge des Tages wird nächsten Monat *zunehmen*.

In looking up a foreign equivalent for an English verb in a dictionary, it is therefore essential to pay careful attention to the abbreviations (*trans.* or *v.a.*) and (*intrans.* or *v.n.*) which may stand after one or other of the words given. In Anglo-American usage almost any verb which used to be intransitive has acquired a more or less metaphorical transitive, often *causative*, meaning, as in *will you run me into town?* This decay of the distinction between the two classes of verbs goes with two other peculiarities of Anglo-American syntax, both pitfalls of translation. In a *passive* construction the object of the active equivalent becomes the subject, e.g. *he struck her* (active form) = *she was struck by him.* Only transitive verbs of other Aryan languages can participate in passive expressions of the latter type, and only the *direct object* (p. 106) of the active equivalent can become the subject when it is changed to the passive construction. Thus we make such changes as:

> *a) he gave me this letter* = *this letter was given to me by him*
> *b) she told me this*   = *this was told me by her*

In contemporary Anglo-American usage it is increasingly common to use an alternative passive construction, in which the *indirect* object (p. 106) of the active verb becomes the subject, e.g.:

> (*a*) *I was given this letter by him.*   (*b*) *I was told this by her.*

In this form we cannot translate them into other European languages. The moral is: use active expressions wherever possible. The reader of *The Loom* will find relatively few passive expressions in the preceding chapters.

If it were permissible to paraphrase the meaning of a verb, it would not be difficult to sidestep the pitfalls of choosing the right one. Unfortunately it is not. Many European peoples, indeed most, depend far more on the use of a large battery of verbs than we ourselves do. In fact there are only two safe rules of verb economy for the beginner who is making a list of verbs essential for self-expression in a Teutonic or Romance language. We need not burden our word list with verbs equivalent to a construction involving an adjective and either *make* (trans.) or *get* (intrans.). The equivalent adjective with the verb listed in Part IV as equivalent to either *make* or *become* serves the purpose. Thus *to tire* means either *to make weary* or *to become* (*get*) *weary*. Similarly *to diminish* means *to make smaller* or *to become* (*get*) *smaller*. *To heat* is *to make hot* or to *become hot*—and so forth.

One danger signal attached to a verb root is the suffix *-ing* mentioned earlier in this chapter. The most idiomatic class of verbs are the helpers, so-called because we commonly use them with other verb derivatives (*infinitive* or *participle*). The English ones are *be,* *shall, will, let, can, do, make, must, may* (after which we never use *to*), *have* and *dare* (after which we sometimes use *to*), and *go, use, ought* (after which we always use *to* in front of the verb). No general rule helps us to recognize idiomatic uses of a helper verb in a foreign language, if we know only its *characteristic* meaning; but we can avoid some pitfalls, if we are clear about the vagaries of helper verbs in our own language.

It would be easy to write a volume about the pathology (and theology) of the verb *to be*. (Some of its vagaries in current English come up for discussion in Chapter IX, p. 387.) Its use as a *copula* linking a thing or person to its attribute or class is an Aryan construction absent in many other languages, cf. the italics for the absent copula in the original of: the Lord *is* my Shepherd. In a large class of English expressions we use the verb *to be* where the equivalent in another closely related language would be the word corresponding to *have*. The fact that a verb which also means to *have* or *possess* may overlap the territory of our verb to *be* is not strange or unreasonable. To say that something *is* red means that it *has* or *possesses* the characteristic or attribute which we describe by that adjective. Thus the literal equivalent of *to be right* in French, German, and in the Scandinavian languages is *to have right*. Similarly, the literal equivalent of *to be wrong* is *to have wrong*. The literal equivalent of *to be warm, hot,* or *cold,* either in French or in Spanish, is to *have warm, hot,* or *cold. Be well,* or *ill,* is another peculiarly English idiom, equivalent to the German *gesund sein,* or *krank sein* (*be healthy* or *sick*). The literal French is equivalent to *to carry oneself well* or *ill* (*se porter bien,* or *se porter mal*); in Swedish, *må väl* or *illa* (*may well* or *ill*); in Norwegian *ha det godt* or *vaere syk* (*have it well,* or *be sick*). The English *be sorry* is equivalent to the Scandinavian *do oneself bad* (*gøre sig ond* in Danish).

Though they look alike on paper, the most characteristic meaning of the helper verbs of two descendants of the same Teutonic root is rarely the same. The meaning of most of them has changed during historic times. The only safeguard against the pitfalls into which this leads us is to recognize which are our most reliable helpers, and to be quite clear about the various uses of the other English ones. The two reliable ones are *can* and *must*. Each has a well-defined territory, which overlaps that of others.

The verb *may* can mean two things. Thus he *may* do this can mean either (*a*) *he is allowed to do this,* or (*b*) *it is possible that he will do this.* We use our English *to have,* like its equivalents in other Indo-European languages, to signify possession, and as a *helper* to indicate past time or completed action (I *have* done this), but it can also do the same job as *must* in *I have to do this*, and replaces the compulsive function of *must* in some expressions which involve past time (*I had to do this*). It is not safe to translate *have* (when it means *must*) by its dictionary equivalent in another language. The combination *have had, has had*, etc., can also signify *arranged* or *allowed* (*let*) where the German uses derivatives of *lassen*, as in *he has had a house built*.

When used in the first person after *I* or *we*, the verb *shall* is equivalent to a particle indicating the indefinite future. Otherwise it retains its old

TEUTONIC HELPER VERBS FROM SAME ROOTS

ENGLISH	SWEDISH	DANISH	DUTCH	GERMAN
I can	jag kan	jeg kan	ik kan	ich kann
I could	jag kunde	jeg kunde	ik kon	ich konnte
I shall	jag skall	jeg skal	ik zal	ich soll
I should	jag skulle	jeg skulde	ik zoude	ich sollte
I will	jag vill	jeg vil	ik wil	ich will
I would	jag ville	jeg vilde	ik wilde	ich wollte
I must	jag måste	.....	ik moet	ich muss
I let	jag låter	jeg lader	ik laat	ich lasse
I may	jag må	jeg maa	ik mag	ich mag
I might	jag måtte	jeg maatte	ik mocht	ich möcht

Teutonic meaning akin to *must* or *have to* (e.g. *thou shalt not commit adultery*). *In the first person* the related form *should* is used after the statement of a condition, as in *I should be glad if he came*. In expressions involving the second or third person, *will* and *would* are generally equivalent to *shall* or *should* involving the first. Otherwise they revert to their original Teutonic meaning illustrated by the adjective *willing*. This distinction is not as clear-cut or universal as armchair grammarians would lead us to suppose. Few English-speaking people recognize any difference between (*a*) *I should do this, if he asked me*, (*b*) *I would do this, if he asked me*.

Since *can* and *must* are the most reliable helpers, it is best to use their equivalents whenever either shares the territory of another such as *shall, have, may*. The use of *can* and *must* is not foolproof, unless the beginner is alert to one pitfall of translation from English into any

Romance or any other Teutonic language. Like *ought, can* and *must* form peculiar combinations with *have* (*could have, must have, ought to have*) for which the literal equivalent in other languages is *have could, have must, have ought*. The easiest to deal with is *can*. It is correct to use the corresponding German (*können*) or French (*pouvoir*) verb in the present or simple past where the English equivalent is either *can-could* or *is able to—was able to*, etc., but *I could have* does not mean the same as *I have been able to*. It is equivalent to *I should have been able to*. To use *can* with safety, the best rule of thumb is to remember that the foreign equivalent for *can-could* always corresponds to our *is* (or *was*) *able to*, but does not correspond to our *can-could* before *have*.

WORD ORDER

Root words, the order in which we arrange them, tone and gesture are the indispensable tools of daily speech. Next to correct choice of words, their order is therefore the most important part of grammar. Comparison of the statement that *men eat fish* with *fish eat men* sufficiently illustrates the importance of word order as a vehicle of meaning in our own language. Armchair grammarians sometimes write as if a rigid pattern of word order is a comparatively late and sophisticated device. It is easy to support this view with spurious evidence. Much of the literature which furnishes case material for our knowledge of the earlier stages of the history of a language is poetry or rhetoric, and such belongs to a period when the gap between the written and the spoken word was much wider than it now is. We all know the obscurities into which poets plunge us by transgressing customary conventions of word order in conformity to the dictates of meter, alliteration, rhyme, or cadence. There is no reason to believe that they were ever less prone to violate the speech pattern of everyday life, and it is difficult to see how human beings could cooperate in daily work, if they took advantage of the license which poets claim. In short, we may reasonably suppose that the importance of word order in modern languages is as old as speech itself. The suggestion made on page 123 applies especially to the next few pages devoted to this topic. It will be wise to *skim it lightly on first reading*, and to return to it later for relevant information as occasion arises.

Rules of word order are like traffic regulations. The only thing rational about them is the rational necessity for uniform behavior as a safeguard against congestion. To discuss word order intelligibly we need some fixed points with reference to which we can speak of constituent words or phrases as *before* or *after*. Verb and *subject* (p. 105) give us such fixed points which are generally easy to recognize in any statement other than newspaper headlines. Two others (p. 106) are respectively called the *direct object* and the *indirect object*. These terms do not describe any definite relation of a thing or person to the process implied in the meaning of a verb. We recognize them by converting a statement into a question, or vice versa.

The grammarian's *subject* is the person or thing which answers the question formed by putting *who* or *what* in front of the verb in an ordinary statement. In this way we get the subject of each clause in the following sentence from a Chartist pamphlet:

> Peoples of all trades and callings forthwith *cease* work until the above document *is* the law of the land.

> First Clause: *Who* cease work? *Peoples of all trades and callings.*

> Second Clause: *What* is the law? *This document.*

The *direct object* is the answer to the question formed by putting *who*, *which* or *what* in front of the verb and the subject behind it. We get the *indirect object* by putting *to whom*, or *to what*, in the same position. To get the two objects of the statement: *I may have told you this joke once too often*, we therefore ask:

> *What may I have told?* . . . THIS JOKE (Direct Object).

> *To whom may I have told this joke?* . . . YOU (Indirect Object).

The general rule for an ordinary Anglo-American statement is that the subject *precedes* the verb. The same rule also applies to French, Spanish, or Italian. In the Celtic languages, the subject comes after the verb, and in Teutonic languages it comes before the verb of a simple statement only when no other word precedes either of them. In German, Danish, Swedish, or Dutch, the subject of a sentence which begins with an expression such as *two years ago* comes immediately *after* a simple verb, or immediately after the helper of a compound verb. Thus the Teutonic word order is illustrated by the following:

Two years ago left a mine explosion (*left*) fifty families
fatherless.

This inversion is very common in Bible English, e.g. *then came he to the ship*. It survives in a few contemporary English idioms such as *here comes the postman, there goes the train, seldom do such inversions occur in our language*, the Wellsian *came the dawn*, and the inevitable *pop goes the weasel*. The Anglo-American student of a Teutonic language will find it helpful to recall the pious idiom of the Pilgrim fathers.

In English and in Scandinavian languages the object, whether direct or indirect, *comes after:* (*a*) the *main verb;* (*b*) the *subject.* The rules for placing the object of a sentence in German or Dutch and in the Romance languages are different. Separate rules apply to the position of verb and object in simple Dutch or German statements and in complex sentences made up of two or more statements connected with link words. We shall come to complex sentences later on (p. 154). In simple statements, the English-Scandinavian rule holds good when there is only one verb. When the verb is compound, the object comes after the helper; and the participle or infinitive form of the verb comes after the object at the end of the sentence. Thus German-Dutch word order is illustrated by the English and German equivalents:

The keeper *has*   *given*   the kangaroo candy.

Der Wärter *hat* dem Känguruh Kandiszucker *gegeben*.

This difference between German-Dutch and Scandinavian-English word order is *very important* to anyone who wants to learn Dutch or German. To read Dutch or to read German with ease, you have to cultivate the habit of looking for the main verb at the end of a long sentence. To speak either of these languages correctly you have to cultivate the trick of recasting any simple sentence in the form illustrated above, if it contains a helper verb. The difficulty may be complicated by the presence of two helper verbs. The second helper verb (*infinitive*) then goes to the end of the statement immediately after the participle form of the main verb. Such sentences usually involve *should have, could have*, etc., and we cannot translate them literally (see pp. 144 and 296).

The Scandinavian-English rule of word order applies to the relative position of the object or objects, the helper verb and the participle or infinitive form of the main verb, in a French, Italian, or Spanish statement, *when the object is a noun*. If the indirect object is a noun, the equivalent of *to* precedes it. The indirect noun object follows the direct object, as when preceded by *to* in English (p. 106). If either or both objects are pronouns, they follow the verb in a positive command or request, i.e., after the *imperative* form of the verb. In a statement they come *between* the verb and its subject. If the verb is compound they come before the helper or first verb. To write or to speak French, Italian, or Spanish, we have to get used to the following changes:

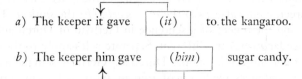

a) The keeper it gave   (*it*)   to the kangaroo.

b) The keeper him gave   (*him*)   sugar candy.

When there are two objects, the Scandinavian-English rule is that the indirect object comes before the direct object unless the latter is preceded by *to* or its (optional) equivalent (*till* in Swedish and *til* in Danish). No such straightforward rule applies to all statements in German and Dutch. Usually the direct object comes first. This is the general rule in Dutch when both objects are nouns; but if both are pronouns, the shorter comes first, as in the English sentence: *I told him everything.* German custom is less simple. It can be summed up in three rules:

a) If one object is a pronoun and the other a noun, the pronoun object comes first.

b) If both are nouns, the indirect object precedes the direct.

c) If both are pronouns, the direct object comes first.

The relative position of two pronoun objects is not the same in all the Romance languages. In Italian and Spanish, the *indirect precedes the direct* object. The French rule is that the *first* person or the *second* person precedes the *third* person. If both objects are pronouns of the third person, the *direct object comes first.* The necessary change is indicated by the following models:

a) She has sent me it   = *Elle me l'a envoyé.*
                 She me it has sent.

b) She has sent you it   = *Elle vous l'a envoyé.*
                 She you it has sent.

c) She has sent him it   = *Elle le lui a envoyé.*
                 She it him has sent.

In addition to the verb, its subject and one or both objects, a simple statement may also contain one or more qualifying expréssions. These are of two kinds, *adjectival* if they refer to a noun, and *adverbial* if they limit or extend the meaning of some other word. Adjectives and adjectival expressions can be used in two ways. One is the *predicative* use after the verb "to be," as in *the baboon was carefree*. The other is the *attributive* use, as in *the perplexed and celibate bishop*. In some languages, e.g. German or Russian, adjectives have different predicative and attributive forms. The position of the predicative adjectival expression calls for no special comment. We recognize whether an attributive adjective or adjectival expression refers to one or other of several nouns by keeping it next to the noun which it qualifies.* The position of *old* and *silk* is sufficient to leave no doubt about whether an American or a Scotsman is discussing the *old underwear of the silk merchant* or the *silk underwear of the old merchant*.

If everybody does the same, it does not matter whether drivers keep to the left as in Britain, or to the right as in the United States. By the same token, it does not matter whether the adjective usually comes after the noun, as in Celtic and Romance, or in front of it, as in Teutonic and Slavonic, languages. The student of a Romance language will find it helpful to recall a few fixed expressions in which the normal English order is reversed, e.g. *lords temporal, malice afore-thought, fee simple, lie direct, retort courteous, cook general, body politic, knight errant*. This rule does not apply to two classes of adjectives. Romance *possessives* and Romance *numerals* precede the noun. Thus a Spaniard says *mi amiga* (my friend) or *tres muchachos* (three boys).

As in English, pointer words, e.g. words equivalent to *this* and *that*, including the "articles" *the* and *a* (*an*), come in front both of the attributive adjective and of the noun in Romance as well as in Teutonic languages. In this connection, we should be on the lookout for two classes of English idioms as pitfalls of translation: (*a*) *such, almost, only*, and *even* precede the article, e.g. *such a woman, almost a father, only a colonel's daughter;* (*b*) any adjective qualified by the particle *so* precedes the article, e.g. *so long a journey*. The English rule for placing a long adjectival expression is not the same as that of other Teutonic languages. *Long* English adjectival expressions often

* This applies to speech whether a language is synthetic or analytical. In synthetic languages, writers may take liberties by relying on concord (p. 322) to label the adjective.

follow the corresponding noun. We do not observe the Swedish or German word order in *a question so sudden and unexpected.*

We use several English words to qualify a noun, an adjective, a verb, or a particle. Four of the most common are *almost, even, only,* and *enough.* The form of these words does not tell us whether they do or do not refer to a noun, i.e., whether equivalent or not equivalent to an adjective of another language. We can indicate which word they qualify by position. In English it is common to place such particles immediately *in front of* the word which they qualify. Unfortunately, this useful device is not universally observed. The English word *enough,* though placed in front of a noun which it qualifies (e.g. *enough bother*), comes after a verb, adjective, or particle (e.g. *sleeping enough, a hard enough time, working long enough*).

What matters about rules of word order is: (*a*) whether we apply them consistently when they do affect the meaning of a statement; (*b*) whether we allow freedom when they do not do so. Some languages have straightforward rules about the order of adverbial particles or qualifying expressions according as they signify *time, place, manner,* or *extent.* For instance, when two adverbial particles occur in a Teutonic language, the one which indicates *time* comes first. A defect of English syntax is that although the accepted order for any particular pair of adverbs conforms to rigid custom, there is no simple rule which applies to *any* situation. Sometimes an adverb of time precedes, and sometimes it follows another adverb as in:

> *a*) He often wept bitterly.
> *b*) He went North today.

Inversion of subject and verb is one way of changing a plain statement into a question in all Teutonic and Romance languages. The same is true of Bible English. It is true of Anglo-American only when the verb is a *helper,* as in *can you face reading the rest of this chapter?* Otherwise Anglo-American has its own peculiar roundabout method of interrogation. We no longer say: *sayest thou?* The modern form of the question is: *do you say?* We use this roundabout form with all verbs except helper verbs other than *let.* We *can* also employ it with *have.* In a few years no one will object to *did he ought?* or *did he use?* When translating a question from modern English into German, Swedish, or French, we have therefore to recast it in Bible English.*

---

* The two forms of interrogation occur consecutively in the Authorized Version, 1 Cor. vi. 2 and 3.

Inversion of verb and subject in Teutonic and Romance languages, and the roundabout Anglo-American expression with *do* or *did*, turn a statement into the general form which implies acceptance or rejection of the situation as a whole. We cannot concentrate attention on the identity of the transaction indicated by the verb itself without either elaborating the question or using italics. In this general form, the answer to the question will be *yes*, *no*, or some noncommittal comment. In English it is immaterial whether we ask it in the positive form (*did the . . . ?*) or negative (*didn't he . . . ?*). In some languages this distinction is important. The English *yes* has to be translated by different French or Scandinavian words when the negative is substituted for the positive form of the question. The English *Yes*, after a positive question, is equivalent to the Scandinavian *Ja*, and the French *Oui*. After a negative question, the English *Yes* is equivalent to the Scandinavian *Jo*, and the French *Si*. The German *Ja* and *Doch* tally with the Scandinavian *Ja* and *Jo*.

The preceding remarks apply to the difference between the form of a question and the form of a statement in so far as the design of the question is to elicit confirmation of the statement as a whole. It may also be designed to elicit new information. It may then begin with an *interrogative particle*, in English, *when*, *why*, *where*, *how*. The interrogative particle precedes other words in the order appropriate to a question designed to check the whole situation. Apart from the use of interrogative pronouns or particles, and inversion of subject and verb, or a combination of both, there are various other ways of putting a question. If we want to ascertain the identity of the subject we have merely to substitute the English interrogative pronouns *who*, *what*, *which*, and equivalent words in a Romance or Teutonic language without any change of word order. The question then takes the form: *who can face reading the rest of this chapter?* To ascertain the identity of the object demands more than the substitution of an interrogative pronoun. The latter comes at the beginning of the question and the subject follows the verb, as in *what can you face reading?*

In English we can make a statement into a question by putting in front of it the clause: *is it true that?* This is roughly equivalent to a common form of French interrogation introduced by *est-ce que* (*is it that*). French permits a peculiar form of interrogation which lays emphasis on the subject without calling for specific interrogation. The following literal translation illustrates it:

Is my father here?	= *Mon père, est-il ici?*
	My father, is he here?

In conversation we often do without devices on which we commonly rely when we put a question in writing. A falling and rising tone suffice to convey interrogation without change of word order appropriate to plain statement. Emphasis on one or another word indicates doubt about the identity of subject, object, or activity denoted by the verb. We can do the same in writing by use of italics, but we have no type convention to signify change of tone in print. In everyday speech, though less in writing, we can convert a statement into a question by judicious or polite afterthought. The formula added is an idiom peculiar to each language. In English we add such expressions as *eh? don't you?* or *isn't it?* The German equivalent is *nicht wahr* (*not true?*). The Swedish is *inte sannt* (*not true?*) or *eller hur* (*or how?*), the French is *n'est-ce pas* (*is this not?*) and the Spanish is *verdad* (*true?*) The English affirmative answer *I did*, etc., is a pitfall for the unwary. In other European languages it is more usual to add a pronoun object, i.e., *it*. Thus in Swedish *I did* is *jag gjorde det* (*I did it = I did so*).

One very important class of rules about word order regulate negation. Rules of negation, like rules of interrogation and the rule for the position of the subject in ordinary statements, draw attention to a fundamental difference between the syntax of Bible English and the syntax of Anglo-American. Subject to a qualification, mentioned later (p. 155), the rule for Bible English is the same as for Scandinavian languages. If the verb is single and has no pronoun object, the negative particles *not, never* (or their Scandinavian equivalents) come immediately after it. If the verb is compound, they come immediately after the helper. For compound verbs with helpers other than *let*, the rule is the same in modern English; and the same rule applies to the helpers *be* and *have* when they stand alone. Otherwise we now use the peculiarly Anglo-American construction with *do* or *did*. Thus a modern translation of the Bible would not say: *I came not to call the righteous, but sinners to repentance.* It would say: *I did not come to call.* . . .

When inversion of subject and verb occurs, as in the negative form of question, the English negative particle comes immediately after the subject, like that of Scandinavian dialects. The negative particle of a Scandinavian statement always comes after the object when the latter is a personal pronoun. This again is the word order of *Mayflower* English. Compare for instance the following:

a) He came unto his own and his own *received him not*
(= did not receive him).

b) The world was made by him and the world *knew him not*
(= did not know him).

This rule does not apply to a noun object, e.g. *ye receive not our witness.* In a negative question, the Scandinavian like the English negative particle comes after the subject and before the noun object. Its position with reference to the subject in Anglo-American is not obligatory. We sometimes say *do you not?* and we sometimes say *don't you?* The rule of word order in Bible English and in Scandinavian languages is the same: (*a*) for a negative command or request; (*b*) for a negative statement. The Bible English or Scandinavian form is: *lead us not into temptation.* The roundabout Anglo-American equivalent is: *do not lead us into temptation.* We use this roundabout form of the negative request or command only with *not.* If the negative particle is *never* we stick to *Mayflower* idiom.

The position of the negative particle in a Dutch or a German sentence is not the same as in Bible English or in Scandinavian languages. When it qualifies the statement as a whole, it comes after the object whether the latter is a pronoun or a noun. In a question it comes at the end of a sentence unless the verb is compound. Then it comes immediately before the participle or infinitive. In the Romance languages the negative particle stands before the verb if the latter is simple, and before the helper verb if it is compound. When one or both objects are pronouns, and therefore stand in front of the simple verb or in front of the helper, the negative particle precedes them. French (pp. 339 and 341) makes use of two particles simultaneously. The *ne* which corresponds to the Italian *non* and the Spanish *no*, occupies the position stated. The second (*pas, point, jamais, guère, que*) comes immediately after the single verb, or after the helper.

In some languages the question form, like negation in Indo-European ones, is expressed by means of a particle. Latin had an interrogative particle, *-ne* equivalent to our *eh?* The Anglo-American *do* or *did* might almost be called interrogative particles, when used in questions. From this point of view the rules of language traffic in Finland are specially interesting, because the Finnish way of expressing question and denial is the mirror image of the common practice in the Indo-European family. Finns express interrogation by putting the interrogative particle *ko*, as we express negation by putting the negative particle *not*, after the pronoun.

To express negation, they attach *e* to the pronoun suffix which they put in front of the verb, instead of after it. That is to say, the negative statement involves an inversion analogous to the inversion in the question form of French or German:

ole-mme-ko	= *are we?*	*emme-ko-ole*	= *are we not?*
ole-mme	= *we are.*	*emme-ole*	= *we are not.*

So far we have considered simple statements, commands, or questions which we cannot split up without introducing a new verb. Link words may connect one or more statements to form compound or complex sentences. Such link words are of two classes. One class, represented by only three *essential* elements of a basic vocabulary for English use, are the so-called *co-ordinate* conjunctions. In contradistinction to these three essential link words (*and*, *or*, and *but*) there are others called *subordinate* conjunctions. The most essential English subordinate conjunctions are:

after	how	so (as) . . . as	when
as (in such a	if	so . . . that	where
way that)	in order that	though	whether
because	than	till	why
before	since		

In addition to the particles given above, we also use the pronouns *who*, *whom*, *what*, and *that* as subordinate link words, e.g. (*a*) this is the house *that* Jack built; (*b*) I know *who* he is.

The distinction between co-ordinate and subordinate link words is useful because the normal rules of word order in some languages are not the same in clauses which begin with the latter. Though we may sometimes leave out *that* in a complex English, and its equivalent in a complex Scandinavian or German sentence, the best definition of a subordinate clause is that it can begin with one of these words. Grammar books sometimes distinguish the *principal* from the subordinate clause or clauses in a complex sentence by the statement that the principal clause is the most important part of the statement. Whether we usually convey any real distinction between the relative importance of the constituent clauses in a complex sentence is at least doubtful.

In relation to *word order*, the distinction between co-ordinate and subordinate clauses is not important to the student of a Romance language. In Romance languages, as in English, the order of words in

each part of a complex sentence is the same. Two minor exceptions
are:

a) in Romance, as in Teutonic languages, the *relative pronoun*
comes at the beginning of a clause even when it is not the
subject, as in: *the readers for whom he wrote this novel* . . .

b) English, like other Teutonic languages, permits subject-verb
inversion instead of the usual sequence after *if*, when a condition is hypothetical, as in: *were he to come = if he came.*

A similar inversion is possible in Scandinavian languages, and is
common in Germany. It is reminiscent of the Chinese idiom of expressing condition by a question. In complex sentences, Scandinavian
is not precisely the same as English word order. In any Scandinavian
subordinate clause the negative particle and any particle indicating
time stands in front of the verb. Scandinavian word order in a complex sentence is illustrated by:

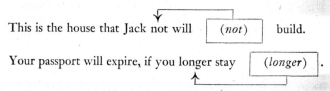

This is the house that Jack not will | (*not*) | build.

Your passport will expire, if you longer stay | (*longer*) | .

The difference between word order of a subordinate clause and of
a simple sentence is much greater in German or Dutch than in Scandinavian languages.

The rules for a simple statement apply to the principal clause of a
complex sentence, i.e., (*a*) the present or past tense form of a simple
or helper verb comes immediately after the German or Dutch subject, when the latter is the first word in the sentence; (*b*) when another word precedes the subject the simple tense form of the Dutch
or German verb precedes its subject; (*c*) the infinitive or participle
which goes with the helper verb always goes to the end of the sentence; (*d*) if there are two helpers (e.g. *I should have come*), the
second helper (infinitive form) follows the infinitive (p. 285). The
rules for placing the German or Dutch verb in a subordinate clause
are:

a) When the verb is simple, it is the last word.

b) The helper also comes at the end immediately after the participle
or infinitive which goes with it.

The following models illustrate both rules:

English word order	*German-Dutch word order*
After I had heard it yesterday, I forgot it again.	After I it yesterday heard had forgot I it again.
When I have seen it, I shall remember it.	When I it seen have, shall I it remember.

It is just as well to bear in mind the fact that conjunctions, especially subordinate conjunctions, are late arrivals in the history of a language. Many living people get on without them. Though they give emphasis to the logical layout of a sequence of statements, they cannot do much to clarify what the content does not itself disclose. In short, we can save ourselves endless trouble with a foreign language if we cultivate the habit of using simple sentences (see p. 166) in our own. We can short-circuit the embarrassment of changing the pattern of word order, if that is necessary and we can steer clear of the troublesome choice of correct case form for the link pronoun of a relative clause. Habitual use of the latter adds to the difficulties of learning a new language and leads to a congested style of writing in the one we customarily use.

It goes without saying that the use of a different pattern for different clauses of a complex sentence adds to the difficulties of learning a language without making the meaning more clear. That it is also a disadvantage for those who are brought up to speak German is clear if we compare the following examples which show how an Englishman and a German may deal with the problem of separating the constituents of a lengthy statement:

a) Since this is an English sentence, it is not difficult to see what changes are necessary if we want to break it up.

This is an English sentence. We may want to break it up. Changes are then necessary. They are not difficult to see.

b) Da dies ein englischer Satz ist, ist es nicht schwer zu sehen, welche Änderungen notwendig sind, wenn wir ihn zerlegen wollen.

Dies ist ein englischer Satz. Wir wollen ihn zerlegen. Änderungen sind dann notwendig. Welche ist nicht schwer zu sehen.

Clearly we have to put much more effort into recasting an involved German sentence as a sequence of simple ones than we spend when we do the same with an English one. This is important because our first impulse in stating a closely knit argument is always to keep the threads together with conjunctions. In a first draft we are therefore prone to construct cumbersome sentences which are not necessarily objectionable in speech. Effective writing demands a different technique. Without the vitality they get from tone and gesture, long and involved sentences call for excessive attention, and are less suitable for rapid reading than a succession of short ones. So we rightly regard the use of the short sentence as a criterion of good style in French or English writing. The rules of word order make it easy for an English or French writer to make the necessary changes in a first draft of an intricate piece of reasoning. The rules of German word order make it difficult to do so. Hence it is not surprising that the style of German technical books and journals is notoriously ponderous and obscure. It is unlikely that Hegel would have taken in three generations of Germans and one generation of Russians if he had been trained to write in the terse English of T. H. Huxley or William James.

The following citation from a book of a German scholar, Carl Bröckelmann (*Grundriss der vergleichenden Grammatik der Semitischen Sprachen*) is a type specimen of Teutonic telescopy. The key to the English translation is that the verb *are* before K. Voller goes with the last two words:

Diese von Th. Nöldeke, *Geschichte des Qôrans*, Göttingen 1860, erstmals dargelegten Grundanschauungen über die Sprache des Qôrans sind von K. Vollers, *Volkssprache und Schriftsprache im alten Arabien*, Strassburg 1906, durch die falsche Voraussetzung, dass die Varianten der spätern Qôranleser, statt Eigentümlichkeiten verschiedener Dialekte vielmehr nur solche der ursprünglichen Qôransprache wiedergaben, übertrieben und entstellt.

These by Th. Nöldeke, *History of the Koran*, Göttingen, 1860, for the first time put forward basic views on the language of the Koran are in K. Voller's *Spoken and Written Language in Ancient Arabia*, Strasbourg, 1906, by the wrong assumption, that the variant readings of the later Koran scholars, instead of (being) peculiarities of different dialects, rather only those of the original Koran language reflected, exaggerated, and distorted.

The vagaries of German word order are not a sufficient reason for the vast gulf between the language which Germans use in the home and the jargon which German scholars write. Accepted standards of such scholarly composition are also the product of a social tradition hostile to the democratic way of life. Intellectual arrogance necessarily fosters long-winded exposition when it takes the form to which W. von Humboldt confesses in the statement: "For my own part, it repels me to unravel an idea for the benefit of somebody else when I have cleared it up." If one has to consult a German work of scholarship or technology, it is reassuring to bear this in mind. When the English-speaking reader meets a sentence like the preceding specimen, it is some comfort to know that German readers also have to *unravel* its meaning for their own benefit.

The fact that people often use a native word order when trying to speak a foreign language sometimes gives rise to comic effects in drama or fiction. It also suggests a useful device for the home student. When learning a language, we have to acquire several types of skill, including the use of the right word and use of the right arrangement. It is rarely good policy to learn two skills at the same time. So the student of a new language may find it helpful to practice the more important tricks of syntax in a foreign language by separate exercises in *syntactical* translations. For instance if you are starting Swedish, the syntactical translation of *didn't you come here yesterday?* is *came you not yesterday hither?* If you are learning German, a syntactical translation of *if I don't come soon, don't wait*, is *if I not soon come wait not*. Models which make use of alliteration or convey novel information are easier to remember than collections of words which have no emotive content. For instance, one of the tricks of Swedish syntax can be memorized by the syntactical translation of *the prophets of the Old Testament did not often wash* as *the prophets of the Old Testament washed themselves not often.*

WORD FORM AND CONTEXT

In Chapter III we learned that many flexional endings, like the *-s* in *he eats,* contribute nothing to the meaning of a statement. Context, and context alone, dictates which we choose. Thus we use *eats* in preference to *eat* if the subject is *he, she, it,* or any noun. In languages which are rich in flexional derivatives, a large part of syntax, including *concord* and the troublesome uses of the subjunctive mood of the verb in subordinate clauses, is made up of rules of this sort.

At one time rules of concord (pp. 100–104) occupied many pages of English grammar, because familiarity with the flexions of Latin and Greek was the greater part of a gentleman's education. The wreckage of the English personal pronouns helps us to get a different perspective. The table on page 160 gives the Old English and modern Icelandic equivalents to emphasize the progressive character of Anglo-American. It also shows our debt to Old Norse, from which we derived *they, them, theirs.* The objective forms (*me, thee, him,* etc.) often called the *accusative,* are really survivals of a dative. The table does not show where *she* and *its* came from. The *she* probably came from the Old English demonstrative *seo* (*that*). *Its* was a later innovation. The 1611 edition of the English Bible uses *his* for *things* and males. This pronoun is a good example of analogical extension. The first person to use it was an Italian in 1598. Englishmen adopted it during the seventeenth century.

Though personal pronouns have retained more of the old flexions than any other class of English words, and therefore account for a large proportion of common errors of English speech catalogued in the grammar books used thirty years ago, we now use only seventeen to do the work of thirty-five distinct forms in Old English. In one way, the use of the pronouns is still changing. Throughout the English-speaking world, people commonly use *they* in speech to avoid invidious sex discrimination, or the roundabout expression *he or she.* Similarly, *them* is common in speech for *him or her,* and *their* for *his or her.* Probably the written language will soon assimilate the

CASE	FIRST PERSON			SECOND PERSON			THIRD PERSON			
	Sing.	Dual.	Plur.	Sing.	Dual.	Plur.	Masc.	Neuter	Fem.	Plural

A. OLD ENGLISH

CASE	Sing.	Dual.	Plur.	Sing.	Dual.	Plur.	Masc.	Neuter	Fem.	Plural
Nominative	ic (I)	wit	we (WE)	þu (THOU)	git	ge (YE)	he (HE)	hit (IT)	heo	hie
Accusative	mec	uncit	usic	þec	incit	eowic	hine	hit (IT)	hie	hie
Dative	me (ME)	unc	us (US)	þe (THEE)	inc	eow (YOU)	him (HIM)	him (HIM)	hire (HER OR HERS)	him
Genitive	min (MINE)	uncer	ure (OUR)	þin (THINE)	incer	eower (YOURS)	his (HIS)	his (HIS)	hire	hira

B. ICELANDIC

CASE	Sing.	Dual.	Plur.	Sing.	Dual.	Plur.	Masc.	Neuter	Fem.	Plural
Nominative	jeg	við	vjer	þu	þið	þjer	hann	það	hun	þau* (THEY)
Accusative	mig	okkur	oss	þig	ykkur	yður			hana	þeim (THEM)
Dative	mjer	okkur	vor	þjer	ykkur	yður	honum	því	henni	
Genitive	min	okkar	vor	þin	ykkar	yðar	hans	þess	hennar	þeirra (THEIR)

* Neuter form only given here.

practice, and grammarians will then say that *they, them,* and *their* are *common gender singular*, as well as plural forms of the third person.

We can already foresee changes which must come, even if rational arguments for language planning produce no effect. Headmasters and headmistresses no longer bother so much about whether we should say *the committee meets* and *the committee disagree*, whether we need be more circumspect than Shakespeare about when we use *who* or *whom*, whether it is low-bred to say *these sort* and *these kind*, whether it is useful to preserve a niche for the archaic dual-plural distinction by insisting on the comparative *better* in preference to the superlative *best of the two*, or whether it is improper to use *me* in preference to the "possessive adjective" when we say: *do you object to my kissing you?*

The conventions of syntax change continually by the process of analogical extension. We use word forms because we are accustomed to use them in a similar situation. Thus our first impulse is to use *were* for *was* in the sentence: *a large group of children was waiting at the clinic.* Whatever old-fashioned grammarians may say about the correct use of *was* and *were* when the subject is the "collective" noun *group*, most of us yield to the force of habit and use *were* for the simple reason that it is usual for *were* to follow children. Since we get used to saying *know* rather than *knows* after *you*, most of us say *none of you know*, unless we have time for a grammatical post-mortem on the agglutinative contraction *not one = none*. So we may be quite certain that everyone will soon look on *none of you knows* as pedantic archaism.

Habits formed in this way give us some insight into the meaningless association of *it* with *rains*, and similar expressions, e.g. *it is usual*. People who speak a language which has equivalents of *is, are, was, were* for the *copula* connecting *attribute* and *topic* (i.e., thing or person) get used to the transition from the explicit statement *the water is hot* to the more economical form, *it is hot*, when the context makes it clear that *it* stands for a real thing. The same remarks apply to the conventional question patterns, *is the water hot?* and *is it hot?* It is a short step to apply the same formula metaphorically when the precise topic is less clearly specified. In spite of the fact that a unit of time is not a heatable object, we also say *the day is hot*. When we make the more economical substitution *it is hot*, in accordance with our habit of dealing with a statement with an explicit and relevant topic, the field of reference of the pronoun embraces the whole setup.

What now compensates for loss of its original function as a snappy substitute for a tangible thing is our habit of interrogation. The customary inversion demands a subject after the verb in the formula *is it hot?* Thus habit and metaphor conspire to encourage intrusion of the pronoun *it* into situations where it merely does the job of an interrogative particle such as *eh?*

Something analogous goes on with words which have the formal peculiarities of nouns and verbs, and we can watch it happening in our own language. *Hammer* is the *name word* for a static object. By assimilating *-ing* it becomes identified with the process of using it, and attracts all the affixes of a weak verb. The converse occurs. A process such as to *sing* is associated with a person or thing by assimilating the affix *-er* of *singer*. Interplay of habit and metaphor works havoc with any attempt to establish a clear-cut relation between word form and word function; and we can see both at work in the most primitive levels of speech. Malinowski sums up the results of his own studies on speech in backward communities as follows:

"The fundamental outlines of grammar are due to the most primitive uses of language. . . . Through later processes of linguistic use and of thinking, there took place an indiscriminate and wholesale shifting of roots and meanings from one grammatical category to another. For according to our view of primitive semantics, each significant root originally must have had its place, and one place only, in its proper verbal category. Thus, the roots meaning *man, animal, tree, stone, water*, are essentially nominal roots. The meanings *sleep, eat, go, come, fall*, are verbal. But as language and thought develop, the constant action of metaphor, of generalization, analogy and abstraction, and of similar linguistic uses build up links between the categories and obliterate the boundary lines, thus allowing words and roots to move freely over the whole field of Language. In analytic languages, like Chinese and English, this ubiquitous nature of roots is most conspicuous, but it can be found even in very primitive languages. . . . The migration of roots into improper places has given to the imaginary reality of hypostatized meaning a special solidity of its own. For, since early experience warrants the substantival existence of anything found within the category of Crude Substance, and subsequently linguistic shifts introduce there such roots as *going, rest, motion*, etc., the obvious inference is that such abstract entities or ideas live in a real world of their own. Such harmless adjectives as *good* or *bad*, expressing the savage's half-animal satisfaction or dissatisfaction in a situation, subsequently intrude into the enclosure reserved for the clumsy, rough-hewn blocks of primitive substance, are sublimated into *Goodness* and *Badness,* and create whole theological worlds, and systems of Thought and Religion." *

What Malinowski calls *"shifting of roots and meanings from one grammatical category to another"* has multiplied words appropriate to situations which have nothing in common and is responsible for 90 per cent of the difficulties of learning a language. One illustration of this is the multiplicity of word forms connected with the subject-object distinction. The lamp illuminates (shines on) the table in the same sense as the lamp illuminates (or shines on) *me.* If so, *I* see the lamp. We do not say that the table *sees* the lamp; and there is a good enough reason for this distinction. The lamp does not stimulate the table as it stimulates my retina; but this difference does not justify the use of two pronouns *I* and *me.* In both statements the pronoun is the goal, and the lamp is the agent as *I* is the agent in *I moved the lamp.* Possibly there was once a real distinction of this kind, if what we should now call *verbs* were only words for action. Today it signifies nothing apart from the context. To know which is the agent and which is the goal of action we need to know the meaning of the verb. If the verb is *hear* the subject is the goal of the process and the object is what initiates it. If the verb is *strike,* the reverse is true. The grammatical object is not necessarily the logical or biological object. It may be the actor or the victim of a performance, the stimulus or a result of a process.

THE HARD LABOR OF GOOD WRITING

The positive rules of syntax which remain when we have cleared away the cobwebs of classical grammar are concerned with the most explicit use of particles, with the rejection of unnecessarily idiomatic expressions, with burial of dead metaphors, and with rules of word order to prevent ambiguity or loss of interest. Syntax, as writers on "semantics" so often forget, is concerned with far more than the problem of meaning. The use of language is a social activity which involves a hearer or reader as well as a speaker or writer. So the art of writing implies the power to grip the attention, and sustain the interest, of the reader. Prolixity, pomposity, and evasion of direct statement are characteristics of writing most inimical to sustained interest; and anyone who is willing to take the trouble can learn to

* Appendix to *The Meaning of Meaning* by C. K. Ogden and I. A. Richards.

avoid bad writing in this sense. Brilliant writing may be a gift, but the power to write simple, lucid, and compelling English lies within the power of any intelligent person who has grown up to speak it.

One important thing to know about the art of writing is that effective and lucid writing is *hard work*. A first draft is never perfect, and a good writer is essentially a good *self-editor*. Indiscriminate exercises in précis are far less helpful than the deliberate application of rules based on the recognition of standard forms of prolixity to which even the best authors are prone. If we apply a few fixed rules we can generally reduce a prose paragraph taken at random from any English classic by 30 or 40 per cent without departing a hair's breadth from the meaning. The important ones are: (*a*) condensation of participial expressions; (*b*) elimination of impersonal formulae; (*c*) translation of the roundabout passive into direct or active form; (*d*) cutting out circumlocutions for which a single particle suffices; (*e*) rejection of *the*, unless absolutely necessary.

One useful recipe for concise writing is to give every *participle* the once-over in a first draft. *The sun having arisen*, then invites the shorter substitute, *after sunrise*. If we are on the lookout for the passive form of statement as another incitement to boredom, we shall strike out the expression *it will be seen from the foregoing figures*, and substitute the snappier, more arresting active equivalent, *the foregoing figures show you*. The last example suggests another general recipe indicated in the last paragraph. The remoteness of the college cloister has cumbered the English language with a litter of *impersonal* constructions which defeat the essentially social character of communication in writing by creating the impression that a statement is for the benefit of the author and the Deity alone. Thus the intrusive *it* of the subject-predicate fetish is another danger signal in a first draft. *It would thus seem that*, or *it would thus appear that*, for *seemingly* or *apparently*, which do the same job when really necessary, are representative exhibits for the prosecution. They should go to the same limbo as *it is said that* (*some people say*), *it is true that* (*admittedly*), the completely redundant *it is this that*, and the analogous circumlocution of which a type specimen is the untrue statement, *'tis love that makes the world go round*.

There are other common literary habits of long-windedness. One is the use of conjunctional and prepositional phrases when a single link word or directive would suffice. The *Times Literary Supplement* and British Civil Service Reports specialize in *the question as to whether*, when *whether* by itself suffices in the same context. *During the time that* generally means the same as *while*. *At an earlier date* is an unnecessarily roundabout way of saying *previously*. *With reference to* is overworked in situations where *about*, or *concerning*, would do as well, and both the latter, though no shorter than *as to*, are more explicit. The reader who has now grasped the importance of using particles explicitly will be on the lookout for these. Another trick which makes writing congested is indiscriminate use of the definite article *the* in situations where it is not really necessary. For instance, we can strike out four inessential articles of the sentence: If *the* war goes on, *the* social services will be cut, *the* income tax will rise, and *the* prices of commodities will soar.

Anyone who wishes to cultivate an agreeable and competent style can practice how to recognize signposts of prolixity by rewriting passages from standard authors or editorial articles in newspapers without recourse to redundant particles, passive expressions, prepositional and conjunctival phrases, or to unnecessary articles. Another type of exercise which helps to develop the habit of *self-editorship* is to rewrite in simple sentences passages from books by authors able to manipulate long and complex ones with more or less effect. Sentences with more than one subordinate clause are nearly always difficult to follow, and complex sentences in general are best kept to round off a fusillade of simple statements, when the habit of writing in simple sentences has been well formed. If we have to use complex sentences, the subordinate clause should generally come first. One of the tasks of self-editing is to see that it does so. The worst type of involved sentence is the one with a clause starting with *that, who,* or *which,* telescoped into another beginning in the same way. *That, who,* and *which* (like participles, passive verbs, *the* and *it*) are therefore danger signals in a first draft. One simple trick which helps in cutting up long and complex sentences is the use of certain adverbial particles or expressions to maintain continuity of meaning. *Meanwhile, first, then, after that,* or *afterwards, in spite of this, in this way, thus, for that reason, consequently, so, therefore,* are therefore useful items of a word list. We can reinforce the habit of self-editorship by practicing the use of such words in dissection of sentences made up to illustrate each of the subordinate conjunctions of page 154. The following example illustrates this type of exercise:

a) COMPLEX SENTENCES:

Although you cannot learn a language without hard work, you may well exaggerate how much effort is necessary. Avoidable discouragement arises *because* many people memorize words and rules which we do not really need *when* we speak or write. There is another thing *which* adds to the burden of learning. Many people do not get *as* much benefit from reading *as* they would *if* they first got a bird's-eye view of grammar in order to recognize rules *which* are not essential for self-expression, *when* they meet them in a fresh setting. *If* we set about our task as the reader of *The Loom of Language* will do, we shall find *that* the effort required is smaller than we think. One of our readers, *who* wanted to learn Swedish, had failed to make much progress, *before* she read *The Loom of Language* in proof. *Since* she followed its plan of study, she has gone ahead quickly. She started reading Swedish newspapers and writing to a boy friend in Sweden after she had got a bird's-eye view of the grammar and was thoroughly familiar with about a hundred essential particles, pronouns, and pointer words. Her vocabulary grew without effort, and her grasp of grammar became firmer, *while* she went on with her daily reading *and* continued her correspondence. She now intends to persevere *till* she is proficient.

b) SIMPLE SENTENCES:

You cannot learn a language without hard work. Still, you can exaggerate the necessary effort. Many people memorize words and rules without asking this question: Do we really need them for speech and writing? Another thing adds to the burden of learning. Many people read without first getting a bird's-eye view of grammar. They meet rules not essential for self-expression. They have not met them before. So they do not recognize them as such. Readers of *The Loom of Language* will set about the task in a different way. They will then find the effort less than our first estimate of it. One of its readers wanted to learn Swedish. She had *previously* failed to make much progress. *Then* she read *The Loom of Language* in proof. She followed its plan of study. *After that* she went ahead quickly. She *first* got a bird's-eye view of the grammar. She also got thoroughly familiar with about a hundred essential particles, pronouns, and pointer words. *Next*, she started reading Swedish newspapers and writing to a boy friend in Sweden. She went on reading daily and continued to correspond. *Meanwhile* her vocabulary grew without effort. She also got a firmer grasp of grammar. *Though not yet* proficient, she intends to persevere.

SPEECH AND WRITING

A difficulty which besets many people when they try to express themselves effectively in writing would be less formidable, if early education did more to encourage the habit of careful and thoughtful speech. Within the domestic circle we can rely on the charity or intelligence of the listener to interpret a half-finished sentence or to sharpen the outline of a loose definition. Since we can usually do so with impunity, many of us never cultivate precise habits of self-expression in everyday life. To write, especially for readers with whom we are not personally acquainted, is another matter. We cannot exploit a common background of domestic associations. We cannot take advantage of associations prompted by surrounding objects or current events. For all we can convey by tone or gesture, conventions of punctuation and of typography (e.g. italics) are the only means at our disposal. If conversation is habitually trivial and confined to a narrow social circle, learning to write is learning a new language.

Maybe, libraries of sound films or phonograph records will eventually supersede the bookshelf as the collective memory of mankind. Meantime, the art of speech, even public speech, cannot be quite the same as the art of writing. There must be a region where the written and the spoken word do not overlap, but we can make it, and should make it, as small as need be. Whether it is relatively large, as in Germany, or small, as in Norway, reflects the extent to which intellectuals are a caste apart from the aspirations and needs of their fellow citizens. Homely writing closely akin to thoughtful speech is a signpost of the democratic way of life. For writing cannot fail to be effective, vibrant with sympathy for the difficulties of the reader.

Where the democratic way of life prevails, public demand for popular science and social statistics discourages literary affectations. Drama and fiction deal more and more with the lives of ordinary people and reflect their speech habits. Since rhetorical prose based on classical models is not adapted to the needs of a public habituated to rapid reading in buses and trains, the vastly increased output of printed matter since the introduction of the linotype machine has also helped to bring the written closer to the spoken word. In our own generation broadcasting has reinforced the trend. Publication of radio talks popularizes a style akin to daily speech, and, as one of our leading phoneticians has said:

"There are signs that the tyranny of print under which we have lived since the days of the Renaissance may give way to a more emancipated era of the spoken word which is now broadcast as freely as print is disseminated. Wireless is making of us a nation of speech critics, and may restore good spoken English to a place of honour."

FURTHER READING

FOWLER — *The King's English.*
GRATTON AND GURREY — *Our Living Language.*
HERBERT — *What a Word.*
JESPERSEN — *Philosophy of Grammar.*
MENCKEN — *The American Language.*
OGDEN AND RICHARDS — *The Meaning of Meaning.*

The Classification of Languages

BEFORE there were comparative linguists, practical men already knew that some European languages resemble one another noticeably. The English sailor whose ship brought him for the first time to Amsterdam, to Hamburg, and to Copenhagen was bound to notice that many Dutch, German, and Danish words are the same, or almost the same, as their equivalents in his own tongue. Where he would have said *thirst, come, good,* the Dutchman used the words *dorst, komen, goed;* the German *Durst, kommnen, gut;* and the Dane, *Tørst, kom, god.* The Frenchman calling on Lisbon, on Barcelona, and on Genoa discovered to his delight that *aimer* (to love), *nuit* (night), *dix* (ten) differ very little from the corresponding Portuguese words *amar, noute, dez;* Spanish *amar, noche, diez;* or Italian *amare, notte, dieci.* In fact, the difference is so small that use of the French words alone would often produce the desired result. Because of such resemblances, people spoke of *related* languages. By the sixteenth century, three units which we now call the *Teutonic,* the *Romance* or *Latin,* and the *Slavonic* groups were widely recognized. If you know one language in any of these three groups, you will have little difficulty in learning a second one. So it is eminently a practical division.

When the modern linguist still calls English, Dutch, German, Danish, Norwegian, Swedish *related* languages, he means more than this. We now use the term in an evolutionary sense. Languages are *related,* if the many features of vocabulary, structure, and phonetics which they share are due to gradual differentiation of what was once a single tongue. Sometimes we have to infer what the common parent was like; but we have firsthand knowledge of the origin of one language group. The deeper we delve into the past, the more French, Spanish, Italian, etc., converge. Finally they become one in Latin, or, to be more accurate, in *Vulgar* Latin as spoken by the common people in the various parts of the Western Roman Empire.

Like the doctrine of organic evolution, this attitude to the study of languages is a comparatively recent innovation. It was wholly alien to European thought before the French Revolution. For more than two thousand years before that time, grammatical scholarship had existed as a learned profession. During the whole of this period scholars had accepted the fact that languages exist without probing into the origins of their diversity. In Greece the growth of a more adventurous spirit was checked by the prevailing social outlook of a slave civilization. When Christianity became the predominant creed of the Western world, Hebrew cosmogony stifled evolutionary speculation in every field of inquiry.

Investigations of Greek philosophers and grammarians suffered at all times from one fundamental weakness. They were strictly confined to the homemade idiom. This was the inevitable consequence of a cultural conceit which divided the world into Greeks and Barbarians. The same social forces which held back the progress of mechanics and of medicine in the slave civilizations of the Mediterranean world held up the study of grammar. To bother about the *taal* of inferior people was not the proper concern of an Athenian or of a Roman gentleman. Even Herodotus, who had toured Egypt and had written on its quaint customs, nowhere indicates that he had acquired much knowledge of the language.

The Alexandrian conquest brought about little change of mind when Greek traders and travelers were roaming far beyond the Mediterranean basin, establishing intimate contact with Bactrians, Iranians, and even with India. Both Greek and Roman civilization had unrivaled opportunities for getting acquainted with changing phases in the idioms of peoples who spoke and wrote widely diverse tongues. They had unrivaled, and long since lost, opportunities to get some light on the mysteries of ancient scripts such as hieroglyphics and cuneiform. They never exploited their opportunities. The Egyptian hieroglyphic writing was a sealed book till the second decade of the nineteenth century. The decoding of cuneiform inscriptions is a work of the last hundred years.

Christianity performed one genuine service to the study of language, as it performed a genuine service to medicine by promoting hospitals. It threw the opprobrious term *Barbarian* overboard, and thus paved the way for the study of all tongues on their own merits. Before it had come to terms with the ruling class, Christianity was truly the faith of the weary and heavy laden, of the proletarian and the slave without property, without fatherland. In Christ there was "neither Scythian, barbarian, bond nor free, but a new creation." Accordingly the early church ignored social rank and cultural frontiers. All idioms of the globe enjoyed equal rights, and the gift of tongues was in high esteem among the miracles of the apostolic age.

Christian salvation was an act of faith. To understand the new religion the heathen must needs hear the gospel in their own vernaculars. So proselytizing went hand in hand with translating. At an early date, Christian scholars translated the Gospels into Syriac, Coptic, and Armenian. The Bible is the beginning of Slavonic literature, and the translation of the New Testament by the West Gothic Bishop, Ulfilas, is the oldest Germanic document extant. Even today the Christian impulse to translate remains unabated. Our Bible societies have carried out pioneer work in the study of African and Polynesian dialects.

The historical balance sheet of Christian teaching and language study also carries a weighty item on the debit side. The story of the Tower of Babel was sacrosanct, and with it, as a corollary, the belief that Hebrew was the original language of mankind. So the emergence and spread of Christianity was not followed by any deeper understanding of the natural history of language. Throughout the Middle Ages the path trod by the Christian scholar was one already beaten by his pagan forerunner. There was no significant progress in the comparative study of languages, but mercantile venture and missionary enterprise during the age of the Great Navigations made a wealth of fresh material accessible through the new medium of the printed page, and encouraged European scholars to break away from exclusive preoccupation with dead languages. For the first time, they began to recognize that some languages are more alike than others.

Joseph Justus Scaliger (1540–1609), variously recognized as *the phoenix of Europe, the light of the world, the bottomless pit of knowledge,* saw as much, and a little more, when he wrote his treatise on the languages of Europe. He arranged them all in eleven main classes, which fall again into four major and seven minor ones. The four major classes he based on their words for *god*, into *deus-, theos-, gott-,* and *bog-* languages, or, as we should say, into Latin (Romance) languages, Greek, Germanic, and Slavonic. The remaining seven classes are made up of Epirotic or Albanian, Tartar, Hungarian,

Finnic, Irish (*that part of it which today is spoken in the mountainous regions of Scotland*, i.e., Gaelic), Old British, as spoken in Wales and Brittany, and finally Cantabrian or Basque.

During the seventeenth century many miscellanies of foreign languages, like the herbals and bestiaries of the time, came off the printing presses of European countries. The most ambitious of them all was the outcome of a project of Leibniz, the mathematician, who was assisted by Catherine II of Russia. The material was handed over to the German traveler, Pallas, for classification. The results of his labor appeared in 1787 under the title, *Linguarum Totius Orbis Vocabularia Comparativa* (Comparative Vocabularies of all the Languages of the World). The number of words on the list circulated was 285, and the number of languages covered was 200, of which 149 were Asiatic and 51 European. In a later edition, this number was considerably increased by the addition of African and of Amerindian dialects from the New World. Pallas' compilation was of little use. He had put it together hastily on the basis of superficial study of his materials. Its merit was that it stimulated others to undertake something more ambitious and more reliable. One of them was the Spaniard, Hervas; another the German, Adelung. Leibniz's suggestions influenced both of them.

Lorenzo Hervas (1735–1809) had lived for many years among the American Indians, and published the enormous number of forty grammars, based upon his contact with their languages. Between 1800 and 1805 he also published a collected work with the title: *Catálogo de las lenguas de las naciones conocidas y numeracion, division y clases de estas segun la diversidad de sus idiomas y dialectos* (Catalogue of the languages of all the known nations with the enumeration, division, and classes of these nations according to their languages and dialects). This linguistic museum contained three hundred exhibits. It would have been more useful if the author's arrangement of the specimens had not been based on the delusion that there is a necessary connection between race and language. A second encyclopedic attempt to bring all languages together, as duly labeled exhibits, was that of the German grammarian and popular philosopher, Adelung. It bears the title, *Mithridates, or General Science of Languages, with the Lord's Prayer in nearly 500 Languages and Dialects*, published in four volumes between 1806 and 1817. When the fourth volume appeared, Adelung's compilation had become entirely obsolete. In the meantime, Bopp had published his revolutionary treatise on the conjugational system of Sanskrit, Greek, Latin, Persian, and German.

Previously, there had been little curiosity about the way in which language grows. In the introduction to *Mithridates* Adelung makes a suggestion, put forward earlier by Horne Tooke, without any attempt to check or explore its implications. This remarkable Englishman was one of the first Europeans to conceive a plausible hypothesis to account for the origin of flexion. In a book called *Diversions of Purley*, published in 1786, Tooke anticipates the central theme of the task which Bopp carried out with greater knowledge and success during the first half of the nineteenth century. Thus he writes:

"All those common terminations, in any language, of which all Nouns or Verbs in that language equally partake (under the notion of declension or conjugation) are themselves separate words with distinct meanings . . . these terminations are explicable, and ought to be explained."

The work of Bopp and other pioneers of comparative grammar received a powerful impetus from the study of Sanskrit. Though Sassetti, an Italian of the sixteenth century, had called Sanskrit a *pleasant, musical* language, and had united *Dio* (God) with *Deva*, it had remained a sealed book for almost two hundred years. Now and then some missionary, like Robertus Nobilibus, or Heinrich Roth, a German who was anxious to be able to dispute with Brahmanic priests, made himself acquainted with it, but this did not touch the world at large. After Sassetti, the first European to point out the staggering similarities between Sanskrit and the European languages was the German missionary, Benjamin Schultze. For years he had preached the Gospel to the Indian heathen, and had helped in the translation of the Bible into Tamil. On August 19, 1725, he sent to Professor Franken an interesting letter in which he emphasized the similarity between the numerals of Sanskrit, German, and Latin.

When English mercantile imperialism was firmly grounded in India, civil servants began to establish contact with the present and past of the country. An Asiatic Society got started at Calcutta in 1784. Four years later, a much-quoted letter of William Jones, Chief-Justice at Fort William in Bengal, was made public. In it the author demonstrated the genealogical connection between Sanskrit, Greek, and Latin, between Sanskrit and German, and between Sanskrit, Celtic, and Persian:

"The Sanskrit language, whatever be its antiquity, is of a wonderful structure; more perfect than the Greek, more copious than the Latin, and more exquisitely refined than either; yet bearing to both of them a stronger affinity, both in the roots of verbs and in the forms of grammar, than could have been produced by accident; so strong indeed, that no philologer could possibly examine all the three without believing them to have sprung from some common source which, perhaps, no longer exists. There is a similar reason, though not quite so forcible, for supposing that both the Gothic and Celtic, though blended with a different idiom, had the same origin with the Sanskrit."

This happened within a few years of the publication of Hutton's *Theory of the Earth*, a book which challenged the Mosaic account of the creation. Custodians of the Pentateuch were alarmed by the prospect that Sanskrit would bring down the Tower of Babel. To anticipate the danger, they pilloried Sanskrit as a priestly fraud, a kind of pidgin classic concocted by Brahmins from Greek and Latin elements. William Jones, himself a scholar of unimpeachable piety, had to make the secular confession:

"I can only declare my belief that the language of Noah is irretrievably lost. After diligent search I cannot find a single word used in common by the Arabian, Indian, and Tartar families, before the admixture of these dialects occasioned by the Mahommedan conquests."

Together with tea and coffee, Napoleon's blockade of England withheld from the Continent Sanskrit grammars and dictionaries which English scholars were now busy turning out. Fortunately the Bibliothèque Nationale in Paris possessed Sanskrit texts. Paris had in custody Hamilton, an Englishman who enlivened his involuntary sojourn in the French capital by giving private lessons in Sanskrit. One of his pupils was a brilliant young German, Friedrich Schlegel. In 1808, Schlegel published a little book, *Über die Sprache und Weisheit der Inder* (On the Language and Philosophy of the Indians). This put Sanskrit on the Continental map. Much that is in Schlegel's book makes us smile today, perhaps most of all the author's dictum that Sanskrit is the mother of all languages. None the less, it was a turning point in the scientific study of language. In a single sentence which boldly prospects the field of future research, Schlegel exposes the new impetus which came from contemporary progress of naturalistic studies:

"Comparative grammar will give us entirely new information on the *genealogy* of language, in exactly the same way in which comparative anatomy has thrown light upon the natural history."

The study of Latin in the Middle Ages had preserved a secure basis for this evolutionary approach to the study of other languages, because the Latin parentage of modern French, Spanish, Portuguese, Italian, and Rumanian is an historically verifiable fact. Unfortunately, history has not been so obliging as to preserve the parent of the Teutonic and the Slavonic groups. To be sure, the present differences between Dutch, German, and the Scandinavian languages diminish as we go back in time. Still, differences remain when we have retraced our steps to the oldest records available. At that point we have to replace the *historical* by the *comparative* method, and to try to obtain by inference what history has failed to rescue. We are in much the same position as the biologist, who can trace the record of vertebrate evolution from bony remains in the rocks, till he reaches the point when vertebrates had not acquired a hard skeleton. Beyond this, anything we can know or plausibly surmise about their origin must be based upon a comparison between the characteristic features of the vertebrate body and the characteristic features of bodily organization among the various classes of invertebrates.

THE BASIS OF EVOLUTIONARY CLASSIFICATION

Biologists who classify animals from an evolutionary point of view make the assumption that characteristics common to all—or to nearly all—members of a group are also characteristic of their common ancestor. Similar reasoning is implicit in the comparative method of studying languages; and those who study the evolution of languages enjoy an advantage which the evolutionary biologist does not share. No large-scale changes in the diversity of animal life on our planet have occurred during the period of the written record, but distinct languages have come into being during comparatively recent times. We can check the value of clues which suggest common parentage of related languages by an almost continuous historical record of what has happened to Latin.

Word similarity is one of the three most important of these clues. It stands to reason that two closely related languages must have a *large* number of recognizably similar words. Comparison of the members of the Romance group shows that this is so. Such resemblance does not signify identity, which may be due to borrowing. Evidence for kinship is strongest if words which are alike are words which are not

TENSES OF THE VERB *BE* IN ROMANCE LANGUAGES

(PRONOUNS ONLY USED FOR EMPHASIS IN BRACKETS)

	ENGLISH	FRENCH	SPANISH	LATIN	ITALIAN
Present	I am	je suis	(yo) soy	(ego) sum	(io) sono
	thou art	tu es	(tú) eres	(tu) es	(tu) sei
	he is	il est	(él) es	(ille) est	(egli) è
	we are	nous sommes	(nosotros) somos	(nos) sumus	(noi) siamo
	you are	vous êtes	(vosotros) sois	(vos) estis	(voi) siete
	they are	ils sont	(ellos) son	(illi) sunt	(essi) sono
Past Imperfect	I was (used to be)	*j'étais*	era	eram	ero
	thou wert	*tu étais*	eras	eras	eri
	he was	*il était*	era	erat	
	we were	*nous étions*	éramos	eramus	erava-mo
	you were	*vous étiez*	erais	eratis	eravate
	they were	*ils étaient*	eran	erant	erano
Past Definite	I was	je fus	fuí	fui	fui
	thou wert	tu fus	fuiste	fuisti	fosti
	he was	il fut	fué	fuit	fu
	we were	nous fûmes	fuimos	fuimus	fummo
	you were	vous fûtes	fuisteis	fuistis	foste
	they were	ils furent	fueron	fuerunt	furono
Future	I shall be	je serai	seré	*ero*	sarò
	thou wilt be	tu seras	serás	*eris*	sarai
	he will be	il sera	será	*erit*	sarà
	we shall be	nous serons	seremos	*erimus*	saremo
	you will be	vous serez	seréis	*eritis*	sarete
	they will be	ils seront	serán	*erunt*	saran-no
	(TO) BE	ÊTRE	SER	ESSE	ESSERE

likely to have passed from one language to the other, or to have been assimilated by both from a third. Such *conservative* words include personal pronouns; verbs expressing *basic* activities or states, such as *come* and *go*, *give* and *take*, *eat* and *drink*, *live* and *die;* adjectives denoting elementary qualities such as *young* and *old*, *big* and *small*, *high* and *deep;* or names which stand for universally distributed objects, such as *earth, dog, stone, water, fire,* for parts of the body such as *head, ear, eye, nose, mouth,* or for blood relationship such as *father, mother, sister, brother.*

If the number of words which two languages share is small, and confined to a special aspect of cultural life, it is almost certain that one is indebted to the other. This applies to word similarities which the Celtic and Teutonic groups do not share with other Aryan languages. The common words of this class are all nouns, some of which are names for metals, tools and vehicles. This does not indicate that there is a particularly close evolutionary relationship between Celtic and Teutonic in the sense defined above. Other features show that a wide gulf separates them. Archaeological evidence suggests that the Teutons took over words with the arts they assimilated from Celtic communities at a higher cultural level.

Through such culture contacts words have wandered from one language to another of a totally different origin. The modern word *bicycle* pedals over linguistic frontiers as the machine used to pedal over national boundaries before passports were obligatory. The word material of all, or nearly all, languages is more or less mongrel. Even in the more exclusive members of the Teutonic group the number of intruders is many times larger than the number of words which the linguist thinks he can trace back to the hypothetical common idiom called primitive Teutonic. When dealing with words for numbers, or weights and measures, we have always to reckon with the possibility of cultural, and therefore *word,* diffusion. If vocabulary is the only clue available, we have to give due consideration to geographical situation. If two languages which share a considerable portion of conservative root words are not geographically contiguous, it is highly probable that they are related.

Word similarity is a good clue. A second is agreement with respect to *grammatical behavior.* French, Spanish and Italian, which we may use as our control group, have a host of common grammatical features such as:

1) A future tense (see pp. 94 and 339) which is a combination of the infinitive and the auxiliary *to have.* (Fr. *aimer-ai, aimer-as;* Ital. *amar-ò, amar-ai;* Span. *amar-é, amar-ás.*)

2) The definite article (Fr. masc. *le,* fem. *la,* Span. *el* or *la,* Ital. *il* or *la*), and pronouns of the third person (Fr. *il* or *elle,* Span. *él* or

ella, Ital. *egli* or *ella*) all derived from the Latin demonstrative *ille, illa.*

3) A twofold gender system in which the masculine noun generally takes the place of the Latin neuter (Fr. *le vin,* the wine; Span. *el vino;* Ital. *il vino;* Latin *vinum*).

Grammatical peculiarities, like words, may be more or less conservative. In the widest sense of the term, grammar includes the study of idiom and sentence construction, or *syntax,* in contradistinction to *accidence,* which deals with the modification of individual words by flexion or root-vowel changes. The syntax of a language is much less conservative than its accidence. When we meet with resemblances of the latter type, it would be far-fetched to attribute them to chance or to borrowing. All the evidence available tends to show that, while words and idioms diffuse freely, peculiarities of *accidence* do not. Now and then a language may borrow a prefix or a suffix, together with a foreign word, and subsequently tack one or the other on to indigenous words, as German did with *-ei* (*Liebelei,* "flirtation"), which is the French *-ie* (as in *la vilenie,* "villainy"); but we know of no language which has incorporated a whole set of alien endings like those of the Latin verb (p. 95).

Absence of grammatical resemblance does not invariably mean that two or more languages are unrelated. Once a parent language has split into several new species, the different fragments may move more or less swiftly along similar or different paths. For example, French has discarded more of the luxuriant system of Latin verb flexions than its Italian sister. English has experienced catastrophic denudation of its Teutonic flexions. Consequently its grammar is now more like that of Chinese than like that of Sanskrit. Grammatical comparison may therefore mislead us, and when the evidence of word similarity does not point to the same conclusion as the evidence from grammatical peculiarities, the latter is of little value.

A third clue which reinforces the testimony of recognizable word similarities arises from *consistent differences* between words of corresponding meaning. We can easily spot such a consistent difference by comparing the English words *to, tongue* and *tin* with their German equivalents *zu, Zunge* and *Zinn.* The resemblance between members of the same pair is not striking if we confine our attention to one pair at a time, but when we look at the very large number of such pairs in which the initial German Z (pronounced *ts*) takes the place of our English T, we discover an immense stock of new word similarities. The fact that changes affecting most words with a particular sound have taken place in one or both of two languages since they began to diverge conceals many word similarities from immediate recognition. This inference is not mere speculation. It is directly supported by what has happened in the recorded history of the Romance group, as illustrated in the following examples showing a vowel and a consonant shift characteristic of French, Spanish and Italian.

LATIN	FRENCH	SPANISH	ITALIAN
*o*vum, (egg)	*œu*f	h*ue*vo	*uo*vo
n*o*vum, (new)	n*eu*f	n*ue*vo	n*uo*vo
m*o*rit, (he dies)	m*eu*rt	m*ue*re	m*uo*re
fa*ct*um, (fact)	fai*t*	he*ch*o	fa*tt*o
lac(-*tis*) (milk)	lai*t*	le*ch*e	la*tt*e
o*ct*o, (eight)	hui*t*	o*ch*o	o*tt*o

If we observe correspondence of this type when we investigate two other languages, such as Finnish and Magyar (Hungarian), we have to conclude that each pair of words has been derived from a single and earlier one. If we notice several types of sound replacement, each supported by a large number of examples, we can regard relationship as certain. This conclusion is of great practical value to anyone who is learning a language. Sound transformations between related languages such as English and German, or French and Spanish, are not mere historical curios, like the sound changes in the earlier history of the Indo-European group. How to recognize them should take its place in the technique of learning a foreign language, because knowledge of them is an aid to memory, and often helps us to spot the familiar equivalent of an unfamiliar word. Use of such rules, set forth more specifically in Chapter VI of *The Loom*, should be part of the laboratory training of the home student who is learning a new language. The reader who takes advantage of the exhibits in the language museum of Part IV can exchange the monotony of learning lists of unrelated items for the fun of recognizing when the rules apply, of noticing exceptions, and of discovering why they are exceptions.

One of the words in the preceding lists illustrates this forcibly. At first sight there is no resemblance between the Spanish word *hecho* and the Latin-English word *fact* or its French equivalent *fait*. Anyone who has been initiated into the sound shifts of the Romance languages recognizes two trademarks of Spanish. One is the *CH* which corresponds to *IT* in words of Old French origin, or *CT* in modern French and English words of Latin descent. The other is the initial silent *H* which often replaces *f*, as illustrated by the Spanish (*hava*) and Italian (*fava*) words for *bean*. If an American or British student of German knows that the initial German *D* replaces our *TH*, there is no need to consult a dictionary for the meaning of *Ding* and *Durst*.

If we apply our three tests—community of basic vocabulary, similarity of grammatical structure, and regularity of sound correspondence—to English, Dutch, German and the Scandinavian languages, all the findings suggest unity of origin. Naturally, it is not possible to exhibit the full extent of word community within the limits of this book; but the reader will find abundant relevant material in the word lists of Part IV. Here we must content ourselves with the illustration already given on page 7, where a request contained in the Lord's Prayer is printed in five Teutonic and in five Romance languages. The reader may also refer to the tables of personal pronouns printed on pages 115 and 116.

The grammatical apparatus of the Teutonic languages points to the same conclusion, as the reader may see by comparing the forms of the verbs *to be* and *to have* displayed in tabular form on pages 89 and below. Three of the most characteristic grammatical features of the Teutonic group are the following:

1) Throughout the Teutonic languages, there is the same type (see table on p. 184) of comparison (English *thin, thinner, thinnest*, German *dünn, dünner, dünnst*; Swedish *tunn, tunnare, tunnaste*)

2) All members of the group form the past tense and past participle of the verb in two ways: (*a*) by modifying the root vowel (English *sing, sang, sung*; German *singen, sang, gesungen*; Danish *synge, sang, sungen*); (*b*) by adding *d* or *t* to the stem (English *punish, punished*; German *strafen, strafte, gestraft*; Danish *straffe, straffede, straffet*).

3) The typical genitive singular case mark is -*s*, as in English *day's*, Swedish *dags*, Danish *Dags*, German *Tages*.

If we follow out our third clue, we find a very striking series of sound shifts characteristic of each language. We have had one example of consonant equivalence in the Teutonic group. Below is a single example of vowel equivalence:

ENGLISH	SWEDISH	GERMAN
bone	ben	Bein
goat	get	Geiss
oak	ek	Eiche
stone	sten	Stein
whole	hel	heil

TO HAVE IN TEUTONIC LANGUAGES

ENGLISH	SWEDISH	DANISH	DUTCH *	GERMAN *
I have	*jag* ⎱	*jeg* ⎱	*ik* heb	*ich* habe
thou hast	*Du* ⎰ har	*Du* ⎰	*jij* hebt	*du* hast
he has	*han* ⎰	*han* ⎰ har	*hij* heeft	*er* hat
we ⎱	*vi* ⎱	*vi* ⎰	*wij* ⎱	*wir* haben
you ⎰ have	*Ni* ⎰ hava	*De* ⎰	*jullie* ⎰ hebben	*ihr* habt
they ⎰	*de* ⎰	*de* ⎰	*zij* ⎰	*sie* haben
I had	*jag, etc.,* hade		*ik* ⎱	*ich* hatte
thou hadst			*jij* ⎰ had	*du* hattest
he ⎱			*hij* ⎰	*er* hatte
we ⎰			*wij* ⎱	*wir* hatten
you ⎰ had	*jag, etc.,* hade	*jeg, etc.,* havde	*jullie* ⎰ hadden	*ihr* hattet
they ⎰			*zij* ⎰	*sie* hatten
I have had	*jag* har haft	*jeg* har haft	*ik* heb gehad	*ich* habe gehabt
I shall have	*jag* skall hava	*jeg* skal have	*ik* zal hebben	*ich* werde haben

* For polite address German has *Sie* + third person plural; Dutch has U + third person singular (p. 138).

THE INDO-EUROPEAN FAMILY

Similarities are comparatively easy to trace in closely related languages such as Swedish and German or French and Italian. We can still detect some, when we compare individual members of these groups with those of others. Centuries back some people felt, though dimly, that the Teutonic group was not an isolated unit. In 1597, Bonaventura Vulcanius observed that twenty-two words are the same in German and Persian. Twenty years later, another scholar stressed the similarities between Lithuanian and Latin. Both were right, though both drew the wrong conclusions from their findings, the former that German had an admixture of Persian, the latter that the Lithuanians were of Roman stock.

Two hundred years later, in 1817, Rasmus Kristian Rask, a brilliant young Dane who had been investigating the origin of Old Norse in Iceland, first drew attention to sound correspondence between Greek and Latin on the one hand, and the Teutonic languages on the other. Textbooks usually refer to this discovery as *Grimm's Law*—after the German scholar who took up Rask's idea. One item of this most celebrated of all sound shifts is the change from the Latin *p* to the Teutonic *f:*

LATIN	ENGLISH	SWEDISH	GERMAN
*p*lenus	*f*ull	*f*ull	*v*oll *
*p*iscis	*f*ish	*f*isk	*F*isch
*p*ed-is	*f*oot	*f*ot	*F*uss
*p*ater	*f*ather	*f*ader	*V*ater

* The German *V* stands for the *f* sound in *far*.

A little later the German scholar Franz Bopp (1791–1867) showed that Sanskrit, Persian, Greek, Latin, and Teutonic in its earlier stages, have similar verb flexions. His studies led him to the conclusion that Aryan verb and case flexion have come about by the gluing on of what were once independent vocables such as pronouns and prepositions. It was a brilliant idea. Bopp's only weakness was that he tried to establish its validity when sufficient evidence was not available. Inevitably, like other pioneers, he made errors. His disciples grossly neglected the important part which *analogy* (pp. 81 and 197) has played in the accretion of affixes to roots. Subsequently a strong reaction set in. Even now, many linguists approach Bopp's agglutination theory squeamishly, as if it dealt with the human pudenda. This attitude is none the less foolish when it affects scientific caution for its justification, because much valid historic evidence to support Bopp's teaching (see especially pp. 87, 109, 339) is available from the relatively recent history of Indo-European languages.

The present tense of "to bear," "to carry," in the following table, where the Teutonic group is represented by Old High German, illustrates obvious affinities of conjugation in the Aryan family:

ENGLISH	SANSKRIT	GREEK (DORIC)	LATIN *	OLD HIGH GERMAN	OLD SLAVONIC
I bear	bharami	phero	fero	biru	bera
(thou bearest)	bharasi	phereis	fers	biris	beresi
he bears	bharati	pherei	fert	birit	beretu
we bear	bharamas	pheromes	ferimus	berames	beremu
you bear	bharata	pherete	fertis	beret	berete
they bear	bharanti	pheronti	ferunt	berant	beratu

* The initial *f* sound in many Latin words corresponds to *b* in Teutonic languages, cf. Latin *frater*, English *brother*.

The singular of the present *optative* of the verb *to be*, correspond-ing to the use of *be* in *if it be*, in three dead languages of the group is:

SANSKRIT	OLD LATIN	GOTHIC
syam	siem	sijau
syas	sies	sijais
syat	siet	sijai

From a mass of phonetic, morphological and word similarities, we thus recognize the unity of the well-defined family called *Aryan* by Anglo-American, *Indo-European* by French, and *Indo-Germanic* by German writers. The last of the three is a misnomer begotten of national conceit. Indeed the family does not keep within the limits indicated by the term *Indo-European*. It is spread out over an enor-mous belt that stretches almost without interruption from Central Asia to the fringes of westernmost Europe. On the European side the terminus is Celtic, and on the Asiatic, *Tokharian*, a tongue once spoken by the inhabitants of Eastern Turkestan and recently (1906) unearthed in documents written over a thousand years ago.

The undeniable similarities between these languages suggest that they are all representatives of a single earlier one which must have been spoken by some community, at some place and at some time in the prehistoric past. The idiom of the far-flung *Imperium Romanum* began as a rustic dialect of the province of Latium; but nobody can tell where the speakers of proto-Aryan lived, whether in Southern Russia, or on the Iranian plateau, or somewhere else. If, as some philologists believe, Old Indic and the Persian of the *Avesta* have the most archaic features of Aryan languages known to us, it is not neces-sarily true that the habitat of the early Aryan-speaking people was nearer to Asia than to Europe. The example of Icelandic shows that a language may stray far away from home and still preserve charac-teristics long ago discarded by those that stayed behind. Only one thing seems certain. When the recorded history of Aryan begins with the Vedic hymns, the dispersal of the Aryan-speaking tribes had al-ready taken place.

From the writings of some German authors we might gain the base-less impression that we are almost as well-informed about the lan-guage and cultural life of the proto-Aryans as we are about Egyptian civilization. One German linguist has pushed audacity so far as to compile a dictionary of hypothetical primitive Aryan, and another has surpassed him by telling us a story in it. Others have asserted that

TEUTONIC COMPARISON

ANGLO-AMERICAN	SWEDISH	DANISH	DUTCH	GERMAN
a) Regular type:				
RICH	rik	rig	rijk	reich
RICHER than	rikare än	rigere end	rijker dan	reicher als
RICHEST	rikast	rigest	rijkst	reichst
b) Irregular forms:				
i) GOOD		god(t) *	goed	gut
BETTER	bättre	bedre	beter	besser
BEST	bäst	bedst	best	
ii) MUCH	mycken(t)	megen(t)	veel	viel
MORE	mera	mere	meer	mehr
MOST		mest	meest	meist
iii) LITTLE	liten(t)	lille	weinig	wenig
	lilla (pl.)			weniger (minder)
LESS		mindre	minder	
LEAST	minst	mindst	minst	wenigst (mindest)

* The -*t* ending is that of the neuter form.

the proto-Aryans were already tilling the soil with the ox and the yoke. The proof adduced is that the word for the *yoke* is common to all Aryan languages (Old Indian *yugam;* Greek *zygon;* Latin *jugum;* Gothic *yuk*). Hence the thing, as well as the name, must have been part of primitive Aryan culture. Arguments of this kind are not convincing. The fact that the word *yoke* occurs in all Aryan languages is explicable without burdening the primitive Aryan dictionary. There is no reason whatsoever why an Aryan-speaking tribe should not have borrowed the yoke from a non-Aryan-speaking community, and then passed it on to others. Though we know little about early culture contacts, common sense tells us that what has happened in historical times must also have happened before.

It has also been said that the primitive Aryan-speaking tribes could count at least as far as one hundred. This does not necessarily follow from the fact that names for 2 or for 3 or for 10, etc., are alike. You cannot exchange goods without being able to count. It is therefore quite possible * that Aryan-speaking tribes borrowed the art of counting from an outside source, or that it diffused from one branch of the

* Philologists sometimes justify emphasis on similarity of number words on the ground that they also share general phonetic features characteristic of a language as a whole. This is also true of words which have undoubtedly been borrowed, and is easily explained by the phonetic habits of a people.

THE TEUTONIC VERB

A. STRONG TYPE

ANGLO-AMERICAN	SWEDISH	DANISH	DUTCH	GERMAN
a) to give	att giva	at give	te geven	zu geben
given (part)	givit	givet	gegeven	gegeben
give(s) (sing.)	giver	} giver	{ geef(t)	gebe (gibt)
(plur.)	giva		geeven	geben
gave (sing.)	gav	} gav	{ gaf	gab
(plur.)	gavo		gaven	gaben
b) to come	att komma	at komme	te komen	zu kommen
come (part.)	kommit	kommet	gekomen	gekommen
come(s) (sing.)	kommer	} kommer	{ kom(t)	komme(t)
(plur.)	komma		komen	kommen
came (sing.)	kom	} kom	{ kwam	kam
(plur.)	komme		kwamen	kamen

B. WEAK TYPE

ANGLO-AMERICAN	SWEDISH	DANISH	DUTCH	GERMAN
a) to work	att arbeta	at arbejde	te arbeiden	zu arbeiten
worked (part.)	arbetat	arbejdet	gearbeid	gearbeitet
work(s) (sing.)	arbetar	} arbejder	{ arbeide(t)	arbeite(t)
(plur.)	arbeta		arbeiden	arbeiten
worked (sing.)	} arbetade	arbejdede	{ arbeidde	arbeitete
(plur.)			arbeidden	arbeiteten
b) to hear	att höra	at høre	te hooren	zu hören
heard (part.)	hört	hørt	gehoord	gehört
hear(s) (sing.)	hör	} hører	{ hoor(t)	höre(t)
(plur.)	höra		hooren	hören
heard (sing.)	} hörde	hørte	{ hoorde	hörte
(plur.)			hoorden	hörten

family to its neighbors. Indeed, numerals are the most indefatigable wanderers among words, as indefatigable as alphabets. In the language of the Gypsies, an Indic tribe, the names for 7, 8, and 9 are modern Greek, whereas those for 5 and 10 are Indic. In the Finno-Ugrian group, the word for 100 is borrowed from Iranian; and Hebrew *schesh* (6) and *scheba* (7) are supposed to be derived from Aryan, while the Hebrew name for 8 is assumed to be Egyptian. But there is no need to go so far back. The English *dozen* and *million* have been taken over in comparatively recent times from the Romance languages.

German philologists have not been content to draw encouraging conclusions from words which are alike and have the same meaning in all the Aryan languages. They have also speculated about the significance of words which do not exist. Of itself, the fact that the Aryan family has no common term for the tiger does not indicate that the proto-Aryans inhabited a region where there were no tigers. Once the hypothetical *Urvolk* started to move, tribes which went into colder regions would no longer need to preserve the word for it. If we are entitled to deduce that the East did not use salt because the Western Aryan word for the mineral does not occur in the Indo-Iranian tongues, the absence of a common Aryan word for milk must force us to conclude that proto-Aryan babies used to feed on something else.

LANGUAGE FAMILIES OF THE WORLD

In a modern classification of the animal kingdom taxonomists unite many small groups, such as fishes, birds and mammals, or crustacea, insects and arachnida (spiders and scorpions) in larger ones such as vertebrates and arthropods. Beyond that point we can only speculate with little plausibility about their evolutionary past. Besides about ten great groups, such as vertebrates and arthropods, embracing the majority of animal species, there are many small ones made up of few species, isolated from one another and from the members of any of the larger divisions. So it is with languages. Thus Japanese, Korean, Manchu, Mongolian, each stand outside any recognized families as isolated units.

We have seen that most of the inhabitants of Europe speak languages with common features. These common features justify the recognition of a single great *Indo-European family*. Besides the Romance or Latin and the Teutonic languages mentioned in the preceding pages, the Indo-European family includes several other well-defined groups, such as the Celtic (Scots Gaelic, Erse, Welsh, Breton) in the West, and the Slavonic (Russian, Polish, Czech and Slovak, Bulgarian and Serbo-Croatian) in the East of Europe, together with the Indo-Iranian languages spoken by the inhabitants of Persia and a large part of India. Lithuanian (with its sister dialect, Latvian), Greek, Albanian, and Armenian are isolated members of the same family.

The Indo-European or Aryan group does not include all existing European languages. Finnish, Magyar, Esthonian and Lappish have common features which have led linguists to place them in a separate group called the *Finno-Ugrian* family. So far as we can judge at present, Turkish, which resembles several Central Asiatic languages (Tartar, Uzbeg, Kirghiz), belongs to neither of the two families mentioned; and Basque, still spoken on the French and Spanish sides of the Pyrenees, has no clear affinities with any other language in the world.

Long before modern language research established the unity of the Aryan family, Jewish scholars recognized the similarities of Arabic, Hebrew and Aramaic which are representatives of a Semitic family. The Semitic family also includes the fossil languages of the Phoenicians and Assyro-Babylonians. The languages of China, Tibet, Burma and Siam constitute a fourth great language family. Like the Semitic, the *Indo-Chinese* family has an indigenous literature. In Central and Southern Africa other languages such as Luganda, Swahili, Kafir, Zulu, have been associated in a *Bantu* unit which does *not* include those of the Bushmen and Hottentots. In Northern Africa Somali, Galla and Berber show similarities which have forced linguists to recognize a *Hamitic* family. To this group ancient Egyptian also belongs. A *Dravidian* family includes Southern Indian languages, which have no relation to the Aryan vernaculars of India. Yet another major family with clear-cut features is the *Malayo-Polynesian*, which includes Malay and the tongues of most of the islands in the Indian and Pacific Oceans.

Something like a hundred language groups, including the Papuan, Australian and Amerindian (e.g. Mexican and Greenlandic) vernaculars, Japanese, Basque, Manchu, Georgian, and Korean, still remain to be connected in larger units. This has not been possible so far, either because they have not yet been properly studied, or because their past phases are not on record. Below is a list of families which are well-defined:

I. INDO-EUROPEAN:

    (*a*) *Teutonic*
        (German, Dutch, Scandinavian, English)
    (*b*) *Celtic*
        (Erse, Gaelic, Welsh, Breton)
    (*c*) *Romance*
        (French, Spanish, Catalan, Portuguese, Italian, Rumanian)
    (*d*) *Slavonic*
        (Russian, Polish, Czech, Slovakian, Bulgarian, Serbo-Croatian, and Slovene)

(e) *Baltic*
(Lithuanian, Lettish)
(f) *Greek*   (g) *Albanian*
(h) *Armenian*   (i) *Persian*   (j) *Modern Indic dialects*

II. FINNO-UGRIAN:
(a) *Lappish*   (b) *Finnish*   (c) *Esthonian*
(d) *Cheremessian, Mordvinian*   (e) *Magyar* (*Hungarian*)

III. SEMITIC:
(a) *Arabic*   (b) *Ethiopian*   (c) *Hebrew*   (d) *Maltese*

IV. HAMITIC:
(a) *Cushite* (*Somali, Galla*)   (b) *Berber* languages

V. INDO-CHINESE:
(a) *Chinese*   (b) *Tibetan*   (c) *Siamese*   (d) *Burmese*

VI. MALAYO-POLYNESIAN:
(a) *Malay*   (b) *Fijian*   (c) *Tahitian*   (d) *Maori*

VII. TURCO-TARTAR:
(a) *Turkish*   (b) *Tartar*   (c) *Kirghiz*

VIII. DRAVIDIAN:
(a) *Tamil*   (b) *Telugu*   (c) *Canarese*

IX. BANTU:
Kafir, Zulu, Bechuana, Sesuto, Herero, Congo, Duala, etc.

GRAMMATICAL CHARACTERISTICS OF LANGUAGE FAMILIES

Because grammatical similarities between different languages furnish one of the three most important indications of evolutionary relationship, it is useful to recognize certain general grammatical features which may be *more or less* characteristic of a language. From this point of view we can classify language types which *may* coincide with genuine evolutionary affinity, if the evidence of grammar is supported by other clues such as the two already discussed. If other clues are not available, the fact that languages are classified in this way does not necessarily point to common origin, because languages which are related may have lost outstanding grammatical similarities, and languages which belong to different families may have evolved similar grammatical traits along different paths. From this point of view, we can divide languages into the following types:—*isolating, flexional, root-inflected* and *classificatory.*

The first and the last are the most clear-cut; and the second, which embraces a great diversity of tongues, depends on grammatical devices which have no common origin. Even when we stretch the limits of all three to the utmost, we are left with many languages in which isolated flexional and classificatory features may be blended without decisive predominance of any one of them, and the language of a single community may traverse the boundaries of such groups in a comparatively short period of its history. Thus the English of Alfred the Great was a typically flexional language, and Anglo-American is predominantly isolating. Basque, which is a law unto itself, the Amerindian dialects, and the speech of the Esquimaux in Greenland, fit into no clearly defined family based on evidence of common ancestry, and we cannot classify them in any of the three grammatical groups mentioned above.

The word of an *isolating* language is an unalterable unit. Neither flexional accretions nor internal changes reveal what part the word plays in the sentence, as do the changes from *house* to *houses, men* to *men's, give* to *gave, live* to *lived*. All the words which we should call verbs are fixed like *must* (p. 112), and all the words we call nouns are fixed like *grouse*. Vernaculars of the Chinese family, usually cited as extreme examples of the isolating type, have other common features which are not necessarily connected with the fact that the word is an unchangeable unit; and the fact that they are difficult to learn has nothing to do with it. We have already touched on the real difficulties, i.e., its script, ambiguities of the many homophones (p. 38) and phonetic subtleties of the tone values; and shall study them at greater length in Chapter X. Here it is important to emphasize that representatives of other language groups, especially languages which have been subject to hybridization resulting from culture contacts through trade, conquest or migration, have evolved far toward the same goal. To the extent that they have done so, they are easier to learn than closely related neighbors.

Malay is one of the Polynesian language group often described as agglutinating languages. In his primer of Malay Winstedt says: "Nouns have no inflexion for gender, number or case . . . there is no article . . . the comparative is formed by using *lĕbeh* (more) before the adjective. The superlative is formed by putting the word *sa-kali* (most) after the adjective. . . . There is no inflexion to mark mood, tense or even voice." To this it may be added that the adjective is invariant and the pronoun has no case form. Malay is therefore an isolating language with none of the peculiar disabilities of Chinese, i.e., tone values and numerous homophones.

AGGLUTINATION AND AMALGAMATION

The *flexional* type includes languages which mainly indicate modification of meaning and grammatical relations by affixes attached to
the same word *root*. According to the degree of fusion between core
and accretion, we can distinguish two sorts of external flexion, *agglutination* and *amalgamation*.

The *words* of agglutinating languages such as Finnish, Magyar
(Hungarian), and Turkish are not exclusively independent and mobile particles like those of Chinese. Affixes loosely joined to the un-
changing root in such a way that the boundary between the core and
its accretion is unmistakable modify the meaning of the former. In

FIG. 26.—COIN OF MACCABEAN TIMES WITH EARLY HEBREW CHARACTERS
On left side: s-q-l j-s-r-l s p (*shekel of Israel year 2*). On right side:
j-r-w-s-j-m h-q-d-w-s-h (*Holy Jerusalem*).

some agglutinating languages, we can recognize many or most of these
affixes as contracted remains of longer words which still enjoy an
independent existence. In others, the affixes do not correspond to
elements which exist apart. What is most characteristic of such languages is that each affix, like an independent word, has a *distinctive*
meaning. So derivatives (see footnote p. 21) of an agglutinating language when classified according to case, mood, etc., have clear-cut
uses, and the method of forming them is also clear-cut. Neither the
use nor the form of derivatives described by the same name admits the
perplexing irregularities of a typically *amalgamating* language such as
Latin, Greek, or Sanskrit.

The term itself implies that *agglutinating* languages form their derivatives by the process of fusion discussed in Chapter III and elsewhere. This is not certainly true of all so-called agglutinating languages, but it is appropriate to those of the Finno-Ugrian family. A
Hungarian example will make this clear. In the Indo-European languages, the case endings are not recognizable as vestiges of individual

words, but in Magyar we can still see how a directive is glued to the noun. From *hajo*, ship, and *hajo-k*, ships, we get:

SINGULAR	PLURAL
hajo-ban (= *hajo* + *benn*), in the ship	*hajo-k-ban*, in the ships
hajo-bol (= *hajo* + *belöl*), out of the ship	*hajo-k-bol*, out of the ships
hajo-ba (= *hajo* + *bele*), into the ship	*hajo-k-ba*, into the ships
hajo-hoz (= *hajo* + *hozza*), toward the ship	*hajo-k-hoz*, toward the ships
hajo-nak (= *hajo* + *nek*), for the ship	*hajo-k-nak*, for the ships

The origin of the affixes is not equally clear in Finnish, but the example cited illustrates a feature common to Finnish and Magyar. Case marks of the singular do not differ from those of the plural in languages of the Finno-Ugrian family. Signs which express plurality remain the same throughout the declension. In contradistinction to that of Greek or Latin, where number and case marks are indissolubly fused, the buildup of the flexional forms of the Finnish or Magyar noun is transparent. The fact that Finnish has fifteen "cases" does not make it difficult to learn, because the case endings in both numbers are the same for all nouns or pronouns and for adjectives,* which mimic the endings of the nouns associated with them. Since an invariable case mark corresponds to the use of a fairly well-defined particle in our own language, the effort spent in learning the case endings of a Finnish noun or pronoun is not greater than the effort involved in learning the same number of independent words.

Analogous remarks apply to the Finnish verb, which has two tense forms, present and past, like ours. The same personal affixes occur throughout, and the change in the final root vowel indicating completed action is the same for *all* verbs. Here is a specimen:

mene-mme—we go	*meni-mme*—we went
mene-tte—you go	*meni-tte*—you went
mene-vät—they go	*meni-vät*—they went

Where we should use a separate possessive pronoun in front of a noun, people who speak a Finno-Ugrian language use an affix attached to the end of a noun as the personal affix is attached to the verb. This personal affix follows the case mark. Thus from *talo* (house) we get:

* In other Finno-Ugrian languages the adjective takes no case affix.

talo-ssa-*mme*—in my house   taloi-ssa-*mme*—in my houses
talo-ssa-*nne*—in your house   taloi-ssa-*nne*—in your houses
talo-ssa-*nsa*—in their house   taloi-ssa-*nsa*—in their houses

The first of the three personal affixes is the same for the Finnish noun and Finnish verb. In Samoyede, a language related to Finnish and Magyar, the same pronoun suffixes appear throughout the conjugation of the verb and the corresponding possessive derivatives of the noun. So the formal distinction between noun and verb is tenuous, as seen by comparing:

lamba-u—my ski   *mada-u* = I cut (my cutting)
lamba-r—thy ski   *mada-r* = thou cuttest (thy cutting)
lamba-da—his ski   *mada-da* = he cuts (his cutting)

The structure of derivative words in languages of the Finno-Ugrian family is not always as schematic as the examples given might suggest. In some languages of the family the vowel of the suffix harmonizes with that of the root word. The result is that one and the same suffix may have two or even three different vowels, according to the company it keeps, e.g. in Finnish *alämä-ssä* means *in the life*, but *talo-ssa* means *in the house*. The modifying suffixes, particularly in Finnish, sometimes adhere more intimately to the root, as in the Indo-European languages. Nonetheless, two essential features are common to all the Finno-Ugrian group. One is *great regularity of the prevailing pattern* of derivatives. The other is *comparative freedom from arbitrary affixes* which contribute nothing to the meaning of a statement. Thus grammatical gender (p. 101) is completely absent.

Where we draw the line between a language which is predominantly agglutinating or isolating depends on where we draw the line between a *word* and an *affix*. If we do not know the history of a language, it is not easy to do so. We do not recognize words such as *except* or *but* as separate entities because they are names of things at which we can point or because they stand for actions we can mimic. We distinguish them from affixes such as *mis-* or *anti-*, *because we can move them about in the sentence*. Now this test is straightforward because of the characteristics of English word order. For example, we put prepositions on the one hand, and pointer words or adjectives on the other, in front of a noun. A pointer word with two or more adjectives, adverbs, and conjunctions can separate a preposition from a noun. When the adjective comes after the noun, as it usually does in French, the distinction is not so sharp, and it is less sharp in some

Indic vernaculars. The Hindustani (p. 416) adjective precedes and the directive *follows* the noun. If these *postpositions*—we cannot rightly call them *prepositions*—never strayed further afield, there would be nothing to distinguish them from case affixes like those of Finnish.

Even the status of a pronoun as an independent element of living speech is difficult to assess by any other criterion. The reader who knows some French will realize that the pronouns *je, me, tu, te, il*, etc., never stand by themselves. When a Frenchman answers a question with a single word, he replaces them by *moi, toi, lui*, etc. We recognize them as *words* by their mobility in the sentence. That *je* or *il* do not always stand immediately in front of the verb is due to certain accidents of the French language, viz. the fact that the pronoun object and the negative particle *ne* precede the verb, and the use of inversion for question formation. By the same token (p. 191) we ought to call the personal suffixes of the Finnish verb, pronouns.

Thus the distinction between an affix and a particle is clear-cut only when the conventions of word order permit the independent mobility of the latter. We are entitled to speak of a language as isolating when, as in Chinese vernaculars, great mobility of unchangeable elements is characteristic of it. When we speak of a language as agglutinating, we usually mean that a clear-cut distinction between particle and affix is impossible because any of the formal elements described by either of these names occurs in a small range of combinations with recognizably separate words, e.g. those we call nouns, adjectives, or verbs. Some grammarians apply the epithet *agglutinative* to any language with a highly regular system of affixes, including the Bantu dialects discussed below. The veteran philologist Jacob Grimm first emphasized the merits of Magyar and commended it as a model to people interested in language planning. The existence of such regularity in natural languages has left a strong impress on projects for a constructed world auxiliary.

At an early stage in the *process* of agglutination many words will share similar affixes, because the latter have not yet suffered *much* modification by fusion with different roots. Hence mere *regularity* of affixes has sometimes been used as a criterion of the agglutinating type; but regularity may also result from an entirely different process. After amalgamation has gone far, lifeless affixes tack themselves on to new words by the process of analogical extension, or old ones may be regularized for the same reason. In this way a language with an amalgamating *past*, e.g. Italian, may approach the regularity of a language in which few words have *yet reached* the stage of true external flexion. So the fact that Turkish or Japanese have regular affixes does not mean that they have evolved in the same way as Hungarian or Finnish. Only the last two, together with *Esthonian*, with the language of the Lapps, and with dialects of a considerable region of northern Siberia constitute a truly related group within the heterogeneous assemblage once called the *Turanian* family.

In a language of the *amalgamating* type, e.g. Sanskrit, Greek, or Latin, modifications of the sense of the word and the place it takes in the sentence depend on affixes intimately fused with the radical (*root*) element. Since fusion between core and affix is intimate, the build-up of words is by no means transparent. Even the grammarian can rarely dissect them. We can always recognize which accretions are characteristic of number or case in the various forms of the Magyar noun (p. 191), because all the plural case forms, as of *hajo* (ship), contain the suffix -*k* immediately after the root; but comparison of singular and plural case forms of an Indo-European noun does not necessarily tell you which part of the suffix attached to the root is characteristic of a particular *case* or of a particular *number*. There is no part of the suffix common to *all plural* in contrast to *all singular* case forms. In a language such as Latin or Sanskrit there is no part of the suffix common to the genitive, singular or plural, in contradistinction to the different *number* forms of all other case forms.

You can see this without difficulty, if you compare the following case forms of a Latin word with our Hungarian example:

nav*is*, a ship	nav*es*, ships
nav*is*, of a ship	nav*ium*, of the ships
nav*i*, to a ship	nav*ibus*, to the ships

English equivalents for different case forms of the Latin for a *ship* or *ships*, as printed above, are those given in textbooks, and the truth is that textbooks conceal the worst from the beginner. Correct choice of case endings in a typical amalgamating language does not always depend on whether the English equivalent would have a particle such as *of* or *to* in front of it. The Latin case ending is much more versatile than in the corresponding Magyar one. The dative *navi* turns up in many situations, where we cannot translate it by *to a ship*, and there is no simple rule which tells us what ending to tack on a Latin noun in one of several dative situations. Compare, for instance, the following with the preceding examples:

port*a*,	a gate	port*ae*,	gates
port*ae*,	of a gate	port*arum*,	of the gates
port*ae*,	to a gate	port*is*,	to the gates

Comparison of the case forms of these two nouns emphasizes the *irregularity* of derivatives in an amalgamating language. Though English is no longer an amalgamating language and is now remarkably regular in comparison with its nearest neighbors, there is no single way in which the plural of all English nouns is formed; and there is no single way in which the past of all English verbs is formed. We can arrange English nouns in families like *man-mouse* or *pan-house*, according to the way in which we derive their plural forms, and verbs in families such as *sing-drink, think-bring, live-bake*, according to the way in which we derive the past tense. In a typical amalgamating language we have to reckon with many noun families (declensions) and many verb families (conjugations). Each declension has its own type of case as well as plural formation. Each conjugation has its own way of building person, time, mood, and voice derivatives.

The two most characteristic features which distinguish languages of the amalgamating from languages of the agglutinating type may therefore be summed up in this way. Amalgamating languages have many derivatives arbitrarily chosen by custom in situations connected by no common thread of meaning, and many different ways of forming the derivative appropriate to a single context in accordance with meaning or conventional usage. The table manners of an agglutinating language are unassuming. You use a spoon because a spoon is the tool appropriate for soup, and there is no difficulty about recognizing what a spoon is, because all the spoons are produced according to a standard pattern. The table manners of an amalgamating language are largely molded by a code of gentlemanly uselessness. You have a large assortment of tools before you. Whether you use a fork with or without a knife or a spoon depends on conventions of social class without regard to the texture of the food.

To all the intrinsic difficulties of learning a language such as Latin, old-fashioned grammarians and schoolmasters have added the distracting pretense that such table manners have a rational basis. This is false. The grammar of an agglutinating language such as Finnish (or

Esperanto) is mainly concerned with meaning. The grammar of an amalgamating language such as Latin is mainly concerned with social ritual. If you hope to master a language such as Latin, the question you have to ask is not what any one of half a dozen different affixes which grammarians describe as trademarks of the *ablative case* signify. They have no *unique* meaning. Each case affix of a Latin noun is the trademark of a shelf of diversely assorted idioms. The business of the learner who succeeds in emerging from the fog of false rationality in textbooks of classical grammar is to find out in what situations Latin or Greek authors use these affixes. The use of Latin case forms is a social habit, like eating asparagus with the fingers. The only reason for making an exception of asparagus is that the people with money do so.

Like the boundary between oil and water in a test tube, the difference between amalgamation and agglutination is not clear-cut. It would be difficult to give good reasons for describing the personal suffixes of the Celtic verb (or the verb of some Indian vernaculars) as amalgamating in contradistinction to agglutinating. Flexions of this kind pass through the stage of agglutination to amalgamation. They then propagate themselves by analogy, as when we stick the -*s* on the *park* in: *he parks his car here.* Conventions of script may greatly exaggerate or hide regularities or irregularities of the spoken language. The literary language of Germany preserves a luxuriance of flexions which are not clearly audible in the daily intercourse of many Germans. The same is more true of French. French script conceals a wealth of contractions which would make a faithful transcription of French speech recall the characteristics of some Amerindian dialects (p. 209). Written English is more isolating than Anglo-American as we speak it, because it frowns on many agglutinative contractions of the pronoun or negative particle (e.g. *who've, won't*) with helper verbs.

A large proportion of the languages of the world got script from alien missionaries bent on spreading the use of sacred texts. The missionary who equips a language with its alphabet uses his own judgment to decide which elements of speech are, or are not, to be treated as separate words, and his judgment is necessarily prejudiced by the grammatical framework of his own education. If he is a classical scholar, he will approach the task with a keen eye for similarities between Latin or Greek and the language which he is learning.

ORIGIN OF FLEXIONS

The value of the distinction between an *isolating* type, which shuns affixation, an *agglutinating* type which favors a variety of highly regular affixes, and an *amalgamating* type which conserves a welter of irregular ones, lies less in the fact that it draws attention to essential differences between different languages, than that it emphasizes the coexistence of *processes* which play a part in the evolution of one and the same language. Though one of these processes may prevail at a given moment, the others are never absent. A language such as modern English or modern French exhibits characteristics which are separated by thousands of years. It is like a bus in which the water diviner sits next to the trained geologist, and the faith healer next to the physician. The vowel chime of *sing, sang, sung*, re-echoes from vaults of time before the chanting of the Vedic hymns, while a considerable class of English verbs such as *cast, hurt, put*, have shed nearly every trace of the characteristics which distinguish the Aryan verb as such. In this and in other ways the grammar of the Anglo-American language is far more like that of Chinese than that of Latin or Sanskrit.

Nobody hesitates to call Chinese *isolating* and Latin *amalgamating*, but neither label attached to French would do justice to it. In the course of the last thousand years or so, French has moved away from its flexional origin and has gradually shifted toward isolation without fully shedding its accretions. French has not gone nearly so far as English along this path, and Italian has lagged behind French, but Italian is much easier to learn, because what has happened to the few surviving flexions of English has happened to the far more elaborate flexional system of Italian. There has been extensive *leveling* of the endings by analogical extension which continually swells the overwhelming majority of English plurals ending in *-s* or English past tense forms ending in *-ed*. To this extent modern Italian has assumed a regularity reminiscent of Finnish, while it has also collected a large battery of new agglutinative contractions for the definite article (p. 361) accompanied by a preposition.

Like other formative processes, leveling or regularization by analogy waxes in periods of illiteracy and culture contact, waning under the discipline of script. The part it has played in the evolution of our remaining flexions will come up for further discussion in Chapter VI.

What applies to flexions, or to derivative affixes such as the -er in baker, applies equally to pronunciation, to word order and to syntax in general. Habit, local or personal limitations of vocabulary and human laziness continually conspire to impose the pattern of the more familiar word or phrase on those we use less often. To the extent that grammarians have set themselves against the popular drift toward (pp. 161 and 264) regularity, their influence has been retrograde. Analogical extension is the process by which natural languages are always striving to assume the orderliness of a constructed auxiliary.

To get rid of the disorder inherent in natural languages was the cardinal *motif* of language planning in the latter half of the nineteenth century. The issue was not entirely novel. The grammarians of antiquity had discussed it and were of two minds. One party, the *anomalists*, took the conservative view. The other, the *analogists*, swam with the stream, and even practiced revision of texts to prune away grammatical irregularities. The controversy went on for several centuries. Among others, Julius Caesar took a hand in it. As a general he favored regimentation. So he naturally took the side of the analogists.

The fact that isolation is the predominant feature of some languages (e.g. Chinese dialects or Malay), regularity of affixes the outstanding characteristics of others (e.g. Finno-Ugrian dialects, Japanese, Turkish) and chaotic irregularity of suffixes the prevailing grammatical pattern of a third group (e.g. Sanskrit, Greek, Latin or Old English) has prompted speculations which take us into the twilight of human speech, without much hope of reaching certainty. Some linguists believe that primitive speech was a singsong matrix from which words emerged with the frayed edges of a Sanskrit noun or verb. According to this view there has been a steady progress from amalgamation, through agglutinative regularity to isolation. Others favor the opposite view. They believe that the speech of our primitive ancestors once consisted of separate root words which were probably monosyllabic, like those of Chinese dialects. If so, words which carried less emphasis than others became attached as modifiers to more meaningful ones. Finally, these accretions got intimately fused, and forfeited their former independence.

Since we can see four processes, isolation, agglutinative contraction, leveling by analogy and flexional fusion, competing simultaneously in English or Italian, these extremes do not exhaust all the conceivable possibilities of evolution. If we hear less about a third, and more likely one, the reason is that most linguists still allow far too little *time* for the evolution of speech. It has taken us long to out-grow Archbishop Ussher's chronology which fixed the date of the creation as October 4, 4004 B.C., at nine o'clock in the morning. Al-though our knowledge of grammar does not extend much further back than three thousand years, human beings like ourselves have existed for at least twenty times as long. We now know that the age of man, as a talking animal, may be as much as a hundred thousand years, perhaps more; and anything we can learn about Sanskrit, old Chinese—or even the ancient Hittite language—can never be more than the last charred pages of a burnt-out bookshelf. Long ago, one philologist saw the implications of this. In his book *Sprachwissen-schaft* Von der Gabelentz (1891) has suggested the possibility that isolation, agglutination, and flexion may succeed one another in a cyclical or spiral sequence:

"Language moves along the diagonal of two forces. The tendency towards economy of effort which leads to a slurring of the sounds, and the tendency towards clearness which prevents phonetic attrition from causing the complete destruction of language. The affixes become fused and finally they disappear without leaving any trace behind, but their functions remain, and strive once more after expression. In the isolating languages they find it in word-order or formal elements, which again suc-cumb in the course of time to agglutination, fusion and eclipse. Mean-while, language is already preparing a new substitute for what is decaying in the form of periphrastic expressions which may be of a syntactical kind or consist of compound words. But the process is always the same. The line of evolution bends back towards isolation, not quite back to the previous path, but to a nearly parallel one. It thus comes to resemble a *spiral*. . . . If we could retrace our steps for a moment to the presump-tive root-stage of language, should we be entitled to say that it is the first, and not perhaps the fourth, or seventh, or twentieth in its history—that the spiral, to use our simile once more, did not already at that time have so and so many turns behind? What do we know about the age of mankind?"

ROOT INFLEXION

While the distinction between agglutination and amalgamation or external flexion is fluid, modification of meaning by root inflexion, such as in *swim-swam-swum*, is sharply defined. This example shows that it exists in the Indo-European group, though it is less typical than addition of suffixes. Its oldest Aryan manifestation, called *Ablaut* by German grammarians, is most characteristic of the verb. We have met with examples in the *strong* class which includes *swim, come, find, sit*. *Ablaut* is common in Sanskrit (*matum*, to measure—*mita*, measured), and in Greek (*trepo*, I turn—*tetropha*, I have turned), but much less so in Latin. Today it is most strongly entrenched in the Teutonic group.

Several types of root vowel change are particularly characteristic of Teutonic, especially German, verbs. One is the existence of pairs of which one member is intransitive (cannot have an object), the other transitive in a *causative* sense. We still have a few such pairs in English, e.g. *fall-fell, lie-lay, sit-set*. Thus we *fall* down (*intrans.*); but we *fell* a tree (i.e., *cause* it to fall). We *lie* down; but we *lay* (*cause* to lie) a book on the table. We *sit* down; but we *set* (*cause* to sit) a flag on a pole.

Umlaut is the technical word for a type of root inflexion peculiar to the Teutonic group. It is specially characteristic of the noun, and is illustrated by the English plurals *man-men, foot-feet*. Such pairs originally had a plural suffix containing the *i* or *j* (p. 71) sound, which modified the vowels *a, o, u* in the stem itself. Thus we get Old High German *gast-gesti* (mod. Germ. *Gast-Gäste*). The process began first in English, and was already complete in documents of the eighth century. Alfred's English had *fot-fet, mus-mys* (pronounce the *y* like the *u* of French or the *ü* of German). In the language of Shakespeare they appear as *fut-fit* and *mous-meis*. Old English had other pairs which have since disappeared. Thus the plural of *boc*, our *book* (German *Buch*) was *bec* (German *Bücher*), and that of *hnutu*, our *nut* (German *Nuss*) was *hnyte* (German *Nüsse*). This trick never be-

ENGLISH	SWEDISH	GERMAN
man-men	man-män	*Mann-Männer*
mouse-mice	mus-möss	*Maus-Mäuse*
louse-lice	lus-löss	*Laus-Läuse*
goose-geese	gås-gäss	*Gans-Gänse*
foot-feet	*fot-fötter*	*Fuss-Füsse*
tooth-teeth	*tand-tänder*	*Zahn-Zähne*

came fashionable in English. During the Middle English period it succumbed almost completely to the custom of making the plural by adding *-es*. Owing to this drift toward the invariant root, the hallmark of a progressive language, English has escaped the fate of German and Swedish. There are a few Swedish, but no German nouns of the *man-men* class; but many Swedish, and far more German, nouns which retain a plural ending also have a modified stem vowel. The German and Swedish equivalents of the *man-men* class are shown on the preceding page.

The same process has affected other types of word derivation in Teutonic languages, especially German. For instance we distinguish between the adjectival and noun forms *foul* and *filth*, or between the verb and adjectival forms *fill* and *full* (German *füllen* and *voll*). Similarly we have noun-verb pairs such as: *gold-gild*, *food-feed* (*Futter-füttern*), *tale-tell* (*Zahl-zählen*), *brood-breed* (*Brut-brüten*). Other related pairs distinguished by stem vowel change are *fox-vixen* and *elder-older*.

In German the shifting of the root vowels went on in historic times, several hundred years after that of English. It did not reach completion before about A.D. 1150. Once the pattern became fashionable it affected words which never had the *i* sound in the succeeding syllable. No drift toward unification had set in before the printing press mummified the grammar of German. Thus vowel change now crops up in the comparative and superlative of nearly all monosyllabic adjectives (e.g. *hoch-höher*), distinguishes the ordinary past of many verbs from the subjunctive (e.g. *ich nahm-ich nähme*), the agent from his activity (e.g. *backen-Bäcker*), the diminutive from the basic word (*Haus-Häuschen*), the noun-abstract from its adjective (*gut-Güte*), the verb from the adjective (e.g. *glatt-glätten, smooth-to smooth*).

In many German dialects such *mutation* appears where standard German does without. Thus we meet *Hünd, Ärm, Täg*, for *Hunde, Arme, Tage*, and Yiddish opposes *tog-teg* to the *Tag-Tage* of com-

GERMAN	OLD ENGLISH	ANGLO-AMERICAN
ich helfe	ic helpe	
du hilfst	thu hilpst	
er hilft	he hilpth	help(s)
wir helfen	we ⎫	
ihr helft	ge ⎬ helpath	
sie helfen	hie ⎭	

mon German. Apart from the disruption caused by an *i* or *j* sound in the succeeding syllable, and the Ablaut inherited from primitive Indo-European, modern German preserves several other vowel mutations. Occasionally the various types come together in the conjugational forms of a single verb. Thus we have *ich sterbe* (I die)—*er stirbt* (he

dies)—*stirb!* (die!)—*er starb* (he died)—*er ist gestorben* (he has died)
—*wenn er stürbe* (if he died). The backwardness of German root
vowel behavior is particularly impressive if we compare it with both
Old English and Modern English, as shown on the preceding page.

In view of the prevailing ideology of the Third Reich, there is an
element of comedy in this peculiarity which puts German apart from
its sister languages. Internal vowel change, which is subsidiary to
external flexion in the group as a whole, is the trademark of the
Semitic family. The Semitic root word consists of three, less often of
two or four, consonants. Thus the consonantal group *sh-m-r* signifies
the general notion of "guarding," and *g-n-b* the general notion of
"stealing." Into this fixed framework fit vowels, which change according to the meaning and grammatical functions of the word.
From the root *sh-m-r* we get *shamar*, he has guarded; *shomer*, guarding; *shamur*, being guarded. From the root *g-n-b* we have *ganab*, he
has stolen; *goneb*, stealing; *ganub*, being stolen. Though Semitic languages form derivatives by addition of prefixes and suffixes, such ad-
ditions have a much smaller range than those of the older Indo-
European languages. It is therefore misleading to lump Semitic
together with the Indo-European languages as flexional types. Semitic
languages constitute a sharply marked type characterized by *root
inflexion*, in contradistinction to *amalgamation*, which is characteristic of the old Aryan languages such as Sanskrit, Latin, or Russian.

The student of German will find it useful to tabulate some essentially Semitic features of the language. Excluding minor irregularities
and such comparatives as *hoch-höher* (high-higher), we can distinguish the following categories:

1) In the conjugation of the second and third person singular of the
present tense and sometimes in the imperative of many strong
verbs, e.g.:

sprechen	(talk)	: *ich spreche*	*er spricht*	*Sprich!*
geben	(give)	: *ich gebe*	*er gibt*	*Gib!*
nehmen	(take)	: *ich nehme*	*er nimmt*	*Nimm!*
lesen	(read)	: *ich lese*	*er liest*	*Lies!*

2) In the formation of the past subjunctive of strong verbs, e.g. *er gäbe*,
er nähme, er läse, when the vowel of the ordinary past is long as
in *er gab, er nahm, er las*.

3) In many couplets of intransitive verbs and transitive ones (p. 141)
with a causative significance, e.g. *trinken-tränken* (drink-give to
drink), *wiegen-wägen* (weigh), *saugen-säugen* (suck-suckle).

4) Plural derivatives of neuter and masculine nouns with the stem vowels, *a, o, u, au*, e.g. *Kalb-Kälber* (calf-calves), *Buch-Bücher* (book-books), *Stock-Stöcke* (stick-sticks), *Haus-Häuser* (house-houses).

5) Adjectival derivatives for materials, e.g. *Holz-hölzern* (wood-wooden), *Erde-irden* (earth-earthen).

6) Adjectival derivatives with the suffixes *-ig, -icht, -isch,* or *-lich*, e.g. *Macht-mächtig* (power-powerful), *Haus-häuslich* (house-domestic), *Stadt-städtisch* (town-urban).

7) Diminutives, e.g. *Mann-Männchen, Frau-Fräulein.*

8) Abstract feminine nouns in *-e*, e.g. *gut-die Güte* (good-goodness), *hoch-die Höhe* (high-the height).

9) Collective neuter nouns, *Berg-Gebirge* (mountain-mountain range), *Wurm-Gewürm* (worm-vermin).

10) Feminine nouns which take *-in*, e.g. *Hund-Hündin* (dog-bitch).

CLASSIFICATORY LANGUAGES

The Bantu languages of Africa illustrate features common to the speech of backward and relatively static cultures throughout the world. One of these gives us a clue to the possible origin of gender in the Indo-European group. The Bantu family includes nearly all the native tongues spoken from the equator to the Cape Province. In this huge triangle, the only exceptions are the dialects of the Bushmen, of the Hottentots, and of the Pygmies of Central Africa. About a hundred and fifty Bantu dialects form a remarkably homogeneous unit. Most of them are not separated by greater differences than those which distinguish Spanish from Italian.

One member has been known to us since the seventeenth century. In 1624, a catechism appeared in Congolese. A generation later the Italian, Brusciotto, published a Congolese grammar. These two documents show that the language has changed little during the last three hundred years, and therefore refute the belief that unwritten languages necessarily change more rapidly than codified ones. One Bantu language already had a script before the arrival of the Christian missionary and the white trader. It is called Swahili, and was originally the dialect of Zanzibar. Today it is the *lingua franca* of the East Coast of Africa. For several centuries before the Great Navigations, Arabs had been trading with Zanzibar, and the native community adopted the unsuitable alphabet of the Moslem merchants.

The Kafir-Sotho group of Bantu languages (South-East Africa) have a peculiarity not shared by other members of the same family. In addition to consonants common to the speech of other peoples, there are characteristic clicks produced by inspiration of air. They resemble the smacking sound of a kiss. It is probable that they are "borrowed" elements from the click languages of the Bushmen and Hottentots.

The existence of the Bantu family as such has been recognized for a century. This is partly because every name word belongs to one of a limited number of prefix-labeled classes analogous to our small word clusters labeled by such suffixes as *-er, -ship, -hood, -dom,* and *-ter* or *-ther* in *father, mother, brother, sister, daughter.* So also in Greek, many animals have names ending in *-x,* e.g. *alopex* (fox), *aspalax* (mole), *dorx* (roe-deer), *hystrix* (porcupine), *pithex* (ape). The analogous German terminal *-chs* also holds together a limited group of animals, e.g. *Dachs* (badger), *Fuchs* (fox), *Lachs* (salmon), *Ochs* (ox). Several German names for animals have another suffix, *-er,* e.g. *Adler* (eagle), *Hamster* (hamster), *Kater* (tomcat), *Sperber* (hawk). Endings such as these are isolated examples of what is a universal characteristic of the Bantu languages. The name of any thing, any person, or any action is labeled by a particular *prefix* which assigns it to one of about twenty classes of words labeled in the same way.

The other outstanding peculiarity of the Bantu family is that the noun prefix colors the entire structure of the sentence. Whatever moves within the orbit of a noun is stamped accordingly. Thus a qualifying adjective or even a numeral carries the prefix of the preceding noun which it qualifies, e.g. *mu-ntu, mu-lotu* (*man handsome = handsome man*), but *ba-ntu ba-lotu* (*men handsome = handsome men*). The pronoun of the third person has a form which more or less recalls the prefix of the noun represented by it. In the sentence *u-lede = he* (*the man*) *is asleep, u-* reflects the *mu-* of *mu-ntu* (*man*), and in *lu-lede = he* (the baby) *is* asleep, *lu-* echoes the classifier *lu-* of *lu-sabila* (baby). In Swahili and many other Bantu languages, the personal pronoun is prefixed to the verb even when the sentence has a noun subject, e.g. *ba-kazana ba-enda* (*the girls they go*). This binding together of the various parts of the sentence produces a kind of alliterative singsong, e.g.:

ba-lavu	*ba-baluma*	*ba-ntu*
the lions	they bit	the men

The type of concord which occurs in a highly inflected Aryan language produces an analogous but rhyming singsong, e.g. in German: *die hübschen amerikanischen Studentinnen machten Sensation* (the pretty American coeds made a hit).

The Bantu prefixes of most classes have distinct singular and plural forms. A singular prefix *mu-* (Subiya), corresponding to a plural prefix *ba-*, signifies human agents. Thus *mu-sisu* means *boy*, and *ba-sisu* means *boys*. Another singular prefix *ki-* (Swahili), corresponding to the plural prefix *vi-*, is largely used for manufactured things, e.g. *ki-funiko, cover*, and *vi-funiko, covers*. The prefix *ma-* (Sotho) is characteristic of a collectivity, of a big number, a liquid, and also of things which occur in pairs, e.g. *ma-naka* (horns of an animal). The prefix *ka-* (Ganda) corresponding to a plural prefix, *tu-*, denotes small size, e.g. *ka-ntu* (small man), *tu-ntu* (small men). With the prefix *bo-* (Duala), abstract nouns are formed, derived from adjectives, verbs and names for things, e.g. *bo-nyaki* (growth, from *nyaka*, grow). The prefix *ku-* (Ganda) serves for the formation of verb nouns or infinitives, e.g. *ku-lagira* (to command, or commanding).

Since there is no precise parallel to this type of concord in our own language, we must fall back on an artificial model to illustrate what it involves. Let us first suppose that every English noun had one of twenty prefixes analogous to the suffix *-er* common to the occupational *fisher-writer-builder* class. We may also suppose that the words *dog* and *sheep* respectively carried the prefixes *be-* and *m'-*. If English also had the same concord system as a Bantu dialect, the sentence *hungry dogs sometimes attack young sheep* would then be *be-hungry be-dogs sometimes be-they-attack m'-young m'-sheep*.

The origin of the Bantu classifiers is not above dispute. It is possible, though not conclusively proved, that they were once independent words with a concrete meaning, standing for groups of allied objects, such as human beings, trees, liquids, things long or short, big or small, weak or strong. When associated with other words they originally marked them as members of one class. According to this view, *be-dog* and *m'-sheep* of the parable used above would be what remains of *beast-dog* and *meat-sheep*. Subsequently the outlines of once-distinct classes became blurred through contamination and fusion, and the classifier sank to the level of a purely grammatical device. If so, the original plan has survived only in the first two classes. With few exceptions these signify human beings.

Only in a relatively static society at a primitive level of culture with little division of labor could classificatory particles retain a clear-cut function. Migration and civilization bring human beings into new situations which call for new vocables. These do not necessarily fall into any pre-existing niche of a classificatory system. In fact, languages of the classificatory type are confined to communities which used neither script nor the plow before contact with white men. The surmise that Bantu classifiers were once concrete words suggests analogy with the *numeratives* which the Chinese and Japanese almost invariably insert between figures and things counted, as when we speak of *three head of cattle*. Thus the Chinese say *two piece man* (= *two men*), *three tail fish* (= *three fish*), *four handle knife* (= *four knives*), *five ornament officials* (= *five officials*). The analogy should not be pushed too far, because Bantu classifiers no longer possess a clear-cut meaning, nor do they survive as independent words.

Particles or affixes used as classifiers are not confined to the Bantu languages. Capell * writes as follows about one of the Papuan dialects:

"In the languages of Southern Bougainville nouns are divided into upwards of twenty classes, and the adjectives and numerals vary in agreement with the class to which the noun belongs. One gets something of the same effect as in the Bantu languages, except that in the Papuan languages it is the *end of the word*, not the beginning, that changes."

In Kiriwinian, a language of the Trobriand Islands, demonstratives as well as adjectives and numerals are coupled with characteristic particles which are common to all members of a particular class of noun, and each noun belongs to such a class. Professor Malinowski, who has given an illuminating account ** of it, describes its essential peculiarities in the following passage:

"Let us transpose this peculiarity of Kiriwinian into English, following the native prototype very closely, and imagine that no adjective, no numeral, no demonstrative, may be used without a particle denoting the nature of the object referred to. All names of human beings would take the prefix 'human.' Instead of saying 'one soldier' we would have to say 'human-one soldier walks in the street.' Instead of 'how many passengers were in the accident?' 'how human-many passengers were in the accident?' Answer, 'human-seventeen.' Or again, in reply to 'Are the Smiths human-nice people?' we should say, 'No, they are human-dull!' Again,

* *Oceania*, 1937.
** *Classificatory Particles in Kiriwina* (Bulletin of the School of Oriental Studies, vol. i, 1917–20).

nouns denoting persons belonging to the female sex would be numbered, pointed at, and qualified with the aid of the prefix 'female'; wooden objects with the particle 'wooden'; flat or thin things with the particle 'leafy,' following in all this the precedent of Kiriwina. Thus, pointing at a table, we would say, 'Look at wooden-this'; describing a landscape, 'leafy-brown leaves on the wooden-large trees'; speaking of a book, 'leafy-hundred pages in it'; 'the women of Spain are female-beautiful'; 'human-this boy is very naughty, but female-this girl is good.' "

Thus the habit of labeling all name words with one of a limited number of affixes is not confined to the Bantu family. It is widely distributed among unrelated languages spoken by static and backward communities throughout the world. The number of such classes may be as many as twenty, as in Bantu dialects; or *it* may be as few as *four*, as in one of the dialects of the Australian aborigines. The classificatory mark is not necessarily a prefix. In the Papuan language cited by Capell, it is a suffix like the gender terminal of an Aryan adjective.

Thus the distinction between the classificatory and the flexional type is not so sharp as it first seems to be. The trademark of the Indo-European adjective as a separate entity is that it carries the suffix determined by one of the three gender classes to which a noun is assigned. We know that what are called adjectives in Aryan languages were once indistinguishable from nouns, and the example of Finnish (p. 191) shows us how easily the ending of the noun gets attached to an accompanying epithet. In each of the three Aryan gender classes we meet with a greater or less proportion of nouns with characteristic affixes limited to one of them, and the notion of sex which an American or an Englishman associates with gender has a very flimsy relation to the classification of Indo-European nouns in their respective gender classes.

Though we have no firsthand knowledge about the origin of gender, we know enough to dismiss the likelihood that it had any essential connection with sex. The most plausible view is that the distinction of gender in the Indo-European family is all that is left of a system of suffixes essentially like the Bantu prefixes. If so, the former luxuriance of such a system has been corroded in turn by nomadic habits and civilized living as primitive Aryan-speaking tribes successively came into contact with new objects which did not fit into the framework of a classification suited to the limited experience of settled life at a low level of technical equipment.

PHONETIC PATTERN OF LANGUAGE FAMILIES

Just as we recognize grammatical processes such as isolation, agglutination, amalgamation, root inflexion, we can also recognize sound patterns which predominate in one or other group. Such phonetic patterns furnish us with an additional clue to linguistic affinities, albeit a clue which too few philologists have followed up. Our last section illustrates one phonetic type which is distributed over a large part of the world. In a multitude of unrelated languages, including Japanese, Malayo-Polynesian, and Bantu dialects, agglutinative regularity coexists with a sound pattern quite unlike that of our own language or of any languages related to it. Jespersen (*Growth and Structure of the English Language*) illustrates the contrast by the following passage from the language of Hawaii, of which the familiar place names (e.g. *Honolulu*) recall the same characteristics as the Japanese *Yokohama, Fujiyama*, etc.: *I kona hiki ana aku ilaila ua hookipa ia mai la oia me ke aloha pumehana loa.*

The syllable in this sample consists of a vowel or of a vowel preceded by a *simple* consonant. That is to say (p. 49) the syllable is like a typical Chinese word. Aryan languages are rich in consonant clusters. In languages as far apart as Norwegian, Welsh, and Greek, we may meet at the beginning of many words any of the consonants *b, d, f, g, k, p*, followed by *l* or *r, t* followed by *r, s* by *l, t*, or *tr*. For this reason alone such words as *sprinkle, sprightly, expression, blaspheme, electrical*, or the German *Zwetschge* (prune), are quite foreign to the pattern of sounds to which many peoples of the world are attuned. They also illustrate another characteristic of the Aryan family. Aryan words are comparatively rich in *closed* (p. 49) syllables; and, if monosyllabic, are commonly of the closed type illustrated by *God* and *man*, or *cat* and *dog*. We have many English monosyllables which illustrate both these trademarks of Aryan word structure, e.g. *breeds, straps, prowled, plump, sprained, smelts, blunts, stinks, floats, proved, stringed.*

Firth * points out that certain combinations of initial consonants illustrated by word counts in dictionaries are characteristic of particular groups within the Aryan family. We shall find that some clusters, e.g. the Greek PS-, Latin -CT-, and Teutonic SN- or SK- are signposts of word origin. Some clusters or elements of a cluster may convey a common thread of meaning in groups of words which exist in

* *Speech* (Benn's Library).

closely related languages. In English there are about a hundred and twenty verbs in which a final *l* suggests repetitive action, as in *wobble, wangle, riddle, coddle, bungle, handle, nestle, snaffle, tipple, sprinkle.*

Among modern Aryan languages Italian has moved furthest from the Aryan pattern, owing to elimination of some Latin medial consonant combinations, e.g. -CT- to -TT- (p. 237), and through the decay of the final consonant of the Latin terminals. Hence almost all Italian words end in a vowel. Conversely English is very rich in words which end with a consonant cluster owing to the decay of the vowel of a terminal syllable, e.g. the short *e* still fairly audible in the plural flexion of *houses* or *princes,* and in the past suffix of *a learned woman.* So it may be no accident that a wealth of compound consonants and closed syllables go with a family whose other diagnostic characteristic, at least that of all its *earliest* representatives Sanskrit, Old Persian, Greek, Latin, of which we have knowledge, is *amalgamation,* i.e., great irregularity of affixation.

At one time comparative linguists distinguished an *incorporating* or *holophrastic* type to accommodate the Amerindian languages, which illustrate another peculiarity of sound pattern. It is extremely difficult to recognize where one word begins and another ends in the language of the Greenland Eskimo. The same is true of a great variety of indigenous, totally unrelated, vernaculars of the American continent. How far people distinguish one word from the next, especially in rapid speech, varies from one dialect to another within a small group. In a large family such as the Aryan, we find examples of highly holophrastic languages such as French or highly staccato languages such as German.

The peculiar sound pattern of the Aryan group which is now custodian of the bulk of modern scientific knowledge has one result relevant (p. 514) to the design of a satisfactory international auxiliary. People who do not speak an Aryan language commonly distort words of Aryan origin when they assimilate them. Extraneous vowels break up consonant clusters, or supplement closed syllables, and familiar more or less related sounds replace foreign ones. Thus the Roman transcription of *football* and *calcium* after passing through the phonetic sieve of Japanese is *fotoboru* and *karushumu* in which *r* deputizes for the alien *l.* Since Japanese does not tolerate a terminal consonant, assimilated words tack on a vowel, e.g. *inki* (ink), *naihu* (knife). In fact, Japanese equivalents for technical terms of Greek origin are reminiscent of Greek transcription in the Cypriotic syllabary (Fig. 14). Mencken has drawn attention to similar distortions by Italian immigrants in the United States, e.g. *atto* (hat), *orso* (horse), *scioppa* (shop), *bosso* (boss).

FURTHER READING

BLOOMFIELD   *Language.*
FINCK   *Die Haupttypen des Sprachbaus.*
FIRTH   *Speech.*
                    The Tongues of Men.
GRAFF   *Language and Languages.*
MEILLET   *Les Langues dans l'Europe nouvelle.*
MEILLET and COHEN   *Les Langues du Monde.*
PEDERSEN   *Linguistic Science in the Nineteenth Century.*
SAPIR   *Language.*
TUCKER   *Introduction to the Natural History of Language.*
WHITNEY   *Life and Growth of Language.*

PART TWO

OUR HYBRID HERITAGE
A COOK'S TOUR ROUND THE TEUTONIC AND ROMANCE GROUPS

How to Learn the Basic Word List

SOME people complain of poor memory, and attribute to it the difficulties of learning a foreign language. If also fond of horticulture or of natural history, they do not complain about the difficulty of memorizing a copious vocabulary of technical terms. So a poor memory is rarely a correct explanation of what holds them back. One of the essential obstacles is that the interest of the beginner is focused exclusively on a remote goal. It is not also directed, like that of the naturalist, to the material itself. To learn with least effort we have to become *language conscious*. If *The Loom of Language* has succeeded in its task so far the reader who has not studied languages before, and the reader who has studied them without thinking much about their family traits, will now be more language conscious. The four chapters which follow are for those who are. They contain a more detailed treatment of some of the languages referred to in previous chapters for the benefit of the home student who may want to start learning to read or to write intelligibly in one or other of them. Anyone who intends to give the method of this book a fair trial must pay careful attention to cross references, including references to relevant tables in Part I. Some practical suggestions which immensely lighten the tedium of traversing the first few milestones when learning a new language have come from the work of scholars who have contributed to the international language movement (see Chapter XI). They have not yet made their way into current textbooks, and the reader who wishes to use *The Loom of Language* as an aid to the study of a foreign language should recall them at this stage.

The most important is to concentrate on learning a relatively small class of words before trying to learn any others. This class includes the *particles, pronouns, pointer words,* and *helper verbs.* There are several reasons for doing this. One is that a battery of about one hundred and fifty of such words *for ready use,* supplemented by a nodding acquaintance with about a hundred others, includes a very high proportion of the words we constantly use or constantly meet on the printed page. A second is that what verbs, adjectives, and nouns we commonly meet, especially the nouns, depends on individual circumstances and tastes. A third is that it is easier to guess the meaning of nouns, adjectives, and verbs when we meet them. This is partly because an increasing proportion of new words of this kind are international, and also because the particles are the most unstable elements in a language. We do not borrow prepositions or conjunctions, but we constantly borrow nouns, verbs, or adjectives, and such borrowed words play an important part in modern life. The word for a telephone or for a museum is recognizably the same in English, Swedish, Serbo-Croat, or Hungarian; but the Dane who learns the word *rabbit* in his first lesson from the English primer commonly used in Danish schools may live ten years in Nottingham or correspond regularly with a friend in New York without getting involved in a discussion about rodents of any kind.

If you learn only ten new words of the group which includes particles, pronouns, and pointer words every day for a fortnight, you will have at your disposal at least 25 per cent of the *total* number of words you use when you write a letter. When you have done this, it is important to have a small vocabulary of essential nouns, adjectives, and verbs ready for *use*. Before you start trying to write or to read in a foreign language, it is best to get a *bird's-eye view* of its grammatical peculiarities. The bird's-eye view is easy to get in an hour's reading, and is not difficult to memorize unless the language, like Russian, has a large number of archaic and useless grammatical devices. Even so, much of the effort commonly put into learning the rules of grammar can be capitalized for use in other ways, if you do not start reading or writing till you have a broad general outlook. It will help you to remember the essentials, if you see them in an evolutionary context. Since it is relatively easy to recall information when prompted by the written word, a student who first gets a bird's-eye view of the grammar of a new language will be able to recognize essential rules when he meets them in newspapers, letters, or books. In this way, reading will help to fix them from the start. Contrariwise, the beginner who starts reading without the bird's-eye view may become *color blind to conventions which are essential* for correct self-expression. Facility in guesswork may then become a hindrance to learning how to write or speak correctly.

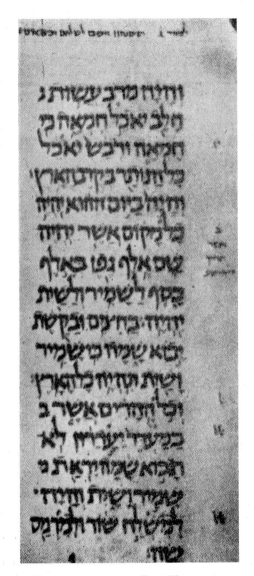

FIG. 27. THREE VERSES FROM THE OLD TESTAMENT IN THE OLDEST
DATABLE MS OF THE HEBREW BIBLE, THE PROPHETEN-CODEX FROM CAIRO

FIG. 28. PAGE FROM THE "CODEX ARGENTEUS" NOW IN UPPSALA

This is a sixth-century edition of the New Testament translated by Bishop Ulfilas into Gothic about A.D. 350. The characters used are mainly drawn from the Greek alphabet supplemented by Roman and Runic letters. Note for instance the Greek symbol Ѱ which stands not for *ps* as in Greek writing but for Þ.

The *Codex Argenteus* now in the University library at Uppsala has 187 of the original 330 leaves of the four gospels intact. Wolfenbuttel and Milan libraries possess other fragments of the gospels, the Pauline epistles, and the Old Testament books Ezra and Nehemiah, together with a part of a Gothic calendar. These are the basis of our earliest knowledge about the Teutonic languages.

To say that the bird's-eye view given in the next few chapters will help the beginner to start writing to a correspondent who will correct gross errors, or to begin reading without becoming color blind to rules of grammar, does not mean that they provide an insurance policy against all possible mistakes, if the rules given are conscientiously applied. Only a series of volumes each nearly as long as this one and each devoted to each of the languages dealt with, could claim to do so. Their aim is to explain what the beginner needs to know in order to avoid serious misunderstandings in straightforward self-expression (see Chapter IV) or the reading of unpretentious prose, and therefore to help the home student to start using a language with as little delay as is possible or advisable. Beyond this point, progress in a foreign, like progress in the home, language depends on trial and error.

It is more easy to form habits than to break them; and it is more difficult to learn by eye alone than by eye and ear together. So it is a bad thing to start memorizing foreign words from the printed page without first learning how to pronounce them recognizably. The spelling conventions (see Chapter II) of different languages are very different, and it is important to learn sufficient about them to avoid *gross* mistakes. Beyond this, further progress is impossible without personal instruction, travel, or gramophone records (such as the Linguaphone or Columbia series) for those who can afford them, and careful attention to foreign broadcasts if such opportunities are not accessible.

Peculiar psychological difficulties beset individuals of English-speaking countries when they approach the study of a foreign language. Some arise from social tradition. Others are due to geographical situation. English-speaking people speak a language which has become world-wide through conquest, colonization, and economic penetration. Partly for this reason and partly because their water frontiers cut them off from daily contact with other speech communities they lack the incentives which encourage a Dane or a Dutchman to acquire linguistic proficiency. Though these extrinsic impediments are undoubtedly powerful, there is another side to the picture. Those who have been brought up to speak the Anglo-American language have one great linguistic advantage. Their word equipment makes it equally easy for them to take up the study of any Teutonic or any Romance language with a background of familiar associations, because modern English is a hybrid language. Indeed, more than one artificial auxiliary language, notably Steiner's *Pasilingua* put forward in 1885, takes as its basis the English stock in trade of words for this reason. It is the object of this chapter to help the reader to become more language conscious by recognizing what it implies.

Examples taken from the Lord's Prayer and printed on page 7 show the close family likeness of the common root words in the Teutonic group, including English. For this reason sentences and expressions made up of such words can be used to illustrate grammatical affinities and differences which an American or a Briton with no previous knowledge of other members of the group can recognize without difficulty. The resemblance between members of the group is so close that many linguists speak of them as the Teutonic *dialects*.* English stands apart from other members of the Teutonic group in two ways. Its grammar has undergone much greater simplification, and it has assimilated an enormous proportion of words from other language groups, more especially the Latin. In fact, if we set out to discover its place in the Indo-European family by merely counting the Teutonic and Latin root words (see p. 2) in a large dictionary, we could make a good case for putting it in the Romance group.

This conclusion would be wrong. Though it is true that more than half the words in a good dictionary are of Latin origin, it is also true that nearly all the root words which we use *most* often—the class referred to on pages 116–117—are Teutonic. However freely we sprinkle our prose with foreign words, we cannot speak or write English without using native (i.e., Teutonic) elements. Native are (*a*) all pronouns, (*b*) all demonstrative and possessive adjectives, (*c*) the articles, (*d*) the auxiliaries, (*e*) the strong verbs, (*f*) nearly all prepositions and conjunctions, (*g*) most of the adverbs of time and place, (*h*) the numerals, except *dozen, million, billion,* and *milliard.* Native also are the few flexions which English has retained. Thus the majority of words on a printed page, even if it is about technical matters which

* The word *dialect* is used in two senses. In everyday life we associate it with local variations of pronunciation and minor local differences of vocabulary within a single *political* unit. Since the members of a single political unit are usually able to understand one another in spite of such local variations, dialect differences also signify differences which do not make it absolutely impossible for people to understand one another. In this sense dialects overrun national boundaries. The "Doric" of Robert Burns differs from Bible English or from Anglo-American both with respect to pronunciation and to spelling conventions, as much as Norwegian differs from Swedish or Danish. Anyone who can read Norwegian can read Swedes or Danish, and Norwegians can understand Swedes or Danes when they speak their own languages. We only speak of them as different *languages* because they are dialects of different *sovereign* states. It is impossible to draw a hard-and-fast line between language and dialect differences.

rely on a large vocabulary of Latin derivatives, are Teutonic; and though it is possible to write good English prose in which all, or nearly all, the vocabulary is based on Teutonic roots, it would be difficult to write a representative specimen of sustained and intelligible English containing a bare majority of Latin-French words.

The basic stratum, i.e., the most common words, of our English vocabulary is derived from a mixture of dialects more closely allied to Dutch than to other existing members of the group, especially to the Dutch of the Frisian Islands. These dialects were the common speech of Germanic tribes, called Angles, Saxons, and Jutes, who came to Britain between 400 and 700 A.D. The Norse invaders, who left their footprints on our syntax, contributed few *specifically* Scandinavian words to Southern English, though there are many Norse words in dialects spoken in Scotland. Norse was the language of the Orkneys till the end of the fourteenth, and persisted in the outermost Shetlands (Foula) till the end of the eighteenth century. Many words in Scots vernaculars recall current Scandinavian equivalents, e.g. *bra* (fine, good), *bairn* (child), and *flit* (move household effects). Scandinavian suffixes occur in many place names, such as -*by* (small town), cf. *Grimsby* or *Whitby*, and the latter survives in the compound *by-law* of everyday speech in South Britain.

When the Norman invaders came in 1066 the language of England and of the South of Scotland was almost purely Teutonic. It had assimilated very few Latin words save those ones which were by then common to Teutonic dialects on the Continent. Except in Wales, Cornwall, and the Scottish highlands, the Celtic of pre-Roman Britain survived only in place names. After the Norman Conquest, more particularly after the beginning of the fourteenth century, the language of England and of the Scottish lowlands underwent a drastic change. It absorbed a large number of words of Latin origin, first through the influence of the Norman hierarchy, and later through the influence of scholars and writers. It shed a vast load of useless grammatical luggage. Norman scribes revised its spelling, and while this was happening important changes of pronunciation were going on.

This latinization of English did not begin immediately after the Conquest. For the greater part of two centuries, there were two languages in England. The overlords spoke Norman French, as the white settlers of Kenya speak modern English. The English serfs still spoke the language in which Beowulf and the Bible of Alfred the Great were written. By the beginning of the fourteenth century a social process was gathering momentum. There were self-governing towns with a burgher class of native English stock. There was a flourishing wool trade with Flanders. There were schools where the sons of prosperous burghers learned French grammar. In the England of Dick Whittington, English again became a written language, but a written language which had to accommodate itself to a world of familiar things for which the Saxon poets had no names. Investment in trading enterprise fostered a new sort of class collaboration depicted in Chaucer's *Canterbury Tales,* and a new type of litigation with an English-speaking clientele. In 1362 Edward III ordered the use of English in the courts, though the *written* law of the land was French till the eighteenth century.

In contradistinction to *Old English*, the purely Teutonic language of Alfred the Great, the English of this period, that of Chaucer and of Wycliff, is called *Middle English*. Scholars refer literary remains to the middle period if written between about A.D. 1150 and 1500. The process of assimilating words of Latin origin received a new stimulus from the rise of classical scholarship at the end of the middle, and has been nursed through the modern, period by the growth of scientific knowledge. One result is that English in its present form has an enormous range of couplets, one member Teutonic like *forgive*, the other Latin or French like *pardon*. Usually the Teutonic one is more intimate, the Latin formal, because Teutonic words are the language of the countryside, Latin or French words the prerogative of lawyers, priests, and scholars. Thus Wamba the jester in *Ivanhoe* points out that the ungulates (*sheep, pig, calf, ox*) have native names while it is still the business of the English people to look after them. When they reach the table of the Norman overlord they have become *mutton, pork, veal, beef,* for which the corresponding French words are *mouton, porc, veau, bœuf.*

Relatively few people learn lists of new words with ease, unless they can connect them with familiar facts, and an adult who has already collected a variegated vocabulary is in a strong position to take advantage of this hybrid character of modern English. To become language conscious in this way we need to know something about the regularities of sound change which have been mentioned in the last chapter (p. 178), and we need a few hints which help us to detect when an Anglo-American word is Teutonic or Latin. This can be done by following up clues suggested in Chapters II and V. The spelling of a word is often a sufficient signpost of its origin, especially if we know a little about the sound changes which have occurred in the history of the Teutonic and Latin families.

How the *sound shifts* mentioned in Chapter V help to build up word associations is illustrated by the German word *Teil* (*part*) or its derivative verb *teilen* (*separate, divide, distribute, share*). Old Teutonic words which begin with the *d* sound begin with the *t* sound in modern German (p. 226). If we apply this rule *Teil* becomes *deil*, which means the same as the Swedish-Danish *del*, with the corresponding derivative verbs *dela* (Swedish) or *dele* (Danish). In its new form it recalls our words *dell* and *deal*. The Oxford Dictionary tells us that the latter comes from Old English *deel*, which also meant a *part*, and to *deal* cards still means to *divide* the pack into *parts*, to *share* or *distribute* them. The word *dell* (or *dale*) has no connection with this root. It has the same meaning as the Swedish-Danish *dal*, German *Tal*, and Dutch *dal*, for *valley*.

If you follow this plan, you can introduce an element of adventure into memorizing a vocabulary, and incidentally learn more about the correct use of English words. It may be helpful to look up some of the unusual words in the *Canterbury Tales*, or the *Faerie Queene*. For instance, the smaller Oxford Dictionary tells us that the Chaucerian *eke* means *also*, and compares it with the contemporary Dutch (*ook*) and German (*auch*) equivalents. The Swedish for *also* is *och* or *också*. You can also compare the Middle English *eke* with the Swedish *och* and Danish *og* for our link word *and*, which we can sometimes replace by *also*.

An example which illustrates how to make associations for memorizing words of Romance origin is *hospitable*. The Oxford Dictionary tells us that this comes from the Latin verb *hospitare* (*to entertain*). The related word *hospite* meant either *guest* or *host*, and it has survived as the latter. Another related Latin word is *hospitale*, a place for *guests*, later for *travelers*. This was the original meaning of *hospital*, and survives as such in *Knights Hospitallers*. In Old French it appears shortened to *hostel*, which exists in English. In modern French *s* before *t* or *p* has often disappeared. That it was once there, is indicated by a circumflex accent (ˆ) over the preceding vowel, as in *hôtel*. The French words *hôte, hôtesse, hôtel, hôpital*, resolve themselves into their English equivalents when we apply this rule. *Hostelry, hospice,* and *hospitality* obviously share the same lineage. A host of other similarities come to life if we are familiar with another sound change. When an accented *é* precedes *t, p,* or *c* at the beginning of a modern

French word it often takes the place of the Latin *s* in English words of Romance origin. Thus *état* (*state*), *étranger* (*stranger, foreigner*) *étoffe* (*stuff*), *éponge* (*sponge*), *épouse* (*spouse, wife*), *épicier* (*grocer*—man who sells *spices*), and *école* (*school*) come to life if we know this.

Even when there is no precise English equivalent containing the same root as a word in one of the Romance languages, we can usually lighten the effort of memorizing the latter by fishing up a related word which does contain it. In the table on page 244 there are twenty-two English words of which eight, or one-third of the total, recall the Romance equivalent. English words of related meaning at once suggest the Romance root in most of the others. Thus our Teutonic *hunger* pairs off with *famine* and *famished* which suggest the French word *faim*. The French word *fil* for our Teutonic *thread* turns up in *filament*. Similarly we associate *fumes* with smoke, *fugitive* with flee, *foliage* with leaves, *factory* production with making things, *filial* piety with son and daughter (more particularly the latter), or *ferrous* metals with iron. That leaves us with a few Italian and French words which are self-explanatory to a naturalist, chemist, or anatomist. Thus *formic* acid is an irritant emitted by ants, *sainfoin* is a leguminous hay substitute, and *Vicia faba* is the botanical name for the common bean.

SOUND SHIFTS IN THE TEUTONIC LANGUAGES

Before studying further examples of the way in which the hybrid character of English word equipment helps anyone who is beginning to learn a Teutonic or Romance language, we need to know more about sound changes such as those mentioned in the preceding paragraphs. The neglect of an enormous volume of relevant research in textbooks for beginners shows how little education is enlightened by Bacon's counsel: "We do ill to exalt the powers of the human mind, when we should seek out its proper helps." *

Let us start with the Teutonic group. We have no direct knowledge of the single ancestor of all Teutonic languages, but our earliest records lead us to infer that it underwent a drastic change some time before the beginning of the Christian era. This change, which involved

---

* English primers of German—perhaps because philology has been cultivated in Germany—refer to such sound changes, but do not disclose equally relevant information of the way in which English pronunciation has changed since it parted company with what is now German. Otherwise it is true to say that the topic is still taboo in elementary teaching.

several consonants, may have come about because tribes speaking an Indo-European language came into contact with people who spoke non-Aryan languages such as the peculiar speech still extant among the Basques. Five of these consonant changes appear below, and we can recognize them in the difference between the English form of an Indo-European word and its Latin or Greek equivalent. Thus the first and second are recognizable in comparison of the Greek or Latin *pater* with our word *father;* the first and last by comparing the Greek root *pod-* or Latin *ped-* with our *foot;* the third by comparing the Latin *genus* and *genu* with our *kin* and *knee;* and the last two by comparing the Greek root *kard-* or Latin *cord-* with *heart:*

1) *p* became *f*
2) *t* became *th* (þ)
3) *g* became *k*
4) *k* became the throaty Scots *ch* in *loch*, and subsequently the simple aspirate *h*
5) *d* became *t*

The reader who knows no Latin and is not likely to acquire more knowledge of Latin than can be got from the next chapter but one, should not find it impossible to detect the same root in some English words of Teutonic and of Latin or Greek origin. Thus we recognize the same root as *foot* in *pedicure*, and the same root as *heart* in *cardiac*, the same root in *trinity* as in *three*, the same root in *fire* as in *pyrex* glass, and the same root in *flat* as in *plateau* or *platitude* (a flat saying).

This primitive or *first* sound shift in the history of the Teutonic-speaking peoples equipped English with sounds for which the Latin alphabet had no precise equivalents. For reasons sufficiently explained in our survey of the alphabet, this fact has its practical application. With the exception of a few words derived from Greek, English words containing *th* are Teutonic. So also are words which begin with *w* or *y* or contain *gh*. These consonant, or combinations of consonant, symbols are therefore signals which tell us whether we are likely to find a recognizably equivalent or related word in a Teutonic language. The following is a list of five signposts of Teutonic word origin:

Words containing *sh*, e.g. *sheep, shield, ship*
Words containing *th*, e.g. *thaw, then, thin*
Words containing *gh*, e.g. *laughter, through, rough*
Words with initial *w*, e.g. *ware, wasp, wash*
Words with initial *sk*, e.g. *skin, skirt, sky*

These five signposts help us to recognize a very large number of words of Teutonic origin as such, and many more can be identified by the presence of characteristically Teutonic prefixes, of which the *be-* (in *belong* or *behead*) is the most reliable, and suffixes of which the adjectival *-some* (in *lonesome*), the diminutive *-ling* and the abstract endings *-dom*, *-hood* or *-head*, *-ship*, *-kind*, and *-craft* are most diagnostic.

When we are able to detect words of Teutonic origin in this way, we can lighten the task of memorizing our word list with a little information about the simultaneous changes of pronunciation which have occurred since the common parent of the Teutonic family split into three main groups—an eastern represented by Gothic, a northern or Scandinavian represented by Old Norse, and a western represented by Old English and Old High German. In what follows we must not confuse *sounds* with their *symbols*. The latter may be arbitrary conventions peculiar to particular languages, or a hang-over from a period when the pronunciation was different. Thus the German *W* is merely another way of writing the sound represented by our *V;* and the sound we usually represent by F and sometimes by GH (e.g. *laugh*) is either F (as in *Fisch*) or V (as in *Vater* for *father*). The letter J used in English for the peculiarly English sound in *jam* or *Gentile* stands in all other Teutonic languages for a different sound represented by our Y in *yeast*. Our own dӡ sound in *jam* has no equivalent in German, Danish, Dutch or Swedish. It is confined to English in the Teutonic clan.

These different conventions of closely allied languages may be due to the whims of scribes who originally sponsored the system of spelling in use today, or, like the German W, to changes of pronunciation since their time. If we want to detect word equivalence on the printed page, what is more important to know is how pronunciation of related dialects had already diverged before writing began, or how it is reflected in subsequent spelling reforms. For instance, the correspondence between the Swedish words *vind*, *väder*, and *vatten* on the one hand and the German words *Wind*, *Wetter*, and *Wasser* or their English equivalents *wind*, *weather*, and *water* on the other, is partly concealed by the fact that Scandinavian spelling incorporates the V-shift which English has resisted.

English has preserved two old Teutonic consonant sounds which have scarcely left a trace in its sister Teutonic dialects other than Icelandic. One of these is the þ sound of *thin*, the other is the ð sound of *then*. Modern Icelandic is more conservative than English in so far as þ is never softened to ð (p. 69) at the beginning of a word. That is illustrated by:

ICELANDIC	ENGLISH
þar	there
þessi	this
þu	thou
þinn	thine
þeirra	their

In other Teutonic languages, þ has changed directly to *t*, or via ð to *d*. This is illustrated by many common words, such as our definite article *the*, with its plural equivalent *de* in Swedish, Danish and Dutch, and *die* in German; the English *that* with its neuter equivalent *det* in Swedish and Danish, or *dat* in Dutch; the English *they* and *theirs*, with modern Scandinavian equivalents, *de* and *deras* (Swedish), *deres* (Danish); or the English *thou* with its equivalent Swedish, Danish, and German *du*.

German equivalents of English words with the initial consonants þ or ð, i.e., either sound represented by *th* in English spelling, start with *d:*

Dank,	thanks	*Ding,*	thing
das,	that	*denken,*	think
dann,	then	*drei,*	three
da,	there	*Durst,*	thirst
dick,	thick	*Distel,*	thistle
Dieb,	thief	*Dorn,*	thorn
dünn,	thin	*Dorf,*	thorp (= village)

In two ways English has changed as some of the Scandinavian dialects have done. One is that a sound which was SK in Old English (then spelt *sc*) has now become SH, as in German, where the spelling convention is SCH, e.g. shade—*Schatten*, shame—*Scham*, (to) shed —*scheiden*. A partial change of this kind has occurred in Swedish, in which the symbol SK, except when it precedes the back vowels *a*, *å*, or *o*, is pronounced ʃ, i.e., *skepp* has the same initial sound as its equivalent *ship*. The following words illustrate the English shift from *sk* to *sh*. In the Swedish equivalents on the left, the symbols have their original (hard) value. Those of the right are paper survivals, the initial sound being the same as in English:

SWEDISH	ENGLISH	SWEDISH	ENGLISH
skaka	shake	skepp	ship
skal	shell	skida	sheath
skall	shall	skimma	shimmer
skam	shame	skinna	shine
skarp	sharp	skjuta	shoot
sko	shoe	sköld	shield
skott	shot	skur	shower
skrika	shriek		

In the evolution of modern English there has also been a weakening of the guttural *g* like the weakening of the guttural *k* illustrated by the words now spelt with the arbitrary combination *sh*. This has had an important grammatical consequence which will appear at a later stage (p. 260). The hard *g* as in *goat* is generally the sound which corresponds to the symbol in German, Dutch, and Danish. In Swedish it is usually softened to our *y* sound unless preceded by a back vowel (*a* in *father*, *aw* in *law*, *oo* in *book*). Swedish spelling does not reflect this softening, but in Danish and Norwegian the softened *g* is replaced by GJ, J or I; and in new Norwegian *y* is substituted for the soft *g* after ø (Swedish or German ö roughly equivalent to our *ir* in *shirk*). Thus in German *eye* is *Auge*, in Swedish it is *öga* and in Norwegian *øye*. So also *way* is *Weg* in German, *väg* in Swedish, *vej* in Danish, *vei* in Norwegian. In many English words of Teutonic origin the *g* has softened in this way, and Y or W are now its gravestones in the written language. The Y may stamp a diphthong as in *eye* or *way*, or it may be equivalent to the soft Scandinavian G or GJ as in *yellow* (German *gelb*, Swedish *gul*). A *W* in place of *g* turns up in the panteutonic word for bird (Swed. *fågel*, German *Vogel*) which we now spell as *fowl*, as also in *bow* (Swed. *båge*, German *Bogen*).

In a large class of English words, the combination *gh* is completely silent. The combination originally stood for a breathy sound represented by *ch* in German, and still pronounced as such in Scots. Thus the Scots words for *night* and *light* are close to the German *Nacht* and *Licht*. This sound, which has disappeared in English elsewhere, is almost absent in Scandinavian. Thus the Scandinavian word for *night* is *natt*, and *ljus* for *light* (Swedish) or *lys* (Danish and Norwegian).

So far as the consonants are concerned, the changes from *w* to *v* and from þ to *t*, or from ð to *d*, are the sound shifts which are most important to anyone who aims at learning Norwegian or Swedish. They are illustrated by:

ENGLISH	SWEDISH	ENGLISH	SWEDISH
waggon, wagon	vagn	thick	tjock
water	vatten	thief	tjuv
weak	vek	thin	tunn
week	vecka	thing	ting
wild	vild	think	tänka
wise	vis	thousand	tusen
work	verk	three	tre
world	värld	thread	tråd
warm	varm	throne	tron
way	väg	thumb	tumme
weather	väder		
well	väl		
west	väster		
wet	våt	that	det
whale	val	them	dem
whistle	vissla	there	där
white	vit	these	dessa
wide	vid	thine	din
willing	villig	thou	du
win	vinna		
witness	vitna		
wood	ved		
worst	värste	brother	broder (bror)
worth	värde	father	fader (far)
wreck	vrak	mother	moder (mor)

In an English-Swedish dictionary there are many other words beginning with *th* or *sh* with Swedish equivalents, recognizable as such when these changes are made. Of course, the family likeness is obvious in a host of words without sounds which have undergone a shift of this type. Even if the English equivalent given in the dictionary does not correspond to a Swedish word, it is often easy to think of a related one which does so. Thus the Swedish word *skara* (cut) reminds us of *shear*, and *veta* (know) is derived from the same Teutonic root as *wit* (German *wissen*), still used as a verb in Bible English and in the expression *to wit*.

Similarities between English words of Teutonic origin and the corresponding ones in other Teutonic languages are most difficult to recognize at sight when the latter is German. From the phonetic point of view, German has wandered furthest afield from the old Teutonic homestead. So the similarities of German and English words are less easy to recognize than the family likeness of English and Swedish ones. In the evolution of German, a compact group of changes called the *second sound shift* took place in middle and south Germany, and these are reflected in German spelling. The most characteristic are the following:

a) At the *beginning* of a word (or in the middle after a consonant) *t* was followed by a hiss, i.e., became *ts* (as in *cats*). This *ts* sound is represented by Z in German script.

b) Inside the word after a vowel the *t* shifted further and became a hiss, now spelt SS.

c) The initial *p* was followed by *f*, and the result is represented by PF-.

d) After a vowel the shift went further, *f* replaced *p*—in script FF-.

Another sound change which took place early in the High German dialects was the shift from *k* to *ch* (as in Scots *loch*) after vowels. This change is illustrated by (*e*) below. Besides the preceding, other sound changes, some of them much later, now distinguish High from Low German dialects (including Old English). The most important are:

f) The early shift of the initial *d* to *t*.

g) The initial *s* before *l, m, n, p, t,* usually becomes *sh* as in *ship* (spelt SCH except before P and T).

h) Between two vowels *v* often becomes *b*.

	ENGLISH	GERMAN		ENGLISH	GERMAN
(a)	tap	Zapfen	(c)	path	Pfad
	ten	zehn		pepper	Pfeffer
	tide (time)	Zeit		pipe	Pfeife
	to	zu		plant	Pflanze
	tongue	Zunge		plaster	Pflaster
	two	zwei	(d)	hope	hoffen
(b)	better	besser		pepper	Pfeffer
	eat	essen		pipe	Pfeife
	foot	Fuss		ape	Affe
	kettle	Kessel		gape	gaffen
	let	lassen		sleep	schlafen
	water	Wasser			

ENGLISH	GERMAN	ENGLISH	GERMAN
(e) book	Buch	(g) sleep	schlafen
break	brechen	smut	Schmutz
make	machen	snow	Schnee
rake (tool)	Rechen	swan	Schwan
reek	riechen	sweat	Schweiss
token	Zeichen	(h) give	geben
weak	weich	have	haben
week	Woche	live	leben
(f) dance	tanzen	liver	Leber
daughter	Tochter	love	lieben
day	Tag	sieve	Sieb
dream	Traum		
drink	trinken		

Some of the words chosen in these examples illustrate more than one sound shift. For instance, we have to make two changes to get our *sweat* from *Schweiss*. When we apply (*b*), *Schweiss* changes to *Schweit*, and this changes to *Sweit* when we apply (*g*). It is then recognizably the same as its English equivalent.

The geographical boundaries between regions where the older or *Low* and the newer or *High* German forms predominate are not the same for all the shifts mentioned above. The process of change reaches its peak in South German, including German Swiss (High Alemanic) dialects. As we go north and northwest, the typical High German sounds fade out and disappear in the plains. The Low German of north and northeast Germany, like Dutch and Flemish which are really Low German dialects with their own spelling rules, remains true to the earlier Germanic sound pattern. A line across Germany divides a region where Low German forms predominate from one where the High German prevail. It runs from the Belgian frontier south of Aachen to Düsseldorf, thence to Cassel, striking the Elbe above Magdeburg, passes north of Luther's Wittenberg, and touches the Polish frontier northeast of Frankfort-on-the-Oder. North of the line we hear *dat Water*, South of it, *das Wasser*.

In what has gone before we have seen that English consonants are conservative. The consonants of English have departed from the Old Teutonic pattern less than those of any Teutonic language except Icelandic. The reverse is true of the vowels. In the middle period during the century in which Chaucer wrote, the English vowels shifted while the spelling remained fixed. This explains why we so often succeed in identifying an English word with a German one when we see the two in print, but fail to do so when they strike our ear. German vowels also shifted between the Middle High German and the Modern High German period, and the evolution of two English and German vowels runs parallel. In both languages a primitive long I (pronounced *ee* as in *bee*) became the diphthong *y* in *fly*. The German spells it as EI (Middle High German *min*, Modern High German *mein*), while English retains the older spelling (Old English *min*, Modern English *mine*). The primitive long *u* (like *oo* in *food*) went through a similar process, but this time the diphthong (*ow* as in *how*) is indicated as such in both languages. The German spells it as AU (Middle High German *hus*, Modern High German *Haus*). In English it is OU or OW (Old English *mus*, *brun*, Modern English *mouse*, *brown*). In all, there were seven characteristic vowel changes in Middle English, including the two mentioned. Not all of them extended to Scotland, where *house* is still pronounced like its Scandinavian equivalent *hus* and a *cow* is a *ku*. Owing to the chaos of English vowel symbols, these sound shifts are not of very great assistance to the beginner. Like Spanish, modern German spelling is very regular compared with our own. The following paragraph summarizes its essential conventions. At a first reading it will be wise to SKIP it, as also to skip the succeeding ones (pp. 231–232) which deal with pronunciation and spelling of Dutch and Scandinavian dialects.

The few exceptions to the rule that one sound has the same German symbol are:

a) The *f*- sound is represented both by F and V, e.g. *füllen* (fill) and *voll* (full).

b) The *i*- sound of *file* is represented by EI, e.g. *mein* (my) or AI, e.g. *MAI* (May).

c) The *oi*- sound of *boy* is represented by EU or AU, e.g. *teuer* (dear), *Häuser* (houses).

d) The *ee*- sound in *bee* is represented by IE or IH, e.g. *Liebe* (love), *Ihr* (your).

e) The use of a silent H or a double vowel symbol to give A, E, O the *long* values of *Ah! Eh! Oh!* e.g. *Jahr* (year)—*Aal* (eel), *mehr* (more)—*Meer* (sea), *bohren* (bore)—*Boot* (boat).

A simple rule decides whether the vowels A, E, I, O are long or short when the long value is not indicated as under (*d*) and (*e*) above. Before two or more consonants they have the *short* values of our word *pat-pet-pit-pot*, e.g. *kalt* (cold), *sechs* (six), *ist* (is), *offen* (open). Otherwise with one exception A, E, O, have the *ah! eh! oh!* values of *Ja* (yes), *dem* (the), *wo* (where). The exception is that a final -E (or the -E in -EN) is slurred like the -ER in *worker*.

The German U has two values, the short one before a double consonant is like *u* in *pull*, e.g. *Luft* (air), the long one like *oo* in *pool*, e.g. *gut* (good). Three German vowel symbols (Ä, Ö, Ü), with *long* and *short* values in accordance with the same rule have special marks; and they do not exactly correspond to any of our own sounds. The short Ä, e.g. in *Länge* (length) is like the short *e* in *pen*. The long Ä, e.g. in *sägen* (saw) is somewhat nearer to the long *e* in *fête*. The Ö and Ü are pronounced with *rounded lips*, long Ö, e.g. in *schön* (beautiful) rather like *u* in *fur*, short Ö, e.g. *könnte* (could), rather like *or* in *work*. The long Ü, e.g. *über* (over) is like the *u* in Scots *guid*. To get the short Ü, e.g. *fünf* (five), make the *i* in *pin* with rounded lips.

The pronunciation of German consonants is straightforward. The only silent symbol is H after a vowel. The English contracted syllable represented by the initial KN of *know* (= Scots *ken*), *knife, knit,* etc., does not exist in other Teutonic dialects. The German KN-, e.g. in *Knabe* (boy) is pronounced as in *darkness*. The symbols F, H, K, M, N, P, T, X have their characteristic English values. In radio or stage pronunciation the voiced consonants *b, d, g*, shift toward their voiceless equivalents *p, t, k* when at the end of a word, e.g. the G of *des Tages* (the day's) is as in *goat*, but of *der Tag* as in *coat*. The stage German R is trilled like the Scots. The main differences between German and English consonant conventions are:

1) CH after a back vowel (A, O, U), e.g. in *Nacht* (night) is hard as in Scots *loch*, but is nearer the sound of *h* in *hew* after the front vowels Ä, E, I, Ö, Ü, e.g. in *nicht* (not).

2) S alone at the beginning of a word, e.g. *See* (lake), or syllable, e.g. *lesen* (read), is the *z* sound of *s* in buys. Before P or T at the beginning of a word, S (= SCH elsewhere) is like *sh* in *ship*. A double SS or a single S at the end of a word is the true *s* sound of *bliss*, e.g. *Fuss* (foot), *das* (the).

3) Z always stands for the *ts* in *cats*, e.g. *Zunge* (tongue). This is a convention peculiar to German.

4) As in Dutch, W = *v* in *voice*, e.g. *Wasser* (water) and either F or V = *f* in *find*, e.g. *Feder* (feather) or *Vater* (father).

5) As in all Teutonic dialects (other than English), J = *y* as in *year*, e.g. in *Ja* (yes).

6) NG is like *ng* in *bing*, e.g. *Finger* is pronounced by analogy to *singer*, not to its English equivalent.

7) CHS = *ks*, e.g. in *Ochs*, ox and QU = *kv*, e.g. in *Quarz* or *Quelle* (spring).

In German, as in all Teutonic languages other than English, the personal pronoun of polite address (*Sie*) in its several guises (*Ihnen*, etc.) begins with a capital letter. In German as in Danish and Norwegian correspondence, the same applies to *Du*, etc. The custom of using a capital for the nominative of the first person singular is peculiarly Anglo-American. In German as in Danish orthography nouns are labeled by an initial capital letter, e.g. *der Schnee* (the snow). This habit, which slows down the speed of typing, did not become fashionable till the middle of the sixteenth century. Luther's Bible follows no consistent plan; e.g. the opening verses of the Old Testament are:

> "Im anfang schuff Gott Himmel und Erden. Und die Erde war wüst und leer, und es war finster auf der Tieffe, Und der Geist Gottes schwebet auf dem Wasser. Und Gott sprach, Es werde liecht, Und es ward liecht. Und Gott sahe, dass das liecht gut war, Da scheided Gott das Liecht von Finsternis, und nennet das liecht, Tag, und die finisternis, Nacht. Da ward aus abend und morgen der Erste tage."

Simple German words and compound nouns are stressed on the first syllable, e.g. *Kóchin* (cook), *árbeiten* (work), *Bíerfass* (beer vat). Foreign words usually carry the stress on the last syllable, e.g. *Organisatión*, *Resultát* (result), *Fabrík* (factory). Words beginning with the prefixes *be-, ge-, er-, emp-, ent-, ver-, zer-, miss-* accent the basic element, e.g. *begléiten* (accompany), *erláuben* (allow), *vergéssen* (forget).

The second sound shift does not exist in the everyday speech of ordinary folk in north Germany. It goes without saying that people who speak Dutch and North German or *Platt* dialects, can understand one another. Anyone who can read German should be able to read Dutch. To do so it is only necessary to recall the sound changes cited above and to know the peculiar spelling conventions of written Dutch. These are as follows:

With the exception of Z, S, and G, Dutch consonant symbols have values like the German ones. At the beginning of a word, e.g. *zoon* (son), Z has its characteristic value (as in *zebra*), but in the middle of a word, e.g. *huizen* (houses), it is like an *s*. By itself the Dutch S has its characteristic value in our *this* or *hiss;* but IS = *iz*. The combination SJ, e.g. in *meisje* (girl), is like *sh* in *ship*. Except before R, the combination SCH is pronounced *s + ch* of *loch*. Otherwise it is like *s*. Thus SCHR = *sr*, e.g. in *schrijven* (write). Dutch G stands for a weaker variety of *ch*.

Before a double consonant, e.g. in *vallen* (fall) or *denken* (think), and in monosyllables, e.g. *man* or *mes* (knife) the single vowel symbols A and E are like their English equivalents in *pat* and *pet*. Before a single consonant, e.g. in *Kamer* (room), or *vrede* (peace), they have their vowel values in *father* and *fête*. The terminal -EN is pronounced like -*er* in *father*. Thus the final *n* in -*en* of the verb plural and infinitive (p. 259) is a paper survival. The single I and O, e.g. in *vinden* (find) or *onder* (under) are respectively pronounced as in our *pit* and *pot*. The U before a double consonant, e.g. in *zuster* (sister) is as in *rust*. Otherwise U or UU are like the Scots *u* in *guid* or the German *ü*.

The double vowel symbols AA, e.g. in *maan* (moon), OO, e.g. in *oom* (uncle), EE, e.g. *twee* (two) are respectively equal to *ah! oh! eh!* The combinations IE (equivalent to Y in words of foreign origin), e.g. in *niet* (not), EI, e.g. in *einde* (end), AU, e.g. in *nauw* (narrow) have the same values as in German. There is a group of combinations peculiar to Dutch:

1) IJ, e.g. *mijn* (my) near to *i* in *file*
2) EU, e.g. *deur* (door) like the French *eu* or English *u, o, e, i* in *fur, worm, pert, fir*
3) OE, e.g. *goed* (good) near to *oo* in *fool*
4) OU, e.g. *oud* (old) near to the *o* in *old*
5) UI, e.g. *huis* (house) rather like *oi* in *foil*

The triple and quadruple groups are pronounced as follows:

AAI, e.g. *fraai* (fine) like *y* in *fly*
OOI, e.g. *hooi* (hay) like *oy* in *boy*
OEI, e.g. *moeilijk* (difficult) roughly *oo-y* (as in *boot* and *pity*)
EEUW, e.g. *leeuw* (lion) roughly *ay-oo* (as in *tray* and *too*)
IEUW, e.g. *nieuw*, roughly *ew* in its English equivalent

Each of the Scandinavian dialects has words peculiar to itself, as Scots Doric contains words which do not occur in the daily speech of Kent or Kansas. The proportion of recognizably common or actually identical words in Swedish, Norwegian, and Danish is enormous. Anyone who can speak or read one of them can be intelligible to someone who speaks either of the other two, and can read all three with little difficulty. The difficulty can be greatly reduced by a few hints about the spelling conventions characteristic of each, and the sound shift peculiar to Danish.

Norwegian has two vowel symbols not in our alphabet. It shares *å* with Swedish (*aa* in Danish) and *ø* with Danish (*ö* in Swedish). The Swedish *ä* is written as *e* in Norwegian except before *r*, when it is *æ*, as always in Danish. The Swedish *ju* is always *y* in Danish and Norwegian words. The initial *hv* of Danish and Norwegian equivalents for English words which begin with *wh* is replaced by *v* alone in Swedish. The double Danish or Norwegian *kk*, which shortens the preceding vowel, is written as *ck* in Swedish. The Swedish and Norwegian *nn* and *ll* are replaced by *nd* and *ld* in Danish. In Danish and in Norwegian a soft Swedish *g*, pronounced like our *y*, is represented by *gj*. The terminal vowel *a* of Swedish words becomes *e* in Danish and Norwegian. The most striking difference

of pronunciation reflected in spelling is the shift from a final voiceless
p, t, k in Swedish or Norwegian to the voiced equivalents *b, d, g* in
Danish, as illustrated by:

ENGLISH	SWEDISH	DANISH
ship	skepp	Skib
foot	fot	Fod
speech	språk	Sprog

The identity of some words is obscured by the spelling of prepositions
used as prefixes, e.g. Swedish *upp* for Danish *op*. When due allowance
is made for all these differences of spelling or of pronunciation, it is
safe to say that 95 per cent of the words of a serviceable vocabulary are
either identical in any of the three Scandinavian dialects mentioned, or
can be appropriately modified in accordance with the rules above.

Scandinavian symbols usually have the same values as those of
German in the preceding table. The notable Swedish exceptions are
as follows:

a) Before *front* vowels, (E, I, Y, Ä, Ö), G softens to *y* as in *yew*, e.g.
   get (goat), K becomes *ch* as in *loch*, e.g. *kära* (dear), SK becomes *sh* as in *ship* (*skepp*).

b) After L or R the final G is like *y* in *bury*, e.g. *berg* (mountain).

c) SJ, e.g. *sju* (seven), SKJ or STJ, e.g. *stjärna* (star) is like *sh* in *ship*.

d) Before R, e.g. *flickor* (girls) and in many monosyllables, e.g. *stol*
   (chair), O is like *oo* in *good*.

e) Å is generally like *oa* in *oar*.

The Danish AA replaces the Swedish Å; Æ and Ø replace the Ger-
man-Swedish Ä and Ö. Other differences are:

a) General tendency of voiceless (P, T, K) to assume the sound values
   of the corresponding voiced consonants (*b, d, g*). Thus *ikke* is
   pronounced like *igger* in *bigger*.

b) Terminal G, final V after L, and initial H before V (where *hv*
   replaces *wh* of the English equivalent, e.g. *hvad* = what) are
   silent.

c) D is silent after L, N, R, e.g. *holde* (hold), *finde* (find) and like ð
   when it follows a vowel.

d) The combination GJ is soft like the Swedish G before *e*.

SOUND CHANGES IN THE LATIN FAMILY

Most English words of Latin origin are of two kinds. First come
words derived from the French of Normandy and Picardy. These

were brought in by the Norman conquerors. When this Norman and Picardian French had ceased to be a spoken language in England, the influx of French words did not stop. A second and even larger wave broke over England. This was partly due to the influence of Paris as a literary center in medieval times. Thus borrowed French words of the

ENGLISH WORDS DERIVED THROUGH FRENCH	ENGLISH WORDS DIRECTLY DERIVED FROM LATIN	LATIN
conceit	concept	conceptu
constraint	constriction	constrictione
couch	collocate	collocare
count	compute	computare
coy	quiet	quieto
dainty	dignity	dignitate
defeat	defect	defecto
dungeon	dominion	dominio
esteem	estimate	aestimare
fashion	faction	factione
feat	fact	facto
frail	fragile	fragili
loyal	legal	legali
mayor	major	majore
penance	penitence	poenitentia
poor	pauper	pauperi
privy	private	privato
royal	regal	regali
rule	regulate	regulare
sir	senior	seniore
strait	strict	stricto
sure	secure	securo
trait	tract	tractu
treason	tradition	traditione

period between Chaucer and Caxton do not come from the same region as the earlier Norman words and they are more distinctively French in the modern sense of the term. Since Caxton's time the introduction of Latin or Neo-Latin (French) roots has never ceased. There are now about two thousand primary Latin roots in English, excluding several times as many derivatives and the enormous variety of technical terms not listed in an ordinary dictionary. Owing to the fact that words of Latin origin have come into English directly from classical sources and indirectly through French, our English vocabulary has a very large number of doublets, illustrated by the list printed above.

French itself has suffered a similar fate. Legions of classical Latin words have marched into the French language since the sixteenth century. The Roman grammarian Varo would have been unable to identify Old French *filz*, *larron*, and *conseil* with Latin *filius*, *latro*, and *consilium* respectively, but would have had no difficulty in detecting the Latin origin of the more modern words of the following list (p. 235). There *as elsewhere* below the printed form of a Latin noun or adjective is usually the *ablative singular*.*

The spelling of many French loan words is identical with that of the corresponding words in modern French, e.g. *figure*, *front*, *fruit*, *gain*, *grace*, *grain*, *tablet*, *torrent*, *torture*, or does not deviate sufficiently to make identification impossible, e.g. *chain* (chaine), *charity* (charité), *color* (couleur). Furthermore, words which look alike or similar in French and English have usually an area of common meaning. On the other hand, there are many which betray the beginner. The reason for this is that the meaning of words often changes in the course of centuries through metaphorical usage, through specialization or through generalization. Even since the time of James I, such words as *crafty* (originally *skilled*) and *cunning* (*knowing*, *wise*), have done so, and many words such as *homely* (*plain* in America, *domesticated* in England) do not mean the same thing on both sides of the Atlantic. So it is not surprising that French *spirituel* means *witty* or that *figure* refers to the face alone.

If we were to ask for *mutton* (mouton) and *mustard* (moutarde), *onions* (oignons) and *vinegar* (vinaigre) in a French inn, we should not be understood unless we indicated our wishes in writing. Sometimes our own pronunciation of a French loan word (e.g. *damage*) is nearer to the original than that of a Frenchman today. Modern French has discarded many words which survive in English, e.g. *able*, *bacon*, *chattel*, *mischief*, *nice*, *noise*, *nuisance*, *pledge*, *plenty*, *random*, *remember*, *revel*. English is thus a museum in which relics of Old and Middle French are exhibited; but English words of Latin origin derived from borrowed French words are far less numerous than English words coined directly from Latin roots, and these are the words which lighten our task in learning a Romance language such as

---

* The case system had decayed in the daily speech (p. 325) of the late empire and the ablative or dative is often the literary case form nearest to the colloquial singular.

Spanish. To take full advantage of our Latin legacy we therefore need to know a little about how the pronunciation of Latin changed when it split up into the daughter dialects which are now spoken, and how the sound changes are reflected in the spelling of each.

LATIN	FRENCH			
	(a) Older		(b) Newer	
causa	CHOSE	(*thing*)	cause	(*cause*)
calculo	CAILLOU	(*pebble*)	calcul	(*calculus*)
calce	CHAUX	(*lime*)	calque	(*tracing*)
carta	CHARTE	(*charter*)	carte	(*card*)
captivo	CHÉTIF	(*wretched*)	captif	(*captive*)
factione	FAÇON	(*style*)	faction	(*faction*)
fabrica	FORGE	(*smithy*)	fabrique	(*factory*)
fragili	FRÊLE	(*frail*)	fragile	(*fragile*)
hospitale	HÔTEL	(*hotel, mansion*)	hôpital	(*hospital*)
parabola	PAROLE	(*speech*)	parabole	(*parable*)
pietate	PITIÉ	(*pity*)	piété	(*piety*)
praedicatore	PRÊCHEUR	(*preacher*)	prédicateur	(*preacher*)
questione	QUÊTE	(*quest*)	question	(*question*)
rigido	RAIDE	(*stiff*)	rigide	(*rigid*)
redemptione	RANÇON	(*ransom*)	rédemption	(*redemption*)

There are several signposts by which English words of Latin or French origin can be recognized. We have already come across one of them (C for the *k* sound) in Chapter II. Another important one is the combination -TI- for the sound represented by *sh* in words of Teutonic parentage. The following is a list of some of the most reliable clues:

1) The combinations CT, TI (pronounced *sh*) and SC, e.g. *action* and *scale*.
2) Words containing the sound ʒ (p. 70) represented by the French J of *jeu* (game) or G of *rouge* (red), e.g. *vision* or *treasure*.
3) Words beginning with J and G pronounced as *J* in *jam*, e.g. *gentle*, *giant*, *jacket*.
4) Nearly all words containing OI, e.g. *boil, moisture, soil*.
5) All words in which OU stands for long *u*, e.g. *group, soup, tour*.
6) Words beginning with CH followed by *a* (where *ch* = *tsh*), e.g. *challenge, change, charm*.

7) Words with final GUE, initial QU, and final QUE, e.g. *fatigue, quarter, brusque.*

8) All words in which final S and T are mute, e.g. *debris, bouquet.*

9) Nearly all words ending in -ANT, -ENT, e.g. *agent, merchant, student.*

10) Most polysyllabic words with end stress, e.g. *buffoon, compaign, elite.*

At one time the habit of attaching Latin affixes to native words or words containing a Greek or Teutonic root was frowned on. So other signposts are several Latin particles, or numerals used as affixes (*contra-, pre-, a-* or *ad-, ante-, per-, multi-, uni-, di-, tri-*). Some of these are easily confused with Greek ones (*a-, anti-, peri-*) which do not mean the same. The abstract noun ending *-ion* in *constipation* is also Latin, as is the termination *-it* in *deposit.* The following is a list of the more common affixes of Latin or French origin and the characteristic meaning of the prefixes:

a) PREFIXES:

ab- (away)	*extra-* (beyond)	*re-* (again)
ad- (to)	*in-* (in)	*retro-* (backward)
ambi- (both)	*in-, ne-, non-* (not)	*semi-* (half)
ante- (before)	*inter-* (between)	*sine-* (without)
bene- (well)	*intra-* (within)	*sub-* (under)
bi- (twice)	*pen-* (almost)	*subter-* (under)
circum- (around)	*per-* (through)	*super-* (above)
contra- (against)	*post-* (after)	*trans-* (across)
con- (with)	*pre-* (before)	*tri-* (three)
de- (from)	*preter-* (beyond)	*ultra-* (beyond)
ex-, e- (out of)	*pro-* (for, forth)	*vice-* (in place of)

b) SUFFIXES:

-able	*-ance*	*-esque*	*-ite*	*-ment*
-acious	*-ary*	*-ess,*	*-ity*	*-mony*
-acy	*-ery* or *-ory*	*-ette*	*-ive*	*-tude*
-age	*-ent, ant*	*-ion*	*-ise*	

Like French, all Romance languages have a stock of old words of a more familiar type derived directly from Vulgar Latin, and a newer, larger stratum of classical Latin words introduced by scholars, clergy, lawyers, or technicians. Words of the second class are easy to recognize. The roots have the same shape as those of our own loan words which belong to the same class. The others, that is to say the older

ones, are less easy to recognize, and therefore more difficult to memorize. The home student can get some fun out of the otherwise dreary
task of memorizing a basic word list by noting the sound shifts which
disguise or even distort beyond recognition the original Latin form.
Illustrative examples of this trick will be the basis of the next few
pages which deal with phonetic changes during the period when
Latin was breaking up into what we now call French, Spanish, Portuguese, and Italian.

When Latin began to break up into these dialects the H had become
silent. Initially the symbol has disappeared in all but four Italian words.
It is soundless in French and in Spanish words, though it survives
in the spelling. Apparently the people of the Roman Empire also
became slack about the use of compound consonants such as *ct, pt, st.*
The first of these has disappeared in all the daughter dialects, except
in Latin words *reintroduced* by scholars. In Italian words other than
those of the last-named type CT = TT, in Spanish CT = CH (as in
much), in Portuguese and Old French CT = IT. In Modern French
the symbol remains -IT, but the T is usually silent. The combination
pt becomes *t* (or *tt*) in old words of all the Romance dialects, though
scholars have sometimes put back an unpronounced *p* or *b* in script,
as in the modern French *sept* for the Old French *set* (seven) or as in
our *debt* derived from the French *dette*.

LATIN	ITALIAN	SPANISH	PORTU-GUESE	FRENCH	ENGLISH
DICTO	detto	dicho	dito	dit	*said*
FACTO	fatto	hecho	feito	fait	*done*
LACTE	latte	leche	leite	lait	*milk*
LECTO	letto	lecho	leito	lit	*bed*
NOCTE	notte	noche	noite	nuit	*night*
OCTO	otto	ocho	oito	huit	*eight*
SEPTEM	sette	siete	sete	sept	*seven*
TECTO	tetto	techo	teto	toit	*roof*

Except in French there was decay of the initial combinations *pl, cl,
fl.* In Italian *l* fades out in the γ- sound represented by I. In Spanish
the *lli* sound of *million*, represented by LL, may replace any one of
the three compounds cited. In Portuguese the three consonant combinations make way for the *sh* sound represented by CH.

LATIN	ITALIAN	SPANISH	PORTU- GUESE	FRENCH	ENGLISH
PLENO	pieno	lleno	cheio	plein	*full*
PLUERE	piovere	llover	chover	pleuvoir	*to rain*
CLAVE	chiave	llave	chave	clef	*key*
FLAMMA	fiamma	llama	chama	flamme	*flame*

In two of its daughter dialects the *medial* and *final l* of a Latin word often takes the soft value of *lli* in *million*. The symbol for this is GL in Italian and LH in Portuguese. In Spanish it gave way to the *ch* in Scots *loch*. This is represented by J. In many French words, including all those in the list below, a Latin L has become the *y* sound in *yes*. This pronunciation, which is Parisian in origin, appears from the seventeenth century on and does not intrude in the written language.

LATIN	ITALIAN	SPANISH	PORTU- GUESE	FRENCH	ENGLISH
AURICULA	orecchio	oreja	orelha	oreille	*ear*
CONSILIO	consiglio	consejo	conselho	conseil	*counsel*
FILIA	figlia	hija	filha	fille	*daughter*
FOLIA	foglia	hoja	fôlha	feuille	*leaf*
OCULO	occhio	ojo	ôlho	œil	*eye*
PALEA	paglia	paja	palha	paille	*straw*
TRIPALIO	travaglio	trabajo	trabalho	travail	*work*

Between vowels *b* and *p* of Latin words were also unstable. Of the two the former softened to the *v* sound even before Vulgar Latin broke up. In French it maintains itself as *v* or has faded out, in Italian and Portuguese words it vacillates between *b* and *v*, and in Spanish it appears uniformly as *b*, but the Spanish Academy Grammar admits that "in the greater part of Spain the pronunciation of *b* and *v* is the same although it ought not to be." Latin *p* between vowels survives in Italian alone. In French it has become *v*, and in Spanish and Portuguese soft *b*.

Another change affected all Latin dialects except *Portuguese*. A short stressed *e* and *o* respectively made way for the compound vowels *ie* and *ue*. In French the latter became a sound like *ö* in German. It is written -EU in the ensuing examples.

In general Latin had fewer compound vowels than its descendants.

LATIN	ITALIAN	SPANISH	PORTU-GUESE	FRENCH	ENGLISH
CAPILLO	capello	cabello	cabelo	cheveu	*hair*
CAPRA	capra	cabra		chèvre	*goat*
LEPORE	lepre	liebre	lebre	lièvre	*hare*
OPERARIO	operaio	obrero	obreiro	ouvrier	*worker*
SAPERE	sapere	saber		savoir	*to know*
SAPORE	sapore	sabor		saveur	*taste*
BIBERE	bevere	beber		boire	*to drink*
CABALLO	cavallo	caballo	cavalo	cheval	*horse*
FEBRE	febbre	fiebre	febre	fièvre	*fever*
HABERE	avere	haber	haver	avoir	*to have*
PROBARE	provare	probar	provar	prouver	*to prove*

LATIN	ITALIAN	SPANISH	PORTU-GUESE	FRENCH	ENGLISH
PEDE	piede	pie	pé	pied	*foot*
PETRA	pietra	piedra	pedra	pierre	*stone*
TENET	tiene		tem	tient	*he holds*
DECEM	dieci	diez	dez	dix	*ten*
MORIT	muore	muere	morre	meurt	*he dies*
POTET	può	puede	pode	peut	*he can*
NOVO	nuovo	nuevo	novo	neuf	*new*
FOCO	fuoco	fuego	fogo	feu	*fire*
PROBA	pruova	prueba	prova	preuve	*proof*

The most prominent one, *au*, has become a simple vowel in all our four Romance languages. Its descendant is spelt O in Italian and Spanish, OU or OI in Portuguese, and O or AU in French.

LATIN	ITALIAN	SPANISH	PORTU-GUESE	FRENCH	ENGLISH
AURO	oro		ouro	or	*gold*
CAUSA	cosa		cousa	chose	*thing*
PAUPERI	povero		pobre	pauvre	*poor*

Another common tendency at work during the period of differentiation of the Romance dialects is reflected in spelling. Spanish,

Portuguese, and French equivalents of classical Latin words beginning with ST, SC, SP, SQ, SL, appropriate a vowel, e.g. Latin *spíritu*, Spanish *espíritu*, Portuguese *espírito*, French *esprit*, or Latin *scribere* (to write), Spanish *escribir*, Portuguese *escrever*, French *écrire*. This e- turns up in Latin inscriptions of the second century A.D., and was once part of the spoken language of the empire. It dropped out in Italian, e.g. *spirito* or *scrivere*. In English words derived from French or Latin this initial e is absent. There are a few exceptions, e.g. *estate*, *esquire*, *espouse*, *especially*. The following list illustrates the contrast and also shows a French peculiarity explained in the next paragraph.

ENGLISH	FRENCH	SPANISH	ENGLISH	FRENCH	SPANISH
scald	échauffer	escaldar	*spine*	épine	espina
scarlet	écarlate	escarlata	*sponge*	éponge	esponja
school	école	escuela	*spouse*	épou	esposo
scripture	écriture	escritura	*stamp*	étampe	estampa
scum	écume	espuma	*standard*	étandard	estandarte
slave	esclave	esclavo	*state*	état	estado
sluice	écluse	esclusa	*stanch*	étancher	estancar
space	espace	espacio	*stomach*	estomac	estómago
spade	épée	espada	*strange*	étrange	estraño
Spain	Espagne	España	*study*	étudier	estudiar
spice	épice	especia	*stuff*	étoffe	estofa

We have now looked at what was happening to Latin dialects simultaneously in different parts of the disintegrated empire during the four or so centuries after the fall of Rome. We shall now look at more local changes. From this viewpoint French stands most apart

ITALIAN	SPANISH	PORTUGUESE	MIDDLE FRENCH	MODERN FRENCH	ENGLISH
	bastardo		bastard	BÂTARD	*bastard*
	bestia	besta	beste	BÊTE	*beast*
chiostro	claustro		cloistre	CLOÎTRE	*cloister*
	costa		coste	CÔTE	*coast*
costare	costar	custar	couster	COÛTER	*(to) cost*
festa	fiesta	festa	feste	FÊTE	*feast*
isola	isla	ilha	isle	ÎLE	*isle*
ostrica	ostra		oistre	HUÎTRE	*oyster*

from its sister languages. We have already met (p. 219) one peculiarity of French. The compound consonant *st* has made way for *t*. The preceding vowel then carries a circumflex accent, as in the examples below. The change began in the eleventh century, but a mute S before T persisted in written French till the reforms of 1740.

Another specifically Old French sound change has also cropped up in preceding tables. The modern French C is a hard (*k*) sound only before *a, o,* and *u*. Otherwise it stands for *s*. Where C preceded *a* in Latin words it softened to the *sh* sound in *ship*, spelt CH in French orthography (cf. *chamois, champagne*), as in the following:

LATIN	ITALIAN	SPANISH	PORTUGUESE	FRENCH	ENGLISH
caballo	cavallo	caballo	cavalo	CHEVAL	*horse*
camisia	camicia	camisa		CHEMISE	*shirt*
capra	capra	cabra		CHÈVRE	*goat*
capite	capo	cabo	cabeça	CHEF *	*head*
caro		caro		CHER	*dear*
causa		cosa	cousa	CHOSE	*thing*

* In a metaphorical sense. The anatomical head is *la tête*.

In many English words derived from French this initial CH conceals correspondence with the Spanish or Italian equivalent. It does so, for instance, in those below:

LATIN	SPANISH	FRENCH	ENGLISH
calefacere	calentar	chauffer	*chafe*
cambio	cambio	change	*change*
campione	campeón	champion	*champion*
cancellario	canciller	chancelier	*chancellor*
cantare	cantar	chanter	*chant*
capitulo	capítulo	chapitre	*chapter*
captiare	cazar	chasser	*chase*
caritate	caritad	charité	*charity*
carta	carta	charte	*chart*
casto	casto	chaste	*chaste*

Another characteristically French sound shift recalls what happened in Middle English and is still going on in Scandinavian dialects. Between two vowels *g* softened to *y* or *i* or disappeared. Hence we get English old-new couplets such as *royal-regal, loyal-legal, frail-fragile.* (The English pronunciation of *royal* and *loyal* is a survival of the Old French stage.) Examples are in the following table.

LATIN	ITALIAN	SPANISH	PORTUGUESE	FRENCH	ENGLISH
augusto		agosto		AOÛT	*August*
castigare	castigare	castigar		CHÂTIER	*to chastise*
integro	intero	entero	inteiro	ENTIER	*entire*
fugire	fuggire	huir	fugir	FUIR	*to flee*
lege	legge	ley	lei	LOI	*law*
ligare	legare	ligar		LIER	*to tie*
negare	negare	negar		NIER	*to deny*
nigro	nero	negro		NOIR	*black*
pacare	pagare	pagar		PAYER	*to pay*
pagano	pagano		pagão	PAYEN	*heathen*
plaga	piaga	llaga	praga	PLAIE	*wound (plague)*
ruga	(*strada*)	(*calle*)	rua	RUE	*street*

Another French consonant shift scarcely conceals the Latin equivalent. A *v* which through phonetic loss has become final hardens to *f*, or is mute, as shown in the next installment for our vocabulary of Romance words. One reason for mentioning this is that it brings to life a grammatical irregularity. The feminine form (p. 357) of adjectives which have the masculine singular ending -*f* takes -*ve* in place of it.

LATIN	ITALIAN	SPANISH	PORTUGUESE	FRENCH	ENGLISH
bove	bove	buey	boi	BŒUF	*ox*
breve		breve		BREF (-*ève*)	*brief*
novo (-*a*)	nuovo	nuevo	novo	NEUF (-*ve*)	*new*
novem	nove	nueve	nove	NEUF	*nine*
clave	chiave	llave	chave	CLEF	*key*
nervo	nervo	nervio	nervo	NERF	*nerve*
ovo	uovo	huevo	ôvo	ŒUF	*egg*
vivo (-*a*)		vivo (-*a*)		VIF (-*ve*)	*alive*

Two vowel shifts are peculiar to French: (*a*) in an open syllable the Latin stressed *a* became an *e* sound, spelt today E, È, É, AI, or -ER; (*b*) in the same position the Latin stressed *e* changed to the diphthong OI. The combination now stands for a sound like *wa* in Scots *we twa.*

French grammarians disapproved of this pronunciation till the Revolution put its seal on it. Examples of these changes are below.

What is most characteristic of modern French words is loss of body through successive elimination of terminal vowels, medial consonants, and final consonants. The consequence is that French has a very large proportion of monosyllables. Indeed, almost every bisyllabic Latin word which has left a direct descendant in modern French is now represented by a single syllable, as illustrated by the following couplets in which a medial consonant has disappeared: lege-LOI (*law*), fide-FOI (*faith*), videt-VOIT (*sees*), credit-CROIT (*believes*), or patre-PÈRE (*father*), matre-MÈRE (*mother*), fratre-FRÈRE (*brother*), sorore-SŒUR (*sister*). In other French words, as in the last four, an unaccented final E exists only on paper.

LATIN	ITALIAN	SPANISH	PORTUGUESE	FRENCH	ENGLISH
a) cantare	cantare	cantar		CHANTER	sing
claro	chiaro	claro		CLAIR	clear
ala		ala		AILE	wing (aisle)
prato	prato	prado		PRÉ	meadow
sale	sale	sal		SEL	salt
patre	padre		pai	PÈRE	father
b) seta	seta	seda		SOIE	silk
me		me		MOI	me
velo	velo	véu		VOILE	veil
tela		tela		TOILE	cloth

The last remark would be equally true about the majority of final consonants, e.g. the silent T in *voit* or *croit*. One result of this is a great gap (see p. 22) between the flexional system of the written and of the spoken language. No other Romance language furnishes comparable examples of drastic shortening, e.g. EAU (pronounced *o*) from *aqua* (water), HAUT (pronounced *o*) from *alto* (high), MI from *medio* (half), AOÛT (pronounced *a-oo* or *oo*) from *augusto* (August), ROND (pronounced *rõ*) from *rotundo* (round), SÛR (pronounced *syr*) from *securo* (safe), HÔTE (pronounced *oat*) from *hospite* (host). Thus the Latin ancestry of most French words, other than those which have been introduced by scholars in comparatively recent times, is far less apparent than that of their Italian or Spanish equivalents.

As a spoken language Spanish has moved further away from Latin than Italian has, but not so far as French. Partly for this reason, but also because the spelling of Spanish words is highly regular, there is

less to say about the sound changes in relation to the appearance of
the printed word. For recognizing the similarity of English words of
Latin origin to their Spanish equivalents, the important ones are few.
Some have turned up in the preceding paragraphs. The most misleading one is still to come. This is the disappearance of the *initial f*, replaced in script by what is now *silent H*, cf. *hacienda*, which comes

LATIN	ITALIAN	SPANISH	PORTUGUESE	FRENCH	ENGLISH
faba	fava	HAVA	fava	fève	*bean*
fabulari	(*parlare*)	HABLAR	falar	(*parler*)	*to speak* *
facere	fare	HACER	fazer	faire	*to make*
falcone	falcone	HALCÓN	falcão	faucon	*falcon*
fame	fame	HAMBRE	fome	faim	*hunger*
farina	farina	HARINA	farinha	farine	*flour*
fendere	fendere	HENDER	fender	fendre	*to split*
foeno	fieno	HENO	feno	foin	*hay*
fervore	fervore	HERVOR	fervor	ferveur	*fervor*
ferro	ferro	HIERRO	ferro	fer	*iron*
fico	fico	HIGO	figo	figue	*fig*
filio	figlio	HIJO	filho	fils	*son*
filia	figlia	HIJA	filha	fille	*daughter*
filo	filo	HILO	fio	fil	*thread*
folia	foglia	HOJA	fôlha	feuille	*leaf*
furca	forca	HORCA	fôrca	fourche	*pitchfork*
forma	forma	HORMA	forma	forme	*form*
formica	formica	HORMIGA	formiga	fourmi	*ant*
fugire	fuggire	HUIR	fugir	fuir	*to flee*
fumo	fumo	HUMO	fumo	fumée	*smoke*
furone	furetto	HURÓN	furão	furet	*ferret*
ficato	fegato	HÍGADO	fígado	foie	*liver*

* Hence *palaver*.

from the Latin word *facienda*. Some linguists attribute this to the
influence of the Moorish occupation, and others to that of the pre-
Aryan population now represented by the Basques, who have no *f*
sound. The first of these suggestions is unlikely, because H at the
beginning of a word crops up at a comparatively late stage in old
documents. The Spanish Jews who emigrated to Salonika about A.D.
1500 still preserve the Latin *f*, e.g. *fierro* for *hierro* (iron) and *favlar*
for *hablar* (to speak). So also do the Portuguese. The change began in
the neighborhood of Burgos on the Spanish border of the Pyrenees,

and in Gascony on the French side. That is to say, it prevailed where Spanish and French communities were in closest contact with the f-less Basques. In the list of words on page 244 are a few characteristic examples of the change from f to h, i.e., the *disappearance* of f.

The disappearance of initial f did not take place in all old Spanish words. It remained intact when followed by r or ue, as is shown in the following:

LATIN	ITALIAN	SPANISH	PORTUGUESE	FRENCH	ENGLISH
fronte	fronte	frente		front	forehead, front
frigido	freddo	frio		froid	cold
fricto	fritto	frito		frit	fried
foco	fuoco	fuego	fogo	feu	fire
forti	forte	fuerte	forte	fort	strong
fortia	forza	fuerza	fôrça	force	force

Many Spanish words have come to look different from equivalent ones in other Romance languages because of the interpolation of an additional consonant:

LATIN	ITALIAN	SPANISH	PORTUGUESE	FRENCH	ENGLISH
fame	fame	hambre	fome	faim	hunger
homine	uomo	hombre	homem	homme	man
legumine	legume	legumbre	legume	légume	vegetable
sanguine	sangue	sangre	sangue	sang	blood
seminare	seminare	sembrar	semear	semer	to sow

The table before the last but one shows that Portuguese does not share this f-less word form. As previous ones have shown, Portuguese differs from Spanish in two other ways. It participated in the b-v shift which Spanish resisted, and it resisted the replacement of e and o by the compounds ie and ue. Portuguese shares with French the tendency to slough off medial consonants. It shares with Spanish elimination of a medial d, as illustrated by the first five, and, with no other Romance language the disappearance of l, as illustrated by the last four examples in the next table. The reader will find other differences between Portuguese and Spanish in Chapter VIII, page 345.

LATIN	ITALIAN	SPANISH	PORTUGUESE	FRENCH	ENGLISH
cadere	cadere	caer	CAIR	choir *	to fall
credere	credere	creer	CRER	croire	to believe
fideli	fedele	FIEL		fidèle	faithful
audire	udire	oir	OUVIR	ouïr †	to hear
laudare	lodare	loar	LOUVAR	louer	to praise
caelo	cielo		CÉU	ciel	sky
colore	colore	color	CÔR	couleur	color
salute	salute	salud	SAÚDE	salut	health
volare	volare	volar	VOAR	voler	to fly

* *archaic;* the usual verb equivalent of *to fall* is *tomber.*
† *archaic;* the usual verb equivalent of *to hear* is *entendre.* The imperative of *ouïr* survives in our law courts as *oyez, oyez* (*hear, oh, hear!*).

THE GREEK CONTRIBUTION

The revolt against papal authority in the sixteenth century went hand in hand with Biblical scholarship and a renewal of interest in Greek philosophy. Greek words, disguised by Latin spelling, came into English usage. At the beginning of the nineteenth century a steady trickle became a torrent. On the whole, medical science had favored Latin more than Greek roots from which to build new technical terms. The introduction of modern chemical nomenclature in the closing years of the eighteenth century set a new fashion. Modern scholarship, whether literary or naturalistic, prefers Greek to Latin; and proprietary products have fallen into line. At no other time in our history have there been so many words of Greek origin on the lips of the English-speaking peoples.

Today Latin as a quarry for word-building material has lost its former importance. In the terminology of modern science, especially in *aeronautics, biochemistry, chemotherapy, genetics,* its place is increasingly taken by Greek. But the inventor of a new process or instrument does not scan the pages of Plato or Aristotle for a suitable name. He goes to the lexicon and creates something which was never heard before. So it happens that the language of Euripides is sending out new shoots in the name of a dental cream, a mouthwash or a patent medicine. A large number of these artificially created scientific and technical terms are becoming common property. When they are of an unwieldy length, everyday speech tends to subject them to a

FIG. 29. RUNE STONE

This remarkable Rune stone now stands in the national park in Stockholm. It was placed over the grave of a young man named Vämod by his father Varin. The rune begins: *To the memory of Vämod stands this stone. But Varin the father engraved it for his dead son.* Then follow many verses of a long elegy.

process of clipping similar to what resulted in *alms*, shortened in the course of centuries from the same Greek root which yields *eleemosy-nary*. What used to take several centuries is now reached in a few decades, if not in a few years. With the same snappiness with which popular parlance has shortened *pepper* (Greek *peperi*) to *pep*, it has changed *photograph* to *photo*, *automobile* to *auto*, *telephone* to *phone*, and *stenographer* to *stenog*.

Most words of Greek origin are easy to recognize in script by certain peculiar consonant combinations introduced by Latin scribes. Of these *ph* pronounced like *f*, in *phonograph*, and *ch* pronounced like *k* in a *Christian chorus*, are infallible. So also is the *rh* in *rheumatism* and *diarrhea*. An initial *ps* pronounced like *s* alone, as in *psychology* or *pseudonym*, is nearly always indicative of Greek origin, as is the vowel combinations *oe* or a *y* pronounced as in *lyre*. The combination *th* for þ represented in Greek by θ is common to Greek and Teutonic root words. Scholars of the Reformation period used Latin spelling conventions such as C for K in Greek roots. This practice is dying out. Though we still write *cycle* and *cyst*, the Greek K is now used at the beginning of some technical words coined from Greek sources, as illustrated by *kinetic*, *kerosene*, or *kleptomaniac*. German and French, like English, adhere to the earlier Latin transliteration PH where Scandinavians, Spaniards, and Italians have adopted the later F. Romance languages other than French render TH by T, RH by R and Y by I, as in the Spanish words *fotografía, teatro, diarrea, síntoma*.

Many words of Greek origin can be recognized at sight by their prefixes, of which the following are specially important. Of the examples given on page 248, the first of each pair is literary, the second a product of the new technical humanism.

To these we should add the numeral prefixes: *mono-* (1) as *monogamy*, *di-* (2), *tri-* (3), *tetra-* (4), *penta-* (5), *hexa-* (6), in *tripod, tetrahedron, pentagon, hexagon; hepta-* (7) as in *heptameter, octo-* (8) as in *octopus* and *octagon, deka-* (10) as in *decalogue, kilo-* (1000) in *kilometer* or *kilogram*. One of the foregoing prefixes, *ex-* or *ec-*, is like its Latin equivalent and is not diagnostic. So also is *pro-*. The only outstanding Greek suffixes are *-ic* or *-ics* in *dialectic* and *mathematics*, with the derivative *-ical* and *ism*, e.g. in *theism*. The last exhibit in the language museum (Part IV) of *The Loom* is a list of Greek words used to build international technical terms.

Both in its ancient and modern form, Greek stands apart from other languages of the Aryan family. Twenty-five hundred years ago,

amphi-	*both* or *around*	as in	*amphitheater,*	*amphibious.*
a- or *an-*	*not*	as in	*amnesty,*	*amorphous.*
ana-	*back, again,*	as in	*anachronism,*	*anabolism.*
anti-	*against*	as in	*antithesis,*	*antiseptic.*
apo-	*away*	as in	*apostasy,*	*apogamy.*
auto-	*by itself*	as in	*autocrat,*	*autoerotic.*
dia-	*through*	as in	*diagonal,*	*diamagnetic.*
dys-	*bad*	as in	*dysgenic,*	*dyspepsia.*
ec-, ex-	*from, out of*	as in	*exodus,*	*ecdysis.*
endo-	*within*	as in	*endogenous,*	*endometrium.*
epi-	*upon*	as in	*epigram,*	*epidiascope.*
eu-	*good*	as in	*eulogy,*	*eugenic.*
hemi-	*half*	as in	*hemisphere,*	*hemicycle.*
hetero-	*different*	as in	*heterodox,*	*heterodyne.*
homo-	*same*	as in	*homophone,*	*homosexual.*
hyper-	*above*	as in	*hyperbole,*	*hypertrophy.*
hypo-	*below*	as in	*hypothesis,*	*hypophosphate.*
iso-	*equal*	as in	*isosceles,*	*isomer.*
kata-	*down*	as in	*catastrophe,*	*catalysis.*
meta-	*after*	as in	*metaphysics,*	*metabolism.*
neo-	*new*	as in	*neologism,*	*neon.*
palaeo-	*old*	as in	*palaeography,*	*palaeolithic.*
pan-	*all*	as in	*pantheism,*	*panchromatic.*
para-	*beside*	as in	*paradox,*	*parameter.*
peri-	*around*	as in	*periphrasis,*	*periscope.*
poly-	*many*	as in	*polytheism,*	*polydactyly.*
pro-	*before*	as in	*prologue,*	*prognosis.*
proto-	*first*	as in	*protocol,*	*protoplasm.*
pseudo-	*false*	as in	*pseudonym,*	*pseudopodium.*
syn-, sym-	*together*	as in	*synchronous,*	*symbiosis.*

closely related dialects were spoken throughout the Balkan Peninsula, the Aegean Islands, including Cyprus and Crete, in the western part of Asia Minor, and in many settlements of the Black Sea. That people who spoke these dialects could understand one another was the only tie between all the constantly warring and rarely united communities called collectively Ancient Greece. By the fourth century B.C., a common standard for written communication based on mainland Attic was accepted. This *koine*, which was officially adopted by the Macedonian kings, supplanted all its local competitors (Ionic, Doric, Aeolic, Arcadian, Corinthian, etc.) except Spartan, which still survives locally in modern Greece as *Tsaconian*. The *koine* spread over the Near and Middle East. After the division of the Macedonian Empire, it disintegrated into regional forms such as the Macedonian Greek of the mainland and the Alexandrian Greek into which the Jews of Egypt translated their Old Testament (Septuaginta). Even in the third century A.D. the Western Church relied mainly on Greek. During the fourth, it began to die out in Gaul, Spain, Italy, and North Africa, and Augustine could not read Plato in the original. When Constantinople fell to the Turks in the fifteenth century Greek survived as a living language only in vernaculars restricted to the southernmost portion of the Balkan Peninsula and its vicinity.

There was little vernacular writing before Greece won its independence from the Turks in 1827. Thereafter classical models had a strong influence on the form adopted. As a written language, modern Greek is therefore a product, and a highly artificial product, of the last century. The gap between the written and the spoken language is greater than in any other European language. While Italian spelling has become more phonetic with the march of time, Greek spelling has relinquished the claims of convenience to cherish an historic memory of departed glory. A modern movement to bring the literary language nearer to the spoken has met with no success. In 1911, students of the University of Athens demonstrated in public against the proposal to translate the Bible into folk Greek. Excluding the vocative, classical Greek had four case forms corresponding to those of Old Norse, Old English, and Old German. Modern Greek, as prescribed in the textbooks used in the schools, retains three case forms of the adjective, noun, and article, and the three gender classes still exist. It has dropped two tense forms (perfect and future) which are replaced by analytical constructions. Otherwise it has not moved far from the elaborate flexional system of ancestral Greek.

PRONUNCIATION OF SPANISH, ITALIAN, AND FRENCH

From various clues such as the study of puns and of meter in Latin literature, or of features common to two or more of its modern descendants, it seems quite clear that the Latin of the Roman Empire had a very regular system of spelling. With few exceptions a particular symbol always stood for a particular sound, or a group of very closely related sounds. This is almost true of Italian or of Spanish today. French spelling is scarcely more regular than that of English. The home student who wishes to learn a Romance language will need to be familiar with its sound patterns and conventions. Other readers

should *skip the rest of the chapter*. There are notes on the pronunciation of Portuguese in Chapter VIII (p. 345).

We have seen that Italian is rich in double consonants such as *tt*, *ll*,
nn, *zz*, etc., and it is necessary to *linger* on them in pronouncing a
word in which one of them occurs. One inconsistency, common to
Italian, Spanish, and French spelling, involves the pronunciation of
the symbols C and G. In Latin they always had their hard values in
cat and *goat*. In its modern descendants they still have them when
they precede the vowels *a*, *o*, and *u*. Thus we meet the same hard C in
costa (Italian and Spanish), *côte* (French) as in its equivalent *coast*.
So also we meet the same hard G in *governo* (Italian), *gobierno*
(Spanish), *gouvernement* (French), for *government*. Before *e* and
i the Italian C is the CH sound in *child*, and the Italian G is the soft
G of *gem*. Before *e* and *i* the Spanish C has the same value as the Spanish Z before *a*, *o* and *u*,* i.e., the TH in *thin*, and the Spanish G has the
value which Spanish J has before *all* vowels, i.e., the guttural sound
of CH in Scots *loch*. Before *e* and *i* the French C is the C in *cinder*
and the French G is the same as the French J (p. 235), which is our
S in *treasure*.

When the hard *c* and *g* sounds precede *e* and *i* in the Italian word
the symbols which stand for them are CH as in *chianti* and GH as in
ghiaccio (ice). The corresponding Spanish and French symbols are
QU as in Fr. *bouquet* and GU as in Fr. *guide*. The symbols CI and
GI before *a*, *o*, *u* in an Italian word have the same values as C or G
before *e* or *i*, corresponding to our CH in *chocolate* (*cioccolata*), and
our J in *journal* (*giornale*). Italian SC before E or I is pronounced like
SH in *ship*, elsewhere like SC in *scope*. SCH has the same value as
SCH in *school*. Similarly the French GE before *a*, *o*, *u* as in *nous
mangeons* (we eat) stands for the soft French J or G alone before *e*
and *i*. A subscript mark called the *cedilla* shows that a French or
Portuguese C before *a*, *o*, *u*, as in *leçon* (lesson) has the value of C in
cinder.

These inconsistencies and conventions draw attention to the chief
differences between the sound values of identical symbols in the
Romance group. Thus the Italian CH of *chianti* has the *k* value in
character, the Spanish CH in *mucho* its value in the equivalent *much*,
and the French CH is the *sh* sound in *chamois* or *champagne*. The
symbol J does not occur in modern Italian. The Spanish J is the

---

* The θ value for the Spanish Z and C before *e* and *i* is Castilian. In Spanish-
speaking America both C and Z have the value of the French C in CIGARETTE.

CH in Scots *loch*, and the French J is the SI sound in *vision*. The Italian Z usually corresponds to *ts*, the Spanish-American to C in *citrus*, and the French Z to our own in *maze*. There is no *z* sound in Spanish. In Italian and in French an S between two vowels as in *easy* stands for *z*, otherwise for the *pure s* sound in *silly*. The Spanish S is always pure, i.e., a hiss as in *case*, never a buzz as in *rose*. The French and Spanish QU is the *k* sound in *lacquer*. The Italian QU is the *kw* sound in *liquid*.

The LLI sound of *billiards* has cropped up earlier in this chapter, in Italian with the symbol GL, in Portuguese with LH, in Spanish with LL. Originally, and today in some dialects, the LL of a French word had the same value, which has otherwise faded to the *y* sound in *yes*. In some French words the LL still stands for an ordinary *l* sound, e.g. *ville* (town) or *village*. The N in some Latin words has undergone a softening analogous to the LLI sound. For this N sound as in *onion*, the Italian and French symbol is GN as in *Mignon*. The Spanish symbol is Ñ, as in *cañón* (tube). The mark is called the *tilde*.

Another feature of the sound pattern of Romance languages mentioned in passing is the total absence of an *h* sound. Though the symbol remains, there is no aspirate in a French word which begins with H, e.g. *herbe* (grass), nor in a Spanish one, e.g. *hombre* (man). The H of French and Spanish is a dead letter and it has disappeared altogether in corresponding Italian words, e.g. *erba* or *uomo*. The four Italian words which cling to it are: *ho* (I have), *hai* (thou hast), *ha* (he has), *hanno* (they have). The initial H of these words distinguishes them from their homophones: *o* (or), *ai* (to the), *a* (to), *anno* (year). Conversely, the symbol R which is often a dead letter in Anglo-American words is always audible in words of Romance languages. The Spanish and Italian R is an R rolled on the tip of the tongue. The more fashionable Parisian variant of the French R is less forcible and somewhat throaty.

Italian and Spanish have stuck to the very thrifty battery of Latin vowels. The simple vowel symbols A, E, I, O, U, are roughly equivalent to *ah*, *eh*, or *e* in *yes*, *ee*, *oh*, *oo* in *too*. Romance vowels are pure vowels. Unlike long English vowels they have no tendency toward diphthongization. To get the correct value it is necessary to keep lips and tongue fixed during articulation. If you do, you will pronounce the Italian O of *dove* (where) correctly like the AW of *law*. Otherwise it will sound like the O of *alone* and be wrong. When in Italian or Spanish two vowels come together, and one of them is *i* or *u*, the other vowel (*a, e, o*) takes the stress, and *i* or *u* are quickly passed over. The vowel equipment of Portuguese (see p. 345) and of French has traveled far from the Latin homestead.

No single French vowel *exactly* corresponds to any English one. All we can attempt to do is to give approximate equivalents which a Frenchman could recognize as such.

Before a double consonant *a* is usually as in *man*, e.g. *patte* (paw). Before a single consonant it is often long as in *far*. The circumflex (^) written above a vowel lengthens it, and is a sign that at one time the vowel was followed by S + consonant, e.g. *château* (castle).

Without an accent E may be short and open like the E of *let*, e.g. *sel* (salt), or is faintly audible like the first E in *veneer*, e.g. *leçon*. A final E without an accent, e.g. *barbe* (beard), is always silent in daily speech, like the *e* in our word *made*. É is pronounced like the AY in *hay*, e.g. *pécher* (to sin). Final -ER and -EZ in verb forms have the sound value of É, e.g. *chasser* (to chase), *payez* (pay!). È sounds like the *ai* in *affair*, e.g. *mère* (mother). Ê has roughly the same open sound of *ea* in *treacherous*, but is longer, e.g. *pêcher* (to fish).

O is generally short as in *long*, e.g. *lot* (lot). Ô sounds like O in *opal*, e.g. *ôter* (remove). The sound represented by U has no equivalent in English. If you speak Scots, pronounce it like the U of *guid;* if you know German, like the Ü of *Hütte*. Otherwise, pout your lips as if you were to pronounce the U of *pool*, but without uttering any sound. Then, with the lips in the same position as before, try to pronounce the E of *flea*, and you *may* obtain the sound of French U in *lune* (moon), or *punir* (punish).

AI may either be pronounced like È, as in *vrai* (true), or like É, as in *je chanterai* (I shall sing). AU and EAU sound like OU in *ought*, e.g. *cause, beau* (beautiful). EU resembles the pronunciation of EA in *heard*, e.g. *Europe*. OU is like the OO of *loot*, e.g. *doux* (sweet). OI sounds like *wa*, e.g. *soir*.

Unless the following word begins with a vowel, final consonants, chiefly T, D, S, X, Z, and less often C, F, L, are usually silent, e.g. *sonnet, nid* (nest), *vers, yeux* (eyes), *nez* (nose), *trop* (too much), *estomac* (stomach), *clef* (key), *fusil* (rifle). Americans and English are familiar with many borrowed French words in which the final consonants are not pronounced, e.g. *ballet, gourmand, chamois, pince-nez*. These silent finals, which preserve continuity with the past of the language, become vocal under certain conditions. When a word ending in a mute consonant precedes one with an initial vowel, French safeguards smoothness of speech by bringing the dead letter back to life. It becomes the beginning of the following word. Thus *on en a pour son argent* (it is worth the money) is pronounced *on en a pour son argent*. For this so-called *liaison* there is no hard-and-fast rule. Common people use it more sparingly than those who affect culture. It is customary between article and noun, e.g. *les enfants* (the children), pointed word or possessive adjective and noun, e.g. *nos amis* (our friends), numeral and noun, e.g. *trois autos* (three motor cars), pronoun and verb, e.g. *ils arrivent* (they arrive). The French have other means of avoiding a clash of two vowels. One is liquidation of the first vowel, e.g. *l'oiseau* for *le oiseau* (the bird), the other is insertion of an auxiliary consonant (*t, s, l*) between the two vowels, e.g. *a-t-il?* (has he?). Unlike French, Spanish is not averse to vowel collision, cf. *la obscuridad* and *l'obscurité* (darkness).

French is a highly nasal language. At an early stage of its evolution the nasal consonants M and N became silent, or almost so, imparting a nasal twang to the preceding vowel. When English-speaking people first try to pronounce a nasal vowel like the one in the French word *son* (sound) they usually say *song*. To make sure that you actually nasalize the O instead of producing an ordinary O followed by a nasal consonant, take the advice of an English phonetician and make the following experiment:

"Pinch the nose tightly so that no air can escape, and then say the sound. If the nasalized vowel is being said, then it can be prolonged indefinitely; but if *ng* is being pronounced, then the sound will come to an abrupt ending."

Modern French has four different nasal vowels which in script are represented by a great variety of vowel-consonant combinations:

1) Nasalized A (*a*), written AN, EN, AM, EM, e.g. *dans* (in) *mensonge* (lie), *ambition, membre.*
2) Nasalized E (*e*), written IN, EN, AIN, EIN, IM, AIM, e.g. *fin, romain, plein* (full), *simple, faim* (hunger), *chien* (dog).
3) Nasalized O (*o*), written ON, OM, e.g. *bon* (good), *corrompu* (corrupt).
4) Nasalized U (*œ*), written UN, UM, e.g. *brun* (brown), *humble.*
   IN- has a nasal sound when prefixed to a word beginning with a consonant, as in *injuste.* When prefixed to a word beginning with a vowel or a mute H, as in *inutile, inhumain,* it is pronounced like the IN- in English *inefficient.*
   Double N does not cause nasalization of the preceding vowel, e.g. *bannir* (banish).

The French H is an empty symbol. It is always soundless, but its presence at the beginning of some words affects pronunciation of its predecessor. From this point of view we can put French nouns with an initial H in two classes. In words of the *mute*-H class it is a dummy, e.g. its succeeding vowel brings to life an otherwise mute final consonant of the preceding word, or suppresses the vowel of the definite article. In a second class of words the initial H, though silent on its own account, protects the following vowel from a tie-up with the preceding consonant, or the suppression of the final vowel of the definite article. The second class consists of Teutonic words, largely those which the Franks left behind them, or of Greek words introduced by scholars.

DUMMY H		BUFFER H	
l'herbe	(grass)	*la hache*	(the axe)
l'heure	(the hour)	*la haie*	(the hedge)
l'hirondelle	(the swallow)	*la haine*	(hate)
l'huile	(oil)	*la harpe*	(the harp)
l'huître	(the oyster)	*la hélice*	(the propeller)
l'habitude	(custom)	*la Hongrie*	(Hungary)
l'homme	(the man)	*le hibou*	(the owl)
l'héritage		*le hareng*	(the herring)
l'historien		*le hasard*	(chance)
l'honneur		*le héros*	(the hero)
l'hiver	(winter)	*le homard*	(the lobster)
l'hôtel	(the hotel)	*le havre*	(the harbor)

The buffer H of *héros* prevents confusion between *les héros* and *les zéros*, when other evidence is lacking.

STRESS.—The way in which the common people of the Roman Empire stressed their words has left a deep mark on the modern Romance langauges. Unlike the Greeks the Romans never stressed the last syllable of a polysyllabic word. Words of two syllables had the stress on the first, e.g. *púro* (pure). Words of more than two had it on the last but one if the vowel was long, e.g. *colōres*. Otherwise it was on the last but two, as in *ásino* (ass). On the whole Spaniards and Italians still place emphasis where it used to be in Vulgar Latin times, as in the Spanish equivalents, *colóres*, *ásno*. Many Italian and even more Spanish words now have stress on the final syllable because what came after it has disappeared, e.g. Spanish *ciudád*, Italian *città* (Latin *civitáte*). In Italian, end stress is indicated by a *grave* (`) accent, the only one in its script, as in *temerità* (temerity). The *grave* accent also serves to distinguish a few monosyllables from words which look alike and sound alike, e.g. *è* (is), *e* (and), or *dà* (he gives), *da* (from; at). Spanish has more words with end stress, and a trickier system of stress marks. Rules of Spanish stress are as follows:

1) Words ending in a vowel, e.g. *salubre*, or in N, e.g. *imagen*, or S, e.g. *martes*, and stressed on the last *but one* syllable, do without the accent.
2) Words ending in a consonant other than N or S, and stressed on the last syllable, do without the accent, e.g. *esperar*, *propriedad*.
3) Words which do not come under these two rules require the acute ('), e.g. *fuí*, *imaginación*.
4) The acute accent also serves to distinguish between words of like spelling but different meaning, e.g. *más* (more), *mas* (but), *el* (the) —*él* (he).

With regard to stress French stands quite apart from her sisters. When, as usual, the unstressed part of an original Latin word has disappeared, we should expect to find the stress on the final syllable, cf. Latin *amico*, French *ami*. In fact, a rule of this sort gives an exaggerated impression. Predominance of the final syllable is slight, and a trifling increase in stress goes with rise of tone. For purpose of emphasis or contrast, stress may fall on a syllable other than the last.

Since C and G are sources of trouble to the student of any Romance language, the following table may prove useful:

C AND G BEFORE E AND I

LATIN		ITALIAN		SPANISH		PORTUGUESE		FRENCH	
LETTER	SOUND	LETTER	SOUND	LETTER	SOUND	LETTER	SOUND	LETTER	SOUND
C centum = 100	*c*old	C cento	*ch*in	C ciento	*th*in	C cento	*c*inder	C cent	*c*inder
G genero = brother- in-law	*g*ift	G genero	*g*em	(y, h)	—	G genro	mea*s*ure	G, J gendre	mea*s*ure

FURTHER READING

BAUGH   *History of the English Language.*
JESPERSEN   *Growth and Structure of the English Language.*
MENCKEN   *The American Language.*
MYERS   *The Foundations of English.*
SKEAT   *A Concise Etymological Dictionary of the English Language.*

The *Linguaphone* and *Columbia* Records.

CHAPTER VII

Our Teutonic Relatives—A Bird's-eye View of Teutonic Grammar

THE object of this chapter is to give a bird's-eye view of the grammar of four Teutonic languages, more especially German, for the benefit of the home student who may wish to learn one of them by using the methods outlined in the preceding chapter. The reader who does *not* intend to do so will find a more detailed treatment of principles already stated in Chapter V. The reader who *does* must pay attention to each cross reference for relevant material printed in another context.

Some striking peculiarities of English are: (*a*) great reduction of its flexional system owing to loss of useless grammatical devices such as gender, number, or case concord of adjectives; (*b*) great regularity of remaining flexions, e.g. the plural -*s*. Both reduction and leveling have taken place in all Teutonic languages, but in no other have these processes gone so far. German is the most *conservative* of those with which we shall deal. It has not gone far beyond the level of English in the time of Alfred the Great. Consequently it is the most difficult to learn. A brief account of the evolution of English grammar will help to bring the dead bones of German grammar to life, and lighten the task of learning for the beginner.

If Alfred the Great had established schools to make the Old English Bible, like the Reformation Bible, accessible to the common people, English-speaking boys and girls would have had much more grammar to learn about than American or British boys and girls now need to know. Like Icelandic and German, Old English was still a highly *inflected* language. The reader of *The Loom* has already met two examples of this difference between the English of Alfred's time and the English of today. Old English had more *case forms* of the personal pronoun (p. 104) and more *personal* forms (p. 84) of the verb.

In modern English the personal pronouns and the relative pronouns (*who*) have three case forms, at least in the singular: the *nominative* (verb subject), the possessive or *genitive*, and the *objective*, which may be the "direct" or "indirect" object of a verb and is always used after a directive. Old English had *four* case forms in the singular and plural, together with corresponding ones of the *dual* number, which has disappeared in all modern Teutonic languages except Icelandic. The original four case forms included a nominative and genitive used as we still use them, an *accusative* or direct object form also used after certain prepositions, e.g. *þurgh* (through—German *durch*), and a *dative* or indirect object form used after the majority of prepositions. The fate of these two *object* or *preposition* case forms has been different in different Teutonic languages. Comparison of the tables printed on pages 160 and 115 shows that the Old English dative eventually displaced the accusative. The Old Norse accusative supplanted the dative, which has disappeared in Swedish, Danish, and Norwegian. These languages have therefore three case forms like English. The same is true of Dutch (p. 115), though a trace of a separate dative persists in the third person plural. German and Icelandic have stuck to the old four case forms. If you want to learn German it is necessary to memorize the rules given in small print below.

Germans still use the acusative case form of the pronoun (or adjective) as the *direct object* and always after some prepositions: *durch* (through), *ohne* (without), *gegen* (against), *um* (around), *für* (for). When the verb expresses motion, the accusative case form *also* comes after the prepositions *in*, *auf*, (on), *über* (over), *unter* (under), *zwischen* (between), *an* (at), *hinter* (behind), *vor* (in front of), *neben* (beside). The dative or *indirect object* form follows: (*a*) these prepositions if the verb indicates rest, (*b*) *aus* (out of), *ausser* (except), *bei* (at, near), *gegenüber* (opposite), *mit* (with), *nach* (after, to), *seit* (since), *von* (of, from), *zu* (to). Prepositions followed by the genitive are: *anstatt* (instead of), *diesseits* (on this side of), *trotz* (in spite of), *während* (during), *wegen* (because of).

What happened to the *verb* after the Battle of Hastings can be seen from the table on the facing page.

This table exhibits several features which Old English shares with German (or Dutch) but not with modern English or with modern Scandinavian dialects. If we leave out of account the ritual *thou* form no longer used in Anglo-American conversation or prose, the only surviving *personal* flexion of its verb is the third person singular -*s* of the present tense. The personal flexion of the Old English plural (*-ath* in the present and *-on* in the past) had already disappeared in *Mayflower* times, but in two ways the English of the Pilgrim Fathers was more like Alfred's English. The Old English flexion of the third person singular, as in the Bible forms *doeth, saith, loveth, hateth, findeth, hungereth* and *thirsteth*, etc., was still current in South Britain; and the Old Teutonic *thou* form with its flexion *-st* was still used, as in

ANGLO-AMERICAN		BIBLE ENGLISH		OLD ENGLISH		GERMAN	
I	} do	I	do	ic	do	ich	tue
you		thou	doest	thu	dest	* du	tust
he	does	he	doeth	he	deth	er	tut
we	} do	we	} do	we	} doth	wir	tun
you		you		ge		* ihr	tut
they		they		hie		sie	tun
I	} did	I	did	ic	dyde	ich	tat
you		thou	didst	thu	dydest	du	tat(e)st
he		he	} did	he	dyde	er	tat
we		we		we	} dydon	wir	taten
you		you		ge		ihr	tatet
they		they		hie		sie	taten
I have done		I have done		ic haebbe gedon		ich habe getan	
I had done		I had done		ic haefde gedon		ich hatte getan	
(to) do		(to) do		don		(zu) tun	

* In German the *du* and *ihr* forms are used only between intimates and relatives. The *Sie* form replaces both in other circumstances (see p. 138). The pronoun *sie* and the possessive *ihr* (with their case forms) are always written or printed with a *capital* if they stand for the second person, and so are *du, ihr*, and *dein, euer* when used in letters.

German. The *-th* terminal of the third person singular present disappeared early in North Britain. The *-s* ending had already replaced it in the fourteenth century. During the eighteenth century, the Northumbrian form came everywhere into its own.

Another difference between the Old and the modern English verb is that the former had a special *infinitive* form. The infinitive, which is the dictionary form of the verb, does not always correspond to the dictionary form of the modern English verb. The latter (except that of the verb *to be*) is also the present tense form of all persons other than the third singular, and is used as an imperative. The Oxford or Webster dictionary verb corresponds to the typical Teutonic infinitive: (*a*) after the preposition *to* (e.g. try to *do* this); (*b*) after certain helper verbs (p. 142), (e.g. I shall *do* so myself, if I cannot make him *do* it). In such situations other Teutonic languages require a form with its own characteristic terminal. In Old English this infinitive ending was *-ian, -an* (or *-n*), corresponding to the Dutch or German *-en* or *-n*.

To us, perhaps, the oddest thing about the Old English verb is its past participle. Like that of modern Dutch or German, it carried the prefix *ge-*. Originally it had nothing to do with past time. It was attached to the beginning of a large class of verb roots in all their derivatives, and survives as such in some current German verbs. Thus the Old English for *to win* is *gewinnan*, equivalent to the German *zu gewinnen*. If, as is probable, it was once a preposition, it had ceased to mean anything much more definite than the *be-* in *behold, belong, believe*. The past participle pattern of these *ge-* verbs infected others, and became its characteristic label, as *be-* has become an adjectival affix in *bedecked, beloved, bewigged, beflagged*. Before Chaucer's time the softening process (p. 224) which changed the pronoun *ge* to *ye* had transformed *gedon* to *y-done*. The vestigial *y*-prefix lingered on in a few archaic expressions used in poetry for several centuries after Chaucer. For instance, we read in Milton, "By heaven *y-clept* (i.e., *called*) Euphrosyne."

In the *Prologue* of Chaucer's *Canterbury Tales* the *y*-inflected participle occurs frequently, as in

> It is ful fair to been *ycleped* "madame,"
> And goon to vigilies al before,
> And have a mantel roialliche *ybore*.

In the opening lines, "the yonge sonne hath in the Ram (i.e., in the sign of Aries) his halve course *yronne*." The story tells "of sondry folk, by aventure *yfalle* in felaweshipe." The Knight "was late *ycome* from his viage." Of the Prioress we learn that

> At mete wel *ytaught* was she with alle:
> She leet no morsel from hir lippes falle.

The Monk "hadde of gold *ywroght* a ful curious pyn." Of the Shipman we are told that "full many a draughte of wyn had he *ydrawe*." The

Plowman had "*ylad* of dong ful many a fother (cartload)." The Steward's hair "was by his erys ful round *yshorn*," and the Host was "boold of his speeche, and wys, and wel *ytaught*."

Such forms are fairly common in Spenser's *Faerie Queene*, e.g.:

> A gentle knight was pricking on the plaine
> *Ycladd* in mightie armes and silver shielde . . .

Grammatical similarities between German and Old English are more striking when we allow for phonetic changes (p. 225) which have occurred in the history of the former (i.e., þ to *d* or *t*, *d* to *t*). When

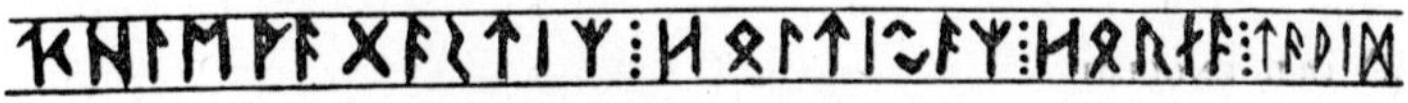

FIG. 30.—EARLIEST TEUTONIC INSCRIPTION

(See p. 62 for translation and Fig. 17 for code of Runic signs.)

we make these substitutions, we see that there is only one essential difference between the flexion of the German and the Old English verb. In German the plural ending *-en*, corresponding to the *-on* of the Old English *past*, is also the corresponding plural * ending of the *present* tense. Otherwise the behavior of the German verb is essentially like that of the English verb in the time of Alfred the Great.

ANGLO-AMERICAN	GOTHIC		GERMAN		DUTCH	
I take	(ik)	nima	ich	nehme	ik	neem
you take	(thu)	nimis	du	nimmst	jij	neemt
it takes	(ita)	nimith	es	nimmt	het	
we (two) take	(wit)	nimos	......		......	
you (two) take	(jut?)	nimats	......		......	
we	(weis)	nimam	wir	nehmen	wij	
you take	(jus)	nimith	ihr	nehmt	jullie nemen	
they	(ija)	nimand	sie	nehmen	zij	

If we go back a little further to the earliest Teutonic document, i.e., the Gothic Bible of Bishop Ulfilas (Fig. 28), we meet a more formidable array of verb flexions. The example printed above shows that the Gothic verb had separate endings for all three persons of the plural as for the singular. It also had *dual* forms of the first and second person.

* Excluding the *familiar* form of the second person.

The separate pronoun, not always used in the written language, is in brackets.

Thus a leveling process has gone on throughout the history of the verb in all the Teutonic languages. In Dutch and in German it has stopped short at the stage which English had reached at the Battle of Hastings. In Norwegian, in Danish, and in *nonliterary* Swedish, it has

OLD ENGLISH AND GERMAN NOUNS

		DAY (masc.)	WATER (neut.)	TONGUE (fem.)	BEAR (masc.)
a) OLD ENGLISH:					
Sing.	Nom.	} daeg	} waeter	tunge	bera
	Acc.			} tungan	beran
	Dat.	daege	waetere		}
	Gen.	daeges	waeteres		
Plur.	Nom.	} dagas	} waeter	} tungan	} beran
	Acc.				
	Gen.	daga	waetera	tungena	berena
	Dat.	dagum	waeterum	tungum	berum
b) GERMAN:					
Sing.	Nom.	} Tag	} Wasser	} Zunge	Bär
	Acc.				} Bären
	Dat.	Tag(e)			
	Gen.	Tages	Wassers		
Plur.	Nom.	} Tage	} Wasser	} Zungen	} Bären
	Acc.				
	Gen.				
	Dat.	Tagen	Wassern		

led to the disappearance of *all* personal flexions. The survival of the third person singular -*s* of the English present tense is offset by the fact that English—unlike the Scandinavian languages—has lost the flexion of its infinitive. As far as the verb is concerned, the grammar of the Teutonic languages offers few difficulties for anyone who knows English. You have to remember sound changes (see p. 226) which dictate the past tense form, and the two following rules about personal endings:

a) In German and Dutch, the Bible English -*th* of *cometh* is hardened to -*t*, and the plural forms of both tenses have the infinitive ending -*en* tacked on to the stem;

b) In modern Scandinavian languages the ending of the invariant present tense is -*er* or -*ar*, the past tense is invariant as in English, and the infinitive ends in -*e* (Danish and Norwegian), or -*a* (Swedish).

For an American or anyone born in the British Isles, the difficulties of a Teutonic language begin with the noun and the adjective, especially the latter. The modern English noun has four forms in writing. Of these, only two are in common use, viz., the ordinary singular form (e.g. *mother*), the ordinary plural (e.g. *mothers*) nearly always derived from the singular by adding -*s*. Nowadays we rarely use the *optional* genitives (e.g. *mother's* and *mothers'*) when the noun stands for an inanimate object such as *chamber* or *pot*. The Old English noun had four *case* forms in the singular and four in the plural, making eight altogether, and the rules for using them were the same as the rules for the corresponding pronouns (p. 258). The nouns chosen as museum exhibits illustrate sound changes described in the preceding chapter. The change from *daeg* to *day* is an example of the softening of the Old English *g*, and *tunge-Zunge, waeter-Wasser* illustrate the shift from T to Z (initial) or SS (medial).

Our table of Old English nouns with their modern German equivalents discloses two difficulties with which our Norman conquerors would have had to deal as best they could, if they had condescended to learn the language of the people. To use a noun correctly they would have had to choose the appropriate case ending, and there was no simple rule to guide the choice. There were several classes (declensions) of noun behavior. If the learner had followed the practice of modern schoolbooks, he (or she) would have to know which declension a noun belonged to before he could decide what ending, singular or plural, the direct object, the indirect object, the possessive, or the form appropriate to the preceding preposition ought to take.

During the two centuries after the Conquest these difficulties solved themselves. The distinction between nominative, accusative, and dative forms was not essential, because it either depends on a quite arbitrary custom of using one or other case form after a particular preposition, or does something which can be expressed just as well by word order (pp. 106 and 147). It had disappeared before the beginning of the fourteenth century. The distinction between the singular and the plural, and the possessive use of the genitive case forms do have a function, and a plural flexion together with a genitive have persisted. For reasons we do not know the English people made the best of a bad job by the chivalrous device of adopting the typical *masculine* nominative and accusative plural ending *-as* (our *-es* or *-s*) to signify plurality. Similarly the typical masculine or neuter genitive singular *-es* (our *'s* or *'*) spread to nouns which originally did not have this genitive ending.

Perhaps, as Bradley suggests, the growing popularity of the *-s* terminal was the survival of the fittest. It gained ground because it was easiest to distinguish. The result was an immense simplification. The words *waeter, tunge,* and *bera* were once representative of large classes of nouns, and there were others with plural endings in *-a, -u,* and *-e.* Today there are scarcely a dozen English nouns in daily use outside the class of those which tack on *-s* in the plural. Such leveling also occurred in Swedish, Danish, and Dutch; but standardization of the plural ending did not go so far as in English. So the chief difficulty with Teutonic, other than German or Icelandic, nouns is the choice of the right plural ending. No such leveling of case forms has taken place in Icelandic; and in German it has not gone so far as in the modern Scandinavian languages or in Dutch. All German nouns have a dative plural ending in *-en* or *-n* corresponding to the common dative plural ending *-um* of Old English nouns. In literary German the dative singular ending *-e,* common to Old English nouns, is still in use, though it is almost dead in speech. German feminine nouns are invariant throughout the singular. Some German nouns still behave much like our Old English *bera*. These always tack on *-n* in the singular except when used as the subject of the verb.

The student who wishes to learn German, or is learning it, should notice more carefully how the German noun as still used resembles the English noun of the Venerable Bede:

a) Just as all Old English nouns took the ending *-um* in the dative plural, all German nouns have the dative plural ending -EN or -N.

b) Just as some Old English masculine nouns such as *bera* (p. 262) added -N for all cases in the singular other than the nominative, one class of German masculine nouns add -EN or -N when used in the singular except as subject of the verb. This class includes nouns with the nominative ending -E and a few others, notably BÄR (*bear*), OCHS (*ox*), TOR (*fool*), DIAMANT (*diamond*), HERR (*gentleman*), PRINZ (*prince*), KAMERAD (*comrade*), SOLDAT (*soldier*), MENSCH (*man*).

c) Other German, like other Old English, masculine, and German neuter, nouns, like Old English neuters, take the characteristic Teutonic genitive singular ending -ES or -S.

d) Just as Old English feminine nouns take the nominative and accusative ending -*an* in the plural, most German feminine nouns take the ending -EN in *all* cases of the plural.

In our last table the gender of each noun is printed after it. Our simple rules for deciding whether to use *he, she* or *it* would not have helped our Norman conquerors to decide that a *day* is masculine. For reasons already indicated (p. 102), the gender class of an Old English noun means much more than how to use pronouns in a reasonable way, when we substitute *he, she* or *it* for a noun. Unlike the modern English adjective and pointer word, both of which (with two exceptions, *this-these* and *that-those*) are *invariant*, the adjective or pointer word of English before the Conquest had singular and plural case endings, not necessarily the same ones, for masculine, feminine, or neuter nouns.

Neither the fact that an adjective had these endings, all of them quite unnecessary if we always put it next to the noun it qualifies, nor the fact that there is no rhyme nor reason in classifying a *day* as masculine, a *child* as neuter, and a *crime* as feminine, were the only grounds for complaint. In the old or less progressive Teutonic languages, the adjective misbehaves in a way which even Greeks and Romans prohibited. *After* another qualifying word such as a demonstrative (*the, this, that*) or a possessive (*my, his, your*, etc.) it does not take the ending appropriate to the same case, the same gender, and the same number when no such *determinative* accompanies it. The next museum exhibit is put in to show you the sort of adjective the Normans found when they landed near Brighton. All the derivatives in the table on page 266 have been leveled down in modern English, and now correspond to the single word *blind*.

The table emphasizes how German lags behind. Like the Old English, the modern German adjective has two declensions, a *strong* one for use *without* an accompanying determinative word, and a *weak* one for use when a determinative precedes it. The strong adjective forms have case and number endings like those of the more typical masculine, neuter, and feminine noun classes. The weak adjective forms are less profuse. German has only two. In Dutch and in *modern* Scandinavian languages (excluding Icelandic), the distinction between masculine and feminine, together with all case differences, has been dropped. The weak plural has merged with a single strong form for use with singular or plural nouns (see p. 276).

To write German correctly we have to choose the right case form of the adjective. The rule usually given in grammar books is that the adjective has to have the same case, number, and gender as the noun with which it goes. Since the strong adjective has more distinct case forms than the German noun, we cannot always recognize the case of the noun by its form. What we mean by the case of the noun is the case of the pronoun which can take its place. The pronoun has retained the four case forms of the adjective.

During the three centuries after the Norman Conquest grammatical simplification of English went on apace. By A.D. 1400 English had outstripped Dutch, and we might now call Anglo-American an *isolating,* as opposed to a *flexional* language. What flexions now persist are

THE OLD TEUTONIC ADJECTIVE

	(i) STRONG FORM				(ii) WEAK FORM			
	MASC. SING.	NEUT. SING.	FEM. SING.	PLURAL	MASC. SING.	NEUT. SING.	FEM. SING.	PLURAL

(a) OLD ENGLISH

	MASC. SING.	NEUT. SING.	FEM. SING.	PLURAL	MASC. SING.	NEUT. SING.	FEM. SING.	PLURAL
NOMIN.	blind	blind	blinde	blinde	blinda	blinde	blinde	blindan
ACCUS.	blindne	blind	blinde	blinde	blindan	blinde	blinde	blindan
DAT.	blindum	blindum	blindre	blindum	blindan	blindan	blindan	blindum
GEN.	blindes	blindes	blindre	blindum	blindan	blindan	blindan	blindra

(b) GERMAN

	MASC. SING.	NEUT. SING.	FEM. SING.	PLURAL	MASC. SING.	NEUT. SING.	FEM. SING.	PLURAL
NOMIN.	blinder	blindes	blinde	blinde	blinde	blinde	blinde	blinden
ACCUS.	blinden	blindes	blinde	blinde	blinden	blinde	blinde	blinden
DAT.	blindem	blindem	blinder	blinder	blinden	blinden	blinden	blinden
GEN.	blindes	blindes	blinder	blinder	blinden	blinden	blinden	blinden

shared by some or all of the surviving Teutonic dialects. So it is true to say that Anglo-American grammar is essentially a Teutonic language. We have already met three features common to all Teutonic dialects, including English (p. 180). Of these the behavior of the verb is the most important. The Teutonic verb has only two tense forms, of which the so-called *present* often expresses future time (e.g. *I go to London tomorrow*). There are two ways of making the simple past. Some verbs (*strong* class) undergo *internal* vowel change. Others (*weak* class) add a suffix with the *d* or *t* sound to the root. The existence of a compact class of verbs which undergo comparable stem vowel changes, and the weak suffix with the *d* or *t* sound are two trademarks of the Teutonic group.

In connection with verb irregularities which confuse a beginner three facts are helpful. One is that all strong verbs are *old*, and all newer ones belong to the weak class, which has now incorporated many verbs which were once strong. This has gone furthest in English. So it is usually safe to bet that if an English verb is strong, its etymological equivalent in another Teutonic language will also be strong. It is often safe to make another assumption. If two verbs undergo the same vowel change in English, equivalent verbs in another Teutonic language undergo a corresponding change. Thus the German verbs *finden* and *binden*, equivalent to our words *find* and *bind*, have similar past tense forms *fand* and *band* with corresponding past participles *gefunden* and *gebunden*. So also the Danish verbs *finde* and *binde* form their past tense forms (*fand* and *band*) and past participles (*fundet* and *bundet*) in the same way. The difference between the weak D and T types (represented by *spilled* and *spelt* in English) is more apparent than real. In the spoken language (see p. 68), a D changes to T after the *voiceless* consonants F, K, P, S, and a T changes to D after the *voiced* consonants V, G, B, Z, M. In English -(E)D is usually, and in German -(E)TE is always the terminal added to the stem of a weak verb in its past tense.

The past participle of all transitive verbs goes with the present or past of Teutonic forms of the verb *have* in combinations equivalent to *have given* or *had given*. The table on page 181 shows the conjugation of *have* in the Teutonic dialects. The use of other helper verbs (see p. 144) displays a strong family likeness. In fact, the same root verbs are used in Danish, Swedish, and Dutch where the English verbs *shall* or *will*, *should* or *would*, are used alone or in front of *have* or *had* or any other verb to express future time or condition.

We have met with one common characteristic of the Teutonic languages in Chapter V where there is a table of the comparison of the adjective. All the Teutonic languages form three classes of derivatives other than those usually called *flexions*. Some of them are important. For instance, it is less useful for the foreigner to know that a *gander*

SIX TEUTONIC STRONG VERBS

(INFINITIVE—PAST TENSE SINGULAR—PAST PARTICIPLE)

ENGLISH	SWEDISH	DANISH	DUTCH	GERMAN
COME	komma	komme	komen	kommen
came	kom	kom	kwam	kam
come	kommit	kommet	gekomen	gekommen
FIND	finna	finde	vinden	finden
found	fann	fand	vond	fand
found	funnit	fundet	gevonden	gefunden
FLY	flyga	flyve	vliegen	fliegen
flew	flög	fløj	vloog	flog
flown	flugit	fløjet	gevlogen	geflogen
RIDE	rida	ride	rijden	reiten
rode	red	red	reed	ritt
ridden	ridit	redet	gereden	geritten
SEE	se	se	zien	sehen
saw	såg	saa	zag	sah
seen	sett	set	gezien	gesehen
SING	sjunga	synge	zingen	singen
sang	sjöng	sang	zong	sang
sung	sjungit	sunget	gezongen	gesungen

is a male *goose* or that the plural of *louse* is *lice*, than to learn the trick of manufacturing numberless new words such as *fisher* or *writer* by tacking -*er* on to a verb. The older Teutonic verbs readily combine with prepositions, e.g. *undergo*, or *overcome* (Swedish *överkomma*), and with other prefixes which have no separate existence. Teutonic languages have many adjectives or adverbs formed from nouns by adding -*ly* (English), -*lig* (Swedish-Danish), -*lijk* (Dutch), and -*lich* (German), corresponding to Old English -*lic*. In modern English this terminal is characteristic of adverbial derivatives (see p. 99) but we will cling to a few adjectives such as *godly, manly, brotherly, kindly*. At least one of the affixes in the accompanying table, though very much alive, is not native. It has no precise English equivalent, recognizable as such. From about the twelfth century onward Ger-

ENGLISH-TEUTONIC AFFIXES

ENGLISH	EXAMPLE	SWEDISH	DANISH	DUTCH	GERMAN
a) Noun:					
-DOM	kingdom	-DOM	-DOM	-DOM	-TUM
-ER	writer	-ARE	-ER	-ER	-ER
-HOOD (-HEAD)	fatherhood	-HET	-HED	-HEID	-HEIT
-ING	warning	-ING	-ING	-ING	-UNG
-LING	darling	-LING	-LING	-LING	-LING
-NESS	kindness	—	—	-NIS	-NIS
-SHIP	friendship	-SKAP	-SKAB	-SCHAP	-SCHAFT
b) Adjective:					
-FUL	wishful	-FULL	-FULD	-VOL	-VOLL
-ISH	hellish	-ISK	-ISK	-ISCH	-ISCH
-LESS	lifeless	-LÖS	-LOS	-LOOS	-LOS
-LY	lonely	-LIK	-LIG	-LIJK	-LICH
-SOME	loathsome	-SAM	-SOM	-ZAAM	-SAM
-Y	dusty	-IK	-IG	-IG	-ICH, -IG
UN-	unkind	O-	U-	ON-	UN-
c) Adverb:					
-WARD	homeward	—	—	-WAARTS	-WÄRTS
-WISE	likewise	-VIS	-VIS	-WIJZE	-WEISE
d) Verb:					
BE-	behold	BE-	BE-	BE-	BE-
—	—	-ERA	ERE	-EEREN	-IEREN
FOR-	forbid	FÖR-	FOR-	VER-	VER-
FORE-	foresee	FÖRE-	FORE-	VOOR-	VOR-
MIS-	mistake	MISS-	MIS-	MIS-	MISS-

man courtly poetry assimilated many French verbs. The infinitive ending *-ier* became Germanized as *-ieren*, and this terminal subsequently attached itself to native roots, as in *halbieren* (halve). The stress on the suffix *-ier-* instead of on the root labels it as an intruder. It turns up later as *-er-* in Scandinavian, and in Dutch it is *-eer-*. It is very prolific. In fact, it can tack itself on to almost any current international root, as of scientific terms, e.g. *telefonera* (Swed.), *telefonere* (Dan.), *telefoneeren* (Dutch), *telefonieren* (German). German and Dutch verbs of this class have past participles without the *ge-* prefix, e.g. *ich habe telegrafiert* (I have telegraphed).

It is possible to avoid some errors of self-expression if our bird's-eye view takes in some of the outstanding *differences* between English and other Teutonic, languages. One of these, the disappearance of grammatical gender, and with it of adjectival concord, has been mentioned more than once. Several syntactical peculiarities of modern English are also pitfalls for the beginner. One common to *Mayflower* English, and to English in its present stage, is the identity of word order in different clauses of a complex sentence (pp. 154–158). The moral of this is to stick to simple sentences when possible, and to recognize the conjunctions listed on page 154 as danger signals when it is not convenient to do so. The way to deal with some other outstanding syntactical peculiarities of Anglo-American when writing or speaking German, Dutch, Swedish, or Danish has been suggested in Chapter IV. *Express yourself in the idiom of the Pilgrim Fathers.* Three important rules to recall are: (*a*) *inversion* of the verb and its subject unless the latter is the first word in a simple statement (p. 147); (*b*) use of the *simple* interrogative, e.g. *what say you?* (p. 151); (*c*) use of the *direct* negative, e.g. *I know not how* (p. 152).

In the same chapter we have met with four other characteristics of Anglo-American usage, and the student of any other Teutonic language should recall them at this stage. They are: (*a*) the economy of English particles; (*b*) the peculiar uses of the English *-ing derivative* as verb-noun or with a helper (p. 130) to signify present time and continued action; (*c*) the disappearance of the distinction (p. 131) between *transitive* and *intransitive* verbs; (*d*) the transference of the *indirect object* to the subject in passive constructions (p. 142).

It is important to note the wide range of the two epithets *all* and *only*. We can use the former before a plural or before a singular noun e.g. *all the water*. Swedish, Danish, Dutch, and German prescribe separate words (see table on p. 280) for *all* before a plural noun and *all the*, e.g. *the whole*. The English word *only* can qualify a verb, adjective, or noun. As an adverb, i.e., qualifier of a verb or adjective, its usual meaning is the same as *merely*. As an adjective its usual meaning is *solitary* or *single*. Swedish, Danish, Dutch, and German prescribe separate words (see pp. 280 and 341) for *only* as adverb meaning *merely* and as *adjective* meaning *single*.

Teutonic verbs include several confusing clusters of near synonyms. At one time all Teutonic dialects had a verb *fara* or *faran*, meaning to

TEUTONIC POINTER WORDS AND LINK PRONOUNS *

ENGLISH	SWEDISH	DANISH	DUTCH	GERMAN †

a) Demonstratives (*see* pp. 136–137).

THIS	denna (c.s.) detta (n.s.) dessa (pl.)	denne (c.s.) dette (n.s.) disse (pl.)	deze (c.s.) dit (n.s.) deze (pl.)	dieser (m.s.) ‡ dieses (n.s.) diese (f.s. & m.n.f.pl.)
THAT	den det de		die dat die	jener jenes jene
WHICH	vilken vilket vilka	hvilken hvilket hvilke	welke welk welke	welcher welches welche

b) Link Pronouns (*see* pp. 136–137).

THAT	ATT	AT	DAT	DASS
WHO, THAT, WHICH (as subject)			DIE (c.s. & c.n.pl.) DAT (n.sg.)	DER (m.) DAS (n.) DIE (f.s. & m.n.f.pl.)
WHOM, THAT, WHICH (as object)	SOM			DEN (m.) DAS (n.) DIE (f.s. & m.n.f.pl.)
TO WHOM TO WHICH	TILL VILKEN (c.) TILL VILKET (n.) TILL VILKA (pl.)	TIL HVILKEN TIL HVILKET TIL HVILKE	AAN WIE (*persons*) WAARAN (*things*)	DEM (m.n.) DER (f.) DEN*en* (c.pl.)
WHOSE, OF WHICH	VEMS	HVIS	VAN WIE (*persons*) WAARVAN (*things*)	DESSEN (m.n.) DEREN (f.s. & m.n.f.pl.)
WHOM, WHICH (after all other prepositions.)	(H)VILKEN (c.) (H)VILKET (n.) VILKA HVILKE (pl.)		*prep.* + WIE (*persons*) WAAR + *prep.* (*things*)	as for WHOM above after prep- ositions on page 259, otherwise as for TO WHOM.
WHAT	VAD	HVAD	WAT	WAS

* *c.* common, *n.* neuter, *m.* masculine, *f.* feminine, gender. *s.* singular, *pl.* plural. For conventions respecting *capitals* (see p. 373).

† Nominative case forms only given here (see p. 291).

‡ In common speech stressed *der, die, das,* replace *dieser,* etc., e.g. *der Mann* with stress on *Mann* means *the man,* but with stress on *der* it means *this man.*

go or to travel. It survives in set English expressions such as *farewell* or "to go far and *fare* worse." The word *ford* comes from the same root. Otherwise *go* and its Dutch equivalent *gaan* have taken over its functions. The Scandinavian equivalent of *go* is more fastidious. We can use the Swedish *gå* when a human being *goes* on foot or when a

TEUTONIC INTERROGATIVES *

ENGLISH	SWEDISH	DANISH	DUTCH	GERMAN
how?	hur	hvordan	hoe	wie
how much? how many?	hur mycket hur många	hvor meget hvor mange	hoeveel	wieviel wieviele
when?	när	naar	wanneer	wann
whence?	varifrån	hvorfra	vanwaar	woher
whither? where?	vart var	hvorhen hvor	waarheen waar	wohin wo
why?	varför	hvorfor	waarom	warum
who?	*VEM*	*HVEM*	*WIE*	*WER*
which?	*VILKEN, VILKET, VILKA*	*HVILKEN, HVILKET, HVILKE*	*WELKE WELK WELKE*	*WELCHER (-ES, -E)*
what?	*VAD*	*HVAD*	*WAT*	*WAS*
whom?	*VEM*	*HVEM*	*WIEN*	*WEN*
to whom?	*TILL VEM*	*TIL HVEM*	*AAN WIE*	*WEM*
whose?	*VEMS*	*HVIS*	*VAN WIE*	*WESSEN*
what kind of . . . ?	vad slags	hvilken slags	wat voor een	was für ein

* Same conventions as on p. 373.

train or other vehicle *goes*, but when we speak of going in a train or other vehicle the right verb is *fara*. Analogous remarks apply to Danish, and to the use of the German verbs *gehen* and *fahren*, but German usage is now less exacting.

Another cluster corresponds to *place, set* or *lay*, for all of which we can usually substitute *put*. The choice of the right word for *put* is perplexing in other Teutonic languages, especially in German. It therefore calls for explanation. We have three English words for bodily orientation, all Teutonic: *stand, sit, lie*. A bottle *stands* on the table if upright or *lies* if fallen; and we *set*, i.e., *make sit*, a flag on a pole. German preserves these distinctions meticulously in the corresponding causative verb forms *stellen* (Swed. *ställa*), *setzen* (Swed. *sätta*), *legen* (Swed. *lägga*) corresponding to *stehen, sitzen, liegen* (Swed. *stå, sitta, ligga*) for *stand, sit, lie*. They are not interchangeable though each equivalent to *put*. The intransitive forms in all Teutonic languages are strong, the causative weak.

German is more exacting than its sister languages in another way. We can combine *put* with a variety of directives. German demands separate derivative verbs, e.g. *aufsetzen* (einen Hut) = to put on (a hat), *anziehen* (einen Rock) = to put on (a coat), *umbinden* (eine Schürze) = to put on (an apron). It is important to remember that the English verb *make* has a wider range than its dictionary equivalent in other Teutonic languages. *Making* in the sense of *compelling* is specifically English. For the correct word see *compel* or *force*.

To complete our bird's-eye view, we have now to ask how the several members of the Teutonic group differ from and resemble one another. For this purpose we may draw a line across the map of Europe corresponding roughly with the fifty-fifth parallel of latitude. North of it, the Teutonic group is represented by Icelandic, Norwegian, Swedish, and Danish, south by Dutch (including Flemish) and High German. This line now splits the Teutonic group into two natural clans with highly characteristic grammatical features.

THE SCANDINAVIAN CLAN

The Scandinavian clan consists of four official languages of which *Icelandic* differs little from Old Norse of the sagas. Icelanders read the latter as we read Shakespeare, if we do so. The others, Swedish, Danish and Norwegian, differ from one another scarcely more than do some dialects within the British Isles. The first is spoken throughout Sweden by over six million people, and by a substantial Swedish minority in Finland. Danish is the official language of Denmark, with a population of three and three-quarter millions. The Norwegian dialects are the vernaculars of about two and three-quarter millions. The official language of Norway is less highly standardized than that of Denmark. Till 1905 when Norway seceded from Sweden, it was still Danish. This official Dano-Norwegian of the ruling clique was then the medium of instruction in all higher education as well as of administrative procedure, and was far removed from the speech of the masses. Since secession, the government has introduced successive changes to make the spelling more phonetic and the accepted grammatical stand-ards nearer to those of common intercourse. To accommodate local sentiment of communities separated by great distances in a vast and thinly populated territory, the newest official spelling and grammar books admit many alternative forms, and as yet no English-Norwegian dictionaries incorporate the changes which came into force in 1938. The net result of all these changes is that written Norwegian is now as close to Swedish as to Danish.

The grammar of Swedish, Danish, and Norwegian is very much simpler than that of German. The word order (see Chapter IV) is essentially like that of the authorized English Bible except that the negative particle or an adverb of time precede the verb in a subordi-nate clause. Illustrations of this are the Swedish and Danish equivalents of the sentence: *he said that he could not come:*

> Han sade att han inte (*or* icke) kunde komma. (*Swed.*)
> Han sagde at han ikke kunde komme.   (*Dan.*)

Personal flexion of the verb has disappeared. The present tense ending for all persons singular and (except in literary Swedish) all persons plural, is the same, -*r* added to the infinitive form: the only exception to this rule is that the present tense of some Swedish verbs ends in -*er* instead of -*ar*. The infinitive ending is -*a* (Swedish) or -*e* (Danish and Norwegian). The past tense of weak verbs ends in -*de* or -*te* (cf. *loved* and *slept*) in accordance with the preceding conso-nant (p. 68) when the end vowel of the stem is omitted. Compound tense forms are analogous to our own. Thus we have (Swedish) *jag kallar* (I call), *jag kallade* (I called), *jag har kallat* (I have called), *jag hade kallat* (I had called), *jag skall kalla* (I shall call), *jag skulle kalla* (I should call). In the Danish equivalent *e* replaces *a* throughout (e.g. *jeg kaller*). Any good dictionary gives a list of the past tenses and past participles of strong verbs.

The *active* past participle used with *hava* or *have* always ends in *t* as above. The *passive* adjectival form is nearly always the same in Nor-wegian, often in Danish, but never in Swedish. The Swedish adjectival form ends in -*d* (sing.) or -*de* (plur.) when the verb is weak, or -*en* (sing.), -*ene* (plur.) when it is strong, as in *given* or *givene* in contradis-tinction to *givit* (given) after *hava*. The many Danish verbs which form a *contracted* past analogous to *dreamt* (in contradistinction to *dreamed*), e.g. *betale-betalt* (pay-paid), have no special adjectival form, and uncontracted verbs have kept the *d* form in the plural only, e.g. *straffet* (punished) in the singular, *straffede* in the plural.

aftur á vald si.
fylkjum í Hopei-héraō.

˙DON í morgun. FÚ.
Óstaōfest fregn frá Tokio
hermir, aō Japanir muni ekki

Smáskæruhópar h.
hafa undanfarna mánuōi
viō í næsta nágrenni höfuōb.

eg
:r á
.ndir
)snaōi,
eōa aō
starf Á-
alfrétta-
klu bet-
s starfs
ōalskrif-
karitari
fá æföa
vinna
ótta-
eira
ng
ō

Sami mokaflinn ennþá
fyrir öllu Norōurlandi

loki.
328
hr
ſ
ł
þr.
Á
mann.
245 ?
F

Um 90 þúsund tunnur saltaōar alls á öllu landinu og í kvöld er búist viō aō 200 þús. mál verōi komin á land í bræōslu

SAMI mokaflinn er ennþá
svo aō segja fyrir öllu
Norōurlandi, enda hefir veriō á-
ntt veiōiveōur. stillur '''

Verksmiōjan á Sólbakka
búin aō fá ˙
af k˖˙

FIG. 31.—CUTTING FROM ICELANDIC NEWSPAPER SHOWING THE TWO *th* SYMBOLS þ (AS IN *thin*) AND ō (AS IN *them*).

One outstanding oddity of the Scandinavian clan is the flexional passive already mentioned on page 109. Any part of the verb can take a passive meaning if we add -*s* to the end of it or if it ends in -*r*, substitute *s* for the latter, e.g. in Swedish:

att kalla to call		*att kallas* to be called	
jag kallar	I call	*jag kallas*	I am called
jag kallade	I called	*jag kallades*	I was called
jag har kallat	I have called	*jag har kallats*	I have been called
jag skall kalla	I shall call	*jag skall kallas*	I shall be called
jag skulle kalla	I should call	*jag skulle kallas*	I should be called

The rule is the same for all three dialects, and it is the easiest way of handling a passive construction. In the spoken language it is more usual to substitute a roundabout construction in which *bliva* (Swed.), *blive* (Dan.), *bli* (Norweg.) takes the place of our *be*, and *vara* or *vaere* (be) replaces to *have*. This passive auxiliary was originally equivalent to the German *bleiben* (remain). Its present tense is *blir* or *bliver*, its past tense *blev* (Norweg. *ble*); past participle *blivit*, *blevit*, or *blitt*. The verb *bliva* takes the *adjective* participle (p. 274), *not* the form used with *hava* in an active construction, when (as always in Swedish) the two are different, e.g.:

jag blir straffad	I am being punished	*jeg bliver straffet*
vi blir (bliva) straffade	we are being punished	*vi bliver straffede*

Similarly we have:

jag skall bliva straffad	I shall be punished	*jeg skal blive straffet*
jag är blivit straffad	I have been punished	*jeg er blevet straffet*
jag var blivit straffad	I had been punished	*jeg var blevet straffet*

The only flexions of the noun are the genitive -*s* (see below) and the plural ending, typically -*er* in Danish, Norwegian, and many Swedish nouns (-*ar* and -*or* in some Swedish). A few nouns form a plural analogous to that of our *ox-oxen*. Two words of this class are common to all three dialects:—ear-ears: *öra-öron* (Swed.), *øre-øren* (Dan., Norweg.), and eye-eyes, *öga-ögon* (Swed.), *øje-øjne* (Dan.), *øye-øyne* (Norweg.). A large class like our *sheep*, with no plural flexion, includes all monosyllabic nouns of neuter gender. A few words (p. 201) like our *mouse-mice*, *man-men* (Swed. *man-män*, Dan. *Mand-Maend*, Norweg. *Mann-Menn*) form the plural by internal vowel change alone. As in German, many monosyllables with the stem vowels *o*, *a*, have modified plurals, e.g. book-books = *bok-böcker* (Swed.), *Bog-Bøger* (Dan.).

The so-called indefinite article (*a* or *an*) has two forms in official Swedish and Danish. Norwegian, like some Swedish dialects, now has three. One, *ett* (Swedish) or *et* (Dan. and Norweg.) stands before nouns classed as neuter. The other, *en*, stands before nouns classed as nonneuter (common gender) in Swedish and Danish, or masculine in Norwegian, which has a feminine *ei* as well. Thus we have *en god fader* (a good father), and *et(t) godt barn* (a good child). The adjective has three forms:

a) root + the suffix -*a* (Sw.) or -*e* (Dan. and Norweg.) when associated with any plural noun or any singular noun preceded by a demonstrative or possessive, e.g.:

	SWEDISH	DANISH
good women	*goda kvinnor*	*gode Kvinder*
my young child	*mitt unga barn*	*mit unge Barn*
this good book	*denna goda bok*	*denne gode Bog*

b) root *alone*, when associated with a *singular nonneuter* noun which is not preceded by a demonstrative or possessive, e.g.:

a good dog	*en god hund*	*en god Hund*

c) root + suffix *-t*, when associated with a *singular neuter* noun not preceded by a demonstrative or possessive, e.g.:

a young child	*ett ungt barn*	*et ungt Barn*

The oddest feature of the Scandinavian clan is the behavior of the definite article. If a *singular* noun is *not* preceded by an adjective, the definite article has the same form as the indefinite but is fused to the end of the noun itself, e.g.:

en bok = a book = *en Bog*   :   *boken* = the book = *Bogen*
ett barn = a child = *et Barn*   :   *barnet* = the child = *Barnet*

If the noun is plural the suffix *-na* (Swed.) or *-ne* (Dan. and Norweg.) is tacked on to it when the last consonant is *r*. If the plural does not end in *-r*, the definite article suffix is *-en* (Swed.) or *-ene* (Dan. and Norweg.), e.g.:

hundar = dogs = *Hunder*   :   *hundarna* = the dogs = *Hunderne*
barn = children = *Børn*   :   *barnen* = the children = *Børnene*

If an adjective precedes a noun the definite article is expressed by the demonstrative *den* (com.), *det* (neut.), *de* (plur.) which otherwise means *that*. In Swedish it is still accompanied by the terminal article, e.g.:

de goda hundarna = the good dogs = *de gode Hunder*

The fusion of the terminal definite article with the noun is so complete that it comes between the latter and the genitive *-s*, e.g.:

a dog's	*en hunds*	*en Hunds*
the dog's	*hundens*	*Hundens*
the dogs'	*hundarnas*	*Hundernes*
a child's	*ett barns*	*et Barns*
the child's	*barnets*	*Barnets*
the children's	*barnens*	*Børnenes*

Comparison of the Scandinavian (p. 184) is like that of the English adjective. Comparatives and superlatives have no separate neuter form. A pitfall for the beginner arises from the fact that our *much* and *many* have the same comparative and superlative forms. Thus we have:

mycket-mera-mesta	much-more-most	*meget-mere-meste*
många-flera-flesta	many-more-most	*mange-flere-fleste*

Scandinavian adverbs are formed from adjectives by adding the neuter suffix *-t* (also by adding *-vis* or *-en*). The *-t* is not added to Danish and Norwegian adjectives which end in *-lig*.

The survival of gender is less troublesome than it would otherwise be because most nouns belong to the nonneuter (*common*) class. The

ie imidlertid blev
.es at rederne fant det
nytteslØst å fortsette så lenge de nor-
ske maskinister stod utenom.

Mange med i biblio-
tekmØtet på Rjukan.

RJUKAN, 8. august.

(AP) Norsk Bibliotekforening holder i disse dager sitt årsmØte på Rjukan. Rjukan offentlige bibliotek feirer samtidig sitt 25 års jubleum. Arsmøtet har fått en usedvanlig stor tilslutning, idet ikke mindre enn 120 bibliotekfolk fra hele landet deltar. SØndag var det åpent fore-dragr '- i Folkets hus, hvor Johan inckel jr. talte om «Publi-
'».
'- med til rapporter og
bl ˻ tr'˻

Fɪɢ. 32.—Cᴜᴛᴛɪɴɢ ꜰʀᴏᴍ ᴀ Nᴏʀᴡᴇɢɪᴀɴ Nᴇᴡꜱᴘᴀᴘᴇʀ ꜱʜᴏᴡɪɴɢ ᴛʜᴇ Sᴄᴀɴ-
ᴅɪɴᴀᴠɪᴀɴ ᴠᴏᴡᴇʟ ꜱʏᴍʙᴏʟꜱ *Ø* ᴀɴᴅ *å*.

neuter class includes *substances, trees, fruits, young animals*, including *barn* (child), *countries, continents*, and all abstract nouns which end in *-ande* or *-ende*. Besides these there is a compact group of common words shown below.

The Scandinavian negative particle is quite unlike the English-Dutch-German *not-niet-nicht*. In Danish and Norwegian it is *ikke*, of which the literary Swedish equivalent (used only in books) is *icke*. In conversation or correspondence Swedes use *inte*, e.g. *jag skall inte se honom* = I shall not see him = *jeg skal ikke se ham*.

There is a much greater gap between the written and spoken language of Sweden than of Denmark and modern Norway. Many flexions which exist in literature have no existence in spoken Swedish or in correspond-

ENGLISH	SWEDISH	DANISH	ENGLISH	SWEDISH	DANISH
animal	djur	Dyr	floor	golv	Gulv
egg	ägg	Aeg	hotel	hotell	Hotel
life	LIV		house	HUS	
people	FOLK		roof	tak	Tag
pig	SVIN		table	BORD	
sheep	får	Faar	window	fönster	Vindue
blood	BLOD		country	LAND	
bone	BEN		language	språk	Sprog
ear	öra	øre	letter	BREV	
eye	öga	øje	light	ljus	Lys
hair	hår	Haar	name	namn	Navn
heart	hjärta	Hjerte	weather	väder	Vejr
leg	BEN		word	ORD	
water	vatten	Vand	year	år	Aar

ence. In literary Swedish the plural of the present tense is identical with the infinitive, and the past of strong verbs has plural forms which end in *o*, some being very irregular, e.g. for *gå* (go) we have the two past forms *gick-gingo* and analogous ones for *få* (may). The plural flexion of the verb is never used in speech. The final *-de* of the past tense form is often silent. The infinitive and the corresponding present tense form of many verbs is contracted as in Norwegian, e.g. *be* (*bedja*), request, *bli* (*bliva*), become, *dra* (*draga*), carry, *ge* (*giva*), give, *ha* (*hava*), have, *ta* (*taga*) take. Similarly *skall* contracts to *ska*, *Eder* to *Er* (you or your), *broder* (brother) to *bror*.

The terminal article and the flexional passive are both highly characteristic of the Scandinavian clan. Another of its peculiarities is a booby trap for the beginner, because English, like Dutch or German, has no equivalent for it. Scandinavian dialects have special forms of the possessive adjective of the third person (analogous to the Latin

TEUTONIC INDEFINITE POINTER WORDS

	SWEDISH	DANISH	DUTCH	GERMAN ‡
A, AN	en (c.) ett (n.)	et (n.)	een	ein (m. & n.) eine (f.)
ALL (pl.) *	alla	alle	al	alle
AS MUCH AS	så mycken (-t) som	saa megen (-t) som	zooveel als	so viel wie
BOTH	båda (bägge)	begge (baade)	beide	
EACH, EVERY, EACH ONE	var	hver	elk (e-), ieder (-e)	jeder (-es, -e)
ENOUGH	nog	nok	genoeg	genug
EVERYONE	ENVAR	ENHVER	IEDEREEN	JEDERMANN (ALLE)
EVERYTHING	ALLT	ALT	ALLES	
FEW	få	faa	weinige	wenige
MANY	många	mange	veele	viele
MUCH	mycken (-t)	megen (-t)	veel	viel
NO, NOT ANY	ingen (c.) intet (n.)		geen	kein (m. & n.) keine (f.)
NOBODY	INGEN		NIEMAND	
NOTHING	INTET		NIETS	NICHTS
ONE (pron.)	MAN (EN)		MEN	MAN
ONLY †	enda	ene	eenigst (-e)	einzig (e)
OTHER	annan annat andra	anden andet andre	ander andere	anderer (m.) anderes (n.) andere (f.)
SEVERAL	flera	flere	verscheidene	mehrere, verschiedene
SOME, ANY	någon något några	nogen noget nogle	eenig	etwas
SOMEONE	NÅGON	NOGEN	IEMAND	JEMAND
SOMETHING	NÅGOT	NOGET	IETS	ETWAS
SUCH	sådan (-t, -a)	saadan (-t, -e)	zulk (-e)	solcher (-es, -e)
THE	den (c.s.) det (n.s.) de (pl.)		de (c.s.) het (n.s.)	der (m.s.) das (n.s.) die (f.s. & m.n.f.pl.)
TOO MUCH	för mycken (-t)	for megen (-t)	te veel	zuviel

* *All* before a singular noun is equivalent to *the whole* (Swed. *hela*, Dan. *hele*, Dutch *geheel*, German *ganz*).

† Not as adverb, see p. 341.

‡ Invariant unless *masculine, neuter,* and *feminine* nominative case forms are in parentheses.

suus) corresponding to the reflexive pronoun *sig*. They are *sin* (sing. common), *sitt* or *sit* (neut. sing.), *sina* or *sine* (plur.) in accordance with the gender and number of the thing possessed. We must *always (and only)* use them when they refer back to the subject of the verb, e.g.:

Jag har hans bok (I have his book).   *Jeg har hans Bog.*
Han har sin bok (He has his book).   *Han har sin Bog.*
Jag besökte hennes bror (I visited her   *Jeg besøgte hendes Broder.*
brother).
Hon elskar sitt barn (She loves her child).   *Hun elsker sit Barn.*

THE SOUTHERN CLAN

The flexional passive of the Scandinavian verb and the terminal definite article of the Scandinavian noun are features which the English and the southern representatives of the Teutonic group have never had at any stage in their common history. The southern clan, which includes Dutch and German, also has positive grammatical characteristics which its members do not share with its northern relatives. Three of them recall characteristics of Old English:

1) The flexional ending of the third person singular of the present tense of a Dutch or German verb is *t*. In accordance with the phonetic evolution of the modern Teutonic languages, this corresponds to the final *-th* in *Mayflower* English (e.g. *saith, loveth*).
2) The infinitive ends in *-en*, as the Old English infinitive ends in *-an* (e.g. Dutch-German *finden*, Old English, *findan*).
3) The past participle of most verbs carries the prefix *ge-*, which softened to *y-* in Middle English, and had almost completely disappeared by the beginning of the seventeenth century.

When the Roman occupation of Britain came to an end, the domain of Low and High German, in contradistinction to Norse, was roughly what it is today, and a process of differentiation had begun. In the Lowlands and throughout the area which is now north Germany there have been no drastic phonetic changes other than those which are also incorporated in the modern Scandinavian dialects (e.g. *w* to *v*, þ to ð or *t* and ð to *d*). To the south, a *second sound shift* (p. 226) occurred before the time of Alfred the Great. The German dialects had begun to split apart in two divisions when west Germanic tribes first invaded Britain.

This division into *Low* or north and *High* or south and middle German cuts across the official separation of the written languages. Dutch (including Belgian Dutch or Flemish) is Low German with its own spelling conventions. What is ordinarily called the German language embodies the High German (*second*) sound shift and an elaborate battery of useless flexions which Dutch has discarded. It is the written language of Germany as a whole, of Austria and of parts of Switzerland. Throughout the same area it is also the pattern of educated and of *public* speech. The country dialects of northern Germany are Low German. This *Plattdeutsch*, which is nearer to Dutch than to the daily speech of south or middle Germany, has its own literature, like the Scots Doric.

The flexional grammar of Dutch is very simple. The chief difficulty is that there are two forms of the definite article, *de* and *het*. The latter is used only before *singular* nouns classed as neuter, e.g. *de stoel* —*de stoelen* (the chair—the chairs), *het boek*—*de boeken* (the book —the books). There is only one indefinite article, *een*. Adjectives have two forms, e.g. *deze man is rijk* and *deze rijke man* for *this man is rich* and *this rich man* respectively. Reduction of the troublesome apparatus of adjectival concord has gone as far as in the English of Chaucer, and the inconvenience of gender crops up only in the choice of the definite article. As in Middle English, the suffix -*e* is added to the ordinary root form of the adjective before a plural noun or a singular noun preceded by an article, demonstrative or possessive.

What is true of many of the dialects of Germany and Switzerland is true of Dutch. The genitive case form of the noun is absent in *speech*. It has made way for the roundabout usage with *van* equivalent to the German *von* (of), e.g. *de vrouw van mijn vriend* (in colloquial German *die Frau von meinem Freund*—the wife of my friend *or* my friend's wife). Thus case distinction survives in Dutch even less than in English. The only noun flexion still important is the plural ending. This has been much less regularized than in English. Alone among the Teutonic languages, Dutch shares with English a class of nouns with the plural terminal -*s*. This includes those that end in -*el*, -*en*, and -*er*, e.g. *tafel-tafels* (table-tables), *kammer-kammers* (room-rooms). The majority of Dutch nouns take -*en* like *oxen*, e.g. *huis-huizen* (house-houses).

With due regard to the sound shift, the Dutch verb is essentially the same as the German. There is one important difference. In Dutch, *zal* (our *shall*) is the auxiliary verb used to express future time. In Cape Dutch or Afrikaans (one of the two official languages of the Union of South Africa) the simple past (e.g. *I heard*), habitually replaced in some German dialects by the roundabout construction with *have* (e.g. *I have heard*), has almost completely disappeared in favor of the latter. This alternative construction is a useful trick in German conversation, because the past tense and past participle of

Teutonic verbs (cf. *gave, given*), are often unlike. So the use of the informal construction dispenses with need for memorizing the past tense forms. The present tense of the Afrikaans verb is invariant and identical with the infinitive, which has no terminal.

The first person singular of the present tense is the *root* (i.e., the *infinitive* after removal of the suffix *-en*). The second and third person singular is formed from the first by adding *-t*, and all persons of the plural are the same as the infinitive. The past tense of weak verbs is formed by adding *-te* or *-de* in the singular, or *-ten* and *-den* in the plural, to the root. Whether we use the *d* (as in *loved*) or *t* form (as in *slept*) is determined (see p. 67) in accordance with pronunciation of a dental after a voiced or voiceless consonant. Thus we have:

ik leer	(I learn)	*ik leerde*	(I learned)
ik lach	(I laugh)	*ik lachte*	(I laughed)

The past participle is formed by putting *ge-* in front of the root and adding *-d* or *-t*. The compound tenses are formed as in English, e.g.:

ik hab geleerd (I have learned)	*ik zal leeren* (I shall learn)

Passive expression follows the German pattern (p. 296) with the auxiliary *word-wordt-worden* (present), *werd-werden* (past).

Owing to the ease with which it is possible to recognize the equivalence of Dutch words and English words of Teutonic stock, as also to the relative simplicity of its flexional system which, with Danish, stands near to English, Dutch would be a very easy language for anyone already at home with Anglo-American if it shared the features of word order common to English, Scandinavian dialects, and French. As we shall now see, the chief difficulties arise in connection with the construction of the sentence.

GERMAN WORD ORDER

The most important difference between English and the two Germanic languages is the *order of words*. It is so great that half the work of translating a passage from a German or Dutch book remains to be done when the meaning of all the individual words is clear, especially if it conveys new information or deals with abstract issues. Were it otherwise, the meaning of any piece of simple Dutch prose would be transparent to an English-speaking reader who had spent an hour or so examining the Table of Particles, etc., elsewhere in *The Loom of Language*. To make rapid progress in reading Dutch or German, it is therefore essential to absorb the word pattern of the printed page. One suggestion which may help the reader to apply the rules given in the preceding paragraph appears on page 158.

How the meaning of the simplest narrative may be obscured by the unfamiliarity of the arrangement of words, unless the reader is attuned to it by the painless effort of previous exercise in *syntactical translation*, can be seen from the following word-for-word translation of a passage from one of Hoffmann's *Tales:*

"Have you now reasonable become, my dear lord Count," sneered the gipsy. "I thought to me indeed that itself the money find would. For I have you indeed always as a prudent and intelligent man known."

"Indeed thou shalt it have, but under one condition."

"And that sounds?"

"That thou now nor never to the young Count the secret of his birth betray. Thou hast it surely not perhaps already done?"

"Aye, there must I indeed a real dunce be," replied Rollet laughing. "Rather had I from me myself the tongue out-cut. No, no, about that can you yourself becalm. For if I him it told had, so would he his way to the Lady mother certainly even without me already found have."

To write German correctly it is necessary to know its archaic system of concord between the noun, pronoun, and adjective (p. 290), as well as to know how to arrange German words in the right way. To read German fluently, the former is unimportant and the latter is all-important. So the word pattern of German is the common denominator, and should be the *first concern* of the beginner who does not share the conviction that all learning must and should be painful. At this stage the reader should therefore read once more the remarks on pages 143–159. To emphasize the importance of German (or Dutch) word order, we shall now bring the essential rules together:

1) Principal clauses, co-ordinate clauses, and simple sentences:
    a) Inversion of verb and subject when another sentence element or a subordinate clause precedes the latter (p. 146):

> *Oft kommt mein Mann nicht nach Hause*
> Often my husband does not come home.

> *Weil es Sonntag ist, koche ich nicht*
> Because it is Sunday, I am not cooking.

Note: In colloquial German inversion is practically confined to questions.

b) Past participle or infinitive go to the end of the sentence or clause:

> *Die Katze hat die Milch nicht getrunken*
> The cat hasn't drunk the milk.

> *Der Hund will mir folgen.*
> The dog wants to follow me.

c) The simple negative follows the object (direct or indirect) when it negates the statement as a whole, but precedes a word or phrase which it negates otherwise:

> *Mein Vater hat mir gestern den Scheck nicht gegeben*
> My father did not *give* me the check yesterday.

> *Mein Vater hat mir nicht gestern den Scheck gegeben*
> My father did not give me the check *yesterday*.

2) Subordinate clauses:

a) The finite verb goes to the end, immediately after the participle or infinitive when it is a helper:

> *Sie kam nach Hause, weil sie kein Geld mehr hatte*
> She came home because she had no more money.

> *Mein Bruder sagte mir, dass er nach Berlin gehen wolle (will)*
> My brother told me that he wanted to go to Berlin.

In all other Teutonic languages, except Dutch, and in all Romance languages, words connected by meaning are placed in close proximity. German, and not only written German, dislocates them. Thus the article may be separated from its noun by a string of qualifiers, and the length of the string is determined by the whims of the writer, e.g. *der gestern Abend auf dem Alexandraplatz von einem Lastauto überfahrene Bäckermeister Müller ist heute morgen seinen Verletzungen erlegen* = the yesterday evening on the Alexandraplatz by a lorry run over master-baker Müller has this morning to his injuries succumbed. The auxiliary pushes the verb to the end of the statement, as in *ich werde dich heute Abend aufsuchen* (I shall you this evening visit). When you get to the end of a sentence you may always fish up an unsuspected negation, e.g. *er befriedigte unsere Wünsche nicht* = he satisfied our wishes not. The dependent clause is rounded up by the verb, e.g. *er behauptet, dass er ihn in Chicago getroffen habe* = he says that he him in Chicago met had; and when the subordinate is placed before the main clause it calls for inversion of the verb in the latter (*da er arbeitslos ist, kann er die Miete nicht bezahlen* = since he unemployed is, can he the rent not pay). Even the preposition may leave its customary place before the noun and march behind it, e.g. *der Dame gegenüber* (opposite the lady)—as was possible in Latin, e.g. *pax vobiscum* (peace be with you).

Other preliminary essentials for a reading knowledge of German are already contained in the tables of pronouns, particles, demonstratives, and helper verbs, together with what has been said about the common features of all the Teutonic languages or of the Germanic clan. Anyone who wishes to write German correctly must also master the concord of noun and adjective. The behavior of nouns, of adjectives, and of pronouns in relation to one another confronts those of us who are interested in the social use of language and its future with an arresting problem.

It is easy to understand why Icelanders can still read the Sagas. The Norse community in Iceland has been isolated from foreign invasion and intimate trade contacts with the outside world, while the speech habits of Britain and some parts of Europe have been eroded by conquest and commerce. The conservative character of German is not such a simple story. The Hanseatic ports once held leadership in maritime trade. There were famous culture centers such as Nuremberg, Augsburg and Mainz. There was the flourishing mining industry of South Germany and Saxony. There were the great international banking houses of the Fugger and Welser. Still, Germany was not yet a nation like fourteenth-century England or sixteenth-century France. It had no metropolis comparable to London, Paris, Rome, or Madrid. The Berlin of today does not enjoy a supremacy which these capitals had earned three hundred years ago. Till the present generation German was not the language of a single political unit in the sense that Icelandic has been for a thousand years. When Napoleon's campaigns brought about the downfall of the Holy Roman Empire, German was the common literary medium of a loose confederation of sovereign states with no common standard of speech. Modern Germany as a political unity begins after the Battle of Sedan. The union of all the High German-speaking peoples outside Switzerland did not come about till Hitler absorbed Austria in the Third Reich.

In the fourteenth century, that is to say about the time when English became the official language of the English judiciary, the secretariat of the chancelleries of the Holy Roman Empire gave up the use of Latin. They started to write in German. The royal chancellery of

Prague set the fashion, and the court of the Elector of Saxony fell into step. This administrative German, a language with archaic features like that of our own law courts, was the only common standard when the task of translating the Bible brought Luther face to face with a medley of local dialects. "I speak," he tells us, "according to the usage of the Saxon chancellery which is followed by all the princes and kings of Germany. All the imperial cities, all the courts of princes, write according to the usage of the Saxon chancellery which is that of my own prince."

Luther's Bible made this archaic German the printed and written language of the Protestant states, north and south. At first, the Catholic countries resisted. In time they also adopted the same standard. Its spread received much help from the printers who had a material interest in using spelling and grammatical forms free from all too obvious provincialisms. By the middle of the eighteenth century Germany already had a standardized literary and written language. During the nineteenth century what had begun as a paper language also came to be a spoken language. Still, linguistic unification has never gone so far in Germany as in France. Most German children are nurtured on local dialects. They do not get their initiation to the spoken and written norm till they reach school; and those who remain in the country habitually speak a local vernacular. In the larger towns most people speak a language which stands somewhere between dialect and what is taught in school, but the pronunciation even of educated people, who deliberately pursue the prescribed model, usually betrays the part of the country from which they come. There are also considerable regional differences of vocabulary, as illustrated by a conversation between a Berliner and a Wiener:

"A Berliner in Vienna goes into a shop and asks for a *Reisemütze* (traveling cap). The assistant corrects him: 'You want a *Reisekappe*,' and shows him several. The Berliner remarks: '*Die bunten liebe ich nicht*' (I don't like those with several colors). The assistant turns this sentence into his own German: '*Die färbigen gefallen Ihnen nicht?*' The Viennese, you see, *loves* (*liebt*) only people; he does not *love* things. Lastly, the Berliner says: '*Wie teuer ist diese Mütze?*' (How much is this cap?), and again is guilty, all innocently, of a most crude Berlinism. *Teuer*, indeed, applies to prices above the normal, to unduly high prices. The Viennese merely says: '*Was kostet das?*' The Berliner looks round for the *Kasse* (cash desk) and finds the sign: *Kassa*. He leaves the shop saying, since it is still early in the day: '*Guten Morgen*,' greatly to the surprise of the Viennese, who uses this form of words on arrival only, and not on leaving.

The Viennese in turn replies with the words: *'Ich habe die Ehre! Guten Tag!'* and this time the Berliner is surprised, since he uses the expression *Guten Tag!* only on arrival, and not when leaving."

(E. Tonnelat: *A History of the German Language*)

THE GERMAN NOUN

The usual practice of textbooks is to exhibit a staggering assortment of tabulations of different declensions of German nouns. This way of displaying the eccentricities of the German noun is useful if we want to compare it with its equivalent in one of the older and more highly inflected representatives of the Teutonic family; but it is not a good way of summarizing the peculiarities which we need to *remember*, because the German noun of today is simpler than the Teutonic noun in the time of Alfred the Great. For instance, a distinctive genitive plural ending has disappeared altogether. In the spoken language the dative singular case ending survives only in set expressions such as *nach Hause* (home) or *zu Hause* (at home). Essential rules we need to remember about what endings we have to add to the nominative singular (i.e., dictionary) form are the following:

A. In the SINGULAR:

   1) Feminine nouns do not change.

   2) Masculine nouns which, like *der Knabe* (boy), have -E in the nominative take -EN in all other cases. A few others (e.g. MENSCH, KAMERAD, SOLDAT, PRINZ, OCHS, NERV) also take -EN.

   3) The other masculine nouns and *all* neuter nouns add -ES or -S (after -EL, -ER, -EN, -CHEN) in the genitive.

   4) Proper names and technical terms derived from foreign roots, such as TELEFON or RADIUM add -S in the genitive and do not otherwise change.

B. The DATIVE PLURAL of ALL nouns ends in -(E)N.

C. In ALL OTHER CASES of the PLURAL:

   1) Add -EN to all polysyllabic feminines (except *Mutter and Tochter*) and to all the masculines mentioned under A(2).

   2) Masculines and neuters in -ER, -EL, -EN, -CHEN (diminutives), do not change, but many of the masculines and all feminines and neuters (diminutives) have root-vowel change (Umlaut) as stated under D.

   3) Many monosyllabic masculines, feminines, and neuters take -E. Some of the masculines and all the feminines have Umlaut, e.g. *der Sohn* (son)—*die Söhne* (sons).

   4) The most common monosyllabic neuters (e.g. Bild, Blatt,

Buch, Ei, Feld, Glas, Haus, Kind, Kleid, Land, Licht, Loch, etc.), and a few masculines of one syllable have -ER (dative -ERN). All nouns of this group have Umlaut.

5) A small number of masculines and neuters show mixed declension, e.g. -(E)S in the genitive singular and -(E)N in the plural. None of them has Umlaut. Examples are: AUGE (eye), BAUER (farmer), BETT (bed), DOKTOR (PROFESSOR, DIREKTOR, REKTOR, etc.), NACHBAR (neighbor), OHR (ear), STAAT (state), STRAHL (ray).

D. The root vowels, *a, o, u,* and the diphthong *au* may change to ä, ö, ü, äu in the plural.

The genitive form of the German noun follows the thing possessed as in *der Hut meines Vaters* (my father's hat). In this example the masculine singular noun carries its genitive terminal. Since no plural and no feminine singular nouns have a special genitive ending, the beginner will ask how to express the same relation when the noun is neither masculine singular nor neuter singular. The answer is that it usually comes after a pointer word or adjective which does carry the case trademark. Thus *my sister's hat* is *der Hut meiner Schwester*. The roundabout method of expression is common in speech, and is easier to handle, e.g. *der Hut von meinem Vater* (the hat of my father), or *der Hut von meiner Schwester.*

To apply the rules given in the preceding and in succeeding paragraphs we need to be able to recognize the *gender class to which a German noun belongs.* Each noun in the museum exhibits of Part IV is so labeled by the definite article (nominative sing.) *der* (m.), *die* (f.), *das* (n.). The following rules are helpful:

1) MASCULINE are:
   a) Names of adult males (excluding diminutives), seasons, months, days, and compass points. Notable exceptions: *Die Nacht* (night), *die Woche* (week), *das Jahr* (year).
   b) Nouns which end in -EN (excluding infinitives so used).

2) FEMININE are:
   a) Names of adult females (excluding diminutives). Notable exception: *das Weib* (wife or woman).
   b) Nouns which end in -EI, -HEIT, -KEIT, -SCHAFT, -IN, and -UNG and foreign words which end in -IE, -IK, -ION, -TÄT.

3) NEUTER are:
   a) Diminutives which end in -LEIN or -CHEN.
   b) Metals.

c) All other parts of speech used as nouns, together with the following common words:

EIS	(ice)	EI	(egg)	BLATT	(leaf)
ENDE	(end)	HUHN	(fowl)	DORF	(village)
FEUER	(fire)	INSEKT		GRAS	(grass)
GAS	(gas)	KANINCHEN	(rabbit)	HAUS	
JAHR	(year)	PFERD	(horse)	HOTEL	
LICHT	(light)	SCHAF	(sheep)	LAND	
WASSER	(water)	SCHWEIN	(pig)	STROH	(straw)
		TIER	(animal)		

BAD	(bath)	BIER	(beer)	AUGE	(eye)
BETT	(bed)	BROT	(bread)	BEIN	(leg)
BILD	(picture)	FETT	(fat)	BLUT	(blood)
BUCH	(book)	FLEISCH	(meat)	HAAR	(hair)
FENSTER	(window)	GEMÜSE	(greens)	HERZ	(heart)
KISSEN	(cushion)	ÖL	(oil)	OHR	(ear)
SCHLOSS	(lock, castle)				
ZIMMER	(room)				

BILLET	(ticket)	BECKEN	(basin)
BOOT	(boat)	GLAS	
DACH	(roof)	KLEID	(dress)
DECK		PAPIER	
DOCK		TUCH	(cloth)
SCHIFF	(ship)		
SEGEL	(sail)		

German verb roots used as nouns without change are generally masculine, e.g. *fallen—der Fall, laufen—der Lauf* (run—course), *sitzen—der Sitz* (sit—seat), *schreien—der Schrei* (cry). If the verb root changes, e.g. by vowel mutation, the noun is usually feminine, e.g. *geben—die Gabe* (give—gift), *helfen—die Hilfe* (help), *schreiben—die Schrift* (write—script).

CONCORD OF THE GERMAN ADJECTIVE

The most difficult thing about German for the beginner is the elaborate flexion of the adjective. Its behavior depends on (*a*) whether it is predicative, i.e., separated from its noun by the verb *be*; (*b*) whether it stands before a noun without any pointer word or possessive adjective in front of it; (*c*) whether it stands between a noun and a pointer word or possessive adjective.

These remarks apply to *ordinary* adjectives. Numerals (other than *ein*) * do not change. Demonstratives (table on p. 271), the articles and possessives (table on p. 116) always behave in the same way in accordance with the number of the noun, its gender class and its *case*. The demonstratives (*dieser, jeder, jener, solcher, mancher, welcher*) behave like the definite article (*der, die, das,* etc.). In the singular the

	MASC. SING.	NEUTER SING.	FEMIN. SING.	PLURAL	MASC.	NEUTER	
Nomin.	DER				EIN		
		DAS	DIE				EINE
Acc.	DEN				EINEN		
Gen.	DES		DER		EINES		
							EINER
Dat.	DEM		DEN		EINEM		

possessives (*mein*, etc.) behave like the indefinite article (*ein*), as also does *kein* (no). In the plural they take the same endings as demonstratives.

In the preceding table the nominative case form is the one which goes with a noun, if subject of the verb. The genitive is the one which goes with a noun used in a possessive sense. The accusative case form goes with a noun which is the direct object, and the dative with a noun which is the indirect object. If a preposition comes before the determinative (demonstrative, possessive or article) we have to choose between the accusative and dative case forms in accordance with the recipe on p. 258. Thus the accusative case form goes with *ohne* (without), *für* (for), and *durch* (through). The dative goes with *mit* (with), *von* (of *or* from), and *in* unless the verb denotes motion. With the neuter, feminine and masculine nouns *das Haus* (house), *die Frau* (woman), *der Hut* (hat), we therefore write:

SINGULAR		PLURAL	
ohne das Haus	*mit dem Haus*	*ohne die Häuser*	*mit den Häusern*
ohne mein Haus	*mit meinem Haus*	*ohne meine Häuser*	*in meinen Häusern*
für die Frau	*von der Frau*	*für die Frauen*	*von den Frauen*
für meine Frau	*von meiner Frau*	*für unsere Frauen*	*von unseren Frauen*
durch den Hut	*in dem Hut*	*durch die Hüte*	*in den Hüten*
durch meinen Hut	*in meinem Hut*	*durch meine Hüte*	*von meinen Hüten*

The rules for choice of endings appropriate to ordinary adjectives fall under four headings:

* *Zwei* and *drei* have genitive forms, *zweier, dreier,* still in use.

1. If predicative, an adjective has the dictionary form *without addition of any* ending. It behaves as all English adjectives behave. We do not have to bother about the number, gender or case of the noun. We use the same word *dumm* to say:

Das ist dumm = this is stupid	*Sie ist dumm* = she is stupid
Er ist dumm = he is stupid	*Wir sind dumm* = we are stupid

2. If the adjective comes after a *demonstrative* or the *definite article* it behaves like nouns of the *weak* class represented by *der Knabe* (p. 288). We then have to choose between the two endings -E and -EN in ac-

	MASCULINE SINGULAR	NEUTER SINGULAR	FEMININE SINGULAR	PLURAL
Nomin.	der blind*E*	das blind*E*	die blind*E*	die blind*EN*
Accus.	den blind*EN*			
Gen.	des blind*EN*		der blind*EN*	
Dat.	dem blind*EN*		den blind*EN*	

cordance with the number, gender, and case of the noun. The ending -E is the form which always goes with a singular subject. It is also the accusative case form for singular nouns of the feminine and neuter classes. Otherwise we have to use the ending -EN. The above table shows the relation of the definite article to an accompanying (*weak*) adjective.

Thus we have to use the weak forms of the adjective in:

von der guten Frau	= from the good woman
mit diesem neuen Geld	= with this new money
ohne die alten Hüte	= without the old hats

3. When no demonstrative, article or possessive stands in front of the adjective, it takes the *strong* endings of the various case forms of the demonstrative. Once we know the case forms of *der, das, die,* we know the strong endings of the adjective. The table on page 293 shows the essential similarity between the strong endings of the adjective and the endings of the *absent* (in brackets) demonstrative.

Accordingly we use the strong forms analogous to the corresponding absent demonstrative in:

ohne rotes Blut
without red blood

mit rotem Blut
with red blood

für gute Frauen
for good women

von guten Frauen
of good women

4. The behavior of an ordinary adjective when it stands alone before the noun and when it follows a demonstrative or the definite article might be summed up by saying that it does not carry the strong ending if pre-

	MASCULINE SINGULAR	NEUTER SINGULAR	SINGULAR FEMININE	PLURAL
Nomin.	(*dER*) rotER	(*daS*) rotES	(*diE*) rotE	
Accus.	(*dEN*) rotEN			
Gen.	(*dES*) rotES		(*dER*) rotER	
Dat.	(*dEM*) rotEM			rotEN (*dEN*)

ceded by another word which has it. This statement includes what happens when it comes after the other class of determinatives, i.e., after *ein*, *kein*, and the possessives *mein*, *sein*, etc. The nominative singular masculine, as well as both the nominative and accusative singular neuter forms of these words lack the strong endings of the other case forms; and the adjective which follows the indefinite article or possessive takes the strong endings of the masculine singular nominative and of both nominative and accusative singular neuter. Otherwise an adjective which follows *ein*, *kein*, *mein*, etc., has the weak endings. The table on page 294 illustrates the partnership.

Accordingly we have to say:

ohne das grosse Haus
ohne ein grosses Haus

ohne die gute Frau
ohne eine gute Frau

Analogous to the difference between the nominative and accusative case forms of *der*, etc., and *ein* is the difference between the possessive pronouns *meiner, meines, mein,* etc. (mine), and the possessive adjective *mein* (my). There are (see p. 116) five ways of saying *it is mine* in German, if the word *it* refers to a masculine noun such as *Hut: es ist meiner;*

	MASCULINE SINGULAR	NEUTER SINGULAR	FEMININE SINGULAR	PLURAL
Nomin.	mein rotER	mein rotES	meine rotE	meine rotEN
Accus.	meinen rotEN			
Gen.	meines rotEN		meiner rotEN	
Dat.	meinem rotEN		meinen rotEN	

es ist der meinige; es ist der meine; er ist mein; er gehört mir. Some nouns derived from adjectives and participles retain the two forms appropriate to the definite and indefinite articles, e.g.:

der Angestellte	(employee)	*ein Angestellter*
der Beamte	(official)	*ein Beamter*
der Fremde	(stranger)	*ein Fremder*
der Gelehrte	(scholar)	*ein Gelehrter*
der Reisende	(traveler)	*ein Reisender*

Unlike the English adverb of manner with its suffix *-ly* and the French one with the suffix *-ment,* most German adverbs belong to our *fast* class (p. 98). They are identical with the uninflected adjective as used alone after the verb, e.g.:

sie hat eine entzückende Stimme	she has a charming voice
sie singt entzückend	she sings in a charming way

This praiseworthy feature of German accidence—or lack of accidence—is one, and perhaps the only one, which we might wish to incorporate in a world auxiliary. Some German adverbs which are not equivalent to the uninflected adjective are survivals of the genitive case form, e.g. *rechts* (to the right), *links* (to the left), *flugs* (quickly), *stets* (always). The genitive case form of the noun is also used to express *indefinite* time, e.g. *eines Tages* (one day), *morgens* (in the morning). The latter must not be confused with *morgen* (tomorrow). The accusative form is used in adverbial expressions involving *definite* time, e.g.:

er lag den ganzen Tag im Bett	he lay the whole day in bed
er geht jeden Tag in den Park	he goes to the park every day

THE GERMAN VERB

With one outstanding exception, and with due allowances for the second sound shift, the High German verb is like the Dutch. The past with *haben* can replace the English simple past or the English past with *have*. The past with *hatte* (*er hatte gehört*—he had heard) is like the English construction. In parts of Germany, the simple past has disappeared in daily speech. A Bavarian housewife says *ich habe Kartoffeln geschält*. Context or the insertion of a particle of time shows whether this means: (*a*) I was peeling potatoes, (*b*) I have just peeled potatoes. The following table summarizes the formation of the simple present and simple past by suffixes added to the stem of a *weak* verb (i.e., what remains after removing the affix -*en* from the infinitive) or by helper verbs. A good dictionary always gives lists of *strong* verbs and their parts. The reader will find some important irregularities of personal flexion in the discussion of internal vowel change on page 201 in Chapter V.

	PRESENT	PAST TENSE		FUTURE	
1st Sing.	-E	⎱	habe	werde	
		-(E)TE			
3rd Sing.	-(E)T	⎰ *or* hat	+ past participle	wird	+ infinitive
Plural	-EN	-(E)TEN haben		werden	

The one exception mentioned in the preceding paragraph is the way in which future time and condition are expressed. In Dutch, as in Scandinavian dialects, the corresponding equivalents *zal* and *zoude* replace *shall* and *should*. At one time the *shall* (SOLL) verb of High German dialects was also a helper to indicate future time. During the fourteenth century it disappeared as a time marker in the Court German of the chancelleries, and reverted to its original compulsive meaning in *thou shalt not commit adultery*. In daily speech future time is usually expressed by the simple present with or without an explicit particle (e.g. *soon*), or adverbial expression (e.g. *next week*) as in all Teutonic languages. In literary German the place of *shall* is taken by WERDEN, the common Germanic helper in passive expressions, e.g.:

ich werde kommen = I shall come
er wird kommen = he will come
wir, Sie, sie werden kommen = we shall come, you, they will come

Similarly, when *should* or *would* are used *after* a condition (e.g. *if he came I should see him*) in contradistinction to situations in which they signify *compulsion* (*you should know*), they are translated by the past, *würde*. If followed by *have*, the latter is translated by *sein* (be), e.g.:

er würde gehen = he would go
er würde gegangen sein = he would have gone

This helper verb *werden* (*worden* in Dutch) is equivalent to the Old English *weorpan* which means *to become*. Its participle has persisted as an affix in *forward, inward,* etc. It is used (like its Dutch equivalent) in passive expressions where we should use *be,* and the German verb *to be* then replaces our verb *to have,* e.g.:

er wird gehört = he is heard
er wurde gehört = he was heard
er ist gehört worden = he has been heard
er war gehört worden = he had been heard

Unfortunately it is not true to say that we can always use the parts of *werden* to translate those of the verb *be,* when it precedes a past participle in what looks like a passive construction. Sometimes the German construction is more like our own, i.e., *sein* (be) replaces *werden*. To know whether a German would use one or other, the best thing to do is to apply the following tests: where it is possible to insert *already* in an English sentence of this type, the correct German equivalent is *sein,* e.g.:

Unglücklicherweise war der Fisch (bereits) gefangen
Unluckily the fish was (already) caught

In all other circumstances use *werden*. It can always be used if the subject of the equivalent active statement is explicitly mentioned.

The German equivalents for some English verbs which take a direct object do not behave like typical *transitive* verbs which can be followed by the accusative case form of a noun or pronoun. The equivalent of the English direct object has the dative case form which usually stands for our indirect object. It cannot become the subject of the verb *werden* in a passive construction. Such verbs include seven common ones: *antworten* (answer), *begegnen* (meet), *danken* (thank), *dienen* (serve), *folgen* (follow), *gehorchen* (obey), *helfen* (help). We have to use these verbs in the active form, either by making the direct object of the English passive construction the German subject when the former is explicitly mentioned, or by introducing the impersonal subject *man*, as in *man dankte mir für meine Dienste* (I was thanked for my service = one thanked me for my service). Reflexive substitutes are not uncommon, e.g. *plötzlich öffnete sich die Tür* (suddenly the door was opened). There is an alternative clumsy impersonal construction involving the passive construction with the indefinite subject *es*, e.g. *es wurde mir gedankt*. Because of all these difficulties, and because Germans themselves avoid passive constructions in everyday speech, the beginner should cultivate the habit of *active* statement.

Though it is true that the German verb *haben* is always equivalent to our *have* when it is used to signify past time, the converse is not true. With many verbs a German uses the parts of *sein* (p. 89). Verbs which go with *haben* are all transitive, e.g. *ich habe gegeben* (I have given), reflexive, e.g. *sie hat sich geschämt* (she felt ashamed), and the helpers *sollen, können, wollen, lassen*, e.g. *er hat nicht kommen wollen* (he did not want to come). The German uses *sein* and its parts when our *have* is followed by an English verb of motion, such as *kommen* (come), *gehen* (go), *reisen* (travel), *steigen* (climb), e.g. *ich bin gegangen* (I have gone). The verbs *bleiben, werden* and *sein* itself also go with *sein*, as illustrated on page 296.

The present tense forms of five English and German helpers are derived from the past of old strong verbs. They have acquired new weak past tense forms. They have singular and plural forms in both, but no specific personal flexions of the third person singular present.

	can	may	shall	will	must
Sing.	*kann*	*mag*	*soll*	*will*	*muss*
Plur.	*können*	*mögen*	*sollen*	*wollen*	*müssen*
	could	might	should	would	......
Sing.	*konnte*	*mochte*	*sollte*	*wollte*	*musste*
Plur.	*konnten*	*mochten*	*sollten*	*wollten*	*mussten*

Though derived from common Teutonic roots the corresponding English and German words do not convey the same meaning. For reasons stated on page 143, this is not surprising. Below is a table to show the correct use of these German helpers, including also *darf-dürfen-durfte*, a sixth form from a root which does not correspond to that of any English auxiliary.

MÜSSEN

necessity (must, have to):

ich muss nun packen
I have to pack now

er musste Amerika verlassen
he had to leave America

es muss interessant gewesen sein
it must have been very interesting

KÖNNEN

(1) *capability* (can, be able):

können Sie tanzen?
can you dance?

wir konnten nicht kommen
we were unable to come

(2) *possibility* (may):

er kann schon am Mittwoch eintreffen
he may arrive (already) on Wednesday

(3) *idiomatic*, e.g.:

er kann Spanisch
he knows Spanish

ich kann nichts dafür
I can't help it

MÖGEN

(1) *possibility* (may):

Sie mögen recht haben
you may be right

(2) *preference* (like to):

ich mag heute nicht ausgehen
I don't like to go out today

mögen Sie ihn?
do you like him?

ich möchte Sie gern besuchen
I should like to look you up

MÖGEN—(*cont.*)

ich möchte lieber hier bleiben
I would rather stay here

WOLLEN

(1) *intention* (will):

ich will und werde ihn zwingen
I will and shall force him

(2) *volition* (wants to, wish to):

er will dich sprechen
he wants to talk to you

(3) *idiomatic:*

ich wollte eben gehen als . . .
I was just leaving when . . .

sie will uns gesehen haben
she pretends having seen us

er will nach Holland
he wants to go to Holland

SOLLEN

(1) *obligation* (shall, be to, ought to):

du sollst nicht stehlen
thou shalt not steal

sag ihm, er soll gehen
tell him to go

Sie sollten ihm kein Geld leihen
you should not lend him any money

Sie hätten früher kommen sollen
you should have come earlier

(2) *idiomatic:*

er soll ihr Geliebter sein
he is said to be her lover

was soll ich tun?
what shall I do?

SOLLEN—(*cont.*)
sollte er vielleicht krank sein?
can he be ill?

DÜRFEN
(1) *permission* (may, be allowed to):

darf (kann) ich nun gehen?
may I go now?

DÜRFEN—(*cont.*)
er hat nicht kommen dürfen
he was not allowed to come

darf ich Sie um ein Streichholz bitten?
may I ask for a match?

(2) *possibility* (may):

das dürfte nicht schwer sein
that shouldn't be difficult

The beginner who is not forewarned may be confused about one use of *lassen*, which is equivalent to *let* in the sense *have a thing done*. After this an infinitive is used where we should put a participle. This construction is common, e.g.:

Er lässt sich ein Haus bauen = *he is having a house built*
Er hat sich ein Haus bauen lassen = *he has had a house built*
Er wird sich ein Haus bauen lassen = *he will have a house built*
Er hat mich warten lassen = *he has kept me waiting*

Broadly speaking we can always translate the dictionary form which also does service for the present tense or the imperative in English by the German infinitive when it is accompanied by a *helper* or preceded by *to*. The latter is equivalent to *zu*, which does not precede the verb if it is accompanied by a helper. We omit the preposition after two verbs (*see*, *hear*) other than helpers listed on page 144, and sometimes after a third (*help*). Germans leave out *zu* after *hören*, *sehen*, and *helfen*, and also do so after a few others. Of these *lernen* (learn) and *lehren* (teach) are most common:

I saw him do it — *ich sah ihn es tun*
I heard him say that . . . — *ich hörte ihn sagen, dass . . .*
Help me (to) find it — *Hilf mir doch es finden*
She taught me *to* dance — *sie lehrte mich tanzen*
I am learning *to* write German — *ich lerne deutsch schreiben*

The helper verbs (*können*, *mögen*, *dürfen*, *wollen*, *sollen*, *müssen*, *lassen*) together with the last named (*sehen*, *hören*, *helfen*) have a second common peculiarity. In their past compound tenses the infinitive form replaces the past participle with the *ge-* prefix, whenever they are accompanied by the infinitive of another verb, e.g.:

er hat nicht gewollt — he didn't want to
er hat nicht hören wollen — he didn't want to listen

The verb *werden* has two past participles, (*a*) *worden* when it is used as a helper in passive expressions, (*b*) when used as an ordinary verb meaning *to become:*

a) *er ist gesehen worden*   he has been seen
b) *die Milch ist sauer geworden*   the milk has become sour

When the English *to* signifies *in order to* the German uses *um zu,* e.g. *er ist auf dem Bahnhof, um seine Frau abzuholen* (he is at the station to meet his wife). The same combination *um . . . zu* must be used when an adjective before the infinitive is qualified by *zu* (too) or *genug* (enough), e.g.:

er war zu schwach um aufzustehen   he was too weak to get up
er hat Geld genug um sich zurückzuziehen   he has money enough to retire

GERMAN SYNTAX

The rules given on page 284 do not exhaust the eccentricities of German word order. The behavior of *verb prefixes* reinforces our impression of dislocation. Both in English and in French the prefix of a verb, e.g. *be-* (in *behold*, etc.) or *re-* (in *reconnaître* = *recognize*) is inseparably married to the root. German has some ten of such inseparable verb prefixes; but it also has others which detach themselves from the root and turn up in another part of the sentence. Of the former, little needs to be said. Some of them are recognizably like English verb prefixes, others are not. None of them except *miss-* has a clear-cut meaning. This class is made up of: *be-, ent, emp-, er-, ge-, miss-, ver, wider-, zer-.* The only useful fact to know about them is that their past participles lack the *ge-* prefix, e.g. *er hat sich betrunken* (he got drunk), *er hat meine Karte noch nicht erhalten* (he has not yet received my card), *er hat mich verraten* (he has betrayed me).

The separable German verbs carry preposition suffixes like those of our words *undergo, uphold, overcome, withstand.* In one group the preposition is always detached, and comes behind the present or simple past tense of the verb of a simple sentence, or of a principal clause, but sticks to the verb root in a *subordinate* clause. This is illustrated by comparison of the simple and complex sentences in the pairs:

a) *Die Dame geht heute aus*
   The lady is going out today

   Die Dame, die gerade ausgeht, ist krank
   The lady who just went out is ill

b) *Der Junge schreibt den Brief ab*
The boy is copying the letter

Der Junge, der den Brief abgeschrieben hat, ist sehr begabt
The boy who has copied the letter is very talented

The past participle of a separable verb which carries the *ge-* prefix is inserted between the *root* and the *preposition-prefix*, e.g. *angebrannt* (burnt), *beigepflichtet* (agreed), *zugelassen* (admitted). After the verb *werden* expressing future time the prefix sticks to the root of the infinitive, e.g.:

ich werde ihm nicht nachlaufen
I shall not run after him

When the preposition *zu* accompanies the infinitive it comes between the prefix and the root, e.g.:

Der Knabe hat die Absicht es abzuschreiben
The boy intends to copy it

Sie bat mich zurückzukommen
She asked me to come back

In the spoken language verbs which always conform to these rules are recognizable by the stress on the prefix, i.e., any one of the following: *an-, auf-, aus-, bei-, in* (= in), *nach-, vor-, zu-*. Unfortunately, another set of verbal prefixes belong to verbs with separable or inseparable forms which do not mean the same thing, or are inseparable when attached to one root and separable when attached to another. Thus *durchreisen*, a separable verb (with stress on the first syllable) means to *travel through without stopping*, but *durchreisen* as an inseparable verb (with the stress on the second syllable), means to *travel all over*. Of such pairs, another example is the separable *unterstehen* (seek shelter) and its inseparable cotwin *unterstehen* (dare). In *unterscheiden* (distinguish) the prefix is inseparable. In *untergehen* (sink) it is separable. These capricious prefixes are: *durch-, hinter-, über, um-, unter-, voll-, wieder-*. The inseparable verbs are usually transitive and form compound tenses with *haben*, the separable ones intransitive, forming compound tenses with *sein* (be).

One great stumbling block of German syntax to the English-speaking beginner is the profusion of particles arbitrarily allocated to particular situations. The single English word *before* can be a conjunction in a temporal sense, a prepositional directive in a spatial or temporal sense, and can replace the adverb *previously*. Where one word suffices, German demands three:

Preposition: before the dawn (temporal) *vor Tagesanbruch*
     before his eyes (spatial) *vor seinen Augen*

Conjunction: before he saw it *ehe er es sah* or *bevor er es sah*

Adverb: you said so before *Sie haben es bereits gesagt*

Similarly our word *after* can be either a preposition or a conjunction, e.g.:

  after his birth *nach seiner Geburt*
  after he was born *nachdem er geboren war*

On the credit side of the German account, German has one word, *während*, for which we have a separate preposition (*during*) and conjunction (*while*), e.g.:

  during dinner *während des Essens*
  while he was eating *während er ass*

For each of the English directives *inside, outside, up,* and *over,* there is a separate German preposition (*in, aus, auf, über*), and *two* adverbs the use of which demands an explanation.

The small number of essential particles in a basic vocabulary for Anglo-American use is partly due to the fact that we have largely discarded distinctions already implicit in the accompanying verb. For instance we no longer make the distinction between *rest* and *motion* (or *situation* and *direction*) explicit in archaic couplets as *here-hither* or *there-thither*. The German dictionary is supercharged with redundant particles or redundant grammatical tricks which indicate whether the verb implies motion, or if so in what (hither-thither) direction. Corresponding to each of the German prepositions mentioned last (*in, aus, auf, über*) there are *here-there* couplets: *herein-hinein, heraus-hinaus, herauf-hinauf, herüber-hinüber,* analogous to *herab-hinab* (down) for which there is no precisely equivalent German preposition.* If the verb is *kommen* (which already indicates motion toward a fixed point), we use the *here* form, *her-*. If the verb is *gehen* (which indicates motion away from a fixed point) we have to use the *there* form *hin-*, e.g.:

* The adverbial form placed *after* the accusative noun does the work of the preposition, as in

  er ging den Hügel hinab he went down the hill
  er kommt die Strasse herab he is coming down the street

Kommen Sie herab = Come down. *Gehen Sie hinab* = Get down.

With *steigen* or *klettern* (both of which mean *climb*) the use of the two forms depends on whether the speaker is at the top or at the bottom of the tree. If at the bottom he (or she) says: *Klettern Sie hinauf*, if at the top, *Klettern Sie herauf*. Both mean *climb up*, and the distinction reveals nothing which is not made explicit by the context.

One way in which the German language indicates location and motion has no parallel in other *modern* Teutonic languages nor in French and Spanish. It is a relic from a very remote past. We have seen (p. 258) that a set of nine prepositions (*an*, up, to *or* at, *auf*, on, *hinter*, behind, *in*, *neben*, near to, *über* over *or* across, *unter* below *or* under, *vor* before, *zwischen* between) sometimes precede a dative and sometimes an accusative case form. If the verb implies *rest* the prescribed case form is the dative, if it implies *motion*, the accusative, e.g.:

er stand unter dem Fenster	he stood below the window
er trat unter das Fenster	he stepped below the window

The distinction is not always so easy to detect, as in

seine Hosen hangen an der Wand	his trousers are hanging on the wall
er hängt das Bild an die Wand	he is hanging the picture on the wall

Still more subtle is the difference between:

Sie tanzte vor ihm	she danced in front of him
Sie tanzte vor ihn	she danced right up to him

Even when the German signs his name, the case form has to obey the movement of the penholder, as in *er schreibt seinen Namen auf das Dokument* (he is writing his name on the document).

Germans often supplement a more or less vague preposition with a more explicit adverb which follows the noun. Such characteristically German prolixity is illustrated by:

er sieht zum Fenster hinaus	he is looking through the window
er geht um den See herum	he is walking round the lake

Thus a simple direction may be supersaturated with particles which are at least 50 per cent redundant, e.g. *vom Dorfe aus gehen Sie auf den Wald zu, und von dort aus über die Brücke hinüber, nach dem kleinen See hin.* (You go up toward the forest and thence across the bridge toward the little lake.) The separable combination *nach . . . hin* within the sentence and the corresponding *nach . . . her*, both meaning *toward*, must be memorized. The preposition *nach* is equivalent to *after* in a purely temporal sense, illustrated previously, as is the *inseparable* adverb *nachher* (afterwards). When *nach* precedes a place name it signifies *to*, e.g. *nach*

Berlin = to Berlin. Thus *nach Hause gehen* means *go home* in contradistinction to *zu Hause sein* (be at home).

The problem of choosing the right word also arises in German—as
in most European languages other than Anglo-American—whenever
we use a verb which may have a transitive or intransitive meaning.
Since most Anglo-American verbs can have both, the choice is one
from which an English-speaking beginner cannot escape. If the ordinary meaning of the verb is transitive, we can use its German equivalent reflexively. This trick is useful when there is no explicit object,
e.g.:

er kühlt die Luft ab	he is cooling the air
die Luft kühlt sich ab	the air is cooling (itself)

This construction is common to German and other Teutonic dialects,
as also to French or Spanish. More usually we have a choice between
two forms of the verb itself. They may be distinguished by internal
vowel changes as on page 202, or by means of the affix *be-*. This prefix,
which has lost any specific meaning in English, converts an intransitive
German verb into its transitive equivalent, i.e., the obligatory form
when there is a direct object, e.g.:

INTRANSITIVE		TRANSITIVE
antworten	(answer)	*beantworten*
drohen	(threaten)	*bedrohen*
herrschen	(rule)	*beherrschen*
trauern	(mourn)	*betrauern*
urteilen	(judge)	*beurteilen*

The German vocabulary is burdened by an enormous number of couplets distinguished by one or another inseparable *prefix*. Besides the *be-*
which gives the intransitive German verb an object in life, one prefix,
miss-, like its English equivalent (cf. understand—misunderstand) has a
clearly defined meaning illustrated by: *achten—missachten* (respect—
despise), *glücken—missglücken* (succeed—fail), *trauen—misstrauen*
(trust—mistrust). Other common prefixes have no single meaning. Both
ent- and *er-* may signify incipient action like the Latin affix *-esc-* in *evanescent*. Thus we have *flammen—entflammen* (blaze—burst into flames)
or *erröten* (turn red), *erkalten* (grow cold). In some verb couplets of this
sort *er-* signifies *getting a result*. Thus we have:

arbeiten	(work)	*erarbeiten*	(obtain through work)
betteln	(beg)	*erbetteln*	(obtain by begging)
kämpfen	(fight)	*erkämpfen*	(obtain by fighting)
haschen	(snatch)	*erhaschen*	(obtain by snatching)

The prefix *ver-* attached to many verbs which can stand on their own legs may have a perfective meaning, e.g.:

brennen	(burn)	*verbrennen*	(burn up)
arbeiten	(work)	*verarbeiten*	(work up)
schiessen	(shoot)	*verschiessen*	(shoot away)
trinken	(drink)	*vertrinken*	(drink away)

In another group of such pairs, the same prefix indicates that the action went awry, e.g.:

biegen	(bend)	*verbiegen*	(spoil by bending)
legen	(put)	*verlegen*	(misplace)
sprechen	(speak)	*sich versprechen*	(commit a slip of the tongue)
hören	(hear)	*sich verhören*	(hear what has not been said)
schreiben	(write)	*sich verschreiben*	(commit a slip of the pen)

The older Teutonic languages had subjunctive verb forms, past and present. In English the only traces of this are (*a*) the use of *were* in conditional clauses, when the condition is *rejected* (i.e., hypothetical or untrue), as in *if I were richer, I could buy it;* (*b*) in diffident statements such as *lest it be lost.* As we might expect, the German subjunctive has been more resistant. The verb *sein* has *present* (*ich* or *er sei, wir* or *sie seien*) and *past* (*ich* or *er wäre, wir* or *sie wären*) subjunctive forms. So has *werden* in the third singular *er werde* of the present, and throughout the past, *würde-würden.* If we exclude the *intimate* forms (with *du* and *ihr*) the only distinct *present* subjunctive form of most other verbs is the third person singular. It ends in -*e* instead of -*t*, e.g. *mache* for *macht* (make) or *finde* for *findet.* The weak verb has no special past subjunctive form. That of strong verbs is formed from the ordinary past by vowel change and the addition of -*e*, e.g. *gab—gäbe* (gave), *flog—flöge* (flew). The subjunctive of the present of strong verbs of the *nehmen-geben* class is formed without the modification of the stem vowel (p. 203). Its use in conditional clauses, as in English, is illustrated by:

> *Wenn ich etwas mehr Geld hätte, würde ich zufriedener sein*
> If I had a little more money I should be happier

> *Wenn ich etwas mehr Geld gehabt hätte, wäre ich zufriedener gewesen*
> If I had had a little bit more money I should have been happier

The German subjunctive is also used in reported speech, e.g.:

In seiner Reichstagsrede erklärte Hitler, er werde bis zum letzten Bluts-tropfen kämpfen; dieser Krieg entscheide über das Schicksal Deutschlands auf tausend Jahre hinaus, etc.

The subjunctive is also used in indirect questions, e.g. *ich fragte ihn, ob er mit der Arbeit fertig sei* (I asked him if he had finished the job). It occurs in certain idiomatic expressions, e.g. the set formula for a qualified statement in which we might use *very nearly:*

Ich wäre fast ums Leben gekommen	I very nearly lost my life

Common idioms are:

da wären wir ja!	here we are!
es koste, was es wolle	cost what it may
es sei denn, dass er gelogen habe	unless he lied about it

The grammar of German is difficult; and the aim of the last few pages has not been to pretend that it is otherwise. If we want to file the innumerable rules and exceptions to the rules in cupboards where we can find them, the best we can do is to label them as representative exhibits of speech deformities or evolutionary relics. Many of them are not essential to anyone who aims at a reading knowledge of the language, or to anyone who wishes to talk or to listen to German broadcasts. For the latter there is some consolation. It is much easier to learn to read, to write, or even to speak most languages correctly than to interpret them by ear alone. This is not true of German. Germans pronounce individual words clearly, and the involved sentences of literary German rarely overflow into daily speech. No European language is more easy to recognize when spoken, if the listener has a serviceable vocabulary of common words. There is therefore a sharp contrast between the merits and defects of German and Chinese. German combines inflation of word forms and grammatical conventions with great phonetic clarity. Chinese unites a maximum of word economy with extreme phonetic subtlety and obscurity.

FURTHER READING

BRADLEY	*The Making of English.*
DUFF AND FREUND	*The Basis and Essentials of German.*
GRUNDY	*Brush up Your German.*
TONNELAT	*A History of the German Language.*
WILSON	*The Student's Guide to Modern Languages* (A Comparative Study of English, French, German, and Spanish).

The primers in simplified Swedish, Danish, Norwegian, German, and Dutch published by Hugo's Language Institute; *Teach Yourself German, Teach Yourself Dutch, Teach Yourself Norwegian* in the Teach Yourself Books (English University Press).

The Latin Legacy

FOUR *Romance* languages, French, Portuguese, Spanish, and Italian, are the theme of the next chapter. Readers of *The Loom of Language* will now know that all of them are descendants of a single tongue, Latin. Twenty-five hundred years ago, Latin was the vernacular of a modest city-state on the Tiber in Central Italy. From there, military conquest imposed it, first on Latium and then upon the rest of Italy. Other related *Italic* dialects, together with Etruscan, with the Celtic of Lombardy, and with the Greek current in the south of the Peninsula and in Sicily, were swamped by the language of Rome itself. The subsequent career of Latin was very different from that of Greek. Outside Greece itself, the Greek language had always been limited to coastal belts, because the Greeks were primarily traders, whose home was the sea. The Romans were consistently imperialists. Their conquests carried Latin over the North of Africa, into the Iberian Peninsula, across Gaul from south to north, to the Rhine and east to the Danube. In all these parts of the empire, indigenous languages were displaced. Only the vernaculars of Britain and Germany escaped this fate. Britain was an island too remote, climatically too unattractive, and materially too poor to encourage settlement. Germany successfully resisted further encroachment by defeating the Romans in the swamps of the Teutoburger Wald.

In Gaul, Romanization was so rapid and so thorough that its native Celtic disappeared completely a few centuries after the Gallic War. The reason for this is largely a matter of speculation; but one thing is certain, Roman overlords did not impose their language upon their subjects by force. *Sprachpolitik*, as once practiced by modern European states, was no part of their program. Since Latin was the language of administration, knowledge of Latin meant promotion and social distinction. So we may presume that the Gaul who wanted to get on would learn it. Common people acquired the racy slang of Roman soldiers, petty officials, traders, settlers, and slaves, while sons of chiefs were nurtured in the more refined idiom of educational establishments which flourished in Marseilles, Autun, Bordeaux, and Lyons.

When parts of Gaul came under Frankish domination in the fifth century A.D., the foreign invaders soon exchanged their Teutonic dialect for the language of subjects numerically stronger and culturally more advanced. Change of language accompanied a change of heart. The Franks embraced the Christian faith, and the official language of the Christian faith was the language of Rome. The impact of Frankish upon Gallo-Roman did not affect its structure, though it contributed many words to its present vocabulary. Several hundreds survive in modern French, e.g. *auberge* (German *Herberge*, inn), *gerbe* (German *Garbe*, sheaf), *haie* (German *Hag*, hedge), *haïr* (German *hassen*, hate), *jardin* (German *Garten*, garden), *riche* (German *reich*, rich). In addition the Franks imported a few suffixes, e.g. *-ard* as in *vieillard* (old man).

The language which diffused throughout the provinces of the empire was not the classical Latin of Tom Brown's schooldays. It was the Latin spoken by the common people. Ever since Latin had become a literary language (in the third century B.C.) there had been a sharp cleavage between popular Latin and the Latin of the erudite. In tracing the evolutionary history of Romance languages from Latin, we must therefore be clear at the outset about what we mean by Latin itself. When we discuss French, Spanish, or Italian, we are dealing with languages which Frenchmen, Spaniards, or Italians *speak*. Latin is a term used in two senses. It may signify a literary product to cater for the tastes of a social elite. It may also mean the living language imposed on a large part of the civilized world by Roman arms before the beginning of the Christian era.

In the first sense, Latin is the Latin of classical authors selected for study in schools or colleges. It was always, as it is now, a *dead* language because it was never the language of daily intercourse. It belongs to an epoch when script was not equipped with the helps which punctuation supplies. Books were not written for rapid reading by a large reading public. For both these reasons a wide gap separated the written from the spoken language of any ancient people. In ancient times what remains a gap was a precipitous chasm.

When we speak of Latin as the common parent of modern Romance languages, we mean the living language which was the common medium of intercourse in Roman Gaul, Roman Spain, and Italy during the empire. For five centuries two languages, each called Latin, existed side by side in the Roman Empire. While the language of the ear kept on the move, the language of the eye remained static over a period as long as that which separates the Anglo-American of Faraday or Mencken from the English of Chaucer and Langland. Naturally, there are gradations of artificiality within the *sermo urbanus,* or cultured manner, as well as gradations of flexibility within the *sermo rusticus,* the *sermo vulgaris,* the *sermo pedestris,* the *sermo usualis,* as its opposite was variously called. The Macaulays of classical prose were less exotic than the Gertrude Steins of classical verse, and the Biglow

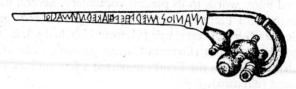

FIG. 33.—VERY EARLY (6TH CENTURY B.C.) LATIN INSCRIPTION OF A FIBULA
(*clasp* or *brooch*)

(Reading from right to left):
MANIOS MED FHEFHAKED NUMASIOI
Manius made me for Numasius
N.B.—In later Latin this would read: *Manius me fecit Numasio.*

Papers of the Golden Age were more colloquial than the compositions of a Roman Burke or a Roman Carlyle.

Unhappily our materials for piecing together a satisfactory picture of Latin as a living language are meager. A few technical treatises, such as the *Mechanics* of Vitruvius, introduce us to words and idioms alien to the writings of poets and rhetoricians, as do inscriptions made by people with no literary pretensions, the protests of grammarians, then as now guardians of scarcity values, expressions which crop up in the comedies of Plautus (264–194 B.C.), occasional lapses made by highbrow authors, and features common to two or more Romance languages alive today.

From all these sources we can be certain that the *Vulgar Latin,* which asserted itself in literature when the acceptance of Christianity promoted a new reading public at the beginning of the fourth century A.D., was the Latin which citizens of the empire had used in everyday life before the beginning of the Christian era. By the largeness of its appeal, Christianity helped to heal the breach between the living and the written language. By doing so, it gave Latin a new lease of life.

FIG. 34. THE OLDEST ROMAN STONE INSCRIPTION—THE LAPIS NIGER FROM THE FORUM (ABOUT 600 B.C.)

The writing is from right to left

The Latin scriptures, or *Vulgate*, arranged by Jerome at the end of the fourth century A.D., made it possible for Latin to survive the barbarian invasions in an age when the Christian priesthood had become a literary craft-union.

As it spread over North Africa, Spain, and Gaul, this living Latin inevitably acquired local peculiarities due to the speech habits of peoples on whom it was imposed, and to other circumstances. For instance, soldiers, traders, and farmers who settled in the various provinces came from an Italy where dialect differences abounded. Though the *Lingua Romana* thus developed a Gallic, a Spanish, and a North African flavor, the language of Gaul and Spain was still essentially the same when the empire collapsed; and it must have had features which do not appear in the writing of authors who were throwing off the traditional code. Where contemporary texts fail us we have the evidence of its own offspring. If a phonetic trick or a word is common to all the Romance languages from Rumania to Portugal and from Sicily to Gaul, we are entitled to assume that it already existed in speech once current throughout the empire. Thus many words which must have existed have left no trace in script, e.g. *ausare* (dare), *captiare* (chase), *cominitiare* (commence), *coraticum* (courage), *misculare* (mix), *nivicare* (snow). By inference we can also reconstruct the Vulgar Latin parent of the pan-Romance word for *to touch* (Italian *toccare*, Spanish *tocar*, French *toucher*).

When the curtain lifts from the anarchy, devastations, and miseries of the Dark Ages, local differences separate languages no longer mutually intelligible in the neighboring speech communities of Spain and Portugal, Provence and northern France, Italy, and Rumania. As a language in this sense, distinct from written Latin, *French* was incubating during the centuries following the disintegration of the Western Roman Empire. The first connected French text is the famous *Oaths of Strasbourg*, publicly sworn in 842 by Louis and Charles, two grandsons of Charlemagne. To be understood by the vassals of his brother, Louis took the oath in Romance, i.e., French, while his brother pledged himself in German. To the same century belongs a poem on the Martyrdom of St. Eulalia. The linguistic unification of France took place during the fourteenth and fifteenth centuries when the literary claims of local dialects such as Picard, Norman, Burgundian, succumbed to those of the dialect of the *Ile-de-France*, i.e., Paris and its surroundings. The oldest available specimens of *Italian* —a few lines inserted in a Latin charter—go back to the second half

of the tenth century. Modern Italian, as the accepted norm for Italy
as a whole, is based on the dialect of Florence, which owes its prestige
to the works of Dante, Petrarch, and Boccaccio and their sponsors,
the master printers. The oldest traces of Spanish occur in charters
and in the *Glosses* (explanatory notes of scribe or reader) of Silos,
dating from the eleventh century. The first literary monument is the
Cid, composed about 1140.

The Romance languages preserve innumerable common traits.
Their grammatical features are remarkably uniform, and they use
recognizably similar words for current things and processes. So it is
relatively easy for anyone who already knows one of them to learn
another, or for an adult to learn more than one of them at the same
time. French has traveled farthest away from Latin. What essentially
distinguishes French from Italian *and* Spanish is the obliteration of
flexions in *speech*. From either it is separated by radical phonetic
changes which often make it impossible to identify a French word as
a Latin one without knowledge of its history. As a written language,
Spanish has most faithfully preserved the Latin flexions, but it is
widely separated from French and Italian by phonetic peculiarities as
well as by a large infusion of new words through contact with Arabic-
speaking peoples during eight centuries of Moorish occupation. On
the whole, Italian has changed least. It was relatively close to Latin
when Dante wrote the *Divina Commedia*, and subsequent changes of
spelling, pronunciation, structure, and vocabulary are negligible in
comparison with what happened to English between the time of Geof-
frey Chaucer and that of Stuart Chase.

Latin did not die with the emergence of the neo-Latin or Romance
languages. It coexisted with them throughout the Middle Ages as the
medium of learning and of the Church. Its hold on Europe as an *interlingua* weakened only when Protestant mercantilism fostered the linguistic autonomy of nation states. Pedanic attempts of the humanists
of the fifteenth and sixteenth centuries to substitute the prolix pomposity of Cicero for the homely idiom of the monasteries hastened its
demise. By reviving Latin, the humanists helped to kill it. The last
English outstanding philosophical work published in Latin was
Bacon's *Novum Organum*, the last English scientific work of importance Newton's *Principia*. As a vehicle of scholarship it survived long-
est in the German universities, then as ever peculiarly insulated from
popular need and sentiment. In the German states between 1681 and
1690, more books were printed in Latin than in German, and Latin

was still the medium of teaching in the German universities. In 1687, Christian Thomasius showed incredible bravado by lecturing in German at Leipzig on the wise conduct of life. This deed was branded by his colleagues as an "unexampled horror," and led to his expulsion from Leipzig. Latin has not wholly resigned its claims as a medium of international communication. It is still the language in which the Pope invokes divine disapproval of birth control or socialism.

CLASSICAL LATIN

Two conclusions are now well established by what we are able to glean about the living language of the Roman Empire from inscriptions and from writings of authors with no pretensions to literary or rhetorical skill. One is that it was *not* so highly inflected as the Latin of the *classics*. The other is that the word order was *more regular*. To emphasize the contrast for the benefit of the reader who has not studied Latin at school, our bird's-eye view of the Romance group will begin with a short account of classical Latin. The next few pages are for cursory reading, and the home student who aims at becoming more language conscious may take the opportunity of recalling English words derived from the Latin roots used in the examples cited. Thus the first example in the ensuing paragraph (*gladiis pugnant*) suggests *gladiator, gladiolus* (why?), *impugn*, and *pugnacity*.

Like the English noun (p. 104 *et seq.*) before the Battle of Hastings, the noun of classical Latin had several singular and plural case forms. Old English (p. 262) had four: *nominative* (subject), *accusative* (direct object), *genitive* (possessive), and *dative* (indirect object). In addition to four case forms with corresponding names, the *singular* noun of classical Latin sometimes had an *ablative* case form distinct from the dative, and occasionally a *vocative* distinct from nominative.

In reality, what is called the ablative plural is always identical with the dative plural, and the singular ablative of many nouns is not distinct from the singular dative. So a grammarian does not necessarily signify a specific form of the noun when he speaks of the ablative case. The ablative case refers to the form of the noun used by classical authors in a variety of situations: e.g. (*a*) with the participle in expressions such as: *the sun having arisen, they set out for home;* (*b*) where we should put in front of an English noun the instrumental directive *with* (glad*iis* pugnant—*they fight with swords*); *from* as the origin of movement (oppid*o* fugit—*he fled from town*); *at* signifying *time* (media nocte—*at midnight*), or *than* (doctior Paulo est—*he is clev-erer than Paul*).

If Latin were the living language of a country in close culture con-tact with the English-speaking world, it might be helpful to empha-size its regularities and to give serviceable rules for recognizing the proper case affix for a Latin noun. Since it is not a living language, the chief reason for discussing the vagaries of the Latin case system is that it helps us to understand some of the differences between noun end-ings of modern Romance languages. Another reason for doing so is that it clarifies the task of language planning for world peace. For three hundred years since the days of Leibniz and Bishop Wilkins, the movement for promoting an interlanguage which is easy to learn has been obstructed by the traditional delusion that Latin is peculiarly lucid and "logical."

In so far as the adjective *logical* means anything when applied to a language as a whole, it suggests that there is a reliable link between the *form* and the *function* of words. If this were really true, it would mean that Latin is an easy language to learn; and there might be a case for reinstating it as a medium of international communication. Though no one could seriously claim that Latin is as easy to learn as Italian, classical scholars rarely disclose the implications of the fact that it is not. The truth is that Italian is simpler to learn, and therefore better suited to international use, because it is the product of a process which was going on in the living language of Italy and the empire, while further progress toward greater flexibility and great regularity was arrested in Roman literature.

In textbooks of Latin for use in schools the Latin case forms are set forth as if the genitive, dative, and ablative derivatives have a definite meaning, like the Finnish case forms, e.g.:

> *hominis* = *of a man*
> *homini* = *to a man*
> *homine* = *with* or *by a man*

In reality no Latin case form has a clear-cut meaning of this sort. The five or—if we include a defunct *locative* (*see below*)—six *possible* distinct case forms, for which few nouns have more than four distinct affixes in each number, could not conceivably do all the work of our English directives. In fact, prepositions were constantly used in classi-cal Latin. Just as Englishmen once had to choose particular case forms (p. 262) of adjective or pronoun after particular prepositions, Latin authors had to choose an appropriate case affix for a noun when a preposition came before it. Thus the use of case was largely a matter of grammatical *context*, as in modern German or Old English.

Even when no preposition accompanies a noun, it is impossible to give clear-cut and economical rules for the choice of the case forms which Latin authors used. We might be tempted to think that the genitive case affix, which corresponds roughly to the *'s* or the apostrophe of our derivatives *father's* or *fathers'*, has a straightforward meaning. Thus some grammar books called the English genitive the *possessive*, but we have seen (p. 104) how little connection it need have to any property relationship. It is even more difficult to define the Latin genitive in all circumstances. Grammarians became aware of this long ago, and split it into a *possessive genitive* (*canis puellae*, the dog of the girl), a *partitive genitive* (*pars corporis*, a part of the body), a *qualitative genitive* (*homo magnae ingenuitatis*, a man of great frankness), an *objective genitive* (*laudator temporis acti*, a booster of bygone times), etc. It is doubtful whether such distinctions help the victim of classical tuition. In Latin, as in the more highly inflected living Indo-European languages such as German and Russian, the genitive is so elusive that Hermann Paul, a famous German linguist, defined it as the case "that expresses *any* relation between two nouns."

The functional obscurities of the cases of classical Latin, in contradistinction to the well-defined meaning of the case affixes in an agglutinating language such as Finnish, would make it a difficult language, even if the case affixes were fixed as they are fixed in Finnish. The truth is that the connection between form and context is as flimsy as the connection between form and function. The irregularity of classical Latin burdens the memory with an immense variety of forms assigned to the same case. Just as English nouns belong to different families based on their plural derivatives such as *man-men*, *ox-oxen*, *house-houses*, Latin nouns form case derivatives in many ways. So if you know the genitive affix of a particular Latin noun, you cannot attach it to another without courting disaster. According to their endings, Latin nouns have been squeezed into five families or *declensions*, each of which has its subdivisions. The first table on page 316 gives a specimen of the nominative and accusative singular and plural case forms of each.

Unlike the Finnish or Hungarian noun, that of Latin has no specific trademark to show if it is singular or plural. In the first declension for instance, a word form such as *rosae* is genitive and dative singular, as well as nominative plural. In the second declension *domino* is dative and ablative singular, and *domini* is genitive singular and nominative plural. The accusative, singular and plural, of a neuter noun is always identical with the nominative, while the dative plural of every Latin noun tallies

	I		II		III	
	SING.	PLUR.	SING.	PLUR.	SING.	PLUR.
NOM.	*rosa* (rose)	*rosae*	*dominus* (master)	*domini*	*dux* (leader)	*duces*
ACC.	*rosam*	*rosas*	*dominum*	*dominos*	*ducem*	

	IV		V	
	SING.	PLUR.	SING.	PLUR.
NOM.	*fructus* (fruit)	*fructus*	*dies*	*dies*
ACC.	*fructum*		*diem*	

with the ablative. Case endings do not always change from one class to another. The word *dominus*, which is of the second declension, has the same ending in the nominative and accusative singular as *fructus*, which is of the fourth, and a word ending in *-er* may belong to the second (*ager*, acre) as well as to the third (*pater*, father); while one in *-es* may be of the third (*fames*, hunger) and of the fifth (*dies*, day). Even within one and the same class the gentive plural may show different endings, e.g. *canum* (of the dogs), *dentium* (of the teeth). Words of the same class with identical endings may suffer other modifications, as shown in the following list:

NOMINATIVE SING.	GENITIVE SING.	NOMINATIVE SING.	GENITIVE SING.
lex (law)	*legis*	*miles* (soldier)	*militis*
judex (judge)	*judicis*	*pulvis* (dust)	*pulveris*
conjux (husband)	*conjugis*	*tempus* (time)	*temporis*
nox (night)	*noctis*	*opus* (work)	*operis*
pes (foot)	*pedis*	*sermo* (speech)	*sermonis*

There are still classical scholars who speak of Latin as an "orderly" or "logical" language. Professor E. P. Morris is much nearer to the truth when he writes (*Principles and Methods in Latin Syntax*):

"The impression of system comes, no doubt, from the way in which we learn the facts of inflexion. For the purposes of teaching, the grammars very properly emphasize as much as possible such measure of system as Latin inflexion permits, producing at the beginning of one's acquaintance with Latin the impression of a series of graded forms and meanings covering most accurately and completely the whole range of expression. But it is obvious that this is a false impression, and so far as we retain it we are building up a wrong foundation. Neither the forms nor the meanings are systematic. . . . A glance at the facts of Latin morphology as they are preserved in any full Latin grammar, or in Brugman's *Grundriss*, or in Lindsay's *Latin Language*, where large masses of facts which defy classification are brought together, furnishes convincing evidence that irregularity and absence of system are not merely occasional, but are the *fundamental* characteristics of Latin form-building."

When Latin became a literary language in the third century B.C., its case system was already withering away. The old *instrumental*, if it ever had a use, had merged with the ablative, when the latter was coalescing with the dative. The *locative*, which used to indicate where something was, or where it took place, had dwindled to a mere shadow. It survived only in place names, e.g. *Romae sum* (I am in Rome), and a few fossilized expressions such as *domi* (at home), *ruri* (in the country). The vocative, which was a kind of noun imperative, e.g. *et tu Brute* (and you, O Brut*us*), as when we use the expression *say, pop*, differed from the nominative only in nouns of the second declension (*Brutus* or *Dominus*, *Brute* or *Domine*). It was often ignored by classical authors.

One great difference between popular Latin and the Latin of the literati and rhetoricians is the extent to which prepositions were used. While the former made ample use of them, classical authors did so with discretion (i.e., their own discretion). In an illuminating passage of his *Essay on Semantics* the French linguist, Bréal, has shown that the tendency to use prepositions where literary style dictated that they should be left out, was not confined to plebeian or rustic speech. Suetonius tells us that the Emperor Augustus himself practiced the popular custom in the interest of greater clarity, and in defiance of literary pedants who considered it more "graceful" and well bred to dispense with prepositions at the risk of being obscure (the prepositions *quae detractae afferunt aliquid obscuritatis, etsi gratiam augent*). In the long run, the prepositional construction was bound to bring about the elimination of the case marks, because there was no point in preserving special signs for relations already indicated, and indicated much more explicitly, by the preposition alone. In literary Latin, decay of the case system was arrested for centuries during which it went on unimpeded in the living language, and ultimately led to an entirely new type of grammar.

The use of the Latin noun, like the use of the English pronoun, involves a choice of endings classified according to case and number. The use of the adjective involved the same choice, complicated, as in Old English or German, by *gender*. So every Latin noun, like every German or Old English noun, can be assigned to one of three genders, masculine, feminine, neuter, according to the behavior of an adjective coupled with it, or of the pronoun which replaces it. This peculiar gender distinction which the Indo-European (pp. 101 and 102) shares with the Semitic family was not based on sex differentiation. Except where gender distinguished actual sex, which was irrelevant to the gender class of most animals, Latin gender referred to nothing in the real world. It was merely a matter of table manners. Nobody, not even a poet, would have been able to say why the wall (*murus*) should be masculine, the door (*porta*) feminine, and the roof (*tectum*) neuter. The singular nominative or dictionary form of many nouns carries no trademark of the gender class to which they belong. *Pirus* (pear tree) was feminine, *hortus* (garden) was masculine, and *corpus* (body) was neuter.

What labels a Latin, like an Old English, noun as masculine, feminine, or neuter is the form of the noun substitute (pronoun) or of the adjective (including demonstratives) which went with it. Excluding participles, nearly all adjectives of classical Latin can be assigned to two types. One type has three sets of case derivatives, e.g. the nominative forms *bonus, bona, bonum* (good). The feminines had endings like those of nouns such as *porta* (door) placed in the first declension, the masculine and neuter respectively like *dominus* (master) and *bellum* (war) in the second declension. To say that a Latin noun is masculine, neuter, or feminine therefore means that a Latin writer would use the masculine, neuter, or feminine forms of such adjectives with it. The flexional modifications of the second type are modeled on the nouns of the third declension. Most adjectives of this type have a common gender form used with either masculine or feminine nouns, and a separate neuter, e.g. *tristis-triste* (sad). Some of them, including present participles, e.g. *amans* (loving), have the same form for all three genders, e.g. *prudens* (prudent), *velox* (quick). The nominative and accusative, singular and plural, of the two chief adjectival types are below:

	(a) *bonus* (good)			(b) *tristis* (sad)	
	MASC.	FEM.	NEUT.	MASC. = FEM.	NEUT.
NOM. SING. ACC. SING.	bonus bonum	bona bonam	} bonum	tristis tristem	} triste
NOM. PLUR. ACC. PLUR.	boni bonos	bonae bonas	} bona	tristes	tristia

It is usually true to say that: (*a*) most Latin nouns of the *porta* (door) type are feminine, (*b*) a large majority of Latin nouns which end in *-us* are masculine, and (*c*) all Latin nouns that end in *-um* are neuter. So it is partly true to say that the noun itself carries the trademark of its gender. One consequence of the fact that a large proportion of Latin nouns are labeled in this way, and that a large class of adjectives have corresponding affixes appropriate to the same gender, is that the Latin adjective very often carries the same suffix as the noun coupled with it, e.g. *alti muri* (high walls), *portae novae* (new doors), *magnum imperium* (great empire). Thus Latin sentences sometimes recall the monotonous singsong of the Bantu dialects (p. 206). The correspondence of the Latin suffixes is less complete than that of the Bantu prefixes, because all Latin adjectives do not have the same gender forms, and all Latin nouns assigned to the same declension do not belong to the same gender.

All these trademarks of the adjective have disappeared in English, and comparison (*black, blacker, blackest*) is now its most characteristic feature. In classical Latin the comparative and superlative derivatives of the adjectives were also formed synthetically, i.e., by adding appropriate suffixes to the ordinary or *positive* root. Originally there must have been a great variety of these accretions, but in written Latin comparative uniformity had been established in favor of *-ior* (m. or f.) or *-ius* (neut.) corresponding to our *-er*, and *-issimus* (*-a, -um*) corresponding to our *-est*, e.g. *fortis* (strong)—*fortior* (stronger)—

fortissimus (strongest). A few of the most common Latin adjectives escaped this regularization. They had comparative and superlative forms derived from stems other than that of the positive, e.g. *bonus* (good)—*melior* (better)—*optimus* (best).

The most backward class of words in modern English is made up of the personal pronouns. In classical Latin (p. 309) the personal pronoun was a relatively rare intruder. There was little need for the nominative forms *I*, *he*, *we*, etc., because person was sufficiently indicated by the terminal of the verb. Thus *vendo* could only mean "I sell," and *vendimus* could only mean "we sell." In modern French, English, or German we can no longer omit the personal pronoun, except when we give a command (*hurry!*) or find it convenient to be abrupt (*couldn't say*). In speech we usually omit personal pronouns of Italian and Spanish, whose verb endings still indicate person and number clearly, e.g. *parlo a voi, signore* (I am speaking to you, sir). When Latin authors used *ego* (I), *tu* (*thou*), etc., they did so for the sole purpose of emphasis or contrast as in Wolsey's disastrously ordered *ego et meus rex* (I and my king). There was no special Latin pronoun of the third person. Its place was taken in classical Latin by the demonstrative *is, ea, id*. This was later replaced by *ille, illa, illud* (that one).

The fundamental difference between the Latin and the English verb system has been pointed out in Chapter III (p. 95 *et seq.*). Like the Old English verb, the Latin verb had four kinds or classes of flexions, of which three might be described as functional and one, mood, depended on context. The first class, based on the personal suffixes, dispensed with need for the pronoun subject, as in Gothic. These flexions had already disappeared in the plural of the Old English verb, and in the singular they were not more useful than our -*s* of the third person singular. Differences between corresponding personal forms, classified in different *tenses*, signified differences of time or aspect. In contradistinction to any of the Teutonic languages, including Gothic, classical Latin has six tenses, *present, imperfect, perfect, pluperfect, future*, and *future perfect*. The conventional meaning attached to these *time* forms or *aspect* forms in textbooks has been explained in Chapter III (pp. 90–96) which deals with the pretensions of verb chronology in antiquity.

In reality the terminology of the Latin verb is misleading. The imperfect form, for instance, is usually said to express an act or process as going on in the past (*monstrabat,* he was showing). It was also used to denote habitual action (*scribebat,* he used to write). The perfect form stood for two things. It indicated completion of an occurrence, as well as the *historic* past. So Latin *scripsi* may be rendered in two ways: *I have written,* and *I wrote.* The pluperfect signified an action prior to some past point specified or implied in the statement, as in

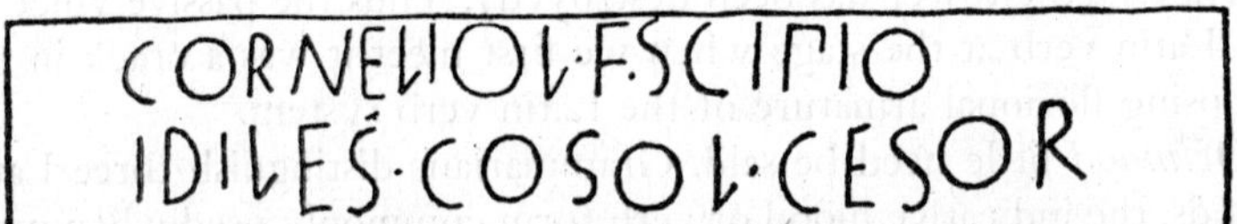

FIG. 35.—FUNERAL INSCRIPTION OF THE CONSUL L. CORNELIUS SCIPIO
IN AN EARLY LATIN SCRIPT (259 B.C.)

English *he had already drunk his beer when we arrived.* The future perfect indicated something anterior to some future action, as in *he will have drunk his beer when we arrive.* The following table gives the *first person* forms of the tenses of the *active* voice in two moods:

I SING.

	INDICATIVE	SUBJUNCTIVE
Present	canto	cantem
Future	cantabo	———
Imperfect	cantabam	cantarem
Perfect	cantavi	cantaverim
Pluperfect	cantaveram	cantavissem
Future Perfect	cantavero	———

Some, but not all of the Latin tenses, each made up of six distinct personal forms, were duplicated for passive use, like the two tenses of the Scandinavian verb (p. 109). There were only three tenses to express meaning in a passive sense, i.e., to replace the active subject by its object. As the Scandinavian passive is recognized by the suffix -*s*, the Latin passive is recognized by the suffix -*r*, e.g. *timeo* (I fear)— *timeor* (I am feared). Classical Latin has no synthetic equivalent of the *passive* perfect, pluperfect, or future perfect. As in English, the passive form of the perfect was a roundabout expression, e.g. *turris deleta est* (the tower has been destroyed). Thus the passive voice of the Latin verb at the stage when we first meet it was a crack in the imposing flexional armature of the Latin verb system.

Of *mood* little need be said. Grammarians distinguish three Latin moods, the indicative mood or verb form commonly used when making an ostensibly plain statement, the imperative mood or verb form used in command or directions, and the subjunctive mood which is variously used in noncommittal statements and in subordinate parts of a sentence. It is sufficient to say that there is no clear-cut difference between the meaning of the indicative and the subjunctive mood. In modern Romance languages the distinction is of little practical importance for conversation or informal writing.

In Latin as in English there were many mansions in the verbal house, and we can classify Latin verbs in families as we can classify English verbs in *weak*, like *love* or *shove*, and *strong* types such as the *sing* and *drink* class, *bind* and *find*, *bring* or *think* classes, according to the way they form past tense forms or participles (*love-loved, sing-sang-sung, drink-drank-drunk, bind-bound, find-found, think-thought, bring-brought*). Schoolbooks arrange Latin verbs in *four* main families, the *amare, monēre, legĕre,* and *audire* types, according to the practice of Priscian, a grammarian who lived in the sixth century A.D.

A considerable class of Latin verbs are excluded from the four so-called regular conjugations of the schoolbooks as irregular verbs. These include some which have tenses formed from different roots, such as *fero*—I carry, I bring—*tuli*, I carried, I brought. This suggests that the uniformity of the regular verb type is greater than it is. The formal similarity of so many Latin verbs placed in the same conjugation is not greater than that of the present tense forms (*catch* and *bring*) corresponding to *caught* and *brought*. Analogy is as bad a guide to Latin conjugation as to Latin declension, particularly as regards the perfect. Of *deleo* (I destroy) the perfect is *delevi*, but of *moneo* (I warn) which appears in the same class, it is *monui*; of *audio* (I hear) it is *audivi*, but of *aperio* (I open) it is *aperui*. The *third* conjugation includes as many different beasts as a Zoo, cf. the following list of perfect-formations:

PRESENT	PERFECT	PRESENT	PERFECT
colligo (I gather)	*collegi*	*ago* (I do, drive)	*egi*
carpo (I pick)	*carpsi*	*frango* (I break)	*fregi*
pono (I put)	*posui*	*rumpo* (I break)	*rupi*
mitto (I send)	*misi*	*curro* (I run)	*cucurri*
ludo (I play)	*lusi*	*tango* (I touch)	*tetigi*

An account of the essential peculiarities of Latin would be incomplete if we left out one of the greatest of all difficulties which confront the translator. Orthodox linguists sometimes tell a story which runs as follows. Relations between Latin words were clearly indicated by flexional marks, and there was therefore no need for fixed word order. Thus the statement *the farmer leads the goat* could be made in six different ways, for instance, *capram agricola ducit—agricola capram ducit—ducit capram agricola*, etc. Which one you chose was largely a question of emphasis. It did not vitally affect the meaning. Such freedom was possible because subject (*agricola*) and object (*capram*) were labeled as such by their affixes. Once the unstressed endings were ruined through phonetic decay, Latin developed auxiliaries and a fixed word order.

Thus far the dominie. Nobody who has wasted a painful youth in bringing together what Latin authors had torn asunder, or in separating what should never have been together, will deny that the word order of *literary* Latin was amazingly "free." In reality, this so-called *free* word order was the greatest impediment to quick grasp of texts, never composed, as are modern books, for rapid reading by working people. The traditional narrative, as told above, omits to mention the circumstance that the Latin of selected school texts existed on wax or papyrus. It was not the language which Romans used when they talked to one another. The crossword puzzles of Cicero and his contemporaries, like the English of Gertrude Stein or James Joyce, had little to do with the character of the language they spoke. It was the exclusive speciality of literary coteries tyrannized by cadence, mesmerized by meter, and enslaved by Greek models. Classical Latin belongs to a period more than a thousand years before the printing press democratized reading and promoted systematic conventions of punctuation, and other devices which have healed the breach between the human eye and the human ear. We do not know the exact nature of the word order which Cicero used when bawling out to his slave; but there can be little doubt that it was as fixed as that of colloquial Italian. The homely Latin of the Vulgate, though not an accurate record of spoken Latin, probably stands nearer to it than the writings of any classical author. Here is a passage from the parable of the prodigal son:

> *Et abiit,   et adhaesit uni*
> And he went and joined one
>
> *civium   regionis illius.   Et misit illum*
> of the citizens of that country. And he sent him
>
> *in villam suam ut pasceret porcos.   Et cupiebat*
> to his farm   to feed the pigs.   And he longed
>
> *implere ventrem suum   de siliquis   quas*
> · to fill his belly   with the husks which
>
> *porci manducabant.   Et nemo illi dabat.*
> the pigs ate.   And nobody gave him anything.
>
> *In se autem reversus,   dixit: quanti*
> After having come to himself he said: How many
>
> *mercenarii   in domo patris mei   abundant panibus,*
> servants in the house of my father have bread enough
>
> *ego autem hic fame   pereo.*
> while I am dying here from hunger.

LATIN AS A LIVING LANGUAGE

By the time the Western Roman Empire collapsed, case distinction of the noun had almost disappeared. Scholars used to discuss whether fixed word order and the use of prepositions led to the elimination of the case marks, or whether slurring and decay of case marks which were *not stressed* brought in prepositions and fixed word order. Undoubtedly the first is nearer the truth than the second. Thus A. D. Sheffield explains in *Grammar and Thinking:*

"Phonetic change . . . was the proximate cause of the 'decay' of inflexions; but no mere physical cause can be viewed as acting upon speech regardless of men's expressive intention in speaking. Before the analytical means of showing sentence-relations had developed, any tendency to slur relating endings would be constantly checked by the speaker's need of making himself understood. The change, therefore, more likely proceeded as follows: Fixed word-order began to appear within the inflected languages simply as a result of growing orderliness of thought. Relating particles were at the same time added to inflected words wherever the inflexional meaning was vague. After word-order had acquired functional value, and the more precise relating-words were current, relating endings lost their importance, and would become assimilated, slurred, and dropped, from the natural tendency of speakers to trouble themselves over no more speech-material than is needed to convey their thought."

The first case casualty was the genitive. Caesar himself had written *pauci de nostris* (a few of ours), which in modern Italian is *pochi dei nostri*. Without doubt this was the way in which common people of Vergil's time talked. Toward the end of the empire the use of the ablative with *de* had universally displaced the old genitive without a

FIG. 36.—OSCAN INSCRIPTION FROM POMPEII
(Reading from right to left.)

preposition, and we come across such modern forms as *de pomis*, equivalent to the modern French *des pommes* (some apples), or *filius de rege*, equivalent to the French *le fils du roi* (king's son). By the beginning of the third century, the noun genitive survived only in set expressions such as *lunae dies*, which is the French *lundi*, our Monday or lunar day.

The dative, or case of giving, though more resistant had a rival at an early date. The accusative had long been used with the preposition *ad* (to). Thus Plautus writes *ad carnuficem dabo* (I shall give to the executioner), where Cicero would have written *carnifici dabo* if he had been discussing so familiar a Roman figure; and a temple regulation of 57 B.C., i.e., during the Golden Era of Latinity, contains *si pecunia ad id templum data erit* (if money should be given to this temple). Eventually a separate *dative* (as opposed to ablative) flexional form of the noun disappeared with the genitive, except in Dacia (Rumania), where traces of it survive today. So popular Latin may be said to have taken the same road as Teutonic languages such as English and Dutch, which have *of* and *to*, or *van* and *aan*, for *de* and *ad* (French *de* and *à*) of Vulgar Latin.

In the later days of the Roman Empire, phonetic decay of the terminals led to further changes. A final *-m* which was the accusative trademark of feminine and masculine nouns, had disappeared at an earlier date. The unstressed vowels *-u* and *-i* of the affixes gave place to *-o* and *-e*. So the distinction between accusative and ablative case forms faded out. Thus *canem* (accus.), *cani* (dat.), and *cane* (ablat.) of *canis* (nomin.) merged in the single *oblique* (p. 105) case form *cane* (dog). Since the first century A.D. the ablative had been confused

	SINGULAR		PLURAL	
	NOM.	OBL.	NOM.	OBL.
I	*luna* (moon)		*lune*	*luna(s)* (moons)
II	*caballu(s)*	*caballu* (horse)	*caballi*	*caballo(s)* (horses)
III	*cani(s)*	*cane* (dog)	*cane(s)* (dogs)	

with the accusative of plural nouns. In an inscription from Pompeii, *cum discentes* (with the pupils) is used for the classical *cum discentibus*.

Before the fall of the empire the five declensions of our Latin grammar books had dwindled to three. The fifth noun family had joined the first (Latin *facies*, figure; Vulgar Latin *facia;* French *face*), and the fourth had joined the second (Latin *fructus*, fruit; Vulgar Latin *fructu;* Italian *frutto*), as *brother* which had joined the *oxen* class (pl. *brethren*) in *Mayflower* times has now joined the same class as *mother* (pl. *mothers*). When the Latin dialects began to diverge after the fall of Rome, Latin declension was probably reduced to the forms as shown in the table above.

In the spoken Latin of Italy a final *s*, like a final *t* had ceased to be heard long before Cicero's time, and no efforts of the grammarian could bring it back. Hence the bracketed *-s* of *lunas* and *caballos* in our table. Partly under the influence of the school, the West preserved it. In spoken French it became silent before the end of the Middle Ages. In Spanish it survives till this day and is now the characteristic mark of the plural. Further simplifications followed. The distinction between nominative and oblique case has disappeared in all modern Romance languages. On Italian territory the oblique form of the plural disappeared. Only the nominative survived (Latin *muri* [nom. pl.]—Italian *muri*). In France, in Spain, and in Portugal the nominative plural disappeared, and the oblique (originally *accusative*) form with a final *s* took its place (Latin acc. pl. *muros*—French *murs*). Case distinction died last in Gaul. In the oldest French and Provençal texts some nouns still preserve the distinction between a subject and an object case as the following table shows:

| | SINGULAR | | PLURAL | |
	NOM.	OBL.	NOM.	OBL.
Vulgar Latin	*murus*	*muru*	*muri*	*muros*
Old French	*murs*	*mur*	*mur*	*murs*
Modern French	*mur*		*murs*	

The case marks of the adjective shared the same fate as those of the noun. Meanwhile separate neuter forms disappeared. There were two reasons why the noun form came nearer to that of the adjective. One is the disappearance of two families of noun behavior owing to the absorption of the fourth and fifth declensions (p. 322) so that the characteristic affixes corresponded to those of one or other remaining families of nouns. The other was regularization of the gender classes. For instance, names of trees assigned to the second declension of classical Latin were feminine, though they had the nominative singular affix *-us* of masculine adjectives. Similarly the first declension, mainly made of feminine nouns such as *regina* (queen) included masculine words such as *nauta* (sailor) and *poeta* (poet). Tree names which were feminine like *populus* (poplar) of which the French is *peuplier* have become masculine in modern Romance languages.

The disappearance of a distinct neuter form of the adjective or, what comes to the same thing, a neuter class of nouns, had already begun in classical times. Authors near to the people would write *dorsus* (back) for *dorsum*, or *caelus* for *caelum*. In so far as all Latin nouns which have the nominative singular affix -*um* were neuter, their character was obliterated by the phonetic decay of the final consonant, -*m*, like the decay of the distinctive masculine or feminine accusative case mark. In late Latin the drift from neuter to masculine became a headlong retreat. Hence most Latin neuter nouns which survive in modern Romance languages are now placed in the masculine gender class; and anyone who has learned a little Latin can usually apply his knowledge of Latin genders with success, i.e., masculine and feminine nouns retain the same gender, and neuters become masculine. Thus *vinum* (wine), *imperium* (empire) and *regnum* (a kingdom) become (*le*) *vin*, (*un*) *empire*, and (*le*) *règne* in French. The exceptions to this rule are few, and some of them are explicable. In so far as the nominative or accusative plural ending of Latin neuter nouns was -*a*, it was the same as the nominative singular of the more typical feminine noun class represented by *porta*. If the meaning of a Latin neuter was such that the plural could be used in a collective sense, or for a pair (cf. *news* or *scissors*), it could be used in a singular context. Thus the Latin neuter plural, *folia* (foliage) becomes the singular feminine *la feuille* for *a leaf* in modern French.

The reader has already had a hint about how knowledge of the forms of the noun in Vulgar Latin throws light on the different types of plural formation in the modern Romance languages. The greater luxuriance of the Latin adjective also helps us to understand the different types of adjective concord which have survived. Latin adjectives for the most part belong to the three-gender type *bonus, -a, -um*, or to the two-gender class *tristis-triste* (sad), *fortis-forte* (strong) or *brevis-breve* (short). The disappearance of the neuter means that survivors of the three-gender class now have only masculine and feminine forms—Spanish *bueno-buena* (sing.), *buenos-buenas* (pl.); Italian *buono-buona, buoni-buone;* French *bon-bonne, bons-bonnes. The* survivors of the two-gender class in French, Spanish, and Italian have only one form. From this class of adjective, gender concord has disappeared, as for all English adjectives.

Unlike Greek, classical Latin did not possess what grammarians call the "definite article." Wherever we find this definite article in modern European languages, it can be traced back to a demonstrative which lost its pointing power in the course of time. Thus our English *the* is a weakened form of *that*, and the unaccented *der* in German *der Óchs* (the ox) began as the *der* we have in *dér Mann* (that man). The definite article of modern languages, including English, French, and Ger-

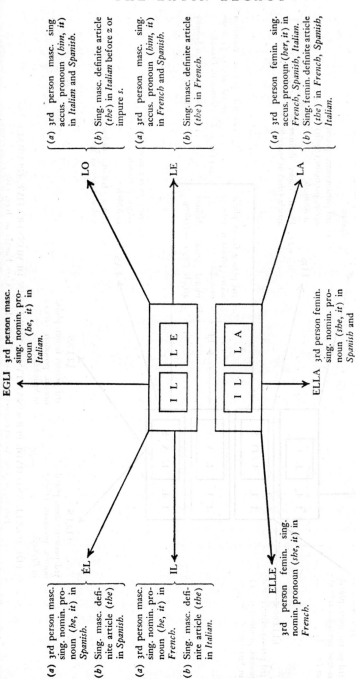

EGLI 3rd person masc. sing. nomin. pronoun (*be*, *it*) in *Italian*.

LO
(*a*) 3rd person masc. sing. accus. pronoun (*him*, *it*) in *Italian* and *Spanish*.
(*b*) Sing. masc. definite article (*tbe*) in *Italian* before z or impure s.

LE
(*a*) 3rd person masc. sing. accus. pronoun (*him*, *it*) in *French* and *Spanish*.
(*b*) Sing. masc. definite article (*tbe*) in *French*.

LA
(*a*) 3rd person femin. sing. accus. pronoun (*ber*, *it*) in *French*, *Spanish*, *Italian*.
(*b*) Sing. femin. definite article (*tbe*) in *French*, *Spanish*, *Italian*.

ILLE

ILLA

ÉL
(*a*) 3rd person masc. sing. nomin. pronoun (*be*, *it*) in *Spanish*.
(*b*) Sing. masc. definite article (*tbe*) in *Spanish*.

IL
(*a*) 3rd person masc. sing. nomin. pronoun (*be*, *it*) in *French*.
(*b*) Sing. masc. definite article (*tbe*) in *Italian*.

ELLE
3rd person femin. sing. nomin. pronoun (*sbe*, *it*) in *French*.

ELLA 3rd person femin. sing. nomin. pronoun (*sbe*, *it*) in *Spanish* and *Italian*.

THE JEKYLL AND HYDE PERSONALITY OF THE LATIN DEMONSTRATIVE (SINGULAR)
PRONOUNS AND ARTICLES DERIVED FROM VULGAR LATIN CASE FORMS OF ILLE, ETC.

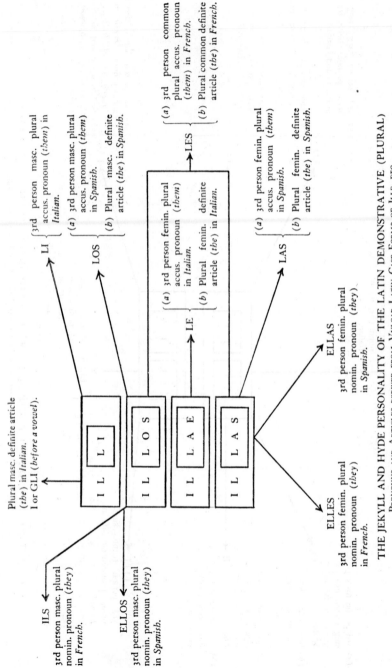

Plural masc. definite article (*the*) in *Italian*.
I or GLI (*before a vowel*).

ILS
3rd person masc. plural nomin. pronoun (*they*) in *French*.

ELLOS
3rd person masc. plural nomin. pronoun (*they*) in *Spanish*.

IL LI

LI
{ 3rd person masc. plural accus. pronoun (*them*) in *Italian*.

IL LOS

LOS
{ (*a*) 3rd person masc. plural accus. pronoun (*them*) in *Spanish*.
(*b*) Plural masc. definite article (*the*) in *Spanish*.

IL LAE

LE
{ (*a*) 3rd person femin. plural accus. pronoun (*them*) in *Italian*.
(*b*) Plural femin. definite article (*the*) in *Italian*.

LES
{ (*a*) 3rd person common plural accus. pronoun (*them*) in *French*.
(*b*) Plural common definite article (*the*) in *French*.

IL LAS

LAS
{ (*a*) 3rd person femin. plural accus. pronoun (*them*) in *Spanish*.
(*b*) Plural femin. definite article (*the*) in *Spanish*.

ELLES
3rd person femin. plural nomin. pronoun (*they*) in *French*.

ELLAS
3rd person femin. plural nomin. pronoun (*they*) in *Spanish*.

THE JEKYLL AND HYDE PERSONALITY OF THE LATIN DEMONSTRATIVE (PLURAL)
Pronouns and Articles derived from Vulgar Latin Case Forms of Ille, etc.

man, rarely lives up to its name. On the contrary, it often has a generalizing, i.e., indefinite function, e.g. *the cat is a domestic animal.* So if we say that Latin had not yet evolved an article, we really mean that the Latin demonstrative had not yet come down in the world. Literary Latin was embarrassingly rich in demonstratives. There were *is-*

ROMANCE PERSONAL PRONOUNS
(First and Second Persons—Unstressed * Forms)

	FRENCH	PORTUGUESE	SPANISH	ITALIAN	LATIN
I	je	eu	yo	io	ego
ME		ME		mi	me (*acc.*) mihi (*dat.*)
(THOU)		TU			
(THEE)		TE		ti	te (*acc.*) tibi (*dat.*)
WE	⎫ ⎬ nous ⎭	nós	nosotros	noi	nos
US		nos		ci	nos (*acc.*) nobis (*dat.*)
YOU (nom.)	⎫ ⎬ vous ⎭	vós	vosotros	voi	vos
(obj.)		vos	os	vi	vos (*acc.*) vobis (*dat.*)

*Unstressed forms = subject, direct object, and indirect object forms. Except when the same as the *stressed* (p. 363), they are *never* used *after* a preposition. The Spanish *nosotros, vosotros* are out of step with their equivalents in Latin, Italian, or French. They date from the late Middle Ages and are combinations of *nos, vos* with *otros* (others). Both have feminine forms—*nosotras, vosotras.* The French also combine *nous* or *vous* with *autres* (others) when they use either in a sense excluding individuals of a second group, e.g. *nous autres Françaises* (we French women). Italians have the same trick (*noi altre,* etc.). In Spanish the combination has replaced the pronoun itself, e.g. *vosotros* = you.

ea- id, for referring to something previously mentioned; *hic- haec-hoc,* for *this near me; iste- ista- istud,* for *that near you,* or *that of yours;* and *ille- illa- illud,* for *that yonder.* The first survives in our abbreviation i.e. for *id est* (that is).

Though the literati may have striven to make a real distinction between the four demonstratives, it is more than doubtful whether the fine shades of meaning which grammarians assign to them played any part in living speech. At least this is certain. When Latin spread beyond Italy and was imposed upon conquered peoples, a distinction ceased to exist. Two of them (*is* and *hic*) completely disappeared. Through use and abuse the meaning of the other pair (*ille* and *iste*) had changed considerably. People used them with less discrimination in the closing years of the empire. They had lost their full power as

ROMANCE PRONOUNS OF THE THIRD PERSON
(UNSTRESSED FORMS)

	FRENCH	PORTUGUESE	SPANISH	ITALIAN
HE	il	êle	él	egli, esso
HIM	le	o	le (*or* lo)	lo
(to) HIM	lui	lhe	le	gli
SHE	elle	ela	ella	ella, essa
HER	la	a	la	
(to) HER	lui	lhe	le	
THEY (masc.)	ils	êles	ellos	essi, loro
THEY (fem.)	elles	elas	ellas	esse, loro
THEM (masc.)	les	os (*or* los)	los	li
THEM (fem.)	les	as (*or* las)	las	le
(to) THEM	leur	lhes	les	SI
Reflexive (himself, herself, itself, themselves)		SE		loro

pointer words. Except in Iberian Latin *iste* disappeared. The same period also gave birth to the indefinite article (*a* or *an* in English) of which the primary function is to introduce something not yet mentioned. For this purpose classical Latin had the word *quidam*, and in popular speech or informal writing, the numeral *unus, una, unum* (e.g. *unus servus*, a slave, a certain slave) was used for it. Only the latter is used in the Vulgate, where it is burdened with as much or as little meaning as the indefinite article of modern French or English.

The fate of the pointer words is mixed up with the history of the personal pronoun. The terminal of a Latin verb sufficiently indicated the pronoun subject, and the nominative pronouns *ego, tu, nos, vos,* were used to give emphasis. In Vulgar as in classical Latin there was no specific emphatic nominative form of the pronoun in the third person analogous to *ego, tu,* etc. When it was necessary to indicate what the personal flexion of the verb could not indicate, i.e., which of several individuals was the subject, a demonstrative, eventually *ille, illa, illud* (i.e., *that one*) took the place of *he, she,* or *it.* The demonstrative was therefore a pronoun as well as a definite article at the time when divergence of the Romance dialects occurred. The result of this split personality is that Romance dialects now contain a group of words which are similar in form, but have different meanings. Thus the word equivalent to *the* in one may be the word equivalent to *her* in another, or to *them* in a third. This curious nexus of elements, which are identical in form but differ in function is illustrated in the highly schematic diagrams on pages 329 and 330.

Like Scandinavian languages, Latin had two possessive forms of the pronoun of the third person. One died intestate. Only the reflexive *suus, sua, suum* left descendants in the modern Romance dialects. Like the Swedish *sin, sitt, sina,* any of its derivative forms could mean *his, her,* or *its.* The gender was fixed by the noun it *qualified,* and not by the noun which it *replaced,* i.e., the feminine case derivative would be used with *mater* or *regina,* a masculine with *pater* or *dominus,* and a neuter with *bellum* or *imperium.*

Another difference between classical and Vulgar Latin is important in connection with the adjective of modern Romance languages. In classical Latin comparison was flexional. There was only one exception. The comparative of adjectives ending in *-uus* (e.g. *arduus,* arduous) was not formed in the regular way by adding the suffix *-ior.* To avoid the ugly clash of three vowels (*u-i-o-r*) the literati used the periphrastic construction *magis arduus* (more arduous) with the corresponding superlative *maxime arduus* (most arduous). Popular speech had employed this handy periphrasis elsewhere. Thus Plautus used *magis aptus* (more suitable), or *plus miser* (more miserable). In the living language there was thus the same competition between synthesis and isolation as we now see in English (cf. *pretty-prettier, handsome-more handsome*). In later Latin the *plus* and *magis* trick became the prevailing pattern.

Rumania, Spain, and Portugal adopted *magis* (Rumanian *mai,* Spanish *más,* Portuguese *mais*), while Italy and Gaul embraced *plus* (Italian *più,* French *plus*). Latin adjectives comparable to English *good,*

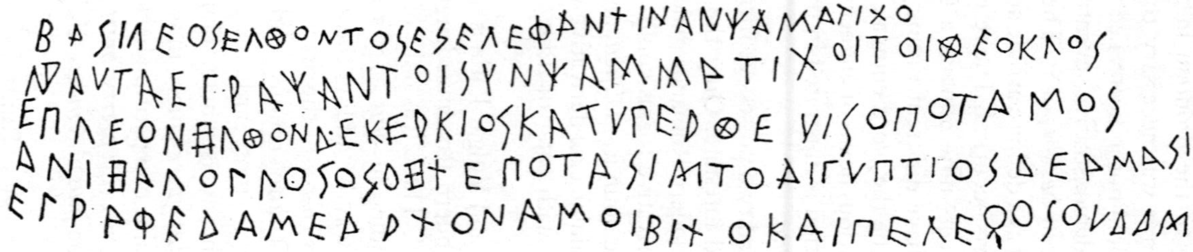

ΒΑΣΙΛΕΟΣΕΛΘΟΝΤΟΣΕΣΕΛΕΦΑΝΤΙΝΑΝΨΑΜΑΤΙΧΟ
ΝΑΥΤΑΕΓΡΑΨΑΝΤΟΙΣΥΝΨΑΜΑΤΙΧΟΙΤΟΙΟΘΕΟΚΛΟΣ
ΕΠΛΕΟΝΗΛΘΟΝΔΕΚΕΡΚΙΟΣΚΑΤΥΠΕΔΘΕΥΙΣΟΠΟΤΑΜΟΣ
ΑΝΙΗΑΛΟΓΛΟΣΟΣΘΤΕΠΟΤΑΣΙΜΤΟΔΙΓΥΠΤΙΟΣΔΕΡΜΑΣΙ
ΕΓΡΑΦΕΔΑΜΕΑΡΤΟΝΑΜΟΙΒΙΧΟΚΑΙΠΕΛΕΦΟΣΟΥΔΑΜ

[βασιλεος ελθοντος ες Ελεφαντιναν Ψαματιχο
ταυτα εγραφαν τοι συν Ψαμματιχοι τοι Θεοκλ(ε)ος
επλεον ηλθον δε Κερκιος κατυπερθε υις ο ποταμος
ανιη αλογλοσος δ ηχε Ποτασιμτο Αγυπτιος δε Αμασις
εγραφε δ αμε Αρχον Αμοιβιχο και Πελεξος ο Υδαμο]

Fig. 37.—Inscription in Early (about 590 b.c.) Greek Lettering from Egypt Chipped on the
Statuary of a Rock Temple by Ionic Mercenaries

It reads:—
When King Psammetik, son of Theokles, came to Elephantine the people of Psammetik wrote this.
They sailed to beyond Kerkis, as far as the river allowed. Potasimpto led the foreigners, Amasis the
Egyptians. This was written by Archon, son of Amoibichos, and by Pelegos, son of Eudamos.

better, best, with comparative and superlative forms derived from other roots, resisted this change, and are now islands of irregularity in an ocean of order. They appear in the table of irregular comparison (p. 336). In all Romance languages the ordinary superlative is formed by putting the definite article in front of the comparative form, e.g. Spanish *más rico* (richer), *el más rico* (the richest). Spanish and Italian have adjectival forms of the same pattern as the Latin superlative with the terminal *-issimus,* but they are not equivalent to *superlatives* in the grammatical sense of the term. The terminal *-ísimo (-a)* of Spanish or *-issimo (-a)* of Italian signifies *exceedingly* as in the exclamation *bravo bravissimo!* or in the mode of address used in letters *carissima* (dearest). These synthetic superlatives reintroduced by the learned should be used sparingly. Spanish *muy* or Italian *molto,* both meaning *very,* replace them adequately in most situations, e.g. Spanish *es muy rico* (he is very rich) for *es riquísimo.*

The Spanish and Italian article before the superlative drops out when the latter follows immediately after a noun. French retains the article, e.g.:

English	the richest man
Spanish	el hombre más rico
Italian	l'uomo più ricco
French	l'homme le plus riche

The comparative particle corresponding to English *than* is *que* in French and Spanish, e.g. French *plus timide qu'un lapin* (shier than a rabbit). Italian uses *di* (Latin *de*), e.g. *è più povero di me* (he is poorer than I). In Spanish and French *de* also occurs, but confined to situations in which *than* is followed by a numeral, e.g. Spanish *menos de cuatro días* (less than four days), French *plus de trois siècles* (more than three centuries).

REGULAR COMPARISON

	FRENCH	SPANISH	LATIN	ITALIAN
hot	chaud	cálido	calidus	caldo
hotter	plus chaud	más cálido	calidior	più caldo
(than)	(que)	(que)	(quam)	(di)
hottest	le plus chaud	el más cálido	calidissimus	il più caldo
	(de)	(de)		(di)
as hot as	aussi chaud que	tan cálido como	tam calidus quam	così caldo come

In Teutonic languages the adverb may be the same as the neuter singular (Scandinavian) or the predicative form of the adjective (German). English alone is encumbered with a special form (p. 99). Classical Latin had several types of adverbs derived from adjectives. In modern Romance languages, nearly all the irregular ones have disappeared. Notable exceptions are *bene* and *male*. In French these have become *bien-mal*, in Italian *bene-male*, and in Spanish *bien-mal*. The previous luxuriance of adverbs formed from adjective roots has given place to a standardized pattern like the English *-ly* derivative. French adverbs are formed by adding *-ment* to the adjective, e.g. *facile-facilement*. The procedure is the same throughout the *Western* Romance languages. In Italian the corresponding forms are *facile-facilmente*, and in Spanish *fácil-fácilmente*.

IRREGULAR COMPARISON OF ROMANCE ADJECTIVES *

ENGLISH	FRENCH	SPANISH	LATIN	ITALIAN
good	bon (*-ne*)	bueno (*-a*)	bon*us* (*-a, -um*)	buono (*-a*)
better	meilleur (*-e*)	mejor (*más bueno*)	melior	migliore (*più buono*)
best	le meilleur	el mejor	optim*us*	il migliore
bad	mauvais (*-e*)	malo	mal*us*	cattivo (*-a*)
worse	plus mauvais (*pire*)	peor (*más malo*)	pejor	peggiore (*più cattivo*)
worst	le plus mauvais (*le pire*)	el peor	pessim*us*	il peggiore
big	grand (*-e*)	grande	magn*us*	grande
bigger	plus grand	más grande (*mayor*)	major	più grande (*maggiore*)
biggest	le plus grand	el más grande	maxim*us*	il più grande
small	petit (*-e*)	pequeño (*-a*)	parv*us*	piccolo (*-a*)
smaller	plus petit (*moindre*)	más pequeño (*menor*)	minor	più piccolo (*minore*)
smallest	le plus petit (*le moindre*)	el más pequeño	minim*us*	il più piccolo

* In italics alternatives which have a more restricted use in common speech. In French only *bon* has no regular comparative.

The germ of this new structure appears in classical Latin. When the Roman wanted to indicate that something was done in a certain way, he sometimes used the ablative (*mente*) of *mens* (mind), and qualified it by means of an appropriate adjective, e.g. *obstinata mente* (with an obstinate mind), or *bona mente* (in good faith). Since *mente* always followed close upon the heels of the adjective, it lost its former independence and became a formative element, eventually used without involving anybody's *mental* processes, e.g. *sola mente* (French *seulement*) in place of *singulariter* (alone). Finally -*mente* fused with the

IRREGULAR COMPARISON OF ROMANCE ADVERBS

ENGLISH	FRENCH	SPANISH	LATIN	ITALIAN
well	bien		bene	bene
better	mieux	mejor	melius	meglio
best	le mieux	lo mejor	(*optime*)	il meglio
badly, ill	mal		male	male
worse	plus mal (*pis*)	peor	pejus	peggio
worst	le plus mal	lo peor	(*pessimum*)	il peggio
little	peu	poco	paucum	poco
less	moins	menos	minus	meno
least	le moins	lo menos	(*minime*)	il meno
very, much	beaucoup	mucho	multum	molto
more	plus	más	plus	più
most	le plus	lo más	(*plurimum*)	il più

adjective, i.e., with its feminine singular form. In Spanish it keeps a trace of its separate identity. The Spaniard usually attaches -*mente* only to the final one when several adverbs follow one another, e.g.: *habla clara, concisa y elegantemente* (he speaks clearly, concisely, and elegantly). This was also the custom in Old French, e.g. *umele et dolce mente* for *humblement et doucement* (humbly and quietly).

One striking difference between the Romance languages and their Teutonic contemporaries is the variety of tense forms which they possess. This is not because the flexional system of the Latin verb escaped the general process of flexional decay common to other classes of words in the living language. In later Latin, verb forms of the classical authors were largely superseded by new ones which remain the basis of conjugation in the Romance languages. The passive flexion disappeared, as it is now disappearing in Scandinavian dialects. Its place was taken partly by the active, partly by a roundabout expression *consistently* made up of the past participle and the auxiliary *esse*, to be. Where classical authors had used the present tense of the latter (*traditus est*, he has been betrayed) to express completed action, later authors used it for action in progress (cf. the French, *il est trahi* = he is being betrayed), and other tenses were used to build up similar con-

PRESENT AND IMPERFECT TENSE FORMS OF ROMANCE VERBS

	FRENCH	SPANISH	LATIN	ITALIAN
I love, etc.	j'aime	amo	amo	amo
	tu aimes	amas	amas	ami
	il aime	ama	amat	ama
	nous aimons	amamos	amamus	amiamo
	vous aimez	amáis	amatis	amate
	ils aiment	aman	amant	amano
I was loving, etc.	j'aimais	amaba	amabam	amavo
	tu aimais	amabas	amabas	amavi
	il aimait	amaba	amabat	amava
	nous aimions	amábamos	amabamus	amavamo
	vous aimiez	amabais	amabatis	amavate
	ils aimaient	amaban	amabant	amavano

structions, e.g. *traditus fuit* (he was betrayed), or *traditus erit* (he will be betrayed).

Two tense forms of classical Latin (future and future perfect) disappeared. A third (*pluperfect*) survived only in Iberian Latin; and a fourth lost some of its former territory. To indicate completion of a process or its final result, Latin, like other Indo-European languages, had a verb form, the *perfect*, which corresponds roughly to our compound past, e.g. from *scribere* (to write), *scripsi* (I have written), but Caesar writes of himself, *Caesar urbem occupatam habet*, which is roughly equivalent to *Caesar has occupied the city*, and Cicero himself writes, *scriptum habeo* (I have written), *satis habeo deliberatum* (I have deliberated enough). In late Latin the old synthetic perfect form (*cantavi* = I have sung) was gradually ousted by the periphrastic construction with *habere* (to have) or *esse* (to be), i.e., *cantavi* by *cantatum habeo*, and *reverti* (I have returned) by *reversus sum*. The synthetic form remained, but came to be confined to the function of a past definite (*cantavi* = I sang). As such it still persists in *literary* French, as in spoken or written Spanish and Italian (he sang: Latin *cantavit*, French *il chanta*, Spanish *cantó*, Italian *cantò*). Frenchmen never use it in conversation or informal writing.

Another tense form which disappeared in the later stages of living Latin was the classical future. While the verb *to have* kept its independence as a helper to indicate past time, the new analytical future

THE FUTURE TENSE OF A ROMANCE VERB

ENGLISH			FRENCH	
love (infin.)			aimer	
I have	I shall		j'ai	j'aimerai
thou hast	thou wilst		tu as	tu aimeras
he has	he will	love	il a	il aimera
we	we shall		nous avons	nous aimerons
you have	you will		vous avez	vous aimerez
they	they will		ils ont	ils aimeront

SPANISH		ITALIAN	
amar		amare	
yo he	yo amaré	io ho	io amerò
tú has	tú amarás	tu hai	tu amerai
él ha	él amará	egli ha	egli amerà
nosotros hemos	nosotros amaremos	noi abbiamo	noi ameremo
vosotros habéis	vosotros amaréis	voi avete	voi amerete
ellos han	ellos amarán	essi hanno	essi ameranno

to which it also contributed formed the basis of a fresh flexional tense form (pp. 93 and 94). This new analytical *future* makes its appearance in the first century A.D. Its predecessor had two entirely different forms. Of *dico* (I say) the future was *dicam* (I shall say), and of *lavo* (I wash) it was *lavabo* (I shall wash). In the second century A.D. the classical future had lost caste, and people resorted to affective circumlocutions such as *volo lavare* (I will wash), *debetis lavare* (you shall wash), *vado* (or *eo*) *lavare* (I am going to wash), or *lavare habeo* (I have to wash). Of these helpers, *habere* prevailed in all of the written Romance languages except in Rumania, where we hear today *voiu cântă.* Elsewhere *habere,* which usually followed the infinitive, got glued to it, as explained on page 94.

In our outline of classical Latin nothing has been said about *nega-tion.* To give a statement a negative meaning, *ne* was used in archaic

FIG. 38.—STONE SLAB FROM LEMNOS WITH EARLY GREEK LETTERING

The language itself, possibly Etruscan, is undeciphered. The writing is from left to right, from right to left, vertically upwards or vertically downwards.

Latin, but it could also label a question * as such. In classical Latin, it is replaced by the stronger *non,* a contraction of *ne* and *unum* (lit. *not one*). In daily speech, Latin-speaking peoples used to strengthen the particle by adding another word for something small or valueless.

* *Cf.* You have *not* understood this?

They said *I can't see a speck* (Latin *punctum*), *we haven't had a crumb* (Latin *micam*), *I won't drink a drop* (Latin *guttam*). In the modern Romance languages the negative particle is still the Latin *non* (Italian *non*, Spanish *no*, Portuguese *não*, Rumanian *nu*), to which some such emphasizing element may be added; and in French a double-barreled negation (*ne-pas*) is obligatory. It arose in the following way. In Old French, *non* had just become *nen*, and later *ne*. It was often strengthened by other words. Some of them tallied with ones used in Vulgar Latin as above. One was new:

je ne vois point	I don't see a speck
je ne mange mie	I don't eat a crumb
je ne bois goutte	I don't drink a drop
je ne marche pas	I don't go a step—from Latin *passus*

The negative value of *ne* in the combinations in this list infected its bedfellows, which lost their original meaning and are now used only as negative particles. Two of them, *mie* and *goutte*, eventually disappeared. Two others, *pas* and *point*, have survived. By the sixteenth century it was the rule to use one of them in any negative statement. Today the most common form is *ne-pas*, and *ne-point* is only for emphasis. If *ne* is accompanied by another negative such as *personne* (nobody), *rien* (nothing), or *jamais* (never), the latter replace *pas* or *point*, e.g. *il ne me visite jamais* (he never looks me up). In popular French the process has gone further. While in Old French the *pas* was more often omitted than not, you now hear French people drop the emasculated *ne* and say *j'aime pas ça* (I don't like it), or *il dort pas* (he doesn't sleep). The French particle *ne* also keeps company with *que* and *guère* in a sense which does not imply negation. When *que* replaces *pas*, it signifies *only*, e.g. *je n'ai que deux sous* (I have only a penny). When *guère* takes its place, it means *scarcely*, e.g. *je ne la connais guère* (I hardly know her). Corresponding to the French *ne . . . que* for *only* we have the Italian *non . . . che*.

If we recall the wide range of *only* in English (p. 271) this construction should not puzzle us. As an adverb *only*, or its equivalent *merely*, involves a qualified negative. It implies *no more (and no less) than*, *no better than* or *not . . . with the exception*. Thus a Frenchman says *il n'a qu'un oeil* (he has no more than one eye, he has only one eye) or *je ne bois qu'aux repas* (I don't drink except at meals, I only drink at meals). This adverbial use of *only* in Romance as in Teutonic (p. 271) languages is quite distinct from that of the adjectival *only* meaning *sole, solitary, single, alone,* or *unique.* For *only* as adjective we have *seul(e)* or, less common, *unique* in French, *solo* or *unico* in Italian (Spanish *solo* or *único*).

Schoolbook knowledge of Latin does not always help us to link up a Romance word with its Latin forerunner. As a living language, Latin had a large stock of words which classical authors never used. Where they would write *equus* for horse, *iter* for journey, *os* for mouth, *ignis* for fire, *comedere* for eat, a citizen of the empire would say *caballus* (French *cheval,* Spanish *caballo,* Italian *cavallo*); *viaticum* (French *voyage,* Spanish *viaje,* Italian *viaggio*); *buca* (French *bouche,* Spanish *boca,* Italian *bocca*); *focus* (French *feu,* Spanish *fuego,* Italian *fuoco*); *manducare,* lit. *to chew* (French *manger,* Italian *mangiare*). In the schoolbooks the Latin word for house is *domus,* which was the name for the house of the well-to-do. Beside it Latin had *casa,* which signified the sort of house with which most Romans had to be content. *Casa* survives in Spanish and Italian, French has *maison* derived from *mansio* (mansion). Many words current in Romance languages go back to diminutive forms which abounded in Vulgar Latin, e.g. *auricula* (little ear) for the classical *auris* (French *oreille,* Italian *orecchio,* Spanish *oreja*), *geniculum* (little knee) for the classical *genu* (French *genou,* Italian *ginocchio*).

Though their common parentage has equipped the Romance dialects with an immense stock of recognizably similar words, some of the more common ones are totally different. For the act of speaking, classical Latin had two words, *loqui* and *fabulari.* The first was high-flown, the second informal. *Loqui* has disappeared, while the latter survives as *hablar* (see p. 244) in Spanish. Italy and France, on the other hand, borrowed a word from church language, *parabulare* (French *parler,* Italian *parlare*). It comes from the Latin word *parabula* (Greek *parobole*). By metaphor the gospel *parables,* i.e., *Christ's word,* came to mean *word* in general. Its semantic journey did not stop there. In its Spanish form (*palabra*) it degenerated from the speech of prophets to the speech of natives in the colonies, hence *palaver.* A similar cleavage is illustrated by the word for *shoulder.* In Spanish it is *hombro,* corresponding with the Latin word *humerus.* The French is *épaule,* and, like the Italian *spalla,* goes back to the Latin equivalent (*scapula*) for the shoulder blade. Classical Latin had two words for *beautiful.* One was *pulcher,* which was ceremonial. The other, *formosus* from *forma,* might be rendered by *shapely.* The former disappeared everywhere. The latter survived in Spain (*hermoso*) and Rumania (*frunos*). The common people of Rome said *bellus* (pretty), instead of *pulcher* or *formosus*. This word lives on in French (*beau* masc., *belle* fem.), in Italian and Spanish (*bello-bella*).

THE IBERIAN DIALECTS

Roman rule extended over more than six hundred years in the Iberian peninsula. Centuries before its end the speech of the conqueror had superseded that of the vanquished. The last reference to it is in the *Annals* of Tacitus. According to him a Tarragonian peasant under torture "cried out in the language of his forefathers." By that time Spain was completely Romanized. Seneca, Quintilian, and Martial were all Spaniards.

A splinter of an earlier type of speech survives as *Basque*, which people still speak on French and Spanish soil at the western end of the Pyrenees. Before the planes of Hitler and Mussolini rained death on them, Basque was the tongue of about half a million people. Spanish Latin has survived all invasions of historic times. At the beginning of the fifth century Germanic hordes, including the Vandals who gave their name to (*v*)Andalusia, overran the peninsula. Then the West Goths ruled for over two centuries, with Toledo as their capital. After them came the Arabs and Moors from Africa. The Muslims who subdued the whole country with the exception of the Asturian mountains, did not interfere with the religion or language of the people, and intermarriage was common under a benign regime. The Spanish national hero, Rodrigo Diez de Bivar, otherwise called the *Cid*, fought both for infidels and Christians. Cruelty and intolerance came with the *reconquista* started by Catholic princes in the unsubdued North.

The Catholic conquest of lost territory slowly spread fanwise toward the South, ending in 1492, when Ferdinand and Isabella appropriated Granada for the sacrament of inquisitorial fire. During the Moorish occupation the speech of the peninsula was still a mixture of dialects descended from Vulgar Latin. In the East, and more closely akin to the Provençal of South France, there was *Catalan;* in the North, *Leonese, Aragonese*, and *Asturian;* in the center *Castilian;* in the West, including Portugal, *Galician*. From Portugal, already a semi-independent province in the eleventh century and foremost as a maritime power under Henry the Navigator, what was originally a Galician dialect was carried to Madeira and the Azores, later to

Brazil. In the neighborhood of fifty million people now speak Portuguese. This figure includes about forty million inhabitants of Brazil, which became a sovereign state in 1822.

In Spain itself the emergence of a common standard was early. At the suggestion of Alfonso X, the Cortes of 1253 made the usage of Toledo the pattern of correct Spanish. Like Madrid and Burgos, Toledo was in Castile. Castilian, at first the vernacular of a handful of folk in the Cantabrian mountains on the Basque border, thus became what is now the official language of about ninety million people, including twenty-three million Spaniards, sixteen million Mexicans, thirteen million Argentinians, thirty million citizens of other South or Central American states, three millions in the Antilles, and one million in the Philippine Islands. American Spanish has some Andalusian features, partly because emigrants to the New World came mainly from the South, and partly because Cadiz was the commercial center of the colonies.

The vocabulary of a territory so repeatedly invaded inevitably has a large admixture of non-Latin words. Germanic tribes left fewer traces than in French, and these few connected with war and feudal institutions. Many hundreds of Arabic words bear testimony to what Spain owes to a civilization vastly superior to its Catholic successor. The sample printed below shows how Arabic infected all levels of the Spanish vocabulary. The ubiquitous *al-* of *algebra* is the Arabic *article* glued on to its noun.

	ARABIC	SPANISH
poor, paltry	misqîn	mezquino
water mill	as-sâniyat	aceña
mayor	al-qâdi	alcalde
constable	al-wazîr	alguacil
suburb	ar-rabad	arrabal
drain	al-ballâ'at	albañal
cistern	al-žubb	aljibe
coffin	at-tâbût	ataúd
young corn	al-qasîl	alcacel
jessamine	yâsamîn	jazmín
alcohol	al-quhl	alcohol
lute	al-'ûd	laúd

Nonetheless, the Spanish vocabulary is essentially a basic stratum of Vulgar with a superstructure of classical Latin. The same is true of Portuguese, which has fewer Basque and more French loan words.

Otherwise the verbal stock in trade of the two Iberian dialects is similar. Needless to say, a few very common things have different Spanish
and Portuguese, as some common things have different Scots, American, and English names, e.g.:

	SPANISH	PORTUGUESE
child	niño	criança, menino (a)
dog	perro	cão
knee	rodilla	joelho
window	ventana	janela
street	calle	rua
hat	sombrero	chapéu
knife	cuchillo	faca

It is not a hard task for anyone who has mastered one of the two
official Iberian languages, and has learned the tricks of identifying
cognate though apparently dissimilar words, to read a newspaper
printed in the other one. A similar statement would not hold good for
conversation. The phonetic differences between Spanish and Portuguese are sharp. The outstanding ones are summarized below:

1) Like French, Portuguese has nasalized vowels, and even (unlike
French) nasalized diphthongs. Nasalization has come about when a vowel
preceded *m* or *n*. These two consonants may be silent, or may have disappeared in writing. The *til* (˜) over the nasal vowel is then the tomb-
stone of one or other, as the French ˆ weeps over a departed *s*, e.g. Spanish
lana (wool), Portuguese *lã;* Spanish *son* (are), Portuguese *são;* Spanish
cristiano (Christian), Portuguese *cristão;* Spanish *pan* (bread), Portuguese *pão;* Spanish *buen* (good), Portuguese *bom;* Spanish *fin* (end),
Portuguese *fim*.
2) Between vowels Portuguese suppresses the Latin *l*, e.g. Latin *caelum*
(sky), Spanish *cielo*, Portuguese *céu;* Latin *salute* (health), Spanish *salud*,
Portuguese *saúde;* Latin *volare* (fly), Spanish *volar*, Portuguese *voar*. The
loss of *l* extends to the definite article and the corresponding unstressed
pronouns of the third person, i.e., *o* and *a, os*, and *as*, for what were once
lo and *la, los* and *las*. Thus *o porto = the* port. Through agglutination of
the article with the preposition *de* or *ad*, we get *do* and *da, dos* and *das*,
or *oa* and *á, aos* and *ás*, which recall the French forms *du, des,* or *au, aux*.
3) The initial Vulgar Latin *cl, fl, pl*, which often becomes *ll* in Spanish,
change to the *ch* (as in *champagne*) of Portuguese, e.g. Spanish *llave*
(key), *lleno* (full), *llama* (flame), Portuguese *chave, cheio, chama* (French
clef, plein, flamme). On this account the equivalence of one small group
of words is impossible to detect without a knowledge of sound shifts.
4) The initial Vulgar Latin *f* which often degenerates to a silent *h* in

Spanish remains in Portuguese, e.g. Portuguese *filho* (son), Spanish *hijo*.

5) While Portuguese stressed vowels *o* and *e* are conservative, they are replaced in Spanish by the diphthongs *ue* and *ie*, e.g. Portuguese *perna* (leg), *nove* (nine), *porta* (door), Spanish *pierna, nueve, puerta*.

6) Portuguese orthography shares with French the accents ‛ , ′ , ˆ , ˌ . The acute accent labels as such an open and stressed vowel, the circumflex a closed and stressed one, e.g. *pó*, powder (Spanish *polvo*), *pôr*, put (Spanish *poner*).

Grammatical differences between the two dialects are trifling. Portuguese discarded *haver* (Spanish *haber*) as a helper verb at an early date. As such it persists only in set expressions. Its modern equivalent is *ter* (Spanish *tener*). Hence *tenho amado* (I have loved), *tenho chegado* (I have arrived), for the Spanish *he amado* and *he llegado*. Both languages favor diminutives. The Spanish favorite is *-ito*, the Portuguese *-inho*. In one way Portuguese still lingers behind modern Spanish, French, or Italian. The agglutination of the infinitive with *habere* to form the future and the conditional is incomplete. In an *affirmative* statement the personal pronoun may slip between the infinitive and the auxiliary, e.g. *dir-me-as* (lit. tell me you have = you will tell me), *dar-vos-emos* (lit. give you we have = we shall give you).

FRENCH

The first Romance language to have a considerable literature was a dialect of the *Midi*, i.e., South of France. This *Provençal* had a flourishing cult of romantic poetry greatly influenced by Moorish culture. Its modern representatives are hayseed dialects of the same region. Closely related to it is the vernacular of the Spanish province of Catalonia, including its capital, Barcelona.

What is now French began as the dialect of the Parisian bourgeoisie. Owing to the political, cultural, and economic predominance of the capital, it spread throughout the monarchy, submerged local dialects and encroached upon Breton, which is a Celtic, and Flemish, which is a Teutonic language. It is now the daily speech of half Belgium, and of substantial minorities in Switzerland and Canada. In 1926 a compact body of forty million European people habitually used French, thirty-seven millions in France itself, excluding the bilingual Bretons, Alsatians, and Corsicans, three million Belgians and nearly a million Swiss. Outside Europe about three and a half millions in the French (or former French) dependencies and a million and a half Canadians use it daily. Canadian French has archaic and dialect peculiarities due to long linguistic isolation and the influence of early emigrants from Normandy.

French has twice enjoyed immense prestige abroad, first during the twelfth and thirteenth centuries when the victorious Crusaders carried it to Jerusalem, Antioch, Cyprus, Constantinople, Egypt, and Tunis, and again in the seventeenth and eighteenth. Five years before the Revolution the Royal Academy of Berlin set the following questions as theme for a prize competition: what has made the French language universal, why does it merit this prerogative, and can we presume that it will keep it? The winner was a French wit and chauvinist, named Rivarol. Rivarol's answer to the first and second was that French owed its prestige to its intrinsic merits, that is to say, to the order and construction of the sentence. ("What is not clear is not French. What is not clear is still English, Italian, Greek, or Latin.")

This is nonsense, as is the plea of some interlinguists, including the late Havelock Ellis, for revival of French as a world auxiliary. Its vogue as a medium of diplomacy was partly due to the fact that it was already a highly standardized language, but far more to a succession of extrinsic circumstances. From the Treaty of Westphalia (1648) till the collapse of Napoleon, France was usually in a position to dictate the terms of her treaties on the Continent. Before the period of enlightenment which preceded the Revolution the Court of Versailles was the cultural citadel of Absolutism. The Encyclopedists were the commercial travelers of English rationalism and the revolutionary wars emblazoned the fame of French culture in a new stratum of European society. The empire reinforced its prestige, but provoked a nationalistic reaction throughout Europe. After the defeat of Bonaparte its influence receded in Scandinavian countries, among the Russian aristocracy in Russia, where official foreign correspondence was conducted in French till about 1840, and in Egypt under the impact of British imperialism. Though it still has ostentation value as a female embellishment in well-to-do circles, unfamiliarity with French no longer stamps a person as an ignoramus among educated people. Neither Lloyd George nor Wilson could converse with the Tiger in his own tongue. That they could discuss the spoils without resource to an interpreter was because Clemenceau had lived in the United States.

ITALIAN AND RUMANIAN

The three Latin dialects discussed in the last few pages have transgressed the boundaries of sovereign states. Italian and Rumanian are essentially national, and other Latin descendants, e.g. Romansch in Switzerland, are local splinters, on all fours with Welsh or Scots Gaelic.

Phonetically Italian has kept closer to Latin than Spanish or French, and its vocabulary has assimilated fewer loan words. The oldest available specimens of Italian (A.D. 960 and 964) occur in Latin documents as formulae repeated by witnesses in connection with the specification of boundaries. Written records are sparse till the thirteenth century. By then Italy again had a literature of its own. The dominant dialect was that of Florence, which owed its prestige less to the poems of Dante, Petrarch, and Boccaccio than to a flourishing textile industry and wealthy banking houses. It has changed remarkably little since Dante's time. In 1926 there were forty-one million Italians in the peninsula, in Sicily, and in Sardinia. Less than a quarter of a million account for Italian minorities either in Switzerland or in Corsica.

Rumania corresponds roughly to the Roman province Dacia under the Emperor Trajan. From one point of view its official language is the English or Persian (p. 414) of the Latin family. Strange-looking words of Vulgar Latin origin mingle with Bulgarian, Albanian, Hungarian, Greek, and Turkish intruders. The Slavonic loan words predominate. Apart from its hybrid character, comparison with English or Persian breaks down. Rumanian grammar has not undergone great simplification. One odd feature mentioned on page 277 is reminiscent of the Scandinavian clan. In the Eastern Empire, Vulgar Latin favored the postposited article, e.g. *homo ille*, rather than the more Western *ille homo*. For that reason, the article is now agglutinated to the end of many Rumanian nouns in such contractions as *homul* = *homo ille* (the man), *lupul* = *lupu ille* (the wolf), *canele* = *cane ille* (the dog). Earliest Rumanian documents do not go back more than four hundred years and are ecclesiastical. Today fifteen million people speak the language.

FURTHER READING

BOURCIEZ   *Eléments de Linguistique Romane.*
GRANDGENT   *An Introduction to Vulgar Latin.*

CHAPTER IX

Modern Descendants of Latin

A BIRD'S-EYE VIEW OF FRENCH, SPANISH, PORTUGUESE, AND ITALIAN GRAMMAR

On the whole, differences between modern descendants of Latin are less than differences between the two main branches of the Teutonic family. The Teutonic dialects had drifted apart before differentiation of the Romance languages began. The Romance languages have many common features which they share with Vulgar Latin, and others which are products of parallel evolution. Because it is the most regular representative of the group, Italian offers the least difficulty to a beginner, especially to anyone who intends merely to get a reading knowledge of it. Our bird's-eye view will therefore deal mainly with Spanish and French. We shall discuss them together. The reader can assemble information appropriate to individual needs from different sections of this chapter, from tables printed elsewhere, or from relevant remarks in other chapters. With the aid of a dictionary, the reader, who is learning Portuguese or intends to do so, will be able to supplement previous tables of essential words (Chapters V and VIII or elsewhere) listing only French, Spanish, and Italian items.

The standpoint of *The Loom of Language* is practical. Our definition of grammar is knowledge essential for intelligible correspondence in a language or for ability to read it, other than information contained in a good dictionary. So we shall not waste space over what is *common* to the idiom of our own language and to that of those dealt with in this chapter. What the home student cannot find in a dictionary are tricks of expression or characteristics of word equivalence *peculiar* to them. There are illustrations of outstanding features of word order in the Romance languages in Chapter IV (p. 145 *et seq.*) and hints about pronunciation of French, Italian, and Spanish in Chapter VI (p. 249 *et seq.*). All there is need to say about comparison of the adjective is in Chapter VIII (pp. 332–336). Other grammatical peculiarities of Spanish, Portuguese, French, or Italian essential for reading or writing knowledge are included in three topics: (*a*) concord of noun and adjective, including plural formation; (*b*) vagaries of the definite article and of the pronoun; (*c*) verb flexion.

Of the Romance dialects dealt with, English-speaking people find Spanish easier than French. Italian is more easy than either. This is so for several reasons: (*a*) the sounds of Spanish (or Italian) are much more like those we ourselves use; (*b*) the spelling conventions of Spanish and Italian are much more consistent than those of French; (*c*) the Latin origin of the older—and therefore many of the more familiar—French words is hard to recognize, and they are therefore difficult to identify with English words of Latin origin (p. 232); (*d*) the entire apparatus of noun-adjective flexion is immensely more regular in Spanish and in Italian than in French. Thus the rules for plural formation of nouns admit less exceptions, and, what is more important, it is easier to detect the gender class of a noun from its ending. Apart from the greater regularity of their flexions, there are other features which bring Spanish or Italian into line with Anglo-American usage. One is a peculiar *durative* construction, equivalent to our own in expressions such as *I was waiting*.

NOUN AND ADJECTIVE

The *only* flexion of the noun now left in Romance languages marks distinction between singular and plural. In comparison with that of Teutonic languages other than English, plural formation of any Romance language is remarkably *regular*. On paper the typical *plural ending of Spanish, Portuguese, and French nouns and adjectives is -s, as in English*. This is partly due to the mastery (p. 327) of the oblique, in competition with the subject, case form. Otherwise the masculine singular form of French nouns might also end in -*s*, as do a few survivors, e.g. *fils* (son) and some proper names such as *Charles*.

Luckily for anyone who intends to learn the language, the regularity of *Italian* noun-adjective concord approaches that of Esperanto. Whether singular or plural, native Italian nouns end in a *vowel*. The subject case (see p. 327) of the Latin noun is the one which has survived in both numbers. Thus most Italian singular nouns end in -*a*, if feminine, or -*o* (cf. *muro* on p. 327) if masculine, according as they come from Latin ones of the first and second declensions. Most of the remainder are survivors of the third, and end in -*e*. In the PLURAL, -*a* changes to -e (Latin -ae) and -o or -e changes to -i. These rules admit *very* few exceptions. The only notable ones are:

a) Three common nouns have irregular plurals: *uomo-uomini* (man-men), *moglie-mogli* (wife-wives), *bue-buoi* (ox-en).

b) Masculine nouns of which the singular ending is an unstressed -a take -i in the plural, e.g. *poeta-poeti* (poet-s), *tema-temi* (theme-s), *dramma-drammi* (drama-s).

c) Some descendants of Latin neuters have singular masculine and plural feminine forms, e.g. *l'uovo-le uova* (the egg-s). We also have to use the plural terminal -a for *braccio, labbro, ginocchio* (arm, lip, knee) as for *il dito-le dita* (the finger-s) when we refer to a *pair*. These have alternate masculine plural forms with the ending -i, as have *frutto* (fruit), *legno* (wood), *dito* (finger), *osso* (bone).

d) Monosyllables, and all nouns which end in a stressed vowel are invariant like our *sheep*, e.g. *la città-le città* (the city—the cities).

e) In conformity with the consistent spelling rules of Italian (p. 354) a hard G before the singular terminals -O or -A becomes GH before the plural -I or -E, e.g. *lago-laghi* (lake-s), *luogo-luoghi* (place-s). Likewise the hard C of the feminine singular becomes CH, e.g. *amica-amiche* (friend-s). Masculine nouns *may* retain the hard sound, e.g. *fuoco-fuochi* (fire-s), *fico-fichi* (fig-s), *stomaco-stomachi*. Many masculines with final -CO have the soft sound of C before I in the plural, e.g. *amico-amici* (friend-s), *medico-medici, porco-porci* (pig-s).

The regular types are illustrated by:

corona	anno	fiore
(crown)	(year)	(flower)
corone	anni	fiori
(crowns)	(years)	(flowers)

Plural formation in Spanish or Portuguese is as regular as in English. All plural Spanish nouns end with -S. There is one noteworthy irregularity. Singular nouns which end in a consonant, in *y*, or an *accented* vowel take -es, e.g.:

corona	año	hombre	flor
(crown)	(year)	(man)	(flower)
coronas	años	hombres	flores
(crowns)	(years)	(men)	(flowers)

The same rule applies to Portuguese nouns, e.g. *livro-livros* (book-books), *pena-penas* (pen-pens). Portuguese nouns which end in -ão change it usually to *oes* in the plural, e.g. *nação-naçoes* (nation-s). Nouns ending in *-al, -el, -ol, -ul*, form the plural in *-ais, -eis, -ois, -uis*, e.g. *papel-papeis* (paper-papers). Nouns ending in *-m* change it to *-ns*, e.g. *homem-homens* (man-men).

There is this difference between French on the one hand and Spanish or Portuguese on the other. The French plural -S, like so many other flexional survivals of the written language, is often nothing more than a convention of the printed or written page. Unless the *next* word begins with a vowel—or a *mute* H (p. 254)—the plural -S is a dead letter. When it does precede a word beginning with a vowel, it sounds like *z*. Otherwise flexional distinction between singular and plural in spoken French is usually guaranteed only by the presence of the definite article *le* (masc. sing.), *la* (fem. sing.), or *les* (plur.); and the French use their definite article far more than we use our own. In fact, it has become a sort of *number-prefix*.

A small group of French nouns has not yet been brought into line with the prevailing pattern. The singular endings *-ail* or *-al* change to *-aux* in the plural, e.g. *émail-émaux, hôpital-hôpitaux*. Apart from these, there are a few vestiges of audible number distinction. The French word for the eye, *l'œil*, has the irregular plural *les yeux*. The ox, *le bœuf*, and the egg, *l'œuf*, lose their final *-f* in the spoken plural—*les bœufs* (pronounced *bö*), *les œufs* (pronounced *ö*). You will not be speaking the French of the textbook if you forget these irregularities and pronounce the plural of *œufs* and *bœufs* like the singular, or say *les œils* for *les yeux*, but you will be understood. You are merely doing what millions of modest Frenchmen themselves do. All that needs to be added is that nouns with the singular endings *-au, -eau, -eu* and *-ou* take *-x* instead of *-s* in the plural (e.g. *cheveux*, hair, *eaux*, waters, *genoux*, knees). This again is a paper distinction. The *x* is silent before a consonant, and pronounced as if it were *z* when the next word begins with a vowel.

To replace a French, Portuguese, Spanish, or Italian noun by the right pronoun, and to choose the right form of the adjective or the article to accompany it, we need to know the gender class to which it belongs. Any noun of a modern Romance language falls into one of two gender classes, masculine and feminine. Sometimes its meaning helps us to identify the gender class of a Romance noun. Three rules apply to the group as a whole: (*a*) male human beings and male domestic animals are masculine, female human beings and female domestic animals feminine; (*b*) names of days, months, and compass bearings are masculine; (*c*) most metals and trees are masculine, most fruits feminine. The reader can turn to the exhibits of Part IV to test these rules and to note exceptions.

Usually, we have to rely as best we can on the *ending*, as already illustrated by reference to Italian nouns. Two clues have turned up in what has gone before:

(*a*) Descendants of Latin masculines and neuters with the nominative singular endings -US and -UM are nearly always masculine. In Spanish, Portuguese, Italian, the corresponding terminal is -O.

(*b*) Descendants of Latin feminines with the nominative singular ending -A are also feminine and retain the same terminal in Spanish and Portuguese, as in Italian. In French it usually makes way for a mute -E. Portuguese nouns ending in -*ção* (Latin -*tione*) are feminine.

These two clues tell us how to deal with the enormous class of Italian, Spanish, and Portuguese nouns which have the singular terminals -O (*masc.*) or -A (*fem.*). Among Latin nouns which did not have the characteristic masculine, neuter, or feminine endings -US, -UM, -A in the nominative singular some had terminals which stamp the gender class of their descendants throughout the group. In the following list the Latin equivalent is the ablative case form.

LATIN	ITALIAN	SPANISH	FRENCH
MASCULINE			
-ALE *canale*	-ALE *canale*		-AL *canal*
-ENTE *accidente*	-ENTE *accidente*		-ENT *accident*
FEMININE			
-IONE *natione*	-IONE *nazione*	-ION *nación*	*nation*
-ATE *libertate*	-A *libertà*	-AD *libertad*	-É *liberté*
-TUDINE *gratitudine*	-TUDINE *gratitudine*	-TUD *gratitud*	-TUDE *gratitude*

Latin abstract nouns with the ablative singular terminal -*ore* were masculine. Their descendants stick to their original gender in Spanish and Italian, but have become effeminate in French:

LATIN	ITALIAN	SPANISH	FRENCH	ENGLISH
clamore	il clamore	el clamor	la clameur	clamor
colore	il colore	el color	la couleur	color
dolore	il dolore	el dolor	la douleur	pain
pudore	il pudore	el pudor	la pudeur	modesty
sapore	il sapore	el sabor	la saveur	taste (savor)
vapore	il vapore	el vapor	la vapeur	steam, vapor

Rules of this sort are not *absolutely* reliable. Even if a noun is masculine or feminine in Latin, its descendant in a daughter dialect does not invariably fall into the same gender class. Consequently knowledge of one Romance language is not an *infallible* guide to gender in another. This is illustrated by the following list:

LATIN		FRENCH	SPANISH	ITALIAN
flore	(*flower*), m.	fleur, f.	flor, f.	fiore, m.
lepore	(*hare*), m.	lièvre, m.	liebre, f.	lepre, f.
limite	(*limit*), m.	limite, f.	límite, m.	limite, m.
pulvere	(*dust*), m.	poudre, f.	polvo, m.	polvere, f.
sanguine	(*blood*), m.	sang, m.	sangre, f.	sangue, m.
aestate	(*summer*), f.	été, m.	estío, m.	estate, f.
dente	(*tooth*), m.	dent, f.	diente, m.	dente, m.
fronte	(*forehead*), f.	front, m.	frente, f.	fronte, f.
arte	(*art*), f.	art, m.	arte, m. *or* f.	arte, f.

A single common exception to the rule that Italian and Spanish -O nouns are masculine is the word for *hand*, which is feminine. Thus the white hand is *la mano blanca* (Span.), *la mano bianca* (Italian). Italian nouns of the *minority* class, i.e., those which do not have the singular terminals -*o* or -*a*, end in -E and are either masculine or feminine. There is an -E class in Spanish and Portuguese, and an even larger group of Spanish and Portuguese nouns which end in a *consonant*. Spanish nouns which have the singular endings -D or -Z are usually feminine.

Spaniards make a peculiar distinction between animate and inanimate objects. When the direct object is a *person* or its pronoun equivalent (demonstrative, interrogative, relative, and indefinite), it must be preceded by the preposition *a*, e.g. *veo a Don Juan* (I see Don Juan); *no he visto a nadie* (I have seen nobody); but *veo la plaza* (I see the square). The preposition *a* may also be used when the object is a familiar animal, e.g. *llama al perro*, he calls the dog. We omit it after *tener* (have) and *querer* (want),

LATIN	ITALIAN	SPANISH	PORTUGUESE	FRENCH	ENGLISH
ovo	uovo	huevo	ôvo	œuf	*egg*
vino	vino	vino	vinho	vin	*wine*
anno	anno	año	ano	an	*year*
aqua	aqua	agua	água	eau	*water*
porta	porta	puerta	porta	porte	*door*
bucca	bocca	boca	bôca	bouche	*mouth*

but not when *tener* means *hold* or *querer* means *love*, e.g. *tengo a mi amiga* (I am holding my friend).

Relatively few French nouns have an explicit gender label like the -*O* or -*A* endings of Spanish, Portuguese, and Italian. The original Latin vowel terminals which help to mark the gender of the Spanish, Portuguese, or Italian noun have disappeared or have changed past recognition. The preceding examples illustrate this.

The following rules are useful to the student of French, and the beginner who is not familiar with Latin or with another Romance language should learn them. French nouns are:

1) MASCULINE if they end in:

    a) -AGE, -AIRE, -ÈGE, -OIRE, -EAU.
    b) -E (*excluding* those ending in -TÉ and TIÉ).
    c) *Consonants* other than those mentioned below.

Examples: *l'héritage*, inheritance   *le laboratoire*, laboratory
          le vestiaire, cloakroom   *le vaisseau*, vessel, ship
          le collége, college   *le congé*, leave

2) FEMININE if they end in:

    a) -TÉ and -TIÉ.
    b) -ÉE.
    c) -E preceded by one or more consonants (e.g. *-ale, -ole, -ule; -be, -ce, -de; -fe, -ne, -pe*).

Examples: *la vanité*, vanity   *l'arrivée*, arrival
          l'amitié, friendship   *la viande*, meat

In all Romance languages the behavior of the adjective tallies closely with that of the noun, and in all of them there are two classes. What is always the larger class is made up of adjectives with four forms, i.e., separate masculine and feminine forms both singular and plural. The smaller class is genderless. Adjectives of this type have only two forms, singular and plural. The *singular* forms of Spanish,

Portuguese, and Italian adjectives of the larger class have the terminals -O (masc.) or -A (fem.). The genderless Italian adjective has the singular terminal -E, as have many genderless Spanish and Portuguese adjectives. Singular forms of other genderless Spanish and Portuguese adjectives end in a consonant. The plural forms of all Italian, Spanish, and Portuguese adjectives follow the same rule: *the plural form of the adjective is like the plural form of a noun with the same singular ending.*

The following examples therefore illustrate all essential rules for use of the Italian adjective:

un libro giallo	(a yellow book)	*un Duce loquace*	(a talkative leader)
libri gialli	(yellow books)	*Duci loquaci*	(talkative leaders)
una nazione ricca	(a rich nation)	*una macchina forte*	(a strong machine)
nazioni ricche	(rich nations)	*macchine forti*	(strong machines)

The Spanish equivalents for *black, poor,* and *common* sufficiently illustrate the use of appropriate forms of the Spanish or Portuguese adjective:

Sing. Masc.	negro		pobre	común
Sing. Femin.	negra			
Plur. Masc.	negros		pobres	comunes
Plur. Femin.	negras			

There is one noteworthy exception to the rules illustrated by these examples. Adjectives signifying *nationality* take the feminine terminals -*a* or -*as*, even if the masculine singular ends in a consonant, e.g. *inglés-inglesa, español-española.*

Representative exhibits of Portuguese noun-adjective concord are:

o navio novo	the new ship	*a pessoa simpática*	the congenial person
os navios novos	the new ships	*as pessoas simpáticas*	the congenial persons

o(a) aluno(a) inteligente	the intelligent pupil
os(as) alunos(as) inteligentes	the intelligent pupils

Genderless Portuguese adjectives ending in -*l* have contracted forms in the plural, e.g. *neutral, fácil, azul* (blue)—*neutraes, fáceis, azuis.*

The genderless class of French adjectives is relatively small. About the time of Agincourt the old genderless adjective got drawn into the orbit of the two-gender class. It assimilated the feminine ending -E, so that *fort* (strong), originally a common gender form, has now separate masculine (*fort*) and feminine (*forte*) singular and corresponding plural forms (*forts-fortes*). Genderless are *brave, large, juste, riche, vide* (empty), *triste* (sad), *facile* (easy), *difficile, rouge* (red), *tiède* (lukewarm), *terrible, humble, capable,* and others which end in *-ble.* The plural suffix of all these is -S *(rouges, faciles,* etc.). This rule applies to the separate masculine or feminine plural forms of most French adjectives which do not belong to the genderless class.

If we want to *write* the feminine equivalent of the masculine singular of most French adjectives, all we have to do is to add -E. What happens in speech is another story. The final consonant (p. 252) of most French words is silent. When the masculine singular form of the paper adjective ends in such a silent consonant (-T, -S, -ER, -N) addition of the -E makes the latter *articulate.* Thus the pronunciation of *vert* (masc.) and *verte* (fem.), meaning green, is roughly *vair-vairt.* Sometimes the final -T or -S is double in the written form of the feminine equivalent, e.g. *net-nette* (clean, distinct), *sot-sotte* (stupid), *gros-grosse* (big), *gras-grasse* (fat). Six adjectives ending in *-et* do not double the final consonant *(complet-complète, concret-concrète, discret-discrète, inquiet-inquiète,* uneasy, *replet-replète,* stout, *secret-secrète).* Those ending in *-er* change to *-ère,* with change of vowel color, e.g. *premier-première, régulier-régulière.* Vowel change also occurs if the masculine singular terminal is -N. This silent consonant symbol labels the preceding vowel as a *nasal* (p. 253). The vowel of the feminine form is not nasal. A silent -N becomes an explicit -NE or -NNE, e.g. *bon-bonne* (good), *plein-pleine* (full). Doubling of the last consonant before the final -E of the written form of the feminine also occurs if the masculine singular ends in the articulate terminals -EL or -UL, e.g. *cruel-cruelle* or *nul-nulle* (no). In the *spoken* language these adjectives belong to the genderless class.

A few irregularities among gender forms of the French adjective recall feminine forms of couplets which stand for persons (e.g. *masseur-masseuse).* Thus *-eux* becomes -EUSE, e.g. *glorieux-glorieuse, fameux-fameuse.* Similarly we have a *berger-bergère* (shepherd-shepherdess) class represented by *premier-première.* As *-eux* becomes *-euse, -aux,* and *-oux* become -AUSSE and -OUSE, e.g. *faux-fausse* (false), *jaloux-jalouse* (jealous). As with the couplet *veuf-veuve* (widower-widow), -F changes to -VE, e.g. *neuf-neuve* (new), *bref-brève.* Four apparent exceptions to rules given depend on the fact that there are alternative masculine singular forms. One which ends in a vowel precedes a word beginning with a consonant. The other precedes a word beginning with a vowel or *h.* These masculine couplets are *nouveau-nouvel* (new), *beau-bel* (beautiful), *vieux-vieil* (old), *mou-mol* (soft), as in *un vieil homme* (an old man), *un vieux* *mur* (an old wall) or *un beau garçon* (a fine boy), *un bel arbre* (a beautiful tree). The feminine derivatives correspond to the second or older number of the couplet in conformity with the rules stated, e.g. *nouvelle, belle, vieille, molle,* i.e., *une vieille femme,* or *une belle dame.*

The few irregular masculine plural forms of the adjective recall those of nouns with the same singular terminals. If the singular ends in *-s* or *-x* there is no change. Thus *il est heureux* = he is happy, and *ils sont heureux* = they are happy. If the masculine singular ends in -EAU or -AL, the masculine plural terminals are respectively -EAUX or -AUX, as in *beau-beaux, nouveau-nouveaux,* or *cardinal-cardinaux.* The corresponding feminine forms are regular, e.g. *nouvelles* or *cardinales.* The masculine plural of *tout* (all) is *tous.* The corresponding feminine forms are regular (*toute-toutes*). When *tous* stands by itself without a noun the final *s* is always articulate.

The position of the epithet adjective in Romance languages is not as rigidly fixed as in English. As a rule (which allows for many exceptions) the adjective comes after the noun. This is nearly always so if the adjective denotes color, nationality, physical property, or if it is longer than the noun. The two ubiquitous Spanish adjectives *bueno* and *malo* usually precede, and the masculine singular forms are then shortened to *buen* and *mal,* e.g. *un buen vino* (a good wine), *un mal escritor* (a bad writer). French adjectives usually placed before the noun are:

beau-belle (beautiful), *joli-jolie* (pretty), *vilain-vilaine* (ugly), *bon-bonne* (good), *mauvais-mauvaise* (bad), *méchant-méchante* (wicked), *meilleur-meilleure* (better), *grand-grande* (great, tall), *gros-grosse* (big), *petit-petite* (small), *jeune* (young), *nouveau-nouvelle* (new), *vieux-vieille* (old), *long-longue* (long), *court-courte* (short).

Both in Spanish and French almost any adjective may be put before the noun for the purpose of emphasis, e.g. *une formidable explosion,* though the same effect is achieved by leaving it at its customary place and stressing it. This shunting of the adjective is much less characteristic of everyday language than of the literary medium which pays attention to such niceties as rhythm, euphony, and length of words. Sometimes a difference of position goes with a very definite difference of meaning. Where there is such a distinction the adjective following the noun has a literal, the adjective preceding it a figurative, meaning. When *gran* appears *before* the Spanish noun it signifies quality, e.g. *un gran hombre,* a great man; when placed *after,* size, *un hombre grande,* a tall man. The same is true of French. In French *un brave homme* is *a decent chap, un homme brave* is *a brave man; un livre triste* is *a sad sort of book, un triste livre* is *a poor sort of book.*

THE ARTICLE IN THE ROMANCE LANGUAGES

All forms of the Romance definite article (as also of the Romance pronoun of the *third* person) come. from the Latin demonstrative ILLE, etc. (p. 329). The form of the definite article depends on the number and gender of the noun, but the choice of the right form is complicated by the initial sound of the noun itself, and by agglutination with prepositions. When it is not accompanied by a preposition, the range of choice is as follows:

	FRENCH	PORTUGUESE	SPANISH *	ITALIAN
Masc. Sing.	LE ⎱ L'	O	EL	IL (or LO) ⎱ L'
Fem. Sing.	LA ⎰	A	LA (or EL)	LA ⎰
Masc. Plur.	⎱ LES	OS	LOS	I (or GLI-GL')
Fem. Plur.	⎰	AS	LAS	LE or L'

Our table shows a bewildering variety of alternatives. So far as Spanish * is concerned, the only choice which calls for explanation is the occasional use of *el* before singular feminine nouns. *La* precedes all feminine singular nouns except those which begin with a *stressed A* (or *HA*), e.g. *el agua—las aguas* (the water-s). This also applies to the indefinite article. For the sake of euphony the masculine form *un* replaces the feminine *una*, e.g. *un aria* (a tune), *un hacha* (an axe). If a Spanish feminine noun begins with an *unstressed A* (*la ambición*), we have to use the ordinary feminine form. If a French *singular* noun of *either gender* or if an Italian singular masculine noun begins with a vowel (or *h* in French) we have to use the truncated *l'*, as in the table that follows. Exceptions to the rule that *l'* precedes words beginning with H are words (p. 254) of Teutonic and of Greek origin (e.g. *héros*). Choice of the Italian article is complicated by: (*a*) the existence of a special singular form *lo* for masculine nouns which begin with Z or with S followed by another consonant (SB, SP, ST) cf. *il padre* (the father) *lo zio* (the uncle); (*b*) the masculine *gli* which replaces *i* before plural nouns beginning

* The table omits one form of the Spanish article. Spanish preserves a separate neuter article, *lo*. It has the sole function of raising a singular adjective, participle, etc., to the status of a noun, e.g. *lo Americano*, what is American; *lo útil*, what is useful; *lo dicho*, what has been said.

with (1) vowels, (2) with Z or with S followed by a consonant. The table illustrates these rules:

ENGLISH	FRENCH	PORTUGUESE	SPANISH	ITALIAN
a) *a field*	un champ	um campo	un campo	un campo
the field	le champ	o campo	el campo	il campo
the fields	les champs	os campos	los campos	i campi
b) *a door*	une porte	uma porta	una puerta	una porta
the door	la porte	a porta	la puerta	la porta
the doors	les portes	as portas	las puertas	le porte
c) *a friend*	un ami	un. amigo	un amigo	un amico
the friend	l'ami	o amigo	el amigo	l'amico
the friends	les amis	os amigos	los amigos	gli amici

Unfortunately, our troubles with the vagaries of the Romance article do not end here. Both the definite articles and the demonstratives of Romance languages are addicted to romantic attachments to prepositions. The preposition of Vulgar Latin was unstressed, like the demonstrative (definite article) which often went with it. So the two got fused. Such agglutination did not go very far in Spanish. It is confined to the singular masculine article and the two prepositions *de* and *a; de + el* became *del* (of the), and *a + el* became *al* (to the, by the), e.g. *el mal humor del maestro* = the bad mood of the teacher (but *de los maestros*); *el bote al faro* = the boat at the lighthouse (but *a los faros*). In written Spanish these two are the only contractions of the kind. In French, agglutination is confined to the same prepositions, but extends to the plural form, as shown in the following table:

	OLD FRENCH	MODERN FRENCH
Sing.	*del* (*de + le*)	*du*
Plur.	*dels* (*de + les*)	*des*
Sing.	*al* (*à + le*)	*au*
Plur.	*als* (*à + les*)	*aux*

In ancient French the masculine singular and plural article also agglutinated with the preposition *en* (Latin *in*) to *el* and *ès*. The former died out. The latter survives in the titles of university degrees such as *docteur ès lettres*, doctor of literature, *docteur ès sciences*, doctor of science.

From this point of view, French is a halfway house between Spanish and Portuguese. Portuguese is a halfway house between French and Italian. The agglutination of Portuguese prepositions to the article, which has lost the initial Latin L, are as follows:

PREPOSITION (Latin equivalent in italics)	DEFINITE ARTICLE			
	O	A	OS	AS
a (= *ad*)	ao	à	aos	às
de	do	da	dos	das
em (= *in*)	no	na	nos	nas
por (= *per*)	pelo	pela	pelos	pelas

The Portuguese prepositions *de* and *em* also agglutinate to the pointer words of which the masculine singular forms are *êste, êsse, aquele*. This gives rise to *dêste, dêsse, daquele*, or *neste, nesse, naquele*, and corresponding feminine singular, masculine plural, or feminine plural forms. Italian has a luxuriant overgrowth of such fusions between preposition and article:

	IL	I	LO	GLI	LA	LE	L'
di, of	del	dei	dello	degli	della	delle	dell'
da, from, by	dal	dai	dallo	dagli	dalla	dalle	dall'
a, to	al	ai	allo	agli	alla	alle	all'
in, in	nel	nei	nello	negli	nella	nelle	nell'
con, with	col	coi	collo	cogli	colla	colle	coll'
su, on	sul	sui	sullo	sugli	sulla	sulle	sull'
per, for	pel	pei	per lo (pello)	per gli (pegli)	per la (pella)	per le (pelle)	per l' (pell')

In modern Romance languages, and in none more than in French, the definite article is now an almost inseparable bedfellow of the noun. Consequently it has lost any personality it once had. We have to use it in many situations where no Anglo-American article occurs. Thus it appears before collective or abstract nouns, e.g. *l'homme* or *la nature*, names of substances, e.g. *le fer* (iron), names of countries, e.g. *le Canada*, names of colors, e.g. *le bleu* (blue) and the generic plural, e.g. *j'aime les pommes* (I like apples). It was not always so. In early French, as in other Romance languages, it was not the custom to put the definite article before an abstract noun, e.g. *covoitise est racine de toz mals* for *la convoitise est la racine de tous les maux* (envy is the root of all evils). This accounts for its absence in some set expressions (see also p. 393) such as: in French, *avoir raison* (be right), *avoir tort* (be wrong), *prendre garde* (take care), *prendre congé* (take leave), *demander pardon* (ask forgiveness); in Spanish, *oir misa* (hear mass), *hacer fiesta* (take a holiday), *dar fin* (finish); in Italian, *far onore* (do honor), *correr pericolo* (run a risk), *prender moglie* (take a wife). Where we use the indefinite article *a* or *an* before names of professions and trades, its equivalent is absent in Romance languages, as in German. Thus the French say *il est médecin* = he is *a* doctor, and the Spaniards say *es médico*.

One of the pitfalls of French is correct use of what grammar books call the *partitive article*. Wherever English-speaking people *can* use *some* or *any* to signify some indefinite quantity of a whole, as in *I had some beer*, the French *must* put before the object the preposition *de* together with the definite article (e.g. *du, de la, des*). Thus the French say: *buvez du lait* (drink milk), *j'ai acheté de la farine* (I have bought flour), *est-ce que vous avez des poires?* (have you pears?), and even abstractly, *il me témoigne de l'amitié* (he shows me friendship). This *article partitif* is a trademark of *modern* French. The habit goes back to late Latin. It occurs in the Vulgate and tallies with the idiom of the *Mayflower* Bible, e.g. *catelli edunt de micis* = the dogs eat *of the* crumbs (Matt. 15, 27). The partitive article may even be prefaced by a preposition, as in *je le mange avec du vinaigre* (I eat it with vinegar). The French *de* is used *alone*, i.e., *without* the definite article:

a) After *beaucoup* (much, many), *peu* (little, few), *pas* (no), *plus* (more), *trop* (too much, too many), e.g. *je n'ai pas de monnaie* (have no money), *j'ai trop de temps* (I have too much time).

b) If the noun is preceded by an adjective, e.g. *j'ai vu de belles maisons* (I have seen some nice houses).

The second of the two rules is generally ignored in colloquial French.

The partitive article occurs also in Italian, e.g. *dammi del vino*. It is NOT compulsory. Spanish and Portuguese usually do without it, but have a peculiar plural equivalent for *some*, not comparable to that of other European languages. The indefinite article has a plural form, e.g.:

	SPANISH	PORTUGUESE
a book	*un libro*	*um livro*
some books	*unos libros*	*uns livros*
a letter	*una carta*	*uma carta*
some letters	*unas cartas*	*umas cartas*

THE ROMANCE PERSONAL PRONOUN

Our tables of personal pronouns (see below and pp. 331 and 332) and possessives (p. 370) do not give equivalents for IT or ITS. The reason is that Romance nouns are either masculine or feminine. What is given as the French, Spanish, or Italian equivalent for SHE is the subject pronoun which takes the place of a female human being, a

ROMANCE PERSONAL PRONOUNS—Stressed * Forms

	ME	(THEE)	HIM	HER	US
FRENCH	MOI	TOI	LUI	ELLE	NOUS
PORTUGUESE	MIM	TI	ÊLE	ELA	NÓS
SPANISH †	MÍ	TÍ	ÉL	ELLA	NOSOTROS
ITALIAN	ME	TE	LUI	LEI	NOI
			(ESSO)	(ESSA)	

	YOU	THEM (m.)	THEM (f.)	REFLEXIVE
FRENCH	VOUS	EUX	ELLES	SOI
PORTUGUESE	VÓS	ÊLES	ELAS	SI
SPANISH †	VOSOTROS	ELLOS	ELLAS	SÍ
ITALIAN	VOI	LORO		SÈ
		(ESSI)	(ESSE)	

* Stressed forms always used when preceded by a preposition.
† There is a stressed neuter Spanish pronoun ELLO (= *it*): *see* footnote page 359. For feminine forms of NOSOTROS, VOSOTROS *see* page 331.

female domestic animal and any group, inanimate object, or abstraction placed in the feminine-gender class. Analogous remarks apply to any other pronoun of the third person. Equivalents of *he, him, his* stand for pronouns which replace a masculine noun; equivalents for *she, her, hers* for pronouns which replace a feminine noun; and what is listed as the equivalent of *he* or *him, she* or *her* would correspond to our *it*, when the latter refers to anything sexless.

The pronoun of Romance, as of other European languages, has been more resistant to flexional decay than the noun, and choice of the correct form is one of the most troublesome things for a beginner. This is so for several reasons:

1) Pronouns of the third person have separate direct object (*accusative*) and indirect object (*dative*) forms.

2) Pronouns of all three persons have separate *unstressed* (conjunctive) forms as subject or object of an accompanying verb and *stressed* (disjunctive) forms for use after a preposition and in certain other situations.

3) The rules of concord for the possessive of the third person have nothing to do with the gender of the possessor.

4) Pronouns may agglutinate with other words.

5) Pronouns of the second person have different *polite* and familiar forms.

The personal flexions of the Portuguese, Spanish, and Italian verb are still intact. It is customary to use Portuguese, Spanish, or Italian verbs without an accompanying subject pronoun, though the latter is handy for emphasis or greater clarity, e.g.:

ENGLISH	FRENCH	PORTUGUESE	SPANISH	ITALIAN
he is good	*il est bon*	*é bom*	*es bueno*	*è buono*

We cannot omit the French subject pronoun. Indeed, it has no separate existence apart from the verb. In answer to a question, the Spaniard, Portuguese, or Italian will use *yo, eu, io*. Except in the legal *je soussigné*, the Frenchman does not use *je* in answer to a question, he uses the stressed *moi* where we usually say *me*, e.g.:

Qui l'a fait?   *Moi.*   Who did it?   Me (= I did).

This rule applies to French pronouns of all persons in so far as there are distinctive stressed forms (*moi, toi, lui, eux*). In the same situation the Italian uses the stressed form for the *third* person (*lui, loro*). The Frenchman uses the stressed forms whenever the pronoun: (*a*) is detached from its verb, (*b*) stands alone. Frenchmen never use them next to the verb, e.g.:

a) Lui, mon ami!   He, my friend!
b) Moi, je n'en sais rien.   I (myself) know nothing about it.
c) Je ferai comme toi.   I'll do as you (do).

There are emphatic French forms of *myself, himself,* etc.: *moi-même, lui-même,* etc. The Spanish equivalent of *même* is *mismo(s)-misma(s)*. The unstressed subject form precedes it, unless it emphasizes a noun, e.g.:

lo hago yo mismo	I do it myself
mi mujer misma	my wife herself

In all the Romance languages dealt with in this chapter the stressed forms are the ones we have to use after a preposition, and they take up the same place in the sentence as the corresponding noun, e.g.:

English	*I came without her.*
French	Je suis venu sans elle.
Portuguese	Tenho vindo sem ella.
Spanish	He venido sin ella.
Italian	Sono venuto senza ella.

The unstressed direct or indirect object form is overshadowed by the verb, which it immediately precedes or follows. We always have to use it when there is no preceding preposition in a statement or question. It always comes before the French verb, and nearly always does so in Spanish and Italian *statements,* e.g. *Je t'aime beaucoup* (French), *Te amo mucho* (Span.), *Ti amo molto* (Ital.) = I love you a lot. Portuguese is out of step with its sister dialects. In simple affirmative Portuguese sentences the object usually follows the verb and a hyphen connects them, e.g.:

êle procura-me	= he is looking for me
dá-me o livro	= he gives me the book

In negative statements of all the four principal Romance languages, the object pronoun (whether direct or indirect) precedes the verb, e.g.:

English	*I don't see it.*
French	Je ne le vois pas.
Portuguese	Não lo vejo.
Spanish	No lo veo.
Italian	Non lo vedo.

The rules on page 148 for placing the object in a statement do not tell us where to put it in a command (or request) on the one hand, and a *question* on the other. The Romance object pronoun always comes *after* the *imperative* verb, if the imperative is affirmative, but *before* the verb if a prohibition, e.g. French *embrace-la* (kiss her), *ne l'embrace pas* (don't kiss her). The direct object is always the accusative unstressed form; but in *French, moi* and *toi* replace *me* and *te* as the *indirect* object, e.g. *donnez-moi de l'eau* (give me some water).

In French and Portuguese, the hyphen indicates the intimate relation of the unstressed form to the verb imperative, as in the following examples, which illustrate agglutination of two pronoun objects (*me-o = mo*) in Portuguese:

> *dê-me un livro* = give me a book
> *dê-mo o senhor* = give it (to) me (sir)

It is customary to write the Spanish and Italian imperative, infinitive and participles without a gap between the verb and the object, e.g.:

ENGLISH	SPANISH	ITALIAN
show me	muéstrame	mostrami
I want to speak to him	quiero hablarle	voglio parlargli

Fusion of verb to its pronoun object goes further in Italian: (*a*) the infinitive (e.g. *parlare*) drops the final E as in the last example; (*b*) the infinitive drops -RE if it ends in -RRE (e.g. *condurre*) as in *condurlo* = to direct him; (*c*) there is doubling of the initial consonant of the pronoun if the imperative ends in a vowel with an accent, e.g. *dammi* = give me, *dillo* = say it. With *con* (with) the stressed Italian pronouns *me, te, se* fuse to form *meco* (with me), *teco* (with thee), *seco* (with him, *or* with her). The three Spanish *stressed* pronouns *mí, tí, sí*, get glued to *con* to form *conmigo, contigo, consigo*. Agglutination goes further in Portuguese. With *com* we have *comigo, contigo, consigo, connosco, convosco* (with me, with thee, etc.). Similarly the unstressed Portuguese *me, te, lhe*, glue on to the direct object of the third person to form *mo-ma-mos-mas, to*, etc., and *lho*, etc., e.g.:

> *Dá-tos* = He gives them to you (thee)

The Portuguese direct object forms of the third person have alternative forms *lo-la-los-las* for use *after* -R, -S, or -Z. If the preceding pronoun is *nos* or *vos*, the latter drop the S:

> *Dá-no-lo* = He gives it to us
> *Dá-vo-lo* = He gives it to you

Thus the same rules for the position of two pronoun objects do not apply to French on the one hand and Spanish or Italian on the other:

a) The Spanish and Italian direct object pronoun follows the indirect, e.g. *no te lo daré* = I shall not give it to you = *non ti lo darò*. This rule applies to statement, question, or command (request), e.g. in Spanish *corregídmelo*, correct it for me.

b) If the French indirect object is a pronoun of the first or second person the same rule holds for a simple *statement*, e.g. *je ne le te donnerai pas* = I shall not give you it.

c) If the French indirect pronoun object is of the third person, it follows the direct object, e.g. *je le lui dirai* = I shall tell him it.

d) The French direct object precedes the indirect one in a *positive* command, and the indirect object has the *stressed* form, e.g. *corrigez-le-moi* = correct it for me.

e) If both Spanish pronoun objects are of the third person SE takes the place of the indirect object which retains its usual place, e.g. *se lo diré* = I shall tell him it.

f) *Negative* commands of all four languages have the same word order as statements.

Our list of unstressed French pronouns should include two peculiar forms which are troublesome. These are *en* and *y*. In colloquial French the former refers to persons and things (or propositions), whereas the latter is generally used for things (and propositions) only. Both are descendants of Latin adverbs of place, *en* from *inde* (thence), *y* from *ibi* (there). Both *en* and *y* may preserve this old locative meaning, *en* for *in, to, from*, etc., and *y* for *here, there, thither*, e.g. *en province* (in the country), *j'y sera* (I shall be there). In Vulgar Latin *inde* and *ibi* often replaced the pronoun of the third person, e.g. *si potis inde manducare*, e.g. lit. *if you can eat (from) it; adjice ibi ovum*, e.g. *add an egg there* (= to it). The French often use the pronoun *en* where we say *some* or *any*, e.g. *en avez-vous?* (have you any?), or where we say *of it, about it, from it*, e.g. *j'en ai assez* (I have enough of it), *nous en parlerons* (we shall talk about it), *il en pourrait mourir* (he might die of it). Also note: *en voilà une surprise!* = what a surprise!

As pronouns equivalent to IT, *en* and *y* keep company with a special class of verbs. The French equivalents for some English verbs which do not precede a preposition always go with *de* (*of* or *from*), e.g. *se servir de* = to use. If the inanimate object IT then accompanies the English verb, we translate it by *en* which always follows another pronoun object, e.g. *je m'en sers* = I use it. Another expression of this class is *avoir besoin de*, e.g. *j'en ai besoin* = I need it. In the same way *y* is the equivalent for *it* or *to it* when the preposition *à* follows the French verb. Since *penser à* means *to think* (*about*), *j'y pensais* means *I was thinking about it*.

The Italian descendant of *inde* is *ne*, as in *quanto ne volete?* how much do you want (of it)? *me ne ricordo,* I remember it. For both functions of the French *y*, Italian has *ci* (Latin *ecce-hic*), *vi* (Latin *ibi*). These are interchangeable, e.g. *ci penserò* (I shall see to it), *vi è stato* (he has been there). Neither *inde* nor *ibi* has left descendants in Spanish or Portuguese. For French *j'y penserai* the Spaniard says *pensaré en ello.*

We have still to discuss the reflexive and possessive forms of Romance personal pronouns. Our own words *myself*, *yourself*, etc., have to do two jobs. We can use them for *emphasis*, and we can use them *reflexively*. Whenever we use them reflexively (e.g. *wash yourself*) in the first or second persons, the equivalent word of a modern Romance dialect is the corresponding unstressed direct object form. For the third person there is a single reflexive pronoun for singular or plural use. It is a current Anglo-American habit to omit the reflexive pronoun when the context shows that we are using a verb reflexively. This is never permissible in Spanish, Portuguese, French, or Italian. The identity of the reflexive and direct object pronoun is illustrated by the first two of the following. The last illustrates the use of the common singular and plural reflexive of the third person:

	FRENCH	SPANISH
I wash	*je me lave*	*me lavo*
we wash	*nous nous lavons*	*nos lavamos*
they wash	*ils se lavent*	*se lavan*

Romance languages have many pseudoreflexive verbs, such as the French verbs *se mettre à* (Italian *mettersi*), to begin, *se promener*, to go for a walk (Spanish *pasearse*), *s'en aller*, to go away (Spanish *irse*), *se souvenir*, remember (Spanish *acordarse*), or the impersonal *il s'agit de* . . . (it is a question of):

elle se mit à pleurer	*allez-vous-en*
she began to cry	go away (beat it)
no me acuerdo de éso	*ella se pasea en el parque*
I don't remember that	she walks in the park

The reflexive pronoun may give the verb a new meaning. In French *je doute qu'il vienne* means: I doubt whether he will come, and *je m'en doute* means: I think so.

The Latin reflexive *se* of the third person is common to Portuguese, Spanish, and French. The unstressed Italian reflexive is *si*, stressed *sè*. The Portuguese reflexive follows the verb like an ordinary Portuguese pronoun object, e.g. *levanto-me* (I get up). The Spanish *se* does two jobs. When the direct and indirect object are *both* of the third person, a Spaniard uses *se* for the indirect object (*le*, *les*), or for the unstressed dative form, e.g. *se lo digo* (I tell it to him = I say so to him).

Possessive pronouns and adjectives (p. 104) of modern Latin dialects are descendants of the old Latin forms *meus* (my), *tuus* (thy), *suus* (his, her, its, their) or of *illorum* (of those), and *noster, voster* (our, your). French and Italian derive the possessive of the third person plural from the Latin genitive *illorum* (French *leur*, Italian *loro*), Spanish and Portuguese from the reflexive *suus*. Like English, Spanish and French have two sets of possessives (cf. *my-mine*), contracted (*possessive adjectives*), which accompany a noun, and fuller ones (*possessive pronouns*) which stand alone. For an English-speaking student of the Romance languages the chief difficulty about possessives is mastery of the gender forms. Our single surviving trace of possessive concord involved in the choice between *his-its-her* refers solely to the *possessor*. Neither the grammatical gender nor the sex of the *possessor* shows up in the form of the Romance possessive adjective or pronoun. In French:

> *son père* = his *or* her father
> *sa mère* = his *or* her mother
> *ses parents* = his *or* her parents

Thus the gender form of the Romance pronoun depends on the thing or person *possessed*. The masculine singular French forms *mon, ton, son*, replace *ma, ta, sa* before a feminine noun beginning with a vowel (or *h*), e.g. *mon amie* (my girl friend) and *mon ami* (my boy friend). Unlike the unstressed *invariant* dative *leur*, the possessive *leur* has a plural (*leurs*), e.g. *leur maison—leurs maisons* = their house(s). The Spanish *su* does the job of *his, her, its, their*, or *your* in any context unless ambiguity might arise; and countless ambiguities can arise from this type of concord. If the Spaniard wishes to make it clear that *su casa* stands for *his house*, he says *su casa de él*, in contradistinction to *su casa de ella* (her house) or *su casa de ellos* (their house). Similarly the Frenchman may say *son père à lui* (his father) or *son père à elle* (her father). The combinations *à moi, à lui*, etc., can replace *le mien, la sienne*, etc., as in *c'est à moi* (it is mine), *c'est à lui* (it is his).

Both in Italian and Portuguese the possessive adjective has the same form as the possessive pronoun. When used attributively, the possessive takes the definite article, e.g. Italian *il mio braccio* (my arm), Portuguese *o meu braço*. The definite article is omitted after *essere* or *ser*, meaning *belong to*, e.g. Italian *la casa è mia* (the house is mine), Portuguese *a casa é minha*. The Spanish possessive adjective has two forms, a shorter which prefaces the noun without the article, e.g. *mi casa*, and a more emphatic one which is put after the noun with the article, e.g. *la casa mía*. The latter also acts as pronoun, and in this capacity takes the article as in French, *ella olvidó el suyo*, i.e., *saco* (she forgot hers, i.e., bag).

ROMANCE POSSESSIVES

	FRENCH	PORTUGUESE	SPANISH	ITALIAN
a) Adjectives:				
MY	*mon* (m.) *ma* (f.) *mes* (pl.)	*meu, minha* *meus, minhas*	*mi*(s)	*mio*, etc.
THY	*ton*, etc.	*teu, tua,* *teus, tuas*	*tu*(s)	*tuo*, etc.
HIS, HER, ITS	*son*, etc.	*seu*, etc. (like *teu*)	*su*(s)	*suo*, etc.
OUR	*notre, nos* (pl.)	*nosso*, etc.	*nuestro*, etc.	*nostro*, etc.
YOUR	*votre, vos* (pl.)	*vosso*, etc.	*vuestro*, etc.	*vostro*, etc.
THEIR	*leur*(s)	*seu*, etc.	*su*(s)	*loro*
b) Pronouns:				
MINE	*le mien,* *la mienne,* *les miens,* *les miennes*	as above preceded by the definite article	*mío*, etc.	as above preceded by the definite article
THINE	*le tien*, etc.		*tuyo*, etc.	
HIS, HERS, ITS	*le sien*, etc.		*suyo*, etc.	
OURS	*le* or *la nôtre* *les nôtres*		(as above)	
YOURS	*le vôtre*, etc.			
THEIRS	*le, la, les* *leur*(s)		*suyo*(s)	

POLITE ADDRESS

One of the booby traps of the Romance languages is choice of pronouns (and possessives) appropriate to intimate or formal address.

Roman citizens addressed one another as *tu*. The *thou* form of French, Spanish, Portuguese, and Italian is now the one used to address husband or wife, children, close relations, and intimate friends. There is a French verb *tutoyer* (German *duzen*) which means *to speak familiarly*, that is, to address a person as *tu* in preference to the more formal *vous* (French *vouzoyer*, German *siezen*).

In the days of the Roman Empire, *nos* (we) often replaced the emphatic *ego* (I). This led to the substitution of *vos* for *tu*. The custom began in the upper ranks of Roman society. Eventually *vos* percolated through the tiers of the social hierarchy till it reached those who had only their chains to lose. So *vous* is now the polite French for *you*. The verb which goes with it has the plural ending, while the adjective or past participle takes the gender and number of the person addressed. Thus the Frenchman says *Madame, vous êtes trop bonne* (how kind of you, Madam), but *Monsieur, vous êtes trop bon*. In spite of the Revolution of 1789, the French often use *Monsieur, Madame* and *Mademoiselle* with the third person, e.g. *Madame est trop bonne*.

Spaniards and Italians have pushed deference further by substituting a less direct form for the original *vos* (Span.) or *voi* (Ital.). The Italian uses *lei* (or more formally *ella*) = she, with the third person singular, e.g. *lei è americano?* (you are American?). *Lei* is the pronominal representative for some feminine noun such as *vossignoria* (Your Lordship). The plural of *lei* is *loro*. In Italian conversation we can often omit *lei* and *loro*. Instead we can use the third person without pronoun, e.g. *ha mangiato?* (have you eaten?).

When a Spaniard addresses a single individual who is not an intimate or a child, he uses *usted* (written *V.* or *Vd.* for short) instead of *tu*. The corresponding pronoun for use when addressing more than one person is *ustedes* (*Vs.* or *Vds.*). *Usted* is a contraction of *vuestra merced* (Your Grace). Consequently the verb appears in the third person, as in Italian, e.g. *cómo se llama usted?* (what is your name?), *cómo se llaman ustedes?* (what are your names?). In very short statements or questions we can omit *usted*, e.g. *qué dice?* (what do you say?).

Portuguese is more extravagant than either Spanish or Italian. The usual equivalent for our *you* when it stands for a male is *o senhor*, and for a female *a senhora*, or (in Brazil) *a senhorita*. So the Portuguese for the simple English *have you got ink?* is *tem o senhor* (or *a senhora*) *tinta?* Our catalogue of polite behavior would be incomplete without the Balkan equivalent. The Rumanian for the polite *you* is the periphrastic *domnia voastra* (Latin *domina vostra*, Your Lordship). The polite forms of our invariant YOU in Italian and Spanish are in the table that follows.

	SPANISH				ITALIAN			
	Singular		Plural		Singular		Plural	
	Masc.	Fem.	Masc.	Fem.	Masc.	Fem.	Masc.	Fem.
Subject (YOU)	USTED		USTEDES		LEI		LORO	
Indirect Object (TO YOU)	LE		LES		LE(GLIE)			
Direct Object (YOU)	LO	LA	LOS	LAS	LA		LI	LE

IMPERSONAL ROMANCE PRONOUNS

Five English words (p. 136) make up a battery of what we shall here call *impersonal pronoun-adjectives*. They are: *this, that, which, what, who(m)*. All except the last (*who* or *whom*) can stand as pointer words alone (*demonstrative pronouns*) or before a noun (*demonstrative adjectives*). In questions the last three can also stand alone (*interrogative pronouns*) or in front of a noun (*interrogative adjectives*). All of them except *this* can introduce a subordinate clause. They are then called *relative* (or *link*) *pronouns*. To this battery of five essential words corresponds a much larger group in any Romance dialect. Choice of the right equivalent for any one of them is complicated by several circumstances, in particular:

a) Romance equivalents of any one of them may have distinct forms as adjectives or as pronouns comparable to the separate adjective and pronoun forms of our possessives (e.g. *my-mine*).

b) The Romance equivalent for any one of them may depend on whether it occurs in a question, whether it links two statements, or whether it is a pointer word.

To help the home student through this maze, there are separate tables (pp. 374–376) in which the same five English impersonal pronouns turn up. Capitals or small letters respectively show whether the Romance equivalent is: (*a*) the pronoun form which stands alone (e.g. *read that*, or *what?*), (*b*) the adjective form before a noun (*read this book*, or *which book?*). Italicized capitals signify that the word can be either. Some are unchangeable, like *what*. Others like *this* or *that* take endings in agreement with the nouns they qualify or replace. If so, the final vowel is italicized to show that it is the masculine singular ending. We then have to choose from one of all four possible *regular* forms. The tables show which ones are irregular, and give appropriate forms in full.

Corresponding to two singular demonstratives *this* and *that* of Anglo-American, some British dialects have *this*, *that*, and *yon*. The three grades of proximity in this series correspond roughly to the Latin sets of which the masculine singular forms were *hic*, *iste*, *ille*. Two of them went into partnership (cf. *this* . . . *here*) with *ecce* (behold), which survives in the French *cet* (Latin *ecce iste*) and *celle* (*ecce illa*).

Spanish and Portuguese preserve the threefold Latin Scots distinction: *este*, *esta*, *estos*, *estas* = this (*the nearer one*), *ese*, *esa*, *esos*, *esas* = that (*the further*), *aquel*, *aquella*, *aquellos*, *aquellas* = yon (remote from both speaker and listener). All three sets can stand alone or with a noun like our own corresponding pointer words. When they stand alone (as pronouns) they carry an accent, e.g. *esta golondrina y aquélla* (this swallow and yonder one). All three, like the article *lo* (p. 359) have neuter forms, *esto*, *eso*, *aquello*, for comparable usage. The corresponding threefold set of Portuguese demonstratives are: *êste* (*-a, -es, -as*), *êsse* (*-a, -es, -as*), *aquele* (*-a, -es, -as*). Spaniards like the Germans, reverse the order for *the former* . . . *the latter* = *éste* (the nearer) . . . *aquél* (the further). The Italian order *quello* . . . *questo* is the same as ours.

The distinction between the adjective and pronoun equivalents of *this-these* and *that-those* in French involves much more than an accent on paper. Where we use them as adjectives the French put *ce* or *cet* (masc. sing.), *cette* (fem. sing.) or *ces* (plur.) in front of the noun, and *ci* (here) or *là* (there) behind it, as in:

ce petit paquet-ci	this little parcel	*ce petit paquet-là*	that little parcel
cette bouteille-ci	this bottle	*cette bouteille-là*	that bottle
ces poires-ci	these pears	*ces poires-là*	those pears

In colloquial French the *là* combination has practically superseded the *ci* form, and serves in either situation.

ROMANCE POINTER WORDS AND RELATIVE PRONOUNS
(see p. 372)

	FRENCH	SPANISH	ITALIAN
a) Demonstratives			
this	CELUI-CI (CECI) CELLE-CI (*f*) ce(t) ....ci ⎫ cette.....ci ⎬ ces ......ci ⎭	ESTE (-*A*, -*OS*, -*AS*)	QUESTO (-*A*, -*I*, -*E*)
that	CELUI-LÀ (CA) CELLE-LÀ (*f*) ce(t) ....là ⎫ cette.....là ⎬ ces ......là ⎭	ESE (-*A*, -*OS*, -*AS*) AQUEL (-*LA*, -*LOS*, -*LAS*)	QUELLO (-*A*, -*I*, -*E*)
which	quel (-*le*, -*s*, -*les*)	cual (-*es*)	quello (-*a*, -*i*, -*e*)

b) Link pronouns—*never omitted*

	FRENCH	SPANISH	ITALIAN
THAT		QUE	CHE
WHAT	CE QUE	⎫	CIÒ CHE
WHO, WHICH (that) (as *subject*)	QUI	⎬ QUE	⎫
WHOM, WHICH (that) (as *object*)	QUE	⎭	⎬ CHE
WHOM (after a preposition)	QUI	⎫	⎭
WHICH (after a preposition)	LEQUEL (LAQUELLE, LESQUELS, LESQUELLES)	⎬ QUIEN (-*ES*)	⎧ IL *or* LA QUALE ⎨ I *or* LE QUALI
WHOSE, OF WHICH	DONT (DE QUI [*persons*] DUQUEL, etc., p. 377 [*things*])	DE QUIEN (-*ES*) (CUYO, -*A*, -*OS*, -*AS*)	IL *or* LA ⎫ I *or* LE ⎬ CUI

To translate the adjective *this-these* (in contradistinction to *that-those*) we can use the simpler form *ce*, etc., without -*ci*, e.g. *ce journal* (this newspaper), *cet ouvrier* (this workman), *cette jeune fille* (this young woman), *ces instruments.*

Where we would say *here* or *there is* (*was* or *were*), *look there goes* or *lo and behold*, French people use the invariant pointers *voici* or *voilà*. Historically they are agglutinations between the singular imperative of *voir* (to see) and the locative particles *ci* (= *ici*) and *là*. So *voici* (Old French *voi ci*) once meant *see here*, and *voilà* (Old French *voi la*) *see there*. Both occur in modern French, but conversational language tends toward using *voilà* without discriminating between *here* and *there*. The following examples show how these gesture substitutes are used: *voici mon chèque* (here is my check), *la voilà* (here or there she is), *le voilà parti* (*off he goes* or *went*), *voilà deux ans que* (it is now two years that).

The Italian equivalent is *ecco* (Latin *eccum*), as in *eccolo* (here he is), *ecco un fiammifero* (here is a match).

The following French examples illustrate the use of the eight pronouns corresponding to *this-these* or *that-those* (see table p. 374), when they refer to (*a*) *le chapeau* (the hat), (*b*) *les chapeaux* (the hats), (*c*) *la noix* (the nut), (*d*) *les noix* (the nuts):

a) *je préfère celui-ci*   *je préfère celui-là*
  I prefer this one   I prefer that one

b) *Ceux-ci sont trop chers*   *Ceux-là sont trop chers*
  These are too dear   Those are too dear

c) *Casse celli-ci*   *Casse celle-là*
  Break this one   Break that one

d) *Elle a acheté celles-ci*   *Elle a acheté celles-là*
  She has bought these   She has bought those

There are two other French pronouns, *ceci* and *cela* (commonly abbreviated to *ça*) corresponding respectively to *this* and *that*, e.g. *ne dites pas ça* = don't say that. We can never use them for persons. *Ce* (*c'*) often stands for *it*, e.g. *c'est vrai* = it is true, *c'est triste* = it is sad. After the invariant *ce*, the adjective can keep the masculine singular form, e.g. *c'est bon* may mean either *il est bon* or *elle est bonne* according as *il* refers to *le vin* or *elle* to *la bière*. This is useful to know, when we are in doubt about the gender of a noun. The French for *the former . . . the latter* is *celui-là . . . celui-ci*.

This is a pointer word pure and simple. *That* can also be a link word, and as such appears twice in the table of link pronouns. It does so because we use it in two ways:

a) THAT so printed occurs after such verbs as *know, doubt, deny, hope, wish, fear, dread.* We can usually omit it, but we can never replace it by *who* or *which.* Its Romance equivalent as given in the table cannot be left out, e.g.:

English	*I know that he is lying.*
French	je sais qu'il ment.
Portuguese	sei que minte.
Spanish	sé que miente.
Italian	so che mente.

b) *that* so printed may refer to some word in the preceding clause and is then replaceable. We can put *who, whom,* or *which* in place of it (e.g. *the house that Jack built = the house which Jack built*).

To translate *that* in all circumstances we therefore need to know equivalents for *who, which, whom,* and *whose* when such words link two clauses. Choice is complicated: (*a*) by case forms like *whom* or *whose* for use with or without an accompanying preposition, (*b*) by the distinction between persons (*who*) and animals or things (*which* or *what*), (*c*) by the existence of interchangeable forms analogous to our own *that-which* couplet. For self-expression we need only know

ROMANCE INTERROGATIVES

(see p. 372)

	FRENCH	SPANISH	ITALIAN
a) Adverbial.			
how?	comment	cómo	come
how much? how many?	combien	cuánto (-*a*, etc.)	quanto (*a*, etc.)
when?	quand	cuándo	quando
where?	où	dónde	dove
why?	pourquoi	por qué	perchè
b) Pronouns and Adjectives.			
which?	quel (etc.) LEQUEL (etc.)	CUÁL (-*ES*)	QUALE (-*I*)
who? whom?	QUI	QUIÉN (-*ES*)	CHI
what? (subject or object)	QUE	QUÉ, QUÉ COSA	CHE, CHE COSA
what? (after a preposition)	QUOI	QUÉ	CHE

one correct substitute, preferably the most common. For illustrations of the use of the table on page 374 we shall confine ourselves to Spanish and French.

As subject or object of a subordinate clause the common Spanish equivalent for *who, whom* or *which* is the invariant QUE, e.g.:

el médico que me ha curado = the doctor who has cured me
los libros que hemos lecho = the books (which) we have read

In all circumstances *que* is the correct Spanish equivalent for the link pronoun *which* or *that*, but it cannot replace *whom* when a preposition accompanies the former of the two. The correct substitute for *whom* is then QUIEN or its plural *quienes*, e.g. *los políticos de quienes hablamos* = the politicians of whom we are talking. A special Spanish relative pronoun CUYO (*-a, -os, -as*) equivalent to *whose* or *of which* can refer alike to persons or things, e.g.:

el tren cuya partida = the train, whose departure. . . .
las islas cuyas rocas = the islands, of which the rocks. . . .

French offers a bewildering choice of possibilities for words of this class, some appropriate to persons only, some to persons and things. The following rules apply to persons or things *alike:*

a) QUI can always replace *who* or *which* as subject of a clause, e.g. *l'homme qui l'a dit* = the man who said it, *le train qui est arrivé* = the train which came in.

b) QUE can always replace *who*(*m*) or *which* as object, e.g. *le médecin que j'ai consulté* = the doctor whom I consulted, *les biscuits que j'ai mangés* = the biscuits I ate.

c) DONT can always replace *whose* or *of which*, e.g. *la femme dont le mari est prisonnier* = the woman whose husband is a prisoner.

d) LEQUEL (*laquelle, lesquels, lesquelles*) can always replace *whom* or *which* preceded by a preposition (or, what comes to the same thing, *that* followed by a preposition at the end of the subordinate clause). *Lequel*, etc., has agglutinative contractions with *à* and *de*, i.e., *auquel, auxquels, auxquelles* (but *à laquelle*), *duquel, desquels, desquelles* (but *de laquelle*).

la femme pour laquelle il a donné sa vie.
the woman for whom he gave his life.

The words *who, whom, whose, which*, as also *what*, can turn up in questions as interrogative pronouns. Both *which* and *what* can also accompany a noun in a question. The choice of the correct French substitute depends on whether they do or do not. The French interrogative adjective is QUEL (*quelle, quels, quelles*), e.g. *quelle route dois-je suivre?* (which road must I follow?). *Quel*, etc., has also an exclamatory use (e.g. *quel dommage!* = what a pity!). When a question involves the verb *to be* followed by a noun, *what* or *which* are really predicative (p. 149) adjectives. So we can say:

quelle est votre opinion?	what is your opinion?
quels sont leurs amis?	which are their friends?

The French *pronoun* substitute for *which?* is LEQUEL (etc.). Like QUI, which can stand for *who?* or *whom? lequel*, etc., can follow a preposition. The French for *what* falls out of step. As subject or object it is QUE. After a preposition the correct equivalent is the stressed form QUOI.* The use of these pronouns is illustrated by:

Lequel de ces enfants est votre fils?	Which of these kids is your boy?
Duquel parles-tu?	Of which are you talking?
Qui l'a dit?	Who said so?
De qui parle-t-il?	Of whom is he talking?
Que dit-il?	What does he say?
De quoi parle-t-il?	What is he talking about?

The Spanish for *who? whom?* is *quién*, for *what? qué*. In conversation we usually replace *qué* by *qué cosa. Which* is *cuál* (plural *cuáles*):

quién canta?	who is singing?
qué ha dicho?	what did he say?
cuál de las viñas?	which of the vineyards?

Cuál takes the place of *qué* (what) before *ser* (to be) when the noun follows, e.g. *cuál es su impresión?* (what is your impression?).

Our list of personal and impersonal pronouns in the tables given makes no allowance for situations in which the agent is *indefinite* or generic (e.g. *you never can tell, one wouldn't think that . . . , they say that . . .*). In medieval Latin, and perhaps in the popular Latin of Caesar's time, the equivalent of our *indefinite* pronouns *one* (*they* or *you*), was *homo* (*man*), e.g. *homo debit considerare* (one must consider). Since *homo* was unstressed in this context, it shrunk. In French it became *on*, in contradistinction to *homme* (man). To avoid a hiatus, *on* becomes *l'on* after *et* (and), *si* (if), *ou* (or), and *où*

---

* Both French *qui* (who?) and *que* (what?) have alternative forms. We may ask *qui est-ce qui?* for *qui?*, or *qu'est-ce que* for *que?* Spoken French favors the longer of the two forms, e.g. *qui est-ce qui veut venir avec moi? = qui veut venir avec moi?* (who wants to come with me?), *qu'est-ce que vous désirez, monsieur? = que désirez-vous, monsieur?* (what do you want?).

ROMANCE INDEFINITE POINTER WORDS *

ENGLISH	FRENCH	SPANISH	ITALIAN
ALL	tout (-e), tous, toutes	todo (-a, -os, -as)	tutto (-a, -i, -e)
AS MUCH (MANY) ... AS	autant de . . . que	tanto (-a, etc.) . . . como	tanto (-a, etc.) . . . come
BOTH	tous (toutes) les deux	ambos (-as)	ambedue
CERTAIN	certain (-e)	cierto (-a)	certo (-a)
EACH, EVERY (adj.)	chaque *	cada *	ogni * ciascuno (-a)
EACH ONE, EVERY ONE	chacun (-e)	cada uno (-a)	ognuno (-a) ciascuno (-a)
ENOUGH	assez de	bastante (-s)	abbastanza *
EVERYTHING	tout	todo	tutto
LITTLE, FEW	peu de	poco (-a)	poco (-a), pochi, poche
MUCH, MANY	beaucoup de	mucho (-a)	molto (-a)
NO (adj.)	aucun (-e)	ninguno (-a)	nessuno (-a)
NOBODY	personne	nadie	nessuno (-a)
NOTHING	rien	nada	niente nulla
OTHER	autre (-s)	otro (-a)	altro (-a)
ONE	on	se	si
ONLY (SOLE)	seul (-e)	único (-a)	solo (-a) unico (-a)
SAME	même (-s)	mismo (-a)	stesso (-a) medesimo (-a)
SEVERAL	plusieurs	varios (-as)	parecchi, parecchie
SOME (A FEW)	quelques (see p. 362)	algunos (-as) unos (-as) (see p. 363)	alcuni (-e) (see p. 361)
SOMEBODY	quelqu'un (-e)	alguien	qualcuno (a)
SOMETHING	quelque chose	algo alguna cosa	qualchecosa
SUCH	tel (-le), tels, telles	tal (-es)	tale (-i)
TOO MUCH (MANY)	trop de	demasiado (-a)	troppo (-a)
WHOEVER	quiconque	cualquiera	chiunque

* Invariable

(where). Parallel evolution has produced the indefinite German, Dutch, or Scandinavian *man*, which is derived from *Mann*, etc. The French equivalent *on* has a far greater range than the English *one*. We *must* always use it as subject of the active verb when there is no definite agent of the equivalent English passive construction. The following examples illustrate its variegated use:

on pourrait dire	one might say
on dit	they say = it is said
on ferme!	closing time—we're locking up!
on demande une bonne	wanted, a maidservant
on sonne	somebody is ringing
si l'on partait	what about leaving?
on pardonne tant que l'on aime	we forgive as long as we love

There is no equivalent idiom in Spanish or Italian. The indefinite pronoun of Spanish or Italian is the reflexive. Thus the Spaniard says *se dice* (or simply *dicen*) for *it is said* (= they say), *se cree* (or *creen*) = *it is believed* (they believe). Similarly the Italian says *si crede* (one believes), *si sa* (one knows).

THE ROMANCE VERB

During the breakup of Vulgar Latin and subsequent evolution of its descendants, simplification of the verb did not go nearly so far as that of the noun. Even today the tense system of the Romance languages is more elaborate than that of the Teutonic languages has ever been. According to the character of their tense or personal endings, the verbs of Romance languages are arranged in classes called *conjugations* (p. 95).

REGULAR FRENCH VERB TYPES

	CHANTER	VENDRE	FINIR	PARTIR
Present	chant-e	vend-s	fin-is	par-s
	chant-es	vend-s	fin-is	par-s
	chant-e	vend	fin-it	par-t
	chant-ons	vend-ons	fin-issons	part-ons
	chant-ez	vend-ez	fin-issez	part-ez
	chant-ent	vend-ent	fin-issent	part-ent
Imperfect	chant-ais	vend-ais	fin-issais	part-ais
	chant-ais	vend-ais	fin-issais	part-ais
	chant-ait	vend-ait	fin-issait	part-ait
	chant-ions	vend-ions	fin-issions	part-ions
	chant-iez	vend-iez	fin-issiez	part-iez
	chant-aient	vend-aient	fin-issaient	part-aient

REGULAR FRENCH VERB TYPES (*continued*)

		CHANTER	VENDRE	FINIR	PARTIR
Past Definite		chant-ai	vend-is	fin-is	part-is
		chant-as	vend-is	fin-is	
		chant-a	vend-it	fin-it	(see *fin-.*)
		chant-âmes	vend-îmes	fin-îmes	
		chant-âtes	vend-îtes	fin-îtes	
		chant-èrent	vend-irent	fin-irent	
Future		chant-erai	vend-rai	fin-irai	part-irai
		chant-eras	vend-ras	fin-iras	
		chant-era	vend-ra	fin-ira	(see *fin-.*)
		chant-erons	vend-rons	fin-irons	
		chant-erez	vend-rez	fin-irez	
		chant-eront	vend-ront	fin-iront	
Con-ditional		chant-erais	vend-rais	fin-irais	part-irais
		chant-erais	vend-rais	fin-irais	
		chant-erait	vend-rait	fin-irait	(see *fin-.*)
		chant-erions	vend-rions	fin-irions	
		chant-eriez	vend-riez	fin-iriez	
		chant-eraient	vend-raient	fin-iraient	
Present Sub-junctive		chant-e	vend-e	fin-isse	part-e
		chant-es	vend-es	fin-isses	part-es
		chant-e	vend-e	fin-isse	part-e
		chant-ions	vend-ions	fin-issions	part-ions
		chant-iez	vend-iez	fin-issiez	part-iez
		chant-ent	vend-ent	fin-issent	part-ent
Imperative		*chant-e	vend-s	fin-is	par-s
		†chant-ez	vend-ez	fin-issez	part-ez
Present Participle		chant-ant	vend-ant	fin-issant	part-ant
Past Participle		chant-é	vend-u	fin-i	part-i

* Singular of familiar form.
† Plural of familiar form, and singular and plural of polite form.

We can group regular French verbs in three conjugations (p. 24). The first, like our weak class, includes the majority of verbs in the language, and nearly all *new* ones. It consists of those (about four thousand) like *chanter* (sing), of which the infinitive ends in -ER.

The second fairly large class (about 350) embraces verbs like *finir* (finish) of which the infinitive ends in -IR. The third is made up of about fifty verbs like *vendre* (sell), of which the infinitive ends in -RE. A small group of about twenty verbs which end in -IR are also worth considering as a separate family. It is made up of words like *partir* (go away), and *dormir* (sleep), which are in constant use. These verbs lack the trademark of the *finir* conjugation. Verbs of the *finir* class have a suffix added to the stem throughout the plural of the present, throughout the imperfect tense and the subjunctive. This suffix, -ISS, comes from the Latin accretion -ISC or -ESC which originally indicated the beginning of a process. Thus the Latin verb for *to burst into flower* is *florescere*. The same suffix, which survives in *evanescent, putrescent, incandescent, adolescent,* lost its meaning through too frequent use in Vulgar Latin.

With the models shown in the table on pages 380 and 381 to guide him (or her) and the *parts* listed in any good dictionary, the home student of French can add to the stem of most (footnote, p. 394) *irregular* verbs the ending appropriate to the context. The overwhelming majority of verbs are regular, and fall into one of the conjugations listed. To write French passably, it is therefore essential to learn a model of each conjugation as given in the table on pages 380 and 381 and to memorize the personal terminals of each tense. To lighten the task the home student may find it helpful to make tables of (*a*) personal terminals common to all tenses, (*b*) personal terminals common to the same tense of all conjugations. *Fortunately, we can get by in real life with much less* (see p. 394). For reading purposes what is most essential is to be able to recognize the tense form.

Within the three conjugations a few deviations from the rule occur: -*er* verbs which have a silent E or an É in the second last syllable, change E or É to È before the endings -*e*, *es*, and -*ent*, e.g. *mener* (lead), *je mène* (I lead), *posséder* (possess), *je possède* (I possess). All verbs ending in -*ler* or -*ter*, double L or T instead of having È, e.g. *appeler* (call), *j'appelle* (I call), *jeter* (throw), *je jette* (I throw). Verbs in -*ayer*, -*oyer*, -*uyer*, substitute I for Y before a silent E or a consonant, e.g. *essayer* (attempt), *j'essaie* (I attempt). If C before A or O has the value of a sibilant, a *cedilla* (ς) is added, e.g. *percer* (pierce), *nous perçons* (we pierce). G in the same situation takes a silent E unto itself, e.g. *manger* (eat), *nous mangeons* (we eat). If the third person singular of the verb in a question has a final vowel and precedes a pronoun beginning with a vowel, a T is inserted to avoid a hiatus, e.g. *aime-t-il, parle-t-on, viendra-t-elle.*

We may also arrange Spanish, Portuguese, or Italian, like French verbs, in three main conjugations, of which there are models set out in tables on pages 383, 384, and 385. The largest Spanish group, corresponding to the *chanter* conjugation in French, is represented by *cantar* with the infinitive ending -AR. *Vender*, like the French (third) *vendre* conjugation, is representative of a second class with the in-

REGULAR SPANISH AND PORTUGUESE VERB TYPES

		a) SPANISH			b) PORTUGUESE		
Present		cant-o	vend-o	part-o	cant-o	vend-o	part-o
		cant-as	vend-es	part-es	cant-as	vend-es	part-es
		cant-a	vend-e	part-e	cant-a	vend-e	part-e
		cant-amos	vend-emos	part-imos	cant-amos	vend-emos	part-imos
		cant-áis	vend-éis	part-is	cant-ais	vend-eis	part-is
		cant-an	vend-en	part-en	cant-am	vend-em	part-em
Imperfect		cant-aba	vend-ía	part-ía	cant-ava	vend-ia	part-ia
		cant-abas	vend-ías	part-ías	cant-avas	vend-ias	part-ias
		cant-aba	vend-ía	part-ía	cant-ava	vend-ia	part-ia
		cant-ábamos	vend-íamos	part-íamos	cant-ávamos	vend-íamos	part-íamos
		cant-ábais	vend-íais	part-íais	cant-aveis	vend-ieis	part-ieis
		cant-aban	vend-ían	part-ían	cant-avam	vend-iam	part-iam
Past Definite		cant-é	vend-í	part-í	cant-ei	vend-i	part-i
		cant-aste	vend-iste	part-iste	cant-aste	vend-este	part-iste
		cant-ó	vend-ió	part-ió	cant-ou	vend-eu	part-iu
		cant-amos	vend-imos	part-imos	cant-ámos	vend-emos	part-imos
		cant-asteis	vend-isteis	part-isteis	cant-astes	vend-estes	part-istes
		cant-aron	vend-ieron	part-ieron	cant-aram	vend-eram	part-iram
Future		cant-aré	vend-er é	part-ir é	cant-arei	vend-erei	part-irei
		cant-arás	vend-erás	part-irás	cant-arás	vend-erás	part-irás
		cant-ará	vend-erá	part-irá	cant-ará	vend-erá	part-irá
		cant-aremos	vend-eremos	part-iremos	cant-aremos	vend-eremos	part-iremos
		cant-aréis	vend-er éis	part-ir éis	cant-areis	vend-ereis	part-ireis
		cant-arán	vend-erán	part-irán	cant-arão	vend-erão	part-irão
Conditional		cant-aría	vend-ería	part-iría	cant-aria	vend-eria	part-iria
		cant-arías	vend-erías	part-irías	cant-arias	vend-erias	part-irias
		cant-aría	vend-ería	part-iría	cant-aria	vend-eria	part-iria
		cant-aríamos	vend-eríamos	part-iríamos	cant-aríamos	vend-eríamos	part-iríamos
		cant-arías	vend-eríais	part-iríais	cant-aríeis	vend-eríeis	part-iríeis
		cant-arían	vender-ían	part-irían	cant-ariam	vend-eriam	part-iriam
Present Subjunctive		cant-e	vend-a	part-a	cant-e	vend-a	part-a
		cant-es	vend-as	part-as	cant-es	vend-as	part-as
		cant-e	vend-a	part-a	cant-e	vend-a	part-a
		cant-emos	vend-amos	part-amos	cant-emos	vend-amos	part-amos
		cant-éis	vend-áis	part-áis	cant-eis	vend-ais	part-ais
		cant-en	vend-an	part-an	cant-em	vend-am	part-am
	*	cant-a	vend-e	part-e	cant-a	vend-e	part-e
	†	cant-ad	vend-ed	part-id	cant-ai	vend-ei	part-i
	‡	cant-ando	vend-iendo	part-iendo	cant-ando	vend-endo	part-indo
	§	cant-ado	vend-ido	part-ido	cant-ado	vend-ido	part-ido

* Imperative singular (familiar form). For imperative of polite address, see p. 402.

† Imperative plural (familiar form).

‡ Present participle (gerund).

§ Past participle.

finitive ending -ER. A third, represented by *partir*, has the infinitive ending -IR.

The student of Spanish, even more than the student of French, has to concentrate on the correct use of the verb. The terminals of the Spanish verb are much closer (p. 176) to those of its Latin parent than are those of the French or Italian verb; but change of stress has led to changes of the stem vowel, and irregularities so produced have been leveled less than in French. So the stem of a verb, whose French equivalent usually has the same vowel throughout, may ring the

REGULAR ITALIAN VERB TYPES

		CANTARE	VENDERE	FINIRE	PARTIRE
Present		cant-o	vend-o	fin-isco	part-o
		cant-i	vend-i	fin-isci	part-i
		cant-a	vend-e	fin-isce	part-e
		cant-iamo	vend-iamo	fin-iamo	part-iamo
		cant-ate	vend-ete	fin-ite	part-ite
		cant-ano	vend-ono	fin-iscono	part-ono
Imperfect		cant-ava	vend-eva	fin-iva	part-iva
		cant-avi	vend-evi	fin-ivi	part-ivi
		cant-ava	vend-eva	fin-iva	part-iva
		cant-avamo	vend-evamo	fin-ivamo	part-ivamo
		cant-avate	vend-evate	fin-ivate	part-ivate
		cant-avano	vend-evano	fin-ivano	part-ivano
Past Definite		cant-ai	vend-ei	fin-ii	part-ii
		cant-asti	vend-esti	fin-isti	part-isti
		cant-ò	vend-è	fin-ì	part-ì
		cant-ammo	vend-emmo	fin-immo	part-immo
		cant-aste	vend-este	fin-iste	part-iste
		cant-arono	vend-erono	fin-irono	part-irono
Future		cant-erò	vend-erò	fin-irò	part-irò
		cant-erai	vend-erai	fin-irai	part-irai
		cant-erà	vend-erà	fin-irà	part-irà
		cant-eremo	vend-eremo	fin-iremo	part-iremo
		cant-erete	vend-erete	fin-irete	part-irete
		cant-eranno	vend-eranno	fin-iranno	part-iranno
Con-ditional		cant-erei	vend-erei	fin-irei	part-irei
		cant-eresti	vend-eresti	fin-iresti	part-iresti
		cant-erebbe	vend-erebbe	fin-irebbe	part-irebbe
		cant-eremmo	vend-eremmo	fin-iremmo	part-iremmo
		cant-ereste	vend-ereste	fin-ireste	part-ireste
		cant-erebbero	vend-erebbero	fin-irebbero	part-irebbero

REGULAR ITALIAN VERB TYPES (*continued*)

		CANTARE	VENDERE	FINIRE	PARTIRE
Present Sub- junctive		cant-i	vend-a	fin-isca	part-a
		cant-i	vend-a	fin-isca	part-a
		cant-i	vend-a	fin-isca	part-a
		cant-iamo	vend-iamo	fin-iamo	part-iamo
		cant-iate	vend-iate	fin-iate	part-iate
		cant-ino	vend-ano	fin-iscano	part-ano
Imperative		cant-a	vend-i	fin-isci	part-i
		cant-ate	vend-ete	fin-ite	part-ite
Present Participle		cant-ando	vend-endo	fin-endo	part-endo
Past Participle		cant-ato	vend-uto	fin-ito	part-ito

changes on O, UE, and U as in: *duermo* (I sleep), *dormimos* (we sleep), *durmiendo* (sleeping). The modern French equivalents are *je dors, nous dormons, dormant.*

Other *internal* irregularities of the written language are purely ortho-graphic, e.g. they are penalties of the regularity of Spanish spelling. Thus a final -C standing for the hard K sound in the stem of a Spanish verb becomes QU, if the verb ending begins with E or I. This change, which conceals the relation of different parts of a verb when we meet them on the written page, adds to the difficulty of using a dictionary. It is made to preserve the rule that the Spanish C before I and E, like the Spanish Z, stands for the TH sound in *thin*. Thus both *toqué* (I touched) and *toco* (I touch) belong to the infinitive *tocar*, as listed in the dictionary. The QU reminds us that the hard K sound of the stem goes through all its derivatives. The most important of these spelling changes are the follow-ing:

1) The letters C and G when to be pronounced hard before E and I, are written QU and GU respectively, e.g. *pagar* (pay), *pago* (I pay), *pagué* (I paid).

2) To indicate that G before A, O, U, stands for the CH in Scots *loch*, J is written instead, e.g. *coger* (gather), *cojo* (I gather).

3) Verbs ending in *-cer* or *-cir*, preceded by a consonant, change C to Z before A and O, e.g. *vencer* (vanquish), *venzo* (I vanquish).

It is not possible to give the precise Anglo-American equivalent of the various tense forms listed in these tables without recourse to roundabout expressions, and there are alternative compound tense forms corresponding to some of them. Before discussing use of simple tenses, we should therefore familiarize ourselves with the Ro-

TO HAVE IN THE ROMANCE FAMILY

		FRENCH	PORTUGUESE	SPANISH	LATIN	ITALIAN
Present		j'ai	hei	he	habeo	ho
		tu as	hàs	has	habes	hai
		il a	hà	ha	habet	ha
		nous avons	havemos	hemos	habemus	abbiamo
		vous avez	haveis or heis	habéis	habetis	avete
		ils ont	hão	han	habent	hanno
Imperfect		j'avais	havia	había	habebam	avevo
		tu avais	havias	habías	habebas	avevi
		il avait	havia	había	habebat	aveva
		nous avions	havíamos	habíamos	habebamus	avevamo
		vous aviez	havieis	habíais	habebatis	avevate
		ils avaient	haviam	habían	habebant	avevano
Past Definite		j'eus	houve	hube	habui	ebbi
		tu eus	houveste	hubiste	habuisti	avesti
		il eut	houve	hubo	habuit	ebbe
		nous eûmes	houvemos	hubimos	habuimus	avemmo
		vous eûtes	houvestes	hubisteis	habuistis	aveste
		ils eurent	houveram	hubieron	habuerunt	ebbero
Future		j'aurai	haverei	habré		avrò
		tu auras	haverás	habrás		avrai
		il aura	haverá	habrá	see	avrà
		nous aurons	haveremos	habremos	p. 176	avremo
		vous aurez	havereis	habréis		avrete
		ils auront	haverão	habrán		avranno
Conditional		j'aurais	haveria	habría		avrei
		tu aurais	haverias	habrías		avresti
		il aurait	haveria	habría	see	avrebbe
		nous aurions	haveriamos	habríamos	p. 176	avremmo
		vous auriez	haverieis	habríais		avreste
		ils auraient	haveriam	habrían		avrebbero
Present Subjunctive		j'aie	haja	haya	habeam	abbia
		tu aies	hajas	hayas	habeas	abbia or abbi
		il ait	haja	haya	habeat	abbia
		nous ayons	hajamos	hayamos	habeamus	abbiamo
		vous ayez	hajais	hayáis	habeatis	abbiate
		ils aient	hajam	hayan	habeant	abbiano
Imperative		aie	hà	hé	habe	abbi
		ayez	havei	habed	habete	abbiate
Present Participle		ayant	havendo	habiendo	habens	avendo
Past Participle		eu	havido	habido	habitum	avuto
Infinitive		AVOIR	HAVER	HABER	HABERE	AVERE

mance idiom appropriate to various situations in which we ourselves use the helper verbs *be* and *have*. This is a long story.

AUXILIARY VERBS

Some Aryan languages have no possessive verb *to have*. Russian has not. It is possible to sidetrack the possessive sense of *to have* by the use of the verb *to be* with a possessive or with a preposition. Thus a Frenchman can say *c'est à moi* (Latin *mihi est*) = this is mine (I possess this). That the Latin verb *habere* is equivalent to our *have* is true in the sense that both denote possession (e.g. *habet duas villas* = he has two farmhouses). Latin authors occasionally used a past participle with *habere*, as when Cicero says *cognitum habeo* (I have recognized). In late Latin *habere* was becoming a helper to express *perfected* action as in Teutonic languages. To say that the Latin verb *esse* corresponds with our verb *to be* is also true in so far as both can:

a) denote *existence* as in the Cartesian catchphrase *cogito ergo sum* (I think, therefore I *am*)

b) act as a *copula* (link) between person or thing and a characteristic of one or the other, as in *leo ferox est* = the lion *is* fierce

c) indicate *location*, as in *Caesar in Gallia est* = Caesar *is* in Gaul

d) state *class membership*, as in *argentum metallum est* = silver *is* a metal

e) go with the past participle in a *passive* construction such as *ab omnibus amatus est* = he was loved by everyone

f) state *pure identity*, as *Augustus imperator est* = Augustus is the emperor

The fate of *habere* is a comparatively simple story. Its modern representatives in Italian (AVERE) and in French (AVOIR) still have a possessive significance. The French and Italians also use parts of *avere* or *avoir* as we use *have* or *had* in compound past tense forms of all verbs other than: (*a*) those which are reflexive (or pseudo-reflexive), (*b*) most intransitive verbs (including especially those which signify motion). This is in keeping (p. 268) with the use of the German *haben* and Swedish *hava*. We can use the Spanish HABER to build up compound past tenses of *all* verbs, but it never denotes possession. The Spanish equivalent for *have* in a possessive sense is TENER (Latin *tenere* = to hold). TENER sometimes invades the territory of the Spanish HABER as a helper. The Portuguese equivalent TER has completely taken over the function of *habere*, both in its original possessive sense and as a helper to signify perfected action. The following examples illustrate the use of modern descendants of *habere* and *tenere* as helpers:

CONJUGATION OF TENER (SPANISH), TER (PORTUGUESE), TENERE (LATIN)

	TENER	TER	TENERE		TENER	TER	TENERE
Present	tengo	tenho	teneo	**Future**	tendré	terei	see p. 339
	tienes	tens	tenes		tendrás	terás	
	tiene	tem	tenet		tendrá	terá	
	tenemos	temos	tenemus		tendremos	teremos	
	ten éis	tendes	tenetis		tendréis	tereis	
	tienen	têm	tenent		tendrán	terão	
Imperfect	tenía	tinha	tenebam	**Conditional**	tendría	teria	see p. 339
	tenías	tinhas	tenebas		tendrías	terias	
	tenía	tinha	tenebat		tendría	teria	
	teníamos	tínhamos	tenebamus		tendríamos	teríamos	
	teníais	tinheis	tenebatis		tendríais	terieis	
	tenían	tinham	tenebant		tendrían	teriam	
Past Definite	tuve	tive	tenui	**Present Subjunctive**	tenga	tenha	teneam
	tuviste	tiveste	tenuisti		tengas	tenhas	teneas
	tuvo	teve	tenuit		tenga	tenha	teneat
	tuvimos	tivemos	tenuimus		tengamos	tenhamos	teneamus
	tuvisteis	tivestes	tenuistis		tengáis	tenhais	teneatis
	tuvieron	tiveram	tenuerunt		tengan	tenham	teneant
Imper.	ten	tem	tene	**Past Part.**	teniendo	tendo	tenendo
	tened	tende	tenete		tenido	tido	tenitum

English	*he has money*	*he has paid*	*he had paid*
French	il a de l'argent	il a payé	il avait payé
Portuguese	tem dinheiro	tem pagado	tinha pagado
Spanish	tiene dinero	ha pagado	había pagado
Italian	ha denaro	ha pagato	aveva pagato

Important set expressions in which *habere* survives in Portuguese as well as in French and Spanish are:

	FRENCH	PORTUGUESE	SPANISH
There is *or* are	il y a	há	hay (ha + y)
There was *or* were	il y avait	havia	había
There will be	il y aura	haverá	habrá
There has (*or* have) been	il y a eu	tem havido	ha habido

Besides denoting possession and indicating time, our own verb *have* expresses necessity, as in *we have to eat before we can philosophize*. So also, the French for *have to* is *avoir à*, the Spanish *haber de*, or (more emphatically) *tener que*, followed by the infinitive, e.g.:

I have to go out = *j'ai à sortir* = *he de* (or *tengo que*) *salir*

What is called the complete conjugations of *esse*, like that of our own verb *to be*, includes derivatives of several different roots. In Vulgar Latin *stare* (to stand) shared some of the territory of *esse*.

Though the French *être* and the Italian *essere* are mainly offspring of *esse*, some of their parts come from *stare*. The Italian *essere*, like its Latin parent, keeps company with the past participle in passive constructions, e.g. *il fanciullo fu lavato* (the child was washed). In French also it is possible to write *il est aimé par tout le monde* (he is loved by everybody); but such passive expressions rarely turn up in daily speech. It is more usual to rely upon:

a) a reflexive construction, e.g. *la propriété se vendra samedi* (the property will be sold on Saturday)

b) an impersonal expression involving the use of *on*, e.g. *on rapporte de Moscou que* (one reports from Moscow that = it is reported from Moscow that)

The French-Italian verb *to be* has an auxiliary use comparable to that of its Teutonic equivalent. That is to say, it takes the place of *to have* in compound past tenses if the verb is *reflexive* or if it is intransitive (especially if it expresses motion):

English:	I washed without soap.	We arrived too late.
French:	Je me suis lavé sans savon.	Nous sommes arrivés trop tard.
Italian:	Mi sono lavato senza sapone.	Siamo arrivati troppo tardi.

The Latin and Italian verb *stare* survives in Spanish and Portuguese as ESTAR. The latter is equivalent to our verb *to be* in three situations, one of which calls for more detailed treatment. Spanish examples will suffice to illustrate the other two, viz.:

a) when our *be* signifies location, ownership, profession, e.g.:

Budapest está en Hungria

b) when our *be* connects a noun with an accidental or temporary attribute, but *never* when *be* precedes a *noun* complement, e.g.:

la señora está enferma = the lady is ill

Italians often use *stare* as the equivalent of our verb *to be*, e.g.:

come sta? = how are you?
sto bene = I am well

A third use of *estar* or of its Italian equivalent *stare*, involves a unique and agreeably familiar construction, peculiar to Spanish, Portuguese, and Italian on the one hand and to Anglo-American on the other. It is a helper equivalent to *be* in expressions which imply *duration*, e.g.:

English:	he is waiting	we were working
Portuguese: ⎫	está esperando	estávamos trabalhando
Spanish: ⎭		estábamos trabajando
Italian:	sta aspettando	stavamo lavorando

It is not correct to couple the French verb *être* with a present participle such as *étudiant* or *travaillant*. To emphasize *continuity* or *duration*, French people can use the idiomatic expression *être en train de* (to be in the process of), as in *je suis en train de manger* (I am busy eating), of if the past is involved, the *imperfect* tense form, e.g. *elle pleurait quand je suis arrivé* (she was crying when I arrived). Customarily there is no distinction between transitory (*elle danse maintenant* = she is dancing now) and habitual (*elle danse bien* = she dances well) action in French. Only the context tells us when *elle parle au canari* means *she is talking to the canary* or *she talks to the canary*.

What is sometimes called the present participle of a Spanish or Portuguese verb (e.g. *trabajando*) is not historically equivalent to the present participle of a French verb. Latin had two verb forms corresponding to the single English one ending in *-ing*. One, the *gerund*, corresponds to the use of the *-ing* form as the name of a process (*we learn by teaching*); the other, the *present participle*, was a verbal adjective (*she died smiling*). Only the latter left a descendant in French, always with the suffix *-ant* (*chantant, vendant, finissant*). This French *-ant* derivative is equivalent to the English *-ing* derivative in three of six ways in which the *latter* is used:

   a) as an ordinary adjective, e.g. *de l'eau courante* (running water)
   b) as a verbal adjective, i.e., an adjective with an object following it, e.g. *cet arbre dominant le paysage* (this tree dominating the scenery)
   c) in adverbial phrases, e.g. *l'idée m'est venue en parlant* (the idea came to me while talking)

Here the correspondence ends. It is not correct to use the French "present participle" to translate the English *-ing* form when accompanied by the auxiliary *be;* and we cannot use it to translate our *-ing* derivative when the latter is an ordinary noun (*spelling is difficult*), or a verbal noun with an object (*spelling English words is difficult*). For the last two French usage corresponds to the alternative English infinitive construction, e.g. *to spell (English words) is difficult* = *épeler (des mots anglais) est difficile.* The Latin gerund and the Latin present participle had a different fate in Spain and Portugal. The present participle, which ended in *-ans, ens,* or *-iens* (nomin.) ceased to be a part of the Spanish verb system. Spanish words which now end in *-ante* or *-iente* are, with few exceptions, simple adjectives or nouns, e.g. *dependiente* (dependent), *estudiante* (student).

The *form* of the Latin gerund survives in the verbal suffix -*ando* (for the regular verb of the first class), and -*iendo* (for all other regular and most irregular verbs). The form of the verb which ends thus is never a pure adjective or verbal noun (see p. 131). It leans upon another verb and remains *invariant*. We can always translate it by the English -*ing* form, though the converse is by no means true.

Accompanied by *estar*, as well as by *ir* (go), and *venir* (come) it expresses present, past, or future continuity (compare English: *he went on talking*). It may also qualify a verb, e.g. *oía sonriendo* (he listened smiling), as also the subject or object of the verb, *veo al muchacho jugando en la plaza* (I see the boy playing in the square). Though never an ordinary

THE SPANISH-PORTUGUESE VERBS *SER* AND *ESTAR*

	SER		ESTAR	
	SPANISH	PORTUGUESE	SPANISH	PORTUGUESE
Present	soy	sou	estoy	estou
	eres	és	estás	estás
	es	é	está	está
	somos	somos	estamos	estamos
	sois	sois	estáis	estais
	son	são	están	estão
Imperfect	era	era	estaba	estava
	eras	eras	estabas	estavas
	era	era	estaba	estava
	éramos	éramos	estábamos	estávamos
	erais	éreis	estabais	estáveis
	eran	eram	estaban	estavam
Past Definite	fuí	fui	estuve	estive
	fuiste	foste	estuviste	estiveste
	fué	foi	estuvo	esteve
	fuimos	fomos	estuvimos	estivémos
	fuisteis	fostes	estuvisteis	estivestes
	fueron	foram	estuvieron	estiveram
Future	seré	serei	estaré	estarei
	serás	serás	estarás	estarás
	será	será	estará	estará
	seremos	seremos	estaremos	estaremos
	seréis	sereis	estaréis	estareis
	serán	serão	estarán	estarão

SPANISH-PORTUGUESE VERBS *SER* AND *ESTAR* (*cont.*)

	SER		ESTAR	
	SPANISH	PORTUGUESE	SPANISH	PORTUGUESE
Con- ditional	sería serías sería seríamos serías serían	seria serias seria seríamos seríeis seriam	estaría estarías estaría estaríamos estaríais estarían	estaria estarias estaria estaríamos estaríeis estariam
Present Sub- junctive	sea seas sea seamos seáis sean	seja sejas seja sejamos sejais sejam	esté estés esté estemos estéis estén	esteja estejas esteja estejamos estejais estejam
Imperative	sé sed	sê sêde	está estad	está estai
Present Participle	siendo	sendo	estando	estando
Past Participle	sido	sido	estado	estado

adjective, Spaniards do use it as a verbal adjective with an object, e.g.
he recibido la carta anunciando su partida (I have received the letter announcing his departure).

Besides the regular verb *estar* there is another Spanish-Portuguese
equivalent of *to be*. It is SER, a mixed verb, mainly descended from
the Latin *esse*, like the French *être*, but partly derived from *sedere*
(to sit). The simple copula between two nouns is always a tense form
of *ser*, as is the copula which connects a noun to an attribute which is
more or less *permanent* or characteristic, e.g. in Spanish

mi hermano era pintor = my brother was a painter
le señora es hermosa = the lady is beautiful

Occasionally *ser* turns up in passive constructions, e.g. *el doctor es
respetado de todos* (the doctor is respected by all), and the participle
then takes the gender and number terminals (*-o, -a, -os, -as*) appropriate to the subject. Both participles are *invariant* in other compound

Spanish-Portuguese tense forms, i.e., (a) HABER or TER with the *past* participle (to signify perfected action), (b) ESTAR with the *present* participle (to signify duration or continuing action). Spaniards, like the French, avoid using passive constructions. So the choice of the right terminal rarely crops up at least in conversation.

When Italians or Frenchmen use ESSERE or ÊTRE to express perfected action (i.e., with the past participle of a reflexive verb or a verb of motion) the participle takes a gender-number terminal appropriate to the subject, e.g.:

l'homme est venu	*la femme est venue*
the man came	the woman came
les hommes se sont suicidés	*les femmes se sont suicidées*
the men committed suicide	the women committed suicide

When coupled with AVERE the Italian past participle (masc. sing. form) is invariant. The same is true of the French past participle when conjugated with AVOIR.

Grammar books often give the rules: (a) it is invariant when the object follows the verb, (b) it takes the terminal appropriate to the number and gender of the *object* if the latter precedes the verb, e.g. *j'ai reçu une carte* (I have received a card) and *la carte que j'ai reçue* (the card which I have received).

In many common expressions our verb *to be* is not equivalent to ÊTRE or ESSERE in French or Italian, nor is it equivalent to the Spanish-Portuguese pair SER and ESTAR. The French for *to be right, wrong, afraid, hot, cold, hungry, thirsty, sleepy*, is *avoir raison, avoir tort, avoir peur, avoir chaud, avoir froid, avoir faim, avoir soif, avoir sommeil*. In the Spanish equivalents *tener* takes the place of the French *avoir* and English *be: tener razón, no tener razón, tener miedo, tener calor, tener frío, tener hambre, tener sed, tener sueño*. When they comment on the weather, Spanish and French people use verbs equivalent to the Latin *facere* (French *faire*, Spanish *hacer*) which means *to do* or *to make*. This usage is traceable to Vulgar Latin, e.g.:

it is cold	il fait froid	hace frío
it is fresh	il fait frais	hace fresco
it is hot	il fait chaud	hace calor
it is windy	il fait du vent	hace viento
it is fine (weather)	il fait beau (temps)	hace buen tiempo
it is daylight	il fait jour	hace luz

USE OF TENSES

Anglo-American, like the Teutonic languages, has only two simple tenses, *present* (e.g. *I have*) and *past* (e.g. *I had*). Otherwise, we indicate time or aspect by particles, adverbial expressions, or compound tenses made up of a participle and a helper verb. Modern Romance languages have at least *four* simple tenses, the *present*, the *future*, and two which refer to the past, the *imperfect* and *perfect* (or *past definite*). It is possible, most of all in French, to lighten the heavy burden of learning such flexional wealth, by resorting to turns which may not be specially recommended by grammar books, but are in harmony with common usage. For everyday French conversation or correspondence it is usually sufficient to know the present tense form, the imperfect, infinitive, present and past participle of an ordinary verb, the present and imperfect of *être* and *avoir*, together with the present of the irregular helpers *aller* (to go)* and *venir* (to come). Of all tenses the present stands first in importance. Apart from expressing what its name implies, it serves in situations analogous to *the show opens tomorrow*, and may legitimately and effectively be used in narrative, e.g. *j'arrive à deux heures du matin, et qu'est-ce que je découvre? Elle est morte, raide morte* (I arrive at two in the morning, and what do I discover? She is dead, stone dead). For the more immediate future conversational French habitually uses *aller* + infinitive (Spanish *ir a* + infinitive), which reduces flexion to a bare minimum and tallies with English *be going to* + infinitive, e.g. French *je vais téléfoner?* Spanish *voy a telefonar*. To indicate the immediate past, as in *I have just swallowed a tooth* (e.g. *have just* + past participle) French and Spanish have their own expressions. The French one is *venir de* + infinitive, the Spanish *acabar de* + infinitive, e.g. he has just gone out = *il vient de sortir* = *acaba de salir*.

In everyday speech French people always use a compound tense form to express what is more remote, e.g. I met him yesterday = *je l'ai rencontré hier*. This construction is made up of the past participle and the present tense of *avoir* (or *être*, if the verb is reflexive or signifies motion). This roundabout way of saying *I came, I saw, I loved* looms as large in French conversation as does the present, and the

---

* The conjugation of ALLER like that of *être*, is built up from several verbs. Two of them, one of which is derived from Latin *vadere*, the other from *ambulare*, form the present tense, e.g., *il va* (he goes), *nous allons* (we go). The third, which is the Latin *ire*, occurs in the future and the conditional, e.g., *j'irai* (I shall go).

English student of French will be wise to use it liberally. The beginner must also acquaint himself with the so-called *imperfect*. This tense implies customary, repetitive, or continuous past action in contrast to a completed process. Thus it is always right to use the *imperfect* when we can substitute *used to* + infinitive for the simple past of an English statement, or when we could alter the English sentence to *was* or *were* + the *-ing* form of the verb, e.g.:

a) *Quand j'avais vingt ans je fumais quarante cigarettes par jour.*
At twenty years of age I *smoked* (= *used to smoke*) forty cigarettes a day.

b) *Elle faisait la cuisine quand je suis arrivé.*
She was cooking when I arrived.

The second of the two statements could also be given the form *Elle était en train de faire la cuisine*, etc. This is useful to know because by resorting to *être en train de* (be in the act of, be busy with) you can get round the imperfect form of the verb.

Another tense form, the *past definite* or *preterite*, has completely disappeared from conversational French, and is now the hallmark of the literary language. It means that the event in question took place once for all at a certain time, and as such corresponds to the simple past of *spoken* and *written* English, and to the compound past of *spoken* French (e.g. *il se rapprocha* for *il s'est rapproché* = he *came* nearer).

In literature it is the tense of sustained narration, hence also called the *past historic*. The first impression of the beginner who reads a French narrative is that alternating use of perfect and imperfect is quite capricious. In reality this is not so. When two actions or processes are going on at one and the same time, the perfect expresses the *pivotal* one. For what is descriptive, explanatory, or incidental to the main theme, the imperfect replaces it. A passage from *Le Crime de Sylvestre Bonnard* by Anatole France illustrates this rule, which applies to all the Romance languages:

J'approchai (past historic) *du foyer mon fauteuil et ma table volante* (I pulled my easy chair and little table up to the fireside), *et je pris* (past historic) *au feu la place qu'Hamilcar deignait* (imperfect) *me laisser* (and occupied so much of my place by the fire as Hamilcar condescended to allow me). *Hamilcar, à la tête des chenets, sur un coussin de plume, était* (imperfect) *couché en rond, le nez entre ses pattes* (Hamilcar was lying in front of the andirons, curled up on a feather cushion, with his nose between his paws). *Un souffle égal soulevait* (imperfect) *sa fourrure épaisse et légère* (his thick, fine fur rose and fell with his regular breath). *A mon approche, il coula* (past historic) *doucement ses prunelles d'agate entre ses paupières mi-closes qu'il referma* (past historic) *presque aussitôt en songeant: "Ce n'est rien, c'est mon maître."* (At my approach his agate eyes glanced at me from between his half-opened lids, which he closed almost at once, thinking to himself: "It is nothing, it is only my master.")

The elimination of the *past definite* from everyday speech is confined to French. In Spanish, Portuguese, and to a lesser degree, in Italian conversation it is still going strong, and the student of Spanish who has previously learned some French will therefore feel tempted to say *he comprado un sombrero* (French *j'ai acheté un chapeau*) where the Spaniard would use the preterite (*compré un sombrero*).

THE INFINITIVE VERB

We have seen (p. 259) that the Anglo-American equivalent of the verb form called the *infinitive* of Teutonic languages is identical with the first person present, and is recognized as such whenever it immediately follows (*a*) the particle *to*, or (*b*) any one of the helper verbs *shall, will, may, must, can, let, make* (meaning *compel*), (*c*) the verbs *see, hear, help,* and (somewhat archaically), *dare.* The infinitive of a modern Romance language, like that of a typical Teutonic language, has its own characteristic terminal and has the same relation to our own usage. That is to say, it is the verb form which occurs after a preposition, or after one of the following auxiliaries, which do not take a preposition:

SPANISH		FRENCH
querer	(want to)	*vouloir*
deber	(shall, must)	*devoir*
poder	(can, be able to)	*pouvoir*
osar	(dare)	*oser*
saber	(know)	*savoir*
hacer	(make, cause)	*faire*
dejar	(let, allow)	*laisser*

The infinitive without a preceding preposition can also occur after other French and Spanish verbs. A second group which do not take a preposition is made up of verbs such as *to come* (French *venir*, Spanish *venir*), and *go* (French *aller*, Spanish *ir, andar*). A third group includes verbs of seeing and hearing, French *voir* (see), *entendre* (hear), *sentir* (feel); Spanish *ver, oir, sentir*. Of the remainder the more important are:

French *aimer mieux* (prefer), *compter* (count on), *désirer* (desire), *envoyer* (send), *espérer* (hope), *faillir* (fail to), *paraître* (appear); Spanish *parecer* (appear), *desear* (desire, want), *temer* (fear), *esperar* (hope).

One of the helper verbs given in the two columns printed above calls for comment. The Spanish-French couplet DEBER-DEVOIR, like the Portuguese DEVER and Italian DOVERE literally mean *to owe;* but they can be used as helpers in a compulsive sense by a process of metaphorical extension parallel to the formation of our word *ought*, originally a past tense form of *owe*. The French present, *je dois*, may mean *I owe* or *I must*, the past *j'ai dû*, I had to, the future *je devrai*, I shall have to, and the conditional *je devrais*, *I ought* to. To use either *devoir* and *pouvoir* or their equivalents in other Romance languages correctly, we have to be on the lookout for a pitfall mentioned in Chapter IV (p. 144). This is the peculiar Anglo-American construction *I should have* (French *j'aurais dû*), *I could have* (French *j'aurais pu*).

The French often resort to a peculiar construction for *must*. It involves the impersonal verb *falloir* (to be necessary that), e.g.:

$$\left.\begin{array}{l} \textit{il faut sortir} \\ \textit{il faut que je sorte} \\ \textit{je dois sortir} \end{array}\right\} \text{ I must go out}$$

When our own equivalent of a Romance infinitive comes after a preposition, the latter is always *to*. Several prepositions may stand immediately before the infinitive of a Romance language. The two chief ones are descendants of the Latin *de* (from *or* of) and *ad* (to). Both in French and in Spanish they survive as *de* and *à* or *a* respectively. The first has become more common, as in the following sentence, which also illustrates the rule that the pronoun object precedes the infinitive: *je suis bien heureux de te voir* (I am very happy to see you). Correct choice of the appropriate preposition depends arbitrarily on the *preceding* main verb, noun, or adjective, and we find it with them in a good dictionary. Where we can replace *to* by *in order to*, Romance equivalents are *pour* (French), *para* (Span.), *per* (Ital.), e.g. I am coming to repair it = *je viens pour le réparer* = *vengo para repararlo* = *vengo per ripararlo*.

Italian has a distinctive preposition *da* derived from the fusion of two Latin ones (*de* + *ad*). In different contexts it can mean *from, at* or *for*. When the infinitive has a *passive* meaning we can usually translate *to* by DA, e.g.:

Egli ha un cavallo da vendere.
He has a horse to sell (= to be sold).

Questa è una regola da imparare a memoria.
This is a rule to learn by heart (= to be learned by heart).

In all Romance, as in Teutonic, languages the infinitive form of the verb (see Chapter IV, p. 130) is the one which replaces our *-ing* form when the latter is a verb-noun, e.g. *voir, c'est croire* (seeing is believing). The Portuguese infinitive has peculiar agglutinative possessive forms equivalent, e.g., to *your seeing* (VEResi), *our doing* (FAZER-mos), *their asking* (PERGUNTARem), with the ending *-es* (your), *-mos* (our), *-em* (their). The following example illustrates this construction:

passei sem me verem = I passed without their seeing me

MOOD

Up till now nearly all our illustrations of Romance verb behavior have appeared in what grammarians call the *indicative* mood. Two other moods, the *subjunctive* and the *conditional*, require special treatment. The latter is still very alive, both in spoken and written French, Spanish, or Italian. The former leads a precarious and uncertain existence in the spoken, that is, the living language, yet is usually given so much space in introductions to French (or German) that the beginner is scared out of his wits. A few facts may help him to regain his confidence. The first is that the subjunctive, except when it replaces the imperative as it does in Spanish or Italian (p. 402) is practically devoid of semantic significance, and for this reason alone no misunderstanding will arise if the beginner should ignore its existence. French grammars, for instance, are in the habit of telling us that the indicative states a fact whereas the subjunctive expresses what is merely surmised, feared, demanded, etc., and then illustrate this assertion by, e.g., *je doute qu'il vienne* (indicative *vient*) = I doubt that he will come. Now this is palpable nonsense. The doubt is not signaled by the subjunctive form *vienne*. It is expressed by *je doute*, and the subjunctive of the dependent clause is as much a pleonasm as is the plural flexion of the verb in *ils se grattent* (they are scratching themselves). There is another source of comfort. Of the two subjunctives in French, the present and the past, the latter has disappeared from the spoken language; the former survives, but is very restricted in its movements. If you should say, for instance, *je ne crois pas qu'il est malade* for . . . *soit malade* as prescribed by grammar, you are merely following what is common usage. You should also not feel unduly intimidated when you wish to express yourself in written French, because it is possible to travel a long distance without calling in the subjunctive, provided you take the following advice: since the subjunctive is a characteristic of dependent or subordinate clauses say what you have to say in simple straightforward statements, and use alternatives for expressions which are usually followed by this troublesome mood. The Spanish subjunctive has a wider range than the French one, in speech as well as in print; besides there are four different forms for the two in French (a present, two past, and a future subjunctive). The reader who wishes to acquaint himself with all the ways, byways and blind alleys of this mood will have to go outside *The Loom* for information. Here it must suffice to say that in all Romance languages grammar prescribes the subjunctive (*a*) after expressions denoting doubt, assumption, fear, order, desire, e.g. French *douter, craindre, ordonner, désirer*, Spanish *dudar, temer, mandar, desear*, Italian *dubitare, temere, mandare, desiderare*, (*b*) after the equivalents of English *it is necessary that* (French *il faut que*, Spanish *es menester que*, Italian *bisogna che*), (*c*) after certain conjunctions of which the most important are:

FRENCH	SPANISH	ITALIAN	ENGLISH
pour que	para que	perchè	in order that
afin que	a fin de que	affinchè	
quoi que	aunque	sebbene	although
bien que	bien que	benchè	
sans que	sin que	senza che	without
pourvu que	con tal que	purchè	provided that
à moins que	a menos que	a meno che	unless
au cas que	en caso que	in caso che	in case that

All you have to do to get the *conditional* of a regular French verb is to add the personal endings of the *imperfect* to the infinitive. To understand its form and *one* of its functions we must go back to Vulgar Latin. Perhaps the reader of *The Loom* has already heard once too often about how Roman citizens of the later empire could express future time by coupling the infinitive with the present tense of *habere*, e.g. *credo quod venire habet* (I believe that he will come); but there is a good enough reason for mentioning it again. For *I believed he would come*, Romans would use past tense forms of *habere* with the infinitive, i.e., *credebam quod venire habebat*, or *credebam quod venire habuit*. Just as the future tense of Romance languages (other than Rumanian) is based on agglutination of the verb infinitive with the present of *habere*, the conditional results from gluing the verb infinitive to *imperfect* (Spanish, Portuguese, French) or *past historic* (Italian) tense forms of the same helper verb. This tells us the original function of the conditional mood, i.e., that we have to use it when we speak about a past event which had not yet happened at the time involved in the preceding statement. Its original past-future function survives in all constructions analogous to those cited above. The following examples show the ordinary future and the past future (i.e., conditional):

English:	he says he will come	he said he would come
French:	il dit qu'il viendra	il disait qu'il viendrait
Spanish:	dice que vendrá	decía que vendría
Italian:	dice che verrà	diceva che venirebbe

The conditional has taken on another function, and derives its name from it. We have to use it in the main clause of French conditional statements when fulfillment is unrealizable, or at least remote, e.g. (*a*) *if he came I should go;* (*b*) *if he had come I should have gone.* Here, as in future-past expressions, illustrated above, the French conditional is equivalent to our construction involving *should* or *would* with the infinitive of the main verb. For our simple past tense form of an ordinary verb of the *if* clause, as in (*a*), or of the helper as in (*b*), the French equivalent is the ordinary imperfect (or pluperfect). The following examples illustrate French conditional statements:

a) *French:*   *Si j'avais de l'argent je l'achèterais.*
   English: If I had money I should buy it.

b) *French:*   *S'il avait eu de l'argent elle l'aurait acheté.*
   English: If he had had money she would have bought it.

Spanish usage is more tricky. Where we use the *would-should* construction, it is always safe to use the *conditional* in the main clause, and Spaniards will not misunderstand a foreigner who uses the ordinary (indicative) present or past in the *if* clause. They themselves resort to the subjunctive form, as we use *were* for *was, is, are:*

Spanish: *Lo darían el premio si fuese más aplicado.*
English: They would give him the prize if he *were* more industrious.

Spanish: *Si tuviera dinero lo compraría.*
English: If I had money I should buy it.

Spanish: *Si habría tenido dinero lo habría comprado.*
English: If I had had money I should have bought it.

The main thing for the beginner to know about the Romance subjunctive is how to leave it alone till he (or she) has mastered all the grammar essential to clear statement. The conditional turns up in many situations which more or less imply condition, e.g. suggestions, and in general where we use *should-would* with the infinitive in a simple statement. For instance, it is a useful form for polite request. In headline idiom the French conditional may indicate uncertainty or even rumor, as illustrated by the last of the ensuing examples:

> *Je ne le ferais pas ainsi.* I shouldn't do it like that.
> *Voudriez-vous bien m'aider un peu?* Would you kindly help me a bit?
> *Que j'aimerais te voir!* How I should love to see you!
> *Darlan rencontrerait Hitler?* Will Darlan meet Hitler?

It is important for anyone who is taking up French to know several common expressions which involve the conditional form of certain helpers, e.g. *vouloir* (to want) and *devoir* (to owe) in the sense *would like to*, and *ought to*, e.g.:

> *Je voudrais bien te visiter.* I should much like to visit you.
> *Il ne devrait point le faire.* He shouldn't do it.

The Latin verb had special forms—the so-called *imperative* mood —to express an *order* or *request*. Such special imperative forms of the verb are rare in modern European languages. What is called the French imperative has two forms, one identical with the first person singular of the present indicative, the other with the second person plural, e.g. *attrape-attrapez* (catch!). Both occur in everyday speech. The first is used in familiar intercourse when addressing one person, the second in the same situation when speaking to more than one. The latter is also the imperative of polite address, singular and plural, e.g. *prenez garde, madame* (take care!). If the verb is reflexive, the reflexive pronoun behaves like any other objective pronoun (p. 366), e.g. it comes *after* the verb in an affirmative command, e.g. *ouvriers de tous les pays, unissez-vous* (workers of the world, unite!), and *before* the verb in a prohibition, e.g. *ne vous en allez pas* (don't go away!). Another way of making a request or recommendation is by employing the infinitive. This is also the Italian and German method, e.g. don't lean out of the window = French *ne pas se pencher en de-*

hors, Italian *non sporgersi*, German *nicht hinauslehnen*. The auxiliaries *avoir*, *être*, *savoir*, and *vouloir* have imperative forms corresponding to the subjunctive (*aie-ayez*, *sois-soyez*, *sache-sachez*, *veuille-veuillez*).

Interrogative expressions may take the place of an imperative. For *venez!* (come!), we may say *voulez-vous venir?* (will you come?), *ne voulez-vous pas venir?* (won't you come?), *vous viendrez, n'est-ce-pas?* (you will come, won't you?), etc.

In Spanish, as in French, the form of a command or a polite request depends upon personal relations between speaker and listener. When speaking to a child, an intimate relation, or a friend, the Spaniard uses an imperative form which is identical with the third person singular of the present indicative, e.g. *tomalo* (take it!). If he addresses more than one he uses a form constructed by substituting *d* for the final *r* of the infinitive, e.g. *corred, niños* (run, boys!). This imperative is not very important, because the beginner will seldom have a chance to use it. The form which we habitually employ is the third person singular of the present subjunctive followed by *usted*, when addressing one person, or the third plural followed by *ustedes* when talking to more than one, e.g. *dispense usted* or *dispensen ustedes* (excuse me).

To make requests or invitations (e.g. *let us be friends again*) the French use the first person plural of the ordinary present tense without the pronoun, as in the *Marseillaise: allons, enfants de la patrie* (let us go forth, children of the fatherland). The Spanish equivalent is the subjunctive first person plural, e.g. *demos un paseo* (let us take a walk). If the request involves someone to whom it is not directly addressed, the *third* person of the subjunctive is used in both languages, e.g. in French, *qu'il attende* (let him wait!), in Spanish *que no entre nadie* (let nobody come in!).

NEGATION AND INTERROGATION

The predominant negative particle of Latin was *non*, which survives as such in Italian. The Spanish equivalent is *no*, Portuguese *não*. The Spanish *no* always precedes the verb and can be separated from it only by a pronoun object or reflexive. In its original form the Latin *non* (like our English *no*) survives in French as an answer to a question or as an interjection. In Spanish, double negation is common. The particle *no* accompanies the verb even when the sentence contains other words which have an explicitly negative meaning, e.g. *ninguno* (no), *nadie* (nobody), *nada* (nothing), *jamás* or *nunca* (never). Thus a Spaniard says *no importa nada* (it doesn't signify nothing = it doesn't matter). Similarly, Italians use *non* with the verb of a sentence which contains *nessuno, niente, nulla*. Such constructions are analogous to the obligatory double-barreled negation of French (*ne . . . pas, ne . . . jamais, ne . . . rien*, etc.) explained in Chapter VIII (p. 341). Double negations (e.g. *I don't want no more nonsense*) were not taboo in *Mayflower* English. The following are illustrative:

English: I do not see anybody. *English:* What does he say? . . .
                                                             Nothing.
French: Je ne vois personne.   *French: Que dit-il?-rien.*
Spanish: No veo a nadie.   *Spanish: Qué dice?-nada.*
Italian: *Non vedo nessuno.*   Italian: *Che dice?-niente.*

The French words which go with the verb preceded by *ne* are: *aucun* (no, none), *nul* (none), *personne* (nobody), *rien* (nothing), *plus* (no more), *jamais* (never), e.g. *il n'avait rien à dire* (he had nothing to say), *aucun des délégués n'est présent* (none of the delegates is present). When they stand alone in answer to a question, *aucun, rien, jamais, personne* are negative, e.g. Who is here? *Personne!* What did he say? *Rien!* In reply to a question demanding a straight *yes* or *no*, Romans repeated the verb of the question. To *fecistine?* (did you do it?), the reply was *sic feci* (so did I), or *non feci* (I did not). In Spanish, *si* derived from *sic* is the affirmative particle (*yes*). French has two, *sí* and *oui* (Old French *oïl*, from Latin *hoc ille*). *Sí*, or stronger, *sí, sí*, denies a negative statement or suggestion, e.g. *tu ne m'aimes plus? Sí, sí!* (You don't love me any more? Yes, yes, I do).

Neither Teutonic nor Romance languages have a single clear-cut and obligatory method of interrogation. Each offers several ways of putting a question. A Latin question to which the answer was *yea, yea* or *nay, nay*, was marked as such by one of several particles (*ne, num, nonne*) equivalent to *eh?* None of these has survived. In spoken French or Spanish a question can be distinguished from an assertion by a device which is both primitive and well-nigh universal, i.e., by change of tone without change of word order, e.g. French *tu ne viens pas?* (you are not coming?). As in Teutonic languages, verb-subject inversion also labels a question, e.g. French *l'as-tu vu?* (have you seen him?), Spanish *tiene el tren un sleeper?* (has the train got a sleeper?).

Such inversion is not invariably interrogative. The Spanish verb often comes before its subject in constructions analogous to *came the dawn*, e.g. *decía la madre a su hija* (said the mother to her daughter).

French interrogation has several peculiarities not shared by Spanish: (1) If the subject is a personal pronoun, it is joined to the verb by a hyphen, e.g. *n'en désirez-vous pas?* (don't you want any?). If the third person of the verb ends in a vowel, a *t* is inserted between verb and pronoun, e.g. *chante-t-elle?* (does she sing?). (2) If the subject is a noun, it remains at the beginning of the sentence, while the interrogative character of the sentence is indicated by the addition of a pleonastic pronoun, e.g. French *ta sœur, est-elle mariée?* (is your sister married?), an arrangement not unknown to Spanish. French has yet a third way of expressing a question. It is by the use of *est-ce que* (is it that), an inversion of *c'est que*. The method began to emerge in the sixteenth century, and is still gaining ground at the expense of simple inversion, e.g. *est-ce que nous sommes loin de Londres?* (are we far from London?). The beginner should use this interrogative form freely because, apart from its popularity, it has the advantage of making inversion unnecessary.

The reader who is learning French may one day meet the common people of France in the flesh. So it is useful to know beforehand that popular speech is amazingly rich in complicated interrogative turns, e.g. *où c'est-il qu'il est?* for *où est-il?* (where is he?), *qu'est que c'est que vous voulez?* for *que voulez-vous?* Fortunately, this goes hand in hand with a tendency of popular French to avoid or to straighten out the irregular verb and regularize it on the pattern of the first conjugation. In this and many other ways, French common people speak what their descendants may write.

ROMANCE AFFIXES

No account of the grammar of a language is complete without reference to affixes other than those of the sort usually called flexions. People who speak Romance languages resort little to noun couplets such as *water power* or compounds such as *rubberneck* or *gumboots*. The French *choux-fleur* (cauliflower) is a representative of a small class which is not gaining much ground. The same is less true of verb-noun couplets represented by the French compounds *porte-monnaie* (purse), *gagne-pain* (livelihood) or the Spanish *mondadientes* (toothpick) and *rascacielos* (skyscraper). Where Anglo-American puts two words together without any intervening link, Romance languages generally require a preposition. To indicate the purpose for which something is meant French uses the particle *à*, Spanish *para*, and Italian *da.* Thus *a teacup* is *une tasse à thé* in French, *hair oil* is *aceite para el pelo* in Spanish, and *a typewriter* is *una macchina da scrivere* in Italian. Inserting of prepositions which we can omit (e.g. trade cycle = cycle of business) makes headlines bulge. Thus the French for *workers' fashion plates* is *planches de gravures de modes pour ouvrières.* Like noun coupling, prefixation is not fashionable. Frenchmen or Spaniards do not lightly make up adjectives like *predigested.* Thus the vocabulary of French is highly conservative. The same is true of Spanish, Portuguese, or Italian if we use Anglo-American as a yardstick; but French is far less flexible than its sister languages, because it has no machinery for deriving words of a class relatively common in the latter.

Many languages have special suffixes to indicate dimensions of, disapproval of, or esteem for the thing or person of the word to which they stick. Almost any German noun which stands for a thing or animal becomes diminutive (and hence endearing or contemptuous) by addition of *-chen,* or less commonly *-lein,* e.g. *Haus-Häuschen, Mann-Männchen.* The prevalence of this trick explains why diminutives are not listed in German dictionaries. In English such couplets as *duck-duckling, goose-gosling,* or *river-rivulet, book-booklet,* are rare, as are French ones, e.g. *maison-maisonette, jardin-jardinet;* and we have to learn them individually. More like German than English or French, Spanish and Italian abound with words of which the suffixes signify *size, appreciation, tenderness, contempt,* according to context; and we are free to make up new ones.

Masculine forms of some Spanish diminutive terminals are *-ito, -ico, -itico, -cito, -illo.* We recognize the feminine equivalent of the last one in *guerrilla* from *guerra* (war). Italian diminutive suffixes are the *-ino* of *bambino,* the *-etto* of *libretto,* also *-ello, -cello,* and *-cino.* Thus we get *floricita* (little flower) from the Spanish *flor,* and *fioretto* (cf. *floret*) from the Italian *fiore.* From the Spanish names *Carlos* and *Juan* we get *Carlito, Juanito* (Charlie and Johnnie). Such terminals can attach themselves to adjectives or adverbs. Hence the Spanish couplets *ahora-ahorita* (now—right now), *adiós-adiosito* (good-bye —bye-bye), or Italian *povero-poverino* (poor—poor dear), *poco-pochino* (little—wee). There is scarcely any limit to usage of this sort.

In Spanish, Portuguese, and Italian alike, the chief augmentative suffix comes from the Latin *-one.* Hence in Spanish *hombre-hombrón* (man—big man), in Italian *libro-librone* (book-tome). The Latin *depreciatory* suffix *-aceus* (or *-uceus*) becomes *-acho* (or *-ucho*) in Spanish, *-accio* in Italian. Thus we have the Spanish couplet *vino-vinacho* (wine—poor wine), or the Italian *tempo-tempaccio* (weather—bad weather). These affixes are fair game for the beginner. *Alfred-accio* is good Italian for *naughty Alfred*. One prefix deserves special mention. It is the Italian *s-*, a shortened form of the Latin *dis-*, e.g. *sbandare* (disband), *sbarbato* (beardless), *sbarcare* (disembark), *sfare* (undo), *sminuire* (diminish).

FURTHER READING

CHARLES DUFF	*The Basis and Essentials of French.*
	The Basis and Essentials of Italian.
	The Basis and Essentials of Spanish.
DE BAEZA	*Brush up Your Spanish.*
HARTOG	*Brush up Your French.*
TASSINARI	*Brush up Your Italian.*

Also French, Italian, Portuguese, Spanish in Hugo's Simplified System, and *Teach Yourself Spanish*, *Teach Yourself French*, *Teach Yourself Italian* in the Teach Yourself Books (English University Press).

PART THREE

THE WORLD LANGUAGE PROBLEM

CHAPTER X

The Diseases of Language

In the remaining chapters of *The Loom* we are going to look at language as a man-made instrument which men and women may sharpen and redesign for human ends. Before we can take an intelligent interest in the technique of language planning for a society which has removed the causes of war, it is helpful to recognize the defects and merits inherent in languages which people now use or have used in the past. The aim of this chapter is to give relevant information about some languages which have been mentioned in passing elsewhere, and about others which have been left out in the cold.

In their relation to the progress of human knowledge we may divide languages into two groups. In one we may put those which have a written record of human achievement extending back over hundreds, if not thousands, of years. To the other belong those with no rich or time-honored secular literature which could be described as indigenous. The first includes representatives of the Hamitic, Semitic, and Aryan families, Chinese and Japanese. The latter is made up of the Bantu languages, the Amerindian dialects, and members of the Malayo-Polynesian group. Though many of them are by now equipped with scripts through the efforts of Buddhist, Moslem, and Christian missionaries, such literature as they possess is largely sacred and derivative. Till quite recently the same remark could have been made with more or less justice about Finno-Ugrian, Turkish, Mongolian, Caucasian, and Basque. After the Revolution of 1917 the educational policy of the Soviet Union made script a vehicle for secular knowledge among Mongols, Mordvinians, Turco-Tartars, Caucasians, and other non-Aryan speech communities.

The 2,000 million people on this globe speak approximately 1,500 different languages. Only about 30 of them are each spoken by more than 10 millions. The daily speech of nearly half of the world's population belongs to the Indo-European family, within which its Anglo-

American representative takes first rank. Anglo-American is now the *mother* language of over 200 millions, not to mention those who habitually use it as a means of cultural collaboration or rely on it for world communication. If we add to the figure for Anglo-American 120 million people who speak cognate languages (German, Dutch and Flemish, Scandinavian), we get the enormous total of about 320 millions for the Teutonic group. Next come the Aryan tongues of India, spoken by some 230 millions, and the Romance languages, spoken by a total of 200 millions. Then follows the Slavonic-speaking people, of whom there are some 190 millions.

The preceding figure for German does not include Yiddish. Yiddish was originally a West German dialect taken to Poland and Baltic countries by Jewish refugees from persecutions of the late Middle Ages. Its phonetic pattern preserves many characteristics of Middle High German. Its vocabulary is still predominantly German with a considerable admixture of Hebrew words, of Polish words, and of words of languages spoken in countries to which emigrants have taken it. Yiddish can boast of a rich international literature, printed in Hebrew characters.

With the exception of the splinter-speech communities which use Basque, Turkish, and Caucasian dialects, all European languages belong to two great families, the Aryan or Indo-European, and the Finno-Ugrian (p. 190). European representatives of the latter are confined to Hungary, Esthonia, Finland, and Lapland. Major contributions to modern science are due to the efforts of men and women who speak languages belonging to the Romance and Teutonic languages, including Anglo-American, which is the hybrid offspring of both. These have been dealt with in Part III. The most ancient literature of the Indo-European family belongs to the Indo-Iranian group, which includes Sanskrit and Old Persian. Of languages spoken in modern Europe, the *Baltic* group which includes Lettish and Lithuanian stands nearest to primitive Aryan, and the *Slavonic*, headed by Russian, stands nearest to the Baltic group. Classical Greek with its parochial descendant, modern Greek, occupies an isolated position as a language clearly related to other Indo-European languages without being more clearly related to any particular group than to another. At the extreme Western geographical limits of the present distribution of the family, we find remains of the once widespread Celtic group with peculiar structural characteristics which separate it from all others. Albanian and Armenian are also Indo-European languages, but because both have assimilated many loan words from Semitic,

Caucasian, or Turkish neighbors, linguists did not generally recognize their relation to other members of the family till the latter half of the nineteenth century.

THE INDIC GROUP

Widely separated branches of the Indo-European family have a long literary past, and we are therefore in a position to recognize similar processes independently at work in the evolution of different groups. The early literature of the Eastern, like that of the Western members of the Indo-European family, introduces us to a complexity of grammatical usage in sharp contrast to that of its modern evolutionary forms. In the Western branch, simplification started first and went furthest in English. In the Eastern branch, simplification of Persian began earlier and has gone almost as far.

The most ancient stage of Indic is known as *Vedic* or *Vedic Sanskrit*, the language of the Vedas, a collection of hymns, litanies, prayers, incantations, in short, the bible of the Brahmanic cult. The oldest part is the *Rig Veda*, based on oral tradition transmitted for several centuries before the introduction of writing. Possibly it is as old as 1000 B.C.—several hundred years before the art of writing reached India. By that time the Old Indic of the original Vedaistic incantations had made way for a language which became the standard among the priestly caste as well as the medium of high-class secular literature. Perhaps to preserve its purity from contamination with low-brow idiom, priestly grammarians drew up a code of correct usage. Sanskrit means *arranged, ordered,* or *correct.*

In this state of arrested development it continued to exist side by side with living dialects, as Latin, the occupational medium of the church and universities, coexisted for centuries with its new evolutionary forms, the Romance languages. In the drama of the classical period of Indian literature, petrified Sanskrit is used, together with a newer *Prakrit,* separated from it by a social barrier. Men of elevated rank, such as kings and priests, speak Sanskrit. The lowly, including women, speak Prakrit. Some of the Prakrit or Middle Indic dialects became literary languages, that is, stagnant, while popular speech moved further. One form of Prakrit, Pāli, was carried by missionaries to Ceylon, where it became the sacred language of the Buddhist cult.

The chief representatives of Indic in its present-day form are *Bengali* (50 millions), *Western Hindi* (72), *Bihari* (34), *Eastern Hindi*

(23), *Marathi* (18), *Panjabi* (16), *Gujarati* (16), *Rahasthani* (13). The language of the Gypsies, who hail from the northwest of India and invaded Western Europe first in the fifteenth century, is also of Indic origin. Closely related to Old Indic is *Old Iranian*. Its earliest stage is represented by two forms, *Zend* or *Avestan*, that is, the sacred language of the Zoroastrian faith, and *Old Persian*, of which the best-known specimen is a rock inscription of Darius I (522–486 B.C.) at Behistun. The next evolutionary phase of Persian is called *Pehlevi* (i.e., *Parthian*). Modern Persian begins with the tenth century. It has changed but little during the last thousand years.

More than two thousand years ago the Vedic texts had already burdened the Brahmanic priesthood with competing versions. They had to harmonize them, to explain archaic forms, and to clarify dim meanings. The Vedic hymns were inviolable. For centuries priests had chanted them with punctilious attention to the time-honored fashion. They believed, and had an interest in making others believe, that correct observance decided whether the gods would dispatch bliss or otherwise. So training in priestcraft, as today, included careful schooling of the ear for sound, for rhythm, and for speech melody. For this reason ritual requirements eventually gave rise to one of the major cultural contributions of Hindu civilization. The Hindu priests were pioneers of the rudiments of a science of phonetics. Subsequently this preoccupation of the priest-grammarian with the sacred texts extended to secular literature. It culminated in the Sanskrit grammar of Panini (*ca.* 300 B.C.). Panini took a step that went far beyond the trivial exploits of Attic Greece, and had a decisive influence upon the course of nineteenth-century investigation when it became known to European scholars. He and presumably his forerunners were the first to take words to pieces and to distinguish roots from their affixes. Hence grammar is called *vayakarana* in Sanskrit, that is, "separation," "analysis."

Owing to this precocious preoccupation with grammar, we have a very clear picture of what Sanskrit was like. With its eight cases and dual number, the flexional apparatus of the Sanskrit noun was even more elaborate than that of Latin or Greek, and the Sanskrit adjective with its three gender forms reflects the luxuriance of its partner. As we retrace our steps to the earliest source of our information about the beginnings of Aryan speech we therefore approach a stage which recalls the state of affairs in Finnish with its fifteen sets of singular and plural postpositions defining the relation of a noun to other words in the same context. It may well be that we should arrive at such a goal if we could go back further; but the fact is that the use of Sanskrit case forms was not clear-cut and the case affixes were not, like those of Finnish, the same for every noun. This is shown by the following examples of Sanskrit genitive case forms:

NOMINATIVE SINGULAR		GENITIVE SINGULAR
devás	(god)	*devásya*
agnís	(fire)	*agnés*
vắri	(water)	*vắrinas*
çátrus	(enemy)	*çátros*
jắs	(progeny)	*jás*
svásā	(sister)	*svásur*

Many pages of this book could be filled if we set out all the flexions of a single Sanskrit or a single Greek verb with respect to *time, person, voice,* and *mood*. The following example illustrates only the personal flexions of one tense (*present*) and of both voices (*active* and *passive*). The mood is indicative, i.e., the form used in simple statements:

		ACTIVE		PASSIVE	
		SANSKRIT	GREEK	SANSKRIT	GREEK
Sing.	1.	dádhāmi	dídōmi	dadhé	dídomai
	2.	dádhāsi	dídōs	dhatsé	dídosai
	3.	dádhāti	dídōsi(n)	dhatté	dídotai
Dual	1.	dadhvás		dádhvahe	
	2.	dhatthás	dídoton	dadháthe	dídosthon
	3.	dhattás	dídoton	dadháte	dídosthon
Plur.	1.	dadhmás	dídomen	dádhmahe	didómetha
	2.	dhatthá	dídote	dháddhve	dídosthe
	3.	dádhati	didóāsi(n)	dádhate	dídontai

The Anglo-American equivalents would be *I, you, we,* or *they give* and *he gives* (active), and *I am, you, we, they are, he is given* (passive), making altogether three forms of the verb *give* and three of *to be,* or six in all to represent the meaning of eighteen Sanskrit words. For eight different forms of a modern English verb we can make above thirty-six corresponding forms of the Sanskrit or Greek verb. The complete Sanskrit verb finite, that is the verb without its infinitives, participles, and verbal adjectives plus their flexions, has 743 different forms, as against the 268 of Greek. From a complete Greek verb we get the enormous number of 507 forms, from a Latin one 143, and from a Gothic verb 94. The English verb usually has four, or at most five forms (e.g. *give, gives, gave, giving, given*). If we add seven forms of *to be*, four of *to have*, together with *shall* or *will* and *should* or *would*, for construction of compound tenses, we can express with twenty words everything for which Sanskrit burdens the memory with nearly forty times as many different vocables.

MODERN LANGUAGES OF THE EAST

During the past two thousand years there has been a universal drift among Aryan languages toward reduction and regularization of flexion. This tendency toward economy of effort is as striking on the Eastern front as on the Western, and in no language more than in modern Persian and Hindustani. After the Islamic conquest, Persian suffered a heavy infiltration of Arabic words. Consequently its present vocabulary is as Semitic as it is indigenous. Even Semitic grammatical forms crept in, but these affect only Arabic words. There can be little doubt that the decay of Persian flexions was accelerated by the Moslem conquest. In fact, Persian and Anglo-American provide an impressive example of parallel evolution from similar beginnings. Both have abandoned the distinction of grammatical gender. If the sex of an animate being is to be explicit, Persian prefixes equivalents to our words *man* or *woman* for human beings, and *male* or *female* for non-human beings.

Like Anglo-American, Persian has discarded the case system. In both languages words which correspond to French or German, Latin or Greek adjectives are invariant, as in Chinese. The comparison of the Persian adjective is quite regular. To form the comparative we have to add *-tar*, to form the superlative, *-tarin*, e.g. *bozorg* (big), *bozorgtar* (bigger), *bozorgtarin* (the biggest). Persian has no distinct adverbial form. The battery of Persian personal pronouns is even smaller than ours, because the single *u* (literary) or *an* (colloq.) stands for *he, she, it* alike. The Persian verb has a present and two simple past tense forms (past and imperfect), with full personal endings which ordinarily do the work of the pronoun subject, as in Spanish and Italian. There is one conjugation, and the personal endings are with one exception the same for all three tenses. Apart from the third person singular they are like the corresponding parts of the verb *to be* (*budan*). The present tense of *budan* is:

am,	I am	*im,*	we are
i,	thou art	*id,*	you are
ast,	he, she, or it is	*and,*	they are

The present and imperfect tense forms have the prefix *mi-* attached to the present stem and past stem respectively. Thus the present tense of the verb *kharidan* (to buy) is:

mikharam	*mikharim*
mikhari	*mikharid*
mikharad	*mikharand*

The corresponding past tenses are: *kharidam, kharidi,* etc. (I bought, you bought, etc.), and *mikharidam, mikharidi,* etc. (I was buying, you were buying, etc.). For perfected action, future time, and the passive voice, constructions involving helper verbs do service: *budan* for the first, *khastan* (to wish) for the second, and *shodan* (to become) for the third.

Though the modern Indic languages of Aryan origin have not covered the same distance as Persian, they have traveled in the same direction. Sir George Grierson, who was in charge of the *Linguistic Survey of India,* writes of the Hindi dialects:

"Some of these dialects are as analytical as English, others are as synthetic as German. Some have the simplest grammar, with every word relationship indicated, not by declension or conjugation, but by the use of help words; while others have grammars more complicated than that of Latin, with verbs that change their forms not only in agreement with the subject, but even with the object."

According to the prevalence of isolating and flexional features, we can divide modern Indo-Aryan vernaculars (17 standard languages with 345 dialects, spoken by some 230 millions) into two classes, one covering the center of the North Indian plain, called Midland, the other, called the Outer, surrounding it in three-quarters of a circle. The former is represented by *Western Hindi, Panjabi, Rajasthani,* and *Gujarati,* the latter by vernaculars such as *Lahnda, Sindhi, Marathi, Bihari, Bengali.* Grierson says:

"The languages of the outer sub-branch have gone a stage further in linguistic evolution. They were once, in their Sanskrit form, synthetic; then they passed through an analytical stage—some are passing out of that stage only now, and are, like Sindhi and Kashmiri, so to speak caught in the act—and have again become synthetic by the incorporation of the auxiliary words, used in the analytical stage, with the main words to which they are attached. . . . The grammar of each of the Inner languages can be written on a few leaves, while, in order to acquire an acquaintance with one of the Outer languages, page after page of more or less complicated declensions and conjugations must be mastered."

Bengali is spoken in the delta of the Ganges, and north and east to it, by a population equivalent to that of France. The gap between the written and the spoken word forces the foreigner to learn two different languages. This complete separation of the spoken from the written medium is the work of the Pundits of Calcutta who recently borrowed an enormous number of Sanskrit words with a spelling fashionable two thousand years ago. The Bengali verb has eight synthetic tenses. There are but three irregular, but only slightly irregular, verbs (*give, come, go*). Bengali developed a synthetic though as yet very rudimentary declension of the noun, e.g. *ghar* (house), genitive *gharer*, agent case *ghare*. It has gender distinction, but Bengali gender is a paragon of orderly behavior in comparison with that of Sanskrit. All male animals are masculine, all female feminine. All inanimate things are neuter. Only masculine and feminine nouns take the plural ending.

Hindustani is a dialect of Western Hindi. It is the daily speech of a population slightly larger than that of England; but it is better known as a *lingua franca*, current over all India. According to the *Linguistic Survey*, it developed as such in the bazaar attached to the Delhi Court. From there, officials of the Mogul Empire carried it everywhere. One form of Hindustani is *Urdu*. Its script is Persian, and it has a strong admixture of Persian and Arabic words. Owing to expansion over a wide area and hence contact with peoples of diverse speech communities Hindustani grammar has shed many irregularities and superfluities. With few exceptions the verb follows one and the same pattern. The present and past forms of a single helper (*hona*, to be) combine with two participles to do most of the daily work of a tense system. Like the Romance languages Hindustani has scrapped the neuter gender; and the case system has completely disappeared. Particles * placed after the noun (*postpositions*) do the job of our prepositions, e.g.:

* In spite of this regularity of the Hindustani word, some Indian and European compilers of Hindustani grammar books still stick to the Sanskrit or Latin pattern and arrange nouns with their postpositions in seven cases. East and West meet in the scholarly tradition of making difficult what is easy.

mard ke	*of man*	mardon ke	*of men*
mard ko	*to man*	mardon ko	*to men*

THE BALTIC AND SLAVONIC GROUPS

Among modern Indo-European languages, those of the Baltic and Slavonic groups have almost entirely escaped this tendency toward easing the flexional burden. They still preserve a welter of flexional forms. The Baltic group survives in a region northeast of Germany. It has two living representatives. *Lithuanian* is the daily speech of some two and a half million people, *Lettish* that of about one and a half million in the neighboring community, Latvia. Of the two surviving members of the Baltic group, Lithuanian is the more archaic. The accompanying table, which gives the singular forms of the Lithuanian word for *son* side by side with the oldest Teutonic (Gothic) equivalents, shows that Lithuanian actually outstrips the latter, as it also outstrips Latin, in the variety of its case derivatives.

		LITHUANIAN	GOTHIC
Nom.	Sing.	sunus	sunus
Acc.	"	sunu	sunu
Gen.	"	sunaus	sunaus
Dat.	"	sunui	sunau
Instr.	"	sunumi	..
Loc.	"	sunuje	..
Voc.	"	sunau	sunau

East and south of the Baltic and Teutonic regions we now find the huge group of Slavonic languages, spoken by some 190 million people. Philologists classify them as follows:

A. EAST SLAVONIC:
1. Great Russian (100 millions)
2. Little Russian (30 millions)
3. White Russian (12 millions)

B. WEST SLAVONIC:
1. Slovak and Czech (12 millions)
2. Polish (23 millions)

C. SOUTH SLAVONIC:
1. Bulgarian (5 millions)
2. Serbo-Croatian and Slovene (12 millions)

At the beginning of our era the Slavs still inhabited the region between the Vistula, the Carpathian Mountains, and the Dnieper. During the fifth and sixth centuries, they swarmed over huge tracts of Central and Western Europe. At one time they were in possession of parts of Austria, Saxony, and the North German plains to the Elbe. During the Middle Ages, Slavonic surrendered all this territory to Germany; but *Polabian*, a Slavonic dialect, persisted in the lower regions of the Elbe up to the eighteenth century, and even today Germany harbors a minute Slavonic language island, the *Sorbian* of Upper Saxony. While Slavonic has had to retreat from the West, it is still gaining ground on the Asiatic continent as the vehicle of a new civilization. Russian is now pushing as far north as the White Sea and as far east as the shores of the Pacific Ocean.

The earliest recorded form of Slavonic is Old Bulgarian, into which two Greek missionaries, Kyrillos and Methodos, both from Salonika, translated the Gospels in the middle of the ninth century. This Bible language, also called *Church Slavonic*, became the official language of the Greek Orthodox Church. It still is. Since the art of writing was then the exclusive privilege of the priest-scribe class, Church Slavonic also became the secular medium of literature. The Russians did not begin to emancipate themselves from the literary tyranny of the Church, and to create a written language of their own, till the end of the eighteenth century. Its basis was the speech current in the region of Moscow. As a hangover from their church-ridden past, citizens of the U.S.S.R. still stick to "Kyrilliza," a modified form of the Greek alphabet (Fig. 12) once current in Byzantium. The Poles and the Slovaks—but not the Serbs or Bulgarians—are free from this cultural handicap. When their forefathers embraced the Roman form of Christianity, an internationally current alphabet was part of the bargain.

Like the Semitic family, the Slavonic group shows comparatively little internal differentiation. Slavonic languages form a clearly recognizable unit, including national languages which differ no more than Swedish and Danish or Spanish and Italian. It is easier for a Pole to understand a Russian than for a German to understand a Swede, or for a Parisian to understand a Spaniard or an Italian. For a long time Slavonic-speaking peoples remained cut off from Mediterranean influence. What reached them was confined to a thin and muddy trickle that percolated through the Greek Orthodox Church. The comparatively late appearance of loan words in the Slavonic lexicon faithfully reflects this retardation of culture contact with more progressive communities. Since the Soviet Union embarked upon rapid industrialization there has been a great change. Assimilation of international technical terms has become a fashion. To this extent linguistic isolation is breaking down. Meanwhile in Russia, as elsewhere, Slavonic languages constitute a fossil group from the grammatical standpoint. They preserve archaic traits matched only by those of the Baltic group. Noun flexion, always a reliable index of linguistic progress, is not the least of these. Slavonic languages carry on a case system as complicated as that of Latin and Greek; Bulgarian alone has freed itself from this incubus.

It would be congenial to announce that *The Loom of Language* can simplify the task of learning a language spoken by more than a twentieth of the world's inhabitants, and used as the vernacular of a union of states which has undertaken the first large-scale experiment in economic planning. Unfortunately we are not able to do so. It is a commonplace that Russian collectivism originated in a country which was in a backward phase of technical and political evolution. It is also, and conspicuously, true that it originated in a country which was in a backward phase of linguistic evolution. Because other Aryan languages such as Danish, Dutch, or Persian have discarded so much of the grammatical luggage which their ancestors had to carry, it is possible to simplify the task of transmitting a working knowledge of them by summarizing the relatively few essential rules with which the beginner must supplement a basic vocabulary. There is no royal road to fluency in a language which shares the grammatical intricacies of Sanskrit, Lithuanian, or Russian. It is therefore impossible to give the reader who wishes to learn Russian any good advice except to take the precaution of being born and brought up in Russia. Some reader may doubt whether this is a fair statement of the case. Let us look at the evidence:

1) Like that of Lithuanian, the Russian noun is burdened with locative and instrumental case-forms which some other Aryan languages had already discarded a thousand years B.C.

2) Russian shares with German and Icelandic the three genders, masculine, feminine, neuter. Like German, Icelandic, and Lithuanian, it possesses *two* adjectival declensions, one for use when the adjective is attributive, the other when it is predicative (*dom nov*, "the house is new"—*novij dom*, "the new house"). The irregularities of adjectival behavior make those of Latin fade into insignificance.

3) The numbers 2, 3, 4 with fully developed case and gender flexions form a declensional class of their own. From 5 to 30 numbers are declined like certain feminine nouns. From 50 to 80 both parts of the number are declined. From 5 upward the things counted must be put into the genitive plural. The numbers 2–10 carry a subsidiary set of forms called collectives for use where we would say, e.g., *we were five of us*, or *she has six sons*.

4) The essential Russian vocabulary, like that of German, is inflated by a wasteful luxuriance of verb forms. Thus there are couplets distinguished by presence or absence of an infix which denotes repetition, or by one of several prefixes which signify completion. For instance, *djelat* and *djelivat* signify *to do once* and *to do repeatedly*, *ya pisál* means *I was writing*, and *ya napisál* means *I have written*. If you say *write to him* (at once) you have to use the perfective form *napishi yemu*. If you say *write better* (in future), you use its imperfective cotwin, *pishi lushje*.

Britain has relinquished the incubus of gender without discarding the bishops' bench, and Americans who have no use for case concord still condone lynching. So it goes without saying that shortcomings of the Russian language reflect no discredit on the Soviet system, still less on the citizens of the U.S.S.R. themselves. What they do signify is the existence of a powerful social obstacle to cultural relations between the Soviet Union and other countries. The archaic character of the Russian language is a formidable impediment to those who may wish to get firsthand knowledge of Russian affairs through foreign travel. Because such difficulties beset a foreigner, it is disappointing to record lack of revolutionary fervor in the attitude of Soviet leaders to the claims of language planning. While the Kremlin curbed the power of the Greek Orthodox Church, it made no attempt to bring itself into line with Europe, America, Africa, Australia, and New Zealand by liquidating the cultural handicap of the Kyrillic alphabet. That there is no insurmountable obstacle to such a break with the past is shown by the example of Turkey, which has replaced Arabic by Latin script. The task of reform was simplified by the pre-existence of illiteracy in Russia, as in Turkey.

Russian has always been, and still remains, a Tower of Babel. Within the boundaries of the Soviet Union we find representatives of the Indo-European, the Finno-Ugrian, the Turco-Tartar, the Mongolian, and the Caucasian families of speech—all in all some hundred languages and dialects, most of which are mutually unintelligible. The situation is deplorable enough if we confine ourselves to the three Russian languages: *Great*

Russian, spoken in the northeast, with Moscow as the center; *Little Russian,* or Ukrainian; and *White Russian,* current in the northwest along the confines of the Baltic group. These languages are separated by such small differences that they are mutually intelligible. Formerly the written language common to all of them was Great Russian. But today the White Russians as well as the Little Russians have written languages of their own.

THE CELTIC TWILIGHT

The unequal decay of flexion in the Indo-European family does not directly reflect the progress of civilization. We can see this by contrasting Russian or Lithuanian with the Celtic languages. Celtic speech is now confined to the western fringe of Europe. It was once possible to hear it over a territory as vast as the Holy Roman Empire. At the time of Alexander the Great, Celtic-speaking tribes inhabited Britain, most of France and Spain, North Italy, South Germany, and the valley of the Danube down to the Black Sea. Hordes from Gaul crossed to Asia Minor, and established themselves in the district still called *Galatia.* Within a short time, Celtic dialects were displaced everywhere except in Gaul. By the middle of the first century, Gaul itself surrendered. The Gauls were Romanized, and Latin wiped out Celtic. Five hundred years later, the Celtic-speaking remnant had reached vanishing point.

Documentary remains of its former existence are place names, a handful of meager inscriptions from France and Lombardy, and individual words which lie embedded in French and other languages. During the four hundred years of Roman rule, the Celtic dialects of Britain escaped the fate of their Continental kin. They were still intact when Emperor Constantine withdrew his legions. After this brief respite, they succumbed to successive waves of Teutonic invaders. Wherever the German hordes settled, Celtic had to make way for the language of the conqueror. It has persisted only in Wales, in North Scotland, and in Ireland.

As it now exists, the Celtic group can be divided into two branches, the *Goidelic* (Gaelic) and *Brythonic* (British). The former includes Irish or *Erse,* said to be spoken by some four hundred thousand people; *Scots-Gaelic* of the "poor whites" in the Western Highlands, and *Manx,* an almost extinct dialect of the Isle of Man. The oldest Irish documents are the so-called *Ogam* runic inscriptions (p. 63), which may go as far back as the fifth century A.D. To the Brythonic dialects belong *Welsh* and *Breton,* each spoken by a million people, and *Cornish,* which disappeared at the death of Dolly Pentreath in the year 1777. Welsh is still a living language. A high proportion (about 30 per cent) of people who live in Wales are bilingual. Breton is not a splinter of the ancient language of Gaul. It is an island Celtic brought over to latinized Brittany by Welsh and Cornish refugees in the fifth and sixth centuries.

Remarkable structural similarities unite the Gaelic and Brythonic dialects. Clear-cut differences distinguish them. Of the latter, one is specially characteristic. Where Old Irish inscriptions exhibit an initial *qu,* represented by a hard *c* in Erse (*qu-* in Scots Gaelic), Welsh has *p.* For this reason the two branches are sometimes called Q and P Celtic. A few examples are given below:

WELSH		ERSE
pa?	(what?)	*ca*
pen	(head)	*ceann*
pedwar	(four)	*cathair*
par	(couple)	*coraid*

Apart from Basque, the Celtic group remained a playing field for fantastic speculations longer than any other European language. Even when most of the European languages were brought together, with Sanskrit and Iranian, in happy family reunion, Celtic stayed out in the cold.* The large number of roots common to Celtic and other Aryan languages now leaves little doubt about the affinities of Celtic, especially to Latin and to other Italic tongues. Were it otherwise, there would be little to betray the Celtic group as a subdivision of the Aryan family.

The Celtic languages lack any trace of many flexions which are common to other members of the Aryan family. In so far as the Celtic verb exhibits flexion with respect to person, the present endings have not passed beyond the stage at which we can recognize them as pronouns fused to the verb root. The same is true of some frontier dialects in India, where the Old Indic personal endings of the verb have disappeared completely and analogous endings have emerged by fusion of the fixed verb stem with existing pronouns. From this point of view, the grammar of Celtic is more like that of Finno-Ugrian languages than that of Sanskrit, Armenian, or Swedish.

---

* A Scotsman, Andrew Murray, wrote in 1801 two remarkable volumes called a *History of European Languages* emphasizing *inter alia* the relation between Gaelic and Sanskrit.

Fig. 39. Stone with Celtic Inscription in Ogam Signs from Aboyne near Aberdeen in Scotland

Two features, which have been illustrated already, emphasize this essentially agglutinative character of Celtic grammar:

a) Among Celtic languages we find a parallel use of a *contracted* or agglutinative form of the verb used *without* an independent pronoun (p. 87), and an *unchangeable* verb root used together *with* a pronoun placed *after* it.

b) In all Celtic languages prepositions fuse with personal pronouns so that directives have personal terminals analogous to those of verbs.

The parallelism between the conjugation of the preposition and the verb is common to the P and Q representatives of the group, and the characteristics of each throw light on the origin of the other. For instance, we have no difficulty in recognizing the origin of the personal flexions of the Gaelic preposition *le* (with) when we compare them with the corresponding usage of the invariant verb *tha* when arranged in parallel columns:

tha mi,	I am	*leam,*	with me	(= le + *mi*)
tha thu,	thou art	*leat,*	with thee	(= le + *thu*)
tha sinn,	we are	*leinn,*	with us	(= le + *sinn*)
tha sibh,	you are	*leibh,*	with you	(= le + *sibh*)
tha iad,	they are	*leotha,*	with them	(= le + *iad*)

We can invert this process of interpretation by using the personal conjugation of the preposition as a clue to the personal flexion of Welsh verbs in the two following examples, which illustrate two types of conjugation corresponding to the two different forms (*fi* and *mi*) of the Welsh pronouns of the first person:

(1)

danaf,	(= *dan + fi*)	under me	*wyf,*	I am	(= *wys + fi*)
danat,	(= *dan + ti*)	under thee	*wyt,*	thou art	(= *wys + ti*)
danoch,	(= *dan + chwi*)	under you	*ych,*	you are	(= *wys + chwi*)
danynt,	(= *dan + hwynt*)	under them	*ynt,*	they are	(= *wys + hwynt*)

(2)

im,	(= *i + mi*)	to me	*bum,*	I was	(= *bu + mi*)
it,	(= *i + ti*)	to thee	*buost,*	thou wert	(= *bu + ti*)
iwch,	(= *i + chwi*)	to you	*buoch,*	you were	(= *bu + chwi*)
iddynt,	(= *i + hwynt*)	to them	*buont,*	they were	(= *bu + hwynt*)

The Celtic languages have many substitutes for the very heterogeneous system of roots which we call the verb *to be*. The Irish *as* or *is*, the Welsh *oes* (cf. our own *am* or *is*, German *ist*, Sanskrit *asmi*), the Gaelic *bu*, Welsh *bod* (cf. our *be*, German *bin*, Persian *budan*, Old

Saxon *bium*, Sanskrit *bhavami*), are common Aryan roots. To these we must add other peculiarly Celtic roots, such as the Gaelic *tha* and Welsh *mae*. The several forms of the verb *to be* are very important in Celtic usage. Like Basic English, Celtic is remarkably thrifty in its use of verbs. Where we should say *I feel*, the Celt would say *there is a feeling in me*. Here is an Irish example of this characteristic Celtic idiom: *creud adhbhar na moicheirghe sin ort?* In our language this reads: *why did you rise so early?* Literally it means *what cause of this early rising by you?* A Scots highlander can use expressions containing the equivalent to *is* to do the work of almost any other verb. In his idiom:

it will surprise you to hear this = there is a surprise for your ears

The Celtic languages have several merits which might commend themselves to the designer of an international auxiliary. One great virtue they share is that they are not highly inflected. There is little trace left of gender or number concord of the adjective and noun. Case distinction of the latter is vestigial. So such flexions as exist are not difficult to learn. A second virtue is a thrifty use of verbs. These conspicuous merits are insignificant when we place on the debit side, a characteristic which isolates Celtic dialects from all other members of the Aryan group and places them among the most difficult of all the Aryan languages for a foreigner to learn.

The flexional derivatives of other Aryan languages depend on *endings*. So they easily accommodate themselves to the convenience of alphabetical order in a standard dictionary. The special difficulty of the Celtic languages is that the initial consonant of a word may change in different contexts. For instance, the Welsh word for "kinsman" may be *car, gar, char,* or *nghar,* e.g. *car agos* "a near kinsman," *ei gar* "his kinsman," *ei char* "her kinsman," *fy nghar* "my kinsman." In short, the beginning and end of a word may change to meet the dictates of Celtic grammar. So the use of the dictionary is an exploit which the foreigner undertakes with imminent sense of danger, and little confidence of success. A quotation from a book by a Breton nationalist will scarcely give the reader an unduly harsh statement of the difficulty: "As for reading, to look up a word in the dictionary, it is enough to know the few consonants which are interchangeable— K, P, T with C'H, F, Z, or with G, B, D; G, D, B, with K, P, T, or with C'H, V, Z; M with V, and GW with W."

THE SEMITIC LANGUAGES

Nine hundred years ago, the Moslem world was the seat of the most progressive culture then existing. China could point to a rich secular tradition of literature coeval with the sacred texts of Aryan India. The Aryan languages did not as yet enjoy the undisputed prestige of Anglo-American, French, and German in our own age. If we go back to more remote antiquity, Aryan, Semitic, and Chinese yield place to the languages of Egypt * and Mesopotamia, where the permanent record of human striving began.

Nearly three thousand years ago, when Aryan-speaking tribes were letterless savages, Semitic trading peoples hit on the device embodied in our own alphabet. Fully a thousand years before the true relationship between the principal European languages and Indo-Iranian was recognized, Jewish scholars, who applied the methods of their Muslim teachers, had already perceived the unity of the Semitic dialects then known. The rabbi's interest in language problems was half-superstitious, half-practical, like that of the Brahmanic priest or the student of the Koran. His aim was to perpetuate the correct form, spelling, and pronunciation of the Sacred Texts; but there was a difference between the Brahmin and the Jew. Because he often lived in centers of Muslim learning such as Damascus, Seville, and Cordova, and also because he had mastered more than one tongue, the rabbi could easily transgress the confines of his own language. Inescapably he was impressed by similarities between Aramaic, Hebrew, and Arabic, and compelled to assume their kinship. Though he used the discovery to bolster his belief that Hebrew was the parent of Arabic, and incidentally of all other languages, he planted the seed of *comparative grammar*.

The linguistic preoccupations of the medieval Jews, and of their teachers the Arabs, were continued by European scholars of the sixteenth century. Protestant scholarship intensified interest in Hebrew, which took its place with the Latin of the Vulgate and New Testa-

---

* Ancient Egyptian was one of the Hamitic languages. They derive their name from Ham, the Biblical brother of Shem. Besides *Ancient Egyptian,* they include *Cushitic* (of which Somali and Galla are the chief representatives), together with the *Berber* dialects of Northwest Africa. Though the Semitic and Hamitic group diverge widely, their kinship is generally recognized. They share more root words than can be explained by borrowing; and they have some common grammatical peculiarities.

ment Greek; and Ethiopian joined the scholarly repertory of known Semitic dialects. Babylonian-Assyrian (Accadian) was not deciphered and identified till the nineteenth century. The family as a whole derives its name from *Shem*, the son of Noah in the Hebrew myth. It is now commonly divided in the following way: *East Semitic*, Babylonian-Assyrian (Accadian); *West Semitic*, (1) Aramaic, (2) the Canaanite dialects (Hebrew, Phoenician, Moabitic); *South Semitic*, (1) Arabic, (2) Ethiopian.

The Semitic languages form a unit far more closely knit than the Aryan family and have changed comparatively little during their recorded history. As a literary language, modern Arabic stands closer to the Arabic of the Koran than does French to the Latin of Gaul in the time of Mohammed. This suggests one of the reasons why the Semitic tongues have repeatedly superseded one another. Three Semitic languages have successfully competed for first place, and have become current far beyond their original homes. They are: Babylonian-Assyrian, Aramaic, and Arabic. The oldest representative of which we possess documents, and the first to assume international importance, was *Accadian*. Accadian was the speech of people who inhabited the plains of Arabia before they invaded the fertile lands of the Euphrates and Tigris. There they came into contact with the Sumerians, and adopted a superior culture, together with a system of syllabic writing, known as *cuneiform*. A wealth of cuneiform inscriptions and libraries of records engraved on cylinders and bricks of burnt clay have preserved the Babylonian-Assyrian language. The oldest assessable document goes back to the time of the great conqueror, Sargon I (*ca.* 2400).

For centuries Accadian was a medium of commercial and diplomatic correspondence throughout the Near and Middle East. We find evidence of its wide currency in letters which Palestinian princes addressed to Amenophis IV in the fifteenth century B.C. They were unearthed at Tel-el-Amarna, in Egypt. By the time of Alexander the Great, Accadian had ceased to exist as a living language. The medium that took its place was *Aramaic*. The Arameans were a trading people. After relinquishing desert life, they came to occupy the so-called Syrian saddle to the northeast of Mesopotamia. Thanks to this strategic position, they were then able to command the commerce that went along the land routes between the Mediterranean and the Middle East. From about the eighth century B.C. onward, they began to filter into the Babylonian and Assyrian empires. With them went their language and script, and in time Aramaic displaced not only Accadian, but also Hebrew and Phoenician. It even penetrated Arabic-speaking regions, and became one of the official languages of the Persian Empire.

Even after the advent of Christianity, Aramaic was an important cultural medium. The famous Nestorian Stone, discovered in 1625 in Sinngan-fu, shows that missionaries carried the Nestorian heresy with later Aramaic (Syriac) gospel texts as far as China. It was erected in A.D. 781, and reports in parallel Chinese and Syriac inscriptions the successes and failures of the Nestorian mission. All that survives today of this once mighty lingua franca is the speech of three small communities near Damascus.

Aramaic, not Hebrew, was the mother tongue of Palestine during the period with which the gospel narrative deals. When the Evangelists quote the words of Christ, the language is Aramaic, not Hebrew. By that time the local Canaanite dialect in which the earlier parts of the Old Testament were written was already a dead language. The decline of Hebrew set in with the destruction of Jerusalem and the Captivity which began in the sixth century B.C. It was soon superseded by Aramaic, which became the literary as well as the spoken medium of the Jews after the Maccabean period. Hebrew survived only as a language of scholarship and ritual, like Latin in medieval Christendom. It never quite ceased to be written or spoken. Its uninterrupted, though slender, continuity with the past has encouraged Zionists to increase the difficulties of existence for Jews by trying to revive it as a living tongue.

Another Canaanite dialect, Phoenician, is closely related to Hebrew. At a very early period the Phoenicians had succeeded in monopolizing the Mediterranean trade, mainly at the expense of Crete and Egypt. Phoenician settlements were to be found in Rhodes, Sicily, Marseilles, and countless places along the North African coast. In the fourth century B.C. Phoenician ships were trading with South Britain, and had even skirted the shores of West Africa. As the result of this vigorous commercial expansion, the Phoenician language, and with it the Phoenician alphabet which became the mother of most of the world's alphabets, was distributed throughout the Mediterranean basin. Only in Carthage, the richest Phoenician colony, did it become firmly established as a medium of speech. Several centuries after it had ceded place to Aramaic in the more ancient Phoenician communities of Tyre and Sidon, it maintained itself in the African colony.

There it persisted till the fourth or fifth century A.D. According to St. Augustine, who came from North Africa, Carthaginian Phoenician, sometimes called *Punic*, differed little from Hebrew. Phoenician is preserved in many but insignificant inscriptions from the home country and from its colonies, and in ten lines which the Roman playwright, Plautus, inserted in his *Poenulus*.

During the four centuries after Mohammed, the spectacular spread of Islam pushed aside nearly all other Semitic languages in favor of Arabic. The Koran had to be read and chanted in the language of the Prophet himself. Unlike Christianity, Muslims never proselytized for their faith by translation. The various Arabic dialects now spoken from Morocco to the Middle East differ greatly, but a common literary language still holds together widely separated speech communities. The Muslim conquests diffused Arabic over Mesopotamia, Syria, Egypt, the north of Africa, and even parts of Europe. Its impact left Persian with a vocabulary diluted by addition of Semitic, almost equal in number to indigenous words. Even European languages retain many to testify to commercial, industrial, and scientific achievements of Muslim civilization. Familiar examples are: *tariff, traffic, magazine, admiral, muslim, alcohol, Aldebaran, nadir, zero, cipher, algebra, sugar.*

Between the beginning of the ninth and the end of the fifteenth century A.D., Europe assimilated the technique of Muslim civilization, as Japan assimilated the technique of Western civilization during the latter half of the nineteenth century. Scholars of Northern Europe had to acquire a knowledge of Arabic as well as of Latin at a time when Moorish Spain was the flower of European culture, a thriving center of world trade, and the sole custodian of all the mechanics, medicine, astronomy, and mathematics in the ancient world. While Arabic scholars of the chief centers of Muslim culture, such as Damascus, Cairo, Cordova, and Palermo, refused to deviate from the classical Arabic of pre-Islamitic poetry and the Koran, the speech of the common people evolved further and split into the several vernaculars of Syria, Tripoli, Iraq, Algeria, Tunis, Egypt, and Morocco. Their common characteristics are a reduction of vowels, the decay of the flexional system, and heavy admixture of non-Arabic words. Today Arabic is spoken by about forty million people.

About the fourth century A.D., Ethiopia responded to the efforts of Coptic missionaries, and embraced the Christian faith. Thereafter Abyssinian Semitic, known as *Ge'ez* or *Ethiopic*, became a medium of literary activity. It died out as a spoken language in the fourteenth century, but like Sanskrit, Latin, and classical Arabic continued to function as a medium of religious practice, and as such is still the liturgical language of the Abyssinian Church. Its living descendants are *Amharic*, *Tigrina* of Northern Abyssinia, and *Tigré* of Eritrea. *Maltese*, which is of Arabic origin, is the language of a Christian community. It is transcribed in the Latin alphabet.

The reader of *The Loom of Language* will now be familiar with two outstanding peculiarities of the Semitic group. One is called *triliteralism* (p. 57). The other is the prevalence of *internal vowel change*. When relieved of affixes and internal vowels the majority of root words have a core of *three consonants*. Within this fixed framework great variety is possible by ringing the changes on different vowel combinations. With only five simple vowels it is possible to make twenty-five different vocables of the pattern *b-g-n*, in the English triliteral grouping: *begin-began-begun*. It is scarcely an exaggeration to say that a Semitic language exhausts most of the conceivable possibilities of internal vowel change consistent with an inflexible triple-consonant frame.

A distinct arrangement of three particular consonants has its characteristic element of meaning. Thus in Arabic, *katala* means "he killed," *kutila* means "he was killed," *katil* means "murder," and *kitl* means "enemy." The range of root inflexion in the Semitic family vastly exceeds what we find in any Aryan language. Within the Aryan group internal vowel change always plays second fiddle to external flexion. Even in German, where it looms large, the variety of derivatives distinguished by affixes is much greater than the variety of derivatives distinguished by modification of a stem vowel. Among the Semitic dialects modification of the vowel pattern is orderly and all-pervading.

The Semitic noun has possessive affixes like those of Finno-Ugrian languages (p. 190). In other ways the grammar of Semitic dialects recalls features more characteristic of the Aryan tribe. The verb has two tense forms, imperfect and perfect, denoting *aspect* (p. 91). The noun has subject and object forms, singular and plural. The older Semitic dialects had dual forms. The Arabic dual disappeared in the seventh century A.D. Pronouns of the second and third person, like adjectives, have endings appropriate to two noun classes, respectively called masculine and feminine, with as much and as little justice as the so-called masculine and feminine nouns of French or

Spanish. Gender distinction has also infected the verb. Thus the third person of the Arabic verb has the suffixes *a* (masculine) and *at* (feminine). The absence of explicit vowel symbols in the old Semitic script adds to the difficulties which this load of grammatical ballast imposes on anyone who wishes to learn Arabic or Hebrew.

CHINESE

Two characteristics make a language more easy to learn than it would otherwise be. One is grammatical regularity. The other is word economy. Nearly all the languages previously discussed in this chapter are overcharged with irregularities or with devices which unnecessarily multiply the number of word forms essential for acceptable communication. The difficulty of learning Chinese and related languages is of a different sort.

Chinese vernaculars make up one of three branches of the great *Indo-Chinese* family. The other two are represented by the *Tibeto-Burmese* group and the *Tai* languages, including *Siamese* and *Annamese*. The several members of the family are geographically contiguous and have two outstanding similarities. One is that they are *tone* languages. Otherwise identical words uttered in different tones may have great diversity of meaning. In fact, tone differences do the same job as the vowel differences in such a series as *pat, pet, pit, pot, put*. Their second peculiarity is not equally characteristic of the Tibeto-Burmese group which has agglutinative features. With this qualification, it is broadly true to say that all the root words—i.e., all words excluding compounds made by juxtaposition of vocables with an independent existence like that of *ale* and *house* in *alehouse*—are *monosyllabic*. For what we can convey by internal or external flexion Chinese languages rely wholly on position, on auxiliary particles and on compounds.

For the common ancestry of all the members of the family one clue is lacking. In their present form they have no clear-cut community of vocabulary; and we have no means of being certain about whether they ever had a recognizably common stock of word material. The literature of China goes back several thousand years, but it does not give us the information we need. Chinese writing is a logographic script (p. 43). It tells us very little about sounds corresponding to the written symbols when writing first came into use. When the Chinese of today read out a passage from one of their classical authors, they pronounce the words as they would pronounce the words of a newspaper or an advertisement.

Some 400 million people of China, Manchuria, and part of Mongolia now speak the vernaculars which go by the name of Chinese. They include: (*a*) the *Mandarin* dialects, of which the *North Chinese* of about 250 million people is the most important; (*b*) the *Kiangsi* dialects; (*c*) the *Central-Coastal* group (Shanghai, Ningpo, Hangkow); (*d*) the *South Chinese* dialects (Foochow, Amoy-

Compound Character		First Component		Second Component	
明	ming² bright	日	rï² sun	月	ywe⁴ moon
好	hao³ good	女	nyü³ daughter	子	dzê³ son
行	shying² walk	彳	chê² left step	亍	chu² right step
林	lin² woods	木	mu⁴ wood	木	mu⁴ wood

FIG. 40.—COMPOUND CHINESE CHARACTERS
WITH TWO MEANING COMPONENTS

(Adapted from Firth's *The Tongues of Men*)

Swatow, Cantonese-Hakka). The dialects north of the Yang-tse-kiang are remarkably homogeneous if we take into consideration their geographical range; but it is misleading to speak of the vernaculars of all China as dialects of a single language. The southerner who knows only his own vernacular cannot converse with the northerner. China has no common medium of *speech* in the sense that Britain, France, or Germany have one; but is now in the process of evolving a common language based on the northern dialects, more especially Pekingese.*

There are very few exceptions to the rule that *all* Chinese words are monosyllabic. Such as they are, some are repetitive or onomatopoeic, e.g. KO-KO (*brother*) or HA-HA (*laughter*), and others

* The examples given in what follows represent Pekingese.

would probably prove to be compounds, if we were able to delve back into the past. Our own language has moved far in the same direction. In the course of a thousand years there has been wholesale denudation of final vowels and assimilation of terminal syllables. The result has been a large increase of our stock in trade of monosyllabic words. *Though it is far from true to say that all our words are now of this class, it is by no means hard to spin out a long strip of them. In fact, you have one in front of your eyes as you read this. If you try*

Compound Character	'Meaning' Component	'Sound' Component
跑 phao³ to run	足 dzu² foot	包 bao¹ wrap
洪 hung² flood	水 shwei³ water	共 gung⁴ common
炸 dza² to fry	火 hwê³ fire	乍 dza⁴ sudden
訪 fang³ to call & ask	言 yen² words	方 fang¹ direction or square

FIG. 41.—COMPOUND CHINESE CHARACTERS WITH MEANING AND PHONETIC COMPONENT

(Adapted from Firth's *The Tongues of Men*)

to do the same, you will find out that the ones you choose are the words you use, or at least the words that most of us use, most of the time. The ones we have most on our lips are just these small words. By the time you get as far as the next full stop you will have met more than six score of them with no break; and it would be quite a soft job to go on a long time in the same strain as the old rhyme Jack and Jill.

This is not the only way in which Anglo-American approaches Chinese. The reader of *The Loom of Language* no longer needs to be told that English has discarded most of the flexions with which it was equipped a thousand years ago or how much we now rely on the use of unchangeable words. True the process did not complete itself; but there are now few ways in which we have to modify word forms. Our stock of essential words includes a small and sterile class with internal changes such as those of *sing-sang* or *foot-feet*. Otherwise the terminal -*s* of the plural noun, the endings -*s*, -*ed* and -*ing* of the verb together with the optional affixes -*er* and -*est* which we tack on to adjectives circumscribe the flexions which usage demands. It is a short step to Chinese vernaculars of which all words are invariant. With very few exceptions the Chinese word is an unalterable block of material. It tolerates neither flexions nor derivative affixes such as the -*er* in *baker*. In general, its form tells us nothing to suggest that it denotes an act, a state, a quality, a thing, or a person.

One and the same word may thus slip from one grammatical niche to another; and what we call the *parts of speech* have little to do with how Chinese words behave. The word SHANG may mean the *above one*, i.e., *ruler*, and then corresponds to an Aryan noun. In SHANG PIEN (*above side*) it does the job of an Aryan adjective. In SHANG MA (*to above a horse*, i.e., *to mount one*) it is a verb equivalent. In MA SHANG (*horse above*, i.e., *on the horse*) it does service as post-posited directive corresponding to one of our prepositions. Here again we are on familiar ground. We *down* a man, take the *down* train and walk *down* the road. We *house* our goods, sell a *house* and do as little *house* work as possible. This is not to say that all Chinese names for things may also denote actions. The word NÜ (*woman*) is never equivalent to an Aryan verb, though JÊN (*man*) may mean *performing the act of a man*, a one-sided way of expressing the act of coitus. Anglo-American provides a parallel. We *man* a boat but we do not *woman* a cookery class. We buy *salt* and *salt* our soup, *bottle* wine and drink from the *bottle*, but we do not as yet *mustard* our bacon or *cupboard* our pants.

Whether a particular Chinese sound signifies thing, attribute, direction, or action depends in part on context, in part on word order, as illustrated above by MA SHANG and SHANG MA. In everyday speech there is an incipient tendency to mark such distinction by affixation as we distinguish the noun *singer* from the verb *sing* or by pronunciation, as we distinguish between the noun *présent* and the verb *presént* (i.e., make a present). For example, the toneless TZU (pronounced *dze*), a literary word for child, attaches itself to other words, forming couplets which stand for *things*, e.g. PEN-TZU (*exercise book*). So TZU is now the signpost of a concrete object in the spoken language, as -*ly* (originally meaning *like*) is now a signpost of an English qualifier (adjective or adverb). In the fourth tone (p. 438) PEI means *the back*, and in the first tone it means *to carry on one's back*. Difference of tone also distinguishes CH'ANG (*long*) from CHANG (*to get long*, i.e., to grow). A strong aspiration after the initial CH further distinguishes the first from the second number of the couplet.

There is no trace of gender in Chinese vernaculars. Thus a single pronoun of the third person does service (T'A in Pekingese) for male or female, thing or person alike. By recourse to separate particles, such as our words *few*, *many*, *several*, plurality becomes explicit for emphasis or when confusion might arise. To express totality Chinese resorts to the age-old and widespread trick of duplication. Thus JÊN-JÊN means *all men* and T'IEN-T'IEN means *everyday*. One plural particle MÊN (*class*) attaches itself to names for persons, e.g. HSIEN SHÊNG MÊN (*teachers*) or to personal pronouns. Thus we have:

WO	*I, me*	WO-MÊN	*we, us*
NI	*thou, thee*	NI-MÊN	*you*
T'A	*he, she, it, him, her*	T'A-MÊN	*they, them*

Like the noun, the Chinese pronoun has no case forms. Before the indirect object the particle KEI which means *give* does the work of *to* in English or of the *dative* terminal in German. Thus WO CHIE KEI LAO-JE LA means *I lend give gentleman finished*, i.e., *I have lent it to the gentleman*. In literary Chinese juxtaposition does the work of the genitive terminal, e.g. MIN LI (*people power*) means the *power of the people*, as *money power* means *power of money* and *mother love* means *love of a mother*. Colloquial Chinese inserts a particle TI between MIN (*people*) and LI (*power*), as we can preposit *of* in the preceding. The postposited particle TI may also attach itself to a pronoun. So WO-TI means *mine, of me*. If Karlgren is right TI began its career as a pointer word, but it no longer exists as an independent word. It is now comparable to a flexional affix such as the *-s* in *people's*.

Needless to say, Chinese has no special marks for person, tense, mood, or voice. As in colloquial Italian and Spanish, it is the usual thing to leave out the personal pronoun when the situation supplies it. In polite or submissive speech a depreciative expression takes the place of the ego (WO in Pekingese), and a laudatory one ("honorific") does service for *you*. Since there is no flexion the same syllable LAI may mean *go, went, going*, etc. In the absence of another word to stress that a process or state is over and done with, or that the issue is closed, the perfective particle LA can follow the verb. LA is a toneless and contracted form of LIAO meaning *complete* or *finished*. Future time can be made explicit: (*a*) with an adverbial particle equivalent to *soon, henceforth, later on*, etc.; (*b*) by the helper YAO which has an independent existence equivalent to *wish* or *want*, the original meaning of our own helper *will*. Thus we may say: T'A LAI *he comes, he is coming;* T'A LAI LA *he has come, he came;* T'A YAO LAI *he will come.* The particle PA (*stop*) is the signal of a peremptory command, e.g. CH'Ü PA (*clear out*); but it is more polite to use YAO exactly as we use *will* and the French use *vouloir* in *will you tell me* or *veuillez me dire*.

It goes without saying that a language with complete absence of flexion and a large number of ambiguous words must have rules of word order no less rigid than those of English. What is surprising is that so many of the syntactical conventions of Chinese agree with our own. In a straightforward statement, the order in both languages is subject—verb—object. This is illustrated by the following:

I do not fear him. WO PU P'A T'A.

He does not fear me. T'A PU P'A WO.

These sentences show that position alone stamps *WO* as what we call the subject of the first and the object of the second. The object is placed for emphasis at the head of the sentence only where misunderstanding is impossible. In such a statement as the following, the subject is still immediately in front of the verb:

CHE-KO HUA WO PU HSIN = $\dfrac{this\ language\ I\ not\ believe}{\text{(i.e., I don't believe that)}}$

The position of the adjective equivalent is the same in Chinese as in Anglo-American. The attributive adjective comes first as in HAO JÊN (*a good man*). The predicative adjective comes after the noun but without a copula equivalent to *be*. Thus JÊN HAO means *the man is good*.

At other points Anglo-American and Chinese rules of syntax diverge to greater or less degree. Conditional statements and interrogation are two of them. Chinese uses *if* sparingly. It gets along by mere juxtaposition as in conversational English:

T'A-MEN   MAN-MAN-TI   SHUO   WO   CHIU   MING-PAI
they   *slowly*   *speak*   *I*   *then*   *understand*
(i.e., if they spoke slowly I should understand)

There is no inversion of word order in a question of the *yes-no* type. A Chinese question may be a plain statement with an interrogative particle equivalent to *eh?* at the end of it, e.g. T'A LAI MO *he comes eh*, i.e., *is he coming?* Instead of adding MO (*eh?*) to T'A LAI (*he is coming*) it is possible to add a *negation* reminiscent of the nursery jingle *she loves me, she loves me not*. Thus T'A LAI PU LAI (*he come, not come*) means the same as T'A LAI MO. One feature of Chinese has no parallel in European languages. What corresponds to a transitive verb must always trail an object behind it. In effect the Chinese say *he does not want to read books* or *he does not want to write characters* where we should simply say *he does not want to read* or *he does not want to write*. Omission of an object confers a passive meaning, e.g. CHE-KO JÊN TA-SSU LA (*this man kill finished*) means *this man has been killed*.

Everything said so far underlines the likeness of the Chinese to our own way of saying something, and there would be nothing left to write about, if the sound pattern of Chinese were comparable to an English purged of polysyllables. With no rules of grammar but a few common-sense directions about the arrangement of words, with no multiplicity of words disguised for different grammatical categories, as we disguise *Bible* in *Biblical* or as German duplicates its transitive and intransitive verbs, a Chinese dialect would be the easiest language to learn. In fact, it is not.

The range of elementary sounds, i.e., simple vowels and consonants, in no language exceeds about forty. So it stands to reason that the number of pronounceable syllables cannot be equal to the number of stars. In Chinese, the possible maximum is reduced by two characteristics of the spoken language. One is that the Chinese syllable never tolerates initial consonant clusters other than TS, DS, and CH, i.e., no Chinese words have the same form as our *spree, clay, plea*. The second is that the monosyllable ends either in a vowel or in one of a small range of consonants. Even in ancient times the terminal consonants were not more than six in number (*p, t, k, m, n, ng*); and in the northern dialect today, only the last two (*n, ng*) occur. That is to say, nearly all words are monosyllables of the *open* type like our words *by, me, so*. Within the framework of these limitations, the number of pronounceable syllables which can be made up is very small compared with the size of our vocabulary. Indeed, it is a tiny fraction of what the vocabulary of a monosyllabic language would be if it admitted closed syllables, like *stamps* or *clubs*, with double or treble consonants at each end.

The reader will not be slow to draw one inference. At an early date Chinese was encumbered with a large number of homophones, i.e., words with the same sound and different meanings. When further reduction of final sounds took place, the number multiplied. At one time the language of North China distinguished between KA (song), KAP (frog), KAT (cut), and KAK (each). Now the four different words have merged in the single open monosyllable KO. This loss of word substance, together with limitations set upon the character of the syllable, means that less than five hundred mono-syllables are now available for all the things and ideas the Chinese may wish to express by single or compound words. Professor Karl-gren describes what this entails as follows:

"A small dictionary, including only the very commonest words of the language, gives about 4,200 simple words, which gives an average of *ten* different words for each syllable. But it is not to be expected that the words should be evenly distributed among the syllables; the number of homophones in a series is therefore sometimes smaller, sometimes larger. Of the common 4,200 words there are only two that are pronounced *jun*, but 69 that have the pronunciation *i*, 59 *shi*, 29 *ku*, and so forth."

Homophones exist in modern European languages though we often overlook their presence because of differences of spelling (*to-too-two*), gender, as in the German words *der Kiefer* (the jaw) and *die Kiefer* (the fir), or both, as in the French words *le porc* (the pork) and *la pore* (the pore). They are particularly frequent in English. Even if we limit ourselves to those homophones which are made up of an initial consonant and a vowel, like a typical Chinese word, we find such familiar examples as *bay* (color), *bay* (tree), *bay* (sea), *bay* (bark);* *sea, see, See* or *so, sew, sow,* or the following pairs:

be,	bee	doe,	dough	roe,	row
boy,	buoy	hie,	high	toe,	tow
bow,	bough	nay,	neigh	we,	wee
die,	dye	no,	know	way,	weigh

* (a) From French *bai;* (b) from Old French *baie,* Latin *bacca* (berry); (c) from French *baie,* Latin *baia;* (d) from Old French *bayer,* Modern French *aboyer.*

This enumeration does not include words which are also homophones because of the silent Anglo-American (as opposed to Scots) *r*, e.g. *maw, more; saw, soar*. In spite of their great number, English homophones cause no embarrassment in speech because the intended meaning is indicated by the sentence in which they occur, and by the situation in which speaker and hearer find themselves. For this reason, no naval decorator has painted the *boys* when asked to paint the *buoys*. No difficulty arises in real life because *flag* signifies a piece of bunting, as well as a harmless English water flower, or because *spirit* stands for an intoxicant and part of a medium's stock in trade.

Though homophones are more abundant in English than in any other European languages, English homophones are few compared with the total number of words in common use. Indeed, we may well ask how it is possible to communicate with only little over four hundred monosyllables, most of which stand for scores of unrelated things. The answer is that Chinese possesses several peculiar safeguards against confusion of sound and meaning. To begin with, most Chinese homophones are not true homophones of the English *by-buy* type. On this page LI (*pear*), LI (*plum*), and LI (*chestnut*) look exactly the same. In speech they are not. Difference of *tone* keeps them apart. Tone differences which go with a difference of meaning exist in other languages, as when we pronounce *yes* or *yeah* in a matter of fact, interrogative, ironical, or surprised manner; but such differences are casual. The tone differences of Chinese are not casual intrusions. Its proper tone is an essential part of the word. The number of tones varies in different Chinese languages. Cantonese is said to have nine. Pekingese has now only four. It is impossible to convey the differences on paper; but we can get a hint from the language of music. The first is the high level tone ♫ the second the high rising ♫ the third the low rising ♫ the fourth the high falling ♫ . In the first tone FU means *husband*, in the second *fortune*, in the third *government office*, and in the fourth *rich*.

Nobody knows how this elaborate system arose. It would be naïve to believe that the Chinese ever became aware of the dangerous turn their language was taking and deliberately started to differentiate homophones by tone. It is more likely that some tones represent the pronunciation of old monosyllables, while other tones are survivals of words which were once disyllabic and as such had an intonation different from that of monosyllabic words. Though the existence of distinct tones greatly reduces the number of genuine homophones, many words spoken in one tone cover a bewildering variety of different notions. For instance, *I* in the first tone means *one, dress, rely on, cure;* in the second *barbarian, soap, doubt, move;* in the third *chair, ant, tail;* and in the fourth *sense, wing, city, translate, discuss.* Evidently, therefore, Chinese must possess other devices besides tone to make effective speech possible. The most important is the juxtaposition of synonyms or near synonyms. An example will make this clear. Our words *expire* and *die* would both be liable to misunderstanding if listed as such in a vocabulary. *Die* may mean: (*a*) *cease to live,* (*b*) a *metallic mold* or *stamp,* (*c*) a small *toy* of *cubical shape. Expire* may mean: (*a*) *breathe outward,* (*b*) *cease to live.* We can make the first meaning of *die* explicit in our word list, if we write *die—expire.* The second meaning of *expire* comes to life in the same way, when we write *expire—die.* This is what the Chinese do when they combine K'AN (*see* or *investigate*) with CHIEN (*see* or *build*) to make K'AN-CHIEN which means *see* alone. We might clarify the second meaning of *die* as given above by writing *die-mold* or *die-stamp* in which the second element is a generic term. This is what the Chinese do when they make up FU-CH'IN from FU which in one tone means *father, oppose, split,* or *belly* and CH'IN (a *kinsman*). The trick of sorting out homophones by making such couplets pervades Chinese speech and asserts itself when the laborer speaks *pidgin,* e.g. *look-see* for *see.*

If we rank *alehouse* and *housemaid* as disyllabic words, colloquial Chinese is rich in disyllables. It is a monosyllable language in the sense that it contains scarcely any trace of syllables which have no independent mobility, e.g. the syllables *-dom* in *wisdom* or *-es* in *houses.* In nearly all such compounds as those illustrated above, one part like the syllable *man* in *postman* may carry a weaker stress, but like *man* still has a verbal life of its own. Daily speech accommodates a few syllables which have as little autonomy as the *-ship* in *friendship.* We have already met TZU (p. 433). Then there is a suffix based on ÊRH, a still extant word for *boy.* Originally it gave the word with which it went a diminutive meaning, and had the same function as the *-ling* in *duckling* or *gosling.* As such it became fused in such contractions as LÜ'RH (little ass) from LÜ (ass), or FERH (light breeze) from FENG (wind). Nowadays it has lost its former diminutive force, and is added to words to indicate that they are thing words, e.g. CHU'RH (owner).

Another trick which helps to reduce misunderstandings is the use of *numeratives*, words which usually follow a numeral, pointer word, or interrogative as *head* follows the numeral in *three head of cattle*. Different classes of words have different classifiers of this sort. We

Parent Chinese Character	KATA-KANA	Sound	Parent Chinese Character	KATA-KANA	Sound	Parent Chinese Character	KATA-KANA	Sound
阿	ア	a	千	チ	chi	牟	ム	mu
伊	イ	i	門津	ツ	tsu	女	メ	me
宇	ウ	u	天	テ	te	毛	モ	mo
江	エ	e	土	ト	to	也	ヤ	ya
於	オ	o	奈	ナ	na	勇油	ユ	yu
加	カ	ka	仁二	ニ	ni	與	ヨ	yo
幾	キ	ki	奴	ヌ	nu	良	ラ	ra
久	ク	ku	子	ネ	ne	利	リ	ri
个計	ケ	ke	乃	ノ	no	流	ル	ru
己	コ	ko	八	ハ	fa(ha)	礼	レ	re
草散左	サ	sa	比	ヒ	fi(hi)	呂	ロ	ro
之	シ	shi	不	フ	fu	日	ワ	wa
須	ス	su	皿邊	ヘ	fe(he)	慧	エ	we
世	セ	se	保	ホ	fo(ho)	伊	井	wi
曾	ソ	so	末	マ	ma	乎	ヲ	wo
多	タ	ta	三美	ミ	mi	—	—	—

Fig. 42.—Parent Chinese Characters of the Katakana (older) Japanese Syllabary

have already met one KO (*piece*) which keeps company with JÊN (*man*) as in SAN-KO JÊN (*three piece men*, i.e., three men). KO is the numerative of the largest class. Others are K'OU (*mouth*) for things with a round opening such as a pot or a well, PA (*handle*) for knives, spoons and the like, FENG (*seal*) for letters and parcels,

KUA (*hanging*) for a *necklace, beard,* and other suspended objects. Classificatory particles of this sort are widely current in the speech of preliterate communities the world over, and are highly characteristic of such (p. 310). Seemingly the numerative of Chinese is not a new device for dealing with the homophones but a very ancient characteristic of human communication kept alive by a new need.

If we disregard tone differences the number of distinct root words in spoken Chinese is little more than four hundred, or slightly over twelve hundred if we make allowance for them. These have to do the work of a much larger number of things, actions, and concepts. The written language (p. 43) is not embarrassed by the plethora of homophones. Each symbol has a particular meaning, and several symbols may therefore stand for the same sound. Thus ten symbols of Chinese script stand for the various meanings of LI in the second tone. Unhappily this advantage has its own penalty. To become proficient in reading and writing the Chinese pupil has to learn a minimum of about three thousand to four thousand characters. This entails several years of exacting work which might otherwise lay the foundations of more useful knowledge. So much thankless toil tempts us to wonder why the Chinese do not discard their archaic script in favor of our own more handy and more thrifty alphabet. Turkey has already given the world an inspiring object lesson. Under the benevolent despotism of Ataturk it has exchanged the involved and unsuitable Arabic for Latin letters. The result is that Turkish boys and girls now master the elements of reading and writing in six months instead of two or three years.

Admittedly Turkey's problem is a simpler one. Turkish is an agglutinative language, adapted as such to regular conventions of spelling; but the Romanization of Chinese script would lead to hopeless confusion, if it followed the customary practice of transcription in maps and Western newspapers. A satisfactory alphabetic orthography has to bring the tones to life; and there are several feasible ways of doing so. We might distinguish the four Pekingese tones by diacritic marks as in the French series: *e, é, è, ê*. In accordance with the system of Sir Thomas Wade we can put a number in the top right-hand corner, as in many primers for European students. A new and much better transcription is the *National Language Romanization* (Gwoyeu Romatzyh) designed by a Chinese scholar for Chinese use. In the *Gwoyeu Romatzyh* the syllable has a basic core which corresponds to its pronunciation in the first tone, and carries a ter-

minal element to distinguish the second, third, and fourth tones respectively. Where Wade gives TA[1], TA[2], TA[3], TA[4] the *Gwoyeu
Romatzyh* puts DA, DAR, DAA, DAH. Compounds are treated as
single units like *playhouse* and *housewife*. Absence of numeral super-
scripts or diacritic marks lightens the job of the stenographer and
keeps down the size of the keyboard. Below is a sentence (*I add yet
another horizontal stroke*) in Wade's system and in the *National
Romanization:*

WOO	TZAY	JIASHANQ	YIGEH	HERNGL
WO[3]	TSAI[4]	CHIA[1]-SHANG[4]	I[2]-KÊ[3]	HÊNG[2]-ÊRH[0]
I	again	add-upon	one-piece	horizontal + dimin-utive affix

The *National Language Romanization* has made a promising start.
Dictionaries, periodicals, and textbooks have been printed in it, and
associations exist to advertise its far-reaching benefits. In the absence
of other obstacles, its adoption in its present or an amended form
would bring the art of reading within the reach of every Chinese
boy and girl. Foreigners could learn Chinese without having to master the intricacies of a wholly alien script. Elimination of illiteracy
would go hand in hand with diminishing prestige of scholars who
have now a vested interest in the survival of worthless traditions.

The present form of writing shuts the door to the internationally
current terminology of modern science and technology. Sometimes
the Chinese assimilate foreign words in print by using the device mentioned in Chapter II (p. 55). To a large extent they rely on *Ersatz*
products for new technical terms which they paraphrase in their own
words. Thus a *vitamin* is *what protects the people's life* and *aniline*, less
informatively, is *foreign red*. *Electricity* is the *lightning air* and *gas* is
air of coal. In short, China is assimilating twentieth-century science
through the medium of a seventeenth-century technique of discourse.

A social obstacle to reform remains while the Roman alphabet continues to be a symbol of foreign exploitation and Western arrogance;
but the advantages of phonetic writing do not necessarily entail the
use of our own letters. A phonetic script based on thirty-nine Chinese
characters has been under discussion since 1913. In 1918 it won a
place on the school syllabus. Missionaries alert to the advantages of
the *Chu-Yin-Tzu-Mu*, as it is called, have used it in adult education.
They claim that Chinese men and women who had never been able

to read or write their own names mastered the use of it after three to six weeks of tuition. One common objection to reform of Chinese writing is the plea that it would cut off China from her literary past. The truth is that contact with the classics through the medium of script has been the prerogative of a very small class for whom a classical education has been the master key to a successful career in the service of the government. The Chinese masses who toil for a handful of rice cannot lose what they have never possessed.

Another objection is less easy to refute. As yet, China has no common spoken language which everybody everywhere understands. The only language common to north and south is the written language, in which literate people of Peking or Canton, Foochow and Shanghai can read the same notices at the railway stations or the same advertisements by the roadside. The fact that they can do so depends upon the fact that the written language is not based directly on the diverse sounds they utter when they read them aloud. Happily the northern speech is gaining ground, and a common Chinese is taking shape, as a common English took shape in the fourteenth century, and as the dialect of Paris became the language of France.

The disabilities arising from the existence of the homophones extend beyond the boundaries of the Indo-Chinese group. Throughout its history Japan has continually borrowed Chinese words. At one time this chiefly affected discussion of religious, artistic, and philosophic topics. Of late years the range of the Chinese loan words has broadened, because the Japanese sometimes build up technical terms from Chinese as we build them from Greek roots. Thus *electricity* is DEN-KI (*light spirit*). The Japanese vocabulary is now supercharged with monosyllabic sounds which mean many different things. When the *Kana* or syllabic writing (p. 54) was new, Japanese writers would use it exclusively without recourse to Chinese characters as such. Gradually the habit of introducing the ideogram gained ground owing to the influence of Chinese models. The result is that modern Japanese is a mixture of two syllabic scripts and a formidable battery of Chinese characters. The syllable signs represent the sound values of the affixes and particles, the ideograms are used for the core of an inflected word. Thus the Japanese pupil has to learn the two syllabaries (*Hiragana* and *Katakana*) together with about fifteen hundred Chinese characters. Educated Japanese acutely realize their handicap, but the ambiguities which would arise from an enormous number of imported homophones are an almost insurmountable obstacle to the plea for exclusive use of one or other of the syllabaries. Consequently there is a movement to introduce the Roman alphabet. It is somewhat more economical than the syllabaries, and it would have two more

Parent Chinese Character	HIRAGANA	Sound	Parent Chinese Character	HIRAGANA	Sound	Parent Chinese Character	HIRAGANA	Sound
安	あ	a	知	ち	chi	武	む	mu
以	い	i	川	つ	tsu	女	め	me
宇	う	u	天	て	te	毛	も	mo
衣	え	e	止	と	to	也	や	ya
於	お	o	奈	な	na	由	ゆ	yu
加	か	ka	仁	に	ni	与	よ	yo
幾	き	ki	奴	ぬ	nu	良	ら	ra
久	く	ku	禰	ね	ne	利	り	ri
計	け	ke	乃	の	no	留	る	ru
己	こ	ko	波	は	fa(ha)	礼	れ	re
左	さ	sa	比	ひ	fi(hi)	呂	ろ	ro
之	し	shi	不	ふ	fu	和	わ	wa
寸	す	su	部	へ	fe(he)	為	ゐ	wi
世	せ	se	保	ほ	fo(ho)	惠	ゑ	we
曾	そ	so	末	ま	ma	遠	を	wo
太	た	ta	美	み	mi			—

FIG. 43.—PARENT CHINESE CHARACTERS OF THE HIRAGANA (LATER) JAPANESE SYLLABARY

substantial advantages. One is the possibility of distinguishing between homophones as we do when we write, wright, right, and rite. The other is that it is impossible to represent the compound consonants of Latin or Greek roots in international technical terms with Kana signs.

Westernization has brought about a new influx of foreign words, mainly from English sources, and Japanese has freely assimilated international technical terms in preference to compounds of Chinese monosyllables. In doing so it distorts them in conformity with its

		M	N	S	Z	P	B	T	D	K	G	Y	R	H	W
A	ア	マ	ナ	サ	ザ	パ	バ	タ	ダ	カ	ガ	ヤ	ラ	ハ	ワ
I	イ	ミ	ニ	シ	ジ	ピ	ビ	チ	ヂ	キ	ギ	イ	リ	ヒ	ヰ
U	ウ	ム	ヌ	ス	ズ	プ	ブ	ツ	ヅ	ク	グ	ユ	ル	フ	ウ
E	エ	メ	ネ	セ	ゼ	ペ	ベ	テ	デ	ケ	ゲ	エ	レ	ヘ	エ
O	オ	モ	ノ	ソ	ゾ	ポ	ボ	ト	ド	コ	ゴ	ヨ	ロ	ホ	ヲ
UN	ン														

FIG. 44.—JAPANESE *Katakana* SYLLABARY

Some of the corresponding sounds are not exactly as indicated in the table, i.e., TI = *chi*, TU = *tsu* and HU = *fhu*. Note that the voiced and voiceless pairs *s-z*, *p-b*, *t-d*, *k-g* are distinguished only by diacritic marks in the top right-hand corner.

own phonetic pattern (Fig. 14 and p. 209). What is *foreign red* in China is *anirin*, and *spirit of coal* is *gazu*. Typical of such distortions are *peju* (page), *basu* (bus), *pondo* (pound), *doresu* (dress), *gurando* (sports ground), *kurimu* (cream), *tuparaita* (typewriter).

Till recent times European scholars did not doubt that the monosyllabic uniformity of Chinese reflected human speech at its lowest level. There is now some evidence for the view that Chinese may not always have been an isolating language of monosyllables. Modern scholars believe that Chinese once had disyllabic words which became shortened through phonetic decay and fusion, as the Old English *lufu* has been reduced to *love*, and the Latin *bestia* (beast) to French *bête*. According to the researches of Professor Karlgren, the personal pronoun had still distinct forms in the nominative and accusative in the latter part of the Chou Dynasty (1122 B.C.–A.D. 249).

Unfortunately the ideographic nature of Chinese script prevents us from getting any information about the phonetic pattern of the language through its ancient literature. Knowledge of the structure and pronunciation of ancient Chinese is largely based on the sister language *Tibetan*, with literary documents dating from the seventh century A.D. These documents were transcribed in an alphabetic script of Hindu origin. From what they disclose, and from evidence based on rhymes, corroborated by comparison of various modern Chinese dialects, scholars now conclude that the language of China has a disyllabic, inflected past. If their reasoning is correct, Chinese and English may be said to have traveled along the same road at different epochs of human history or prehistory.

This prompts us to ask whether the future evolution of Anglo-American may lead to greater similarities between the two languages, and if so, with what consequences. We have seen that Chinese has one gross defect. It has an immense number of homophones, and it is not sympathetic to the manufacture of new vocables by the use of affixes, or to importation of technical terms of alien origin. Fortunately, there is no likelihood that English would reproduce these defects, if it came still closer to Chinese by dropping its last vestiges of useless flexions. English has two safeguards against impoverishment of meaning by depletion of its vocable resources. One is that it is constantly coining new technical terms by combination of borrowed affixes with native or alien roots. The other is that its inherent phonetic peculiarities permit an immense variety of monosyllables. So its stock of separate pronounceable elements would still be relatively enormous, even if all of them were monosyllables.

CONTACT VERNACULARS

In various parts of the world, intercourse between Europeans and indigenous peoples has given birth to *contact* vernaculars. The best known are *Beach-la-Mar* of the Western Pacific, *pidgin English* of the Chinese ports, Gambia, Sierra Leone, Liberia, etc., and the French *patois* of Mauritius, Madagascar, and the west coast of Africa. The formative process has been the same for each of them. Partly from contempt, partly from an ill-founded belief that he is making things easier for the native, the white man addresses the latter in the truncated idiom of mothers—or lovers. Some people drop into such tricks of expression when talking to a foreigner who is not at home in their own language. Thus a Frenchman will say to an American tourist *moi, beaucoup aimer les américains*, i.e., *j'aime bien les américains*. On their side, natives of subject communities react to the white man by re-echoing the phraseology in which they receive their orders. Everywhere the new speech product consists of more or less deformed European words strung together with a minimum of grammar.

In pidgin English, grammatical reduction does not amount to much, because English has met Chinese halfway. French, which clings to more remnants of its flexional past, offers more to bite on. Thus the noun of French, as it is spoken by descendants of African slaves in Mauritius, has lost its gender. If the adjective has different masculine and feminine forms, the Creole eliminates one, e.g. *éne bon madame* (= *une bonne madame*). The demonstrative *ça* stands for *ce, cet, ces*, as well as for *ceci, cela, celui, celle, ceux, celles*. *Mo* (= *moi*) means *I* before a verb, and *my* before a noun. *Li* (= *lui*) means *he* or *him*. Simplification of the verbal apparatus is pushed to the uttermost. The Creole verb is the form most often used, i.e., the past participle or the imperative, e.g. *vini* (= *venir*), *manzé* (= *manger*). To indicate time or aspect, the Creole relies on helpers. Thus *va* (or *pour*) points to the future, e.g. *li va vini* (*he will come*). The helper which signifies the simple past is *té* or *ti* (= *été*), e.g. *mo té manzé* (I ate). In the same way *finé* or *fini* expresses completed action, e.g. *mo finé causé* (I have spoken, and won't say more). The form *té* or *ti*, which combines with the invariant verb stem, is all that is left of the conjugation (or usage) of *être*. There is no copula. For *je suis malade*, the Mauritian Creole says *mo malade* (I sick). Since *té* or *ti* has no other function, there is no literal equivalent for the Cartesian claptrap *I think, therefore I am*.

Orthodox linguists have paid scant attention to these vernaculars. Consequently there is little available information about them. To the student of language planning for world co-operation, they have salutary lessons. Above all, they open a new approach to the question: what are minimal grammatical requirements of communication at a particular cultural level? Apart from Steiner, the inventor of *Pasilingua* (1885), none of the pioneers of language planning seems to have considered them worthy of sympathetic study.

Pioneers of Language Planning

OUR last chapter was about the diseases of natural languages. This one is about the pathology of artificial languages. To many people the last two words, like *interlanguage* or *world-auxiliary*, are terms synonymous with *Esperanto*. In reality Esperanto is only one among several hundred languages which have been constructed during the past three hundred years; and many people who are in favor of a world-auxiliary would prefer to choose one of the languages which a large proportion of the world's literate population already use. The merits of such views will come up for discussion at a later stage.

Language planning started during the latter half of the seventeenth century. The pioneers were Scottish and English scholars. Several circumstances combined to awaken interest in the problem of international communication at this time. One was the decline of Latin as a medium of scholarship. For more than a thousand years Latin made learned Europeans a single fraternity. After the Reformation, the rise of nationalism encouraged the use of vernaculars. In Italy, which had the first modern scientific academy, Galileo set a new fashion by publishing some of his discoveries in his native tongue. The scientific academies of England and France followed his example. From its beginning in 1662, the Royal Society adopted English. According to Sprat, the first historian of the Society, its statutes demanded from its members *a close, naked, natural way of speaking . . . preferring the language of the artisans, countrymen, and merchants before that of wits and scholars.* About thirty years later the Paris Académie des Sciences followed the example of its English counterpart by substituting French for Latin.

The eclipse of Latin meant that there was no single vehicle of cultural intercourse between the learned academies of Europe. Another contemporaneous circumstance helped to make European scholars language conscious. Since the sixteenth-century Swiss naturalist,

Conrad Gessner, had collected samples of the Lord's Prayer in twenty-two different tongues, an ever-increasing variety of information about strange languages and stranger scripts accompanied miscellanies of new herbs, new beasts, and new drugs with cargoes coming back from voyages of discovery. Navigation and missionary fervor fostered new knowledge of Near and Middle Eastern languages, including Coptic, Ethiopic, and Persian. It made samples of Amerindian, of Dravidian, of Malay, and of North Indic vernaculars available to European scholars. In becoming Bible conscious, Europe became Babel conscious.

One linguistic discovery of the seventeenth century is of special importance, because it suggested a possible remedy for the confusion of tongues. The labors of Jesuit missionaries diffused new knowledge about Chinese script. To seventeenth-century Europe Chinese, a script which substituted words for sounds, was a wholly novel way of writing. Still more novel was one consequence of doing so. To the reader of *The Loom* it is now a commonplace that two people from different parts of China can read the same texts without being able to converse with one another. To seventeenth-century Europe it was a nine days' wonder, and the knowledge of it synchronized with a spectacular innovation. Symbolic algebra was taking new shapes. The invention of logarithms and the calculus of Leibniz, himself in the forefront of the linguistic movement, gave mankind an international vocabulary of computation and motion.

Without doubt, the novelty of mathematical symbolism and the novelty of Chinese logographic writing influenced the first proposals for a system of international communication through script. Leibniz corresponded with Jesuit missionaries to find out as much as possible about Chinese; and Descartes, the French philosopher-mathematician, outlined a scheme for a constructed language in 1629. Thanks to our Hindu numerals, anyone—and by *anyone* Descartes meant anyone except the common people of his time—can master the art of naming all possible numbers which can exist in any language in less than a day's work. If so, the ingenuity of philosophers should be up to the job of finding equally universal symbols for *things and notions* set out in a systematic way. These would be the bricks of a language more logical, more economical, more precise, and more easy to learn than any language which has grown out of the makeshifts of daily intercourse. At least, that is what Descartes believed. He did not put his conviction to the test by trying to construct a universal catalogue of things and notions. Forty years later the dream materialized. In 1668 Bishop Wilkins published the *Essay towards a Real Character and a Philosophical Language.*

Wilkins was not first in the field. George Dalgarno, of Aberdeen, also author of a language for the deaf and dumb, and inventor of a new type of shorthand *applicable to all languages,* had undertaken the same task a few years before Wilkins. In 1661 Dalgarno published the *Ars Signorum,* or *Universal Character and Philosophical Language.* Dalgarno claimed that people who spoke any language could use his for intelligible conversation or writing after two weeks. Essentially, this *Art of Symbol* was a lexicon based on a logical classification of "notions." All knowledge, or what Dalgarno and his contemporaries thought was knowledge, was distributed among seventeen main pigeonholes, each indicated by a *consonant,* e.g. *K* = political matters, *N* = natural objects. Dalgarno divided each of the seventeen main classes into subclasses labeled by a Latin or Greek *vowel* symbol, e.g. *Ke* = judicial affairs, *Ki* = criminal offenses, *Ku* = war. Further splitting of the subclasses into groups indicated by consonants and vowels successively led to a pronounceable polysyllable signifying a particular thing, individual, process, or relation.

Thus the four mammals, called *éléphant, cheval, âne,* and *mulet* in French, *Elefant, Pferd, Esel,* and *Maulesel* in German, or *elephant, horse, donkey,* and *mule* in English, are respectively *Nηka, Nηkη, Nηke,* and *Nηko* in Dalgarno's language. The ambition of its engineer was to design something that would be speakable as well as writable; and the grammatical tools he forged for weaving the items of his *catalanguage* into connected statements included genuinely progressive characteristics. The verb is absorbed in the noun, as in headline idiom (p. 120). Case goes into the ash can. The single suffix *-i* shows the plural number of all names. To show how it works, Dalgarno concludes the book with a translation of the first chapter of Genesis, five Psalms, and two of Aesop's *Fables.* Here is a specimen: *Dam semu Sava samesa Nam tηn Nom* = In the beginning God created the heaven and the earth.

Two features of this pioneer enterprise are of special interest today. One is Dalgarno's recognition that all grown languages, including Latin, are irrational, irregular, and uneconomical. The other is explicit in the introduction to his *Didascalocophus* or the *Deaf and Dumb Man's Tutor* (1680), which contains eloquent testimony to the author's Baconian faith in the inventiveness of man:

"About twenty years ago I published . . . a Synopsis of a Philosophical Grammar and Lexicon, thereby showing a way to remedy the difficulties and absurdities which all languages are clogged with ever since the Confusion, or rather since the Fall, by cutting off all redundancy, rectifying all anomaly, taking away all ambiguity and equivocation, contracting the primitives (primary words) to a few number, and even those not to be of a mere arbitrary, but a rational institution, enlarging the bounds of derivation and composition, for the cause both of copia and emphasis. In a word, designing not only to remedie the confusion of language, by giving a much more easie medium of communication than any yet known, but also to cure even Philosophy itself of the diesease of Sophisms and Logomachies; as also to provide her with more wieldy and manageable instruments of operation, for defining, dividing, demonstrating, etc."

The Council of the Royal Society shared this faith. In 1664 the Royal Society appointed a committee for improving the English language. A minute of December 7th runs:

"It being suggested that there were several persons of the Society whose genius was very proper and inclined to improve the English tongue, and particularly for philosophical purposes, it was voted that there be a committee for improving the English language; and that they meet at Sir Peter Wyche's lodgings in Gray's Inn."

What the suggestions of the committee were we do not know. Apparently, no report was handed in, but we know from a letter addressed by the Royal Chancellery to Dalgarno that his language was recommended to the King for support by several Cambridge and Oxford dons, who stressed its value

"for facilitating the matter of Communication and Intercourse between people of different Languages, and consequently a proper and effectual Means of advancing all the parts of Real and Useful knowledge, Civilizing barbarous Nations, Propagating the Gospel, and increasing Traffique and Commerce."

In conclusion the letter observes that if the project of the Aberdonian was properly supported mankind would later on look back upon his age with admiration and, fired by its example, endeavor

"to proceed in a further repairing the Decayes of Nature, until Art have done its last, or, which is most probable, Nature cease to be, or be Renewed."

The letter is an impressive example of the Baconian faith in the unlimited power of man over nature. Nearly three hundred years ago it began to dawn upon a few human minds that language, instead of being left to the hazards of a slow evolution, could be intelligently interfered with and directed toward a desirable goal.

Dalgarno's *Ars Signorum* stimulated Bishop Wilkins to undertake something similar, but on a vastly more ambitious scale. The Royal Society published the outcome of his efforts. Wilkins was one of its founders, an ardent Parliamentarian, husband of Cromwell's sister, Robina, a man of great versatility and social idealism. He was the first man to popularize Galileo's ideas in England, and did so in a scientific fantasy, published in 1642. In it he described a journey to the moon by rocket. Undoubtedly he was a genius. It would be pleasant to add that he acknowledged his indebtedness to an obscure Scots schoolmaster. He did not.

Bishop Wilkins starts from the fact that we already possess such symbols as +, −, ×, ♀, ♂, ⊙, in the language of mathematics and astronomy. Though pronounced in different ways in different countries, these symbols are the same on paper, and everywhere signify the same thing to the educated. From this he draws the Cartesian conclusion:

"If to every thing and notion there were assigned a distinct Mark, together with some provision to express Grammatical Derivations and Inflexions; this might suffice as to one great end of a Real Character, namely, the expression of our Conceptions by Marks which should signify things, and not words."

Wilkins realizes that if the number of marks is to be kept inside manageable limits some classification of things and notions is indispensable. He therefore compiles, as Dalgarno did, a systematic catalogue as the foundation of his language. The whole body of contemporary knowledge is fossilized in a hierarchy of forty different classes, such as plants, animals, spiritual actions, physical actions, motions, possessions, matters naval, matters ecclesiastical, etc. Each of the forty pigeonholes has its subdivisions with the exception of the fifth class, which encloses HIM. The Bishop aptly remarks that the capitalized (and much hymned to) Him is not divisible into any subordinate species.

The world lexicon of Wilkins is a potpourri of Aristotelean fiction, theological superstition, naturalistic fancy, and much factual matter. The anthropomorphic outlook of the author and the low level of contemporary knowledge embodied in the catalogue are illustrated by his treatment of *Substance Inanimate*. He divides it into *vegetative* and *sensitive.* The *vegetative* splits into *imperfect,* such as *minerals,* and *perfect,* such as *plants.* The *imperfect vegetative* distributes what we should now call the materials of inorganic chemistry between *stone* and *metal.* *Stones* take the labels *vulgar, middle-prized,* and *precious.* Wilkins divides the last into *less transparent* and *more transparent.*

Having completed his hierarchy of knowledge, Wilkins now gets to grips with symbols for visual or auditory recognition. He begins with the *Real Character,* or written language, which everybody will be able to understand without learning how to speak the Philosophical language itself. The real character is to be like Chinese. Each word signifies a notion, not a sound. Wilkins is confident that about two thousand symbols will cover all requirements. The form of this new ideographic writing and its relation to the catalogue is best illustrated by the *commentar* which Wilkins appends to the word *father* in his attempted translation of the Lord's Prayer into Real Character:

" ∠ꝫ⌐ This next character being of a bigger proportion, must therefore represent some Integral Notion. The genius of it, viz. ⊥ is appointed to signifie Oeconomical *Relation.* And whereas the transverse Line at the end toward the *left* hand hath an affix making the *acute* angle with the *upper* side of the Line, therefore doth it refer to the *first* difference of that Genus, which according to the Tables, is relation of Consanguinity: And there being an affix making a *Right Angle* at the other end of the same line, therefore doth it signifie the second species under this Difference, by which the notion of *Parent* is defined. . . . If it were to be rendered Father in the strictest sense, it would be necessary that the Transcendental Note of male should be joyned to it, being a little hook on the top over the middle of the Character after this manner '. And because the word Parent is not here used according to the strictest sense but Metaphorically, therefore might the Transcendental Note of *Metaphor* be put over the head of it after this manner ∠ꝫ⌐ ."

So far the Bishop's catalogue and its written form. To use words in rational discourse a grammar is necessary. The minimum requirements of communication must be fixed. It would be an exaggeration to say that Wilkins made any outstanding contribution to grammatical analysis. He was still far too much under the spell of Greek, Latin, and Hebrew. Indeed, he held that flexion is "founded upon the philosophy of speech and such natural grounds, as do necessarily belong to Language." Nonetheless, he recognized that classical languages were not the last word; and Latin came in for a veritable *trommelfeuer* of criticism. He criticized its abundance of different flexions for one and the same function, the ambiguities and obscurities of its prefixes, the intrusion of grammatical gender into sex relations, its welter of exceptions to all rules of conjugation and declension, the difficulties of concord, and so forth.

Wilkins keeps his own grammatical apparatus within the limits set by forty signs, consisting of circles and dots for particles, and hooks, loops, etc., for terminals. For the time, this was thrifty. Where the dictionary form of an English verb such as *fear* has only three derivative forms (*fears, feared, fearing*), a single Greek verb may appear in over two hundred, and a Latin one in over one hundred costumes. The forty grammatical categories of all sorts in the philosophical language are a sufficient indictment of the irregularities, anomalies, and superfluities of the two classical languages.

Though less interested in mere talk, Wilkins had the ambition to make his language audible. To do this he apes Dalgarno's plan, in his own way. Each of his forty classes or *genera* has a simple sound combination consisting of an open syllable of the Japanese sort. The fifth major class (*God*) is labeled by the "root" *Da*, the thirteenth (*shrub*) by *Gi*, the thirty-ninth (*naval*) by *So*, and the last (*ecclesiastical*) by *Sy*. Subdivisions follow the same plan. To form those of the first order we have to add a consonant to the root. Thus we get words such as *Bab, Bad, Bag*, etc. If you want to understand what is hitting your eardrum, you must therefore be *au fait* with the whole classificatory setup. You may then have no difficulty in diagnosing *De* as "elementary," *Det* as "meteor," and *Deta* as "halo."

To attack the Bishop's project in the light of our incomparably greater scientific and linguistic knowledge would be equally fatuous and unchivalrous. The great defect of it is not that it imposes on the memory the almost superhuman burden of the Chinese characters. That would be bad enough. Its greater weakness is at the base, the catalogue of human knowledge. A Dalgarno or a Wilkins can construct such a catalogue only in the light of information available to his own contemporaries. Thereafter any addition to knowledge, a single discovery, a fresh interpretation, calls for a complete overhaul of the catalogue. The reference symbols of "each thing and notion" specified after the item added to it would call for revision. Had Wilkins's plan come into use among scientific men, science would have been fossilized at the level it had reached in 1650, as Chinese culture was petrified in a logographic script several thousand years before Wilkins wrote.

With all his awareness of what is "improper and preternatural" in Latin, Wilkins failed to apply to its grammatical categories the test of functional relevance. So he never grasped the simplest grammatical essentials of effective communication. His Continental contemporary Leibniz, famous for introducing the modern symbolism of the infinitesimal calculus, did so. Leibniz knew something of Dalgarnian as well as Wilkinsian, and rejected both of them for not being "philosophical" enough. Since the age of nineteen he had dreamed of a language which was to be "an algebra of thought" in the service of science and philosophy. He had little concern for its value as a medium of international communication. His own efforts to collect all existing notions, analyze them, reduce them to simple elements, and arrange them in a logical and coherent system is of no interest to people who live in the twentieth century. It was another wild-goose chase. What is more significant to our time are the conclusions he reached. When he took up the task of providing his dictionary or conceptual catalogue with a grammar, he broke new ground.

Unfortunately he never put his views into book form. They remained unnoticed by all his successors with the exception of Peano, a twentieth-century mathematical logician who also invented *Interlingua*. What puts Leibniz far in advance of his time is that he recognized the scientific basis of intelligent language planning. What the inventors of Volapük and the Esperantists never grasped, Leibniz saw with Leibnizian lucidity. The factual foundations of language planning must be rooted in comparative analysis of natural languages, living and dead. From the data such analysis supplies we can learn why some languages are more easy to master than others. The versatile linguistic equipment of Leibniz supported him well in the task. He could learn lessons from the lingua franca, a jargon spoken by sailors and street urchins of the Mediterranean ports; and he had an experimental guinea pig to hand. The guinea pig was Latin.

As Leibniz himself says, the most difficult task for the student of a foreign language is to memorize gender, declension, and conjugation. So gender distinction goes overboard because "it does not belong to rational grammar." Besides getting rid of gender, Leibniz advocates other reforms. Conjugation can be simplified. Personal flexion is a redundant device, because person is indicated by the accompanying subject. In all this Leibniz says nothing to startle the readers of *The Loom*, though he is way in front of Esperanto. He shoots ahead of many of our own contemporaries—Peano apart—when he discusses the number flexion of the noun. What he intended to substitute we do not know, most probably equivalents to *some, several, all*, etc. Unlike the Esperantist adjective, which continues to execute the archaic antics of concord, that of Leibniz, like that of English, surrenders a battery of meaningless terminals which accompany a Bantu tribal chant to the corresponding noun.

What remains for discussion is case, mood, and time flexion. Very properly Leibniz casts doubt on the raison d'être of the first two with the following argument. As things are, case and mood flexions are useless repetitions of particles. Either case and mood flexions can do without prepositions and conjunctions, or prepositions and conjunctions can do without case and mood terminal. Besides, it is impossible for flexion to express the immense variety of relations which we can indicate by means of particles. After some wavering between a highly synthetic medium and an analytical one, Leibniz comes out in favor of the latter. When all this sanitary demolition is over, the only thing left with the verb is time flexion. Leibniz considers this essential, but wishes to extend it to adjectives (as in Japanese), to adverbs, and to nouns. Thus the adjective *ridiculurus* would qualify an object which *will be* ridiculous, the noun *amavitio* would signify the fact of *having* loved, and *amaturitio* the disturbing certainty of *going to* love. Leibniz's next and most revolutionary step is to reduce the number of parts of speech. Clearly, the adverbs can be merged with adjectives because they have the same relation to the verb as adjectives have to a noun, i.e., they qualify its meaning.

For reasons sufficiently familiar to readers of *The Loom* (p. 114), distinction between adjective and substantive is also "of no great importance in a rational language." The only logical difference between the two is that the latter implies the idea of substance or existence. Every substantive is equivalent to an adjective accompanied by the word *Ens* (Being) or *Res* (Thing). Thus *Idem est Homo quod Ens humanum* (Man is the same thing as Human Being). Similarly (as in Celtic idiom) every verb can be reduced to the single verb substantive *to be* and an adjective: *Petrus scribit, id est: est scribens* (Peter writes, i.e., is writing). So the irreducible elements of discourse boil down to the single noun *Ens* or *Res*, the single verb *est* (is), together with a congeries of adjectival qualifiers and particles which bind the other parts of a statement together by exposing relations between them. A complete vocabulary is exhausted by a lexicon of roots and a list of affixes each with its own and sharply defined meaning.

All this tallies with the fruits of research in comparative grammar two hundred years later. Leibniz was far ahead of his time in other ways. He was alive to what Malinowski calls "the sliding of roots and meanings from one grammatical category to another" (p. 163), and anticipates Ogden's Basic (p. 479) by embarking on an analysis of the *particles* to ascertain their meaning and the requisite minimum number. He regarded this as a task of the utmost importance, and carried it out with particular care. Notably modern in this context is a shrewd guess. Leibniz suggests that metaphorical extension has expanded the field of reference of prepositions, all of which originally had a *spatial* significance. Thus we give them a chronological value, when we say: *between* the nineteenth and twentieth centuries, *in* the future, *before* 1789, etc.

The projects of Dalgarno and Wilkins had this in common with others put forward during the eighteenth and the first half of the nineteenth century. They started from a preconceived logical system without reference to living speech. As late as 1858 a committee report of the French Société Internationale de Linguistique denounced the design of an international auxiliary built of bricks taken from natural languages. The reason given was that all natural languages, classical and modern, dead and living, are embedded in cultural levels which modern man had left behind him. A language "clear, simple, easy, rational, logical, philosophical, rich, harmonious, and elastic enough to cater for all the needs of future progress" must also be a language made out of whole cloth.

The vogue of a priori languages conceived in these terms is easy to understand. Language planning was cradled by the needs of a scholar caste cut off from the common aspirations of ordinary people, without the guidance of a systematic science of comparative linguistics. Inevitably the movement initiated by Dalgarno and Wilkins shared the fate of proposals for number reform put forward by Alexandrian mathematicians from Archimedes to Diophantus. Proposals for an international language with any prospect of success must emerge from the experience of ordinary men and women, like the Hindu number system which revolutionized mathematics after the eclipse of Alexandrian culture.

Still it is not fair to say that the efforts of Dalgarno, Wilkins, or

Leibniz were fruitless. It may well be true that international reform of scientific nomenclature initiated by the *Systema Naturae* of Linnaeus was catalyzed by controversy which his more ambitious predecessor provoked. The movement which came to a focus in the *Systema Naturae* encouraged revision of chemical terminology with results which its author could not have foreseen. It created an international vocabulary of Latin and Greek (p. 246) roots. In a sense, though unwittingly, revision of chemical terminology realized Wilkins's dream of a *real character*. Modern chemistry has a vocabulary of ideographic and pictographic symbols for about a quarter of a million pure substances now known.

The efforts of the catalinguists were not stillborn. They continued to stimulate other speculations for fully a century. Diderot and D'Alembert, joint editors of the French *Encyclopédie*, allotted an article to the same theme. The author was no less a personage than Faiguet, Treasurer of France. Its title was *Nouvelle Langue* (1765). Though merely a sketch, it anticipated and outdistanced proposals of more than a hundred years later. Like his forerunners in England, Faiguet recognized the wasteful and irrational features common to Western European languages, and had enough historical knowledge to notice the analytical drift in the history of his mother tongue. The outcome was a highly regularized skeleton of grammar for a universal a posteriori language, i.e., one which shares features common to, and draws on, the resources of existing languages. In contrast to Faiguet's mother tongue, the New Language had no article and no gender concord. The adjective was to be invariant, as in English, or, as the designer says, a sort of adverb. Case distinction, which has disappeared in nouns of French and other Romance languages, made way for free use of prepositions.

In all this Faiguet had a far better understanding of what is and what is not relevant than the inventor of *Esperanto* with its dead ballast of a separate object case (p. 469) and its adjectival plural. Perhaps because his own language gave him little guidance, Faiguet made no very radical suggestions for simplifying the verb system. It was to consist of a *single* regular conjugation without personal flexions. This cleansing of Augean stables was offset by the terminals -*a* for the present, -*u* for the future, -*é* for the imperfect, -*i* for the perfect, and -*o* for the pluperfect. In addition there were three different infinitive forms (present, past, future), and a subjunctive which was indicated by an -*r* added to the indicative. Still, it was not a bad attempt for its time. Perhaps Faiguet would have used the axe more energetically if he had been inspired by the needs of humanity at large. Like his predecessors he was chiefly at pains to provide "the learned academies of Europe" with a new means of communication.

Faiguet did not compile a vocabulary, and none of his contemporaries took up the task. Alertness to the waste and inconvenience of language confusion was still confined to the scholarly few. It did not become acute and widespread till steam power revolutionized transport, and the ocean cable annihilated distance. Language planning received a new impulse in a contracting planet. Where the single aim had been to cater to the needs of international scholarship, the needs of international trade and internationally organized labor became tenfold more clamorous.

Humanitarian sentiment reinforced more material considerations. The inventor of Volapük, and many of its ardent advocates, regarded linguistic differences as fuel for warmongers and hoped that an interlingua would help to seal the bonds of brotherhood between nations. In fifty odd ephemeral auxiliaries which cropped up during the second half of the nineteenth century, several common features emerge. With few exceptions each was a one-man show, and few of the showmen were sufficiently equipped for the task. With one exception they were continental Europeans bemused by the idiosyncrasies of highly inflected languages such as German, Russian, or one of the offshoots of Latin. Each of them created a language of his own image. They did not look beyond the boundaries of Europe. If the inventor was a Frenchman the product must needs have a subjunctive; and when the Parisian votaries of Volapük objected to Schleyer's *ä*, *ö*, and *ü*, their Teutonic brothers in arms took up the defense with a zeal befitting the custody of the Holy Grail of the Nordic Soul.

The nineteenth-century pioneers of language planning did not appreciate the fact that China's four hundred millions contrive to live and die without the consolation of case, tense, and mood distinction, indeed without any derivative apparatus at all. Why they ignored Chinese and new hybrid vernaculars such as *Beach-la-Mar*, *Creole French*, and *Chinook*, etc., is easy to understand. What still amazes us is that they could not profit by the extreme flexional simplicity of English, with its luxuriant literature, outstanding contributions to science, and world-wide imperial status. They had little or no knowledge of the past, and were therefore unable to derive any benefit from research into the evolution of speech. Almost alone, Grimm saw what

lessons history has to teach. A few years before his death, Grimm re-
canted his traditional loyalty to the flexional vagaries of the older
European languages, and laid down the essential prerequisites of intelligent language planning. The creation of a world-auxiliary is not
a task for peremptory decisions:

"There is only one way out: to study the path which the human mind
has followed in the development of languages. But in the evolution of all
civilized languages fortuitous interference from outside and unwarranted
arbitrariness have played such a large part that the utmost such a study can
achieve is to show up the danger-rocks which have to be avoided."

Wise words!

VOLAPÜK

The first constructed language which human beings actually spoke,
read, wrote, and printed was *Volapük* (1880). Its inventor was Johann
Martin Schleyer, a German Catholic priest, zealous alike in the cause
of world trade and universal brotherhood. Hence his motto: *Menade
bal puki bal* (For one humanity one language). According to his disciples, he knew an amazing number of tongues. If so, he benefited
little from his learning. It was evidently a handicap. It prevented him
from understanding the difficulties of Volapük for less gifted linguists.

The new medium spread very rapidly, first in Germany, then in
France, where it found an able apostle in Auguste Kerckhoffs, Professor of Modern Languages at the Paris High School for Commercial Studies. There was a French Association for the propagation of
Volapük, there were courses in it—and diplomas. Maybe with an eye
on the annual turnover, a famous departmental store, Les Grands
Magasins du Printemps, also espoused the cause. Success in France
encouraged others, especially in the United States. By 1889, the year
of its apogee, Volapük had about two hundred thousand adherents,
two dozen publications, supported by three hundred societies and
clubs. Enthusiastic amateurs were not the only people who embraced
the new faith. Academically trained linguists also flirted with it.

Volapük petered out much faster than it spread. When its partisans
had flocked together in Paris for the third Congress in 1889, the committee had decided to conduct the proceedings exclusively in the new
language. This lighthearted decision, which exposed the inherent difficulties of learning it or using it, was its death knell. A year later the

movement was in full disintegration. What precipitated collapse was a family quarrel. Father Schleyer had constructed the grammar of his proprietary product with the redundant embellishments of his own highly inflected language. Professor Kerckhoffs, supported by most of the active Volapükists, spoke up for the plain man and called for reduction of the frills. In the dispute which ensued, Schleyer took the line that Volapük was his private property. As such, no one could amend it without his consent.

It is impossible to explain the amazing, though short-lived success of Volapük in terms of its intrinsic merits. There was a monstrous naïveté in the design of it. A short analysis of its sounds, grammar, and vocabulary suffices to expose its retreat in the natural line of linguistic progress. Part of the comedy is that Schleyer had the nerve to claim that he had taken spoken English as his model, with due regard to any merits of German, French, Spanish, and Italian. The vowel battery of Schleyer's phonetic apparatus was made up of *a, e, i, o, u,* together with the German *ä, ö, ü,* of which the last is notoriously difficult for English-speaking people to pronounce. In conformity with his German bias, the consonants included the guttural *ch* sound. Out of chivalrous consideration for children, elderly people, and China's four hundred million, Schleyer discarded the *r* sound in favor of *l* (absent in Japanese) and other substitutes. This happened before anyone drew Schleyer's attention to the fact that the Chinese have an *r*. By then he had changed our English *red* or German *rot* to *led*. Similarly *rose* becomes *lol*.

In the grammar of Volapük the noun, like the noun of German and unlike that of Anglo-American or of any Romance language, trailed behind it case marks with or without the uniform plural -S. In this way *father* becomes:

	SINGULAR	PLURAL
Nomin.	fat	fats
Acc.	fati	fatis
Gen.	fata	fatas
Dat.	fate	fates

There was no grammatical gender. Where sex raised its ugly head the simple noun form represented the male, which could assimilate the ladylike prefix *ji-*, as in *blod-jiblod* (brother-sister) and *dog-jidog* (dog-bitch). The adjective was recognizable as such by the suffix *-ik*, e.g. *gudik* (good), supplemented by *-el* when used as a noun, e.g.

gudikel (the good man), *jigudikel* (the good woman). Gain on the roundabouts by leveling the personal pronoun (*ob* = I, *ol* = thou, *obs* = we, *ols* = you, etc.) was lost on the swings, because each person had four cases (e.g. *ob, obi, oba, obe*). From the possessive adjective derived from the pronoun by adding the suffix *-ik*, e.g. *obik* (my), you got the possessive pronoun by an additional *-el*, e.g. *obikel* (mine). Conjugation was a bad joke. In what he had to learn about the vagaries of the Volapük verb, the Chinese paid a heavy price for the liquidation of *r*. Whether there was or was not an independent subject, the personal pronoun stuck to the verb stem. So *fat löfom* literally meant *the father love he.* There were six tenses, as in Latin, each of them with its own characteristic vowel prefixed to the stem, presumably in imitation of the Greek augment:

löfob	I love	*ilöfob*	I had loved
älöfob	I loved	*olöfob*	I shall love
elöfob	I have loved	*ulöfob*	I shall have loved

Strange to say, the prefix *a-* of the imperfect and the *o-* of the future also appeared on adverbs formed from *del* (day), *adela* (yesterday), *adelo* (today). There were characteristic suffixes for a subjunctive and a potential mood, and each with all six tense forms, e.g. *elöfomla* (that he has loved). By prefixing *p-* you could change the active to the passive, and interpolate an *i* immediately after the tense mark to signify habitual action. So it was possible to make one word to say of a woman that *she had been loved all the time.* The Schleyer imperative, like the Schleyer deity, was threefold, with a gentle *will-you-please* form in *-ös*, a normal one in *-öd*, and a categorical of the *won't-you-shut-up* sort in *öz*. The mark of interrogation was a hyphenated *li*, prefixed or suffixed, and the negative particle was *no* placed before the verb, e.g. *no-li elöfons-la?* (will you not have loved?). If admittedly more regular than either, Volapük had almost as many grammatical impedimenta as Sanskrit or Lithuanian.

The Volapükists rightly claimed that the root material of their language was taken from English, German, Latin, and its modern descendants. Unluckily, the roots suffered drastic castigation from Father Schleyer's hands before they became unrecognizable in the Volapük lexicon. The memory of the beginner had nothing to bite on. All roots had to conform with a set of arbitrary conditions. To take on several prefixes and suffixes, they had to be monosyllabic, and even so the enormous length to which such a word could grow forced

Schleyer to italicize the root itself. He had to alter all words which ended in a sibilant (*c*, *s*, *z*, etc.) to accommodate the plural *s;* and every root had to begin and end with a consonant. From this German sausage machine, *knowledge* emerged as *nol*, *difficulty* as *fikul*, and *compliment* as *plim*, the German word *Feld* as *fel*, *Licht* as *lit*, and *Wunde* as *vun*. The name of the language itself illustrates the difficulties of detection. Even geographical names did not escape punishment. *Italy*, *England*, and *Portugal* became *Täl*, *Nelij*, and *Bödugän*. *Europe* changes to *Yulop*, and the other four continents to *Melop*, *Silop*, *Fikop*, and *Talop*. Who would guess that *Vol* in *Volapük* comes from *world*, and *pük* from *speech?*

The method of word derivation was as fanciful, as illogical, and as silly as the maltreatment of roots. In the manner of the catalanguages, there was a huge series of pigeonholes, each labeled with some affix. For instance, the suffix *-el* denotes *inhabitants* of a country or *person-agents.* So *Parisel* (Parisian) wore the same costume as *mitel* (butcher). The suffix *-af* denoted some animals, e.g. *suplaf* (spider), *tiaf* (tiger), but *lein* (lion) and *jeval* (horse) were left out in the cold. The names of birds had the label *-it*, e.g. *galit* (nightingale), the names of diseases *-ip*, e.g. *vatip* (hydropsy), and the names of elements *-in*, e.g. *vatin* (hydrogen). The prefix *lu-* produced something ambiguously nasty. Thus *luvat* (more literally *dirty water*) stood for *urine*. *Lubien* (a nasty bee) was a Volapük *wasp*. Schleyer's technique of building compounds of Teutonic length turned the stomachs of his most devoted French disciples. As a sample, the following is the opening of Schleyer's translation of the Lord's Prayer:

"O Fat obas, kel binol in süls, paisaludomöz nem ola!
Kömomöd monargän ola! Jenomöz vil olik, äs in sül, i su tal!"

We can understand the success of Volapük only if we assume that it satisfied a deep, though still uncritical, longing equally acute in humanitarian and commercial circles. So it was a catastrophe that a German parish priest provided this longing with ephemeral satisfaction at such a low technical level. For a long time to come the naïvetés of Volapük and its well-deserved collapse discredited the artificial language movement. Curiously enough it found many disciples in academic circles, including language departments of universities, always the last refuge of lost causes. The American Philosophical Society, founded by Benjamin Franklin, though sympathetic to proposals for a world-auxiliary, was not taken in. It appointed a committee in 1887 to assess the merits of Schleyer's interlanguage. In a very enlightened report the committee formulated principles of which some should be embodied in any future constructed world-auxiliary. It rejected Volapük because its grammatical structure turns back on the analytical drift of all the more modern European languages, and because its vocabulary is not sufficiently international. The committee suggested the issue of an invitation to all learned societies of the world with a view to starting an international committee for promoting a universal auxiliary based on an Aryan vocabulary consonant with the "needs of commerce, correspondence, conversation, and science." About two thousand learned bodies accepted this invitation of Franklin's Society to a Congress to be held in London or Paris. The Philological Society of London declined the invitation with thanks, for reasons equally fatuous. One was that there was no common Aryan vocabulary. The other was that Volapük was used all over the world. It was therefore too late in the day to offer a substitute.

After the third Congress of 1889, votaries of Volapük washed their hands of the whole business, or ratted. Many of those who ratted followed the rising star of Esperanto. Some regained confidence and continued to tinker with Schleyer's system. Before the final collapse St. de Max had proffered *Bopal* (1887), and Bauer *Spelin* (1888). Thereafter came Fieweger's *Dil* (1893), Dormoy's *Balta* (1893), W. von Arnim's *Veltparl* (1896), and Bollack's *Langue Bleue* (1899). There were several other amendments to Volapük with the same basic defects. The stock in trade of all was a battery of monosyllabic roots, cut to measure from natural languages, and that past human recognition, or cast in an even less familiar mold from an arbitrary mixture of vowels and consonants. The root was a solitary monolith surrounded by concentric stone-circles of superfluous, if exquisitely regular, flexions. There was declension and conjugation of the traditional type, and a luxuriant overgrowth of derivative affixes. The essential problem of word economy was not in the picture. Indeed, the inventor of *La Langue Bleue* (so-called because the celestial azure has no frontiers) boasted that 144,139 different words were theoretically possible within the framework of his phonetics.

Before Volapük, far better artificial languages had appeared on the market without attracting enthusiastic followers. One was Pirro's *Universal-Sprache*, a purely a posteriori system of a very advanced type. The noun, like the adjective, is invariant. Prepositions take over any function which case distinction may retain in natural languages. The outward and visible sign of number is left to the article or other determinants. The personal pronoun with a nominative and an accusative form has no sex differentiation in the third person. A verb without person or number flexions has a simple past with the suffix *-ed*, a future with *-rai*, and compound tenses built with the auxiliary *haben*. Unlike so many before and after him, Pirro did not shirk the task of designing a vocabulary. His lexicon consisted of seven thousand words, largely Latin, hence international, but partly Teutonic. The number of affixes for derivatives was small, but since he took them over from natural languages they were not particularly precise. The merits of the following specimen of the Universal-Sprache speak for themselves:

Men senior, I sende evos un gramatik e un varb-bibel de un nuov glot nomed universal glot. In futur I scriptrai evos semper in did glot. I pregate evos responden ad me in dit self glot.

Though it discouraged some, Volapük also stimulated others to set out along new paths. More than one disillusioned Volapükist recovered to undertake the task which Schleyer had executed with maladroit results. One ex-Volapük enthusiast, Julius Lott, invented *Mundolingue* (1890). It was a neo-Latin language. A moderately well-educated person can quite easily read it, as the following specimen shows:

Amabil amico,
Con grand satisfaction mi ha lect tei letter de le mundolingue. Le possibilitá de un universal lingue pro le civilisat nations ne esse dubitabil, nam noi ha tot elements pro un tal lingue in nostri lingues, sciences, etc.

Another language which owed its existence to Volapük renegades was *Idiom Neutral* (1903). It was designed by members of the Akademi Internasional de Lingu Universal. This body came into being at the Second Volapük Congress. When it developed heretic doctrines the great *Datuval* (inventor) unsuccessfully excommunicated the rebels. The claim of Idiom Neutral in its own time was that it had a vocabulary based on the principle of greatest international currency. The reader who compares Schleyer's version of the opening words of the Lord's Prayer (p. 7) with the following can see how completely it had grown apart from Volapük:

Nostr patr kel es in sieli! Ke votr nom es sanktifiked; ke votr regnia veni; ke votr volu es fasied, kuale in siel, tale et su ter.

ESPERANTO

The collapse of Volapük left the field clear for Esperanto. Esperanto was the child of Dr. Ludwig Lazarus Zamenhof, a Russian-Polish Jew (1859–1917). He put forward his first proposals when Father Schleyer's invention was at the height of its popularity. Zamenhof had spent his early youth at Bielostock, where Russians, Poles, Germans, and Jews hated and ill-treated one another. Reinforced by a humanitarian outlook, this distasteful experience stimulated the young pioneer to reconcile racial antagonisms by getting people to adopt a neutral medium of common understanding. Incubation was long and painful. He was still at grammar school when inspiration dawned. So it was natural to seek a solution in revival of one or other of the two classical languages. Slowly Zamenhof learned to recognize the chaotic superfluity of forms in natural speech. It was English which opened young Zamenhof's eyes:

"I learnt French and German as a child, and could not then make comparisons or draw conclusions; but when, in the fifth class at the academy, I began to study English, I was struck by the simplicity of its grammar, the more so owing to the sudden change from that of Latin and Greek. I came to see that richness of grammatical forms is only a historical chance occurrence, and is not necessary for a language. Under the influence of this idea I began to look through my language and to cast out unnecessary forms, and I perceived that the grammar melted away in my hands, till it became so small as to occupy, without any harm to the language itself, not more than a few pages."

The design of a simplified grammar did not detain him long; but he was held up when he began to construct a vocabulary. Then it dawned on him that we can make an unlimited number of new words by means of derivative affixes added to a single root. The manufacture of suitable affixes led him back to Wilkins's theme, analysis of notional relations. His first idea was to make up his own stock in trade of roots. He soon realized the difficulty of learning the arbitrary root forms of Volapük and began to see that living languages work with a high proportion of common or international words. A preliminary Romano-Teutonic lexicon was born of this recognition. In its final form the project appeared in 1887 under the pseudonym *Linguo Internacia de la Doktoro Esperanto* (International Language by Dr. Hopeful).

Unlike Schleyer, Zamenhof sustained a sensible humility toward his own creation. He did not look upon it as final. He invited criticism. His intention was to collect, discuss, and publish the objections raised, then to amend its shortcomings in the light of the findings. The public ignored Zamenhof's request for sympathetic and enlightened criticism. Esperanto remained unchanged till 1894, when its author himself initiated a drastic reform. It found its first adherents in Czarist Russia where the authorities suppressed its organ, *La Esperantisto*, because it published an article by Tolstoi. From Russia it spread to the Scandinavian countries, to Central Europe, thence to France, where it had strong support in university circles. In 1905 the government of the French Republic made Zamenhof an Officer of the *Légion d'Honneur*. In 1909 H.M. King Alfonso conferred upon him the honor of Commander in the Order of Isabella the Catholic. After a brief eclipse during the Great War of 1914–18, the wave of pacifist sentiment which subsequently swept over the world gave it new momentum.

We should accept figures about its spread and popularity, when given by Esperantists themselves, with the caution we should adopt toward data about the vitality of Erse or Gaelic when those who supply them are Celtic enthusiasts. According to a report published by the General Secretariat of the League of Nations (but based upon data provided by Esperantists), Esperanto could boast of about four thousand publications, consisting of original works, translations, textbooks, propaganda items, etc. In Albania it became a compulsory subject in secondary and higher education. In China the University of Peking offered courses. Madrid, Lisbon, and several German towns placed it on the curriculum of police schools. In Great Britain it was popular in labor colleges, and got some encouragement from such publicists as Lord Bryce, H. G. Wells, Lord Robert Cecil, and Arthur Henderson. In the U.S.S.R., the People's Commissariat for Public Education appointed a commission to examine its claims in January, 1919, and to report on the advisability of teaching an international language in Soviet schools. The commission decided for Esperanto, though Zinoviev favored Ido. Five German towns made Esperanto a compulsory subject in primary schools under the Weimar Republic, and the National Esperanto Institute for the training of teachers at Leipzig received official recognition from the Ministry of the Interior. During the winter 1921–22 there were 1,592 courses in Germany for about 40,000 adults, half of them working-class people. On June 8, 1935, the National Socialist Minister of Education, Bernhard

Rust, decreed that to teach Esperanto in the Third Reich was henceforth illegal. The reason he gave was that *the use of artificial languages such as Esperanto weakens the essential value of national peculiarities.*

Esperanto just failed to gain support which might have made history. In spite of wire pulling and high-grade publicity management, its promoters were not able to persuade the League of Nations to come out unequivocally in favor of its use as *the* international language. Whether this was a calamity the reader may judge from what follows. Let us first look at its phonetic buildup.

Though Esperanto uses all the letters of the Roman alphabet except three (Q, X, V), its aspect is unfamiliar on the printed page. This is due to its five accented consonants, Ĉ, Ĝ, Ĥ, Ĵ, Ŝ, a novelty open to more than one criticism, more particularly that such symbols impede recognition of international roots and slow down the speed of writing. The corresponding sounds are equally open to unfavorable comment. The H (like *h* in *horn*) and the Ĥ (like *ch* in Scots *loch*) are difficult sounds for people brought up to speak Romance languages. Other sounds which cause embarrassment to many nationals are represented by such combinations as SC (= *sts*), KC (= *kts*), and NKC, e.g. *funkcio* (function). In contradistinction to the practice of Volapük, which had end stress appropriate to the importance of its suffixes, the accent of an Esperanto word falls invariably on the last syllable but one, e.g. *virbóvo* (bull).

With many other artificial auxiliaries, Esperanto shares the dubiously useful grammatical trick of labeling each of the "parts of speech" with its own trademark. The noun singular must end in -*o*, the adjective in -*a*, the derived adverb in -*e*, the infinitive in -*i*. The official defense is this: a reader can recognize at once which words express the main theme of an Esperanto sentence and which merely express qualifications. The ubiquitous vocalic endings of Esperanto, like those of Italian, make the spoken language sonorous and prevent accumulation of consonantal clusters which are difficult to pronounce, e.g. in English: *economists expect spread of slumps throughout civilized world.*

Zamenhof learned nothing from the obliteration of subject-object distinction in the English and Romance noun. Esperanto has an object case form ending in -*n* both for *nouns* and pronouns, e.g. *ni lernas Esperanton* (we are learning Esperanto). Esperantists claim that people who speak or write Esperanto enjoy greater freedom of word order, and can therefore reproduce that of the mother tongue without making a statement unintelligible in writing. If *the goat eats the cabbage*, we can also say that *the cabbage eats the goat*, because the *n* of the Esperanto cabbage shows that it is harmless. The Esperanto object case form is also an accusative of direction in the Latin style. Instead of the preposition *al* (to) you may use the accusative and say, e.g. *mi iras Londonon* (nom. *Londono*) = I am going to London. Apparently the Esperanto for our verb *go* does not sufficiently express locomotion.

To make the plural of an Esperanto noun we add *-j* to the singular, e.g. *kato* (cat)—*katoj* (cats), accus. *katon*—*katojn*. There is no grammatical gender, but for some reason difficult to fathom Zamenhof could not break away from the institution of adjectival concord. His adjective has to trail behind it the case and number terminals of the noun, e.g. nomin. *bela rozo* or obj. *belan rozon* (beautiful rose)— *belaj rozoj* or *belajn rozojn* (beautiful roses). Without regard for feminist sentiment, names of females come from names for males by interpolation of *-in* before the trademark *-o* of the noun, e.g. *patro* (father), *patrino* (mother), *frato* (brother), *fratino* (sister). Without deliberate deference to feminine sentiment Zamenhof reverses the process to manufacture the novel product *fraŭlo* (unmarried young man) by analogy with *fraŭlino* (German *Fräulein* = Miss).

The Esperanto verb has, like that of most of the more recent artificial languages, a single regular conjugation, without flexion of number or person, e.g. *mi skribas* (I write), *li skribas* (he writes), *ni scribas* (we write). It sticks to affixation for tense and mood, and there is no shortage of them. We have to learn the *-i* for the infinitive, *-as* for the present indicative, *-is* for the past indicative, *-os* for the future, *-u* for the subjunctive and imperative, and *-us* for the conditional. There is only one auxiliary, *esti* (to be). By chasing it through the different tenses and moods (*estas, estis, estos*, etc.) and then combining it with the three active participles (*amanta* loving, *aminta* having loved, *amonta* going to love), you can manufacture eighteen different compound constructions, and then double the number by substituting passive participles for the active ones (*amata* loved, *amita* having been loved, *amote* going to be loved).

Zamenhof's vocabulary consists of a collection of arbitrarily chosen roots, which grow by addition of about fifty derivative prefixes, suffixes, and infixes. The most glaring defect of the Esperantist stock of words is that it is not consistently international. To be sure, Zamenhof did choose some roots which are pan-European. In this category we find *atom, aksiom, tabak, tualet*. He also chose roots which are partially international, i.e., common to a large number of European languages. In this class we meet, e.g. *ankr* (anchor), *emajl* (enamel). These international and semi-international words had to comply with Zamenhof's sound and spelling conventions. They also had to take on Esperanto terminals. As often as not they are therefore unrecognizable, or at best difficult to recognize, e.g. *kafo* (coffee), *venko* (victory), *koni* (know), *kuri* (run). What is worse, they are often misleading. Thus *sesono* does not mean season, as we might suppose. It means *one-sixth*. So also *fosilo* stands for a *spade*, not for a *fossil*. Not even the starchy food called *sago* escaped mutilation. Its rightful name was changed to *saguo* presumably because *sago* (Latin *sagitta*) was badly needed to designate the Esperanto *arrow*.

Zamenhof rejected an enormous number of internationally current words. He dismissed hundreds ending in *-ation*, *-ition*, and *-sion*, or distorted them, e.g. *nacio* for *nation*, *nacia* for *national*. A large class of words in the Esperanto dictionary are not international in any sense. To coax the susceptibilities of Germans, or Russians who do not or did not then welcome addition of international terms derived from Latin or Greek roots, Zamenhof included words which add to the difficulties of a Frenchman or a Spaniard without appreciably lightening the burden for a Dutchman or a Bulgarian. This compromise was responsible for roots such as *bedaur* (German *bedauern* = regret), *flug* (German *Flug* = flight), *knab* (German *Knabe* = boy), *kugl* (German *Kugel* = sphere).

Striking illustrations of Zamenhof's fear of national susceptibility, and his desire to keep an even balance, are the Esperanto words for *dog, year, hair*, and *school*. For *dog*, one naturally expects *kano* (*cane* in Italian, *cão* in Portuguese, *chien* in French) corresponding to our adjective *canine*. In deference to German and Scandinavian sentiment, it is *hundo*. For *year* the Swedish equivalent is *år*, German *Jahr*, French *an*, Italian *anno*, Spanish *año*, Portuguese *ano*. There is clearly no agreement between the Romance and the Teutonic word form; but the root *ann-* is common to *annual* (English), *annuel* (French), *Annalen* (German). Zamenhof selected the German form, *jar*. The word for *hair* illustrates the same absurdity. In Swedish it is *hår*, German *Haar*, Italian *capello*, Spanish *cabello*, Portuguese *cabelo*, French *cheveu*. Again we have an international root in our technical words

FIG. 45. POSTAGE STAMP OF KEMAL ATATURK TEACHING (P. 441) THE
TURKS TO USE THE ROMAN ALPHABET

Reproduced from a stamp kindly lent by Stanley Gibbons, Ltd.

Some people say that we cannot change people's language habits by Act of
Parliament. This picture shows it can be done.

FIG. 46. MONGOLS LEARNING THE LATIN A B C

capillary or *capillarity*, corresponding to the German *Kapillar—* (*Kapillargefäss, Kapillarität*). Zamenhof chose the purely Teutonic form *har*. One of the most international words in daily speech is *school* (Latin *schola*, Italian *scuola*, French *école*, German *Schule*, Swedish *skola*). Zamenhof chose *lernejo*.

From such roots as raw materials of his dictionary, the Esperantist builds new words by simple juxtaposition, as in *vaporŝipo* (steamboat), *fervojo* (railway), or by adding prefixes and suffixes. Some of the affixes come from other languages with a native halo of vagueness. Others are whims of Dr. Zamenhof himself. Thus the prefix *bo-* signifies relation through marriage, as in *bopatro* (father-in-law), the suffix *-et* is diminutive, as in *venteto*, breeze (from *vento*, wind), and *-eg* is augmentative, as in *ventego* (gale). Even among the votaries the prefix *mal-* has never been popular. The uninitiated European would naturally assume that it means *ill* or *bad*, as in many international words. In Esperanto *mal-* denotes *the opposite of*, hence such strange bedfellows as *malbona* (bad), *malamiko* (enemy), *malfermi* (to open). The derivative affixes of Esperanto have a characteristic absent from other constructed languages. They can lead their own lives if protected by an ending to signify a part of speech deemed suitable for philosophic abstractions. This trick is encouraging to philosophers who indulge in *the in-ness of a one-ship which fills the us-dom with anti-ty*.

Esperanto claims to be an auxiliary which satisfies human needs on an international scale, yet is easier to learn than any natural language. One should think that such a claim involves existence of a vocabulary free from redundancies and local oddities. The sad truth is that neither Zamenhof nor his disciples have ever made an intelligent attempt at rationalization of word material. Unless one is a gourmet, a horticulturist, or a bird watcher, it is difficult to see why a thirty-six-page English-Esperanto dictionary should be encumbered by entries such as artichoke = *artiŝoko*, artichoke (Jerusalem) = *helianto*, nightshade (deadly) = *beladono*, nightshade (woody) = *dolĉamaro*. In the same opus nursing of the sick (Esperanto *flegi*, from German *pflegen*) is differentiated from nursing of children (Esperanto *varti*, from German *warten*) when an Esperanto equivalent of *to look after* would have covered both. The *Key to Esperanto* pushes specialization further by listing *kiso* = kiss, and *ŝmaco* = noisy kiss. If I shake a bottle Esperanto calls it *skui*, but if I shake my friend's hand it is *manpremi*.

When a chamois leaps into the Esperanto world it turns into a *ĉamo*, but the stuff with which I get the dirt off my window is not a compound of *chamois* and *leather*, as you might think, it is *ŝamo*.

Esperanto fostered several rival projects, and their appearance gave rise to anxiety. The year 1900 saw the foundation of the Delegation of the Adoption of an International Auxiliary Language. This body, which had the support of leaders in the academic world, including the chemist Ostwald, the philologist Jespersen, the logician Couturat, approached a large number of scientific bodies and individual men of science with the suggestion that some competent institution, preferably the International Association of Academies, should take over the task of pronouncing judgment on rival claimants. The association refused to do so, and the delegation itself eventually appointed a committee with this object in 1907. Initially discussion focused on two schemes, Esperanto itself and *Idiom Neutral* (p. 465). The delegates then received a third proposal under the pseudonym *Ido*. The author of this bolt from the blue was Louis de Beaufront, till then a leading French Esperantist. The committee decided in favor of Esperanto with the proviso that reforms were necessary on the lines suggested by Ido. The Esperantists officially refused to collaborate with the delegation in the work of reform, and the delegation then adopted the reformed product which took the pseudonym of its author. In some ways Ido is better, but it has the same defective foundations as Esperanto. It has dropped adjectival concord but retains the accusative form of the noun as an optional device. The accented vowels of Esperanto have disappeared. The vocabulary of Ido contains a much higher proportion of Latin roots, and is well-nigh free of Slavonic ingredients. The roots themselves are less distorted. The system of derivative affixes has been pruned of some glaring absurdities, but inflated by a fresh battery based on quasi-logical preoccupations. In place of the six prefixes and twenty-two suffixes of Esperanto, Ido has sixteen prefixes and forty suffixes.

There have been other bitter feuds between orthodox Esperantists and reformist groups. After Ido came *Esperantido* by René de Saussure. The three following equivalent sentences illustrate the family likeness of Esperanto, Ido, and Esperantido:

ESPERANTO

Por homo vere civilizita, filosofo au juristo, la kono de la latina linguo estas dezirebla, sed internacia linguo estas utila por moderna interkomunicado de lando al alia.

IDO

Por homo vere civilizita, filozofo od yuristo, la konoco di Latina esas dezirinda, ma linguo internaciona esas utila por la komunicado moderna de un lando al altra.

ESPERANTIDO

Por homo vere civilizita, filozofo or yuristo, la kono de la latina linguo estas dezirebla, sed internacia linguo estas utila por moderna interkomunicado dey un lando al alia.

INTERLINGUA

No rival successfully arrested the spread of Esperanto, though several of its competitors were immeasurably superior. Every new project made for more internationality of the basic word material. Coming from different directions, pioneers of language planning were converging to a single focus. Some searched the living European representatives of the Aryan family for terms common to the greatest number of them, and inevitably arrived at a vocabulary essentially Latin in its character. Others took the outcome for granted, and went straight to the neo-Latin languages for bricks and straw. A third group extracted from classical Latin what remains alive, i.e., its vocabulary, and discarded what is dead, i.e., its grammar. The most interesting, and till now the most enlightened, attempt to modernize Latin is *Latino sine Flexione* (*Interlingua*), devised by the Italian mathematician, Giuseppe Peano. In 1908 Peano became Director of the Academia pro Interlingua, formerly the Akademi de Lingu Universal, and at a still earlier stage in its career, the Kadem bevünetik Volapüka, founded by the second and third Volapük Congress. The Academia was a meeting ground for people interested in applied linguistics. Any enthusiast could join and contribute to its organ in any artificial language which his fellow travelers could easily understand. The aim was to discover what is most international among the existing welter of European languages.

Since 1903 Peano had been publishing his research in a simplified form of Latin. He did not know that Leibniz (p. 456) had proposed something similar, till one of his pupils came across the German philosopher's observations on rational grammar and a universal language. On January 3, 1908, Peano did something quite unprofessorial. He read a paper to the Academia delle Scienze di Torino. It began in conventional Latin and ended in Peanese. Citing Leibniz, he emphasized the superfluities of Latin grammar. As he discussed and justified each innovation he advocated, he incorporated it in the idiom of his discourse forthwith. Grammar-book Latin underwent a metamorphosis on the spot. What emerged from the chrysalis was a language which any well-educated European can read at first sight.

Interlingua aims at a vocabulary of Latin elements which enjoy widest currency in the living European languages of today. It therefore includes all words with which we ourselves are already familiar, together with latinized Greek stems which have contributed to international terminology. Of itself this does not distinguish Interlingua from some other auxiliaries. Five out of six words in the Esperanto dictionary have roots taken from Latin, directly or indirectly. The Latin bias of Ido, Occidental, or Romanal is even stronger. What distinguishes Interlingua from Esperanto and its relatives is the garb which the international root word wears. In Zamenhof's scheme the borrowed word had to conform with the author's ideas about spelling, pronunciation, and flexional appendices. After clipping and adding, the end product often defies recognition on an international scale. Peano followed a different plan. He did not mutilate his pickings. The Latin word has the stem form, that is, roughly the form in which we meet it in modern languages.

What Peano regards as the stem of a noun, adjective, or pronoun is the ablative (p. 314) form, e.g. *argento, campo, arte, carne, monte, parte, plebe, principe, celebre, audace, novo*. Every one of these words occurs in Italian, Spanish, and Portuguese. We ourselves are familiar with them in: *argentine, camp, artist, carnivorous, mountain, part, plebeian, principal, celebrity, audacious, novelty*. In this way Latin words preserve their final vowels. The stem form of the Peano *verb* is the Latin imperative, or the infinitive without *-re*. So we get *ama (amare), habe (habere), scribe (scribere), audi (audire), i (ire)*. Interlingua has *no* mobile derivative affixes to juggle with. It is wholly analytical, like Chinese or, we might almost add, Anglo-American. What prefixes and suffixes remain stick firmly to the Latin or Greek loan word with all their diversity of meaning, contradictions, and obscurities in English, French, or Spanish usage.

The grammar of Interlingua will not delay us long. Its supreme virtue is its modesty. In Peano's own words, *the minimum grammar is no grammar at all*. No pioneer of language planning has been more iconoclastic toward the irrelevancies of number, gender, tense, and mood. It is Chinese with Latin roots, but because the roots are Latin (or Greek) there is no surfeit of ambiguous homophones. What Latin labels by several different genitive case marks, Interlingua binds together with the "empty" word *de*, equivalent to our word *of*. Thus Latin *vox populi, vox dei*, becomes *voce de populo, voce de Deo*. Number indication is *optional*, an innovation which no future planner can ignore. What is now familiar to the reader of *The Loom*, Peano first grasped. He saw that number and tense intrude in situations where they are irrelevant, and we become slaves of their existence. Whether we like it or not, we have to use two irrelevant Anglo-American flexions when we say: *there were three lies in yesterday's broadcast*. The plural *s* is redundant because the number *three* comes before the noun. The past *were* is irrelevant because what happened *yesterday* is over and done with. Interlingua reserves the *optional* and international plural affix *-s* (Latin *matres*, Greek *meteres*, French *mères*, Spanish *madres*, Dutch *moedres*) for situations in which there is no qualifier equivalent to *many, several*, etc., or nothing in the context to specify plurality, e.g. *the father has sons = patre habe filios*, but *three sons = tres filio*. It is almost an insult to Peano's genius to add that Interlingua has no gender apparatus or that the adjective is *invariant*. If sex is relevant to the situation, we add *mas* for the male, and *femina* for the female, e.g. *cane femina = a bitch*. There is no article, definite or indefinite. The distinction *I—me, he—him*, etc., which almost all Peano's predecessors preserved, dies an overdue death. *Me* stands for *I* and *me, illo* for *he* and *him*.

Demolition of the verb edifice is equally thorough. There are no flexions of person or number. Thus *me habe* = I have, *te habe* = you have, *nos habe* = we have. There is also no obligatory tense distinction. This is in line with the analytical drift of modern European languages (cf. especially *Afrikaans*, p. 282) which rely on helpers or particles to express time or aspect. The *-ed* like the *-s* in *two rabbits escaped yesterday* is redundant. We have no need for either of them when we say: *two sheep hurt themselves yesterday*. The Interlinguist says *heri me es in London* (yesterday I BE in London), *hodie illos es in Paris* (today they BE in Paris), *cras te es in New York* (tomorrow you BE in New York). Peano's attitude to tense is on all fours with his attitude to number. Where explicit particles, or context do not already specify past time, the helper *e* before the verb does so. Similarly *i* (from *ire*) indicates the future as in the French construction *je vais me coucher* (I am going to bed). Thus the Interlinguist says *me i bibe* = I am going to drink, or *me e bibe* = I drank.

Though one of the most attractive projects yet designed, Peano's Interlingua has several weak points. Some of them spring from the fact that its author had his eyes glued on the European *mise-en-scène*, and more particularly, on the cultural hierarchy. So he never asked himself whether Interlingua was free from sounds likely to cause difficulties to linguistic communities outside Europe. There is another grave but easily remediable omission. A completely flexionless language such as Interlingua calls for rigid rules of word order. Peano bothered little about the necessary traffic regulations. The capital weakness of Interlingua is that its vocabulary is too large. Its author ignored the interests of the peoples of Africa and Asia, as he also ignored the plain man in Europe. Had he had more sympathy with their needs he would have worked out a *minimum* vocabulary sufficient for everyday purposes. He did not. The 1915 edition of Peano's *Vocabulario Commune* contains fourteen thousand words which have currency in leading European languages. Here is a sample of Interlingua:

Televisione, aut transmissione de imagines ad distantia, es ultimo applicatione de undas electrico. In die 8 februario 1928, imagines de tres homine in Long Acre apud London es transmisso ad Hartsdale apud New York, et es recepto super uno plano, de 5 per 8 centimetro, ubi assistentes vide facies in London ad move, aperi ore, etc.

NOVIAL

Bacon has said that the true and lawful goal of science is to endow human life with new powers and inventions. Throughout his long and distinguished career (1860–1943), the great Danish linguist Jespersen had the courage and originality to emphasize that philology has the same "true and lawful goal" as any other science. As a young man he espoused in turn Volapük and Esperanto. Later he helped to shape Ido. In 1928 he put forward a project of his own making, but like many other Esperanto renegades did not succeed in shedding the larval skin of his highly inflected past. He called it *Novial.*

Novial is the latest arrival. It is not the last word in language planning. Naturally, it is better than Esperanto or Ido. Because it had the advantage of coming later, it could scarcely be otherwise. Besides, Jespersen was the greatest living authority on English grammar. It would be surprising if a constructive linguist failed to recognize the cardinal virtues of a language so dear to him. What Jespersen calls the best type of international language is one: *which in every point offers the greatest facility to the greatest number.* When he speaks of the greatest number he refers *only to Europeans and those inhabitants of the other continents who are either of European extraction or whose culture is based on European civilization.* This sufficiently explains why Novial retains so many luxuries common to Western European languages.

For instance, the Novial adjective has a *conceptual neuter* form, ending in *-um.* From what is otherwise the invariant *ver* we get *verum,* which means *true thing.* In defiance of decent thrift, Novial has two ways of expressing possessive relations, an analytical one by means of the particle *de,* and a synthetic by means of the ending *-n.* Thus *Men patron kontore* is Novial for: *my (mine)* father's office. Jespersen's treatment of the verb conforms to the analytical technique of Anglo-American. This at least is an enormous advance upon Esperanto, Russian, Lithuanian, and other difficult languages; but is not particularly impressive if we apply the yardstick of Pekingese or Peanese. Future and conditional are expressed by the auxiliaries *sal* and *vud,* perfect and pluperfect by the auxiliaries *ha* and *had.* Novial departs from English usage in one particular. The dictionary form does the work of our past participle in compound past tenses, e.g. *me protekte,* I protect, *me ha protekte,* I have protected, *me had protekte.* This recalls the class of English verbs to which *cut, put,* or *hurt* belong. What simplification results from this is nullified by the superfluous existence of two ways of expressing past time, a synthetic one which ends in the Teutonic weak *-d,* e.g. *me protekted* (I protected), and an analytical one involving an equivalent nonemphatic Chaucerian helper *did,* e.g. *me did protekte.* There are no flexions of mood; but the student of Novial has to learn how to shunt tense forms appropriate to indirect speech.

Like Esperanto, Novial has a bulky apparatus of derivative affixes for coining new words. They recall forms which exist in contemporary European languages; but Jespersen was at pains to give each a clear-cut meaning. There are many whimsicalities in the choice of them. A special suffix denotes action, another indicates the result of an action, and a third is for use *when the product of the action is specially meant, as distinct from the way in which it is done.* (Got it?) In the list of prefixes we meet an old acquaintance, the Esperanto *bo-.* This indicates relation by marriage, e.g. *bopatro* (father-in-law), *bomatra* (mother-in-law), *bofilia* (daughter-in-law). How long the mother-in-law will continue to be a menace to monogamy, or how long monogamy will continue to be the prevailing mores of civilized communities, we cannot say. Meanwhile it is just as easy to make a joke about the analytical English or Chinese equivalent of Jespersen's *bomatra*.

In building up his vocabulary Jespersen aimed at choosing the most international words. Since there are many things and notions for which there are no full-fledged international (i.e., European) terms Jespersen embraced the eclecticism of his predecessors. The result is a mongrel pup. The following story illustrates its hybrid character:

Da G. Bernard Shaw.

Un amiko de me kel had studia spesialim okulali kirurgia, examinad in un vespre men vidpovo e informad me ke lum esed totim non-interessant a lo, pro ke lum esed "normal." Me naturim kredad ke tum signifikad ke lum esed simil a omni altren; ma lo refusad ti interpretatione kom paradoxal, e hastosim explicad a me ke me esed optikalim exeptional e tre fortunosi persone, pro ke "normali" vido donad li povo tu vida koses akuratim e ke nor dek pro sent del popule posesed to povo, konter ke li restanti ninanti pro sent esed non-normal. Me instantim deskovrad li explikatione de men, non-sukseso kom roman-autore. Men mental okule kom men korporal okule esed "normal"; lum vidad koses altriman kam li okules de altri homes, e vidad les plu bonim.

(Traduktet kun permisione de autore.)

THE ANGLO-AMERICAN REACTION

With one exception, G. J. Henderson, who published two proposals, *Lingua* in 1888 and *Latinesce* a few years later, none of the promoters of constructed languages during the nineteenth century were American or British. With few exceptions, no Continental linguists of the nineteenth century, and none of the leaders of the world-auxiliary movement, recognized the fact that one existing language, that of the largest civilized speech community, is free from several defects common to all outstanding projects for an artificial medium, before the publication of Peano's *Interlingua*.

This is not altogether surprising. Because English spelling teems with irregularities, and still more because of the vast resources of its hybrid vocabulary, learning English is not an easy task for anyone who aims to get a *wide reading knowledge*. So academic linguists trained in sedentary pursuits overlooked the astonishing ease with which a beginner can get a good working knowledge of the Anglo-American interlanguage as a vehicle of unpretentious *self-expression*. C. K. Ogden and his colleague, I. A. Richards, are largely responsible for the growing recognition of the merits which won high tribute from Grimm. Ogden and Richards chose Anglo-American usage as the case material of *The Meaning of Meaning*, a handbook of modern logic. What began as an academic examination of how we *define* things, led one of the authors into a more spacious domain. Hitherto we had thought of English as the language with the large dictionary. Ogden's work has taught us to recognize its extreme *word economy*.

To resolve this paradox the reader needs to know the problem which Ogden and Richards discuss in their book. Latent in the theme of *The Meaning of Meaning* is the following question: what is the absolute *minimum number of words we need to retain*, if we are to give an intelligible definition of all other words in Webster's or the Oxford Dictionary? The answer is, about eight hundred, or between two and three months' work for anyone willing to memorize *twelve* new words a day. This great potential word economy of Anglo-American is due to the *withering away of word forms dictated by context without regard to meaning*. We have had many examples of this process, especially in Chapters III, IV, and VII. Our natural interlanguage has shed redundant contextual distinctions between particles and between transitive and intransitive verbs. We can now do without a battery of about four hundred special verb forms which are almost essential to ordinary self-expression in French or German. This is not disputed by critics who carp at the absence of names for everyday objects in Ogden's 850 Basic Word List, and it is not necessary to remind readers of *The Loom* that Anglo-American has another supreme merit which pioneers of language planning, other than the great linguist Henry Sweet, were slow to realize.

Academic British grammarians, with few notable exceptions such as Bradley, have always been apologetic about the flexional "poverty" of English, and disposed to fondle any surviving flexions they could fish up. In fact, there are only three surviving *obligatory* flexions which we need to add to our items for a serviceable vocabulary of new words: (*a*) -*s* for the third person singular of the present tense, or for the plural form of the noun, (*b*) -*d* or -*ed* for the past tense or participle of verbs, (*c*) -*ing*, which can be tacked on to almost any word which signifies an action or process. The genitive -*s* is optional, as are the -*er* and -*est* of essential comparatives or superlatives. The seven forms of the verb *be*, four or five forms of a few—not more than a dozen—common *strong* verbs, and half a dozen irregular noun plurals, round up the essentials of Anglo-American grammar other than rules of word order.

Thus the essential grammar of Anglo-American is much simpler than that of the only two artificial languages which have hitherto attracted a considerable popular following. The language itself is the most cosmopolitan medium of civilized intercourse, and it can boast of a copious literature produced at low cost. It is the exclusive Western vehicle of commercial transactions in the Far East, and the common tongue of business enterprise on the American continent. It is also a lingua franca for the publication of a large bulk of scientific research carried on in Scandinavia, Japan, China, and in countries other than France, Germany, or Italy. For all these and for other reasons, the movement to promote Anglo-American as a world-auxiliary has eclipsed the enthusiasms with which former generations espoused proposals for constructed languages.

Whatever fate has in store for Ogden's system of Basic English, everyone who is interested in the interlanguage problem must acknowledge a debt to its author for clarifying the problem of word economy and specifying the principles for making the dictionary of a satisfactory world-auxiliary. What is not beyond dispute is whether his particular solution of the problem is the best one. To avoid the inflation of a basic vocabulary with separate verbs, Ogden takes advantage of the enormous number of distinctive elements which can be replaced by one of about sixteen common English verbs in combination with other essential words. Thus we can make the following combinations with *go* followed by a directive:

go around (circumscribe, encircle, surround); *go across* (traverse); *go away* (depart); *go after* (follow, pursue); *go again* (return); *go against* (attack); *go before* (precede); *go by* (pass); *go down* (descend); *go for* (fetch); *go in* (enter); *go on* (continue); *go out* (leave); *go through* (penetrate); *go to* (visit); *go up* (ascend); *go with* (fit, suit, accompany).

We can also manufacture many verb equivalents by combining some common English verbs with nouns or adjectives, in accordance with the precedent of Bible English: *make clean, make wet, make whole, make well, make a fire of, make a fuss about, make trouble.*

Reliance on such combinations is the method of verb economy peculiar to Basic English. The Basic Word List contains only the verbs: *come, go, get, give, keep, let, make, put, seem, take, be, do, have, say, see, send, may, will.* It is possible to say anything in effective English which does not offend accepted conventions of grammar without introducing any verbs not included in this list.

We could make any language more easy to learn by lopping off its useless flexions and regularizing those which are useful, and if we deprived French of its preposterous encumbrance of personal flexions (50 per cent *unpronounced*) and the still more preposterous burden of gender or number concord, Frenchmen might still decipher the product, as we can decipher pidgin English. It is doubtful whether this would help a foreigner to read French books, and the great practical advantage of a living, in contradistinction to a constructed, language is the amenity of cheap books already available. Besides, no Frenchman would agree to learn a mutilated form of his own language as an auxiliary for peaceful communication.

This is not the result at which Ogden aims. Spelling reform or simplification of Anglo-American grammar, beyond the elimination of optional survivals for which accepted isolating constructions already exist, would lead to something different from the Anglo-American in which millions of cheaply produced books come out yearly. So Ogden accepts all the few obligatory flexions and irregularities inherent in correct usage and rejects only those (e.g. the optional genitive) which we need not use. He has proved his claims for Basic as a means of self-expression by translating technical works and narratives for educational use into a terse idiom which is not unpleasing to most of us. The prose style of J. B. S. Haldane is often almost pure Basic. Basic is not *essentially* a different sort of English from Anglo-American as we usually understand the term. It would be better to describe it as a system by which a beginner can *learn* to express himself clearly and correctly according to accepted standards with no more effort than learning a constructed language entails.

The recently published New Testament in Basic is a sufficient refutation of the criticism that Basic is a pidgin English. The word list of the Basic New Testament contains some special Bible words which make the total up to a round thousand. The following is a fair sample for comparison with the King James (Authorized) Bible (*Mark* x. 21–24 and *Acts* iv. 32):

KING JAMES BIBLE

BASIC NEW TESTAMENT

Then Jesus beholding him loved him, and said unto him, One thing thou lackest: go thy way, sell whatsoever thou hast, and give to the poor, and thou shalt have treasure in heaven: and come, take up the cross, and follow me. And he was sad at that saying, and went away grieved: for he had great possessions. And Jesus looked round about, and saith unto his disciples, How hardly shall they that have riches enter into the kingdom of God! And the disciples were astonished at his words. But Jesus answereth again, and saith unto them, Children, how hard is it for them that trust in riches to enter into the kingdom of God!

And the multitude of them that believed were of one heart and one soul: neither said any of them that ought of the things which he possessed was his own; but they had all things common. . . . Neither was there any among them that lacked: for as many as were possessors of lands or houses sold them, and brought the prices of the things that were sold, and laid them down at the apostles' feet: and distribution was made unto every man according as he had need.

And Jesus, looking on him, and loving him, said, There is one thing needed: go, get money for your goods, and give it to the poor, and you will have wealth in heaven: and come with me. But his face became sad at the saying, and he went away sorrowing: for he was one who had much property. And Jesus, looking round about, said to his disciples, How hard it is for those who have wealth to come into the kingdom of God! And the disciples were full of wonder at his words. But Jesus said to them again, Children, how hard it is for those who put faith in wealth to come into the kingdom of God!

And all those who were of the faith were one in heart and soul: and not one of them said that any of the things which he had was his property only; but they had all things in common. . . . And no one among them was in need; for everyone who had land or houses, exchanging them for money, took the price of them, and put it at the feet of the Apostles for distribution to everyone as he had need.

Some critics of Basic will say that it is tainted with the philosophical preoccupations of Wilkins, Leibniz, and Bentham—the armchair view that the main business of language is to "transmit ideas." To be sure, transmission of ideas is an unnecessarily charitable description of the everyday speech of people who have to eat, dress, buy cigarettes, pay rent, mate, or excrete. Admittedly a large part of the daily intercourse of intellectuals themselves deals with situations in which it is not convenient to define a beefsteak as a cut from the back end of a male cow kept on the fire long enough with the right things —and so forth. Advocates of Basic may reasonably reply that this concern for our common humanity is spurious, that early training by the method of definition would do much to raise the general intellectual level of mankind, and that the main thing for the beginner is to get self-confidence as soon as possible, at the risk of a little long-windedness.

The focus of intelligent criticism is the form of verb economy which Ogden has chosen. His critics point out that those who have used Basic idiom as a substitute for the more usual type of Anglo-American in examples such as those cited above already know English and have no doubt about the meaning of such combinations as *get for* or *go with*. Is the correct idiomatic construction for the verb of another language equally obvious, if we do not already know English? Is it certain that a foreigner will deduce from its literal meaning the idiomatic verb in the sentence *Martha had her hands full of the work of the house?* This difficulty comes out in three ways of translating into Basic idiom each of the highly indefinite native verbs (*a*) *try*, (*b*) *ask:*

a) attempt = make an attempt at
   test = put to the test
   judge = be the judge of

b) question = put a question about
   request = make a request
   invite = give an invitation

Though it is quite correct English to *put a question* and *make a request*, it is difficult to see why a Chinese should prefer these forms to *making a question* or *putting a request*. Indeed the Chinese would be at home in his native idiom if he took advantage of the fact that *attempt, test, judge, request, question* can all be used as verbs or nouns, and that we *request the presence* of a person when we *invite* him. By exploiting this most remarkable feature of English word economy it would be easy to devise a word list no longer than that of the official Basic 850 without recourse to this bewildering multiplicity of idioms. We could also include a few words such as *purchase*, which can be verb (*to purchase*), noun (*the purchase of*), or adjective (*purchase price*), without such periphrases as *give money for* when we have to refer to an activity of daily occurrence. This way of solving the problem of verb economy has another advantage. The Basic construction is long-winded. The Chinese trick is snappy.

It goes without saying that any attempt to simplify Anglo-American within the framework of generally accepted conventions has a ready welcome where there is continuous contact between British administrators and Oriental or African populations with a multitude of local vernaculars. Owing to the influence of American trade and medicine, and to that of American universities and philanthropic foundations in the Far East, the influence of their common language extends far beyond the bounds of the British Empire or the United States. As a lingua franca in China and Japan, it has no formidable European competitor. Esperanto or any form of rehabilitated Aryan would have no prospect of outstripping Anglo-American unless it first established itself by general agreement as the official medium of a United Europe. In more than one respect Esperanto is inferior, and in none superior, to English. With its wealth of flexions it limps far behind several European languages; and it would be a bold boast to say that its vocabulary is more international than that of English.

There is already a large educational publishing clientele for proposals which aim at promoting the use of Anglo-American as the lingua franca of technology and trade in backward and subject communities. Basic is not the only proposal of this sort. From Toronto comes West's method. This is based on word counts, and presumably, therefore, aims to cater for the needs of those whose immediate goal is rapid progress in reading facility. Miss Elaine Swensen of the Language Research Institute at New York University has devised another system, H. E. Palmer of the Institute for Research in English Teaching in Tokio a third (*Iret*). In *American Speech* (1934), Dr. Jane Rankin Aiken has put forward *Little English*, with an essential vocabulary of eight hundred words, i.e., fifty less than Basic. Others exist and will come.

THE PROSPECTS FOR LANGUAGE PLANNING

The first desideratum of an interlanguage is the ease with which people can learn it. If we apply this test to rival claimants, two conclusions emerge from our narrative. One may well doubt whether any constructed language with the support of a mass movement is superior to Anglo-American, especially if we consider the needs of the Far East or of the awakening millions of Africa. At the same time, it would be easy to devise an artificial language vastly superior to Anglo-American by taking full advantage of neglected lessons from comparative linguistics and of the shortcomings of our predecessors in the same endeavor. If historical circumstances favor the adoption of a living one as a world language, Anglo-American has no dangerous rival; and practical reasons which make people prefer Anglo-American to any artificial interlanguage, however wisely conceived, will inevitably check any bid to supersede the Anglo-American dictionary. Simplified English, whether Basic or Iret, Swensen or Aiken—not to mention more to come—can scarcely aspire to be other than a passport to the more ample territory of the great English-speaking community, and a safe-conduct to its rich treasury of technical literature.

To these conclusions it is reasonable to add another. No artificial interlanguage movement sponsored by voluntary effort can hope to swamp the claims of Anglo-American in the East. Thus our hopes for a neutral constructed language stand or fall with the prospects for a Europe united by a democratic constitution based on intelligent prevision of linguistic problems which democratic co-operation must surmount. The choice before us may be settled for many decades to come by historical circumstances over which we have no control. If historical circumstances do allow us to cast our vote, it will be supremely important to recognize the implications of a decision in favor of Anglo-American or of a new start in language planning.

If advocates of constructed languages have been peculiarly blind to the *intrinsic* merits of Anglo-American, those who champion its claims as a world-auxiliary have been equally deaf to its *extrinsic* disabilities. Though Anglo-American is not a national language, it is not a politically neutral language. If a victorious alliance of the English-speaking people attempts to make it the official medium of a united Europe, its use will make the British nation a *Herrenvolk*. It will perpetuate all the discords which arise when one speech community enjoys a privileged position in the cultural and social life of a larger group. There is only one basis of equality on which nations can co-operate in a peaceful world order without the frictions which arise from linguistic differences. A new European order, or a new world order in which no nation enjoys favored treatment will be one in which every citizen is bilingual, as Welsh or South African children are brought up to be bilingual. The common language of European or world citizenship must be the birthright of everyone, because the birthright of no one.

History has not yet given its verdict. It may not be too late to forestall disasters of a maladroit decision. For that reason the last chapter of *The Loom of Language* will deal with principles which must dictate a wholly satisfactory solution of the world-language problem. Whatever final decision blind fate or intelligent prescience imposes on the future of the most widely distributed and the only talking animal on this planet, this much is clear. The efforts of the pioneers of language planning and the work of men like Ogden will not have been for nothing. Ogden's principle of word economy must influence the design of any satisfactory artificial language of the future. Some features of the later interlanguages, such as Jespersen's and Peano's, will inevitably influence the teaching of Anglo-American, if it is destined to be the auxiliary language of the whole world.

FURTHER READING

COUTURAT	*Histoire de la langue universelle.*
GUÉRARD	*A Short History of the International Language Movement.*
JESPERSEN	*An International Language.*
LOCKHART	*Word Economy.*
OGDEN	*Basic English versus Artificial Languages.*
PANKHURST	*Delphos or the Future of Language.*
RICHARDS	*Basic English and Its Uses.*

Language Planning for a New Order[*]

As far as we can see into the future, there will always be a multiplicity of regional languages for everyday use. Those who advocate the introduction of an international medium do not dispute this. What they do assert is the need for a *second* language as a common medium for people who speak mutually unintelligible tongues. They envisage a world, or at least federations of what were once sovereign states, where people of different speech communities would be bilingual. Everyone would still grow up to speak one or other of existing national languages, but everyone would also acquire a single *auxiliary* for supranational communication. This prospect is not incompatible with the mental capacities of ordinary human beings; nor does it involve a total break with existing practice. Bilingualism exists already in Wales, Belgium, South Africa, and many other parts. Throughout the English-speaking world all secondary-school children study at least one foreign language, that is, French, Spanish, or German; and in some countries pupils who leave school with a smattering of a foreign language are in the majority.

In Britain they are not. Most of the children enter the labor market with a knowledge of no language other than their own. Consequently millions of adult workers are excluded from direct communication with their Continental comrades. Postponement of the school-leaving age will provide an opportunity for bringing the curriculum for elementary instruction in Britain into line with that of many other countries. Thus the adoption of an international auxiliary implies no more than regularization of existing educational practice, i.e., universal in-

[*] The views expressed in this chapter are the outcome of joint discussion between the author and the editor. The latter has attempted to give them shape in a project, *Interglossa*, published recently by Penguin Books Ltd.

struction in a second language and agreement to use one and the same *second* language everywhere. Creation of conditions for uniformity of educational practice by international agreement, as a prelude to universal bilingualism, as defined above, is not a language problem. *It is a political problem.*

Many well-informed people still doubt whether the social need for a single universal second language will prove strong enough to override human laziness. At first sight the plight of modern language teaching in Great Britain and elsewhere lends some support to pessimism. Hitherto our schools have produced poor results. After years of travail the British public-school product may have mastered enough French to get in Paris what Paris is only too willing to sell without French. This need not make us hopeless. Any society ripe for adopting an interlanguage will be faced with a new set of problems. Pupils who now take French or German as school subjects rarely have a clear-cut idea of the purpose for which they are learning them and, more rarely still, the chance of using what knowledge they acquire. The future is likely to provide incentives and opportunities hitherto unknown. Fantastic delays, misunderstandings and waste due to the absence of a single common language for international co-operation will impress even those who are not knowingly affected by it at present.

A hundred years ago, Europe witnessed perhaps less than a dozen international congresses in the course of a whole decade. Delegates were invariably drawn from the upper class. So communication was easy enough. Deliberations were in French. When international congresses became more numerous, they assumed a more gaudy linguistic character. Consequently procedure had often to be conducted in two or more "official" languages. One could choose delegates who were able to compete with the polyglot attendant of an international sleeping car, but the delegate with the best linguistic equipment would rarely be one with the best understanding of relevant issues. This obstacle to international communication becomes more formidable as time goes on. People of new strata and more diverse speech habits discover community of interest, and no single language enjoys the prestige of French during the eighteenth century.

In short, the prospects for language planning depend on the extent to which the impulse to international co-operation keeps in step with the new potential of prosperity for all. Socialist planning, that is planning for the common needs of peoples belonging to different nations or cultural units, will bring about incessant contact between medical officers of health, town-planning experts, electrical engineers, social statisticians, and trade-union representatives. Increased leisure combined with improved traveling facilities will give to a large floating section of the population opportunities to establish new social contacts through the medium of an interlanguage; and its adoption would find a ready ally in the radio. Even those who stay at home perpetually would be tempted to avail themselves of opportunities to learn more of large-scale social enterprise in neighboring communities of the supranational state.

The choice for those of us who cherish this hope lies between a constructed language and an already established medium, either in its existing shape or in some simplified form, such as Basic English. The second involves nothing more than agreement between educational authorities expressing the will of the people. On account of its grammatical simplicity, its hybrid vocabulary, its vast literature, and, above all, its wide distribution over the planet, the claims of Anglo-American would undoubtedly exclude those of any other current language which could conceivably have a large body of promoters in the near future; but political objections to such a choice are formidable. It is most unlikely that a socialist Continent would decide for Anglo-American as its interlanguage if Britain remained hostile to the new order. The chances might improve if a Britain free of its imperial incubus entered into close co-operation with its neighbors next door to build up a world without class, war, and want. Even so there is much to say for the adoption of a *neutral* medium cleansed from the all too evident defects of existing natural languages.

Some linguists meet the plea for a constructed auxiliary with the assertion that language is a product of growth. It is less easy to detect the relevance than to recognize the truth of this assertion. Admittedly it is beyond human ingenuity to construct a live skylark, but the airplane has advantages which no flying animal possesses. Apple trees and gooseberry bushes are also products of growth, and no reasonable man or woman advances this trite reflection as sufficient reason for preventing geneticists from producing new varieties of fruit by combining inherited merits of different strains or allied species. The work accomplished by pioneers of the science of synthetic linguistics shows that it is also possible to produce new language varieties combining the inherent merits of different forms of natural speech. In the light of their achievements and shortcomings we can now prescribe the essential features of a constructed language which would be free from the conspicuous defects of any natural, or of any previously constructed, language.

Professional linguists, who do not dispute the possibility of constructing a language to meet the requirements of international communication, sometimes raise another objection. They say that the adventure would be short-lived, if ever attempted; that no auxiliary could remain intact for long. Even if confined to the territory of Europe itself, it would split into dialects. Each speech community would locally impose its own phonetic habits and its own system of stress; and the Tower of Babel would come crashing down on the builders. Only a perpetual succession of international congresses could thus prevent a new disaster. Such is the gloomy view which Professor Wyld of Oxford takes. There are three sufficient reasons why it need not intimidate us.

To begin with there is nothing inherently absurd in a suggestion for setting up a permanent interlinguistic commission to check the process of disintegration. For three centuries the *forty immortals* of the Académie Française have tried, not without success, to keep literary French in a strait jacket; and Norway has changed its spelling and grammar by three Acts of Parliament in less than forty years. If national governments can control the growth of national languages, an international authority could also maintain an accepted standard for its own medium of communication. Though international committees to supervise scientific terminology, e.g. the International Commission on Zoological Nomenclature, are already in existence, our universities cling to the conviction that intelligent language planning on a world-wide scale is out of the question.

By the nature of their training academic linguists are unduly preoccupied with times when few people could travel beyond a day's journey on horseback or by cart, when reading and writing, like stenography today, were crafts confined to a few, when there were no mechanical means for distributing news or information. It is true that languages have broken up time and again in the past, because of dispersion over a wide area, geographical isolation, absence of a written standard, and other disintegrating agencies. Those who entertain the hope of international communication by an auxiliary envisage a future in which these agencies will no longer operate. Indeed, we have experience to sustain a more hopeful view than is customary in academic quarters. During the centuries which have followed the introduction of printing, the gradual dissolution of illiteracy, and revolutionary changes in our means of communication, English has established itself as the language of North America and of Australasia. It is not true to say that the three main Continental varieties of the common Anglo-American language are drifting further apart. It is probably more true to say that universal schooling, the film, and the radio are bringing them closer together. In any case, experience shows that geographical isolation during several centuries has not made the speech of New England unintelligible to people in Old England, or vice versa. Experience should therefore encourage, rather than discourage, us in pressing for an international auxiliary.

The primary desiderata of an international auxiliary are two. First, it must be an efficient instrument of communication, embracing both the simple needs of everyday life and the more exacting ones of technical discussion. Secondly, it must be easy to learn, whatever the home language of the beginner may be. To be an efficient instrument of communication it must be free from ambiguities and uncertainties arising from grammatical usage or verbal definition. The vocabulary must be free from duplication and unnecessary overlapping. It must shun all that is of purely regional importance. The design of it can turn for guidance to two diverse sources: the pioneer-work of Ogden and recognition of defects which vocabularies of hitherto constructed languages share with natural speech. We can best see what characteristics make it easy to learn a constructed language if we first ask what features of natural languages create difficulties for the beginner. Difficulties may arise from a variety of causes: structural irregularities, grammatical complexities of small or no functional value, an abundance of separate words not essential for communication, unfamiliarity with word forms, difficulty of pronunciation or auditory recognition of certain sounds or sound groups, and finally conventions of script.

Progress of comparative linguistics and criticism provoked by successive projects for a constructed auxiliary have considerably clarified these difficulties during the past fifty years. Consequently there is a wide field of general agreement concerning the essential features of satisfactory design. Though several interlanguages still claim a handful of enthusiastic supporters, it is probably true to say that most people who now advocate an artificial language approach the prospect with a ready ear for new proposals. The plethora of projects touched on in the preceding chapter should not make us despair of unanimity. On the contrary, failure brings us nearer to accord. As Jespersen remarks in the beginning of his book on his own constructed auxiliary (Novial):

"All recent attempts show an unmistakable family likeness, and may be termed dialects of one and the same type of international language. This shows that just as bicycles and typewriters are now nearly all of the same type, which was not the case with the earlier makes, we are now in the matter of interlanguage approaching the time when one standard type can be fixed authoritatively in such a way that the general structure will remain stable, though new words will, of course, be constantly added when need requires."

This family likeness will become increasingly apparent in what . follows. We shall now examine principles of design with due regard to the measure of agreement to which Jespersen draws attention and to later issues which have emerged, more especially from discussion of the merits and defects of simple English. One of the conspicuous defects of Anglo-American in its present form is the difficulty mentioned at the end of the last paragraph but one. Its script, particularly the spelling of its *inherited* stock of monosyllables, has become well-nigh ideographic; and this is the most striking difference between any form of authentic English and any modern constructed language. All advocates of a constructed international auxiliary agree that it must have consistent, simple, straightforward spelling rules, based on the use of the Roman alphabet. Since existing languages such as Italian, Spanish, and Norwegian furnish models of orderly behavior, there has never been any practical difficulty about prescribing a system of phonetic spelling. A representative international committee of experts entrusted with the task of laying the foundations of a constructed world-auxiliary would waste few days in reaching agreement about its spelling conventions.

Spelling raises only one outstanding issue for discussion. Consistent spelling may mean either or both of two proposals: (*a*) that every sound has one symbol and one only; (*b*) that every symbol stands for a single sound. To insist too rigorously on the first has a disadvantage touched on in Chapter II. Different languages have different conventions of alphabetic script, and the imposition of a rule limiting one sound to one symbol alone would therefore mutilate otherwise familiar roots beyond easy recognition. For example, we should not recognize the root *chrom-* in *panchromatic* or *polychrome* as easily if we spelled it with an initial *k*, and the retention of two symbols for some sounds, e.g. CH or K for *k* would not appreciably add to the difficulties of learning.

ESSENTIAL GRAMMAR

It is also safe to say that grammar no longer provides much fuel for controversy among interlinguists. We have moved far since the days of Volapük; and the main outlines of an international grammar are now clear enough. The reader of *The Loom of Language* no longer needs to be told that the multiplication of word forms by flexions is foremost among obstacles to learning a language. In Chapters III, V, X, XI, we have seen that the difficulties are of two sorts:

1) Some flexions (e.g. gender, number accord between noun and adjective) have no semantic value at all and their existence is an arbitrary imposition on the memory.
2) Even when meaningful, flexions which do the same type of work may show widely different forms.

Thus language planners meet on common ground in recognizing that a satisfactory auxiliary must have: (*a*) no *useless* flexions; (*b*) *regularity* of what flexions it retains. About what constitutes regularity advocates of a constructed language do not differ. To say that flexion must be regular means that if we retain a plural, we must form the plural of all nouns in the same way; if we retain a past tense every verb must take the same past tense affix. In short: *a single pattern of conjugation—a single pattern of declension*. To the extent that this measure of agreement exists, any constructed language offers fewer grammatical obstacles to a beginner than do such languages as French, Russian, or German.

Unanimity with reference to what flexions are useful has come about slowly; and is not yet complete. At the time when Volapük and Esperanto took shape, and long after, planners were enthusiastic amateurs blinded by peculiarities of European languages they knew best. Nineteenth-century linguists made the same assumptions as nineteenth-century biologists. They took for granted that what exists necessarily has a use. Awareness of the universal drift from flexional luxuriance toward analytical simplicity in the history of Aryan languages was not yet part of their intellectual equipment. None of them recognized the many similarities between English, which has traveled furthest on the road, and Chinese, which consists wholly of unchangeable independently mobile root words. Professional philologists, who could have enlightened them, were not interested in constructive linguistics. In this setting it was a bold step to sacrifice gender or mood; and the accepted grammatical goal seemed to be a language of the agglutinative type illustrated (Chapter V) by Turkish, Hungarian, or Japanese.

Intellectual impediments to a more iconoclastic attitude were considerable, and we need not be surprised by the tenacity with which earlier pioneers clung to grammatical devices discarded by their successors. The history of *case* illustrates their difficulties. Since the Reformation, generations of schoolboys have been drilled to submit to instruction which assumes a universal subject-order distinction faithfully reflecting something in the real world. Since the grammatical subject is often the actor or agent which initiates the process specified by the verb, and the grammatical object is often the victim or goal, a judicious choice of illustrations (e.g. *the teacher punishes the boy*), presented at an impressionable age, makes it easy to implant the suggestion that this is always so. If the teacher acts in accordance with the last example, this bestows the reassuring conviction that there is a simple rule for choice of the nominative or accusative case form of a Latin or Greek noun. The pupil in whom the teacher has firmly implanted this suggestion will overlook the fact that the grammatical subject is not the agent which initiates the *seeing* process in *I see him;* and is not likely to worry about the fact that the grammatical object is what really does so. In such situations the pupil still applies the rule correctly, because the nominative-accusative forms of the Latin noun tally with our own use of *I—me* and *he—him*. In this way we come to accept local likeness of speech habits as a universal necessity of discourse.

Interlinguists started, like the comparative philologists, with the handicap of a load of misconceptions inherent in traditional methods of teaching Greek or Latin. It has taken us long to recognize that case can be as useless as gender, and we are only beginning to see that no flexional device is an *essential* vehicle of lucid expression. While everyone concedes that a roundabout turn is preferable to passive flexion, most interlinguists still cling to the flexional plural and the flexional past. Thus it is common ground that a world-auxiliary must be at least as isolating as English. Indeed, there is a close family likeness between Novial and English, each with a hybrid vocabulary of Romance and Teutonic roots.

In short, what has happened to the flexional systems of the Aryan family during the past twenty-five hundred years of its known history has happened to the accepted pattern of an artificial interlanguage during the past half-century. There has been a drift toward *isolation*. Jespersen recognized the parallel. He banned the noun accusative terminal of Esperanto or Ido, as Zamenhof vetoed the dative of Volapük, on the ground that it was out of step with linguistic evolution; and cited the fact that Italian, Spanish, French, Portuguese, English, Dutch, and Scandinavian languages have scrapped it. By the same token we may be skeptical about the possessive case terminal which turns up in Novial. Absent in modern Romance languages, it is already vestigial in English, and still more so in Dutch and in many German dialects. Number and tense are the only flexions which no Aryan language has completely discarded.

Unlike gender or the object-case category, flexion of number has a clear-cut meaning. Still it is not an indispensable device. We can always use a separate word to forestall doubt about whether the topic is one sheep or more than one sheep. Indeed it is wasteful to tack on a plural mark when the statement as a whole, or the presence of a qualifier such as *all, many, several, five*, makes it clear that the word stands for more than one of a kind. To some extent, Turkish recognizes such uneconomical behavior. The Turkish noun drops the plural affix (*-tar* or *-ter*) when accompanied by a numeral, e.g. *ev* = house, *evter* = houses, *dört ev* = four houses. The same usage occurs in German, but remains in a very rudimentary stage, e.g. *drei Mann*.

Similar remarks apply to *tense*. We express plurality once and completed action once, and both explicitly, when we say: *two deer cut through the thicket yesterday*. We express plurality twice and completed action twice when we say *two rabbits escaped yesterday*. The flexion -*s* does nothing which the numeral *two* has not already done. The flexion -*ed* does only what the particle *yesterday* does more explicitly. We can use the singular form of the noun in a collective or generic sense without the slightest danger of misunderstanding, for instance, when we say in French *le lapin est bon marché* (*rabbit is cheap*). Context is often sufficient to safeguard the distinction between singular and plural, past or present. When it is not, we can fall back on an appropriate numeral, pointer word, or particle of time.

One serious objection to flexion as a functional device is that familiarity breeds contempt. By too often using a flexional form in a context which makes it redundant we become careless about its meaning. This process of semantic erosion has not gone far enough to

make the plural flexion a positive nuisance, but clear functional outlines of tense distinction have been blurred in many languages, including English (p. 90).

Thus there is no formidable argument for retaining any flexional
frills in a constructed language, designed with due regard to the needs
of the Chinese, Japanese, and other non-Aryan speech communities
to which our own flexional system is alien and confusing. In any case,
a plural form of the noun and a past form of the verb are the only
two likely to find any large body of supporters among interlinguists
other than fanatical adherents of Esperanto. A constructed auxiliary
now designed in the light of defects and merits of previous proposals
would therefore be almost, if not quite, as free of flexions as Chinese
or Peano's Interlingua. This leaves us with the following question:
Would it be also free from other types of word modification? An
international language would not be practicable if it listed as many
words as the *Concise Oxford Dictionary* or *Webster's*. Our limited
learning capacities demand something more economical. So there is
another need for which the planner has to cater. Apart from being
economical, the vocabulary must allow for expansion made necessary
by the incessant emergence of new articles, inventions, and ideas.

Many pioneers of language planning have tried to kill two birds
with one stone by composing a restricted set of basic or root words
from which other words can be derived by a rich battery of prefixes
and suffixes. They do what we do when we derive *bookish* from *book*,
or *systematize* from *system*. Till now the prevailing attitude toward
such derivative affixes has been on all fours with the attitude of
Schleyer, Zamenhof, and Jespersen toward flexions. They have been
less critical of their functional importance than of their erratic behavior. For instance, the Esperanto suffix -EC for the abstract idea is
an incitement to people the world with new fictions comparable to
the definition of love as *the ideality of the relativity of the reality of
an infinitesimal portion of the absolute totality of the Infinite Being*.

Irregularities, formal and functional, of English derivative affixes
are typical of other Aryan languages. The prefix *re-* may, and often
does, connote repetition when attached to a new word; but it is quite
lifeless in *receive, regard, respect*. The negative prefixes *un-, in-, im-,
ir-* attach themselves to a root without regard to phonetic or philological etiquette, as in *unable—impossible, inert—unconscious, insensitive—irresponsible*. The Teutonic suffixes *-dom, -ship* and *-head* or
-hood turn up in abstract nouns of the same general class (*wisdom—*

friendship, lordship—fatherhood). If we tack on *-er* to some verb roots we get a member of the agent class represented by *fisher, writer, reader, teacher, manufacturer*. We may also get a means of transport (*steamer*) or a compartment in one (*smoker, sleeper*). To all these irregularities we have to add those inherent in borrowed Latin roots which contain such uncertain prefixes as *e-* or *ex-*, and *in-*, the last of which may signify either enclosure (*insert*) or negation (*innocuous*). Clearly a language with a regular system of derivative affixes for such clear-cut categories as *repetition, occupation, negation,* etc., would be free from one obstacle which confronts anyone who sets out to learn one of the existing Aryan languages.

This advantage does not meet the objection: *are such derivative affixes really necessary?* To do justice to it we must distinguish between different classes of derivative affixes. One class may be called *semantic* or meaningful. The affix either modifies the meaning of the root to which it is attached or does the work of a compound formation. Clear-cut qualifying affixes such as those which express repetition, negation, precedence, etc., merely usurp the function of necessary mobile items already on the word list. Thus to *re*state is to state *again, post*natal means *after* birth, to *mis*judge means to judge *wrongly,* and the *man* in *bakeman* could do as much work as the accretion *-er* in *baker*. Compounds such as *textile workers, steel workers, wood workers,* etc., are admittedly longer than words of the *fisher, writer, baker* class, but *postman, milkman, iceman, dustman, dairyman* show that compounds made from independent words need not be more long-winded than derivatives. By using derivative affixes of the Esperanto or Novial type we add a new burden to learning without much gain of space or any additional clarity.

Affixes of the other class merely label the grammatical behavior of a word. Thus the *-dom* in *wisdom* or the *-ment* in *arrangement* respectively endow an attribute which would otherwise behave as an adjective, or a process which would otherwise behave as a verb, with the grammatical prerogatives of a *thing*. For instance, we can speak of *wisdom* in contradistinction to *wise,* as *it,* and we can put the article *an* or *the,* which never stand immediately in front of *arrange,* before *arrangement*. This shunting disguises the fact that *wisdom* remains within the adjectival world and means nothing more than *wise behavior*. Some interlanguages carry this much further, having a special affix for each of the parts of speech.

At first sight there seems to be little in favor of this device. A

plausible excuse is that there is a rough-and-ready, if far from perfect, correspondence between parts of speech in an Aryan language
and the three pigeonholes into which we squeeze the physical world.
Although we meet many exceptions to any functional definition of
the parts of speech, it is approximately true to say that a noun label
usually points to what is thing or person, an adjective label to what
is a property, a verb label to what is action in a statement. Such affixes
therefore give the beginner a clue to the layout of a sentence which
contains unfamiliar words. They are signposts of sentence landscape. To that extent they lighten the task of spotting the meaning.

One reply to this is that isolating languages or near-isolating languages which have no (or few) labels to mark what are the parts of
speech in a flexional language can use other devices for guiding us
through the sentence landscape. Four examples from our own language illustrate them: (*a*) the articles label an object with or without
accompanying attributes; (*b*) the pronoun usually labels the succeeding word as a verb in the absence of any flexional marks on the latter;
(*c*) the copula *is, are, was, were* separates the thing or person from
what the statement predicates; (*d*) without recourse to the adverb
terminal *-ly*, the insertion of *and* in *fast and sinking ship* makes it clear
that *fast* does not qualify *sinking*. All these examples imply the existence of definite *word order*. Rules of word order, with whatever
safeguards such particles as *of, the,* and other literally *empty* words
provide, constitute all the grammar of a language, if its vocabulary
consists exclusively of unchangeable independently mobile elements.

Since interlinguists now lean far toward the isolating pattern, we
might expect satisfactory rules of word order to be a threadbare
theme. This is far from true. In the *Key to, and Primer of, Interlingua,*
for instance, the subject is dealt with and dismissed in a few sentences,
the first of which contrives to state the truth upside down:

"The order of words in Interlingua presents no great difficulties, grammar and inflection having been reduced to a minimum. It is so nearly
similar to the English order of words that one may safely follow that
usage without fear of being misunderstood or being too greatly incorrect."

In fact, no author of a project for a constructed auxiliary has paid
much attention to this problem, and those who advocate simple
methods of teaching Anglo-American with a view to its use as an
international language are singularly silent about the pitfalls into
which the vagaries of English word order can lure the beginner.

These vagaries illustrate some of the issues involved in designing satisfactory rules.

While it is true that Anglo-American usage favors the method of grouping together what is thought of together, there is no uniformity about placing the qualifying expression immediately before or immediately after what it qualifies. Thus we place the qualifier *enough* in front of the word it qualifies in *enough fat sheep* and behind in *fat enough sheep*. Neither is consistent with more common procedure, the first because *enough* is not *immediately* in front of the sheep it qualifies, the second because it *follows* and qualifies the word *fat*. Unless we have some flexional mark such as the much-abused English *-ly* to label the adverb as qualifier of the succeeding adjective, a rigid rule concerning the position of two qualifiers is the only way of showing if one qualifies the other or both may qualify a third. English has rigid rules of word order, but the rules are not simple. For every combination of a particular adverb of place with a particular adverb of time usage is fixed, but no straightforward regulation of precedence in favor of one or the other covers all cases.

A constructive conclusion which emerges from the preceding discussion is the need for a comparative study of word order both as a safeguard of meaning and as an aid to ready recognition. At present we have little material evidence to guide a decision about: (*a*) the advantages of *pre-* and *post-* position of directives or qualifiers; (*b*) the most satisfactory way of distinguishing which word is qualified by each of a sequence of qualifiers; (*c*) how best to express interrogation, in speech and in script; (*d*) what latitude of word order for purpose of emphasis is consistent with clarity and ease of recognition; (*e*) what empty words are necessary *signposts of sentence landscape*. These are themes to clarify before the grammar of an interlanguage pruned of flexional irrelevance and redundancy assumes a firm outline.

In this and other ways, a more sympathetic attitude toward the need for a constructed auxiliary would open fields of inquiry which have been neglected by linguists in the past. Because they accept languages as products of growth our scholars have for too long sacrificed the study of functional efficiency to the task of recording what is irregular, irrational, and uneconomical in speech. A more lively interest in language planning would direct their efforts toward new tasks. One which is of special importance has been formulated by Edward Sapir in *International Communication:*

"It is highly desirable that along with the practical labour of getting wider recognition of the international language idea, there go hand in hand comparative researches which aim to lay bare the logical structures that are inadequately symbolized in our present-day languages, in order that we may see more clearly than we have yet been able to see how much of psychological insight and logical rigour have been and can be expressed in linguistic form. One of the most ambitious and important tasks that can be undertaken is the attempt to work out the relation between logic and usage in a number of national and constructed languages, in order that the eventual problem of adequately symbolizing thought may be seen as the problem it still is."

AN INTERDICTIONARY

Among the many pioneers who have put forward proposals for a constructed interlanguage, few have undertaken the task of giving to a skeleton of grammar the flesh and bones of a full-fledged vocabulary. Its execution brings us face to face with the two major difficulties of memorizing a vocabulary, i.e., unfamiliarity with the auditory or visual shape of words, and superfluity of separate forms. Elimination of unnecessary items came to the fore in the classificatory projects of Dalgarno and of Wilkins; and it has once more become a live issue owing to the popularity of Ogden's method for teaching and using a simplified yet acceptable form of Anglo-American. Between the publication of the *Real Character* of Wilkins and *The Meaning of Meaning* by Ogden and Richards, no author of a constructed language has come to grips with the problem of word wastage. Those who have not shirked the labor of constructing a lexicon have invariably concentrated on the more immediate and inescapable problem of word form. Thus Peano's *Interlingua* accepts the *entire* bulk of English words derived from Latin.

To reduce the mnemonic burden of language learning to a minimum, it is essential to work with familiar materials, i.e., with roots taken from existing languages. Most of the languages hitherto constructed pay lip service to this principle, so stated; but there is less unanimity about the best way of choosing familiar material, i.e., a stock of roots with wide international currency. Indeed, there has been much confusion between two issues—proportional representation of different speech communities in the total stock in trade of roots, and widest possible international currency of each individual root.

Up to date no one has consistently followed either plan. Out-and-out application of an eclectic solution, on an international scale, would suffice to demonstrate its inherent absurdity. A vocabulary drawn from Teutonic, Romance, Slavonic, Chinese, Japanese, Arabic, and Indian vernaculars, Mongolian, Polynesian, and Bantu dialects, with due regard to the size of each contributory speech community, would be largely foreign to the eye and ear of individuals belonging to any major one; and it would contain scarcely a trace of roots familiar to individuals using dialects of a small one. The acid test of basing choice on a count of heads has never been carried out. The pioneers of language planning have been Europeans primarily concerned with the needs of travel, commerce, and technics. Their outlook has been limited by requirements and difficulties of nations within the pale of Western civilization. So their first concern has been to accommodate the claims of countries where official speech is a language of the Teutonic and Romance groups. Within this framework compromise leads to a hybrid vocabulary very much like that of English. This shows up in comparison of a random sample of English words and their equivalents in Jespersen's *Novial:*

NOVIAL	ENGLISH
danka (Teutonic)	to thank
demanda (Romance)	to demand
dentiste (Romance)	dentist
diki (Teutonic)	thick
dishe (Teutonic)	dish
distribu (Romance)	distribute
dorne (Teutonic)	thorn

There is a further objection to the eclectic principle. A few, yet by no means isolated, examples suffice to illustrate what it is. A Frenchman or an Italian will link up the root *alt-* with *altitude* (French) and *altura* (Italian), suggesting height. The German will recall his own *alt* (old) and go wrong. The Italian or Spaniard will at once recognize the root *calid-* in the Italian word *caldo* and Spanish *caliente,* both meaning *hot.* A German is more likely to associate it with *kalt* (cold). Even if he is a student of Latin or familiar with such words as *Kalorie* or *Kalorimeter,* a language based on a mixture of Romance and Teutonic materials will supply no clue to the correct meaning. Clearly, there is only one way of getting over the difficulties arising from unfamiliar material and of making a vocabulary with roots which readily suggest their meaning to men and women of different nationalities. Our first concern should be to choose roots present in words which people of different nations use.

Is this plan practicable? It is possible to answer this question without going to the trouble of making statistical word counts in different languages. The impact of scientific discovery on human society has affected our speech, as it has affected other social habits. Though a few speech communities in Europe, notably Iceland and to a lesser extent Germany and Holland, have shut their ears to the growing stock of internationally current terms for machinery, instruments, chemicals, electrical appliances, and manufactured products, the vocabulary of modern technics is equally the word material of the United States and of the U.S.S.R., of modern Iran and of Italy. It is already invading the Far East and must do so more and more, if China and India emerge from their present miseries as free and modernized societies.

The world-wide and expanding lexicon of modern technics follows the dictates of international scientific practice. It grows by combination of roots drawn almost exclusively from two languages—Greek and Latin. To the extent that the lexicon of many projects, e.g. Esperanto, Ido, Occidental, Novial, is largely or, like *Romanal* and Peano's Interlingua, almost exclusively based on material of recognizably Latin origin, all recent interlanguages display the family likeness to which Jespersen refers in the passage quoted. In fact they do include a considerable proportion of words based on roots which individually enjoy a high measure of international currency.

The international vocabulary of technics contains a large proportion of Latin roots; but Greek has furnished for a long time the basis of the *majority of new scientific words*. For instance, the new terminology which Faraday and his successors designed for the description of electrochemical phenomena is exclusively derived from Greek roots, as in: *electrolyte, electrode, cathode, anode, cation, anion*, and *ion*. Yet the Greek contribution to the vocabulary of languages hitherto constructed has been small. Indeed the *Concise Oxford Dictionary* has a far higher proportion (p. 2) of Greek roots than any hitherto constructed language. If interlinguists utilize them at all, they confine themselves to those assimilated by Latin. In short, none of the pioneers of language planning has paid due regard to the profound revolution in scientific nomenclature which took place in the closing years of the eighteenth and the beginning of the nineteenth century. Nor did they see the implications of a fact which disturbed the English philologist Bradley. The language of invention now becomes the idiom of the street corner before the lapse of a generation. Bradley gave expression to his alarm at this process of internationalization in words which the partisans of past projects might well have heeded:

"At present our English dictionaries are burdened with an enormous and daily increasing mass of scientific terms that are not English at all except in the form of their terminations and in the pronunciations inferred from their spelling. The adoption of an international language for science would bring about the disappearance of these monstrosities of un-English English. . . ."

Partly because of the tempo of invention, partly because of more widespread schooling, partly because of the expanding volume of books and articles popularizing new scientific discoveries, this infiltration of what Bradley was pleased to call *abstruse* words has increased enormously of recent years. Nineteenth-century interlinguists with a conventional literary training and outlook could scarcely foresee a time when schoolboys would chatter about *heterodyne* outfits, *periscopic* sights, or *stratosphere* flying as lightheartedly as they had discussed kites or marbles. Wherever there are gasoline pumps and women's journals with articles on modern standards of nutrition, anyone with a good school education—American or Russian, French or German—will recall and understand words compounded with *thermo-*, *kine-*, *hydro-*, *phon-*, *phot-*, *geo-*, or *chromo-*. The table on page 504 illustrates neglect of this Greek building material in favor of the Latin one. The first column lists some forty Greek bricks which frequently appear in international words; the second and third exhibit Esperanto and Novial words which have basically the same meaning as the Greek element in the first column. With the exception of a few marked by an asterisk, all of them are of Romance origin. The exceptions (other than *mikri* = small) are neither Latin nor Greek.

Thus no existing project can claim to provide for maximum ease of recognition or memorization of vocabulary; but if no existing project is wholly satisfactory, it is not difficult to point to the basis of a better solution. What remains to be done is not an insurmountable task. The discovery of a common international *denominator* does not call for the elaborate and tedious word counts which have occupied the

	GREEK ELEMENT		ESPERANTO	NOVIAL
hetero	different	heterosexual	difera	diferenci
homo	same	homosexual	same *	sami *
iso	equal	isosceles	egala	egali
micro	small	microscope	malgranda	mikri *
mono	alone, single	monoplane	sola	soli
neo	new	neolithic	nova	novi
palaeo	old	palaeology	malnova	oldi *
pan	all	panchromatic	tuta	toti
poly	many	polygamous	multa	multi
pseudo	false	pseudonym	malvera	falsi
therm	heat	thermometer	varma *	varmi *
derma	skin	dermatitis	hauto *	pele
hypno	sleep	hypnosis	dormo	dormio
chron	time	chronometer	tempo	tempo
chrom	color	chromosome	koloro	kolore
tele	distance	television	malproksima	distanti
erg	work	allergic	laboro	labore
demo	people	democracy	popolo	popule
bio	life	biology	vivo	vivo
physi	nature	physiology	naturo	nature
krati	government	autocracy	rego	regiro
kosmo	world	cosmopolitan	mondo	monde
helio	sun	heliotropic	suno *	sune *
morph	form	morphology	formo	forme
astr	star	astronomy	stelo	stele
phon	sound	phonetics	sono	suone
geo	earth	geology	tero	tere
hydr	water	hydrodynamics	akvo	hidra
anthrop	man	anthropology	viro	viro
gyne	woman	gynaecology	virino	fema
akoust	hearing	acoustics	audi	audi
graph	writing	telegraph	skribi	skripte
skop	seeing	telescope	vidi	vide
kine	moving	kinetic	movi	mova
ball	throwing	ballistics	jeti	lansa
phob	fearing	xenophobia	timi	tima
phil	loving	philately	ami	ama
game	marrying	polygamy	edzigo *	mariteso
phag	eating	phagocyte	mangi	manja
mnemo	remembering	mnemonic	memori	memora

* See explanation, p. 503.

efforts—and wasted the time—of some enthusiasts. We can start with the fact that a growing vocabulary of international terms is a by-product of the impact of scientific invention on modern society. Hence our first need is a classified synopsis of technical words which have filtered into the everyday speech of different language communities. These we can resolve into their constituent parts. We can then form a picture of which roots enjoy wide international circulation. The overwhelming majority will be Greek or Latin. For constructing an economical, yet adequate, vocabulary there will be no lack of suitable building material.

What constitutes an adequate vocabulary in this sense enters into the problem of word economy. For the present it suffices to say that an international vocabulary need cater only for communication within the confines of our common international culture. Commerce and travel have equipped us with such words as *sugar, bazaar, samovar, sultanas, fjord, café, skis,* and there is no reason why an international language should not take from each nation or speech community those words which describe their own specific amenities and institutions.

An analysis of the geographical distribution of roots derived from scientific and technical terms, such as *telegraph, megaphone, micrometer, microscope, cyclostyle, thermoplastics,* will certainly reveal wide international currency of some Latin and Greek roots of the same meaning. This prompts the question: which should we prefer? If one enjoys much wider distribution than the other, we should generally decide in its favor; but if the difference is not great we might take into consideration other criteria of merit. For instance, the existence of a Latin *and* a Greek root with the same meaning would enable us to avoid homophones. Thus the Latin syllable *sol* is common to *solar, solitary, solitude,* and *solstice.* While there is no equally common Greek root to suggest the meaning of *alone,* there is the suggestive *helio* of *heliograph, helium, perihelion, heliotropism,* and other technical words for the *sun.* We can therefore keep *sol* for *alone* and take *helio* for the *sun.* Many Latin words which are international, at least in the European and American sense, have widely divergent meanings in different countries. By substituting Greek for Latin we could avoid possible misunderstanding. For instance, the French word *conscience* is often equivalent to our word *consciousness,* and the German praises somebody for being *consistent* by applying the epithet *konsequent.* Another criterion which might well influence our decision will come up for discussion later on. We can also take into account the *relative ease with which it is possible for people of different tongues to pronounce* a Latin root or its Greek equivalent.

The raw materials of our lexicon will be: (*a*) a dual battery of cosmopolitan Latin and Greek roots; (*b*) a list of the necessary items which make up an adequate vocabulary for ordinary communication. We then have all the data from which a representative body could prescribe the details of a satisfactory interlanguage. If free from grammatical irrelevancies, people of moderate intelligence and a secondary-school education should be able to read it with little previous instruction and learn to write and speak it in far less time than any ethnic language requires. Admittedly, the intervocabulary outlined above would be almost exclusively Western in origin. But we need not fear that our Eastern neighbors will reject it for that reason. The word invasion of medicine and engineering need not be a corollary of political oppression and economic exploitation. Besides, Europe can say to China: I take your *syntax*, and you take my *word*.

WORD ECONOMY

The next question which arises is: *what words* are essential? This is what C. K. Ogden and Miss L. W. Lockhart call the problem of *word economy*. The expression *word economy* may suggest two, if not three, quite different notions to a person who meets it for the first time. One is ability to frame different statements, questions, or requests with the least number of different vocables. Another is ability to frame the same utterance in the most compact form, i.e., with the least number of vocables, different or otherwise. Economy of the first sort implies a minimum vocabulary of *essential* words. Economy of the second calls for a large vocabulary of *available* words. Since it is not difficult to multiply words, the fundamental problem of word economy from our viewpoint is how to cut down those which are not essential for self-expression. There remains a third and more primitive way in which economy may be achieved. We can save breath or space by contracting the volume of a word or word sequence, as in *U.S.S.R.* for *Union of Socialist Soviet Republics*, or *Gestapo* for *Geheime Staatspolizei* (Secret State Police).

At first sight it may seem a hopeless task to construct a vocabulary that would cover all the essential needs of intercommunication, yet contain not more than, say, a thousand basic words. A modern newspaper assumes acquaintance with perhaps twenty thousand, and in the English section of a very humble English-French pocket dictionary some ten thousand are listed. It requires no lengthy scrutiny to discover that a large portion of the material is not essential. A rationally constructed word list would discard many synonyms or near synonyms, of which Anglo-American is chock-full, e.g. *little—small, big—large, begin—commence*. It need not tolerate such functional overlapping, as *band—ribbon—strip*. It would also steer clear of over-specialization by making one word do what in natural languages is often done by three or more. Thus the outer cover of the human body is called *la peau* in French, that of the onion *la pelure*, and that of the sausage *la cotte*. Though less fastidious than the French, we ourselves overburden the dictionary with the corresponding series *skin—rind—jacket—peel*. When we distinguish between *thread—twine—cord—string—rope—tow* we are merely heaping name upon name for what is ultimately a difference in size.

Since our interlanguage pursues strictly utilitarian ends and seeks perfection in precision, it can do without some of the verbal gewgaws and falderals of poetic and "cultured" speech. There is no need to incorporate a large number of words to express subtleties of attitude. We could safely replace the existing plethora of vocables denoting approval or disapproval by a bare handful of names. But rejection of such would not keep us within the thousand-word limit. We have to look elsewhere for help; and here we can apply with profit, if we apply it with temperance, the basic principle of Dalgarno's *Art of Symbols* and Wilkins's *Real Character*. All European languages have words which embrace the meaning of a group. Thus the general term *clothes* (with the bedfellows *vesture, garment, apparel, dress*) includes two main classes: *under clothes* including *vest, shirt, knickers, petticoat*, and *outer clothes* including *frock, skirt, trousers, coat*. In the same way *building* covers *school, theater, prison, villa, hospital, museum*, and *drink* or *beverage* includes nonalcoholic and alcoholic, to the latter of which we assign *wine, cider, beer, whisky, gin*.

A careful comparative investigation would probably reveal that modern English is far better equipped with words of the *food, drink, container, instrument* class than French or Spanish for instance. It is almost self-evident that classifying words of this sort must play an important part in the buildup of an economical vocabulary, because they enable us to refer to a maximum number of different things, operations, and properties with a minimum of separate names. In a given context or situation *drink* will usually deputize well enough for the more specific *wine*. It is also self-evident that there are limits to the use of master key words, if we aim at excluding vagueness and ambiguity. It is not enough to have a general word *animal* distinguishable as *wild* or *domestic*. In real life we need words for *cat, cow, dog, horse, pig*. So one important problem which confronts us is this: which *animals, drinks, garments*, etc., have claim to a place on a list of essential words? The answer is not quite simple. We would not hesitate to provide a special niche for *wine, cow, shoe;* but can we ignore *cider, bull,* or *brassière?* Let us see how we can extricate ourselves from the difficulty of having no such words. One way is to choose a more general term and leave the rest to the situation. Another is to extract a definition or use a substitution by juggling with material already to hand. Thus we can define *cider* as a *drink made from apples,* a *bull* as the *male of the cow,* and a *brassière* as *support for the breasts.*

At bottom, word economy depends on judicious selection of *general* terms and descriptive periphrase for *specific* uses. With reference to what constitutes judicious selection we have to remember two things. Definition is often cumbersome, and the aptitude for picking out features which make for identification in a given situation is the product of training. In short, the difficulty of fishing out an appropriate definition may be much greater than the effort of memorizing an extra word. Therefore it is a doubtful advantage to cut out single names for things or processes to which we constantly refer. On the other hand, we can clearly dispense with separate names for an immense number of things and processes to which we do not continually refer; and the process of definition, when context calls for closer definition, need not be as wordy as the idiom of English or other Aryan languages often prescribes. Even within the framework of acceptable Anglo-American we can substitute *apple drink* and *breast support* for *cider* and *brassière* without committing an offense against usage. Making compounds of this sort is not the same as exact definition, but definition need never be more fastidious than context requires. From a purely pedantic point of view *limewater* might stand for the water we sprinkle on the soil for the benefit of lime trees, but it is precise enough in any real context in which it might occur.

In general the combination of a generic name with another word as in *limewater* suffices to specify a particular object or process in a way which is easy to recall because sufficiently suggestive. Here English usage provides some instructive models. Ordinarily a *house* is a private residence, the sort of building to which we refer most often, but it is also the generic basis of *alehouse, playhouse, greenhouse, poorhouse, bakehouse*. While it may be as difficult to construct a definition of a *theater* as to learn a separate word for it, it is not easier to learn a new word than to recall a compound as explicit as *playhouse*, in which both elements are items of an essential vocabulary. Another model for the use of such generic words is the series *handwear, footwear, neckwear, headwear*. Clearly, we could reduce the size of our essential vocabulary by adopting the principle of using such generic terms as *-house, -wear, -man, -land*, for other classes such as *vessels, fabrics, filaments*. With each generic term we could then learn sufficiently suggestive couplets such as *postman, highland*, or *handwear* for use when context calls for additional information. Economical compounding of this sort involves two principles. First, the components must be elements of the basic minimum of essential words. Second, the juxtaposition of parts must sufficiently indicate the meaning. We cannot let metaphor have a free hand to prescribe such combinations as *polly seed, rubber neck*, or *waffle bottom*.

How much license we allow to metaphor in other directions is a matter of particular interest in relation to the merits and defects of Basic English. There is no hard-and-fast line between metaphorical usage as in *elastic demand* and generic names such as *elastic* for *rubber;* and we cannot eliminate the use of suggestive metaphors which may point the way to unsuspected similarities. Nonetheless, we have to set some limit, and one is not hard to see. Our essential list should contain separate names for physical and personal or social attributes with as little obvious connection as the drought in *dry goods* and *dry humor*. If we prescribe the same word *sharp* for a tooth, for a twinge, for a temper, and for a telling reply, we might as well replace all names of qualities by two vocables respectively signifying general approval and disapproval. In this field of word choice the *apparent* economies of Basic English, as of Chinese, may raise our hopes unduly.

The dictionary of our ideal interlanguage would naturally list internationally current words such as *cigarette, coffee, tram, bus, hotel, taxi, post, international, tobacco, soya, valuta*. Fixation in print would have two advantages. It might discourage local differences of pronunciation which lead to confusion between the French word *coco*, variously used as a term of endearment, for coconut or for cocaine, and

the English word *cocoa*. It might also promote international accept-
ance of a single word for such world-wide commodities as *petrol*
(Engl.), *gasoline* (Amer.), *essence* (French), *Benzin* (Germ. and
Swed.).

One important contribution of Ogden's Basic to the problem of
word economy in a constructed language is his treatment of the verb.
The Basic equivalent of a verb is a general term (*operator*) and some
qualifying word or expression. By combining the general notion of
space change in *go* with another word or group of words we dispense
with all the various names now restricted to particular types of transport, e.g. *walk* = *go on foot, ride* = *go on a horse*, or *go on a bicycle*,
etc. By the same method we avoid the use of different names for particular manners of moving, e.g. *run* = *go very fast, wander* = *go from
place to place without aim*. We can also do without all *causative-
intransitive* couplets which signify *producing* or *acquiring* a condition, by combining equivalents of *make* or *get* with one of the basic
adjectives, e.g. *increase* = *make* or *get bigger, clarify* = *make* or *get
clear, accelerate* = *make* or *get faster*. By combining sixteen fundamental verb substitutes (*come, get, give, go, keep, let, make, put,
seem, take, be, do, have, say, see, send*) with other essential items of
the word list Basic English thus provides an adequate *Ersatz* for four
thousand verbs in common use.

Before Ogden devised the basic method of teaching English, pioneers of language planning had paid scant attention to the minimum
vocabulary required for effective communication. Consequently, the
English pattern has stimulated as well as circumscribed subsequent
discussion. Though it is desirable to keep down the necessary minimum number of verbs by the same device, a constructed language
could not advantageously incorporate equivalents of Ogden's sixteen
operators and use them in the same way. The word economy of Basic
is a word economy that has to conform with a standard acceptable to
educated English-speaking people. Otherwise we should be at a loss
to justify the inclusion of *come* in a sixteen-verb catalogue already
equipped with *go*. With due regard to the economies which are possible if we combine *go, make, get*, or equivalent "operators" with
other basic elements, it is difficult to recognize some Basic combinations such as *go on, make up, get on* as subspecies of single classes. In
fact, they are idioms of standard Anglo-American usage. The beginner has to learn them as if they were separate items in a list of verbs.

This raises the possibility of including in our word list operators which have a wide range like *make* and *get* or *give* and *take*, but do not coincide with current Anglo-American usage. Some verb couplets are redundant because they express different general relations to the same state or process. Thus *to give life* is *to bear*, *to take life* is *to kill, to get life* is *to be born*. So also *to give instruction* is *to teach* and *to take* (or *get*) *instruction* is *to learn*. *To give credit* is *to lend* and *to get credit* is *to borrow*. It is easy to see how we might make similar economies, if we had an everyday equivalent for the biological *stimulus—response* contrast analogous to the acquisitive *give—get*. The word *give* sufficiently covers the operation of stimulating, but Basic offers nothing which expresses *to make the response appropriate to* implicit in the somewhat archaic *heed*. The addition of an operator with this functional value would explicitly dispense with the need for one member of such pairs as *question—answer, information—interest, command—obedience, defeat—surrender, writing—reading, buy—sell*. Thus *to answer* is to make the response appropriate to a *question* and *to obey* is to heed a *command*.

Other possibilities of word economy in a constructed auxiliary are illustrated by the large number of grammatically inflated abstractions in our language. Since we do not need separate link-word forms for the directives *after* and *before*, we do not need a separate link word *while* corresponding to the directive *during*. Since we can speak of the *above* remarks for the remarks printed or written *higher* on the page, we should also be able to speak of the *previous* letter as the *before* letter without misgiving. Since some people discuss the *Beyond*, we might just as well call the *sequel* the *after* and the *past* the *before*. In fact, every directive is the focus of a cluster of different word forms with the same basic function. In a language with rigid word order and empty words as signposts of the sentence layout, we could generalize without loss of clarity a process which has already gone far in Anglo-American and much further in Chinese.

Broadly speaking, for every one of our directives we can find an adverbial qualifier, an adjective, a noun, and often even a conjunction, with the same fundamental meaning. Each of these may itself be one of a cluster of synonyms. It is merely their different *grammatical* behavior which prevents us from recognizing that *semantically* they are comrades in arms. Why cannot a single word do all the work of *after, since, afterward, subsequent(ly), succeed(ing), sequel, aftermath*, or of *before, previous(ly), preced(ing), past, history?* We could then make about forty temporal, spatial, motor, instrumental, and associative directives do the job of about two hundred words and three or four times as many synonyms or near synonyms sufficiently distinguishable by context and situation alone. Partly for this reason, and partly because this class of words covers all the territory of auxiliaries which express time and aspect (pp. 90–92), it might be an advantage to extend the range corresponding to the Basic English battery of directives by making more refined distinctions. Such distinctions may occur in one language, but be absent in another. For instance, a special word symbolizing physical contact is nonexistent in Anglo-American, but exists in German and would deserve inclusion in an improved set of directives. For generations we have had chairs of comparative philology, but investigations dictated by an instrumental outlook are as rare today as in Grimm's time. If it were not so we should now be able to specify what relations and concepts tentatively or fully expressed in this or that existing medium can justify their claim to a place on the essential word list of a properly constructed language.

Basic English gives us another clue to word economy. As formal distinction between noun and verb, when both stand for processes or states, is an unnecessary complication, formal distinction between noun and adjective is superfluous when both symbolize a property. If we can go out in the *dark* or the *cold*, we have no need of such distinctions as *warm—warmth*, *hot—heat*, *dry—dryness*. If we can discuss the *good*, the *beautiful*, and the *true*, *goodness*, *beauty*, and *truth* are too much of a good thing. At the same time, we need a consistent rule about fusion of such word forms. We cannot endorse such inconsistencies as exist in Anglo-American. It may or may not be important to distinguish between *good actions* and *good people* when we speak of *the good*, but if we do so we should be entitled to use *the unclean* for *uncleanliness* as well as for the *unclean individuals*. The misery of all existing speech is that useful devices remain halfexploited. Grammarians say that analogical extension has not gone far enough. English has now a simple and highly regularized flexional system, but in its linguistic expression of concepts and relations it is as chaotic as any other language, including Esperanto. This is what foreigners mean when they say: English is simple at the start, but, etc.

While we can design a language to achieve a high level of word economy in Ogden's sense, and therefore to lighten the load which the *beginner* has to carry, there is no reason for restricting the vocabulary of an interlanguage constructed with this end in view to the bare minimum of words *essential* for lucid communication; and we have no need to exclude the possibility of ringing the changes on synonyms which safeguard style against monotony. We might well add to our interdictionary an *appendix* containing a *reserve* vocabulary of compact alternatives. Even so, a *maximum* vocabulary of roots, *excluding all strictly technical terms and local names for local things or local institutions*, need scarcely exceed a total of three thousand.

INTERPHONETICS

It would be easy to formulate the outstanding desiderata of an ideal language on the naïve assumption that phonetic considerations are of prior importance; and it would not be difficult to give them practical expression. To begin with, we have to take stock of the fact that the consonant clusters (p. 208) so characteristic of the Aryan family are almost or completely absent in other languages, e.g. in Chinese, Japanese, Bantu, and in Polynesian dialects. So clusters of two or three consonants such as in *blinds*, and, more serious, quadruple combinations as in *mustnt*, are foreign to the ear and tongue of most peoples outside Europe, America, and India. Then again, few people have a range of either simple consonants or simple vowels as great as our own. A fivefold battery of vowels with values roughly like those of the Italian and Spanish *a, e, i, o, u* suffices for many speech communities. Several of our own consonants are phonetic rarities, and many varieties of human speech reject the voiceless series in favor of the voiced, or vice versa. A battery of consonants with very wide currency would not include more than nine items—*l, m, n, r*, together with a choice between the series *p, t, f, k, s*, and the series *b, d, v, g, z*. Even this would be a liberal allowance. The Japanese have no *l*.

A universal alphabet of five vowels and of eight or nine consonants would allow for between fifteen hundred and two thousand pronounceable roots made up of open syllables like the syllables of Japanese, Bantu, and Polynesian words. Supplemented with forty-five monosyllables and a limited number of trisyllables, this would supply enough variety for a maximum vocabulary of sufficient size. The word material of a language constructed in accordance with this principle would be universally, or well-nigh universally, pronounceable and recognizable without special training of ear or tongue. It would offer none of the difficulties with which the French nasal vowels, the English *th* and *j* sounds, or the German and Scots *ch* confront the beginner. Against these admitted merits we have to weigh the fact that a language so designed from whole cloth would perpetuate one of the greatest of all obstacles to learning a new language. The beginner would have to wrestle with the total *unfamiliarity of its word material.* Each item of the vocabulary would be a fresh load with no mnemonic associations to give it buoyancy.

Grammar and memorization of the word list are the two main difficulties of learning a new language, and the only way of reducing the second to negligible dimensions is to make each word the focus of a cluster of familiar associations like the root *tel* common to *telegraph, telescope, telepathy.* We have seen that scientific discovery is solving this problem for mankind by distributing an international vocabulary of roots derived from Latin and Greek. Anything we can do to simplify the phonetic structure of a satisfactory interlanguage has to get done *within that framework.* The framework itself is exacting because Aryan languages in general are rich in variety of simple consonants and of consonantal combinations—Greek more than most. Thus the greatest concession we can make to the phonetic ideal is to weigh the claims of equivalent Latin and Greek roots, with due regard to ease of pronunciation and recognition, when both enjoy international currency.

While it would be foolish to deny the difficulties of achieving a universal standard of pronunciation for an interlanguage based on Latin-Greek word material, and therefore on sounds and combinations of sounds alien to the speech habits of Africa and the Far East, it is possible to exaggerate this disability. People who indulge in the witless luxury of laughing at the foreigner who says *sleep* instead of *slip* condone equally striking differences between the vowel values of London and Lancashire, Aberdeen (Scotland) and Aberdeen (South Dakota). Although obliteration of the distinction between the *p, t, k, f* and the *b, d, g, v* series makes homophones of such couplets as *pup—pub, write—ride, pluck—plug, proof—prove,* the fact that very many Americans discard the voiceless in favor of the voiced consonants does not prevent British audiences from flocking to gangster sound films.

Most of us are not trained phoneticians, and most people without some phonetic training are insensitive to comparatively crude distinctions, if interested in what the speaker is saying. Fastidious folk, who foresee fearful misunderstandings because people of different nations will inevitably give slightly, or even sometimes crudely, different values to the same sound symbols, may well reflect on the following remarks of the English phonetician, Lloyd James, in *Historical Introduction to French Phonetics:*

"A recent experiment proved that the sounds *s*, *f*, *th* are often indistinguishable to listeners when broadcast in isolation by wireless transmission. Nevertheless, despite this fact, listeners understand perfectly what is said. It follows, then, that up to a certain point, it is quite unnecessary to hear each and every sound that the speaker utters. We know that this is so from our experience in listening to speakers in large halls, or theatres. If we are at some distance from the speaker, we miss many of his sounds, but provided we get a certain number, or a certain percentage of the whole, then we understand what he is saying. The point to remember is that there is, or there would appear to be, in language an acoustic minimum necessary for intelligibility, and provided the listener gets this, it is all that he requires. The rest is superfluous. The speaker may utter it, but as far as the listener is concerned, it is quite immaterial to him whether he hears it or not. The more familiar we are with a language, the smaller is the fraction of its sounds, etc., that we require to catch in order to understand what is said. Much of the acoustic matter that is graphically represented in the written language is unnecessary for intelligibility, while, on the contrary, intelligibility requires that certain acoustic features of the language must be present in speech which have no representation whatever in the written language. Educated speech differs from uneducated speech mainly in providing a greater acoustic minimum."

Although the Greek range of consonants, and more especially its consonantal combinations, offers difficulties for most non-Aryan-speaking peoples and for some people who speak Aryan languages, the vowel range of a Latin-Greek vocabulary is not a serious drawback. We need only five simple vowels and their derivative diphthongs. As Jespersen rightly remarks: "It is one of the beauties of an international language that it needs only five vowels, and therefore can allow a certain amount of liberty in pronouncing these sounds without misunderstanding arising." Whether different citizens of a socialist world order pronounce *a* as in the English word *father*, as in the French *la*, German *Vater*, or Danish *far*, is immaterial to easy communication. In fact, the differences are not greater than between *glass* as people respectively pronounce it in Dundee and Dorchester, or between *girl* in Mayfair and Old Kent Road, and far less than between *tomato* as people severally pronounce it in Boston and Birmingham.

We may take it for granted that the difficulty which the Greek θ sound presents to people of many nations, the preference of Germans for voiceless and of Danes for voiced consonants, the partiality of the Scot and the Spaniard for a trilled *r*, and the reluctance of an Englishman to pronounce *r* at all, will not prevent people of different speech communities from using as an efficient and satisfactory medium of communication an interlanguage liable to get color from local sound. Indeed, we need not despair of the possibility of reaching a standard in the course of time. More and more the infant discipline of phonetics, which has lately received a new impulse from the needs of radio transmission and long-distance telephone conversation, will influence the practice of school instruction. In an international community with a single official medium of intercommunication, the radio and the talkie will daily tune the ear to a single speech pattern. We have no reason to fear that discourse through a constructed interlanguage will involve greater difficulties than English conversation between a French Canadian and a South African Boer, a Maori and a New Zealander of Scots parentage, a Hindu Congress member and a Bantu trade-union leader from Johannesburg, or Winston Spencer Churchill and Franklin Delano Roosevelt.

INTERLANGUAGE LEARNING WITHOUT TEARS

We may now sum up the outstanding features of a constructed language designed with due regard to criticisms provoked by a succession of earlier projects and to the efforts of those who aim at adapting English to international use:

1) It would be essentially an *isolating* language. The beginner would not have to plod through a maze of useless and irregular flexions common to Aryan languages such as French or Spanish, German or Russian. With the possible exception of a plural terminal, it would have no flexional modifications of word form. Apart from a few simple rules for the use of *operators* like our words *make* and *get*, formation of compounds like *toothbrush*, and insertion of empty words like *of* to show up the layout of the sentence, its rules of grammar would be rules of word order. These would be as uniform and as few as possible. In short, the grammar of the language could be set forth fully with examples in half a dozen pages of print.

2) It would be essentially a language with Latin-Greek word

material, so chosen that the beginner could associate items of the basic word list with syllables of internationally current words.

3) It would have *word economy* at least as great as that of Basic English. That is to say, the entire list of words essential for ordinary discussion, news, and self-expression (not counting compound formations, words common to the popular talk of the East as well as to the West, and the specialized vocabulary of the scientist and technician) might be not more than a thousand, and could be printed on one sheet of paper.

4) It would have *regular spelling* based on the characters of the Latin alphabet. Having the limited range of simple vowels, it would call for no diacritic marks (like ˆ, ′, and ‵) which reduce the speed of writing and add to the cost of printing.

5) Because of its great word economy it could be easily equipped with the type of simplified *alphabetic* shorthand embodied in R. Dutton's ingenious system of *Speedwords*.

Grammatically such a language would be much simpler than Esperanto, and some other pioneer efforts, though not much simpler than Novial (if we exclude Jespersen's elaborate machinery of word derivation!). Its syntax would be decidedly simpler than that of Anglo-American, because shedding of flexions and leveling of the few surviving ones have not been accompanied by a proportionate simplification and standardization of word order. Its word material would be far more international than that of any hitherto constructed language. Unlike Esperanto, Interlingua, Novial, etc., it would annex Greek roots which are in general circulation wherever scientific discovery is changing human habits. It would be more universal than Basic English because it would be free from Teutonic roots. Like Basic English it would not be encumbered with hundreds of redundant verbs, and the task of learning would not be made unnecessarily difficult by the fantastic irregularities of English, or French spelling. Because the word material would be transparent it would be easy to memorize. Each item would be a peg for attaching relevant semantic associations.

A language purged of irregular spelling, irregular and irrelevant grammar, unusual word collocations (i.e., idioms), and redundant word forms would take its place unobtrusively in a program of general elementary instruction in semantics and etymology. Learning it would be learning to associate roots common to different words and to gain facility in the art of definition. Proficiency would thus come with little effort in a small fraction of the time now devoted to the teaching of foreign languages. Since its adoption presupposes a stable, supranational organization in which children and adults are collaborating with a hitherto unknown intensity of interest and effort, the climate of school tuition would be very different from that of the French class in an American or the Latin class in a Scottish high school. Progress in the world's first true Interlingua would be a passport to a wider international culture made actually or psychologically ubiquitous by broadcasting, the modern cinema, and air travel.

Of itself, no such change can bring the age-long calamity of war to an end; and it is a dangerous error to conceive that it can do so. We cannot hope to reach a remedy for the language obstacles to international co-operation on a democratic footing, while predatory finance capital, intrigues of armament manufacturers, and the vested interest of a rentier class in the misery of colonial peoples continue to stifle the impulse to a world-wide enterprise for the common wealth of mankind. No language reform can abolish war, while social agencies far more powerful than mere linguistic misunderstandings furnish fresh occasion for it. What intelligent language planning can do is to forge a new instrument for human collaboration on a planetary scale, when social institutions propitious to international strife no longer thwart the constructive task of planning health, leisure, and plenty for all.

PART FOUR

LANGUAGE MUSEUM

APPENDIX I

Basic Vocabularies for the
Teutonic Languages

USE OF ROMANCE AND TEUTONIC WORD LISTS

THE number of items in the ensuing word lists exceeds the *minimum* requirements of the beginner in search of a battery adequate for self-expression. They contain assortments of common nouns to meet *individual* requirements, such as those of the traveler or of the motorist, together with many useful English words which *share recognizable roots* with their foreign equivalents. The items in the English column of the Romance and Teutonic word lists do not tally throughout. One reason for discrepancies is the advisability of learning Teutonic words together with English words of Teutonic origin and Romance words together with English words of Latin origin.

The verb lists do not follow this plan consistently. The reason for this is that the meaning of an English verb of Latin origin is usually more sharply defined than that of its Teutonic twin. For many common English verbs less usual but more explicit (see p. 26) synonyms appear in the column at the extreme left. English verb forms printed in italics correspond to Romance or Teutonic verbs of the *intransitive* or *reflexive* type. In the Teutonic word list German verbs printed in italics take the dative case. For a reason explained on page 17, the verb lists contain few items which signify *acquiring* or *conferring* a quality listed as an *adjective*. For instance, we do not need a transitive or intransitive equivalent for *widen*. To widen means to *make wide* (trans.) or to *become wide* (intrans.). We can use French or Spanish, German or Swedish equivalents of *make* and *become* with an adjective in the same way.

The reader who turns to these lists for case material illustrating family likeness or laws of sound shift should remember that the words listed are nearly always the ones in *common* use. By choosing highbrow, pedantic, and somewhat archaic synonyms or near synonyms, it would be easy to construct lists giving a much more impressive picture of genetic relationship.

TEUTONIC WORD LISTS

1. NOUNS

a) CLIMATE AND SCENERY

ENGLISH	SWEDISH	DANISH	DUTCH	GERMAN
air	luft	Luft	lucht	die Luft
bank (river)	strand	Bred	oever	das Ufer
bay	vik	Bugt	baai	die Bucht
beach	strand	Strand	strand (n)	der Strand
bush	buske	Busk	struik	das Gebüsch
cloud	moln (n)	Sky	wolk	die Wolke
coast	kust	Kyst	kust	die Küste
country (not town)	land (n)	Land (n)	platteland (n)	das Land
current	ström	Strøm	stroom	die Strömung
darkness	mörker (n)	Mørke (n)	duisternis	die Dunkelheit
dew	dagg	Dug	dauw	der Tau
dust	dam (n)	Støv (n)	stof (n)	der Staub
earth	jord	Jord	aarde	die Erde
east	öster	Øst	oosten (n)	der Osten
field	fält	Mark	veld (n)	das Feld
foam	skum (n)	Skum (n)	schuim (n)	der Schaum
fog	dimma	Taage	mist	der Nebel
forest	skog	Skov	bosch (n)	der Wald
frost	frost	Frost	vorst	der Frost
grass	gräs (n)	Graes (n) *	gras (n)	das Gras
hail	hagel (n)	Hagl	hagel	der Hagel
hay	hö (n)	Hø (n)	hooi (n)	das Heu
heath	hed	Hede	heide	die Heide
high tide	flod	Flod	vloed	die Flut
hill	kulle	Bakke	heuvel	der Hügel
ice	is	Is	ijs (n)	das Eis
island	ö	Ø	eiland (n)	die Insel
lake	sjö	Sø	meer (n)	der See
light	ljus (n)	Lys (n)	licht (n)	das Licht
lightning	blixt	Lyn (n)	bliksem	der Blitz
low tide	ebb	Ebbe	eb	die Ebbe
meadow	äng	Eng	weide	die Wiese
moon	måne	Maane	maan	der Mond
mountain	berg (n)	Bjerg (n)	berg	der Berg
mud	mudder (n)	Dynd (n)	slijk (n)	der Schlamm

* Danish *æ* is represented throughout by *ae*.

ENGLISH	SWEDISH	DANISH	DUTCH	GERMAN
nature	natur	Natur	natuur	die Natur
north	norr	Nord	noorden (n)	der Norden
peninsula	halvö	Halvø	schiereiland (n)	die Halbinsel
plain	slät	Slette	vlakte	die Ebene
pond	dam	Dam	vijver	der Teich
rain	regn (n)	Regn	regen	der Regen
rainbow	regnbåge	Regnbue	regenboog	der Regenbogen
river	flod	Flod	rivier	der Fluss
rock	klippa	Klippe	rots	der Felsen
sand	sand	Sand (n)	zand (n)	der Sand
sea	hav (n)	Hav (n)	zee	die See
				das Meer
shadow, shade	skugga	Skygge	schaduw	der Schatten
sky	himmel	Himmel	lucht	der Himmel
snow	snö	Sne	sneeuw	der Schnee
south	söder	Syd	zuiden (n)	der Süden
spring (water)	källa	Kilde	bron	die Quelle
star	stjärna	Stjerne	ster	der Stern
storm	storm	Storm	storm	der Sturm
stream	bäck	Baek	beek	der Bach
sun	sol	Sol	zon	die Sonne
thaw	töväder (n)	Tøvejr (n)	dooi	das Tauwetter
thunder	åska	Torden	donder	der Donner
valley	dal	Dal	vallei	das Tal
view	utsikt	Udsigt	uitzicht (n)	die Aussicht
water	vatten (n)	Vand (n)	water (n)	das Wasser
fresh water	sötvatten (n)	Ferskvand (n)	zoet water (n)	das Süsswasser
salt water	saltvatten (n)	Saltvand (n)	zout water (n)	das Salzwasser
waterfall	vattenfall (n)	Vandfald (n)	waterval	der Wasserfall
wave	bölja	Bølge	golf	die Welle
weather	väder (n)	Vejr (n)	weer (n)	das Wetter
west	väster	Vest	westen (n)	der Westen
wind	vind	Vind	wind	der Wind
world	värld	Verden	wereld	die Welt

b) HUMAN BODY

arm	arm	Arm	arm	der Arm
back	rygg	Ryg	rug	der Rücken
beard	skägg (n)	Skaeg (n)	baard	der Bart
belly	buk	Bug	buik	der Bauch
bladder	blåsa	Blaere	blaas	die Blase
blood	blod (n)	Blod (n)	bloed (n)	das Blut
body	kropp	Legeme (n)	lichaam (n)	der Körper
bone	ben (n)	Knokkel	been (n)	der Knochen
brain	hjärna	Hjerne	hersenen (pl.)	das Gehirn

ENGLISH	SWEDISH	DANISH	DUTCH	GERMAN
breath	ande	Aande	adem	der Atem
calf	vad	Laeg	kuit	die Wade
cheek	kind	Kind	wang	die Wange
chest	bröst (n)	Bryst (n)	borst	die Brust
chin	haka	Hage	kin	das Kinn
cold	förkylning	Forkølelse	verkoudheid	die Erkältung
cough	hosta	Hoste	hoest	der Husten
ear	öra (n)	Øre (n)	oor (n)	das Ohr
elbow	armbåge	Albue	elleboog	der Ellbogen
eye	öga (n)	Øje (n)	oog (n)	das Auge
eyebrow	ögonbryn (n)	Øjenbryn (n)	wenkbrauw	die Augenbraue
eyelid	ögonlock (n)	Øjenlaag (n)	ooglid (n)	das Augenlid
face	ansikte (n)	Ansigt (n)	gezicht (n)	das Gesicht
fever	feber	Feber	koorts	das Fieber
finger	finger (n)	Finger	vinger	der Finger
flesh	kött (n)	Kød (n)	vleesch (n)	das Fleisch
foot	fot	Fod	voet	der Fuss
forehead	panna	Pande	voorhoofd (n)	die Stirn
gums	tandkött (n)	Tandkød (n)	tandvleesch (n)	das Zahnfleisch
hair	hår (n)	Haar (n)	haar (n)	das Haar
hand	hand	Haand	hand	die Hand
head	huvud (n)	Hoved (n)	hoofd (n)	der Kopf
headache	huvudvärk	Hovedpine	hoofdpijn	die Kopf- schmerzen (pl.)
heart	hjärta (n)	Hjerte (n)	hart (n)	das Herz
heel	häl	Hael	hiel	die Ferse
hip	höft	Hofte	heup	die Hüfte
intestines	inelvor (pl.)	Involde (pl.)	ingewanden (pl.)	die Einge- weide (pl.)
jaw	käft	Kaebe	kaak	der Kiefer
kidney	njure	Nyre	nier	die Niere
knee	knä (n)	Knae (n)	knie	das Knie
leg	ben (n)	Ben (n)	been (n)	das Bein
lip	läpp	Laebe	lip	die Lippe
liver	lever	Lever	lever	die Leber
lung	lunga	Lunge	long	die Lunge
moustache	mustasch	Overskaeg (n)	snor	der Schnurrbart
mouth	mun	Mund	mond	der Mund
muscle	muskel	Muskel	spier	der Muskel
nail	nagel	Negl	nagel	der Nagel
neck	hals	Hals	nek	der Hals
nerve	nerv	Nerve	zenuw	der Nerv
nose	näsa	Naese	neus	die Nase
pain	smärta	Smerte	pijn	der Schmerz
rib	revben (n)	Ribben (n)	rib	die Rippe
shoulder	skuldra	Skulder	schouder	die Schulter

ENGLISH	SWEDISH	DANISH	DUTCH	GERMAN
skin	skinn (n)	Skind (n)	huid	die Haut
sole	fotsula	Fodsaal	voetzool	die Fussohle
spine	ryggrad	Rygrad	ruggegraat	das Rückgrat
stomach	mage	Mave	maag	der Magen
tear	tår	Taare	traan	die Träne
thigh	lår (n)	Laar (n)	dij	der Schenkel
throat (internal)	strupe	Strube	keel	der Hals
				die Kehle
thumb	tumme	Tommelfinger	duim	der Daumen
toe	tå	Taa	teen	die Zehe
tongue	tunga	Tunge	tong	die Zunge
tooth	tand	Tand	tand	der Zahn
toothache	tandvärk	Tandpine	kiespijn	die Zahn-
				schmerzen
				(pl.)
wound	sår (n)	Saar (n)	wond	die Wunde
wrist	handled	Haandled (n)	pols	das Handgelenk

c) ANIMALS

animal	djur (n)	Dyr (n)	dier (n)	das Tier
ant	myra	Myre	mier	die Ameise
badger	grävling	Graevling	das	der Dachs
bat	flädermus	Flagermus	vleermuis	die Fledermaus
beak	näbb	Naeb (n)	bek	der Schnabel
bear	björn	Bjørn	beer	der Bär
bee	bi (n)	Bi	bij	die Biene
beetle	skalbagge	Bille	tor	der Käfer
bird	fågel	Fugl	vogel	der Vogel
blackbird	koltrast	Solsort	merel	die Amsel
bull	tjur	Tyr	stier	der Stier
				der Bulle
butterfly	fjäril	Sommerfugl	vlinder	der Schmetter-
				ling
calf	kalv	Kalv	kalf (n)	das Kalb
carp	karp	Karpe	karper	der Karpfen
cat	katt	Kat	kat	die Katze
caterpillar	larv	Kaalorm	rups	die Raupe
claw	klo	Klo	klauw	die Klaue
cock	tupp	Hane	haan	der Hahn
cod	torsk	Torsk	kabeljauw	der Kabeljau
cow	ko	Ko	koe	die Kuh
crab	krabba	Krabbe	krab	die Krabbe
crayfish	kräfta	Krebs	kreeft	der Krebs
crow	kråka	Krage	kraai	die Krähe
cuckoo	gök	Gøg	koekoek	der Kuckuck

ENGLISH	SWEDISH	DANISH	DUTCH	GERMAN
dog	hund	Hund	hond	der Hund
donkey	åsna	Aesel (n)	ezel	der Esel
duck	anka	And	eend	die Ente
eagle	örn	Ørn	arend	der Adler
eel	ål	Aal	aal	der Aal
feather	fjäder	Fjer	veer	die Feder
fin	fena	Finne	vin	die Flosse
fish	fisk	Fisk	visch	der Fisch
flea	loppa	Loppe	vloo	der Floh
fly	fluga	Flue	vlieg	die Fliege
fox	räv	Raev	vos	der Fuchs
frog	groda	Frø	kikvorsch	der Frosch
fur	päls	Pels	pels	der Pelz
gill	gäl	Gaelle	kieuw	die Kieme
gnat	mygga	Myg	mug	die Mücke
goat	get	Ged	geit	die Ziege
goose	gås	Gaas	gans	die Gans
grasshopper	gräshoppa	Graeshoppe	sprinkhaan	der Grashüpfer
hare	hare	Hare	haas	der Hase
hen	höna	Høne	kip	das Huhn
			hen	die Henne
heron	häger	Hejre	reiger	der Reiher
herring	sill	Sild	haring	der Hering
hoof	hov	Hov	hoef	der Huf
horn	horn (n)	Horn (n)	hoorn	das Horn
horse	häst	Hest	paard (n)	das Pferd
lamb	lamm (n)	Lam (n)	lam (n)	das Lamm
lion	lejon (n)	Løve	leeuw	der Löwe
lobster	hummer	Hummer	kreeft	der Hummer
louse	lus	Lus	luis	die Laus
mackerel	makrill	Makrel	makreel	die Makrele
mole	mullvad	Muldvarp	mol	der Maulwurf
monkey	apa	Abe	aap	der Affe
moth	nattfjäril	Møl (n)	mot	die Motte
mouse	råtta	Mus	muis	die Maus
owl	uggla	Ugle	uil	die Eule
ox	oxe	Okse	os	der Ochs
oyster	ostron (n)	Østers	oester	die Auster
parrot	papegoja	Papegøje	papegaai	der Papagei
partridge	rapphöna	Agerhøne	patrijs	das Rebhuhn
paw	tass	Pote	poot	die Pfote
pig	svin (n)	Svin (n)	varken (n)	das Schwein
pigeon	duva	Due	duif	die Taube
pike	gädda	Gedde	snoek	der Hecht
plaice	flundra	Rødspaette	schol	die Scholle
rabbit	kanin	Kanin	konijn (n)	das Kaninchen
rat	råtta	Rotte	rat	die Ratte

ENGLISH	SWEDISH	DANISH	DUTCH	GERMAN
salmon	lax	Laks	zalm	der Lachs
scale	fjäll (n)	Skael (n)	schub	die Schuppe
sea gull	mås	Maage	meeuw	die Möwe
seal	säl	Sael	zeehond	der Seehund
shark	haj	Haj	haai	der Hai
sheep	får (n)	Faar (n)	schaap (n)	das Schaf
snail	snigel	Snegl	slak	die Schnecke
snake	orm	Slange	slang	die Schlange
sole	sjötunga	Tunge	tong	die Seezunge
sparrow	sparv	Spurv	musch	der Sperling
spider	spindel	Edderkop	spin	die Spinne
starling	stare	Staer	spreeuw	der Star
stork	stork	Stork	ooievaar	der Storch
swallow	svala	Svale	zwaluw	die Schwalbe
tail	svans	Hale	staart	der Schwanz
toad	padda	Tudse	pad	die Kröte
trout	forell	Forel	forel	die Forelle
turkey	kalkon	Kalkun	kalkoen	der Truthahn
wasp	geting	Hveps	wesp	die Wespe
weasel	vessla	Vaesel	wezel	das Wiesel
whale	valfisk	Hval	walvisch	der Walfisch
wing	vinge	Vinge	vleugel	der Flügel
wolf	varg	Ulv	wolf	der Wolf
worm	mask	Orm	worm	der Wurm

d) FRUIT AND TREES

apple	äpple (n)	Aeble (n)	appel	der Apfel
apple tree	äppleträd (n)	Aebletrae (n)	appelboom	der Apfelbaum
apricot	aprikos	Abrikos	abrikoos	die Aprikose
ash	ask	Ask	esch	die Esche
bark	bark	Bark	schors	die Rinde
beech	bok	Bøg	beuk	die Buche
berry	bär (n)	Baer (n)	bes	die Beere
birch	björk	Birk	berk	die Birke
blackberry	björnbär (n)	Brombaer (n)	braam	die Brombeere
branch	gren	Gren	tak	der Ast
cherry	körsbär (n)	Kirsebaer (n)	kers	die Kirsche
chestnut	kastanje	Kastanie	kastanje	die Kastanie
currant	vinbär (n)	Ribs (n)	aalbes	die Johannis-beere
elm	alm	Elm	olm	die Ulme
fig	fikon (n)	Figen	vijg	die Feige
fir	gran	Gran	den	die Tanne
fruit	frukt	Frugt	vrucht	die Frucht

ENGLISH	SWEDISH	DANISH	DUTCH	GERMAN
gooseberry	krusbär (n)	Stikkelsbaer (n)	kruisbes	die Stachelbeere
grapes	vindruva	Vindrue	druif	d'e Traube
hazelnut	hasselnöt	Hasselnød	hazelnoot	die Haselnuss
kernel	kärna	Kaerne	pit	der Kern
larch	lärkträd (n)	Laerk	lariks	die Lärche
leaf	blad (n)	Blad (n)	blad (n)	das Blatt
lemon	citron	Citron	citroen	die Zitrone
lime tree	lind	Lind	linde	die Linde
oak	ek	Eg	eik	die Eiche
orange	apelsin	Appelsin	sinaasappel	die Orange die Apfelsine
peach	persika	Fersken	perzik	der Pfirsich
pear	päron (pl.)	Paere	peer	die Birne
pine	tall	Fyr	pijnboom	die Kiefer
pineapple	ananas	Ananas	ananas	die Ananas
plum	plommon (n)	Blomme	pruim	die Pflaume
poplar	poppel	Poppel	populier	die Pappel
raspberry	hallon (n)	Hindbaer (n)	framboos	die Himbeere
root	rot	Rod	wortel	die Wurzel
strawberry	jordgubbe	Jordbaer (n)	aardbei	die Erdbeere
tree	träd (n)	Trae (n)	boom	der Baum
tree trunk	stam	Stamme	stam	der Stamm
vine	vinstock	Vinstok	wijnstok	der Weinstock
walnut	valnöt	Valnød	walnoot	die Walnuss
willow	pil	Pil	wilg	die Weide

e) CEREALS AND VEGETABLES

asparagus	sparris	Asparges	asperge	der Spargel
barley	korn (n)	Byg	gerst	die Gerste
bean	böna	Bønne	boon	die Bohne
brussels sprouts	brysselkål	Rosenkaal	Brusselsch spruitje	der Rosenkohl
cabbage	kål	Kaal	kool	der Kohl
carrot	morot	Gulerod	peen	die Karotte
cauliflower	blomkål	Blomkaal	bloemkool	der Blumenkohl
cucumber	gurka	Agurk	komkommer	die Gurke
garlic	vitlök	Hvidløg (n)	knoflook (n)	der Knoblauch
horse-radish	pepparrot	Peberrod	mierikswortel	der Meerrettich
lentil	lins	Linse	linze	die Linse
lettuce	sallad	Salat	sla	der Kopfsalat
mint	mynta	Mynte	kruizemunt	die Minze
mushroom	svamp	Svamp	paddestoel	der Pilz
oats	havre	Havre	haver	der Hafer
onion	lök	Løg (n)	ui	die Zwiebel

ENGLISH	SWEDISH	DANISH	DUTCH	GERMAN
parsley	persilja	Persille	peterselie	die Petersilie
pea	ärta	Aert	erwt	die Erbse
potato	potatis	Kartoffel	aardappel	die Kartoffel
radish	rädisa	Radise	radijs	das Radieschen
rice	ris (n)	Ris	rijst	der Reis
rye	råg	Rug	rogge	der Roggen
spinach	spenat	Spinat	spinazie	der Spinat
stalk	stjälk	Stilk	stengel	der Stengel
			steel	der Stiel
turnip	rova	Roe	knol	die Rübe
wheat	hvete (n)	Hvede	tarwe	der Weizen

f) MATERIALS

alloy	legering	Legering	allooi (n)	die Legierung
brass	mässing	Messing (n)	geelkoper (n)	das Messing
brick	mursten	Mursten	baksteen	der Ziegelstein
cement	cement (n)	Cement	cement (n)	der Zement
chalk	krita	Kridt (n)	krijt (n)	die Kreide
clay	lera	Ler (n)	klei	der Lehm
				der Ton
coal	kol (n)	Kul (n)	kool	die Kohle
concrete	betong	Beton	beton	der Beton
copper	koppar	Kobber (n)	koper (n)	das Kupfer
glass	glas (n)	Glas (n)	glas (n)	das Glas
gold	guld (n)	Guld (n)	goud (n)	das Gold
iron	järn (n)	Jern (n)	ijzer (n)	das Eisen
lead	bly (n)	Bly (n)	lood (n)	das Blei
leather	läder (n)	Laeder (n)	leer (n)	das Leder
lime	kalk	Kalk	kalk	der Kalk
marble	marmor	Marmor (n)	marmer (n)	der Marmor
mercury	kvicksilver (n)	Kviksølv (n)	kwikzilver (n)	das Quecksilber
metal	metall	Metal (n)	metaal (n)	das Metall
rubber	gummi (n)	Gummi	rubber (n)	der Gummi
silver	silver (n)	Sølv (n)	zilver (n)	das Silber
steel	stål (n)	Staal (n)	staal (n)	der Stahl
stone	sten	Sten	steen	der Stein
tar	tjära	Tjaere	teer (n)	der Teer
tin	tenn (n)	Tin (n)	tin (n)	das Zinn
wood	trä (n)	Trae (n)	hout (n)	das Holz

g) BUILDINGS

barn	lada	Lade	schuur	die Scheune
barracks	kasern	Kaserne	kazerne	die Kaserne
bridge	bro	Bro	brug	die Brücke

ENGLISH	SWEDISH	DANISH	DUTCH	GERMAN
building	byggnad	Bygning	gebouw (n)	das Gebäude
castle	slott (n)	Slot (n)	slot (n)	das Schloss
			kasteel (n)	
cathedral	katedral	Katedral	kathedraal	die Kathedrale
cemetery	kyrkogård	Kirkegaard	kerkhof (n)	der Friedhof
church	kyrka	Kirke	kerk	die Kirche
cinema	biograf	Biograf	bioscoop	das Kino
consulate	konsulat (n)	Konsulat (n)	consulaat (n)	das Konsulat
factory	fabrik	Fabrik	fabriek	die Fabrik
farm	bondgård	Bondegaard	boerderij	der Bauernhof
fountain	brunn	Brønd	fontein	der Brunnen
hospital	sjukhus (n)	Hospital (n)	hospitaal (n)	das Kranken-
				haus
hut	hydda	Hytte	hut	die Hütte
inn	värdshus (n)	Kro	herberg	das Wirtshaus
lane (town)	gränd	Straede (n)	steeg	die Gasse
legation	legation	Legation	legatie	die Gesandt-
				schaft
library	bibliotek (n)	Bibliotek	bibliotheek	die Bibliothek
market	marknad	Torv (n)	markt	der Markt
monument	minnesvård	Monument (n)	gedenkteeken	das Denkmal
			(n)	
movies		(see cinema, above)		
path (country)	stig	Sti	pad (n)	der Pfad
pavement (side-	trottoar	Fortov (n)	trottoir (n)	der Bürgersteig
walk)				das Trottoir
police station	polisstation	Politistation	politiebureau	die Polizei-
			(n)	wache
port	hamn	Havn	haven	der Hafen
prison	fängelse (n)	Faengsel (n)	gevangenis	das Gefängnis
public toilets	toilet	Toilet (n)	toilet (n)	der Abort
road (highway)	lands väg	Landevej	landweg	die Landstrasse
school	skola	Skole	school	die Schule
square	torg (n)	Plads	plein (n)	der Platz
street	gata	Gade	straat	die Strasse
suburb	förstad	Forstad	voorstad	die Vorstadt
theater	teater	Teater (n)	schouwburg	das Theater
tower	torn (n)	Taarn (n)	toren	der Turm
town	stad	By	stad	die Stadt
town hall	rådhus (n)	Raadhus (n)	stadhuis (n)	das Rathaus
university	universitet (n)	Universitet (n)	universiteit	die Universität
village	by	Landsby	dorp	das Dorf

b) THE FAMILY

birth	födelse	Fødsel	geboorte	die Geburt
boy	gosse	Dreng	jongen	der Junge

ENGLISH	SWEDISH	DANISH	DUTCH	GERMAN
brother	broder	Broder	broeder	der Bruder
brothers and sisters	syskon (pl.)	Søskende (pl.)	broers en zusters	die Geschwister (pl.)
child	barn (n)	Barn (n)	kind (n)	das Kind
Christian name	förnamn (n)	Fornavn (n)	voornaam	der Vorname
cousin	kusin (m. & f.)	Faetter (male)	neef (male)	der Vetter (male)
		Kusine (female)	nicht (female)	die Kusine (female)
daughter	dotter	Datter	dochter	die Tochter
death	död	Død	dood	der Tod
divorce	skilsmässa	Skilsmisse	echtscheiding	die Scheidung
family	familj	Familie	familie	die Familie
father	fader	Fader	vader	der Vater
gentleman	herre	Herre	heer	der Herr
girl	flicka	Pige	meisje (n)	das Mädchen
grandfather	farfar (patern.) morfar (matern.)	Bedstefader	grootvader	der Grossvater
grandmother	mormor (mat.) farmor (pat.)	Bedstemoder	grootmoeder	die Grossmutter
husband	man	Mand	man	der Mann der Gatte
lady	dam	Dame	dame	die Dame
man	man	Mand	man	der Mann
marriage	äktenskap (n)	Aegteskab (n)	huwelijk (n)	die Ehe
mother	moder	Moder	moeder	die Mutter
parents	föräldrar	Foraeldre	ouders	die Eltern
relative	slägting	Slaegtning	bloedverwant	der Verwandte
sister	syster	Søster	zuster	die Schwester
son	son	Søn	zoon	der Sohn
surname	tillnamn (n)	Efternavn (n)	achternaam	der Familienname
twin	tvilling	Tvilling	tweeling	der Zwilling
wife	hustru	Hustru	vrouw	die Frau die Gattin
woman	kvinna	Kvinde	vrouw	die Frau

i) Dress and Toilet

belt	bälte (n)	Baelte (n)	ceintuur	der Gürtel
boot	känga	Støvle	laars	der Stiefel
braces (suspenders)	hängslen (pl.)	Seler (pl.)	bretels (pl.)	die Hosenträger (pl.)
brush	borste	Børste	borstel	die Bürste

ENGLISH	SWEDISH	DANISH	DUTCH	GERMAN
button	knapp	Knap	knoop	der Knopf
cap	mössa	Kasket	pet	die Mütze
cigar	cigarr	Cigar	sigaar	die Zigarre
cigarette	cigarrett	Cigaret	sigaret	die Zigarette
clothes	kläder	Klaeder	kleeren	die Kleider
coat	jacka	Jakke	jas	der Rock
collar	krage	Flip	boord	der Kragen
comb	kam	Kam	kam	der Kamm
cotton	bomull	Bomuld (n)	katoen (n)	die Baumwolle
cotton wool (absorbent cotton)	bomull	Vat (n)	watten	die Watte
dress	klädning	Kjole	jurk	das Kleid
fashion	mod (n)	Mode	mode	die Mode
glove	handske	Handske	handschoen	der Handschuh
handkerchief	näsduk	Lommetør- klaede (n)	zakdoek	das Taschen- tuch
hat	hatt	Hat	hoed	der Hut
knickers	damkalsonger	Dameben- klaeder	directoire	die Schlupfhose
match	tändsticka	Taendstik	lucifer	das Streichholz
needle	nål	Naal	naald	die Nadel
overcoat	överrock	Frakke	overjas	der Überzieher
pants (under- wear)	kalsonger (pl.)	Underbukser (pl.)	onderbroek	die Unterhose
petticoat	underkjol	Underkjole	onderjurk	der Unterrock
pin	knappnål	Knappenaal	speld	die Stecknadel
pipe	pipa	Pibe	pijp	die Pfeife
pocket	ficka	Lomme	zak	die Tasche
safety pin	säkerhetsnål	Sikkerhedsnaal	veiligheidsspeld	die Sicherheits- nadel
shirt	skjorta	Skjorte	overhemd (n)	das Hemd
shoe	sko	Sko	schoen	der Schuh
shoelace	skoband (n)	Skobaand (n)	schoenveter	das Schuhband
silk	silke (n)	Silke	zijde	die Seide
skirt	kjol	Nederdel	rok	der Rock
sleeve	ärm	Aerme (n)	mouw	der Ärmel
slipper	toffel	Tøffel	pantoffel	der Pantoffel
soap	tvål	Saebe	zeep	die Seife
sock	strumpa	Sok	sok	die Socke
spectacles	glasögonen (pl.)	Briller (pl.)	bril (sg.)	die Brille (sg.)
sponge	svamp	Svamp	spons	der Schwamm
stick	käpp	Stok	stok	der Stock
stocking	strumpa	Strømpe	kous	der Strumpf
thread	tråd	Traad	garen (n)	der Faden
tie	halsduk	Slips	das	der Schlips
toothbrush	tandborste	Tandbørste	tandenborstel	die Zahnbürste

ENGLISH	SWEDISH	DANISH	DUTCH	GERMAN
toothpaste	tandpasta	Tandpasta	tandpasta	die Zahnpasta
trousers	byxor (pl.)	Bukser (pl.)	broek	die Hosen (pl.)
umbrella	paraply (n)	Paraply	paraplu	der Regen-schirm
vest	undertröja	Undertrøje	hemd (n)	das Unterhemd
waistcoat	väst	Vest	vest (n)	die Weste
watch	klocka	Ur (n)	horloge (n)	die Uhr
wool	ull	Uld	wol	die Wolle

j) THE HOME

alarm clock	väckarklocka	Vaekkeur (n)	wekker	der Wecker
armchair	länstol	Laenestol	leuningstoel	der Lehnstuhl
ash	aska	Aske	asch	die Asche
ash tray	askopp	Askebaeger (n)	aschbakje (n)	der Aschen-becher
balcony	balkong	Balkon	balkon (n)	der Balkon
basket	korg	Kurv	korf	der Korb
bath	bad (n)	Bad (n)	bad (n)	das Bad
bed	säng	Seng	bed (n)	das Bett
bedroom	sovrum (n)	Sovekammer (n)	slaapkamer	das Schlafzim-mer
bell (door)	ringklocka	Klokke	bel	die Klingel
blanket	filt	Taeppe (n)	deken	die Decke
blind (roller)	rullgardin	Rullegardin (n)	rolgordijn (n)	die Rollgardine
box (chest)	kista	Kiste	kist	die Kiste
broom	kvast	Kost	bezem	der Besen
bucket	ämbar (n)	Spand	emmer	der Eimer
candle	ljus (n)	Lys (n)	kaars	die Kerze
carpet	matta	Taeppe (n)	tapijt (n)	der Teppich
ceiling	tak (n)	Loft (n)	plafond (n)	die Decke
cellar	källare	Kaelder	kelder	der Keller
chair	stol	Stol	stoel	der Stuhl
chamber pot	nattkärl (n)	Natpotte	kamerpot	der Nachttopf
chimney	skorsten	Skorsten	schoorsteen	der Schornstein
corner	hörn (n)	Hjørne (n)	hoek	die Ecke
cupboard	skåp (n)	Skab (n)	kast	der Schrank
curtain	gardin	Gardin (n)	gordijn (n)	der Vorhang die Gardine
cushion	kudde	Pude	kussen (n)	das Kissen
denatured alco-hol		(see methylated spirit, below)		
door	dörr	Dør	deur	die Tür
drawer	låda	Skuffe	lade	die Schublade
fire	eld	Ild	vuur (v)	das Feuer
flame	flamma	Flamme	vlam	die Flamme

ENGLISH	SWEDISH	DANISH	DUTCH	GERMAN
flat	våning	Lejlighed	étage-woning	die Wohnung
floor	golv (n)	Gulv (n)	vloer	der Fussboden
flower	blomma	Blomst	bloem	die Blume
furniture	möbler (pl.)	Møbler (pl.)	meubelen (pl.)	die Möbel (pl.)
garden	trädgård	Have	tuin	der Garten
ground floor	nedersta	Stueetage	gelijkvloers (n)	das Erdgeschoss
	våning			
hearth	eldstad	Arnested (n)	haard	der Herd
house	hus (n)	Hus (n)	huis (n)	das Haus
iron (flat)	strykjärn (n)	Strygejern (n)	strijkijzer (n)	das Bügeleisen
kerosene		(see paraffin, below)		
key	nyckel	Nøgle	sleutel	der Schlüssel
kitchen	kök (n)	Køkken (n)	keuken	die Küche
lamp	lampa	Lampe	lamp	die Lampe
lavatory	W.C. (pron.	Toilet (n)	W.C. (pron.	der Abort
(toilet)	vay-say)		vay-say)	die Toilette
lock	lås (n)	Laas	slot (n)	das Schloss
mattress	madrass	Madras	matras	die Matraze
methylated	denaturerade	Sprit	brand-spiritus	der Brenn-
spirit	sprit			spiritus
mirror	spegel	Spejl (n)	spiegel	der Spiegel
oven	ugn	Ovn	oven	der Ofen
pantry	skafferi (n)	Spisekammer	provisiekamer	die Speisekam-
		(n)		mer
paper basket	papperskorg	Papirkurv	prullemand	der Papierkorb
paraffin	fotogen (n)	Petroleum	petroleum	das Petroleum
(kerosene)				
picture	tavla	Billede (n)	schilderij (n)	das Bild
pillow	huvudkudde	Pude	oorkussen (n)	das Kopfkissen
pipe (water,	rör (n)	Rør (n)	buis	die Röhre
etc.)				
roof	tak (n)	Tag (n)	dak (n)	das Dach
room	rum (n)	Vaerelse (n)	kamer	das Zimmer
scales	våg	Vaegt	weegschaal	die Wage
sheet	lakan (n)	Lagen (n)	laken (n)	das Bettuch
				das Bettlaken
shovel	skyffel	Skovl	schop	die Schaufel
smoke	rök	Røg	rook	der Rauch
stairs	trappa	Trappe	trap	die Treppe
steam	ånga	Damp	stoom	der Dampf
story, storey	våning	Etage	verdieping	der Stock
table	bord (n)	Bord (n)	tafel	der Tisch
tap	kran	Hane	kraan	der Hahn
toilet (fixture)		(see lavatory, above)		
towel	handduk	Haandklaede	handdoek	das Handtuch
		(n)		
wall (structure)	mur	Mur	muur	die Mauer

ENGLISH	SWEDISH	DANISH	DUTCH	GERMAN
wall (partition)	vägg	Vaeg	wand	die Wand
window	fönster (n)	Vindue (n)	raam (n)	das Fenster
yard	gård	Gaard	binnenplaats	der Hof

k) Food and Drink

ENGLISH	SWEDISH	DANISH	DUTCH	GERMAN
bacon	fläsk (n)	Bacon	rookspek (n)	der Speck
beef	oxkött (n)	Oksekød (n)	rundvleesch (n)	das Rindfleisch
beer	öl (n)	Øl (n)	bier (n)	das Bier
beverage	dryck	Drik	drank	das Getränk
brandy	konjak	Cognac	cognac	der Kognak
bread	bröd (n)	Brød (n)	brood (n)	das Brot
breakfast	frukost	Morgenmad	ontbijt (n)	das Frühstück
butter	smör (n)	Smør (n)	boter	die Butter
cake	kaka	Kage	koek	der Kuchen
cheese	ost	Ost	kaas	der Käse
chicken	kyckling	Kylling	kip	das Huhn
cider	äppelvin (n)	Aeblevin (n)	appelwijn	der Apfelwein
coffee	kaffe (n)	Kaffe	koffie	der Kaffee
cream	grädde	Fløde	room	der Rahm
whipped cream	vispadgrädde	Flødeskum (n)	slagroom	die Schlagsahne
egg	ägg (n)	Aeg (n)	ei (n)	das Ei
boiled egg	koktaägg	kogt Aeg	gekookt ei	gekochtes Ei
fried egg	stäkta ägg	Spejlaeg	gebakken ei	Spiegelei
evening meal	aftonmål	Aftensmad	avondeeten (n)	das Abendessen
fat	fett (n)	Fedt (n)	vet (n)	das Fett
flour	mjöl (n)	Mel (n)	meel (n)	das Mehl
ham	skinka	Skinke	ham	der Schinken
honey	honing	Honning	honing	der Honig
ice cream	glace	Is	roomijs (n)	das Eis
jam	sylt (n)	Syltetøj (n)	jam	die Konfitüre
meat	kött (n)	Kød (n)	vleesch (n)	das Fleisch
midday meal	middag	Middag	middagmaal (n)	das Mittagessen
milk	mjölk	Maelk	melk	die Milch
mustard	senap	Sennop	mosterd	der Senf der Mostrich
mutton	fårkött (n)	Faarekød (n)	schapenvleesch (n)	das Hammel fleisch
oil	olja	Olie	olie	das Öl
pepper	peppar	Peber (n)	peper	der Pfeffer
pork	fläsk (n)	Svinekød (n)	varkenvleesch (n)	das Schweine- fleisch
roll	bulle	Rundstykke (n)	broodje (n)	das Brötchen die Semmel
salad	sallad	Salat	salade	der Salat

ENGLISH	SWEDISH	DANISH	DUTCH	GERMAN
salt	salt (n)	Salt (n)	zout (n)	das Salz
sandwich	smörgås	Smørrebrød (n)	boterhammetje (n)	das belegte Brötchen
sauce	sås	Sauce	saus	die Sosse
sausage	korv	Pølse	worst	die Wurst
soup	soppa	Suppe	soep	die Suppe
sugar	socker (n)	Sukker (n)	suiker	der Zucker
tea	te (n)	Te	thee	der Tee
veal	kalvkött (n)	Kalvekød (n)	kalfsvleesch (n)	das Kalbfleisch
vegetables	grönsaker (pl.)	Grønsager (pl.)	groente	das Gemüse
vinegar	ättika	Edikke	azijn	der Essig
wine	vin (n)	Vin (n)	wijn	der Wein

l) Eating and Cooking Utensils

basin	skål	Kumme	bekken (n)	das Becken
bottle	flaska	Flaske	flesch	die Flasche
can opener	burköpsnarre	Daaseoplukker	blikopener	der Büchsen-öffner
coffee pot	kaffekanna	Kaffekande	koffiepot	die Kaffee-kanne
corkscrew	korkskruv	Proptraek-ker	kurkentrekker	der Kork-zieher
cup	kopp	Kop	kopje (n)	die Tasse
dish	fat (n)	Fad (n)	schotel	die Schüssel
fork	gaffel	Gaffel	vork	die Gabel
frying pan	stekpanna	Stegepande	braadpan	die Bratpfanne
glass	glas (n)	Glas (n)	glas (n)	das Glas
jug	kruka	Kande	kruik	der Krug
kettle	kittel	Kedel	ketel	der Kessel
knife	kniv	Kniv	mes (n)	das Messer
lid	lock (n)	Laag (n)	deksel (n)	der Deckel
napkin	servet	Serviet	servet (n)	die Serviette
plate	tallrik	Tallerken	bord (n)	der Teller
saucepan	kastrull	Kasserolle	stoofpan	der Kochtopf
saucer	tefat (n)	Underkop	schoteltje (n)	die Untertasse
spoon	sked	Ske	lepel	der Löffel
table cloth	borddukk	Borddug	tafellaken (n)	das Tischtuch
teapot	tekanna	Tepotte	theepot	die Teekanne
tin (can) opener	burköppsnare	Daaseopluk-ker	blikopener	der Büchsen-öffner

m) Tools

axe	yxa	Økse	bijl	die Axt
board	bräde (n)	Braet (n)	plank	das Brett

ENGLISH	SWEDISH	DANISH	DUTCH	GERMAN
cartridge	patron	Patron	patroon	die Patrone
chisel	mejsel	Mejsel	beitel	der Meissel
file	fil	Fil	vijl	die Feile
gimlet	borr	Bor (n)	boor	der Bohrer
gun	gevär (n)	Gevaer (n)	geweer (n)	das Gewehr
hammer	hammare	Hammer	hamer	der Hammer
hoe	hacka	Hakke	schoffel	die Hacke
hook (fishing)	metkrok	Medekrog	vischhaak	der Angel-haken
ladder	stege	Stige	ladder	die Leiter
line (fishing)	metrev	Medesnøre (n)	vischlijn	die Angelleine
nail	spik	Søm (n)	spijker	der Nagel
net	nät (n)	Net (n)	net (n)	das Netz
nut	mutter	Møtrik	moer	die Mutter
pincers	tång	Tang	nijptang	die Zange
plane	hyvel	Høvl	schaaf	der Hobel
plow, plough	plog	Plov	ploeg	der Pflug
rod (fishing)	metspö (n)	Medestang	hengel	die Angelrute
saw	såg	Sav	zaag	die Säge
scissors	sax	Saks	schaar	die Schere
screw	skruv	Skrue	schroef	die Schraube
screw driver	skruvmejsel	Skruetraekker	schroevedraaier	der Schrau-benzieher
scythe	lie	Le	zeis	die Sense
spade	spade	Spade	spade	der Spaten
spanner	skruvnyckel	Skruenøgle	schroefsleutel	der Schrauben-schlüssel
spring	fjäder	Fjeder	veer	die Feder
string	snöre (n)	Snor	koord	die Schnur
tools	verktyg (n)	Vaerktøj (n)	werktuig (n)	das Werkzeug
wire	tråd	Traad	draad	der Draht
wrench		(*see* spanner, *above*)		

n) VOCATIONS AND SHOPS

actor	skådespelare	Skuespiller	tooneelspeler	der Schau-spieler
author	skrifställare	Forfatter	schrijver	der Schrift-steller
baker	bagare	Bager	bakker	der Bäcker
bank	bank	Bank	bank	die Bank
bookseller	bokhandlare	Boghandler	boekhandelaar	der Buch-händler
bookshop	boklåda	Boghandel	boekwinkel	die Buch-handlung
butcher	slaktare	Slagter	slager	der Fleischer der Metzger

ENGLISH	SWEDISH	DANISH	DUTCH	GERMAN
café	café (n)	Kafé	café (n)	das Café
				das Kaffeehaus
chemist (pharmacist)	apotekare	Apoteker	apotheker	der Apotheker
chemist's shop	apotek (n)	Apotek	apotheek	die Apotheke
clergyman	präst	Praest	geestelijke	der Pfarrer
				der Geistliche
clerk	kontorist	Kontorist	klerk	der Angestellte
confectionery	konditori (n)	Konditori (n)	suikerbakkerij	die Konditorei
cook (female)	kokerska	Kokkepige	keukenmeid	die Köchin
customer	kund	Kunde	klant	der Kunde
dairy	mjölkbod	Mejeri (n)	melkinrichting	das Milchgeschäft
dentist	tandläkare	Tandlaege	tandarts	der Zahnarzt
doctor	läkare	Laege	dokter	der Arzt
				der Doktor
druggist		(see chemist, above)		
drug store		(see chemist's shop, above)		
engineer	ingeniör	Ingeniør	ingenieur	der Ingenieur
gardener	trädgårdsmästare	Gartner	tuinman	der Gärtner
hairdresser	hårfrisör	Frisør	kapper	der Frisör
				der Haarschneider
jeweler	juvelerare	Juvelér	juwelier	der Juwelier
journalist	journalist	Journalist	journalist	der Journalist
judge	domare	Dommer	rechter	der Richter
laundry	tvättinrättning	Vaskeri (n)	wasscherij	die Waschanstalt
lawyer	advokat	Sagfører	advocaat	der Rechtsanwalt
mail man		(see postman, below)		
mechanic	montör	Mekaniker	mecanicien	der Mechaniker
merchant	köpman	Købmand	koopman	der Kaufmann
milliner	modist	Modehandlerinde	modiste	die Modistin
				die Putzmacherin
musician	musiker	Musiker	muzikant	der Musiker
notary	notarie	Notar	notaris	der Notar
nurse (hospital)	sjuksköterska	Sygeplejerske	verpleegster	die Krankenschwester
officer	officer	Officer	officier	der Offizier
official	ämbetsman	Embedsmand	ambtenaar	der Beamte
painter	målare	Maler	schilder	der Maler
peasant	bonde	Bonde	boer	der Bauer
photographer	fotograf	Fotograf	fotograaf	der Photograph

ENGLISH	SWEDISH	DANISH	DUTCH	GERMAN
policeman	poliskonstapel	Politibetjent	politieagent	der Schutz-mann der Polizist
postman	brevbärare	Postbud	postbode	der Briefträger
publisher	förläggare	Forlaegger	uitgever	der Verleger
servant	tjänare	Tjener	dienstbode	der Dienstbote
shoemaker	skomakare	Skomager	schoenmaker	der Schuh-macher
shop (store)	butik	Butik	winkel	der Laden
singer	sängare	Sanger	zanger	der Sänger
smith	smed	Smed	smid	der Schmied
soldier	soldat	Soldat	soldaat	der Soldat
stationery store	pappershandel	Papirhandel	kantoorboek-handel	die Schreibwa-renhandlung
surgeon	kirurg	Kirurg	chirurg	der Chirurg
tailor	skräddare	Skraedder	kleermaker	der Schneider
teacher	lärare	Laerer	onderwijzer	der Lehrer
traveler	resande	Rejsende	reiziger	der Reisende
typist (female)	maskinskri-verska	Maskinskri-verske	typiste	die Stenotypistin
watchmaker	urmakare	Urmager	horlogemaker	der Uhrmacher
workman	arbetare	Arbejder	arbeider	der Arbeiter

o) Countries and Peoples

Africa	Afrika	Afrika	Afrika	Afrika
America	Amerika	Amerika	Amerika	Amerika
an American	en amerikan	en Amerikaner	een Amerikaan	ein Amerikaner
Argentine	Argentina	Argentina	Argentinië	Argentinien
an Argentine	en Argentinare	en Argentiner	een Argentijn	ein Argentinier
Asia	Asien	Asien	Azië	Asien
Austria	Österrike	Østrig	Oostenrijk	Österreich
Belgium	Belgien	Belgien	België	Belgien
a Belgian	en belgier	en Belgier	een Belg	ein Belgier
Brazil	Brasilien	Brasilien	Brazilie	Brasilien
a Brazilian	en Brasilianare	en Brasilianer	een Braziliaan	ein Brasilianer
China	Kina	Kina	China	China
a Chinese	en kines	en Kineser	een Chinees	ein Chinese
Denmark	Danmark	Danmark	Denemarken	Dänemark
a Dane	en dansk	en Dansker	een Deen	ein Däne
England	England	England	Engeland	England
an Englishman	en engelsman	en Englaender	een Engelsch-man	ein Engländer
Europe	Europa	Europa	Europa	Europa
a European	en europé	en Europaeer	een Europeaan	ein Europäer

ENGLISH	SWEDISH	DANISH	DUTCH	GERMAN
France	Frankrike	Frankrig	Frankrijk	Frankreich
a Frenchman	en fransman	en Fransk-	een Fransch-	ein Franzose
		mand	man	
Germany	Tyskland	Tyskland	Duitschland	Deutschland
a German	en tysk	en Tysker	een Duitscher	ein Deutscher
Great Britain	Storbritanien	Storbritannien	Groot-	Grossbritan-
			Brittanië	nien
Greece	Grekland	Graekenland	Griekenland	Griechenland
a Greek	en grek	en Graeker	een Griek	ein Grieche
Holland	Holland	Holland	Holland	Holland
a Dutchman	en holländare	en Hollaender	een Hollander	ein Holländer
			een Nederlander	
Hungary	Ungern	Ungarn	Hongarije	Ungarn
India	Indien	Indien	Indië	Indien
Ireland	Irland	Irland	Ierland	Irland
an Irishman	en irländare	en Irlaender	een Ier	ein Ire
an Italian	en italienare	en Italiener	een Italiaan	ein Italiener
Italy	Italien	Italien	Italië	Italien
Japan	Japan	Japan	Japan	Japan
a Japanese	en japanes	en Japaner	een Japanees	ein Japaner
Norway	Norge	Norge	Noorwegen	Norwegen
a Norwegian	en norrman	en Nordmand	een Noor	ein Norweger
Poland	Polen	Polen	Polen	Polen
a Pole	en polak	en Polak	een Pool	ein Pole
Portugal	Portugal	Portugal	Portugal	Portugal
a Portuguese	en portugis	en Portugiser	een Portugees	ein Portugiese
Russia	Ryssland	Rusland	Rusland	Russland
a Russian	en ryss	en Russer	een Rus	ein Russe
Scotland	Skottland	Skotland	Schotland	Schottland
a Scotsman	en skotte	en Skotte	een Schot	ein Schotte
Spain	Spanien	Spanien	Spanje	Spanien
a Spaniard	en spanior	en Spanier	een Spanjaard	ein Spanier
Sweden	Sverige	Sverrig	Zweden	Schweden
a Swede	en svensk	en Svensker	een Zweed	ein Schwede
Switzerland	Schweiz	Svejts	Zwitserland	die Schweiz
a Swiss	en schweizare	en Svejtser	een Zwitser	ein Schweizer
Turkey	Turkiet	Tyrkiet	Turkije	die Türkei
United States	Förenta Sta-	de forenede	de Vereenigde	die Vereinig-
	terna	Stater	Staten	ten Staaten

p) READING AND WRITING

address	adress	Adresse	adres (n)	die Adresse
				die Anschrift
blotting paper	läskpapper	Traekpapier	vloeipapier (n)	das Lösch-
	(n)	(n)		papier

ENGLISH	SWEDISH	DANISH	DUTCH	GERMAN
book	bok	Bog	boek (n)	das Buch
copy (of book, etc.)	exemplar (n)	Eksemplar (n)	exemplaar (n)	das Exemplar
copy (of letter, etc.)	kopia	Kopi	copie	die Kopie
date	datum (n)	Datum	datum	das Datum
dictionary	ordbok	Ordbog	woordenboek (n)	das Wörter-buch
edition	upplaga	Oplag (n)	uitgave	die Auflage
envelope	kuvert (n)	Konvolut	enveloppe	das Kuvert der Briefum-schlag
eraser (rubber)	gummi (n)	Viskelaeder (n)	gummi	der Radier-gummi
fountain pen	reservoir-penna	Fyldepen	vulpenhouder	die Füllfeder
ink	bläck (n)	Blaek (n)	inkt	die Tinte
letter	brev (n)	Brev (n)	brief	der Brief
mailbox, letter box	brevlåda	Brevkasse	brievenbus	der Briefkasten
map	karta	Landkort (n)	landkaart	die Karte
newspaper	tidning	Avis	krant	die Zeitung
novel	roman	Roman	roman	der Roman
page	sida	Side	bladzijde	die Seite
paper	papper (n)	Papir (n)	papier (n)	das Papier
parcel	paket (n)	Pakke	pakje (n)	das Paket
pen	penna	Pen	pen	die Feder
pencil	blyertspenna	Blyant	potlood (n)	der Bleistift
periodical	tidskrift	Tidsskrift (n)	tijdschrift (n)	die Zeit-schrift
postage	porto (n)	Porto (n)	porto (n)	das Porto die Postgebühr
postcard	brevkort (n)	Brevkort (n)	briefkaart	die Postkarte
post office	postkontor (n)	Posthus (n)	postkantoor (n)	das Postamt
shorthand	stenografi	Stenografi	snelscrift (n)	die Kurzschrift
signature	underskrift	Underskrift	handteekening	die Unter-schrift
stamp	frimärke (n)	Frimaerke (n)	postzegel	die Briefmarke
typewriter	skrivmaskin	Skrivemaskine	schrijf-machine	die Schreib-maschine

q) HOTEL AND RESTAURANT

bath	bad (n)	Bad (n)	bad (n)	das Bad
bill	räkning	Regning	rekening	die Rechnung

ENGLISH	SWEDISH	DANISH	DUTCH	GERMAN
chambermaid	städerska	Stuepige	kamermeid	das Zimmer-mädchen
change	småpengar (pl.)	Smaapenge (pl.)	kleingeld (n)	das Kleingeld
cloakroom	garderob	Toilet	garderobe	die Garderobe
dining room	matsal	Spisesal	eetzaal	der Speisesaal
elevator		(see lift, below)		
hotel	hotel (n)	Hotel (n)	hotel (n)	das Hotel
lift	hiss	Elevator	lift	der Lift
				der Fahrstuhl
manager	direktör	Bestyrer	directeur	der Direktor
menu	matsedel	Spiseseddel	spijskaart	die Speise-karte
office	kontor (n)	Kontor (n)	Kantoor (n)	das Büro
porter	portier	Portier	portier	der Portier
receipt	kvitto (n)	Kvittering	kwitantie	die Quittung
restaurant	restaurant	Restaurant	restaurant (n)	das Restaurant
tip	drickspengar (pl.)	Drikkepenge (pl.)	fooi	das Trinkgeld
waiter	kypare	Tjener	kellner	der Kellner

r) TRAIN AND RAILWAY

arrival	ankomst	Ankomst	aankomst	die Ankunft
baggage	bagage (n)	Bagage	bagage	das Gepäck
baggage car	bagagevagn	Bagagevogn	bagagewagen	der Gepäck-wagen
booking office	biljettkontor (n)	Billetkontor (n)	plaatsbureau (n)	der Fahrkar-tenschalter
cloakroom	garderob	Garderobe	bagage-depot (n)	die Gepäckab-gabe
coach, car	vagn	Waggon	wagon	der Wagen
compartment	kupé	Kupé	coupé	das Kupee das Abteil
connection	förbindelse	Forbindelse	aansluiting	der Anschluss
customs	tull	Told	douane	das Zollamt
departure	avresa	Afgang	vertrek (n)	die Abfahrt
engine	lokomotiv (n)	Lokomotiv (n)	locomotief	die Lokomo-tive
entrance	ingång	Indgang	ingang	der Eingang
exit	utgång	Udgang	uitgang	der Ausgang
frontier	gräns	Graense	grens	die Grenze
guard	konduktör	Konduktør	conducteur	der Schaffner
information bu-reau, inquiry office	upplysnings-kontor (n)	Oplysnings-kontor (n)	informatie-bureau (n)	die Auskunfts-stelle
passenger	passagerare	Passager	passagier	der Passagier

ENGLISH	SWEDISH	DANISH	DUTCH	GERMAN
passport	pass (n)	Pas (n)	paspoort (n)	der Pass
platform	perrong	Perron	perron (n)	der Bahnsteig
porter	bärare	Drager	kruier	der Gepäck-träger
railway	järnväg	Jernbane	spoorweg	die Eisenbahn
seat	plats	Plads	plaats	der Platz
signal cord	nödbroms	Nødbremse	noodrem	die Notbremse
sleeping car	sovvagn	Sovevogn	slaapwagon	der Schlaf-wagen
smokers	rökare	Rygere	rookcoupé	das Raucherab-teil
station	station	Station	station (n)	der Bahnhof
station master	stationsin-spektor	Stationsfor-stander	stationschef	der Bahnhof-vorsteher
stop	halt	Holdeplads	halte	die Haltestelle
suitcase	kappsäck	Haandkuffert	valies (n)	der Handkoffer
ticket	biljett	Billet	kaartje (n)	die Fahrkarte
return	retur	retur	retour	retour
ticket office		(see booking office, *above*)		
time table	tidtabell	Køreplan	spoorboekje (n)	der Fahrplan
train	tåg (n)	Tog (n)	trein	der Zug
fast train	snelltåg	Iltog Eksprestog	sneltrein	der Eilzug der D-zug
slow train	persontåg	Persontog	boemeltrein	der Personen-zug
trunk	koffert	Kuffert	koffer	der Koffer
visa	visa	Visum (n)	visum (n)	das Visum
waiting room	väntsal	Ventesal	wachtkamer	der Wartesaal

s) SHIP

anchor	ankare (n)	Anker (n)	anker (n)	der Anker
boat	båt	Baad	boot	das Boot
bow	bog	Bov	boeg	der Bug
bridge	brygga	Bro	brug	die Brücke
cabin	kajuta	Kahyt	kajuit	die Kabine
captain	kapten	Kaptajn	kapitein	der Kapitän
compass	kompass	Kompas (n)	kompas (n)	der Kompass
crew	besättning	Mandskab (n)	bemanning	die Mannschaft
deck	däck (n)	Daek (n)	dek (n)	das Deck
dock	docka	Dok	dok (n)	das Dock
flag	flagg	Flag (n)	vlag	die Flagge
gangway	landgång	Landgang	loopplank	die Laufplanke
hold	lastrum (n)	Lastrum (n)	scheepsruim (n)	der Laderaum
keel	köl	Køl	kiel	der Kiel

544   THE LOOM OF LANGUAGE

ENGLISH	SWEDISH	DANISH	DUTCH	GERMAN
lifebelt	räddnings-bälte (n)	Rednings-baelte (n)	reddingsgordel	der Rettungs-gürtel
lifeboat	räddningsbåt	Redningsbaad	reddingsboot	das Rettungs-boot
lighthouse	fyrtorn (n)	Fyrtaarn (n)	vuurtoren	der Leuchtturm
mast	mast	Mast	mast	der Mast
oar	åra	Aare	roeiriem	das Ruder
propeller	skruv	Skrue	schroef	die Schraube
purser	intendent	Hovmester	hofmeester	der Zahlmeister
rope	rep (n)	Reb (n)	touw (n)	das Tau
rudder	roder (n)	Ror (n)	roer (n)	das Ruder
sail	segel (n)	Sejl (n)	zeil (n)	das Segel
sailor	sjöman	Sømand	zeeman	der Seemann
seasickness	sjösjuka	Søsyge	zeeziekte	die Seekrank-heit
ship	skepp (n)	Skib (n)	schip (n)	das Schiff
stern	akter	Agterende	achtersteven (n)	der Hinter-steven
tug	bogserbåt	Bugserbaad	sleepboot	der Schlepper
wharf	kaj	Kaj	kaai	der Kai

t) CYCLING AND AUTOMOBILING

automobile		*(see* car, *below)*		
axle	axel	Aksel	as	die Achse
bearing	lager (n)	Leje (n)	drager	das Lager
bend (road)	kurva	Sving (n)	hoek	die Kurve
bicycle	cykel	Cykle	fiets	das Fahrrad
bonnet	motorhuv	Motorhjælm	motorkap	die Haube
brake	broms	Bremse	rem	die Bremse
bulb	lampa	Paere	lamp	die Birne
bumper	kofångare	Kofanger	schokbreker	der Stossfänger
car	bil	Bil	auto	das Auto / der Wagen
carburetor	förgasare	Karburator	carburator	der Vergaser
chain	kedja	Kaede	ketting	die Kette
clutch	koppling	Kobling	koppeling	die Kupplung
crossroad	korsväg	Korsvej	kruispunt (n)	die Strassen-kreuzung
curve		*(see* bend, *above)*		
distributor	fördelare	Fordeler	verdeeler	der Verteiler
driving license	körkort (n)	Koretilladelse	rijbewijs (n)	der Führer-schein
fine	böter (pl.)	Bøde	boete	die Geldstrafe
gasoline		*(see* petrol, *below)*		
gear	växel	Gear	gier	der Gang

ENGLISH	SWEDISH	DANISH	DUTCH	GERMAN
grade crossing	järnvägsöver-gång	Togoverskaer-ing	overweg	der Bahnüber-gang
headlight	strålkastare	Forlygte	koplicht (n)	der Schein-werfer
hood	sufflett	Kaleche	kap	das Verdeck
horn	signalhorn (n)	Signalhorn (n)	claxon	die Hupe
horsepower	hästkraft	Hestekraft	paardekracht	die Pferde-stärke
ignition	tändning	Taending	ontsteking	die Zündung
insurance	försäkring	Forsikring	verzekering	die Versiche-rung
jack	domkraft	Donkraft	krik	der Heber
license plate	nummerplåt	Nummerplade	numberbord (n)	das Nummern-schild
motorcycle	motorcykel	Motorcykle	motorfiets	das Motorrad
mudguard	stänkskärm	Staenkskaerm	spatbord (n)	der Kotflügel
pedal	pedal	Pedal	pedaal (n)	das Pedal
petrol	bensin	Benzin	benzine	das Benzin
piston	pistong	Stempel (n)	piston	der Kolben
plug	tändstift (n)	Taendrør (n)	bougie	die Kerze
pressure	tryck (n)	Tryk (n)	druk	der Druck
pump	pump	Pumpe	pomp	die Pumpe
radiator	kylare	Køler	koeler	der Kühler
saddle	sadel	Sadel	zadel (n)	der Sattel
spark	gnista	Gnist	vonk	der Funke
speed	fart	Fart	snelheid	die Geschwin-digkeit
speed limit	hastigheds-gräns	Hastigheds-graense	snelheidsgrens	die Höchstge-schwindig-keit
starter	självstartare	Selvstarter	starter	der Anlasser
starting handle (crank)	startväv	Startsving (n)	slinger	die Hand-kurbel
steering wheel	ratt	Rat (n)	stuurrad (n)	das Steuerrad
tank	tank	Tank	reservoir (n)	der Behälter
truck	lastbil	Lastvogn	vrachtauto	das Lastauto
tube	inerring	Slange	binnenband	der Schlauch
tire	ring	Daek (n)	band	der Reifen
valve	ventil	Ventil	ventiel	das Ventil
wheel	hjul (n)	Hjul (n)	wiel (n)	das Rad

u) GENERAL

ENGLISH	SWEDISH	DANISH	DUTCH	GERMAN
accident (mis-hap)	olyckshän-delse	Ulykkestil-faelde (n)	ongeval (n)	der Unfall
accident (chance event)	händelse	Tilfaelde (n)	toeval (n)	der Zufall

ENGLISH	SWEDISH	DANISH	DUTCH	GERMAN
account (report)	berättelse	Beretning	bericht (n)	der Bericht
action	handling	Handling	handeling	die Handlung
advantage	fördel	Fordel	voordeel (n)	der Vorteil
advertisement	annons	Annonce	annonce advertentie	die Annonce das Inserat
advice	råd (n)	Raad (n)	raad	der Rat
age (length of life)	ålder	Alder	leeftijd	das Alter
allusion	hänsyftning	Hentydning	zinspeling	die Anspielung
amount	belopp (n)	Beløb (n)	bedrag (n)	der Betrag
anger	vrede	Vrede	toorn	der Ärger der Zorn
angle	vinkel	Vinkel	hoek	der Winkel
answer	svar (n)	Svar (n)	antwoord (n)	die Antwort
apology	ursäkt	Undskyld- ning	verontschuldig- ing	die Entschuldi- gung
approval	bifall (n)	Bifald (n)	bijval	der Beifall
army	armé	Haer	leger (n)	die Armee das Heer
art	konst	Kunst	kunst	die Kunst
attack	anfall (n)	Angreb (n)	aanval	der Anfall der Angriff
attempt	försök (n)	Forsøg (n)	poging	der Versuch
attraction	dragnings- kraft	Tiltraeknings- kraft	aantrekkings- kracht	die Anziehungs- kraft
average	genomsnitt (n)	Gennemsnit (n)	gemiddelde (n)	der Durch- schnitt
ball (round thing)	boll	Kugle	kogel	die Kugel
battle	slag (n)	Slag (n)	veldslag	die Schlacht
beauty	skönhet	Skønhed	schoonheid	die Schönheit
beginning	begynnelse	Begyndelse	begin (n) aanvang	der Beginn der Anfang
behavior	uppförande (n)	Opførsel	gedrag (n)	das Benehmen das Betragen
belief	tro	Tro	geloof (n)	der Glaube
birth	födelse	Fødsel	geboorte	die Geburt
blindness	blindhet	Blindhed	blindheid	die Blindheit
blot	fläck	Plet	vlek	der Fleck
blow	slag (n)	Slag (n)	slag	der Schlag
bottom	botten	Grund	bodem	der Grund der Boden
boundary, limit	gräns	Graense	grens	die Grenze
bow (arc)	båge	Bue	boog	der Bogen
breed, race	ras	Race	ras (n)	die Rasse
cause (grounds)	orsak	Aarsag	oorzaak	die Ursache

ENGLISH	SWEDISH	DANISH	DUTCH	GERMAN
caution (care)	omsorg	Forsigtighed	vootzichtigheid	die Vorsicht die Sorgfalt
center	midt	Midte	midden (n)	die Mitte
change (alteration)	förändring	Forandring	verandering	die Veränderung
chapter	kapitel (n)	Kapitel (n)	hoofdstuk (n)	das Kapitel
choice	val (n)	Valg (n)	keus	die Wahl
circle	cirkel	Cirkel	cirkel	der Kreis
circumference	omkrets	Omfang (n)	omtrek	der Umfang
collection	samling	Samling	verzameling	die Sammlung
color	färg	Farve Kulør	kleur	die Farbe
combustion	förbränning	Forbraending	verbranding	die Verbrennung
command (order)	befallning	Befaling	bevel (n)	der Befehl
committee	kommitté	Komité	comité (n)	das Komitee der Ausschuss
comparison	jämförelse	Sammenligning	vergelijking	der Vergleich
competition (business)	konkurrens	Konkurrence	concurrentie	die Konkurrenz der Wettbewerb
condition (stipulation)	vilkor (n)	Betingelse	voorwaarde	die Bedingung
condition (state)	tillstånd (n)	Tilstand	toestand	der Zustand die Lage
confidence (trust)	förtroende (n)	Tillid	vertrouwen (n)	das Vertrauen
connection	förbindelse	Forbindelse	verbinding	die Verbindung
consequence	följd	Følge	gevolg (n)	die Folge
consolation	tröst	Trøst	troost	der Trost
contempt	förakt (n)	Foragt	verachting	die Verachtung
contents	innehåll (n)	Indhold (n)	inhoud	der Inhalt
continuation	fortsättning	Fortsaettelse	voortzetting	die Fortsetzung
country (nation)	land (n)	Land (n)	land (n)	das Land
courage	mod (n)	Mod (n)	moed	der Mut
cowardice	feghet	Fejghed	lafheid	die Feigheit
crime	brott (n)	Forbrydelse	misdaad	das Verbrechen
criticism	kritik	Kritik	kritiek	die Kritik
cross	kors (n)	Kors (n)	kruis (n)	das Kreuz
crowd	mängd	Maengde	menigte	die Menge
cry (call)	rop (n)	Raab (n)	roep	der Ruf
cube	tärning	Terning	kubus	der Würfel
custom	sedvana	Saedvane	gewoonte	die Sitte die Gewohnheit

ENGLISH	SWEDISH	DANISH	DUTCH	GERMAN
cut (incision)	snitt (n)	Snit (n)	snit	der Schnitt
damage	skada	Skade	schade	der Schaden
danger	fara	Fare	gevaar (n)	die Gefahr
death	död	Død	dood	der Tod
debt	skuld	Gaeld	schuld	die Schuld
decay	förfall (n)	Forfald (n)	verval (n)	der Verfall
decision	beslut	Beslutning	besluit (n)	der Beschluss
defeat	nederlag (n)	Nederlag (n)	nederlaag	die Niederlage
defense	försvar (n)	Forsvar (n)	verdediging	die Verteidigung
degree (scale)	grad	Grad	graad	der Grad
depth	djup (n)	Dybde	diepte	die Tiefe
description	beskrivning	Beskrivelse	beschrijving	die Beschreibung
desire	önskan	Ønske (n)	wensch	der Wunsch die Verzweiflung
despair	förtvivlan	Fortvivlelse	wanhoop	die Zerstörung
destruction	förödelse	Ødelaeggelse	vernieling	die Vernichtung
detail	detalj	Enkelthed	detail (n)	die Einzelheit das Detail
development	utveckling	Udvikling	ontwikkeling	die Entwicklung
diameter	diameter	Diameter	middellijn	der Durchmesser
digestion	matsmältning	Fordøjelse	spijsvertering	die Verdauung
direction (course)	riktning	Retning	richting	die Richtung
discovery	upptäckt	Opdagelse	ontdekking	die Entdeckung
discussion	diskussion	Drøftelse	bespreking	die Erörterung die Diskussion
disease	sjukdom	Sygdom	ziekte	die Krankheit
disgust	äckel (n)	Vaemmelse	walging	der Ekel
disk (slice)	skiva	Skive	schijf	die Scheibe
distance	avstånd (n)	Afstand	afstand	die Entfernung der Abstand
distribution	fördelning	Fordeling	verdeeling	die Verteilung
doubt	tvivel (n)	Tvivl	twijfel	der Zweifel
dozen	dussin (n)	Dusin (n)	dozijn (n)	das Dutzend
dryness	torrhet	Tørhed	droogte	die Trockenheit
duty	plikt	Pligt	plicht	die Pflicht
edge (border)	rand	Rand	rand	der Rand
education	uppfostran	Opdragelse	opvoeding	die Erziehung
effect	verkning	Virkning	uitwerking	die Wirkung

ENGLISH	SWEDISH	DANISH	DUTCH	GERMAN
effort	ansträngning	Anstrengelse	inspanning	die Anstren-gung die Anspan-nung
encounter (meeting)	möte (n)	Møde (n)	ontmoeting	die Begegnung
end	ände	Ende	einde (n)	das Ende
enemy	fiende	Fjende	vijand	der Feind
enmity	fiendskap (n)	Fjendskab (n)	vijandschap	die Feindschaft
entertainment (amusement)	underhålling	Under-holdning	vermaak (n)	die Unter-haltung
environment	omgivning	Omgivelse	omgeving	die Umgebung
envy	avund (n)	Misundelse	nijd	der Neid
equilibrium	jämvikt	Ligevaegt	evenwicht (n)	das Gleich-gewicht
event	händelse	Tildragelse	gebeurtenis	das Ereignis
example	exempel (n)	Eksempel (n)	voorbeeld (n)	das Beispiel
exception	undantag (n)	Undtagelse	uitzondering	die Ausnahme
exhibition	utställning	Udstilling	tentoonstelling	die Ausstellung
existence	tillvaro	Eksistens	bestaan (n)	das Vorhan-densein das Bestehen
expansion	utvidgning	Udvidelse	uitzetting	die Ausdeh-nung
experience	erfarenhet	Erfaring	ondervinding	die Erfahrung
explanation	förklaring	Forklaring	verklaring	die Erklärung
fact (what is true)	faktum (n)	Kendsgerning Faktum (n)	feit (n)	die Tatsache
fall (drop)	fall (n)	Fald (n)	val	der Fall der Sturz
fear	fruktan	Frygt	vrees	die Furcht die Angst
feeling	känsla	Følelse	gevoel (n)	das Gefühl
flight (air)	flykt	Flugt	vlucht	der Flug
flight (escape)	flykt	Flugt	vlucht	die Flucht
fleet	flotta	Flaade	vloot	die Flotte
fold (thing folded)	fåll	Fold	vouw	die Falte
food	näring	Naering	voedsel (n)	die Nahrung
force	kraft	Kraft	kracht	die Kraft
fracture	brott (n)	Brud (n)	breuk	der Bruch
freedom	frihet	Frihed	vrijheid	die Freiheit
friend	vän	Ven	vriend	der Freund
friendship	vänskap	Venskab (n)	vriendschap	die Freund-schaft
fuel	bränsle (n)	Braendsel (n)	brandstof	das Brenn-material

ENGLISH	SWEDISH	DANISH	DUTCH	GERMAN
future	framtid	Fremtid	toekomst	die Zukunft
game (play)	lek	Spil (n)	spel (n)	das Spiel
gathering	församling	Forsamling	vergadering	die Versammlung
gift (present)	gåva	Gave	geschenk (n)	das Geschenk die Gabe
government	regering	Regering	regeering	die Regierung
gratitude	tacksamhet	Taknemmelighed	dankbaarheid	die Dankbarkeit
greeting	hälsning	Hilsen	groet	der Gruss
growth	växt	Vaekst	groei	das Wachstum
guilt	skuld	Skyld	schuld	die Schuld
half	hälft	Halvdel	helft	die Hälfte
hardness	hårdhet	Haardhed	hardheid	die Härte
haste	hast	Hast	haast	die Hast die Eile
hate	hat (n)	Had (n)	haat	der Hass
health	sundhet	Sundhed	gezondheid	die Gesundheit
hearing (sense of)	hörsel	Hørelse (n)	gehoor (n)	das Gehör
heat (physics)	värme	Varme	warmte	die Wärme
height	höjd	Højde	hoogte	die Höhe
help	hjälp	Hjaelp	hulp	die Hilfe die Unterstützung
history	historia	Historie	geschiedenis	die Geschichte
hole	hål (n)	Hul (n)	gat (n)	das Loch
honor	heder	Aere	eer	die Ehre
hope	hopp (n)	Haab (n)	hoop	die Hoffnung
hunger	hunger	Sult	honger	der Hunger
idea	idé	Ide	idee (n)	die Idee
imitation	efterhärmande (n)	Efterligning	imitatie	die Nachahmung
income	inkomst	Indkomst	inkomen (n)	das Einkommen
increase	tilltagande (n)	Tiltagen (n)	toename	die Zunahme die Vermehrung
industry (application)	flit	Flid	vlijt	der Fleiss
innocence	oskuld	Uskyld	onschuld	die Unschuld
instruction (teaching)	undervisning	Undervisning	onderwijs (n)	der Unterricht
intention	avsikt	Hensigt	voornemen (n)	die Absicht
interest (attention)	intresse (n)	Interesse	belangstelling	das Interesse
invention	uppfinning	Opfindelse	uitvinding	die Erfindung

ENGLISH	SWEDISH	DANISH	DUTCH	GERMAN
investigation	undersökning	Undersøgelse	onderzoek (n)	die Untersuchung
invitation	bjudning	Indbydelse	uitnoodiging	die Einladung
jealousy	svartsjuka	Skinsyge	jaloezie	die Eifersucht
journey	resa	Rejse	reis	die Reise
joy	glädje	Glaede	vreugde	die Freude
judgment	dom	Dom	oordeel (n)	das Urteil
juice	saft	Saft	sap (n)	der Saft
jump	språng (n)	Spring (n)	sprong	der Sprung
justice	rättfärdighet	Retfaerdighed	gerechtigheid	die Gerechtigkeit
kick	spark	Spark (n)	schop	der Fusstritt
			trap	
kind (sort)	art	Art	soort	die Art
			slag (n)	die Sorte
knot	knut	Knude	knoop	der Knoten
knowledge	kunskap	Kundskab	kennis	die Kenntnis
				das Wissen
language	språk (n)	Sprog (n)	taal	die Sprache
laughter	skratt (n)	Latter	lach	das Lachen
			gelach (n)	das Gelächter
law	lag	Lov	wet	das Gesetz
lawsuit	process	Proces	proces (n)	der Prozess
laziness	lättja	Dovenskab	luiheid	die Trägheit
				die Faulheit
lecture	föredrag (n)	Foredrag (n)	voordracht	der Vortrag
leisure	ledighet	Fritid	vrije tijd	die freie Zeit
				die Musse
length	längd	Laengde	lengte	die Länge
lesson	lexa	Lektie	les	die Lektion
level	nivå	Niveau (n)	niveau (n)	das Niveau
lie	lögn	Løgn	leugen	die Lüge
life	liv (n)	Liv (n)	leven (n)	das Leben
line	linie	Linie	lijn (n)	die Linie
liquid	vätska	Vaedske	vloeistof	die Flüssigkeit
list	lista	Liste	lijst	das Verzeichnis
				die Liste
load	last	Laes (n)	last	die Last
look	blick	Blik (n)	blik	der Blick
loss	förlust	Tab (n)	verlies (n)	der Verlust
love	kärlek	Kaerlighed	liefde	die Liebe
luck (chance)	lycka	Held (n)	geluk (n)	das Glück
			kans	die Chance
luxury	lyx	Luksus	luxe	der Luxus
man (human being)	menniska	Menneske (n)	mensch	der Mensch
manager	ledare	Leder	leider	der Leiter

ENGLISH	SWEDISH	DANISH	DUTCH	GERMAN
mark, sign	tecken (n)	Tegn (n)	teeken (n)	das Zeichen
mass	massa	Masse	massa	die Masse
measure	mått (n)	Maal (n)	maat	das Mass
member	medlem	Medlem (n)	lid (n)	das Mitglied
memory	minne (n)	Hukommelse	geheugen (n)	das Gedächtnis
mistake	misstag	Fejl	fout	der Fehler
mixture	blandning	Blanding	mengsel (n)	die Mischung
money	pengar (pl.)	Penge (pl.)	geld (n)	das Geld
mood (temper)	lynne (n)	Stemning	stemming	die Stimmung
		Lune (n)		die Laune
movement	rörelse	Bevaegelse	beweging	die Bewegung
name	namn (n)	Navn (n)	naam	der Name
necessity	nödvändighet	Nødvendighed	noodzakelijk-	die Notwen-
			heid	digkeit
news	nyhet	Nyhed	tijding	die Nachricht
			nieuws (n)	die Neuigkeit
noise (sound)	ljud (n)	Støj	geluid (n)	das Geräusch
noise (din)	buller (n)	Larm	geraas (n)	der Lärm
number (No.)	nummer (n)	Nummer (n)	nummer (n)	die Nummer
number (nu-	tal (n)	Tal (n)	getal (n)	die Zahl
meral)				
number	antal (n)	Antal (n)	aantal (n)	die Anzahl
(amount)				
observation	iakttagelse	Iagttagelse	opmerking	die Beobach-
				tung
occasion	tillfälle (n)	Lejlighed	gelegenheid	die Gelegen-
				heit
occupation	yrke (n)	Stilling	beroep (n)	der Beruf
(profession)				
opening	öppning	Aabning	opening	die Öffnung
opinion	mening	Mening	meening	die Meinung
				die Ansicht
order (arrange-	ordning	Ordning	orde	die Ordnung
ment)				
origin	ursprung (n)	Oprindelse	oorsprong	der Ursprung
owner	egare	Ejer	eigenaar	der Eigentü-
				mer
pain	smärta	Smerte	pijn	der Schmerz
part (of	del	Del	deel (n)	der Teil
whole)				
part (in play,	roll	Rolle	rol	die Rolle
etc.)				
party (faction)	parti (n)	Parti (n)	partij	die Partei
past	det förflutna	Fortid	verleden (n)	die Vergangen-
				heit
payment	betalning	Betaling	betaling	die Bezahlung
peace	fred	Fred	vrede	der Friede

ENGLISH	SWEDISH	DANISH	DUTCH	GERMAN
people (community)	folk (n)	Folk (n)	volk (n)	das Volk
permission	tillåtelse	Tilladelse	vergunning	die Erlaubnis
picture	bild	Billede (n)	beeld (n)	das Bild
piece (fragment)	stycke (n)	Stykke (n)	stuk (n)	das Stück
place (spot)	ställe	Sted (n)	oord (n)	der Ort
		Plads	plaats	die Stelie
				der Platz
plan (project)	plan	Plan	plan (n)	der Plan
pleasure	nöje (n)	Fornøjelse	vermaak (n)	das Vergnügen
point (sharp end)	spets	Spids	punt	die Spitze
point (in space or time)	punkt	Punkt (n)	punt (n)	der Punkt
poison	gift (n)	Gift	vergif (n)	das Gift
politeness	hövlighet	Høflighed	beleefdheid	die Höflichkeit
politics	politik	Politik	politiek	die Politik
practice	övning	Øvelse	oefening	die Ubung
prejudice	fördom	Fordom	vooroordeel (n)	das Vorurteil
press	press	Presse	pers	die Presse
pressure	tryck (n)	Tryk (n)	druk	der Druck
pretext	förevändning	Paaskud (n)	voorwendsel (n)	der Vorwand
price, prize	pris (n)	Pris	prijs	der Preis
product	produkt	Produkt (n)	product (n)	das Erzeugnis
				das Produkt
progress	framsteg (n)	Fremskridt (n)	vordering	der Fortschritt
promise	löfte (n)	Løfte (n)	belofte	das Versprechen
proof (evidence)	bevis (n)	Bevis (n)	bewijs (n)	der Beweis
property (quality)	egenskap	Egenskab	eigenschap	die Eigenschaft
property (things owned)	egendom	Ejendom	eigendom (n)	das Eigentum
protection	beskyld (n)	Beskyttelse	bescherming	der Schutz
publicity (advertising)	reklam	Reklame	reclame	die Reklame
pull	drag (n)	Traek (n)	trek	der Zug
punishment	straff (n)	Straf	straf	die Strafe
purchase	köp (n)	Køb (n)	koop	der Kauf
purpose (aim)	mål (n)	Hensigt	doel (n)	der Zweck
				das Ziel
push	stöt	Stød (n)	stoot	der Stoss
question	fråga	Spørgsmaal (n)	vraag	die Frage
ray	stråle	Straale	straal	der Strahl

ENGLISH	SWEDISH	DANISH	DUTCH	GERMAN
reason (power of thought)	förnuft	Fornuft	vernuft (n)	die Vernunft
recollection	erinring	Erindring	herinnering	die Erinnerung
relation	förhållande (n)	Forhold (n)	verhouding	die Beziehung das Verhältnis
remainder	rest	Rest	rest	der Rest
remark	anmärkning	Bemaerkning	opmerking	die Bemerkung
rent (of house, etc.)	hyra	Leje	huur	die Miete
repetition	upprepning	Gentagelse	herhaling	die Wieder- holung
reproach	förebråelse	Bebrejdelse	verwijt (n)	der Vorwurf
resistance	mötstand (n)	Motstand	tegenstand	der Wider- stand
respect	aktning	Agtelse	achting	die Achtung
rest (repose)	vila	Ro	rust	die Ruhe
revenge	hämnd	Haevn	wraak	die Rache
reward	belöning	Belønning	belooning	die Belohnung
right (just claim)	rätt	Ret	recht (n)	das Recht
risk	risk	Risiko	risico (n)	das Risiko
rule (regulation)	regel	Regel	regeling	die Regel
rumor	rykte (n)	Rygte (n)	gerucht (n)	das Gerücht
safety	säkerhet	Sikkerhed	veiligheid	die Sicherheit
sale	försäljning	Salg (n)	verkoop	der Verkauf
sample	mönster (n)	Monster (n)	monster (n)	das Muster
science	vetenskap	Videnskab	wetenschap	die Wissen- schaft
scratch	skråma	Ridse	schram	die Ritze die Schramme
screen	skärm	Skaerm	scherm (n)	der Schirm
seat	säte (n)	Saede (n)	zitting	der Sitz der Platz
secret	hemlighet	Hemmelighed	geheim (n)	das Geheimnis
sensation (stir)	uppseende (n)	Røre (n)	sensatie	das Aufsehen die Sensation
sense (meaning)	betydelse	Betydning	beteekenis	die Bedeutung
sense (smell, touch, etc.)	sinne	Sans	zintuigen	der Sinn
sentence (group of words)	sats	Saetning	volzin	der Satz
sex	kön (n)	Køn (n)	geslacht (n)	das Geschlecht
shape	form	Form	vorm	die Form die Gestalt
share	andel	Andel	aandeel (n)	der Anteil
side	sida	Side	zijde	die Seite
size	storlek	Størrelse	grootte	die Grösse
sleep	sömn	Søvn	Slaap	der Schlaf

ENGLISH	SWEDISH	DANISH	DUTCH	GERMAN
smell	lukt	Lugt	reuk	der Geruch
smile	smålöje (n)	Smil (n)	glimlach	das Lächeln
society	sällskap (n)	Selskab (n)	maatschappij	die Gesellschaft
song	sång	Sang	lied (n)	das Lied
sound	ljud	Lyd	geluid (n)	der Laut
space	rum (n)	Rum (n)	ruimte	der Raum
speech (address)	tal	Tale	redevoering	die Rede
speed	hastighet	Fart	snelheid	die Geschwindigkeit
square	fyrkant	Firkant	vierkant (n)	das Rechteck
state	stat	Stat	staat	der Staat
stay (sojourn)	uppehåll (n)	Ophold (n)	verblijf (n)	der Aufenthalt
step (pace)	steg	Skridt (n)	stap	der Schritt
story	berättelse	Fortaelling	verhaal (n)	die Erzählung die Geschichte
strike	strejk	Strejke	staking	der Streik
struggle	kamp	Kamp	strijd	der Kampf
study	studium (n)	Studium (n)	studie	das Studium
substance	stoff (n)	Stof (n)	stof	der Stoff die Substanz
success	framgång	Success	succes	der Erfolg
suggestion (proposal)	förslag (n)	Forslag (n)	voorstel (n)	der Vorschlag
sum	summa	Sum	som	die Summe
surface	yta	Overflade	oppervlakte	die Oberfläche
surprise	överraskning	Overraskelse	verrassing	die Überraschung
suspicion	misstanke	Mistanke	achterdocht	der Verdacht
swindle (fraud)	bedrägeri	Bedrag (n)	bedrog (n)	der Betrug der Schwindel
sympathy (compassion)	medlidande (n)	Medlidenhed	medelijden (n)	das Mitleid
task	syssla	Opgave	taak	die Aufgabe
taste	smak	Smag	smaak	der Geschmack
tax	skatt	Skat	belasting	die Steuer
tendency	tendens	Tendens	neiging	die Neigung die Tendenz
tension	spänning	Spaending	spanning	die Spannung
test	prov (n)	Prøve	beproeving	die Prüfung die Probe
thanks	tack	Tak	dank	der Dank
theft	stöld	Tyveri (n)	diefstal	der Diebstahl
thing	ting	Ting	ding (n)	das Ding
	sak	Sag	zaak	die Sache
thirst	törst	Tørst	dorst	der Durst
thought	tanke	Tanke	gedachte	der Gedanke

ENGLISH	SWEDISH	DANISH	DUTCH	GERMAN
tie (bond)	band (n)	Baand (n)	band	das Band
time	tid	Tid	tijd	die Zeit
top (summit)	topp	Top	top	die Spitze
				der Gipfel
touch (contact)	beröring	Berøring	aanraking	die Berührung
trade	handel	Handel	handel	der Handel
trade union	fackförening	Fagforening	vakvereeniging	die Gewerk-
				schaft
translation	översättning	Oversaettelse	vertaling	die Überset-
				zung
treatment	behandlande	Behandling	behandeling	die Behandlung
triangle	trekant	Trekant	driehoek	das Dreieck
trick	knep (n)	Kneb (n)	truc	der Kniff
trouble (worry)	sorg	Sorg	zorg	die Sorge
truth	sanning	Sandhed	waarheid	die Wahrheit
turn	vändning	Vending	wending	die Wendung
				die Drehung
unemployment	arbetslöshet	Arbejdsløs-	werkloosheid	die Arbeits-
		hed		losigkeit
unit	enhet	Enhed	eenheid	die Einheit
use (application)	bruk	Brug	gebruik (n)	der Gebrauch
				die Anwendung
vacation, holi-	ferier (pl.)	Ferie	vacantie	die Ferien (pl.)
days				
value	värde (n)	Vaerd (n)	waarde	der Wert
vanity	fåfänga	Tomhed	ijdelheid	die Eitelkeit
vehicle	åkdon	Køretøj (n)	voertuig (n)	das Fahrzeug
vermin	ohyra	Utøj (n)	ongedierte (n)	das Ungeziefer
vessel (container)	behållare	Beholder	vat (n)	das Gefäss
				der Behälter
victory	seger	Sejr	overwinning	der Sieg
visit	besök	Besøg (n)	bezoek (n)	der Besuch
	visit	Visit	visite	die Visite
voice, vote	stämma	Stemme	stem	die Stimme
wages	lön	Løn	loon (n)	der Lohn
walk (stroll)	spatsergång	Spadseretur	wandeling	der Spazier-
				gang
want (lack)	brist	Mangel	gebrek (n)	der Mangel
war	krig	Krig	oorlog	der Krieg
warning	varning	Advarsel	waarschuwing	die Warnung
waste	slöseri (n)	Ødelaeggelse	verkwisting	die Verschwen-
				dung
way	väg	Vej	weg	der Weg
wealth	rikedom	Rigdom	rijkdom	der Reichtum
weapon	vapen (n)	Vaaben (n)	wapen (n)	die Waffe
weight	vikt	Vaegt	gewicht (n)	das Gewicht
width	bredd	Bredde	breedte	die Breite

ENGLISH	SWEDISH	DANISH	DUTCH	GERMAN
will	vilja	Villie	wil	der Wille
wish	önskan	Ønske (n)	wensch	der Wunsch
word	ord (n)	Ord (n)	woord (n)	das Wort
work (labor)	arbete (n)	Arbejde (n)	werk (n)	die Arbeit
youth	ungdom	Ungdom	jeugd	die Jugend
zeal	iver	Iver	ijver	der Eifer

2. DIVISION OF TIME

a) GENERAL TERMS

afternoon	eftermiddag	Eftermiddag	namiddag	der Nachmittag
century	århundrade (n)	Aarhundrede (n)	eeuw	das Jahrhundert
Christmas	Jul	Jul	Kerstmis	Weihnachten
day	dag	Dag	dag	der Tag
dawn	daggryning	Daggry (n)	dageraad	der Tagesanbruch
dusk	skymning	Tusmørke (n)	schemering	die Dämmerung
Easter	Påsk	Paaske	Paschen	Ostern
evening	afton	Aften	avond	der Abend
fortnight	fjorton dagar	fjorten Dage	veertien dagen	vierzehn Tage
holiday (public)	helgdag	Festdag	vacantiedag	der Festtag
hour	timme	Time	uur (n)	die Stunde
half an hour	en halvtimme	en halv Time	een half uur	eine halbe Stunde
a quarter of an hour	en kvart	et Kvarter (n)	een kwartier	eine Viertelstunde
an hour and a half	en och en halv timme	halvanden Time	anderhalfuur	anderthalb Stunden
leap year	skottår (n)	Skudaar (n)	schrikkeljaar (n)	das Schaltjahr
midnight	midnatt	Midnat	middernacht	die Mitternacht
minute	minut	Minut (n)	minuut	die Minute
month	månad	Maaned	maand	der Monat
morning	morgon	Morgen	morgen	der Morgen
night	natt	Nat	nacht	die Nacht
noon	middag	Middag	middag	der Mittag
season	årstid	Aarstid	jaargetijde (n)	die Jahreszeit
second	sekund	Sekund (n)	seconde	die Sekunde

ENGLISH	SWEDISH	DANISH	DUTCH	GERMAN
sunrise	soluppgång	Solopgang	zonsopgang	der Sonnen-aufgang
sunset	solnedgång	Solnedgang	zonsondergang	der Sonnen-untergang
time	tid	Tid	tijd	die Zeit
week	vecka	Uge	week	die Woche
year	år (n)	Aar (n)	jaar (n)	das Jahr

b) Seasons, Months, and Days

spring	vår	Foraar (n)	lente	der Frühling
summer	sommar	Sommer	zomer	der Sommer
autumn	höst	Efteraar (n)	herfst	der Herbst
winter	vinter	Vinter	winter	der Winter
January	januari	Januar	Januari	Januar
February	februari	Februar	Februari	Februar
March	mars	Marts	Maart	März
April	april	April	April	April
May	maj	Maj	Mei	Mai
June	juni	Juni	Juni	Juni
July	juli	Juli	Juli	Juli
August	augusti	August	Augustus	August
September	september	September	September	September
October	oktober	Oktober	October	Oktober
November	november	November	November	November
December	december	December	December	Dezember
Monday	måndag	Mandag	Maandag	Montag
Tuesday	tisdag	Tirsdag	Dinsdag	Dienstag
Wednesday	onsdag	Onsdag	Woensdag	Mittwoch
Thursday	torsdag	Torsdag	Donderdag	Donnerstag
Friday	fredag	Fredag	Vrijdag	Freitag
Saturday	lördag	Lørdag	Zaterdag	Samstag Sonnabend
Sunday	söndag	Søndag	Zondag	Sonntag

3. NUMERALS

one	en, ett (n)	en, et (n)	een	ein, eine (f)
two	två	to	twee	zwei
three	tre	tre	drie	drei
four	fyra	fire	vier	vier

ENGLISH	SWEDISH	DANISH	DUTCH	GERMAN
five	fem	fem	vijf	fünf
six	sex	seks	zes	sechs
seven	sju	syv	zeven	sieben
eight	åtta	otte	acht	acht
nine	nio	ni	negen	neun
ten	tio	ti	tien	zehn
eleven	elva	elleve	elf	elf
twelve	tolv	tolv	twaalf	zwölf
thirteen	tretton	tretten	dertien	dreizehn
fourteen	fjorton	fjorten	veertien	vierzehn
fifteen	femton	femten	vijftien	fünfzehn
sixteen	sexton	sejsten	zestien	sechzehn
seventeen	sjutton	sytten	zeventien	siebzehn
eighteen	aderton	atten	achttien	achtzehn
nineteen	nitton	nitten	negentien	neunzehn
twenty	tjugo	tyve	twintig	zwanzig
twenty-one	tjugoen	en og tyve	een en twintig	einund-zwanzig
twenty-two	tjugotvå	to og tyve	twee en twintig	zweiund-zwanzig
thirty	trettio	tredive	dertig	dreissig
forty	fyrtio	fyrre	veertig	vierzig
fifty	femtio	halvtres	vijftig	fünfzig
sixty	sextio	tres	zestig	sechszig
seventy	sjuttio	halvfjers	zeventig	siebenzig
eighty	åttio	firs	tachtig	achtzig
ninety	nittio	halvfems	negentig	neunzig
hundred	hundra	hundrede	honderd	hundert
thousand	tusen	tusinde	duizend	tausend
million	en million	en million	een millioen	eine Million
first	den första	den første	de eerste	der erste
second	andra	anden	tweede	zweite
third	tredje	tredje	derde	dritte
fourth	fjärde	fjerde	vierde	vierte
fifth	femte	femte	vijfde	fünfte
sixth	sjette	sjette	zesde	sechste
seventh	sjunde	syvende	zevende	siebente
eighth	åttonde	ottende	achtste	achte
half	en halv	en halv	een helft	ein Halb
one-third	en tredjedel	en Tredjedel	een derde	ein Drittel
one-fourth	en fjärdedel	en Fjerdedel	een vierde	ein Viertel
one-fifth	en femtedel	en Femtedel	een vijfde	ein Fünftel
once	en gång	een Gang	eenmaal	einmal
twice	två gånger	to Gange	tweemaal	zweimal
three times	tre gånger	tre Gange	driemaal	dreimal

4. ADJECTIVES

ENGLISH	SWEDISH	DANISH	DUTCH	GERMAN
able (capable)	duglig	dygtig	bekwaam	fähig
absent	frånfarande	fravaerende	afwezig	abwesend
accidental	tillfällig	tilfaeldig	toevallig	zufällig
agreeable	behaglig	behagelig	aangenaam	angenehm
alive	levande	levende	levend	lebend
ambiguous	tvetydig	tvetydig	dubbelzinnig	doppelsinnig
amusing	rolig	morsom	vermakelijk	amüsant
				unterhaltend
angry	vred	vred	toornig	böse
			boos	aufgebracht
artificial	konstlad	kunstig	kunstmatig	künstlich
attentive	uppmärksam	opmaerksom	aandachtig	aufmerksam
avaricious	girig	gerrig	gierig	geizig
awake	vaken	vaagen	wakker	wach
bad	dålig	daarlig	slecht	schlecht
beautiful	skön	smuk	mooi	schön
bent	böjd	bøjet	gebogen	gebogen
bitter	bitter	bitter	bitter	bitter
black	svart	sort	zwart	schwarz
blind	blind	blind	blind	blind
blue	blå	blaa	blauw	blau
blunt (not sharp)	slö	sløv	stomp	stumpf
brave	tapper	tapper	dapper	tapfer
	modig	modig	moedig	mutig
bright (full of light)	ljus	lys	helder	hell
broad (wide)	bred	bred	breed	breit
brown	brun	brun	bruin	braun
careful (cautious)	försiktig	forsigtig	voorzichtig	vorsichtig
charming	förtjusande	fortryllende	bekoorlijk	reizend
				bezaubernd
cheap	billig	billig	goedkoop	billig
clean	ren	ren	schoon	rein
				sauber
clear (not clouded)	klar	klar	klaar	klar
cold	kall	kold	koud	kalt
comfortable	bekväm	bekvem	behaagelijk	bequem
continual	ständig	bestandig	gestadig	fortwährend
				beständig

ENGLISH	SWEDISH	DANISH	DUTCH	GERMAN
continuous	oavbruten	uafbrudt	onafgebroken	ununterbroch-en
contrary	motsatt	modsat	tegengesteld	gegenteilig
cool	kylig	kølig	koel	kühl
cruel	grym	grusom	wreed	grausam
daily	daglig	daglig	dagelijksch	täglich
dangerous	farlig	farlig	gevaarlijk	gefährlich
dark	mörk	mørk	donker	dunkel
dead	död	død	dood	tot
deaf	döv	døv	doof	taub
deaf and dumb	dövstum	døvstum	doofstom	taubstumm
dear (beloved)	kär	kaer	liet	lieb
dear (expensive)	dyr	dyr	duur	teuer
deep	djup	dyb	diep	tief
different (dif-fering)	olik	forskellig	verschillend	verschieden
difficult	svår	vanskelig	moeilijk	schwer schwierig
dirty	smutsig	snavset	vuil	schmutzig
disagreeable	obehaglig	ubehagelig	onaangenaam	unangenehm
distinct (clear)	tydlig	tydelig	duidelijk	deutlich
domestic	huslig	huslig	huiselijk	häuslich
double	dubbel	dobbelt	dubbel	doppelt
drunk	drucken	drukken	dronken	betrunken
dry	torr	tør	droog	trocken
dumb	stum	stum	stom	stumm
dusty	dammig	støvet	stoffig	staubig
early	tidig	tidlig	vroeg	früh
eastern	östlig	østlig	oostersch	östlich
easy	lätt	nem	gemakkelijk	leicht
edible	ätbar	spiselig	eetbaar	essbar
empty	tom	tom	ledig	leer
equal	lika	lige	gelijk	gleich
extreme	ytterst	yderst	uiterste	äusserst
faithful	trogen	tro	trouw	treu
false	falsk	falsk	valsch	falsch
famous	berömd	berømt	beroemd	berühmt
fast (firm)	fast	fast	vlug	fest
fast (speedy)	snabb	hurtig	spoedig	schnell
fat (of meat)	fet	fed	vet	fett
favorable	gynnsam	gunstig	gunstig	günstig
female	kvinlig	kvindelig	vrouwelijk	weiblich
fertile	fruktbar	frugtbar	vruchtbaar	fruchtbar
flat	flat	flad	vlak	flach
foreign	utländsk	udenlandsk	buitenlandsch	ausländisch
fragile	skör	skør	broos	zerbrechlich
free	fri	fri	vrij	frei

ENGLISH	SWEDISH	DANISH	DUTCH	GERMAN
fresh	frisk	frisk	versch	frisch
friendly	vänlig	venlig	vriendelijk	freundlich
full	full	fuld	vol	voll
furious	rasande	rasende	woedend	wütend
future	framtida	fremtidig	toekomstig	zukünftig
generous	frikostig	gavmild	vrijgevig	freigebig
genuine	äkta	aegte	echt	echt
good	god	god	goed	gut
gray	grå	graa	grijs	grau
great, large	stor	stor	groot	gross
green	grön	grøn	groen	grün
guilty	skyldig	skyldig	schuldig	schuldig
happy	lycklig	lykkelig	gelukkig	glücklich
hard	hård	haard	hard	hart
harmful	skadlig	skadelig	schadelijk	schädlich
healthy	sund	sund	gezond	gesund
heavy	tung	tung	zwaar	schwer
high	hög	høj	hoog	hoch
hollow	ihålig	hul	hol	hohl
honest	ärlig	aerlig	eerlijk	ehrlich
hot	het	hed	heet	heiss
human	mänsklig	menneskelig	menschelijk	menschlich
hungry	hungrig	sulten	hongerig	hungrig
ill	sjuk	syg	ziek	krank
important	viktig	vigtig	belangrijk	wichtig
impossible	omöjlig	umulig	onmogelijk	unmöglich
industrious	flitig	flittig	vlijtig	fleissig
inner	inre	indre	binnen	inner
innocent	oskyldig	uskyldig	onschuldig	unschuldig
inquisitive	nyfiken	nysgerrig	nieuwsgierig	neugierig
insane	vansinnig	sindssyg	krankzinnig	geistesgestört irr
intelligent	klok intelligent	klog intelligent	knap intelligent	klug intelligent
interesting	intressant	interessant	interessant	interessant
just (fair)	rättfärdig	retfaerdig	rechtvaardig	gerecht
kind	godhjärtad	godhjertet	goedig	gütig freundlich
last	sist	sidst	laatst	letzt
late	sen	sen	laat	spät
lazy	lat	doven	lui	träge faul
lean	mager	mager	mager	mager
left	vänster	venstre	linker	link
light (in weight)	lätt	let	licht	leicht
liquid	flytande	flydende	vloeibaar	flüssig
long	lång	lang	lang	lang

ENGLISH	SWEDISH	DANISH	DUTCH	GERMAN
loose (slack)	lös	løs	los	lose
loud	högjudd	høj	luid	laut
low	låg	lav	laag	niedrig
lukewarm	ljum	lunken	lauw	lauwarm
male	manlig	mandlig	mannelijk	männlich
married	gift	gift	gehuwd	verheiratet
mean (average)	medel	gennemsnitlig	gemiddeld	mittler durchschnitt- lich
medical	medicinsk	medicinsk	geneeskundig	medizinisch
military	militärisk	militaer	militair	militärisch
mobile	rörlig	bevaegelig	beweegbaar	beweglich
modest	blygsam	beskeden	bescheiden	bescheiden
moist	fuktig	fugtig	vochtig	feucht
mutual	ömsesidig	gensidig	wederzijdsch	gegenseitig
naked	naken	nøgen	naakt	nackt
narrow	smal	smal	nauw	schmal
natural	naturlig	naturlig	natuurlijk	natürlich
necessary	nödvändig	nødvendig	noodig	nötig notwendig
new	ny	ny	nieuw	neu
next	näst	naest	naast	nächst
northern	nordlig	nordlig	noordelijk	nördlich
obedient	lydig	lydig	gehoorzaam	gehorsam
occupied (of seat, etc.)	upptaget	optaget	bezet	besetzt
old	gammal	gammel	oud	alt
only	endast	eneste	eenig	einzig
open	öppen	aaben	open	offen
ordinary (current)	vanlig	saedvanlig	gewoon	gewöhnlich
original (first)	ursprunglig	oprindelig	oorspronkelijk	ursprünglich
outer	yttre	ydre	buiten	äusser
own (one's)	egen	egen	eigen	eigen
painful	smärtful	smertelig	pijnlijk	schmerzhaft
pale	blek	bleg	bleek	bleich
past	förgangen	forbigangen	verleden	vergangen
patient	talig	taalmodig	geduldig	geduldig
personal	personlig	personlig	persoonlijk	persönlich
pointed	spetsig	spids	puntig	spitz
poisonous	giftig	giftig	giftig	giftig
polite	hövlig	høflig	beleefd	höflich
poor	fattig	fattig	arm	arm
popular	populär	populaer	populair	populär
possible	möjlig	mulig	mogelijk	möglich
practical	praktisk	praktisk	practisch	praktisch
pregnant	havande	svanger	zwanger	schwanger

ENGLISH	SWEDISH	DANISH	DUTCH	GERMAN
present	närvarande	naervaerende	tegenwoordig	gegenwärtig
pretty	vacker	køn	aardig	hübsch
principal	huvudsaklig	hovedsagelig	hoofdzakelijk	wichtigst
				hauptsächlichst
probable	sannolik	sandsynlig	waarschijnlijk	wahrscheinlich
proud	stolt	stolt	trotsch	stolz
public	offentlig	offentlig	publiek	öffentlich
quiet (calm)	lugn	rolig	rustig	ruhig
rare	sällsynt	sjaelden	zeldzaam	selten
raw (not cooked)	rå	raa	rauw	roh
ready	färdig	faerdig	klaar	bereit
				fertig
real	verklig	virkelig	werkelijk	wirklich
reasonable (rational)	förnuftig	fornuftig	verstandig	vernünftig
red	röd	rød	rood	rot
regular	regelbunden	regelmaessig	regelmatig	regelmässig
responsible	ansvarig	ansvarlig	verantwoordelijk	verantwortlich
rich	rik	rig	rijk	reich
ridiculous	löjlig	latterlig	belachelijk	lächerlich
right (correct)	riktig	rigtig	juist	richtig
right (hand)	höger	højre	rechter	recht
rigid	styv	stiv	stijf	steif
ripe	mogen	moden	rijp	reif
rough (not smooth)	skrovlig	ru	ruw	rauh
round	rund	rund	rond	rund
rude	ohövlig	uhøflig	onbeleefd	unhöflich
rusty	rostig	rusten	roestig	rostig
sad	bedrövad	bedrøvet	treurig	traurig
				betrübt
satisfied	nöjd	tilfreds	tevreden	zufrieden
scientific	vetenskaplig	videnskabelig	wetenschappelijk	wissenschaftlich
secret	hemlig	hemmelig	geheim	geheim
sensitive	känslig	følsom	gevoelig	empfindlich
separate	skiljd	saerskilt	afzonderlijk	getrennt
serious	allvarsam	alvorlig	ernstig	ernst
shallow	grund	lav	ondiep	untief
				seicht
sharp	skarp	skarp	scherp	scharf
short	kort	kort	kort	kurz
shut	stängt	lukket	dicht	geschlossen
shy	skygg	sky	schuw	scheu
similar	likartad	lignende	soortgelijk	ähnlich

ENGLISH	SWEDISH	DANISH	DUTCH	GERMAN
simple	enkel	enkelt	eenvoudig	einfach
sleepy	sömnig	søvnig	slaperig	schläfrig
slim	smärt	slank	slank	schlank
slow	långsam	langsom	langzaam	langsam
small, little	liten	lille	klein	klein
smooth	slät	glat	glad	glatt
sober	nykter	aedru	nuchter	nüchtern
soft	mjuk	blød	zacht	weich
solid (not liquid)	fast	fast	vast	fest
sour	sur	sur	zuur	sauer
southern	sydlig	sydlig	zuidelijk	südlich
special	särskild	saeregen	bijzonder	besonder
square	fyrkantig	firkantet	vierkant	viereckig
steep	brant	stejl	steil	steil
sticky	klibbig	klaebrig	kleverig	klebrig
straight	rak	lige	recht	gerade
strange (peculiar)	egendomlig	ejendommelig	eigenaardig	eigentümlich sonderbar
strong	stark	staerk	sterk	stark
stupid	dum	dum	dom	dumm
sudden	plötslig	pludselig	plotseling	plötzlich
sufficient	tillräcklig	tilstraekkelig	voldoende	genügend
suitable (appropriate)	passande	passende	passend	passend geeignet
sure (certain)	säker	sikker	zeker	sicher
sweet	söt	sød	zoet	süss
talkative	pratsam	snaksom	spraakzaam	gesprächig
tame	tam	tam	tam	zahm
thankful	tacksam	taknemmelig	dankbaar	dankbar
thick (not thin)	tjock	tyk	dik	dick
thick (dense)	tät	taet	dicht	dicht
thin	tunn	tynd	dun	dünn
thirsty	törstig	tørstig	dorstig	durstig
tight (close-fitting)	trång	taet	nauw	eng
tired	trött	traet	moe	müde
topmost	överst	øverst	bovenste	oberst
tough	seg	sejg	taai	zäh
transparent	genomskinlig	gennemsigtig	doorzichtig	durchsichtig
true	sann	sand	waar	wahr
ugly	ful	grim	leelijk	hässlich
unconscious	medvetslös	bevidstløs	bewusteloos	bewusstlos
unemployed	arbetslös	arbejdsløs	werkeloos	arbeitslos
urgent	brådskande	indtraengende	dringend	dringend
useful	nyttig	nyttig	nuttig	nützlich
vain	fåfäng	forfaengelig	verwaand	eitel
valid	giltig	gyldig	geldig	gültig

ENGLISH	SWEDISH	DANISH	DUTCH	GERMAN
valuable	värdefull	vaerdifuld	kostbaar	wertvoll
visible	synlig	synlig	zichtbaar	sichtbar
vulgar	gemen	gemen	ordinair	gemein
warm	varm	varm	warm	warm
weak	svag	svag	zwak	schwach
western	vesterlig	vestlig	westelijk	westlich
wet	våt	vaad	nat	nass
white	vit	hvid	wit	weiss
whole	hel	hel	geheel	ganz
wild	vild	vild	wild	wild
wrong (incorrect)	oriktig	urigtig	verkeerd	unrichtig falsch
yearly	årlig	aarlig	jaarlijksch	jährlich
yellow	gul	gul	geel	gelb
young	ung	ung	jong	jung

5. VERBS

be able to	kunna	kunne	kunnen	können
absorb	insuga	indsuge	opzuigen	absorbieren
accept	mottaga	modtage	aannemen	annehmen
accompany	följa	ledsage	begeleiden	begleiten
accuse	anklaga	anklage	aanklagen	anklagen
act upon	verka på	virke paa	werken op	wirken auf
add to	tillfoga	tilføje	bijvoegen	hinzufügen
add up	addera	addere	optellen	addieren zusammen-zählen
admire	beundra	beundre	bewonderen	bewundern
advertise	annonsera	avertere	adverteeren	annoncieren
advise	råda	raade	raden	*raten*
be afraid of	vara rädd för	vaere bange for	bevreesd zijn voor	sich fürchten vor
be in agreement with	hålla med	stemme over-eens med	overeen-stemmen met	übereinstim-men mit
take aim at	sikta på	sigte paa	mikken op	zielen auf
alight from	stiga ur .	stige ud	uitstijgen	aussteigen
allow	tillåta	tillade	veroorloven	*erlauben*
amuse (oneself)	roa (sig)	more (sig)	(zich) ver-maken	(sich) unter-halten
annoy	plåga	plage	ergeren	ärgern
answer (reply)	svara	svare	antwoorden	*antworten*
apologize	ursäkta sig	undskylde sig	zich veront-schuldigen	sich entschul-digen

ENGLISH	SWEDISH	DANISH	DUTCH	GERMAN
arrange	ordna	ordne	regelen	regeln
arrest (take in custody)	arrestera	arrestere	arresteeren	festnehmen
arrive	ankomma	ankomme	aankomen	ankommen
be ashamed of	skämmas för	skamme sig over	zich schamen over	sich schämen (gen.)
ask (put a question)	fråga	spørge	vragen	fragen
ask (beg)	bedja	bede	vragen verzoeken	bitten ersuchen
associate with	umgås med	omgaas med	omgaan met	umgehen mit
assure	försäkra	forsikre	verzekeren	versichern
astonish	förvåna	forbavse	verbazen	überraschen
attack	angripa	angribe	aanvallen	angreifen
attempt	försöka	forsøge	beproeven	versuchen
attract	tildraga	tiltraekke	aantrekken	anziehen
avoid	undvika	undgaa	vermijden	vermeiden
bathe, take a bath	bada	bade	baden	baden
beat (give blows)	slå	slaa	slaan	schlagen
become	bliva	blive	worden	werden
begin	börja	begynde	beginnen	beginnen
behave	uppföra sig	opføre sig	zich gedragen	sich betragen sich benehmen
believe	tro	tro	gelooven	*glauben*
belong to	tillhöra	tilhøre	behooren	*gehören*
bend	böja	bøje	buigen	biegen
bend down (stoop)	böja sig	bøje sig	zich bukken	sich bücken
bet	slå vad	vaedde	wedden	wetten
bite	bita	bide	bijten	beissen
blame (reproach)	tadla	dadle	laken	tadeln
blow	blåsa	blaese	blazen	blasen
blow one's nose	snyta sig	pudse sin Naese	zijn neus snuiten	sich die Nase putzen sich schneuzen
boast	skryta	prale	zich beroemen	sich rühmen
boil } boil }	koka	koge	koken	kochen
bore (drill)	borra	bore	boren	bohren
bore (tire)	uttråka	kede	vervelen	langweilen
be born	vara född	vaere født	geboren zijn	geboren werden
borrow	låna (av)	lanne (af)	leenen (van)	borgen (von)
bother oneself about	bry sig om	bryde sig om	zich bekommeren om	sich kümmern um
break } break }	bryta	braekke	breken	zerbrechen

ENGLISH	SWEDISH	DANISH	DUTCH	GERMAN
breathe	andas	aande	ademen	atmen
breed (rear)	avla	avle	fokken	züchten
	uppföda	opdrage	opvoeden	aufziehen
breed	avla	yngle	voortbrengen	sich vermehren
bring	hämta	bringe	brengen	bringen
broadcast	utsända	udsende	uitzenden	rundfunken
brush	borsta	børste	borstelen	bürsten
build	bygga	bygge	bouwen	bauen
burn ⎱ *burn* ⎰	bränna	braende	branden	brennen
burst	brista	briste	barsten	platzen
bury (inter)	begrava	begrave	begraven	begraben
be busy with	sysselsätta sig med	beskaeftige sig med	zich bezig houden met	sich beschäftigen mit
buy	köpa	købe	koopen	kaufen
calculate	beräkna	beregne	berekenen	berechnen
call (name)	kalla	kalde	noemen	nennen
call (shout for)	ropa	raabe	roepen	rufen
be called	heta	hedde	heeten	heissen
carry	bära	baere	dragen	tragen
catch (capture)	fånga	fange	vangen	fangen
cease (stop)	upphöra	ophøre	ophouden	aufhören
celebrate	fira	fejre	vieren	feiern
change (alter)	förändra	forandre	veranderen	ändern
change (money)	växla	veksle	wisselen	wechseln
change	förändras	forandre sig	veranderen	sich verändern
chew	tugga	tygge	kauwen	kauen
choke	kväva	kvaele	worgen	würgen
choke	kvävas	kvaeles	stikken	ersticken
choose, elect	välja	vaelge	kiezen	wählen
clean	göra ren	gøre ren	schoonmaken	reinigen putzen
climb	klättra	klatre	klimmen	klettern
collect	samla	samle	verzamelen	sammeln
comb	kamma	kaemme	kammen	kämmen
come	komma	komme	komen	kommen
compare	jämföra	sammenligne	vergelijken	vergleichen
compel	tvinga	tvinge	dwingen	zwingen
compete	konkurera	konkurrere	mededingen	konkurrieren
complain (about)	klaga (över)	klage (over)	klagen (øver)	klagen (über)
concern (impersonal)	angå	angaa	betreffen	betreffen angehen
condemn	döma	dømme	veroordeelen	verurteilen
confess	erkänna	bekende	bekennen	gestehen
confuse	förvirra	forvirre	verwarren	verwirren

ENGLISH	SWEDISH	DANISH	DUTCH	GERMAN
congratulate	gratulera	gratulere	gelukwenschen feliciteeren	*gratulieren* beglückwün- schen
connect	förbinda	forbinde	verbinden	verbinden
conquer (terri- tory)	erövra	erobre	veroveren	erobern
consent	samtycka	samtykke	toestemmen inwilligen	zustimmen einwilligen
console (com- fort)	trösta	trøste	troosten	trösten
contain	innehålla	indeholde	bevatten	enthalten
continue	fortsätta	fortsaette	voortzetten	fortsetzen fortfahren mit
contradict	motsäga	modsige	tegenspreken	*widersprechen*
contribute	bidraga	bidrage	bijdragen	beitragen
control	kontrolera	kontrolere	controleeren	kontrollieren
converge	löpa samman	løbe sammen	samenloopen	zusammen- laufen konvergieren
convince	övertyga	overtyde	overtuigen	überzeugen
cook	koka	koge	koken	kochen
copy	kopiera	kopiere	copieeren	kopieren
correct	rätta	rette	verbeteren	verbessern korrigieren
correspond to	motsvara	svare til	beantwoorden aan	entsprechen
cost	kosta	koste	kosten	kosten
cough	hosta	hoste	hoesten	husten
count (find number)	räkna	taelle	tellen	zählen
cover	täcka	daekke	bedekken	bedecken
creep	krypa	krybe	kruipen	kriechen
criticize	kritisera	kritisere	critiseeren	kritisieren
crush	krossa	knuse	verpletteren	zerdrücken
cure	bota	helbrede	genezen	heilen
cut	skära	skaere	snijden	schneiden
cycle	cykla	cykle	fietsen	radeln
damage	skada	beskadige	beschadigen	beschädigen
dance	dansa	danse	dansen	tanzen
dare	vaga	vove	durven	wagen
dazzle	blända	blaende	verblinden	blenden
deceive	bedraga	bedrage	bedriegen	betrügen
decide	besluta	beslutte	beslissen	beschliessen
decorate	pryda	smykke	tooien	schmücken
deduce (infer)	sluta	slutte	besluiten	schliessen folgern

ENGLISH	SWEDISH	DANISH	DUTCH	GERMAN
defeat	besegra	besejre	verslaan	besiegen
				schlagen
defend	försvara	forsvare	verdedigen	verteidigen
defy	utfordra	udfordre	uitdagen	herausfordern
demand	fordra	fordre	verlangen	fordern
				verlangen
deny (say that	förneka	benaegte	loochenen	leugnen
thing is untrue)				
depart	avresa	afrejse	vertrekken	abreisen
depend upon	bero av	afhaenge af	afhangen van	abhängen von
describe	beskriva	beskrive	beschrijven	beschreiben
deserve	förtjäna	fortjene	verdienen	verdienen
design (plan)	planlägga	planlaegge	ontwerpen	entwerfen
despair of	förtvivla om	fortvivle over	wanhopen aan	verzeifeln an
despise	förakta	foragte	verachten	verachten
destroy	förstöra	ødelaegge	vernielen	zerstören
detain (delay)	uppehålla	opholde	ophouden	aufhalten
develop	utveckla	udvikle	ontwikkelen	entwickeln
develop	utveckla sig	udvikle sig	zich ontwikkel-	sich ent-
			en	wickeln
die	dö	dø	sterven	sterben
dig	gräva	grave	graven	graben
digest	smälta	fordøje	verteeren	verdauen
disappear	försvinna	forsvinde	verdwijnen	verschwinden
disappoint	svika	skuffe	teleustellen	enttäuschen
discharge (dis-	afskeda	afskedige	ontslaan	entlassen
miss)				
discover	upptäcka	opdage	ontdekken	entdecken
disinfect	desinficiera	desinficere	desinfecteeren	desinfizieren
dissolve	upplösa	opløse	oplossen	auflösen
distinguish	åtskilja	skelne mellem	onderscheiden	unterscheiden
between	mellan		tusschen	zwischen
distribute	fördela	fordele	verdeelen	verteilen
disturb	oroa	forstyrre	storen	stören
dive	dyka	dykke	duiken	tauchen
divide	dela	dele	deelen	teilen
divorce (get di-	skilja sig	skille fra	scheiden	sich scheiden
vorced from)				
do	göra	gøre	doen	tun
doubt (of)	tvivla (på)	tvivle (paa)	twijfelen (om)	zweifeln (an)
				bezweifeln
draw (sketch)	rita	tegne	teekenen	zeichnen
dream	drömma	drømme	droomen	träumen
dress oneself	kläda sig	klaede sig	zich aankleeden	sich ankleiden
drink	dricka	drikke	drinken	trinken
drive (vehicle)	köra	køre	rijden	fahren
drown	drunkna	drukne	verdrinken	ertrinken

ENGLISH	SWEDISH	DANISH	DUTCH	GERMAN
dry	torka	tørre	drogen	trocknen
dye	färga	farve	verven	färben
earn	förtjäna	fortjene	verdienen	verdienen
eat (of animals)	äta	aede	vreten	fressen
eat (of man)	äta	spise	eten	essen
educate (train)	uppfostra	opdrage	opvoeden	erziehen
embrace	omfamna	omfavne	omarmen	umarmen
emphasize	betona	laegge Vaegt paa	nadruk leggen op	betonen Nachdruck legen auf
empty	tömma	tømme	ledigen	leeren
encourage	uppmuntra	opmuntre	aanmoedigen	ermutigen
endeavor	bemöda sig	bestraebe sig	streven	sich bemühen sich bestreben
become engaged to	förlova sig med	forlove sig med	zich verloven met	sich verloben mit
enjoy	njuta	nyde	genieten	geniessen
envy	misunna	misunde	benijden	beneiden
escape	undvika	undvige	ontvluchten	entkommen entweichen
estimate	uppskatta	vurdere	schatten	schätzen
evaporate	avdunsta	fordampe	verdampen	verdunsten
exaggerate	överdriva	overdrive	overdrijven	übertreiben
examine (investigate)	undersöka	undersøge	onderzoeken	untersuchen
excite	uppega	pirre	opwinden	aufregen
exclude	utestänga	udelukke	uitsluiten	ausschliessen
excuse	ursäkta	undskylde	verontschuldigen	entschuldigen
exhibit	utställa	udstille	tentoonstellen	ausstellen
exist	existera	eksistere	bestaan	bestehen existieren
expect	vänta	forvente	verwachten	erwarten
explain	förklara	forklare	uitleggen	erklären
exploit	utnyta	udbytte	uitbuiten	ausbeuten
express oneself	uttrycka sig	udtrykke sig	zich uitdrukken	sich ausdrücken
extinguish	utsläcka	udslukke	uitdooven	auslöschen
faint (swoon)	svimma	besvime	in onmacht vallen	in Ohnmacht fallen
fall	falla	falde	vallen	fallen
fall in love with	förälska sig	forelske sig	verliefd worden op	sich verlieben in
fasten (fix)	fästa	gøre fast	vastmaken	befestigen
feed (animals)	fodra	fodre	voeden	füttern
feed (people)	nära	(er) naere	voeden	(er) nähren
feel	känna sig	føle	zich voelen	sich fühlen

ENGLISH	SWEDISH	DANISH	DUTCH	GERMAN
fetch	hämta	hente	halen	holen
fight	kämpa	kaempe	vechten	kämpfen
fill	fylla	fylde	vullen	füllen
find	finna	finde	vinden	finden
finish (con- clude)	sluta	slutte	besluiten	schliessen
finish (com- plete)	fullända	fuldende	voltooien	vollenden fertigmachen
fish	fiska	fiske	visschen	fischen
fit (make to fit)	passa	tilpasse	aanpassen	anpassen
flatter	smickra	smigre	vleien	*schmeicheln*
flee (run away from)	fly	flygte	vluchten	fliehen
flow	flyta	flyde	vloeien	fliessen
fly	flyga	flyve	vliegen	fliegen
fold	fålla	folde	vouwen	falten
follow	följa	følge	volgen	*folgen*
forbid	förbjuda	forbyde	verbieden	verbieten
forecast (predict)	förutsäga	forudsige	voorspellen	voraussagen
foresee	förutse	forudse	voorzien	voraussehen
forget	glömma	glemme	vergeten	vergessen
forgive	förlåta	tilgive	vergeven	verzeihen
freeze	frysa	fryse	bevriezen	zum Gefrieren bringen
freeze	frysa	fryse	bevriezen	gefrieren
frighten	skrämma	forskraekke	verschrikken	erschrecken
gather (pick)	plocka	plukke	plukken	pflücken
gather (come together)	församla sig	forsamles	vergaderen	sich versam- meln
get up (rise)	stiga upp	staa op	opstaan	aufstehen
give	giva	give	geven	geben
go (on foot)	gå	gaa	gaan	gehen
go (in vehicle)	fara	køre	rijden	fahren
govern	regera	regere	regeeren	regieren
greet	hälsa	hilse	groeten	grüssen
grind (crush)	mala	male	malen	mahlen
groan	stöna	stønne	steunen	stöhnen
grow	växa	vokse	groeien	wachsen
grumble	brumma knorra	brumme knurre	morren knorren	murren brummen
guess	gissa	gaette	gissen	erraten
hang } *hang*	hänga	haenge	hangen	{ hängen hangen
happen (imper- sonal)	hända	ske	gebeuren	geschehen sich ereignen
harvest (reap)	skörda	høste	oogsten	ernten
hate	hata	hade	haten	hassen

ENGLISH	SWEDISH	DANISH	DUTCH	GERMAN
have	hava	have	hebben	haben
hear	höra	høre	hooren	hören
help	hjälpa	hjaelpe	helpen	*helfen*
hesitate	tveka	tøve	aarzelen	zögern
hide	dölja	skjule	verbergen	verbergen
hide (from)	gömma sig (för)	skjule sig (for)	zich verbergen (voor)	sich verbergen (vor)
hinder	hindra	hindre	hinderen	hindern
hire	hyra	hyre	huren	mieten
hit (strike)	träffa	traeffe	treffen	treffen
hold	hålla	holde	houden	halten
hope	hoppas	haabe	hopen	hoffen
hunt	jaga	jage	jagen	jagen
hurry	skynda sig	skynde sig	zich haasten	sich beeilen eilen
hurt (injure)	skada	saare	bezeeren	verletzen
illuminate (light up)	upplysa	oplyse	verlichten	Licht machen
imagine (form picture)	föreställa sig	forestille	zich voorstellen	sich vorstellen
imitate	efterhärma	efterligne	nabootsen	nachahmen
import	införa	indføre	invoeren	einführen
incline	böja	bøje	neigen	neigen
include	inneslutta	indeslutte	insluiten	einschliessen
infect	smitta inficiera	smitte inficere	besmetten infecteeren	anstecken infizieren
inflate	uppblåsa	opblaese	opblazen	aufblasen
inherit	ärva	arve	erven	erben
inquire (about)	fråga (efter)	spørge (efter)	vragen (naar)	fragen (nach)
insult	förolämpa	fornaerme	beleedigen	beschimpfen
insure	försäkra	forsikre	verzekeren	versichern
interest	intressera	interessere	belangstellen	interessieren
interfere (with)	blanda sig (in)	blande sig (i)	zich bemoeien (met)	sich einmi- schen (in)
introduce (person)	föreställa presentera	forestille	voorstellen	vorstellen
invent	uppfinna	opfinde	uitvinden	erfinden
invite	inbjuda	indbyde	uitnoodigen	einladen
join (unite)	förena	forene	vereenigen	vereinigen
joke (jest)	skämta	spøge	schertsen	scherzen spassen
judge	döma	dømme	beoordeelen	beurteilen
jump	hoppa	springe	springen	springen hüpfen
keep (preserve)	bevara	bevare	bewaren	(auf) bewah- ren
keep (retain)	behålla	beholde	behoeden	behalten

ENGLISH	SWEDISH	DANISH	DUTCH	GERMAN
kick	sparka	sparke	schoppen	mit dem Fusse stossen
kill	döda	draebe	dooden	töten
kiss	kyssa	kysse	kussen	küssen
kneel	knäböja	knaele	knielen	knien
knock (at door)	knacka	banke	kloppen	klopfen
know	känna	kende	kennen	kennen
	veta	vide	weten	wissen
land	landa	lande	landen	landen
last	vara	vare	duren	dauern während
laugh	skratta	le	lachen	lachen
laugh at	utskratta	udle	uitlachen	auslachen
lead	föra	føre	voeren	führen
lean on	luta på	laene sig til	leunen op	sich lehnen an
learn	lära sig	laere	leeren	lernen
leave behind	lemna efter	efterlade	achterlaten	zurücklassen
lend	låna	laane	leenen	leihen
let (house, etc.)	uthyra	udleje	verhuren	vermieten
lie (tell lie)	ljuga	lyve	liegen	lügen
lie (position)	ligga	ligge	liggen	liegen
lie down	lägga sig	laegge sig	gaan liggen	sich nieder- legen
lift	lyfta	løfte	tillen	heben
light (cigarette, etc.)	tända	taende	aansteken	anzünden anstecken
like	tycka om	synes om	gaarne hebben houden van	gern haben mögen
limp	halta	halte	hinken	hinken
listen to	lyssna till	lytte til	toehooreṇ	zuhören
live (be alive)	leva	leve	leven	leben
live (dwell)	bo	bo	wonen	wohnen
look after (take care of)	se efter	se efter	oppassen	achten auf
look (have ap- pearance of)	se ut	se ud	uitzien	aussehen
look at	se på	se paa	aanzien	ansehen
	beskåda	betragte	aankijken	betrachten
lose	tappa	tabe	verliezen	verlieren
love (person)	älska	elske	beminnen	lieben
lubricate	smjöra	smøre	smeren	schmieren
make	göra	gøre	maken	machen
make a mistake	taga fel	tage Fejl	een fout maken	einen Fehler machen
manage (direct)	sköta	lede	besturen	leiten
manufacture	fabricera	fabrikere	fabriceeren	fabrizieren
march	marschera	marchere	marcheeren	marschieren

ENGLISH	SWEDISH	DANISH	DUTCH	GERMAN
marry (get married)	gifta sig med	gifte sig med	huwen trouwen met	heiraten sich verheiraten mit
mate	para	parre sig	paren	paaren
measure } *measure* }	mäta	maale	meten	messen
meet (encounter)	möta träffa	møde traeffe	ontmoeten	*begegnen* treffen
melt } *melt* }	smälta	smelte	smelten	schmelzen
mend	reparera	reparere	repareeren	reparieren
milk	mjölka	malke	melken	melken
mix	blanda	blande	mengen	mischen
mourn	beklaga	beklage	betreuren	beklagen
move (shift)	röra	rykke	verschuiven	rücken verschieben
move (change residence)	flytta	flytte	verhuizen	umziehen
move (budge)	röra sig	røre sig	zich bewegen	sich bewegen
multiply	multiplicera	multiplicere	vermenigvuldigen	multiplizieren
need	behöva	behøve	noodig hebben	brauchen nötig haben
neglect	försumma	forsømme	veronachtzamen	vernachlässigen
nurse (sick)	sköta	pleje	verplegen	pflegen
obey	lyda	adlyde	gehoorzamen	*gehorchen*
offend	förolämpa	fornaerme	beleedigen	beleidigen
offer	erbjuda	tilbyde	aanbieden	anbieten
omit (leave out)	utelemna	udelade	weglaten	auslassen
open	öppna	aabne	opendoen.	öffnen aufmachen
oppose (withstand)	motstå	modsaette sig	weerstaan	*sich widersetzen*
oppress	förtrycka	undertrykke	onderdrukken	unterdrücken
order (goods)	beställa	bestille	bestellen	bestellen
organize	organisera	organisere	organiseeren	organisieren
owe	vara skyldig	skylde	schuldig zijn	schulden
pack	packa	pakke	pakken	packen
paint	måla	male	schilderen	malen
pay	betala	betale	betalen	bezahlen
peel	skala	skraelle	pellen	schälen
perform (carry out)	utföra	udføre	uitvoeren	ausführen
persecute	förfölja	forfølge	vervolgen	verfolgen
persuade	övertala	overtale	overreden	überreden
pick up	plocka upp	tage op	oprapen	auflesen

ENGLISH	SWEDISH	DANISH	DUTCH	GERMAN
pity	ömka	ynke	medelijden hebben met	bemitleiden Mitleid haben mit
plan	planera	planere	plannen	planen
plant	plantera	plante	planten	pflanzen
play (game)	leka	lege	spelen	spielen
play (instrument)	spela	spille	spelen	spielen
please	behaga	behage	behagen	gefallen
plow, plough	plöja	pløje	ploegen	pflügen
plunder	plundra	plyndre	plunderen	plündern
poison	förgifta	forgifte	vergiftigen	vergiften
possess	besitta	besidde	bezitten	besitzen
postpone	uppskjuta	udsaette	uitstellen	verschieben
pour	gjuta	øse	gieten	giessen
practice (exercise oneself)	praktisera	øve	oefenen	üben sich üben
praise	berömma	rose	roemen	loben rühmen
pray	bedja	bede	bidden	beten
precede	gå förut	gaa foran	voorafgaan	vorangehen
prefer	föredraga	foretraekke	verkiezen	vorziehen
prepare	förbereda	forberede	voorbereiden	vorbereiten
press	trycka	trykke	drukken	drücken
pretend (feign)	föregiva	foregive	voorgeven	vorgeben
prevent	hindra	forhindre	verhinderen	verhindern
print	trycka	trykke	drukken	drucken
profit (from)	draga fördel (av)	profitere (af)	profiteeren (van)	profitieren (von)
promise	lova	love	beloven	versprechen
pronounce	uttala	udtale	uitspreken	aussprechen
propose (suggest)	föreslå	foreslaa	voorstellen	vorschlagen
protect	beskydda	beskytte	beschermen	beschützen
protest	protestera	protestere	protesteeren	protestieren
prove	bevisa	bevise	bewijzen	beweisen
publish (of publisher)	förlägga	udgive	uitgeven	verlegen herausgeben
pull	draga	traekke	trekken	ziehen
pump (water)	pumpa	pumpe	pompen	pumpen
pump (inflate)	pumpa upp	oppumpe	oppompen	aufpumpen
punish	straffa	straffe	straffen	(be)strafen
push	stöta	støde	stooten	stossen
put	sätta	saette	zetten	setzen
	ställa	stille	stellen	stellen
	lägga	laegge	leggen	legen
quarrel	gräla	skaendes	twisten	zanken
be quiet (silent)	var tyst	tie	zwijgen	schweigen
quote	citera	citere	citeeren	zitieren

ENGLISH	SWEDISH	DANISH	DUTCH	GERMAN
rain	regna	regne	regenen	regnen
react	reagera	reagere	reageeren	reagieren
read	läsa	laese	lezen	lesen
receive	mottaga	modtage	ontvangen	empfangen
				erhalten
recite	recitera	recitere	reciteeren	rezitieren
				vorlesen
recognize	känna igen	genkende	erkennen	erkennen
recommend	rekommen-	anbefale	aanbevelen	empfehlen
	dera			
recover (get	tillfriskna	komme sig	herstellen	sich erholen
better)				
reflect (light)	reflektera	kaste tilbage	reflecteeren	zurückwerfen
				reflektieren
refuse to	vägra att	naegte at	weigeren te	sich weigern
				zu
regret	beklaga	beklage	spijten	bedauern
reject	förkasta	afvise	verwerpen	zurückweisen
rejoice (be glad)	glädja sig	glaede sig	zich verheugen	sich freuen
	fröjdas			
release (let go)	släppa	løslade	loslaten	loslassen
rely on	lita på	stole paa	vertrouwen op	sich verlassen
				auf
remain	förbliva	forblive	blijven	bleiben
remember	komma ihåg	mindes	zich herin-	sich erinnern
	erinra sig	huske	neren	
remind	påminna	erindre	herinneren	erinnern
renew	förnya	forny	vernieuwen	erneuern
repeat	upprepa	gentage	herhalen	wiederholen
report (news)	meddela	meddele	berichten	berichten
				melden
represent (stand	föreställa	forestille	voorstellen	vorstellen
for)				
resemble	likna	ligne	gelijken	*gleichen*
reserve (seat)	reservera	reservere	reserveeren	reservieren
respect	akta	agte	achten	achten
restrict	inskränka	indskraenke	beperken	einschränken
rest (take rest)	vila	hvile	rusten	ruhen
				sich ausruhen
reveal	uppenbara	aabenbare	openbaren	enthüllen
revenge oneself	hämnas	haevne sig	zich wreken	sich rächen
review (books)	recensera	anmelde	bespreken	besprechen
			recenseeren	rezensieren
revise	revidera	revidere	herzien	revidieren
revolt (rise)	uppresa sig	rejse sig	opstaan	sich erheben
reward	belöna	belønne	beloonen	belohnen
ride	rida	ride	rijden	reiten

ENGLISH	SWEDISH	DANISH	DUTCH	GERMAN
be right	hava rätt	have Ret	gelijk hebben	Recht haben
ring	ringa	ringe	bellen	klingeln
			luiden	läuten
ring	ringa	klinge	luiden	läuten
risk (incur risk)	riskera	risikere	gevaar loopen	Gefahr laufen
			riskeeren	riskieren
roast	steka	stege	braden	braten
roll ⎱	rulla	rulle	rollen	rollen
roll ⎰				
rot (decay)	ruttna	raadne	rotten	faulen
row	ro	ro	roeien	rudern
rub	gnida	gnide	wrijven	reiben
ruin	ruinera	ruinere	ruineeren	ruinieren
				verderben
run	löpa	løbe	rennen	rennen
			loopen	laufen
sail	segla	sejle	zeilen	segeln
save (from)	rädda (från)	redde (fra)	redden (van)	retten (von)
save (money)	spara	spare	sparen	sparen
saw	såga	save	zagen	sägen
say, tell	säga	sige	zeggen	sagen
scatter (sprinkle)	strö	strø	strooien	streuen
scrape	skrapa	skrabe	schrapen	schaben
scratch	riva	kradse	schrabben	kratzen
scream	skrika	skrige	gillen	schreien
screw	skruva	skrue	schroeven	schrauben
search	ransaka	ransage	fouilleeren	durchsuchen
secrete	avsöndra	afsondre	afscheiden	ausscheiden
see	se	se	zien	sehen
seek (look for)	söka	søge	zoeken	suchen
seem	tyckas	synes	schijnen	scheinen
seize (grasp)	gripa	gribe	grijpen	ergreifen
				packen
sell	sälja	saelge	verkoopen	verkaufen
send	sända	sende	zenden	senden
				schicken
separate	skilja	skille	separeeren	trennen
	separera	separere		
serve	tjäna	tjene	dienen	*dienen*
serve (meals)	servera	servere	serveeren	servieren
sew	sy	sy	naaien	nähen
shake	skaka	ryste	schudden	schütteln
share with	dela med	dele med	deelen met	teilen mit
shave	raka sig	barbere sig	zich scheren	sich rasieren
shine	skina	skinne	schijnen	scheinen
shoot	skjuta	skyde	schieten	schiessen
shoot dead	skjuta ihjäl	ihjelskyde	doodschieten	erschiessen

ENGLISH	SWEDISH	DANISH	DUTCH	GERMAN
show	visa	vise	toonen	zeigen
shut (close)	stänga	lukke	sluiten	schliessen
			dichtdoen	zumachen
shut in	instänga	indelukke	insluiten	einschliessen
side with	hålla med	holde med	partij kiezen	Partei nehmen
			voor	für
sigh	sucka	sukke	zuchten	seufzen
sign	underteckna	underskrive	onderteekenen	unterschreiben
				unterzeichnen
signify (mean)	betyda	betyde	beduiden	bedeuten
sin	synda	synde	zondigen	sündigen
sing	sjunga	synge	zingen	singen
sink	sänka	saenke	doen zinken	versenken
sink	sjunka	synke	zinken	sinken
sit	sitta	sidde	zitten	sitzen
sit down	sätta sig	saette sig	gaan zitten	sich setzen
skate	åka skridskor	løbe paa	schaatsen	Schlittschuh
		Skøjter	rijden	laufen
slander	baktala	bagtale	lasteren	verleumden
sleep	sova	sove	slapen	schlafen
slip	halka	glide ud	uitglijden	ausgleiten
smear	smörja	smøre	smeren	schmieren
smell	lukta	lugte	ruiken	riechen
smell of	lukta av	lugte af	rieken naar	riechen nach
smile	småle	smile	glimlachen	lächeln
smoke } *smoke*	röka	ryge	rooken	rauchen
sneeze	nysa	nyse	niezen	niesen
snore	snarka	snorke	snorken	schnarchen
snow	snöa	sne	sneeuwen	schneien
soak	blöta	bløde	weeken	einweichen
sob	snyfta	hulke	snikken	schluchzen
soil	smutsa	tilsøle	bezoedelen	beschmutzen
solve	upplösa	løse	oplossen	lösen
sow	så	saa	zaaien	säen
speak	tala	tale	spreken	sprechen
spell	stava	stave	spellen	buchstabieren
spend (money)	kasta ut	give ud	uitgeven	ausgeben
spend (time)	tillbringa	tilbringe	besteden	verbringen
			doorbrengen	zubringen
spit	spotta	spytte	spuwen	spucken
				speien
split	klyva	spalte	splijten	spalten
spread out	utbreda	sprede	uitbreiden	ausbreiten
squeeze out	pressa	trykke ud	uitpersen	auspressen
stand	stå	staa	staan	stehen

ENGLISH	SWEDISH	DANISH	DUTCH	GERMAN
stay (reside with)	stanna hos	bo	logeeren	wohnen bei
steal	stjäla	stjaele	stelen	stehlen
stick (glue)	klibba	klaebe	kleven	kleben
stimulate	stimulera	stimulere	aansporen	anregen stimulieren
sting	sticka	stikke	steken	stechen
stink	stinka	stinke	stinken	stinken
stop (cause to stop)	stoppa	stoppe	aanhouden	anhalten
stop (make a halt)	stanna	standse	stoppen	anhalten
strike (be on strike)	stryka	strejke	staken	streiken
stroke (caress)	strejka	stryge	strijken	streicheln
struggle	streta	kaempe	vechten	ringen
study	studera	studere	studeeren	studieren
subtract	afdraga subtrahera	fradrage subtrahere	aftrekken	abziehen subtrahieren
succeed (be successful in doing)	lyckas	lykkes	gelukken	gelingen glücken
suck	suga	suge	zuigen	saugen
suffer (from)	lida (av)	lide (af)	lijden (aan)	leiden (an)
suit (be fitting)	passa	passe	passen	passen
support (back up)	understödja	understøtte	ondersteunen	unterstützen
support (prop up)	stötta	støtte	steunen	stützen
suppose (assume)	antaga	antage	aannemen	annehmen
surprise (take by surprise)	överraska	overraske	verrassen	überraschen
surpass	överträffa	overgaa	overtreffen	übertreffen
surround	omgiva	omgive	omringen	umgeben
swear (take oath)	svärja	svaerge	zweren	schwören
swear (curse)	svära	bande	vloeken	fluchen
sweat	svettas	svede	zweeten	schwitzen
sweep	sopa	feje	vegen	fegen kehren
swell	svullna	svulme	opzwellen	anschwellen
swim	simma	svømme	zwemmen	schwimmen
swing	svänga	svinge	schommelen	schwingen
sympathize	sympatisera	sympatisere	medevoelen	mitfühlen
take	taga	tage	nemen	nehmen
take away (remove)	taga bort	tage bort	wegnemen	wegnehmen
talk (chat)	prata	snakke	praten babbelen	plaudern schwatzen

ENGLISH	SWEDISH	DANISH	DUTCH	GERMAN
taste	smaka	smage	proeven	versuchen probieren
taste of	smaka på	smage af	smaken naar	schmecken nach
teach	lära	undervise	onderwijzen	lehren
tear	riva sönder	rive itu	verscheuren	zerreissen
tell (narrate)	berätta	fortaelle	vertellen	erzählen
test	prova	prøve	toetsen	prüfen
thank	tacka	takke	danken	*danken*
think (believe)	tänka	taenke	denken	glauben
think (ponder)	tänka efter	taenke efter	nadenken	nachdenken
threaten	hota	true	bedreigen	bedrohen
throw	kasta	kaste	werpen	werfen
thunder	åska	tordne	donderen	donnern
tickle	kittla	kilde	kittelen	kitzeln
tie (bind)	binda	binde	binden	binden
tolerate (endure)	tåla	taale	dulden	dulden leiden
touch	vidröra	berøre	(aan)raken	berühren
trade	handla	handle	handelen	handeln
translate	översätta	oversaette	vertalen	übersetzen
travel	resa	rejse	reizen	reisen
tread on	träda på	traede paa	treden op	treten auf
treat	traktera	behandle	behandelen	behandeln
tremble	darra	ryste	beven	zittern
turn over	vända	vende	wenden	wenden
type	maskinskriva	maskinskrive	typen	tippen
underline	understryka	understrege	onderstreepen	unterstreichen
understand (comprehend)	förstå	forstaa	verstaan begrijpen	verstehen begreifen
undertake	företaga	foretage	ondernemen	unternehmen
undress	kläda av sig	klaede sig af	ontkleeden	sich ausziehen
unpack	packa upp	pakke ud	uitpakken	auspacken
upset	stöta omkull	støde om	omverstooten	umstossen
urinate	kasta vatten	lade Vandet	urinieren	urinieren das Wasser abschlagen
use (employ)	bruka	bruge	gebruiken	gebrauchen
vaccinate	vaccinera	vaccinere pode	inenten vaccineeren	impfen
visit	besöka	besøge	bezoeken	besuchen
vomit	kräkas	kaste op	braken	sich erbrechen
vote	rösta	stemme	stemmen	stimmen
wait (for)	vänta (på)	vente (paa)	wachten (op)	warten (auf)
wake	väcka	vaekke	wekken	wecken
wake	vakna	vaagne op	ontwaken	erwachen

ENGLISH	SWEDISH	DANISH	DUTCH	GERMAN
go for a walk	promenera	spadsere	wandelen	spazieren gehen
				bummeln
wander about	fara omkring	strejfe om	omzwerven	umherschwei-
				fen
want to	vilja	ville	willen	wollen
warn	varna	advare	waarschuwen	warnen
wash	tvätta	vaske	wasschen	waschen
wash	tvätta sig	vaske sig	zich wasschen	sich waschen
waste (food,	slösa	spilde	verkwisten	vergeuden
money, etc.)				verschwenden
wave (hand)	vinka	vinke	wenken	winken
wear (clothes)	bära	have paa	dragen	tragen
weave	väva	vaeve	weven	weben
weep	gråta	graede	weenen	weinen
weigh } *weigh*	väga	veje	wegen	wiegen
whisper	viska	hviske	fluisteren	flüstern
whistle	vissla	fløjte	fluiten	pfeifen
win	vinna	vinde	winnen	gewinnen
wind around	vinda	vinde	winden	winden
wind up (spring)	draga upp	traekke op	opwinden	aufziehen
wish	önska	ønske	wenschen	wünschen
wonder	undra	undre sig	zich verwon-	sich wundern
			deren	
work	arbeta	arbejde	werken;	arbeiten
			arbeiden	
worship	dyrka	dyrke	vereeren	verehren
be worth	vara värd	vaere vaerd	waard zijn	wert sein
wrap up	inpacka	pakke ind	inpakken	einpacken
write	skriva	skrive	schrijven	schreiben
be wrong	hava orätt	have Uret	ongelijk	Unrecht haben
			hebben	
yawn	gäspa	gabe	gapen	gähnen
yield (give way)	giva efter för	give efter	toegeven	nachgeben

6. ADVERBS

a) PLACE AND MOTION

above, upstairs	ovanför	ovenpaa	boven	oben
away	bort	bort	weg	weg
				fort
back	tillbaka	tilbage	terug	zurück
behind	bakom	bagefter	achter	hinten

ENGLISH	SWEDISH	DANISH	DUTCH	GERMAN
below, down- stairs	nedanför	nedenunder	beneden	unten
down (wards)	ned	nedad	naar beneden	hinab nach unten
elsewhere	annorstädes	andetstets	elders	anderswo
everywhere	överallt	overalt	overal	überall
far	långt	langt	ver	weit
forward	framåt	fremad	voorwaarts	vorwärts
hence	härifrån	herfra	van hier	von hier
here	här	her	hier	hier
hither	hit	hid	hierheen	hierher
home (wards)	hem	hjem	naar huis	nach Hause
at home	hemma	hjemme	thuis	zu Hause
inside	innanför	indenfor	binnen	drinnen
near	nära	naer	dichtbij	nah
nowhere	ingenstädes	intetsteds	nergens	nirgends
out	ut	ud	uit	aus
outside	utanför	udenfor	buiten	draussen
past	förbi	forbi	voorbij	vorbei
somewhere	någonstädes	nogensteds	ergens	irgendwo
thence	därifrån	derfra	vandaar	von dort
there	där	der	daar	dort
thither	dit	derhen	daarheen	dorthin
through	igenom	igennem	door	hindurch
to the left	till vänster	til venstre	links	links
to the right	till höger	til højre	rechts	rechts
underneath	inunder	derunder	daaronder	darunter
upward	uppät	opad	op naar boven	hinauf nach oben

b) TIME

afterward	efteråt	derefter	naderhand	nachher
again	igen	igen	weder	wieder
ago	för ... sedan	for ... siden	geleden	vor
already	redan	allerede	reeds	schon bereits
always	alltid	altid	altijd	immer stets
as soon as	så snart som	saa snart som	zoodra als	so bald als
at first	först	først	vooreerst	zuerst
at last	ändtligen	endelig	eindelijk	endlich
at once	genast	straks	terstond opeens	sofort sogleich
at present	närvarande	nu for Tiden	tegenwoordig	gegenwärtig
constantly	beständig	bestandig	voortdurend	beständig fortwährend

ENGLISH	SWEDISH	DANISH	DUTCH	GERMAN
early	tidigt	tidligt	vroeg	früh zeitig
ever	någonsin	nogensinde	ooit	je
formerly	fordom	forhen	vroeger	früher
from time to time	tid eften annan	fra Tid til anden	nu en dan	von Zeit zu Zeit
in future	framdeles	i Fremtiden	toekomstig	zukünftig
in the evening	i afton	om Aftenen	's avonds	abends am Abend
in the morning	i morgen	om Morgenen	's morgens	morgens am Morgen
in time	i tid	i Tide	op tijd	rechtzeitig beizeiten
last night	i går kvåll	sidste Nat	gisteravond	gestern abend
last week	förra veckan	sidste Uge	verleden week	letzte Woche
late	sent	sent	laat	spät
meanwhile	emellertid	imitlertid	intusschen	inzwischen unterdessen
monthly	månatligen	maanedlig	maandelijks	monatlich
never	aldrig	aldrig	nooit	nie
next week	nästa vecka	naeste Uge	aanstaande week	nächste Woche
not yet	ännu icke	endnu ikke	nog niet	noch nicht
now	nu	nu	nu	nun
nowadays	nu för tiden	nu til dags	heden ten dage	heutzutage
often	ofta	ofte	dikwijls	oft
once	engång	en Gang	eens	einst einmal
recently	nyligen	nylig	onlangs	neulich kürzlich
repeatedly	gång pa gång	gentagne Gange	herhaaldelijk	wiederholt
seldom	sällan	sjaelden	zelden	selten
sometimes	ibland	untertiden	soms	manchmal zuweilen
soon	snart	snart	spoedig	bald
still, yet	ännu	endnu	nog	noch
the day before yesterday	i förgår	iforgaars	eergisteren	vorgestern
the day after tomorrow	i övermorgon	iovermorgen	overmorgen	übermorgen
then (at that time)	då	da	toen	dann
thereafter	därpå	derpaa	daarop	darauf
this afternoon	i eftermiddag	i Eftermiddag	vanmiddag	heute nach- mittag

ENGLISH	SWEDISH	DANISH	DUTCH	GERMAN
this evening	i afton i kväll	iaften	vanavond	heute abend
this morning	i morse	imorges	vanochtend	heute morgen
today	idag	idag	heden vandaag	heute
tomorrow	imorgon	imorgen	morgen	morgen
tomorrow evening	i morgon afton	i Morgen Aften	morgen avond	morgen abend
tomorrow morning	i morgon bittida	i Morgen tidlig	morgen ochtend	morgen früh
tonight	i natt	inat	vannacht	heute nacht
weekly	engång i veckan	ugentlig	wekelijks	wöchentlich
yearly	årligen	aarlig	jaarlijks	jährlich
yesterday	igår	igaar	gisteren	gestern
what is the time?	vad är klockan?	hvad er Klokken?	hoe laat is het?	wie spät ist es? wieviel Uhr ist es?
it is five o'clock	klockan är fem	Klokken er fem	het is vijf uur	es ist fünf Uhr
it is half past five	klockan är halv sex	Klokken er halv seks	het is half zes	es ist halb sechs Uhr
it is a quarter to five	klockan är en kvart i fem	Klokken er et kvarter i fem	het is kwart voor vijven	es ist ein Viertel vor fünf Uhr (or: drei Viertel auf fünf)
it is a quarter past five	klockan är en kvart över fem	Klokken er et kvarter over fem	het is kwart over vijven	es ist ein Viertel nach fünf Uhr (or: ein Viertel auf sechs)
it is twenty minutes to five	klockan är tjugo minuter i fem	Klokken er tyve minuter i fem	het is twintig minuten voor vijven	es ist zwanzig Minuten vor fünf Uhr
it is twenty minutes past five	klockan är tjugo minuter över fem	Klokken er tyve minuter over fem	het is twintig minuten over vijven	es ist zwanzig Minuten nach fünf Uhr

c) Manner, Quantity, Affirmation and Negation

about	omkring	omtrent	ongeveer	ungefähr etwa
a little	en smula	lidt	een beetje	ein wenig ein bisschen

ENGLISH	SWEDISH	DANISH	DUTCH	GERMAN
almost	nästan	naesten	bijna	fast
				beinah
also, too	också	ogsaa	ook	auch
apparently	synbarligen	tilsyneladende	schijnbaar	scheinbar
				anscheinend
as a matter of	faktiskt	i Virkelighe-	feitelijk	tatsächlich
fact		den		wirklich
as much	så mycket	ligesaa meget	zooveel	so viel
at least	åtminstone	i det mindste	ten minste	wenigstens
				mindestens
at most	på det högsta	i det højeste	hoogstens	höchstens
badly	dåligt	daarligt	slecht	schlecht
besides	dessutom	desuden	bovendien	überdies
				zudem
by chance	tillfälligtvis	tilfaeldigvis	toevallig	zufällig
by heart	utantill	udenad	van buiten	auswendig
by no means	ingalunda	ingenlunde	geenszins	keineswegs
by the way	i förbigående	apropos	à propos	beiläufig ge-
		for Resten		sagt
chiefly	havudsakligen	hovedsagelig	voornaamelijk	hauptsächlich
completely	fullständigt	fulstaendig	volkomen	vollkommen
				vollständig
deliberately	avsikligt	forsaetligt	opzettelijk	absichtlich
				bewusst
directly	direkt	direkte	direct	direkt
easily	lätt	let	licht	leicht
enough	nog	nok	genoeg	genügend
even	även	selv	zelfs	selbst
exactly	precis	akkurat	precies	genau
exclusively	uteslutande	udelukkende	uitsluitend	ausschliesslich
extraordinarily	utomordentlig	overordentlig	buitengewoon	ungewöhnlich
extremely	ytterst	yderst	uiterst	höchst
				äusserst
fortunately	lyckligtvis	lykkeligvis	gelukkig	glücklicher-
				weise;
				zum Glück
gradually	småningom	gradvis	trapsgewijze	allmählich
				nach und nach
gratis	gratis	gratis	gratis	gratis
				umsonst
hardly	knappast	naeppe	nauwelijks	kaum
indeed	faktisk	faktisk	inderdaad	tatsächlich
				in der Tat
in vain	förgäves	forgaeves	tevergeefs	vergebens
less and less	mindre och	mindre og	minder en	immer weniger
	mindre	mindre	minder	

ENGLISH	SWEDISH	DANISH	DUTCH	GERMAN
loud	högt	højt	hard	laut
more and more	mer och mer	mer og mer	meer en meer	immer mehr
namely		(see viz., below)		
no	nej	nej	neen	nein
not	inte	ikke	niet	nicht
not at all	inte alls	slet ikke	in't geheel niet	durchaus nicht
not even	inte ens	ikke engang	niet eens	nicht einmal
obviously	påtagligen	øjensynlig	blijkbaar	offensichtlich augenschein- lich
of course	naturligtvis	naturligvis	natuurlijk	natürlich
only	bara	kun	slechts	nur
on the contrary	tvärtom	tvaertimod	integendeel	im Gegenteil
partly	delvis	delvis	deels	teilweise teils
perhaps	kanske	maaske	misschien	vielleicht
preferably	hellre	hellere	liever	lieber
probably	sannolikt	sandsynligvis	waarschijnlijk	wahrscheinlich
quickly	raskt fort	hurtigt	gauw spoedig	schnell rasch
quietly	lugnt	rolig	rustig	ruhig
really	verkligen	virkelig	werkelijk	wirklich
slowly	långsamt	langsomt	langzaam	langsam
so, thus	så	saa	zoo	so
so much the better	så mycket bättre	saa meget des bedre	des te beter	um so besser
so to speak	så at såga	saa at sige	om zoo te zeggen	so zu sagen
specially	särskilt	saerskilt	bijzonder	besonders
suddenly	plötsligt	pludseligt	plotseling	plötzlich
together	tillsammans	tilsammen	samen tegelijk	zusammen
too, too much	för	for	te	zu
undoubtedly	utan tvivel	uden Tvivl	ongetwijfeld	ohne Zweifel
unfortunately	olyckligen	ulykkeligvis	bij ongeluk	zum Unglück unglücklicher- weise
usually	vanligtvis	saedvanligvis	gewoonlijk	gewöhnlich
very	mycket	meget	zeer	sehr
viz.	nämlig	nemlig	namelijk te weten	nämlich das heisst
voluntarily	frivilligt	frivillig	vrijwillig	freiwillig
well	bra	godt	goed	gut
willingly	gärna	gerne	gaarne	gern
yes	ja jo	ja jo	ja	ja

7. SOCIAL USAGE

ENGLISH	SWEDISH	DANISH	DUTCH	GERMAN
Good morning!	God morgon!	God Morgen!	Goeden morgen!	Guten Morgen!
Good evening!	God afton!	God Aften!	Goeden avond!	Guten Abend!
Good night!	God natt!	God Nat!	Goeden nacht!	Gute Nacht!
Good day!	God dag!	God Dag!	Goeden dag!	Guten Tag!
Good-bye!	Adjö!	Farvel!	Tot ziens!	Auf Wiedersehen!
Good health!	Skål!	Skaal!	Proost!	Prosit!
Thank you! (accepting offer)	Ja, Tack!	Ja, Tak!	Alstublieft! Graag!	Bitte! Bitte schön!
No, thank you! (refusing offer)	Nej, Tack!	Nej, Tak!	Dank U! Nee, dank U!	Danke! Danke schön!
Thanks! (for favor done)	Tack!	Tak!	Dank U!	Danke!
Don't mention it!	Ingen orsak!	Aa jeg beder!	Alstublieft!	Bitte! Bitte schön!
Excuse me!	Ursäkta!	Undskyld mig!	Excuseer!	Entschuldigen Sie!
I beg your pardon!	Förlåt!	Omforladelse!	Pardon!	Verzeihung!
Please, show me . . .	Var så god och visa mig . . . !	Vaer saa god at vise mig . . . !	Wijs mij . . . alstublieft!	Bitte, zeigen Sie mir . . . !
How are you?	Hur står det till?	Hvordan har De det?	Hoe gaat het?	Wie geht's (Ihnen)?
Very well, thank you	Tack, utmärkt	Tak, udmaerket	Goed, dank U	Gut, danke
Come in!	Stig in!	Kom ind!	Binnen!	Herein!

Basic Vocabularies for the Romance Languages

ROMANCE WORD LISTS

1. NOUNS

a) CLIMATE AND SCENERY

ENGLISH	FRENCH	SPANISH	PORTU-GUESE	ITALIAN
air	l'air (m)	el aire	o ar	l'aria
bank (of river)	la rive	la orilla	a margem	la riva
bay	la baie	la bahía	a baía	la baia
beach	la plage	la playa	a praia	la spiaggia
cape	le cap	el cabo	o cabo	il capo
cave	la caverne	la cueva	a caverna	la caverna
climate	le climat	el clima	o clima	il clima
cloud	le nuage	la nube	a nuvem	la nube
coast	la côte	la costa	a costa	la costa
country (not town)	la campagne	el campo	o campo	la campagna
current	le courant	la corriente	a corrente	la corrente
darkness	l'obscurité (f)	la obscuridad	a escuridão	l'oscurità (f)
desert	le désert	el desierto	o deserto	il deserto
dew	la rosée	el rocío	o orvalho	la rugiada
dust	la poussière	el polvo	o pó	la polvere
earth	la terre	la tierra	a terra	la terra
east	l'est (m)	el este	o leste	l'est (m)
field	le champ	el campo	o campo	il campo
foam	l'écume (f)	la espuma	a espuma	la schiuma
forest	la forêt	el bosque	a floresta	il bosco
frost	la gelée	la helada	a geada	il gelo
grass	l'herbe (f)	la hierba	a erva	l'erba
hail	la grêle	el granizo	o granizo	la grandine
hay	le foin	el heno	o feno	il fieno
hill	la colline	la colina	a colina	la collina
horizon	l'horizon (m)	el horizonte	o horizonte	l'orizzonte (m)
ice	la glace	el hielo	o gêlo	il ghiaccio
island	l'île (f)	la isla	a ilha	l'isola
lake	le lac	el lago	o lago	il lago
light	la lumière	la luz	a luz	la luce
lightning	l'éclair (m)	el relámpago	o relâmpago	il fulmine
meadow	le pré	el prado	o prado	il prato

ENGLISH	FRENCH	SPANISH	PORTU-GUESE	ITALIAN
mist	le brouillard	la niebla	a neblina	la nebbia
moon	la lune	la luna	a lua	la luna
full moon	la pleine lune	la luna llena	a lua cheia	il plenilunio
mountain	la montagne	la montaña	a montanha	la montagna
mouth (river)	l'embouchure (f)	la desemboca-dura	a foz	l'imboccatura
mud (river, etc.)	la vase	el barro	o lôdo	il fango
north	le nord	el norte	o norte	il nord
peninsula	la péninsule	la península	a península	la penisola
plain	la plaine	el llano	a planície	il piano
pond	l'étang (m)	el estanque	a lagôa	lo stagno
rain	la pluie	la lluvia	a chuva	la pioggia
rainbow	l'arc-en-ciel (m)	el arco iris	o arco iris	l'arcobaleno
river (large)	le fleuve	el río	o rio	il fiume
rock	le rocher	la roca	a rocha	lo scoglio
sand	le sable	la arena	a areia	la sabbia
sea	la mer	el mar	o mar	il mare
shadow	l'ombre (f)	la sombra	a sombra	l'ombra
sky	le ciel	el cielo	o céu	il cielo
snow	la neige	la nieve	a neve	la neve
south	le sud	el sur	o sul	il sud
spring (water)	la source	la fuente	a nascente	la sorgente
star	l'étoile (f)	la estrella	a estrêla	la stella
storm	la tempête	la tormenta	a tempestade	il temporale
straits	le détroit	el estrecho	o estreito	lo stretto
stream	le ruisseau	el arroyo	o riacho	il ruscello
sun	le soleil	el sol	o sol	il sole
thunder	le tonnerre	el trueno	o trovão	il tuono
tide	la marée	la marea	a maré	la marea
high tide	la marée haute	la pleamar	a preamar	l'alta marea
low tide	la marée basse	la bajamar	a baixamar	la bassa marea
town	la ville	la ciudad	a cidade	la città
valley	la vallée	el valle	o vale	la valle
view	la vue	la vista	a vista	la vista
village	le village	la aldea	a aldeia	il villaggio
vineyard	le vignoble	la viña	a vinha	la vigna
water	l'eau (f)	el agua (f)	a água	l'acqua
waterfall	la cascade	la cascada	a cascata	la cascata
wave	la vague	la ola	a onda	l'onda
weather	le temps	el tiempo	o tempo	il tempo
west	l'ouest (m)	el oeste	o oeste	l'ovest (m)

b) HUMAN BODY

ankle	la cheville	el tobillo	o tornozelo	la caviglia
arm	le bras	el brazo	o braço	il braccio
				le braccia (pl.)

ENGLISH	FRENCH	SPANISH	PORTU-GUESE	ITALIAN
artery	l'artère (f)	la arteria	a artéria	l'arteria
back	le dos	la espalda	o dorso	il dorso
beard	la barbe	la barba	a barba	la barba
belly	le ventre	el vientre	o ventre	il ventre
bladder	la vessie	la vejiga	a bexiga	la vescica
blood	le sang	la sangre	o sangue	il sangue
body	le corps	el cuerpo	o corpo	il corpo
bone	l'os (m)	el hueso	o ôsso	l'osso le ossa (pl.)
brain	la cervelle	el cerebro	o cérebro	il cervello
breast	le sein	el seno	o seio	il seno
calf	le mollet	la pantorrilla	a barriga	il polpaccio
cheek	la joue	la mejilla	a face	la guancia
chest	la poitrine	el pecho	o peito	il petto
chin	le menton	la barba	a barba	il mento
cold	le rhume	el resfriado	a constipação	il raffreddore
complexion	le teint	la tez	a tez	la carnagione
cough	la toux	la tos	a tosse	la tosse
disease	la maladie	la enfermedad	a enfermidade	la malattia
ear	l'oreille (f)	la oreja	a orelha	l'orecchio
elbow	le coude	el codo	o cotovêlo	il gomito
eye	l'œil (m) les yeux (pl.)	el ojo	o ôlho	l'occhio
eyebrow	le sourcil	la ceja	a sobrancelha	il sopracciglio
eyelid	la paupière	el párpado	a palpebra	la palpebra
face	le visage	la cara	a cara	la faccia
fever	la fièvre	la fiebre	a febre	la febbre
finger	le doigt	el dedo	o dedo	il dito le dita (pl.)
fist	le poing	el puño	o punho	il pugno
flesh	la chair	la carne	a carne	la carne
foot	le pied	el pie	o pé	il piede
forehead	le front	la frente	a testa	la fronte
gum	la gencive	la encía	a gengiva	la gengiva
hair (of head)	les cheveux	el cabello	o cabelo	i capelli
hand	la main	la mano	a mão	la mano
head	la tête	la cabeza	a cabeça	la testa
health	la santé	la salud	a saúde	la salute
heart	le cœur	el corazón	o calcanhar	il cuore
heel	le talon	el talón	o tacão	il tallone
hip	la hanche	la cadera	o quadril	l'anca
jaw	la mâchoire	la quijada	a queixada	la mascella
kidney	le rein	el riñón	o rim	il rene
knee	le genou	la rodilla	o joelho	il ginocchio le ginocchia (pl.)
leg	la jambe	la pierna	a perna	la gamba

ENGLISH	FRENCH	SPANISH	PORTU-GUESE	ITALIAN
lip	la lèvre	el labio	o lábio	il labbro
				le labbra (pl.)
liver	le foie	el hígado	o fígado	il fegato
lung	le poumon	el pulmón	o pulmão	il polmone
moustache	la moustache	el bigote	o bigode	i baffi
mouth	la bouche	la boca	a bôca	la bocca
muscle	le muscle	el músculo	o músculo	il muscolo
nail	l'ongle (m)	la uña	a unha	l'unghia
neck	le cou	el cuello	o pescoço	il collo
nerve	le nerf	el nervio	o nervo	il nervo
nose	le nez	la nariz	o nariz	il naso
palm	la paume	la palma	a palma	la palma
pulse	le pouls	el pulso	o pulso	il polso
rib	la côte	la costilla	a costella	la costola
shoulder	l'épaule (f)	el hombro	o hombro	la spalla
skeleton	le squelette	el esqueleto	o esqueleto	lo scheletro
skin	la peau	la piel	a pele	la pelle
skull	le crâne	el cráneo	o crânio	il cranio
sole	la plante	la planta	a planta	la pianta
spine	l'épine dorsale (f)	la espina dorsal	a espinha dorsal	la spina dorsale
stomach	l'estomac (m)	el estómago	o estômago	lo stomaco
tear	la larme	la lágrima	a lágrima	la lagrima
temple	la tempe	la sien	a fonte	la tempia
thigh	la cuisse	el muslo	a coxa	la coscia
throat (internal)	la gorge	la garganta	a garganta	la gola
thumb	le pouce	el pulgar	o polegar	il pollice
toe	l'orteil (m)	el dedo del pie	o dedo do pé	il dito del piede
tongue	la langue	la lengua	a língua	la lingua
tooth	la dent	el diente	o dente	il dente
vein	la veine	la vena	a veia	la vena
wound	la blessure	la herida	a ferida	la ferita
wrist	le poignet	la muñeca	o pulso	il polso

c) ANIMALS

animal	l'animal (m)	el animal	o animal	l'animale (m)
ant	la fourmi	la hormiga	a formiga	la formica
beak	le bec	el pico	o bico	il becco
bear	l'ours (m)	el oso	o urso	l'orso
bee	l'abeille (f)	la abeja	a abelha	l'ape (f)
bird	l'oiseau (m)	el pájaro	o pássaro	l'uccello
blackbird	le merle	el mirlo	o melro	il merlo
bull	le taureau	el toro	o touro	il toro

ENGLISH	FRENCH	SPANISH	PORTU-GUESE	ITALIAN
butterfly	le papillon	la mariposa	a borboleta	la farfalla
calf	le veau	el ternero	a vitela	il vitello
cat	le chat	el gato	o gato	il gatto
caterpillar	la chenille	la oruga	a lagarta	il bruco
claw (cat, etc.)	la griffe	la garra	a garra	l'artiglio
cock	le coq	el gallo	o galo	il gallo
cockroach	le cafard	la cucaracha	la barata	lo scarafaggio
cod	la morue	el bacalao	o bacalhau	il merluzzo
cow	la vache	la vaca	a vaca	la vacca
crayfish	l'écrevisse (f)	el cangrejo	o caranguejo	il gambero
crow	le corbeau	el cuervo	o corvo	il corvo
dog	le chien	el perro	o cão	il cane
donkey	l'âne (m)	el burro	o burro	il ciuco
duck	le canard	el pato	o pato	l'anitra
eagle	l'aigle (m)	el águila (f)	a águia	l'aquila
eel	l'anguille (f)	la anguila	a enguia	l'anguilla
elephant	l'éléphant (m)	el elefante	o elefante	l'elefante (m)
feather	la plume	la pluma	a pena	la penna
fin	la nageoire	la aleta	a barbatana	la pinna
fish	le poisson	el pez	o peixe	il pesce
flea	la puce	la pulga	a pulga	la pulce
fly	la mouche	la mosca	a môsca	la mosca
fox	le renard	el zorro	a raposa	la volpe
frog	la grenouille	la rana	a rã	il ranocchio
gill	la branchie	la branquia	o barranco	la branchia
goat	la chèvre	la cabra	a cabra	la capra
goose	l'oie (f)	el ganso	o ganso	l'oca
grasshopper	la sauterelle	el saltamontes	o gafanhoto	la cavaletta
hare	le lièvre	la liebre	a lebre	la lepre
hen	la poule	la gallina	a galhina	la gallina
herring	le hareng	el arenque	o arenque	l'aringa
hoof	le sabot	la pezuña	o casco	lo zoccolo
horn	la corne	el cuerno	o corno	il corno
horse	le cheval	el caballo	o cavalo	il cavallo
insect	l'insecte (m)	el insecto	o insecto	l'insetto
lamb	l'agneau (m)	el cordero	o cordeiro	l'agnello
lark	l'alouette (f)	la alondra	a cotovia	l'allodola
lion	le lion	el león	o leão	il leone
lobster (spiny)	la langouste	la langosta	a lagosta	l'aragosta
louse	le pou	el piojo	o piolho	il pidocchio
mackerel	le maquereau	el escombro	a cavala	lo sgombro
monkey	le singe	el mono	o macaco	la scimmia
mosquito	le moustique	el mosquito	o mosquito	la zanzara
mouse	la souris	el ratón	o rato	il topo
mule	le mulet	el mulo	a mula	il mulo
mussel	la moule	la almeja	o mexilhão	il pidocchio

ENGLISH	FRENCH	SPANISH	PORTU-GUESE	ITALIAN
nightingale	le rossignol	el ruiseñor	o rouxinol	l'usignuolo
octopus	la pieuvre	el pulpo	o polvo	il polpo
owl	le hibou	el buho	o mocho	il gufo
ox	le bœuf	el buey	o boi	il bue
oyster	l'huître (f)	la ostra	a ostra	l'ostrica
parrot	le perroquet	el loro	o papagaio	il pappagallo
partridge	la perdrix	la perdiz	a perdiz	la pernice
pig	le cochon	el cerdo	o porco	il porco
pigeon	le pigeon	el pichón	o pombo	il piccione
pike	le brochet	el sollo	o lúcio	il luccio
rabbit	le lapin	el conejo	o coelho	il coniglio
rat	le rat	la rata	o rato	il sorcio
salmon	le saumon	el salmón	o salmão	il salmone
scale	l'écaille (f)	la escama	a escama	la squama
sea gull	la mouette	la gaviota	a gaivota	il gabbiano
seal	le phoque	la foca	a foca	la foca
shark	le requin	el tiburón	o tubarão	il pescecane
sheep	le mouton	la oveja	a ovelha	la pecora
skin (fur)	la peau	la piel	a pele	la pelle
slug	la limace	la babosa	a lesma	la lumaca
snail	le colimaçon	el caracol	o caracol	la chiocciola
snake	le serpent	la serpiente	a serpente	il serpente
	la couleuvre	la culebra	a cobra	la biscia
sole	la sole	el lenguado	o linguado	la sogliola
sparrow	le moineau	el gorrión	o pardal	il passero
spider	l'araignée	la araña	a aranha	il ragno
squirrel	l'écureuil (m)	la ardilla	o esquilo	lo scoiattolo
swallow	l'hirondelle (f)	la golondrina	a andorinha	la rondine
tail	la queue	la cola	a cauda	la coda
tiger	le tigre	el tigre	o tigre	la tigre
toad	le crapaud	el sapo	o sapo	il rospo
trout	la truite	la trucha	a truta	la trota
tuna, tunny	le thon	el atún	o atum	il tonno
wasp	la guêpe	la avispa	a vespa	la vespa
whale	la baleine	la ballena	a baleia	la balena
wing	l'aile (f)	el ala (f)	a asa	l'ala
wolf	le loup	el lobo	o lobo	il lupo
worm	le ver	el gusano	o bicho	il verme

d) FRUIT AND TREES

almond	l'amande (f)	la almendra	a amêndoa	la mandorla
apple	la pomme	la manzana	a maçã	la mela
apple tree	le pommier	el manzano	a macieira	il melo
apricot	l'abricot (m)	el albaricoque	o damasco	l'albicocca

ENGLISH	FRENCH	SPANISH	PORTU-GUESE	ITALIAN
ash	le frêne	el fresno	o freixo	il frassino
bark	l'écorce (f)	la corteza	a casca	la corteccia
beech	le hêtre	el haya (f)	a faia	il faggio
berry	la baie	la baya	a baga	la bacca
birch	le bouleau	el abedul	o vidoeiro	la betulla
branch	la branche	la rama	o ramo	il ramo
cherry	la cerise	la cereza	a cereja	la ciliegia
cherry tree	le cerisier	el cerezo	a cerejeira	il ciliegio
chestnut	la châtaigne	la castaña	a castanha	la castagna
	le marron			
chestnut tree	le châtaignier	el castaño	o castanheiro	il castagno
currant	la groseille	la grosella	a groselha	il ribes
cypress	le cyprès	el ciprés	o cipreste	il cipresso
date	la datte	el dátil	a tâmara	il dattero
elm	l'orme (m)	el olmo	o olmo	l'olmo
fig	la figue	el higo	o figo	il fico
fig tree	le figuier	la higuera	a figueira	il fico
fir	le sapin	el abeto	o abeto	l'abete (m)
fruit	le fruit	la fruta	a fruta	la frutta
grapes	le raisin	la uva	a uva	l'uva
hazelnut	la noisette	la avellana	a avelã	la nocciuola
laurel	le laurier	el laurel	o loureiro	l'alloro
leaf	la feuille	la hoja	a fôlha	la foglia
lemon	le citron	el limón	o limão	il limone
lime tree	le tilleul	el tilo	a tília	il tiglio
melon	le melon	el melón	o melão	il melone
mulberry tree	le mûrier	la morera	a amoreira	il gelso
oak	le chêne	el roble	o carvalho	la quercia
olive	l'olive (f)	la aceituna	a azeitona	l'oliva
olive tree	l'olivier (m)	el olivo	a oliveira	l'olivo
orange	l'orange (f)	la naranja	a laranja	l'arancia
orange tree	l'orangier (m)	el naranjo	a laranjeira	l'arancio
peach	la pêche	el melocotón	o pêssego	la pesca
pear	la poire	la pera	a pera	la pera
pear tree	le poirier	el peral	a pereira	il pero
pine	le pin	el pino	o pinheiro	il pino
pineapple	l'ananas (m)	la piña	o ananás	l'ananasso
plum	la prune	la ciruela	a ameixa	la susina
poplar	le peuplier	el álamo	o álamo	il pioppo
raspberry	la framboise	la frambuesa	a framboesa	il lampone
root	la racine	la raíz	a raiz	la radice
strawberry	la fraise	la fresa	o morango	la fragola
tree	l'arbre (m)	el árbol	a árvore	l'albero
tree trunk	le tronc	el tronco	o tronco	il tronco
vine	la vigne	la parra	a videira	la vite
walnut	la noix	la nuez	a noz	la noce

ENGLISH	FRENCH	SPANISH	PORTU-GUESE	ITALIAN
walnut tree	le noyer	el nogal	a nogueira	il noce
willow	le saule	el sauce	o salgueiro	il salcio

e) Cereals and Vegetables

ENGLISH	FRENCH	SPANISH	PORTU-GUESE	ITALIAN
artichoke	l'artichaut (m)	la alcachofa	a alcachofa	il carciofo
asparagus	l'asperge (f)	el espárrago	o aspargo	l'asparago
barley	l'orge (f)	la cebada	a cevada	l'orzo
bean (broad)	la fève	el haba (f)	a fava	la fava
bean (kidney)	le haricot	la judía	o feijão	il fagiuolo
cabbage	le choux	la col	a couve	il cavolo
carrot	la carotte	la zanahoria	a cenoura	la carota
cauliflower	le chou-fleur	la coliflor	a couve flor	il cavolfiore
celery	le céleri	el apio	o aipo	il sedano
chives	la ciboulette	la cebollana	o cebolinho	la cipollina
corn	*(see* maize, *below)*			
cucumber	le concombre	el pepino	o pepino	il cetriolo
eggplant	l'aubergine (f)	la berenjena	a beringela	la melanzana
garlic	l'ail (m)	el ajo	o alho	l'aglio
herb	l'herbe (f)	la hierba	a herva	l'erba
horse-radish	le raifort	el rábano picante	o rabo de cavalo	la barbaforte
lentil	la lentille	la lenteja	a lentilha	la lenticchia
lettuce	la laitue	la lechuga	a alface	la lattuga
maize	le maïs	el maíz	o milho	il granturco
mint	la menthe	la menta	a hortelã	la menta
mushroom	le champignon	la seta	o cogumelo	il fungo
oats	l'avoine (f)	la avena	a aveia	l'avena
onion	l'oignon (m)	la cebolla	a cebola	la cipolla
parsley	le persil	el perejil	a salsa	il prezzemolo
pea	le pois	el guisante	a ervilha	il pisello
potato	la pomme de terre	la patata	a batata	la patata
pumpkin	le potiron	la calabaza	a abóbora	la zucca
radish	le radis	el rábano	o rábano	il ravanello
rice	le riz	el arroz	o arroz	il riso
rye	le seigle	el centeno	o centeio	la segale
sage	la sauge	la salvia	a salva	la salvia
seed	la graine	la semilla	a semente	il seme
spinach	les épinards (m)	la espinaca	o espinafre	gli spinacci
tomato	la tomate	el tomate	o tomate	il pomodoro
turnip	le navet	el nabo	o nabo	la rapa
wheat	le froment	el trigo	o trigo	il frumento

f) MATERIALS

ENGLISH	FRENCH	SPANISH	PORTU-GUESE	ITALIAN
brass	le laiton	el latón	o latão	l'ottone (m)
brick	la brique	el ladrillo	o tijolo	il mattone
chalk	la craie	la greda	a greda	la creta
clay	l'argile (f)	la arcilla	a argila	l'argilla
concrete	le béton	el hormigón	o formigão	il calcestruzzo
copper	le cuivre	el cobre	o cobre	il rame
cork	le liège	el corcho	a cortiça	il sughero
glass	le verre	el vidrio	o vidro	il vetro
gold	l'or (m)	el oro	o ouro	l'oro
iron	le fer	el hierro	o ferro	il ferro
lead	le plomb	el plomo	o chumbo	il piombo
leather	le cuir	el cuero	o couro	il cuoio
lime	la chaux	la cal	a cal	la calce
marble	le marbre	el mármol	o mármore	il marmo
metal	le métal	el metal	o metal	il metallo
rubber	le caoutchouc	el caucho	a borracha	la gomma
silver	l'argent (m)	la plata	a prata	l'argento
steel	l'acier (m)	el acero	o aço	l'acciaio
stone	la pierre	la piedra	a pedra	la pietra
tar	le goudron	el alquitrán	o alcatrão	il catrame
tin (metal)	l'étain (m)	el estaño	o estanho	lo stagno
tin (sheet)	le fer-blanc	la hojalata	a fôlha de lata	la latta
wood	le bois	la madera	a madeira	il legno

g) BUILDINGS

barn	la grange	el granero	o celeiro	il granaio
barracks	la caserne	el cuartel	o quartel	la caserna
bridge	le pont	el puente	a ponte	il ponte
building	le bâtiment	el edificio	o edifício	l'edificio
castle	le château	el castillo	o castelo	il castello
cathedral	la cathédrale	la catedral	a catedral	il duomo
cemetery	le cimetière	el cementerio	o cemitério	il cimitero
church	l'église (f)	la iglesia	a igreja	la chiesa
consulate	le consulat	el consulado	o consulado	il consolato
corner (street)	le coin	la esquina	a esquina	il canto
courtyard	la cour	el patio	o pátio	il cortile
dock	le bassin	la dársena	a doca	il bacino
embassy	l'ambassade (f)	la embajada	a embaixada	l'ambasciata
factory	l'usine (f)	la fábrica	a fábrica	la fabbrica
farm	la ferme	la granja	a granja	la fattoria

ENGLISH	FRENCH	SPANISH	PORTU-GUESE	SPANISH
fountain	la fontaine	la fuente	a fonte	la fontana
hospital	l'hôpital (m)	el hospital	o hospital	l'ospedale (m)
hut	la hutte	la cabaña	a cabana	la capanna
inn	l'auberge (f)	la posada	a estalagem	l'osteria
lane (town)	la ruelle	la calleja	o beco	il vicolo
library	la bibliothèque	la biblioteca	a biblioteca	la biblioteca
market	le marché	el mercado	o mercado	il mercato
ministry	le ministère	el ministerio	o ministério	il ministero
museum	le musée	el museo	o museu	il museo
palace	le palais	el palacio	o palácio	il palazzo
path (country)	le sentier	la senda	a caminho	il sentiero
pavement	le trottoir	la acera	o passeio	il marciapiede
pier	le jetée	el muelle	o molhe	il molo
police station	le commissariat le poste	la comisaría	a esquadra da polícia	la questura
port	le port	el puerto	o porto	il porto
prison	la prison	la prisión	a prisão	la prigione
road	le chemin	la carretera	a estrada	il cammino
(highway)	la route	la vía	o via	la via
school	l'école (f)	la escuela	a escola	la scuola
square	la place	la plaza	a praça	la piazza
stable (cattle)	l'étable (f)	la cuadra	o estábulo	la stalla
street	la rue	la calle	a rua	la strada
theater	le théâtre	el teatro	o teatro	il teatro
tower	la tour	la torre	a torre	la torre
town hall	l'hôtel de ville la mairie	el ayuntamiento	a câmara municipal	il municipio
university	l'université (f)	la universidad	a universidade	l'università (f)

b) THE FAMILY

aunt	la tante	la tía	a tia	la zia
boy	le garçon	el muchacho	o rapaz	il ragazzo
brother	le frère	el hermano	o irmão	il fratello
child	l'enfant (m.f.)	el (la) niño(a)	o (a) menino (a)	il (la) fanciullo (a)
Christian name	le prénom	el nombre de pila	o nome de baptismo	il nome di battesimo
cousin	le (la) cousin (e)	el (la) primo (a)	o (a) primo (a)	il (la) cugino (a)
daughter	la fille	la hija	a filha	la figlia
divorce	le divorce	el divorcio	o divórcio	il divorzio
family	la famille	la familia	a família	la famiglia
father	le père	el padre	o pai	il padre

ENGLISH	FRENCH	SPANISH	PORTU-GUESE	ITALIAN
gentleman	le monsieur	el señor	o senhor	il signore
girl	la fille *	la muchacha	a rapariga	la ragazza
	la jeune fille	la chica		
grandfather	le grand-père	el abuelo	o avô	il nonno
grandmother	la grand'mère	la abuela	a avó	la nonna
husband	le mari	el marido	o marido	il marito
	l'époux	el esposo	o espôso	lo sposo
lady	la dame	la señora	a senhora	la signora
man	l'homme	el hombre	o homem	l'uomo
marriage	le mariage	el matrimonio	o matrimónio	il matrimonio
mother	la mère	la madre	a mãe	la madre
parents	père et mère	padre y madre	pãe e mai	padre e madre
	les parents	los padres	os pais	i genitori
relation	le (la) parent (e)	el (la) pariente	o (a) parente	il (la) parente
sister	la sœur	la hermana	a irmã	la sorella
son	le fils	el hijo	o filho	il figlio
surname	le nom	el apellido	o apelido	il cognome
twins	les jumeaux	los gemelos	os gémeos	i gemelli
uncle	l'oncle	el tío	o tio	lo zio
wife	la femme	la mujer	a mulher	la moglie
	l'épouse	la esposa	a espôsa	
woman	la femme	la mujer	a mulher	la donna

i) DRESS AND TOILET

apron	le tablier	el delantal	o avental	il grembiale
boot	la botte	la bota	a bota	lo stivale
braces	les bretelles (f)	los tirantes	os suspensórios	le bretelle
brush	la brosse	el cepillo	a escôva	la spazzola
button	le bouton	el botón	o botão	il bottone
cigar	le cigare	el puro	o charuto	il sigaro
cigarette	la cigarette	el cigarillo	o cigarro	la sigaretta
cloth	l'êtoffe (f)	la tela	a fazenda	la stoffa
clothes	les vêtements (m)	la ropa	as roupas	gli abiti
collar	le faux-col	el cuello	o colarinho	il colletto
comb	le peigne	el peine	o pente	il pettine
cotton	le coton	el algodón	o algodão	il cotone
drawers (men's)	le caleçon	los calzoncillos	as ceroulas	le mutande
dress	la robe	el vestido	o vestido	l'abito

* *une fille* (a girl) may only be used in contrast to *un garçon* (a boy). In other situations use *une jeune fille*. *Fille* without the adjective signifies a prostitute.

ENGLISH	FRENCH	SPANISH	PORTU-GUESE	ITALIAN
fashion	la mode	la moda	a moda	la moda
glove	le gant	el guante	a luva	il guanto
handbag	la sacoche	el bolso	a bôlsa	la borsa
handkerchief	le mouchoir	el pañuelo	o lenço	il fazzoletto
hat	le chapeau	el sombrero	o chapéu	il cappello
jacket	le veston	la chaqueta	a jaqueta	la giacchetta
match	l'allumette (f)	la cerilla	o fósforo	il fiammifero
needle	l'aiguille (f)	la aguja	a agulha	l'ago
overcoat	le pardessus	el abrigo	o sobretudo	il soprabito
pin	l'épingle (f)	el alfiler	o alfinête	lo spillo
pipe	la pipe ·	la pipa	o cachimbo	la pipa
pocket	la poche	el bolsillo	a algibeira	la tasca
powder	la poudre	los polvos	o pó	la cipria
raincoat	l'imperméable (m)	el impermeable	o impermeável	l'impermeabile (m)
razor blade	la lame	la hoja de afeitar	a lamina	la lama
shirt	la chemise	la camisa	a camisa	la camicia
shoe	le soulier	el zapato	o sapato	la scarpa
shoelace	le lacet	el cordon	o atacador	il laccio
silk	la soie	la seda	a sêda	la seta
skirt	la jupe	la falda	a saia	la gonna
sleeve	la manche	la manga	a manga	la manica
soap	le savon	el jabón	o sabão	il sapone
sock	la chaussette	el calcetín	a peúga	il calzettino
spectacles	les lunettes (f)	las gafas	os óculos	gli occhiali
sponge	l'éponge (f)	la esponja	a esponja	la spugna
stick	la canne	el bastón	a bengala	il bastone
stocking	le bas	la media	a meia	la calza
suit	le complet	el traje	o fato	l'abito completo
tie	la cravate	la corbata	a gravata	la cravatta
toothbrush	la brosse à dents	el cepillo de dientes	a escôva dos dentes	la spazzolina da denti
trousers	le pantalon	los pantalones	as calças	i pantaloni
umbrella	le parapluie	el paraguas	o guarda-chuva	l'ombrello
waistcoat	le gilet	el chaleco	o colete	il panciotto
watch	la montre	el reloj	o relógio	l'orologio
wool	la laine	la lana	a lã	la lana

j) THE HOME

alarm clock	le réveil	el despertador	o despertador	la sveglia
armchair	le fauteuil	el sillón	a poltrona	la poltrona
ash	la cendre	la ceniza	a cinza	la cenere

ENGLISH	FRENCH	SPANISH	PORTU-GUESE	ITALIAN
ash tray	le cendrier	el cenicero	o cinzeiro	il portacenere
balcony	le balcon	el balcón	o balcão	il balcone
basement	le sous-sol	el sótano	a cave	il sottosuolo
basket	le panier	el cesto	o cesto	il paniere
bath	le bain	el baño	o banho	il bagno
bed	le lit	la cama	a cama	il letto
bedroom	la chambre à coucher	la alcoba	o quarto de dormir	la camera da letto
bell (door)	la sonnette	la campanilla	a campaínha	il campanello
blanket	la couverture	la manta	o cobertor	la coperta
blind	le store	la persiana	a persiana	la persiana
box	la boîte	la caja	a caixa	la scatola
broom	le balai	la escoba	a vassoura	la scopa
bucket	le seau	el balde	o balde	il secchio
candle	la bougie	la vela	a vela	la candela
carpet	le tapis	la alfombra	o tapete	il tappeto
ceiling	le plafond	el techo	o teto	il soffitto
chair	la chaise	la silla	a cadeira	la sedia
chamber pot	le vase de nuit	el vaso de noche	a bacia de cama	il vaso da notte
chimney	la cheminée	la chimenea	a chaminé	il camino
coal	le charbon	el carbón	o carvão	il carbone
corner	le coin	el rincón	o canto	l'angolo
cupboard	l'armoire (f)	el armario	o armário	l'armadio
curtain	le rideau	la cortina	a cortina	la cortina
cushion	le coussin	el cojín	a almofada	il cuscino
denatured alcohol	*(see* methylated spirit, *below)*			
door	la porte	la puerta	a porta	la porta
drawer	le tiroir	el cajón	a gaveta	il cassetto
flame	la flamme	la llama	a châma	la fiamma
flat	l'appartement (m)	el piso	o aposento	l'appartamento
floor	la plancher	el suelo	o soalho	il pavimento
flower	la fleur	la flor	a flor	il fiore
furniture	les meubles (m)	los muebles	os móveis	i mobili
garden	le jardin	el jardín	o jardim	il giardino
ground floor	le rez-de-chaussée	la planta baja	o rés-do-chão	il pianterreno
hook	le crochet	el gancho	o gancho	l'uncino
house	la maison	la casa	a casa	la casa
iron (flat)	le fer à repasser	la plancha	o ferro de engomar	il ferro da stirare
kerosene	*(see* paraffin, *below)*			
key	la clef	la llave	a chave	la chiave

ENGLISH	FRENCH	SPANISH	PORTU-GUESE	ITALIAN
kitchen	la cuisine	la cocina	a cozinha	la cucina
ladder	l'échelle (f)	la escalera	a escada	la scala
lamp	la lampe	la lámpara	o candieiro	la lampada
lock	la serrure	la cerradura	a fechadura	la serratura
mattress	le matelas	el colchón	o colchão	il materasso
methylated spirit	l'alcool dénaturé (m)	el alcohol metílico	o alcool desnaturado	l'alcool denaturato
mirror	le miroir	el espejo	o espelho	lo specchio
pantry	le garde-manger	la despensa	a despensa	la dispensa
paraffin	le pétrole	el petróleo	o petróleo	il petrolio
picture	le tableau	el cuadro	o quadro	il quadro
pillow	l'oreiller (m)	la almohada	a almofada	il guanciale
pipe (water, etc.)	le tuyau	el tubo	o cano	il condotto
poker	le tisonnier	el atizador	o atiçador	l'attizzatoio
record (gramophone)	le disque	el disco	o disco	il disco
roof	le toit	el techado	o telhado	il tetto
room	la chambre la pièce	el cuarto la habitación	o quarto a camara	la camera la stanza
sheet	le drap	la sábana	o lençol	il lenzuolo
shovel	la pelle	la pala	a pá	la pala
sideboard	le buffet	el aparador	o aparador	la credenza
sitting room	le salon	la sala	a sala	il salotto
smoke	la fumée	el humo	o fumo	il fumo
stairs	l'escalier (m)	la escalera	a escada	la scala
story, storey	l'étage (m)	el piso	o andar	il piano
stove	le poêle	la estufa	a estufa	la stufa
switch (electric)	le commutateur	el conmutador	o comutador	l'interruttore
table	la table	la mesa	a mesa	la tavola
tap	le robinet	el grifo	a torneira	il rubinetto
toilet (W.C.)	le cabinet	el retrete	o retrete	il gabinetto
towel	la serviette	la toalla	a toalha	l'asciugamano
vacuum cleaner	l'aspirateur (m)	el aspirador	o aspirador	l'aspiratore (m)
wall (house)	le mur	el muro	o muro	il muro
wall (room)	la paroi	la pared	a parede	la parete
window	la fenêtre	la ventana	a janela	la finestra

k) FOOD AND DRINK

bacon	le lard	el tocino	o toucinho	il lardo
beef	le bœuf	la carne de vaca	a carne de vaca	il manzo

ENGLISH	FRENCH	SPANISH	PORTU-GUESE	ITALIAN
beer	la bière	la cerveza	a cerveja	la birra
beverage	la boisson	la bebida	a bebida	la bevanda
biscuit	le biscuit	el bizcocho	o biscoito	il biscotto
bread	le pain	el pan	o pão	il pane
breakfast	le petit déjeuner	el desayuno	o pequeno almôço	la prima colazione
brandy	le cognac	el coñac	a aguardente	il cognac
butter	le beurre	la mantequilla	a manteiga	il burro
cake	le gâteau	el pastel	o bolo	la torta
cheese	le fromage	el queso	o queijo	il formaggio
chicken	le poulet	el pollo	o frango	il pollo
chop	la côtelette	la chuleta	a costeleta	la costoletta
coffee	le café	el café	o café	il caffè
cream	la crème	la crema	a nata	la panna
dessert	le dessert	el postre	a sobremesa	la frutta
dinner	le dîner	la comida	o jantar	il pranzo
egg	l'œuf (m)	el huevo	o ôvo	l'uovo
fried eggs	des œufs sur le plat	huevos fritos	óvos assados	uova al tegame
soft-boiled eggs	des œufs à la coque	huevos pasados por agua	óvos quentes	uova sode
fat	la graisse	la grasa	a gordura	il grasso
flour	la farine	la harina	a farinha	la farina
ham	le jambon	el jamón	o prezunto	il prosciutto
honey	le miel	la miel	o mel	il miele
jam	la confiture	la jalea	a compota	la marmellata
lunch	le déjeuner	el almuerzo	o almôço	la colazione
meal	le repas	la comida	a refeição	il pasto
meat	la viande	la carne	a carne	la carne
milk	le lait	la leche	o leite	il latte
mustard	la moutarde	la mostaza	a mostarda	la mostarda
mutton	le mouton	la carne de carnero	a carne de carneiro	la carne di montone
oil	l'huile (f)	el aceite	o azeite	l'olio
omelet	l'omelette (f)	la tortilla	a omeleta	la frittata
pepper	le poivre	la pimienta	a pimenta	il pepe
pork	le porc	la carne de cerdo	a carne de porco	il maiale
roast	le rôti	el asado	o assado	l'arrosto
roll	le petit pain	el panecillo	o pãozinho	il panino
salad	la salade	la ensalada	a salada	l'insalata
salt	le sel	la sal	o sal	il sale
sauce	la sauce	la salsa	o môlho	la salsa
sausage	la saucisse	la salchicha	a salchicha	la salsiccia
soda water	l'eau de Seltz	el agua de Seltz	a soda	l'acqua minerale

ENGLISH	FRENCH	SPANISH	PORTU-GUESE	ITALIAN
soup	la soupe	la sopa	a sopa	la minestra
stew	le ragoût	el guisado	o guisado	lo stufato
sugar	le sucre	el azúcar	o açúcar	lo zucchero
supper	le souper	la cena	a ceia	la cena
tea	le thé	el té	o chá	il tè
veal	le veau	la ternera	a carne de vitela	la carne de vitello
vegetable	la légume	la legumbre	o legume	il legume
vinegar	le vinaigre	el vinagre	o vinagre	l'aceto
wine	le vin	el vino	o vinho	il vino

l) EATING AND COOKING UTENSILS

basin	le bol	el tazón	a tejela	la catinella
bottle	la bouteille	la botella	a garrafa	la bottiglia
coffee pot	la cafetière	la cafetera	a cafeteira	la caffettiera
colander	la passoire	el colador	o passador	il passino
corkscrew	le tire-bouchon	el sacacorchos	o saca-rôlhas	il cavatappi
cup	la tasse	la taza	a chávena	la tazza
dish	le plat	el plato	o prato	il piatto
fork	la fourchette	el tenedor	o garfo	la forchetta
frying pan	la poêle	la sartén	a frigideira	la padella
glass	le verre	el vaso	o copo	il bicchiere
jug	la cruche	la jarra	o jarro	la brocca
kettle	la bouilloire	la caldera	a chaleira	il calderotto
knife	le couteau	el cuchillo	a faca	il coltello
lid	le couvercle	la tapa	a tampa	il coperchio
napkin	la serviette	la servilleta	o guardanapo	il tovagliolo
plate	l'assiette (f)	el plato	o prato	il piatto
saucer	la soucoupe	el platillo	o pires	il piattino
saucepan	la casserole	la cacerola	a caçarola	la casseruola
spoon	la cuiller	la cuchara	a colhér	il cucchiaio
tablecloth	la nappe	el mantel	a toalha	la tovaglia
teapot	la théière	la tetera	o bule	la teiera

m) TOOLS

axe	la hache	el hacha (f)	o machado	l'ascia
board	la planche	la tabla	a tábua	la tavola
chisel	le ciseau	el cincel	o cinzel	lo scalpello
cord	la corde	la cuerda	a corda	la corda
file	la lime	la lima	a lima	la lima
gimlet	la vrille	la barrena	a verruma	il succhiello

ENGLISH	FRENCH	SPANISH	PORTU-GUESE	ITALIAN
gun	le fusil	la escopeta	a espingarda	il fucile
hammer	le marteau	el martillo	o martelo	il martello
hoe	la houe	la azada	a enxada	la zappa
hook (fishing)	le hameçon	el anzuelo	o anzol	l'amo
line (fishing)	la ligne	el cordel	o fio	la lenza
nail	le clou	el clavo	o prego	il chiodo
net	le filet	la red	a rede	la rete
nut	l'écrou (m)	la tuerca	a porca	la madrevite
pincers	les tenailles (f)	las tenazas	as tenazes	le tanaglie
plane	le rabot	el cepillo	a pleina	la pialla
pliers	les pinces (f)	los alicates	o alicate	le pinzette
plow, plough	la charrue	el arado	o arado	l'aratro
rod (fishing)	la canne	la caña	a cana	la canna
saw	la scie	la sierra	a serra	la sega
scissors	les ciseaux (m)	las tijeras	as tesouras	le forbici
screw	la vis	el tornillo	o parafuso	la vite
screw driver	le tournevis	el destorni-llador	a chave de parafusos	il cacciavite
scythe	la faux	la guadaña	a foice	la falce
spade	la bêche	la pala	a pá	la pala
spanner	la clef	la llave	a chave	la chiave
tool	l'outil (m)	la herramienta	a ferramenta	l'arnese (m)
wire	le fil de fer	el alambre	o arame	il filo di ferro
wrench		(see spanner, above)		

n) VOCATIONS AND SHOPS

actor	l'acteur	el actor	o actor	l'attore
actress	l'actrice	la actriz	a actriz	l'attrice
author	l'auteur	el autor	o autor	l'autore
baker	le boulanger	el panadero	o padeiro	il fornaio
baker's shop	la boulangerie	la panadería	a padaria	la panetteria
bank	la banque	el banco	o banco	la banca
boarding house	la pension	la casa de huéspedes la pensión	a pensão	la pensione
bookseller	le libraire	el librero	o livreiro	il libraio
bookshop	la librairie	la librería	a livraria	la libreria
businessman	le commerçant	el comerciante	o comerciante	il commerci-ante
butcher	le boucher	el carnicero	o carniceiro	il macellaio
butcher's shop	la boucherie	la carnicería	o talho	la macelleria
chemist (chem-istry)	le chimiste	el químico	o químico	il chimico

ENGLISH	FRENCH	SPANISH	PORTU-GUESE	ITALIAN
chemist (pharmacy)	le pharmacien	el farmacéutico	o farmacêutico	il farmacista
cook (female)	la cuisinière	la cocinera	a cozinheira	la cuoca
dairy	la crèmerie	la lechería	a leitaria	la latteria
dentist	le dentiste	el dentista	o dentista	il dentista
doctor	le docteur	el doctor	o doutor	il dottore
	le médecin	el médico	o médico	il medico
druggist	(see chemist [pharmacy], above)			
employee	l'employé	el empleado	o empregado	l'impiegato
engineer	l'ingénieur	el ingeniero	o engenheiro	l'ingegnere
fisherman	le pêcheur	el pescador	o pescador	il pescatore
gardener	le jardinier	el jardinero	o jardineiro	il giardiniere
hairdresser	le coiffeur	el peluquero	o cabeleireiro	il parrucchiere
	la coiffeuse	la peluquera	a cabeleireira	la parrucchiera
jeweler	le bijoutier	el joyero	o joalheiro	il gioielliere
journalist	le (la) journaliste	el (la) periodista	o (a) jornalista	il (la) giornalista
judge	le juge	el juez	o juiz	il giudice
laundry	la blanchisserie	el lavadero	a lavandaria	la lavanderia
lawyer	l'avocat	el abogado	o advogado	l'avvocato
mail man	(see postman, below)			
mechanic	le méçanicien	el mecánico	o mecânico	il meccanico
milliner	la modiste	la modista	a modista	la modista
musician	le musicien	el músico	o músico	il musicista
notary	le notaire	el notario	o notário	il notaio
nurse (hospital)	l'infirmière	la enfermera	a enfermeira	l'infermiera
official	le fonctionnaire	el funcionario	o funcionário	l'ufficiale
optician	l'opticien	el óptico	o oculista	l'ottico
painter	le peintre	el pintor	o pintor	il pittore
peasant	le paysan	el labrador	o lavrador	il contadino
photographer	le photographe	el fotógrafo	o fotógrafo	il fotografo
policeman	l'agent	el policía	o polícia	la guardia
postman	le facteur	el cartero	o carteiro	il portalettere
priest (parish)	le curé	el cura	o cura	il prete
publisher	l'éditeur	el editor	o editor	l'editore
scientist	l'homme de science	el hombre de ciencia	o scientista	lo scienziato
servant	le (la) domestique	el (la) criado (a)	o (a) criado (a)	il (la) domestico(a)
shoemaker	le cordonnier	el zapatero	o sapateiro	il calzolaio
shop, store	le magasin	la tienda	a loja	il negozio
singer	le chanteur	el cantor	o cantor	il (la) cantante
	la chanteuse	la cantora	a cantora	

ENGLISH	FRENCH	SPANISH	PORTU-GUESE	ITALIAN
stationery store	la papeterie	la papelería	a papelaria	la cartoleria
student	l'étudiant	el estudiante	o estudante	lo studente
surgeon	le chirurgien	el cirujano	o cirurgião	il chirurgo
tailor	le tailleur	el sastre	o alfaiate	il sarto
teacher	l'instituteur (m) l'institutrice (f)	el maestro la maestra	o mestre a mestra	il maestro la maestra
typist	la (le) dactylographe	la (el) mecanógrafa (o)	a (o) dactilógrafa (o)	la (il) dattilografa (o)
watchmaker	l'horloger	el relojero	o relojoeiro	l'orologiaio
workman	l'ouvrier	el obrero	o obreiro	l'operaio

o) COUNTRIES AND PEOPLES

Africa	l'Afrique (f)	el África (f)	a África	l'Africa
America	l'Amérique (f)	la América	a América	l'America
an American	un Américain	un americano	um americano	un Americano
Argentine	l'Argentine (f)	la Argentina	a Argentina	l'Argentina
an Argentine	un Argentin	un argentino	um argentino	un Argentino
Asia	l'Asie (f)	el Asia (f)	a Ásia	l'Asia
Austria	l'Autriche (f)	el Austria (f)	a Austria	l'Austria
Belgium	la Belgique	la Bélgica	a Bélgica	il Belgio
a Belgian	un Belge	un belga	um belga	un Belga
Brazil	le Brésil	el Brasil	o Brasil	il Brasile
a Brazilian	un Brésilien	un brasileño	um brasileiro	un Brasiliano
China	la Chine	la China	a China	la Cina
a Chinese	un Chinois	un chino	um chinês	un Cinese
a Dane	un Danois	un dinamarqués	um dinamarquês	un Danese
Denmark	le Danemark	la Dinamarca	a Dinamarca	la Danimarca
Egypt	l'Egypte (f)	el Egipto	Egipto	l'Egitto
empire	l'empire (m)	el imperio	o império	l'impero
England	l'Angleterre (f)	la Inglaterra	a Inglaterra	l'Inghilterra
an Englishman	un Anglais	un inglés	um inglês	un Inglese
Europe	l'Europe (f)	la Europa	a Europa	l'Europa
a European	un Européen	un europeo	um europeo	un Europeo
Finland	la Finlande	la Finlandia	a Finlândia	la Finlandia
a Finn	un Finnois	un finlandés	um finlandês	un Finlandese
a foreigner	un étranger	un extranjero	o estrangeiro	un forestiere
France	la France	la Francia	a França	la Francia
a Frenchman	un Français	un francés	um francês	un Francese
a German	un Allemand	un aleman	um alemão	il Tedesco
Germany	l'Allemagne (f)	la Alemania	a Alemanha	la Germania
Great Britain	la Grande-Bretagne	la Gran Bretaña	Grã-Bretanha	la Gran-Bretagna

ENGLISH	FRENCH	SPANISH	PORTU-GUESE	ITALIAN
Greece	la Grèce	la Grecia	a Grécia	la Grecia
a Greek	un Grec	un griego	um grego	il Greco
Holland	la Hollande	la Holanda	a Holanda	l'Olanda
a Dutchman	un Hollandais	un holandés	um holandês	un Olandese
a Hungarian	un Hongrois	un húngaro	um húngaro	un Ungherese
Hungary	la Hongrie	la Hungría	a Hungria	l'Ungheria
Ireland	l'Irlande (f)	la Irlanda	a Irlanda	l'Irlanda
an Irishman	un Irlandais	un irlandés	um irlandês	un Irlandese
Italy	l'Italie (f)	la Italia	a Itália	l'Italia
an Italian	un Italien	un italiano	um italiano	un Italiano
Japan	le Japon	el Japón	o Japão	il Giappone
a Japanese	le Japonais	un japonés	um Japonês	un Giapponese
kingdom	le royaume	el reino	o reino	il regno
Norway	la Norvège	la Noruega	a Noruega	la Norvegia
a Norwegian	un Norvégien	un noruego	um norueguês	un Norvegese
Poland	la Pologne	la Polonia	a Polónia	la Polonia
a Pole	le Polonais	un polaco	um polaco	un Polacco
Portugal	le Portugal	el Portugal	Portugal	il Portogallo
a Portuguese	le Portugais	un portugués	um português	un Portoghese
republic	la république	la república	a república	la repubblica
Russia	la Russie	la Rusia	a Russia	la Russia
a Russian	un Russe	un ruso	um russo	un Russo
Scotland	l'Ecosse (f)	la Escocia	a Escócia	la Scozia
a Scotsman	un Écossais	un escocés	um escocês	uno Scozzese
Spain	l'Espagne (f)	España	a Espanha	la Spagna
a Spaniard	un Espagnol	un español	um espanhol	uno Spagnuolo
Sweden	la Suède	la Suecia	a Suécia	la Svezia
a Swede	un Suédois	un sueco	um sueco	uno Svedese
a Swiss	un Suisse	un suizo	um suiço	uno Svizzero
Switzerland	la Suisse	Suiza	a Suiça	la Svizzera
a Turk	un Turc	un turco	um turco	un Turco
Turkey	la Turquie	Turquía	a Turquia	la Turchia
U.S.A.	les États-Unis	los Estados Unidos	os Estados Unidos	gli Stati Uniti

p) READING AND WRITING

address	l'adresse (f)	las señas	o enderêço	l'indirizzo
addressee	le destinataire	el destinatario	o destinatário	il destinatario
blotting paper	le papier buvard	el papel secante	o mataborrão	la carta sugante
book	le livre	el libro	o livro	il libro
date	la date	la fecha	a data	la data
dictionary	le dictionnaire	el diccionario	o dicionário	il dizionario
envelope	l'enveloppe (f)	el sobre	o envelope	la busta

ENGLISH	FRENCH	SPANISH	PORTU-GUESE	ITALIAN
eraser (rubber)	la gomme	la goma	o apagador	la gomma
fountain pen	le stylo (graphe)	la pluma estilográfica	a caneta de tinta permanente	la penna stilografica
ink	l'encre (f)	la tinta	a tinta	l'inchiostro
letter	la lettre	la carta	a carta	la lettera
mail	le courrier	el correo	o correio	il corriere
mail box, letter box	la boîte aux lettres	el buzón	a caixa do correio	la buca da lettere
map	la carte	el mapa	o mapa	la carta
news	les nouvelles (f)	las noticias	as notícias o jornal	le notizie il giornale
newspaper	le journal	el periódico	a novela	il romanzo
novel	le roman	la novela	a página	la pagina
page	la page	la página	o papel	la carta
paper	le papier	el papel	o pacote	il pacco
parcel	le paquet	el paquete	a pena	la penna
pen	la plume	la pluma	o lápis	la matita
pencil	le crayon	el lápiz	a revista	la rivista
periodical	la revue	la revista	o porte	l'affrancatura
postage	le port	el franqueo	o bilhete postal	la cartolina postale
postcard	la carte postale	la tarjeta postal	o correio	l'ufficio postale
post office	le bureau de poste	la oficina de correos	a leitura	la lettura
reading	la lecture	la lectura	o remetente	il mittente
sender	l'expéditeur (m)	el remitente	a assinatura	la firma
signature	la signature	la firma	o sêlo	il francobollo
stamp	le timbre-poste	el sello		
typewriter	la machine à écrire	la máquina de escribir	a máquina de escrever	la macchina da scrivere

q) HOTEL AND RESTAURANT

bathroom	la salle de bain	el cuarto de baño	o quarto de banho	la sala da bagno
bill	l'addition (restaurant) la note (hotel)	la cuenta	a conta	il conto
chambermaid	la fille de chambre	la criada	a criada	la cameriera
change	la monnaie	el cambio	o trôco	gli spiccioli
chef	le chef	el jefe	o chefe	il capocuoco
cloakroom	le vestiaire	el vestuario	o guarda-roupa	la guardaroba

ENGLISH	FRENCH	SPANISH	PORTU- GUESE	ITALIAN
dining room	la salla à manger	el comedor	a sala de jantar	la sala da pranzo
elevator	l'ascenseur (m)	el ascensor	o ascensor	l'ascensore
hotel	l'hôtel (m)	el hotel	o hotel	l'albergo
manager	le directeur	el director	o director	il direttore
	le gérant	el gerente	o gerente	il gerente
menu	la carte	la lista	a lista	la lista
office	le bureau	las oficinas	o escritório	l'ufficio
restaurant	le restaurant	el restaurant	o restaurante	il ristorante
staff	le personnel	el personal	o pessoal	il personale
tip	le pourboire	la propina	a gorgeta	la mancia
waiter	le garçon	el camarero	o criado	il cameriere

r) Train and Railway Station

arrival	l'arrivée (f)	la llegada	a chegada	l'arrivo
baggage	les bagages (m)	el equipaje	a bagagem	il bagaglio
baggage car	le fourgon	el furgón	o furgão	il bagagliaio
cloak-room	la consigne	la sala de equipajes	a sala de bagagem	il deposito
coach, car	la voiture	el coche	a carruagem	vettura
	le wagon	el vagón	o vagão	il vagone
compartment	le comparti-ment	el departa-mento	o comparti-mento	lo scomparti-mento
connection	la correspon-dance	el empalme	a ligação	la coincidenza
customs	la douane	la aduana	a alfândega	la dogana
delay	le retard	el retraso	o atrazo	il ritardo
departure	le départ	la partida	a pa tida	la partenza
dining car	le wagon-restaurant	el coche comedor	o vagão-res-taurante	il vagone ristorante
engine	la locomotive la machine	la locomotora	a locomotiva	la locomotiva
entrance	l'entrée (f)	la entrada	a entrada	l'entrata
exit	la sortie	la salida	a saída	l'uscita
guard	le conducteur	el guarda	o condutor	il capotreno
information bu-reau, inquiry office	le bureau de renseigne-ment	la oficina de información	o escritório de informações	l'ufficio in-formazioni
lavatory	le cabinet	el retrete	a retrete	la ritirata
passenger	le voyageur	el pasajero	o passageiro	il passegiere
passport	le passeport	el pasaporte	o passaporte	il passaporto
platform	le quai	el andén	a plataforma	la piattaforma
porter	le porteur	el mozo	o porteiro	il facchino

ENGLISH	FRENCH	SPANISH	PORTU-GUESE	ITALIAN
railway	le chemin de fer	el ferrocarril	o caminho de ferro	la ferrovia
seat	le place	el asiento	o lugar	il posto
sleeping car	le wagon-lit	el coche cama	o vagão leito	la vettura letto
smoking permitted	fumeurs	fumadores	fumadores	fumatori
station	la gare	la estación	a estação	la stazione
station master	le chef de gare	el jefe de estación	o chefe da estação	il capo-stazione
stop	l'arrêt (m)	la parada	a paragem	la fermata
suitcase	la valise	la maleta	a mala de mão	la valigia
ticket	le billet	el billete	o bilhete	il biglietto
return ticket	le billet d'aller et retour	el billete de ida y vuelta	o bilhete de ida e volta	il biglietto d'andata e ritorno
ticket collector	le contrôleur	el revisor	o revisor	il controllore
ticket office	le guichet	la taquilla	a bilheteira	lo sportello
time table	l'indicateur (m)	el horario	o horário	l'orario
train	le train	el tren	o combóio	il treno
fast train	le rapide l'express (m)	el rápido el expreso	o rápido o expresso	il treno rapido
slow train	le train omnibus	el mixto	o mixto	il treno omnibus
trunk	la malle	el baúl	o baú	il baule
waiting room	la salle d'attente	la sala de espera	a sala de espera	la sala d'aspetto

5) SHIP

anchor	l'ancre (f)	el ancla (f)	a âncora	l'ancora
boat (small)	le bateau	la barca	o barco	la barca
boiler	la chaudière	la caldera	a caldeira	la caldaia
bows	l'avant (m)	la proa	a prôa	la prua
bridge	la passerelle	el puente	a ponte	il ponte di comando
cabin	la cabine	el camarote	o camarote	la cabina
captain	le capitaine	el capitan	o capitão	il capitano
compass	la boussole	la brújula	a bússola	la bussola
crew	l'équipage (m)	la tripulación	a equipagem	l'equipaggio
deck	le pont	la cubierta	a coberta	il ponte
flag	le pavillon	el pabellón	a bandeira	la bandiera
funnel	la cheminée	la chimenea	a chaminé	il fumaiolo
hold	la cale	la cala	o porão	la stiva
hull	la coque	el casco	o casco	lo scafo

ENGLISH	FRENCH	SPANISH	PORTU-GUESE	ITALIAN
keel	la quille	la quilla	a quilha	la chiglia
lighthouse	le phare	el faro	o farol	il faro
mast	le mât	el mástil	o mastro	l'albero
oar	la rame	el remo	o remo	il remo
propeller	la hélice	la hélice	a hélice	l'elice (f)
purser	le commissaire	el contador	o comissário	il commissario
rudder	le gouvernail	el timón	o leme	il timone
sail	la voile	la vela	a vela	la vela
seaman	le marin	el marino	o marinheiro	il marinaio
seasickness	le mal de mer	el mareo	o enjôo	il mal di mare
ship	le bateau	el barco	o navio	il bastimento
stern	l'arrière (m)	la popa	a pôpa	la poppa
tug	le remorqueur	el remolcador	o rebocador	il rimorchia-tore

t) Cycling and Automobiling

ENGLISH	FRENCH	SPANISH	PORTU-GUESE	ITALIAN
airplane	l'avion (m)	el avión	o avião	l'aeroplano
automobile	l'auto(mobile) (f)	el auto(móvil)	o auto(móvel)	l'auto(mobile) (f)
axle	l'essieu (m)	el eje	o eixo	l'asse (f)
bearing	le coussinet	el cojinete	a chumaceira	il cuscinetto
bend (road)	le virage	la curva	a curva	la svolta
bicycle	la bicyclette	la bicicleta	a bicicleta	la bicicletta
brake	le frein	el freno	o travão	il freno
bulb	l'ampoule (f)	la ampolleta	a lâmpada	l'ampolla
bumper	le pare-chocs	el tope	o para-choques	il paraurti
chain	la chaîne	la cadena	a cadeia	la catena
clutch	l'embrayage (m)	el embrague	a embraiagem	la frizione
damage	l'avarie (f)	la avería	a avaria	l'avaria
engine	le moteur	el motor	o motor	il motore
fine	l'amende (f)	la multa	a multa	la contravven-zione
gasoline	l'essence (f)	la gasolina	a gasolina	la benzina
gears	l'engrenage (m)	el engranaje	a engrenagem	l'ingranaggio
grade crossing	le passage à niveau	el paso a nivel	a passagem de nível	il passaggio a livello
headlight	le phare	el faro	a lanterna	il faro
hood	la capote	la capota	a capota	la cappotta
horn	le claxon	la bocina	a buzina	la tromba
horsepower	le cheval vapeur	el caballo de fuerza	a força de cavalo	il cavallo vapore

ENGLISH	FRENCH	SPANISH	PORTU-GUESE	ITALIAN
ignition	l'allumage (m)	el encendido	a ignição	l'accensione (f)
jack	le cric	el cric	o macaco	il cricco
lever	le levier	la palanca	a alavanca	la leva
motorcycle	la moto-cyclette	la motocicleta	a motocicleta	la motocicletta
mudguard	l'aile (f)	el guarda barro	o guarda-lama	il parafango
one way	sens unique	dirección única	direcção obri-gatória	senso unico
pump	la pompe	la bomba	a bomba	la pompa
puncture	la crevaison	el pinchazo	o furo	la bucatura
spark	l'étincelle (f)	la chispa	a faísca	la scintilla
spark plug	la bougie	la bujía	a vela	la candela
spring	le ressort	el muelle	a mola	la molla
starter	le démarreur	el arranque	o arranque	l'avviamento
steering wheel	le volant	el volante	o volante	il volante
tire	le pneu	el neumático	o pneumático	la gomma
trolley car, tram	le tramway	el tranvía	o carro eléc-trico	il tranvai
truck	le camion	el camión	o camião	l'autocarro
tube	la chambre à air le boyau	la cámara de aire	a câmara	la camera d'aria
valve	la soupape	la válvula	a válvula	la valvola
wheel	la roue	la rueda	a roda	la ruota

2. DIVISION OF TIME

a) GENERAL TERMS

afternoon	l'après-midi (m)	la tarde	a tarde	il pomeriggio
antiquity	l'antiquité (f)	la antigüedad	a antiguidade	l'antichità (f)
century	le siècle	el siglo	o século	il secolo
Christmas	Noël (m)	Navidad (f)	Natal (m)	il Natale
day	le jour	el día	o dia	il giorno
daybreak	le point du jour	el amanecer	a madrugada	lo spuntar del giorno
dusk	la tombée de la nuit	el anochecer	o anoitecer	il far della notte
Easter	Pâques (m.pl.)	Pascua	Páscoa	la Pasqua
evening	le soir	la tarde	a tarde	la sera
fortnight	quinze jours la quinzaine	quince días la quincena	quinze dias a quinzena	quindici giorni la quindicina

ENGLISH	FRENCH	SPANISH	PORTU-GUESE	ITALIAN
hour	l'heure (f)	la hora	a hora	l'ora
half an hour	une demi-heure	media hora	meia hora	una mezz' ora
a quarter of an hour	un quart d'heure	un cuarto de hora	um quarto de hora	un quarto d'ora
an hour and a half	une heure et demi	hora y media	uma hora e meia	un' ora e mezzo
leap year	l'année bis-sextile	el año bi-siesto	o ano bissexto	l'anno bi-sestile
Middle Ages	le moyen âge	la edad media	a idade média	il medio evo
midnight	le minuit	medianoche	meia noute	la mezzanotte
minute	la minute	el minuto	o minuto	il minuto
month	le mois	el mes	o mês	il mese
morning	le matin	la mañana	a manhã	la mattina
night	la nuit	la noche	a noute	la notte
noon	le midi	mediodía	o meio dia	mezzodì
season	la saison	la estación	a estação	la stagione
second	la seconde	el segundo	o segundo	il secondo
New Year	le nouvel an	el año nuevo	o ano novo	il capo d'anno
sunrise	le lever du soleil	la salida del sol	o nascer do sol	il levar del sole
sunset	le coucher du soleil	la puesta del sol	o pôr do sol	il tramonto
time	le temps	el tiempo	o tempo	il tempo
week	la semaine	la semana	a semana	la settimana
	huit jours	ocho días	oito dias	otto giorni
year	l'an (m)	el año	o ano	l'anno

b) Seasons, Months, and Days

spring	le printemps	la primavera	a primavera	la primavera
summer	l'été (m)	el verano	o verão	l'estate (f)
autumn	l'automne (m)	el otoño	o outono	l'autunno
winter	l'hiver (m)	el invierno	o inverno	l'inverno
January	janvier	enero	janeiro	Gennaio
February	février	febrero	fevereiro	Febbraio
March	mars	marzo	março	Marzo
April	avril	abril	abril	Aprile
May	mai	mayo	maio	Maggio
June	juin	junio	junho	Giugno
July	juillet	julio	julho	Luglio
August	août	agosto	agôsto	Agosto
September	septembre	septiembre	setembro	Settembre
October	octobre	octubre	outubro	Ottobre

ENGLISH	FRENCH	SPANISH	PORTU-GUESE	ITALIAN
November	novembre	noviembre	novembro	Novembre
December	décembre	diciembre	dezembro	Dicembre
Monday	lundi	el lunes	segunda-feira	Lunedì
Tuesday	mardi	el martes	terça-feira	Martedì
Wednesday	mercredi	el miércoles	quarta-feira	Mercoledì
Thursday	jeudi	el jueves	quinta-feira	Giovedì
Friday	vendredi	el viernes	sexta-feira	Venerdì
Saturday	samedi	el sábado	sábado	Sabato
Sunday	dimanche	el domingo	domingo	Domenica

3. NUMERALS

one	un, une	uno, un, una	um, uma	uno, un, una
two	deux	dos	dois, duas	due
three	trois	tres	três	tre
four	quatre	cuatro	quatro	quattro
five	cinq	cinco	cinco	cinque
six	six	seis	seis	sei
seven	sept	siete	sete	sette
eight	huit	ocho	oito	otto
nine	neuf	nueve	nove	nove
ten	dix	diez	dez	dieci
eleven	onze	once	onze	undici
twelve	douze	doce	doze	dodici
thirteen	treize	trece	treze	tredici
fourteen	quatorze	catorce	catorze	quattordici
fifteen	quinze	quince	quinze	quindici
sixteen	seize	diez y seis	dezasseis	sedici
seventeen	dix-sept	diez y siete	dezassete	diciassette
eighteen	dix-huit	diez y ocho	dezóito	diciotto
nineteen	dix-neuf	diez y nueve	dezanove	diciannove
twenty	vingt	veinte	vinte	venti
twenty-one	vingt et un	veinte y uno	vinte e um	ventuno
twenty-two	vingt-deux	veinte y dos	vinte e dois	ventidue
thirty	trente	treinta	trinta	trenta
forty	quarante	cuarenta	quarenta	quaranta
fifty	cinquante	cincuenta	cinqùenta	cinquanta
sixty	soixante	sesenta	sessenta	sessanta
seventy	soixante-dix	setenta	setenta	settanta
eighty	quatre-vingts	ochenta	oitenta	ottanta
ninety	quatre-vingt-dix	noventa	noventa	novanta

ENGLISH	FRENCH	SPANISH	PORTU- GUESE	ITALIAN
hundred	cent	ciento, cien	cem	cento
thousand	mille	mil	mil	mille
million	un million	un millón	um milhão	un milione
first	premier	primero	primeiro	primo
second	second, deuxième	segundo	segundo	secondo
third	troisième	tercero	terceiro	terzo
fourth	quatrième	cuarto	quarto	quarto
fifth	cinquième	quinto	quinto	quinto
sixth	sixième	sexto	sexto	sesto
seventh	septième	séptimo	sétimo	settimo
eighth	huitième	octavo	oitavo	ottavo
half	un demi	un medio	um meio	un mezzo
one-third	un tiers	un tercio	um têrço	un terzo
one-fourth	un quart	un cuarto	um quarto	un quarto
one-fifth	un cinquième	un quinto	um quinto	un quinto
once	une fois	una vez	uma vez	una volta
twice	deux fois	dos veces	duas vezes	due volte
three times	trois fois	tres veces	três vezes	tre volte

a) General

accident (chance event)	l'accident (m)	el acaso	o acaso	il caso
accident (mishap)	l'accident (m)	la desgracia	o acidente	la disgrazia
account (bill)	le compte	la cuenta	a conta	il conto
action	l'action (f)	la acción	a acção	l'azione
advantage	l'avantage (m)	la ventaja	a vantagem	il vantaggio
advertisement	l'annonce (f)	el anuncio	o anúncio	l'annunzio
advice (counsel)	le conseil	el consejo	o conselho	il consiglio
age (length of life)	l'âge (m)	la edad	a idade	l'età (f)
amusement	l'amusement (m)	la diversión	o divertimento	il divertimento
anger	la colère	la cólera	o enfado	la collera
angle	l'angle (m)	el ángulo	o ângulo	l'angolo
answer	la réponse	la respuesta	a resposta	la risposta

The correspondence English -tion, French -tion, Spanish -ción, Portuguese -ção, Italian -zione also occurs in the Romance equivalents to *ambition, association, attention, condition, direction, imitation, nation, relation*, etc.

ENGLISH	FRENCH	SPANISH	PORTU-GUESE	ITALIAN
apology	l'excuse (f)	la disculpa	a satisfação	la scusa
apparatus	l'appareil (m)	el aparato	o aparelho	l'apparecchio
appetite	l'appétit (m)	el apetito	o apetite	l'appetito
army	l'armée (f)	el ejército	o exército	l'esercito
art	l'art (m)	el arte (m)	a arte	l'arte (f)
assistance	l'aide (f)	la ayuda	a ajuda	l'aiuto
attack	l'attaque (f)	el ataque	o ataque	l'attacco
authority	l'autorité	la autoridad	a autoridade	l'autorità (f)

The correspondence English *-ty*, French *-té*, Spanish *-dad*, Portuguese *-dade*, Italian *-tà*, also occurs in the Romance equivalents to *difficulty, liberty, quality, society, tranquillity*, etc.

average	la moyenne	el término medio	o têrmo médio	la media
bag	le sac	el saco	o saco	il sacco
ball	la boule	la bola	a bola	la palla
battle	la bataille	la batalla	a batalha	la battaglia
beauty	la beauté	la belleza	a beleza	la bellezza
beginning	le commence-ment	el principio	o princípio	il principio
birth	la naissance	el nacimiento	o nascimento	la nascita
blot	la tache	el borrón	o borrão	lo sgorbio
blow (hit)	le coup	el golpe	o golpe	il colpo
bottom	le fond	el fondo	o fundo	il fondo
burn	la brûlure	la quemadura	a queimadura	la bruciatura
business (trade)	les affaires (f)	los negocios	os negócios	gli affari
care	le soin	el cuidado	o cuidado	la cura
case (instance)	le cas	el caso	o caso	il caso
cause (grounds)	la cause	la causa	a causa	la causa
change (alteration)	le changement	el cambio	a mudança	il cambia-mento
chemistry	la chimie	la química	a química	la chimica
choice	le choix	la elección	a escolha	la scelta
circle	le cercle	el círculo	o círculo	il circolo
cleanliness	la propreté	la limpieza	a limpeza	la pulizia
color	la couleur	el color	a côr	il colore
committee	le comité	el comité	o comité	il comitato
company	la compagnie	la compañía	a companhia	la compagnia
competition (commercial)	la concurrence	la competencia	a concorrência	la concorrenza
competition (sport, etc.)	le concours	el concurso	o concurso	il concorso
compromise	le compromis	el compromiso	o compromisso	il compromesso
conclusion (end)	la fin	el fin	o fim	la fine
conduct	la conduite	la conducta	a conduta	la condotta

ENGLISH	FRENCH	SPANISH	PORTU-GUESE	ITALIAN
confidence (trust)	la confiance	la confianza	a confiança	la fiducia
conquest	la conquête	la conquista	a conquista	la conquista
contact	le contact	el contacto	o contacto	il contatto
contempt	le mépris	el desprecio	o desprêzo	lo sprezzo
contents	le contenu	el contenido	o conteúdo	il contenuto
country (nation)	le pays	el país	o país	il paese
courage	le courage	el valor	a coragem	il coraggio
cowardice	la lâcheté	la cobardía	a cobardia	la codardia
crack (fissure)	la fente	la hendedura	a fenda	la fessura
crime	le crime	el crimen	o crime	il delitto
crisis	la crise	la crisis	a crise	la crisi
criticism	la critique	la crítica	a crítica	la critica
cross	la croix	la cruz	a cruz	la croce
crowd	la foule	la muchedumbre	a multidão	la folla
cruelty	la cruauté	la crueldad	a crueldade	la crudeltà
cry	le cri	el grito	o grito	il grido
cube	le cube	el cubo	o cubo	il cubo
curve	la courbe	la curva	a curva	la curva
custom (habit)	la coutume	la costumbre	o costume	il costume
cut	la coupure	el corte	o corte	il taglio
damage	le dommage	el daño	o dano	il danno
dance	la danse	el baile	o baile	il ballo
danger	le danger	el peligro	o perigo	il pericolo
death	la mort	la muerte	a morte	la morte
debt	la dette	la deuda	a dívida	il debito
defeat	la défaite	la derrota	a derrota	la disfatta
defect	le défaut	el defecto	o defeito	il difetto
defense	la défense	la defensa	a defesa	la difesa
degree	le degré	el grado	o grau	il grado
depth	la profondeur	la profundidad	a profundidade	la profondità
design (sketch)	le dessin	el diseño	o desenho	il disegno
desire	le désir	el deseo	o desejo	il desiderio
detail	le détail	el detalle	o detalhe	il dettaglio
development	le développement	el desarrollo	o desenvolvimento	lo sviluppo
disaster	le désastre	el desastre	o desastre	il disastro
discovery	la découverte	el descubrimiento	o descobrimento	la scoperta
disgust	le dégoût	la repugnancia	o desgôsto	lo schifo
distance	la distance	la distancia	a distância	la distanza
doubt	le doute	la duda	a dúvida	il dubbio
dream	le rêve	el sueño	o sonho	il sogno
drop (water, etc.)	la goutte	la gota	a gota	la goccia

ENGLISH	FRENCH	SPANISH	PORTU-GUESE	ITALIAN
duration	la durée	la duración	a duração	la durata
duty	le devoir	el deber	o dever	il dovere
edge (border)	le bord	el borde	a borda	l'orlo
effort	l'effort (m)	el esfuerzo	o esfôrço	lo sforzo
electricity	l'électricité (f)	la electricidad	a electricidade	l'elettricità
employment	l'emploi (m)	el empleo	o emprêgo	l'impiego
encounter (meeting)	la rencontre	el encuentro	o encontro	l'incontro
end (extremity)	le bout	el extremo	a extremidade	l'estremità
enemy	l'ennemi (m)	el enemigo	o inimigo	il nemico
enterprise	l'entreprise (f)	la empresa	a emprêsa	l'impresa
entrance	l'entrée (f)	la entrada	a entrada	l'entrata
environment	le milieu	el ambiente	o ambiente	l'ambiente (m)
envy	l'envie (f)	la envidia	a inveja	l'invidia
equality	l'égalité (f)	la igualdad	a igualdade	l'eguaglianza
error	l'erreur (f)	el error	o êrro	l'errore (m)
event	l'événement (m)	el aconteci-miento	o aconteci-mento	l'avvenimento
examination	l'examen (m)	el examen	o exame	l'esame (m)
example	l'exemple (m)	el ejemplo	o exemplo	l'esempio
exchange	l'échange (m)	el cambio	a troca	il cambio
exhibition	l'exposition (f)	la exposición	a exposição	l'esposizione
existence	l'existence (f)	la existencia	a existência	l'esistenza

The correspondence English -ence, French -ence, Spanish -encia, Portuguese -ência, Italian -enza also occurs in the Romance equivalents to *experience, impudence, indifference, patience*, etc.

expense	les frais (m)	los gastos	os gastos	le spese
explanation	l'explication (f)	la explicación	a explicação	la spiegazione
fact	le fait	el hecho	o facto	il fatto
fall (of price, temperature, etc.)	la baisse	la baja	a baixa	la caduta
fear	la peur / la crainte	el temor / el miedo	o receio / o medo	la paura
flight (air)	le vol	el vuelo	o vôo	il volo
fold	le pli	el pliegue	a dobra	la piega
food	la nourriture	el alimento	o alimento	il cibo
force	la force	la fuerza	a fôrça	la forza
friend	l'ami (e)	el(la) amigo(a)	o(a) amigo(a)	l'amico(a)
friendship	l'amitié (f)	la amistad	a amizade	l'amicizia
front	le front	el frente	a frente	il fronte
frontier	la frontière	la frontera	a fronteira	la frontiera
fuel	le combustible	el combustible	o combustível	il combustibile

ENGLISH	FRENCH	SPANISH	PORTU-GUESE	ITALIAN
future	l'avenir (m)	el porvenir	o porvir	l'avvenire (m)
game (play)	le jeu	el juego	o jôgo	il giuoco
gesture	le geste	el gesto	o gesto	il gesto
gland	la glande	la glándula	a glândula	la glandola
government	le gouverne-ment	el gobierno	o govêrno	il governo
gratitude	la reconnais-sance	la gratitud	a gratidão	la gratitudine
group	le groupe	el grupo	o grupo	il gruppo
growth	la croissance	el crecimiento	o crescimento	il crescimento
half	la moitié	la mitad	a metade	la metà
happiness	le bonheur	la felicidad	a felicidade	la felicità
haste	la hâte	la prisa	a pressa	la fretta
hate	la haine	el odio	o ódio	l'odio
health	la santé	la salud	a saúde	la salute
heap	le tas	el montón	o mantão	il mucchio
hearing (sense of)	l'ouïe (f)	el oído	o ouvido	l'udito
heat	la chaleur	el calor	o calor	il calore
height	la hauteur	la altura	a altura	l'altura
history	l'histoire (f)	la historia	a história	la storia
hole	le trou	el agujero	o buraco	il buco
honor	l'honneur (m)	el honor	a honra	l'onore (m)
hope	l'espoir (m)	la esperanza	a esperança	la speranza
hunger	la faim	el hambre	a fome	la fame
idea	l'idée (f)	la idea	a ideia	l'idea
improvement	l'amélioration (f)	el mejora-miento	o melhora-mento	il migliora-mento
impulse	l'impulsion (f)	el impulso	o impulso	l'impulso
inhabitant	l'habitant (m)	el habitante	o habitante	l'abitante
instrument	l'instrument (m)	el instrumento	o instrumento	lo strumento

The correspondence English *-ment,* French *-ment,* Spanish *-mento,* Portuguese *-mento,* Italian *-mento* also occurs in the Romance equivalents to *argument, document, element, fragment, monument,* etc.

insurance	l'assurance (f)	el seguro	o seguro	l'assicura-zione (f)
interest (atten-tion)	l'intérêt (m)	el interés	o interêsse	l'interesse (m)
interest (return)	l'intérêt (m)	el rédito	o juro	l'interesse (m)
jealousy	la jalousie	los celos	o ciume	la gelosia
joke (jest)	la plaisanterie	la broma	o gracejo	lo scherzo
journey	le voyage	el viaje	a viagem	il viaggio
joy	la joie	la alegría	a alegria	la gioia
judgment	le jugement	el juicio	o juízo	il giudizio

ENGLISH	FRENCH	SPANISH	PORTU-GUESE	ITALIAN
jump	le saut	el salto	o salto	il salto
kind (species)	l'espèce (f)	la especie	a espécie	la specie
	le genre	el género	o género	il genere
kiss	le baiser	el beso	o beijo	il bacio
knot	le nœud	el nudo	o nó	il nodo
knowledge	la connais-sance	el conoci-miento	o conheci-mento	la conoscenza
language (tongue of a commu-nity)	la langue	la lengua el idioma	a língua o idioma	la lingua
language (style of expression)	le langage	el lenguaje	a linguagem	il linguaggio il riso
laughter	le rire	la risa	o riso	
laziness	la paresse	la pereza	a preguiça	la pigrizia
law	la loi	la ley	a lei	la legge
lecture	la conférence	la conferencia	a conferência	la conferenza
length (space)	la longueur	la longitud	o comprimento	la lunghezza
lesson	la leçon	la lección	a lição	la lezione
level	le niveau	el nivel	o nível	il livello
lie	le mensonge	la mentira	a mentira	la bugia
life	la vie	la vida	a vida	la vita
line	la ligne	la línea	a linha	la linea
liquid	le liquide	el líquido	o líquido	il liquido
list	la liste	la lista	a lista	la lista
load	la charge	la carga	a carga	il carico
look (glance)	le regard	la mirada	a olhadela	lo sguardo
loss	la perte	la pérdida	a perda	la perdita
love	l'amour (m)	el amor	o amor	l'amore (m)
luxury	le luxe	el lujo	o luxo	il lusso
machine	la machine	la máquina	a máquina	la macchina
majority	la majorité	la mayoría	a maioria	la maggior-anza
manager	le directeur	el director	o director	il direttore
manner	la manière	la manera	a maneira	la maniera
	la façon	el modo	o modo	il modo
mark	la marque	la marca	a marca	la marca
mass	la masse	la masa	a massa	la massa
material	le matériel	el material	o material	il materiale
matter	la matière	la materia	a matéria	la materia
means	le moyen	el medio	o meio	il mezzo
measure	la mesure	la medida	a medida	la misura
meeting (assem-bly)	la réunion	el mitin	a reunião	la riunione
member	le membre	el miembro	o membro	il membro
memory	la mémoire	la memoria	a memória	la memoria
method	la méthode	el método	o método	il metodo

ENGLISH	FRENCH	SPANISH	PORTU-GUESE	ITALIAN
middle	le centre	el centro	o centro	il centro
	le milieu	el medio	o meio	il mezzo
minority	la minorité	la minoría	a menoridade	la minorità
mixture	le mélange	la mezcla	a mistura	la mistura
money	l'argent (m)	el dinero	o dinheiro	il denaro
mood (temper)	l'humeur (f)	el humor	o humor	l'umore (m)
movement	le mouvement	el movimiento	o movimento	il movimento
native land	la patrie	la patria	a pátria	la patria
nature	la nature	la naturaleza	a natureza	la natura
navy	la marine	la marina	a marinha	la marina
noise	le bruit	el ruido	o ruído	il rumore
notice (warning)	l'avis (m)	el aviso	o aviso	l'avviso
number (amount)	le nombre	el número	o número	il numero
number (No.)	le numéro	el número	o número	il numero
object	l'objet (m)	el objeto	o objecto	l'oggetto
offer	l'offre (f)	la oferta	a oferta	l'offerta
order (arrange-ment)	l'ordre (m)	el orden	a ordem	l'ordine (m)
order (com-mand)	l'ordre (m)	la orden	a ordem	l'ordine (m)
order (goods)	la commande	el pedido	a encomenda	l'ordinazione (f)
origin	l'origine (f)	el origen	a origem	l'origine (f)
owner	le propriétaire	el propietario	o proprietário	il proprietario
pain (suffering)	la douleur	el dolor	a dor	il dolore
painting	la peinture	la pintura	a pintura	la pittura
part (of whole)	la partie	la parte	a parte	la parte
party (faction)	le parti	el partido	o partido	il partito
past	le passé	el pasado	o passado	il passato
peace	la paix	la paz	a paz	la pace
people (persons)	les gens	la gente	a gente	la gente
people (com-munity)	le peuple	el pueblo	o povo	il popolo
person	la personne	la persona	a pessoa	la persona
piece (fragment)	le morceau	el pedazo	a peça	il pezzo
place (spot)	l'endroit (m)	el lugar	o lugar	il luogo
plant	la plante	la planta	a planta	la pianta
pleasure	le plaisir	el placer	o prazer	il piacere
poetry	la poésie	la poesía	a poesia	la poesia
point (dot)	le point	el punto	o ponto	il punto
point (sharp end)	la pointe	la punta	a ponta	la punta
poison	le poison	el veneno	o veneno	il veleno
politeness	la politesse	la cortesía	a cortesia	la cortesia
politics	la politique	la política	a política	la politica

ENGLISH	FRENCH	SPANISH	PORTU-GUESE	ITALIAN
population	la population	la población	a população	la popolazione
poverty	la pauvreté	la pobreza	a pobreza	la povertà
power	le pouvoir	el poder	o poder	il potere
practice (exercise)	l'exercice (f)	el ejercicio	o exercício	l'esercizio
prejudice	le préjugé	el perjuicio	o prejuízo	il pregiudizio
present (gift)	le cadeau	el regalo	o presente	il regalo
	le présent	el obsequio	a dádiva	
pressure	la pression	la presión	a pressão	la pressione
price	le prix	el precio	o preço	il prezzo
prize	le prix	el prémio	o prêmio	il premio
problem	le problème	el problema	o problema	il problema
product	le produit	el producto	o produto	il prodotto
profit	le profit	el provecho	o lucro	il profitto
progress	le progrès	el progreso	o progresso	il progresso
proof	la preuve	la prueba	a prova	la prova
property	la propriété	la propiedad	a propriedade	la proprietà
protest	la protestation	la protesta	o protesto	la protesta
punishment	la punition	el castigo	o castigo	la punizione
purchase	l'achat (m)	la compra	a compra	la compera
purpose	le but	el objeto	o propósito	il proposito
question	la question	la pregunta	a pergunta	la domanda
race (breed)	la race	la raza	a raça	la razza
ray	le rayon	el rayo	o raio	il raggio
reason	la raison	la razón	a razão	la ragione
receipt (paper)	le reçu	el recibo	o recibo	la ricevuta
recollection	le souvenir	el recuerdo	a lembrança	il ricordo
refusal	le refus	la negativa	a recusa	il rifiuto
remainder	le reste	el resto	o resto	il resto
remedy	le remède	el remedio	o remédio	il remedio
report (account)	le rapport	el informe	a relação	il rapporto
request	la demande	la petición	a petição	la ricchiesta
respect	le respect	el respeto	o respeito	il rispetto
rest (repose)	le repos	el descanso	o descanso	il riposo
result	le résultat	el resultado	o resultado	il resultato
revenge	la vengeance	la venganza	a vingança	la vendetta
reward	la récompense	la recompensa	a recompensa	la ricompensa
right (just claim)	le droit	el derecho	o direito	il diritto
risk	le risque	el riesgo	o risco	il rischio
rule (regulation)	la règle	la regla	a regra	la regola
sadness	la tristesse	la tristeza	a tristeza	la tristezza
safety	la sureté	la seguridad	a segurança	la sicurezza
sale	la vente	la venta	a venda	la vendita
sample	l'échantillon (m)	la muestra	a amostra	il campione
scale (measure)	l'échelle (f)	la escala	a escala	la scala

ENGLISH	FRENCH	SPANISH	PORTU-GUESE	ITALIAN
science	la science	la ciencia	a sciência	la scienza
sense (meaning)	le sens	el sentido	o sentido	il senso
sentence (group of words)	la phrase	la frase	a frase	la frase
sex	le sexe	el sexo	o sexo	il sesso
shame	la honte	la vergüenza	a vergonha	la vergogna
side	le côté	el lado	o lado	il lato
sight (sense of)	la vue	la vista	a vista	la vista
sign	le signe	la señal	o sinal	il segno
size	la grandeur	el tamaño	o tamanho	la grandezza
sleep	le sommeil	el sueño	o sono	il sonno
smell	l'odeur (f)	el olor	o cheiro	l'odore (m)
smile	le sourir	la sonrisa	o sorriso	il sorriso
song	la chanson	la canción	a canção	la canzone
sound	le son	el sonido	o som	il suono
space	l'espace (m)	el espacio	o espaço	lo spazio
speech (power of)	la parole	el habla (f)	a fala	la parola
speech (discourse)	le discours	el discurso	o discurso	il discorso
speed	la vitesse	la velocidad	a velocidade	la velocità
sport	le sport	el deporte	o desporte	lo sport
square (geometrical)	le carré	el cuadrado	o quadrado	il quadrato
state (government)	l'état (m)	el estado	o estado	lo stato
step	le pas	el paso	o passo	il passo
strike	la grève	la huelga	a greve	lo sciopero
struggle	la lutte	la lucha	a luta	la lotta
study	l'étude (f)	el estudio	o estudo	lo studio
success	le succès	el éxito	o êxito	il successo
suggestion	la suggestion	la sugestión	a sugestão	il suggeri-mento
sum	la somme	la suma	a soma	la somma
summary	le résumé	el resumen	o sumário	il sommario
summit	le sommet	la cumbre	o cume	la cima
surface	la surface	la superficie	a superfície	la superficie
surprise	la surprise	la sorpresa	a surpresa	la sorpresa
suspicion	le soupçon	la sospecha	a suspeita	il sospetto
swindle (fraud)	l'escroquerie (f)	la estafa	a burla	lo scroccone
system	le système	el sistema	o sistema	il sistema
task	la tâche	la tarea	a tarefa	il compito
taste	la goût	el gusto	o gôsto	il gusto
tax	l'impôt (m)	el impuesto	o imposto	la tassa
test	l'épreuve (f)	la prueba	a prova	la prova

ENGLISH	FRENCH	SPANISH	PORTU-GUESE	ITALIAN
thanks	les remerci-ments (m)	las gracias	as graças	le grazie
theft	le vol	el robo	o furto	il furto
thing	la chose	la cosa	a coisa	la cosa
thirst	la soif	la sed	a sêde	la sete
tone	le ton	el tono	o tom	il tono
touch (sense of)	le toucher	el tacto	o toque	il tatto
toy	le jouet	el juguete	o brinquedo	il giuocattolo
trade	le commerce	el comercio	o comércio	il commercio
translation	la traduction	la traducción	a tradução	la traduzione
transport	le transport	el transporte	o transporte	il trasporto
treatment	le traîtement	el tratamiento	o tratamento	il trattamento
treaty	le traité	el tratado	o tratado	il trattato
trial (law)	le procès	el proceso	o processo	il processo
truth	la vérité	la verdad	a verdade	la verità
use (employ-ment)	l'emploi (m)	el uso	o uso	l'uso
value	la valeur	el valor	o valor	il valore
vessel (receptacle)	le vaisseau	la vasija	o vaso	il vaso
victory	la victoire	la victoria	a vitória	la vittoria
voice	la voix	la voz	a voz	la voce
wages	le salaire	el salario	o salário	il salario
walk (stroll)	la promenade	el paseo	o passeio	la passeggiata
want (lack)	le manque	la falta	a falta	la mancanza
war	la guerre	la guerra	a guerra	la guerra
wealth	la richesse	la riqueza	a riqueza	la ricchezza
weapon	l'arme (f)	el arma (f)	a arma	l'arma
weight	le poids	el peso	o pêso	il peso
width	la largeur	la anchura	a largura	la larghezza
will	la volonté	la voluntad	a vontade	la volontà
word	le mot	la palabra	a palavra	la parola
work (achieve-ment)	l'œuvre (f)	la obra	a obra	l'opera
work (exertion)	le travail	el trabajo	o trabalho	il lavoro
world	le monde	el mundo	o mundo	il mondo
youth (early life)	la jeunesse	la juventud	a juventude	la gioventù
zeal	le zèle	el celo	o zêlo	lo zelo

4. ADJECTIVES

able (capable)	capable	capaz	capaz	capace
absent	absent,e	ausente	ausente	assente

ENGLISH	FRENCH	SPANISH	PORTU-GUESE	ITALIAN
acid	acide	ácido	ácido	acido

The correspondence English -id, French -ide, Spanish, Portuguese, Italian -ido also occurs in the Romance equivalents to *liquid, rapid, solid, timid*, etc.

admirable	admirable	admirable	admirável	ammirabile
aerial	aérien,ne	aéreo	aéreo	aereo
agreeable	agréable	agradable	agradável	gradevole
alone	seul,e	solo	só	solo
ambiguous	ambigu,ë	ambiguo	ambíguo	ambiguo
amusing	amusant,e	divertido	divertido	divertente
ancient	ancien,ne	antiguo	antigo	antico
angry	fâché,e	enfadado	enfadado	adirato
annual	annuel,le	anual	anual	annuale

The correspondence English -al, French -el, Spanish -al, Portuguese -al, Italian -ale also occurs in the Romance equivalents to *artificial, gradual, material, natural, universal, usual, sexual*, etc.

astonished	étonné,e	atónito	surpreendido	sorpreso
avaricious	avare	avaro	avaro	avaro
bad	mauvais,e	malo	mau	cattivo
beautiful	beau, belle	bello	belo	bello
		hermoso	formoso	
bent (curved)	courbé,e	curvo	curvo	curvo
bitter (in taste)	amer,ère	amargo	amargo	amaro
black	noir,e	negro	prêto	nero
blind	aveugle	ciego	cego	cieco
blue	bleu,e	azul	azul	azzurro
blunt (not sharp)	émoussé,e	embotado	desafiado	smussato
boiling	bouillant,e	hirviente	fervente	bollente
bright (shining)	brillant,e	brillante	brilhante	brillante
brown	brun,e	moreno	moreno	marrone
busy	occupé,e	ocupado	ocupado	occupato
cautious	prudent,e	cauto	cauto	cauto
cheap	bon-marché	barato	barato	a buon mercato poco caro
cheerful	gai,e	alegre	alegre	allegro
chemical	chimique	químico	químico	chimico
circular	circulaire	circular	circular	circolare

The correspondence English -ular, French -ulaire, Spanish, Portuguese -ular, Italian -olare also occurs in the Romance equivalents to *molecular, muscular, perpendicular, popular, secular*, etc.

clean	propre	limpio	limpo	pulito
clear	clair,e	claro	claro	chiaro
closed	fermé,e	cerrado	fechado	chiuso

ENGLISH	FRENCH	SPANISH	PORTU-GUESE	ITALIAN
cold	froid,e	frío	frio	freddo
comfortable	confortable	cómodo	cómodo	comodo
comic	comique	cómico	cómico	comico

The correspondence English -ic, French -ique, Spanish, Portuguese, Italian -ico also occurs in the Romance equivalents to *domestic, elastic, electric, energetic, scientific,* etc.

commercial	commercial,e	comercial	comercial	commerciale
common (general)	commun,e	común	comum	comune
complete	complet,ète	completo	completo	completo
complicated	compliqué,e	complicado	complicado	complicato
content	content,e	contento	contente	contento
continuous	continu,e	continuo	contínuo	continuo
cooked	cuit,e	cocido	cozinhado	cotto
cool	frais, fraîche	fresco	fresco	fresco
correct	correct,e	correcto	correcto	corretto
covered	couvert,e	cubierto	coberto	coperto
cruel	cruel,le	cruel	cruel	crudele
cunning	rusé,e	astuto	astuto	astuto
curious (inquisitive)	curieux,se	curioso	curioso	curioso

The correspondence English -ous, French, -eux, Spanish -oso, Portuguese -oso, Italian -oso also occurs in the Romance equivalents to *delicious, famous, furious, generous, industrious,* etc.

daily	quotidien,ne	diario	diário	quotidiano
damp	humide	húmedo	húmido	umido
dangerous	dangereux,se	peligroso	perigoso	pericoloso
dark	obscur,e	obscuro	escuro	oscuro
dead	mort,e	muerto	morto	morto
deaf	sourd,e	sordo	surdo	sordo
dear (beloved)	cher,ère	querido	querido	caro
deep	profond,e	profundo	profundo	profondo
delicate (easily damaged)	délicat,e	delicado	delicado	delicato
dense (thick)	épais,se	denso	denso	denso
different	différent,e	diferente	diferente	differente

The correspondence English -ent, French -ent, Spanish, Portuguese and Italian -ente also occurs in the Romance equivalents to *excellent, frequent, innocent, intelligent, patient, permanent, transparent, urgent,* etc.

difficult	difficile	difícil	difícil	difficile
direct	direct,e	directo	directo	diretto
dirty	sale	sucio	sujo	sporco
disagreeable	désagréable	desagradable	desagradável	sgradevole
discreet	discret,ète	discreto	discreto	discreto

ENGLISH	FRENCH	SPANISH	PORTU-GUESE	ITALIAN
dishonest	malhonnête	deshonesto	deshonesto	disonesto
distant	lointain,e	lejano	distante	lontano
distinct	distinct,e	distinto	distinto	distinto
double	double	doble	dobre	doppio
doubtful	douteux,se	dudoso	duvidoso	dubbioso
drunk	ivre	borracho	embriagado	ubbriaco
	soûl,e	ebrio	ébrio	brillo
dry	sec, sèche	seco	sêco	secco
dumb	muet,te	mudo	mudo	muto
easy	facile	fácil	fácil	facile
edible	comestible	comestible	comestivel	commestibile
educated	instruit,e	instruído	instruido	istruito
elegant	élégant,e	elegante	elegante	elegante
employed	employé,e	empleado	empregado	impiegato
empty	vide	vacío	vazio	vuoto
energetic	énergique	enérgico	enérgico	energico
enormous	énorme	enorme	enorme	enorme
entire	entier, ère	entero	inteiro	intiero
equal	égal,e	igual	igual	eguale
exact	exact,e	exacto	exacto	esatto
expensive	cher,ère	caro	caro	caro
external	externe	externo	externo	esterno
extreme	extrême	extremo	extremo	estremo
fair (blond)	blond,e	rubio	loiro	biondo
faithful	fidèle	fiel	fiel	fedele
false	faux,sse	falso	falso	falso
fat	gras,se	gordo	gordo	grasso
feeble (weak)	faible	débil	débil	debole
female (sex)	femelle	hembra	fêmea	femmina
fertile	fécond,e	fecundo	fecundo	fecondo
firm (fixed)	ferme	firme	firme	fermo
flat	plat,te	llano	plano	piano
following	suivant,e	siguiente	seguinte	seguente
foolish	sot,te	tonto	tolo	sciocco
	bête	estúpido	estúpido	stupido
	stupide			
forbidden	défendu,e	prohibido	proibido	vietato
foreign	étranger,ère	extranjero	estrangeiro	straniero
frank	franc,che	franco	franco	franco
free	libre	libre	livre	libero
fresh (new)	frais, fraîche	fresco	fresco	fresco
fried	frit,te	frito	frito	fritto
friendly	aimable	amigable	amigável	amichevole
full	plein,e	lleno	cheio	pieno
future	futur,e	futuro	futuro	futuro
general	général,e	general	geral	generale

ENGLISH	FRENCH	SPANISH	PORTU-GUESE	ITALIAN
good	bon,ne	bueno	bom	buono
grateful	reconnais-sant,e	agradecido	agradecido	riconoscente grato
grave	grave	grave	grave	grave
gray	gris,e	gris pardo	cinzento pardo	grigio bigio
green	vert,e	verde	verde	verde
guilty	coupable	culpable	culpável	colpevole
half	demi,e	medio	meio	mezzo
happy	heureux,se	feliz	feliz	felice
hard	dur,e	duro	duro	duro
harmful	nuisible	nocivo	nocivo	nocivo
healthy (whole-some)	sain,e	sano	são	sano
heavy	lourd,e	pesado	pesado	pesante
high	haut,e	alto	alto	alto
high up	élevé,e	elevado	elevado	elevato
historical	historique	histórico	histórico	storico
hollow	creux,se	hueco	ôco	cavo
honest	honnête	honrado	honesto	onesto
human or humane	humain,e	humano	humano	umano
humble	humble	humilde	humilde	umile
ill	malade	enfermo	enfermo	ammalato
important	important,e	importante	importante	importante
impossible	impossible	imposible	impossível	impossibile
inclined (dis-posed)	disposé,e	dispuesto	disposto	disposto
inconvenient	incommode	incómodo	incómodo	incomodo
incredible	incroyable	increíble	incrível	incredibile
inferior	inférieur,e	inferior	inferior	inferiore
ingenuous	ingénu,e	ingenuo	ingênuo	ingenuo
intact	intact,e	intacto	intacto	intatto
interesting	intéressant,e	interesante	interessante	interessante
internal	interne	interno	interno	interno
just (fair)	juste	justo	justo	giusto
kind	bon,ne aimable	bondadoso amable	bondoso benévolo	buono amabile
known	connu,e	conocido	conhecido	conosciuto
large	grand,e gros,se	grande	grande	grande
last	dernier,ère	último	último	ultimo
late (tardy)	tardif,ve	tardío	tardio	tardo
lazy	paresseux,se	perezoso	mandrião	pigro
lean	maigre	magro	magro	magro
left	gauche	izquierdo	esquerdo	sinistro

ENGLISH	FRENCH	SPANISH	PORTU-GUESE	ITALIAN
light (in weight)	léger,ère	ligero	ligeiro	leggero
light (in color)	clair,e	claro	claro	chiaro
living	vivant,e	vivo	vivo	vivo
long	long,ue	largo	comprido	lungo
loose (slack)	lâche	flojo	frouxo	sciolto
lost	perdu,e	perdido	perdido	perduto
low	bas,se	bajo	baixo	basso
mad	fou, folle	loco	louco	pazzo
male (sex)	mâle	macho	macho	maschio
married	marrié,e	casado	casado	sposato
maximum	maximal,e	máximo	máximo	massimo
mean (average)	moyen,ne	medio	médio	medio
mild	doux,ce	suave	suave	mite
minimum	minimal,e	mínimo	mínimo	minimo
mixed	mêlé,e	mezclado	misturado	misto
mobile	mobile	móvil	móvel	mobile
monthly	mensuel,le	mensual	mensal	mensile
naked	nu,e	desnudo	nu	nudo
narrow	étroit,e	estrecho	estreito	stretto
national	national,e	nacional	nacional	nazionale
near	proche	cercano	próximo	prossimo
necessary	nécessaire	necesario	necessário	necessario
		preciso	preciso	
neighboring	voisin,e	vecino	vizinho	vicino
new	nouveau, nou-velle	nuevo	novo	nuovo
nice (of people)	gentil,le	amable	amável	gentile
	sympathique	simpático	simpático	simpático
numerous	nombreux,se	numeroso	numeroso	numeroso
obstinate	obstiné,e	obstinato	obstinado	ostinato
official	officiel,le	oficial	oficial	ufficiale
old	vieux, vieille	viejo	velho	vecchio
only (sole)	seul,e	único	único	solo
	unique	solo		unico
open	ouvert,e	abierto	aberto	aperto
opposite (con-trary)	opposé,e contraire	opuesto contrario	oposto contrário	opposto contrario
other	autre	otro	outro	altro
own (one's)	propre	propio	próprio	propio
painful	douloureux,se	doloroso	doloroso	doloroso
pale	pâle	pálido	pálido	pallido
parallel	parallèle	paralelo	paralelo	parallelo
past	passé,e	pasado	passado	passato
perfect	parfait,e	perfecto	perfeito	perfetto
personal	personel,le	personal	pessoal	personale
physical	physique	físico	físico	fisico

ENGLISH	FRENCH	SPANISH	PORTU-GUESE	ITALIAN
pink	rose	rosado	côr de rosa	rosa
pointed	pointu,e	puntiagudo	ponteagudo	appuntato
poisonous	vénéneux	venenoso	venenoso	velenoso
polite	poli,e	cortés	cortês	cortese
political	politique	político	político	politico
poor	pauvre	pobre	pobre	povero
possible	possible	posible	possível	possibile
pregnant	enceinte	encinta	grávida	incinta
present (of time)	actuel,le	actual	actual	attuale
present (of place)	présent,e	presente	presente	presente
pretty	joli,e	lindo	lindo	grazioso
	gentil,le	bonito	bonito	bellino
previous	précédent,e	previo	prévio	previo
	préalable	precedente	precedente	precedente
private (not public)	particulier, ère	particular	particular	particolare
	privé,e	privado	privado	privato
probable	probable	probable	provável	probabile
proud	fier,ère	orgulloso	orgulhoso	orgoglioso
public	public,que	público	público	pubblico
pure	pur,e	puro	puro	puro
quiet (calm)	tranquille	tranquilo	tranqùilo	tranquillo
rare	rare	raro	raro	raro
raw	cru,e	crudo	cru	crudo
ready	prêt,e	listo	pronto	pronto
real	réel,le	real	real	reale
reasonable	raisonnable	razonable	razoável	ragionevole
recent	récent,e	reciente	recente	recente
red	rouge	rojo	vermelho	rosso
regular	régulier,ère	regular	regular	regolare
responsible	responsable	responsable	responsável	responsabile
rich	riche	rico	rico	ricco
ridiculous	ridicule	ridículo	ridículo	ridicolo
rigid	raide	rígido	rígido	rigido
right (not left)	droit,e	derecho	direito	destro
ripe	mûr,e	maduro	maduro	maturo
rough (not smooth)	raboteux,se	áspero	áspero	ruvido
round	rond,e	redondo	redondo	rotondo
rude	grossier,ère	grosero	grosseiro	rozzo
	impoli,e	descortés	descortês	scortese
rusty	rouillé,e	oxidado	ferrugento	arrugginito
sad	triste	triste	triste	triste
safe (secure)	sauf,ve	seguro	seguro	sicuro
salt (salty)	salé,e	salado	salgado	salato

ENGLISH	FRENCH	SPANISH	PORTU-GUESE	ITALIAN
same	même	mismo	mesmo	stesso
satisfied	satisfait,e	satisfecho	satisfeito	soddisfatto
seated	assis,e	sentado	sentado	seduto
secret	secret,ète	secreto	secreto	segreto
sensible	sensé,e	sensato	sensato	sensato
sensitive	sensible	sensible	sensível	sensibile
separate	séparé,e	separado	separado	separato
serious (earnest)	sérieux,se	serio	sério	serio
severe	sévère	severo	severo	severo
shallow	peu profond,e	somero	baixo	basso
sharp (keen edge)	tranchant,e	afilado	afiado	affilato
short	court,e	corto	curto	corto
silent (mute)	silencieux,se	silencioso	silencioso	silenzioso
similar	semblable	semejante	semelhante	simile
simple	simple	sencillo	simples	semplice
sincere	sincère	sincero	sincero	sincero
slow	lent,e	lento	vagaroso	lento
small, little	petit,e	pequeño	pequeno	piccolo
smooth	lisse	liso	liso	liscio
sober	sobre	sobrio	sóbrio	sobrio
social	social,e	social	social	sociale
soft (not hard)	mou,molle	blando	brando	molle
sour	aigre	agrio	azêdo	agro
special	spécial,e	especial	especial	speciale
square	carré,e	cuadrado	quadrado	quadro
steep	escarpé,e	escarpado	escarpado	ripido
sticky	collant,e	pegajoso	pegajoso	appiccica-ticcio
straight	droit,e	derecho	direito	diritto
strange (peculiar)	étrange	extraño	raro	strano
strong	fort,e	fuerte	forte	forte
sudden	soudain,e	repentino	repentino	subitaneo
sufficient	suffisant,e	suficiente	suficiente	sufficiente
suitable (appropriate)	convenable	apropriado	apropriado	conveniente
superior	supérieur,e	superior	superior	superiore
supreme	suprême	supremo	supremo	supremo
sure (certain)	sûr,e	cierto	certo	certo
sweet	doux,ce	dulce	doce	dolce
tender	tendre	tierno	tenro	tenero
tepid	tiède	tibio	tépido	tiepido
terrible	terrible	terrible	terrível	terribile
thick (not thin)	épais,se gros,se	espeso grueso	espêsso grosso	spesso grosso

ENGLISH	FRENCH	SPANISH	PORTU-GUESE	ITALIAN
thin	mince	delgado	delgado	sottile
tight (close-fitting)	serré,e	cerrado	apertado	stretto
tired	fatigué,e	cansado	cansado	stanco
true	vrai,e	verdadero	verdadeiro	vero
ugly	laid,e	feo	feio	brutto
uneasy	inquiet,ète	inquieto	inquieto	inquieto
unequal	inégal,e	desigual	desigual	ineguale
unfaithful	infidèle	infiel	infiel	infedele
unfortunate	infortuné,e	desgraciado	desgraçado	sfortunato
ungrateful	ingrat,e	ingrato	ingrato	ingrato
unhappy	malheureux,se	infeliz	infeliz	infelice
unjust	injuste	injusto	injusto	ingiusto
unknown	inconnu,e	desconocido	desconhecido	sconosciuto
useful	util,e	útil	útil	utile
useless	inutile	inútil	inútil	inutile
usual	usuel,le	usual	usual	usuale
vain (persons)	vaniteux,se	vanidoso	vaidoso	vanitoso
violent	violent,e	violento	violento	violento
vulgar	vulgaire	vulgar	vulgar	volgare
warm	chaud,e	caliente	quente	caldo
wet (of persons and objects)	mouillé,e	mojado	molhado	bagnato
white	blanc,che	blanco	branco	bianco
wicked	méchant,e	malo	malvado	cattivo
wide (broad)	large	ancho	largo	largo
wild (not domesticated)	sauvage	salvaje	selvagem	selvaggio
wise	sage	sabio	sábio	saggio
wrong	faux,sse	falso	errado	falso
yellow	jaune	amarillo	amarelo	giallo
young	jeune	joven	novo	giovane

5. VERBS

be able to	pouvoir	poder	poder	potere
absorb	absorber	absorber	absorver	assorbire
abuse (revile)	injurier	injuriar	injuriar	ingiuriare
accept	accepter	aceptar	aceitar	accettare
accompany	accompagner	acompañar	acompanhar	accompagnare
accuse (of)	accuser (de)	acusar (de)	acusar (de)	accusare (di)
get accustomed (to)	s'accoutumer (à)	acostumbrarse (a)	acostumar-se (a)	avvezzarsi (a)

ENGLISH	FRENCH	SPANISH	PORTU-GUESE	ITALIAN
add (to)	ajouter (à)	añadir (a)	juntar (a)	aggiungere (a)
add up	additionner	sumar	somar	sommare
admire	admirer	admirar	admirar	ammirare
advance	avancer	adelantar	adiantar	avanzare
advertise (goods)	annoncer	anunciar	anunciar	annunziare
advise (counsel)	conseiller	aconsejar	aconselhar	consigliare
be afraid (of)	avoir peur (de)	tener miedo (de)	ter mêdo (de)	aver paura (di)
	craindre	temer	temer	temere
be in agreement (with)	être d'accord (avec)	concordar (con)	concordar (com)	essere d'accordo (con)
alight (from)	descendre (de)	apearse (de)	apear-se (de)	scendere (da)
allow (to)	permettre (de)	permitir	permitir	permettere (di)
amuse	divertir	divertir	divertir	divertire
amuse oneself	s'amuser	divertirse	divertir-se	divertirsi
apologize	s'excuser	disculparse	desculpar-se	scusarsi
appear	apparaître	aparecer	aparecer	apparire
approach	s'approcher (de)	acercarse (a)	aproximar-se (de)	avvicinarsi (a)
arm	armer	armar	armar	armare
arrest (seize)	arrêter	arrestar	prender	arrestare
arrive	arriver	llegar	chegar	arrivare
ascend (go up)	monter	subir	subir	salire
be ashamed (of)	avoir honte (de)	avergonzarse (de)	envergonhar-se (de)	aver vergogna (di)
ask (a question)	demander	preguntar	perguntar	domandare
ask for	demander	pedir	pedir	chiedere
astonish (amaze)	étonner	asombrar	assombrar	sbalordire
be astonished	s'étonner	asombrarse	assombrar-se	stupirsi
attack	attaquer	atacar	atacar	attaccare
attempt (to)	essayer (de)	tratar (de)	tentar (de)	tentare
attract	attirer	atraer	atrair	attirare
avoid	éviter	evitar	evitar	evitare
bathe	baigner	bañar	banhar	bagnare
bathe, take bath	se baigner	bañarse	banhar-se	bagnarsi
beat (thrash)	battre	golpear	bater	battere
become	devenir	hacerse	fazer-se	divenire
begin	commencer	empezar	começar	cominciare
begin (to)	commencer (à) se mettre à	ponerse (a)	pôr-se (a)	mettersi (a)
behave	se conduire	conducirse	conduzir-se	condursi
believe	croire	creer	crer	credere
belong to	appartenir à	pertenecer a	pertenecer a	appartenere a
bend	courber	curvar	curvar	curvare
bend	se courber	encorvarse	curvar-se	curvarsi

ENGLISH	FRENCH	SPANISH	PORTU-GUESE	ITALIAN
bet	parier	apostar	apostar	scommettere
bite	mordre	morder	morder	mordere
blame	blâmer	culpar	culpar	incolpare
blossom	fleurir	florecer	florescer	fiorire
blow	souffler	soplar	soprar	soffiare
blow one's nose	se moucher	sonarse	assoar-se	soffiarsi
boast (of)	se vanter (de)	jactarse (de)	gabar-se (de)	vantarsi (di)
boil	faire bouillir	hacer hervir	fazer ferver	far bollire
boil	bouillir	hervir	ferver	bollire
bore (tire)	ennuyer	aburrir	enfastiar	annoiare
be born	naître	nacer	nascer	nascere
borrow	emprunter	pedir prestado	pedir emprestado	prendere a prestito
brake	freiner	enfrenar	travar	frenare
break	briser	romper	romper	rompere
	casser	quebrar	quebrar	spezzare
	rompre			
break	se casser	romperse	romper-se	rompersi
breathe	respirer	respirar	respirar	respirare
breed *or* bring up	élever	criar	criar	allevare
breed	se multiplier	multiplicarse	multiplicar-se	moltiplicarsi
bring	apporter	traer	trazer	portare
broadcast	diffuser	difundir	difundir	radio diffondere
brush	brosser	cepillar	escovar	spazzolare
build	bâtir	edificar	edificar	costruire
burn	brûler	quemar	queimar	bruciare
burn	brûler	arder	arder	ardere
burst	crever	reventar	rebentar	scoppiare
bury (inter)	enterrer	enterrar	enterrar	sotterrare
busy oneself with	s'occuper de	ocuparse de	ocupar-se de	occuparsi di
buy	acheter	comprar	comprar	comprare
calculate	calculer	calcular	calcular	calcolare
call (give name)	appeler nommer	llamar	chamar	chiamare
be called	s'appeler	llamarse	chamar-se	chiamarsi
call (cry to)	appeler	llamar	chamar	chiamare
caress	caresser	acariciar	acariciar	accarezzare
carry	porter	llevar	levar	portare
catch (animal)	attraper	coger	apanhar	prendere
catch cold	s'enrhumer	resfriarse	constipar-se	raffreddarsi
cause	causer	causar	causar	causare
cease (to)	cesser (de)	cesar (de)	cessar	cessare (di)
celebrate	célébrer	celebrar	celebrar	celebrare

ENGLISH	FRENCH	SPANISH	PORTU-GUESE	ITALIAN
change (alter)	changer	cambiar	alterar	cambiare
change	changer	mudar	mudar	cambiarsi
chase away	chasser	echar	enxotar	scacciare
chew	mâcher	masticar	mastigar	masticare
choke (suffocate)	suffoquer	sofocar	sufocar	soffocare
choose	choisir	escoger	escolher	scegliere
clean	nettoyer	limpiar	limpar	pulire
close *or* shut	fermer	cerrar	fechar	chiudere
collect (gather)	rassembler	recoger	colher	raccogliere
comb	peigner	peinar	pentear	pettinare
comb	se peigner	peinarse	pentear-se	pettinarsi
come	venir	venir	vir	venire
come back	revenir	volver	voltar	rivenire
compare (with)	comparer (à)	comparar (a)	comparar (com)	confrontare (con)
compel (to)	obliger (à) forcer (à)	obligar (a) forzar (a)	obrigar (a) forçar (a)	obbligare (a) forzare (a)
complain (about)	se plaindre (de)	quejarse (de)	queixar-se (de)	lagnarsi (di)
concern (be important to)	regarder	concernir	concernar	riguardare
condemn (to)	condamner (à)	condenar (a)	condenar(a)	condannare (a)
confess	avouer	confesar	confessar	confessare
confuse	confondre	confundir	confundir	confondere
congratulate	féliciter	felicitar	felicitar	felicitare
conquer (take by force)	conquérir	conquistar	conquistar	conquistare
console	consoler	consolar	consolar	consolare
contain	contenir	contener	conter	contenere
continue (to)	continuer (à)	continuar	continuar (a)	continuare (a)
contradict	contredire	contradecir	contradizer	contraddire
convince	convaincre	convencer	convencer	convincere
cook	faire cuire	cocinar	cozinhar	cucinare
copy	copier	copiar	copiar	copiare
correct	corriger	corregir	corrigir	correggere
correspond to	correspondre à	corresponder a	corresponder a	corrispondere a
cost	coûter	costar	custar	costare
cough	tousser	toser	tossir	tossire
count	compter	contar	contar	contare
cover (with)	couvrir (de)	cubrir (con)	cobrir (de)	coprire (con)
criticize	critiquer	criticar	criticar	criticare
cross (street, etc.)	traverser	atravesar	atravessar	attraversare
crush	écraser	quebrantar	esmagar	schiacciare
cure (heal)	guérir	curar	curar	guarire

ENGLISH	FRENCH	SPANISH	PORTU-GUESE	ITALIAN
cut	couper	cortar	cortar	tagliare
dance	danser	bailar	dançar	ballare
dare (venture)	oser	atreverse (a)	atrever-se (a)	osare
deceive	tromper	engañar	enganar	ingannare
decide (to)	se décider (à)	decidirse (a)	decidir-se (a)	decidersi (a)
decorate	décorer	decorar	decorar	decorare
deduce (infer)	déduire	deducir	deduzir	dedurre
defend	défendre	defender	defender	difendere
define	définir	definir	definir	definire
demand (insist upon)	exiger	exigir	exigir	esigere
deny (say that thing is un-true)	nier	negar	negar	negare
depart (leave)	partir	partir	partir	partire
depend upon	dépendre de	depender de	depender de	dipendere da
deprive of	priver de	privar de	privar de	privare di
descend	descendre	descender	descer	discendere
describe	décrire	describir	descrever	descrivere
desert	abandonner	abandonar	abandonar	abbandonare
deserve	mériter	merecer	merecer	meritare
desire	désirer	desear	desejar	desiderare
despair (of)	désespérer (de)	desesperar (de)	desesperar (de)	disperare (di)
despise	mépriser	despreciar	desprezar	disprezzare
destroy	détruire	destruir	destruir	distruggere
determine	déterminer	determinar	determinar	determinare
detest	détester	detestar	detestar	detestare
develop (grow)	se développer	desarrollarse	desenvolver-se	svilupparsi
die (from)	mourir (de)	morir (de)	morrer (de)	morire (di)
digest	digérer	digerir	digerir	digerire
diminish	diminuer	disminuir	diminuir	diminuire
dine	dîner	comer	jantar	pranzare
dip (plunge)	plonger	sumergir	mergulhar	immergere
disappear	disparaître	desaparecer	desaperecer	sparire
discover	découvrir	descubrir	descobrir	scoprire
discuss	discuter	discutir	discutir	discutere
disguise oneself	se déguiser	disfrazarse	disfarçar-se	travestirsi
disinfect	désinfecter	desinfectar	desinfetar	disinfettare
dismiss (fire)	congédier saquer (fam.)	despedir	despedir	licenziare
displease	déplaire	desagradar	desagradar	dispiacere
dissolve	dissoudre	disolver	dissolver	dissolvere
distinguish	distinguer	distinguir	distinguir	distinguere
distribute (deal out)	distribuer	distribuir	distribuir	distribuire

ENGLISH	FRENCH	SPANISH	PORTU-GUESE	ITALIAN
disturb	déranger	incomodar	encomodar	disturbare
dive	plonger	zambullirse	mergulhar	tuffarsi
diverge (from)	diverger (de)	divergir (de)	divergir (de)	divergere (di)
divide (into)	diviser (en)	dividir (en)	dividir (em)	dividere (in)
do or make	faire	hacer	fazer	fare
do without	se passer de	pasarse sin	passar sem	fare a meno di
doubt	douter	dudar	duvidar	dubitare
draw (sketch)	dessiner	dibujar	debuxar	disegnare
dream	rêver	soñar	sonhar	sognare
dress	habiller	vestir	vestir	vestire
dress	s'habiller	vestirse	vestir-se	vestirsi
drink	boire	beber	beber	bere
drive (vehicle)	conduire	conducir	guiar	guidare
drop (let fall)	laisser tomber	dejar caer	deixar cair	lasciar cadere
drown	se noyer	ahogarse	afogar-se	annegarsi
dry	sécher	secar	secar	seccare
dye	teindre	teñir	tingir	tingere
earn	gagner	ganar	ganhar	guadagnare
eat	manger	comer	comer	mangiare
educate (instruct)	instruire	instruir	instruir	istruire
elect	élire	elegir	eleger	eleggere
embrace	embrasser	abrazar	abraçar	abbracciare
emphasize	souligner	recalcar	acentuar	accentuare
employ (labor)	employer	emplear	empregar	impiegare
empty	vider	vaciar	despejar	votare
enter	entrer dans	entrar en	entrar em	entrare in
envy	envier	envidiar	invejar	invidiare
erase (cancel)	biffer	borrar	cancelar	cancellare
evaporate	s'évaporer	evaporarse	evaporar-se	svaporarsi
exaggerate	exaggérer	exagerar	exagerar	esagerare
examine (investigate)	examiner	examinar	examinar	esaminare
exclude	exclure	excluir	excluir	escludere
exhibit	exposer	exhibir	exibir	esporre
exist	éxister	existir	existir	esistere
expect	attendre	esperar	esperar	aspettare
explain	expliquer	explicar	explicar	spiegare
exploit	exploiter	explotar	explorar	sfruttare
extend	s'étendre	extenderse	estender-se	stendersi
extinguish	éteindre	apagar	apagar	spegnere
faint	s'évanouir	desmayarse	desmaiar	svenirsi
fall	tomber	caer	cair	cadere
fall asleep	s'endormir	dormirse	adormecer	addormentarsi
fall ill	tomber malade	caer enfermo	cair enfermo	ammalarsi

ENGLISH	FRENCH	SPANISH	PORTU-GUESE	ITALIAN
fall in love (with)	tomber amoureux (de)	enamorarse (de)	enamorar-se (de)	innamorarsi (di)
fasten (fix)	fixer	fijar	fechar	fissare
feed	nourir	alimentar	alimentar	alimentare
feel (well, etc.)	se sentir	sentirse	sentir-se	sentirsi
fill (with)	remplir (de)	llenar (de)	encher (de)	riempire (di)
find	trouver	hallar	achar	trovare
finish	finir	acabar	acabar	finire
fish	pêcher	pescar	pescar	pescare
fit (adjust)	ajuster	ajustar	ajustar	aggiustare
flatter	flatter	adular	lisonjear	lusingare
flee (run away)	s'enfuir	huir	fugir	fuggire
flow (of liquid)	couler	correr	correr	colare
fly	voler	volar	voar	volare
fold	plier	doblar	dobrar	piegare
follow	suivre	seguir	seguir	seguire
forbid	défendre	prohibir	proibir	vietare proibire
forecast (predict)	prédire	predecir	predizer	predire
foresee	prévoir	prever	prever	prevedere
forget	oublier	olvidar	esquecer	dimenticare
forgive	pardonner	perdonar	perdoar	perdonare
found (establish)	fonder	fundar	fundar	fondare
freeze *freeze*	geler ⎱ geler ⎰	helar	gelar	gelare
frighten	effrayer	asustar	assustar	spaventare
furnish	meubler	amueblar	mobilar	ammobigliare
gather (pick)	cueillir	recoger	colher	cogliere
get rid of	se débarrasser de	librarse de	desembaraçar-se de	sbarazzarsi di
give	donner	dar	dar	dare
go	aller	ir andar	ir andar	andare
go away	s'en aller	irse	ir-se	andar via
go out	sortir	salir	sair	uscire
go to bed	se coucher	acostarse	deitar-se	coricarsi
govern	gouverner	gobenar	governar	governare
greet	saluer	saludar	saudar	salutare
grind (reduce to powder)	moudre	moler	moer	macinare
groan	gémir	gemir	gemer	gemere
grow	cultiver	cultivar	cultivar	coltivare
grow (of plants, etc.)	croître	crecer	crescer	crescere

ENGLISH	FRENCH	SPANISH	PORTU-GUESE	ITALIAN
guess	deviner	adivinar	adivinhar	indovinare
guide	guider	guiar	guiar	guidare
handle (tool, etc.)	manier	manejar	manejar	maneggiare
hang (person)	pendre	ahorcar	enforcar	impiccare
hang up	suspendre	colgar	pendurar	sospendere
hang down	pendre	colgar	colgar	penzolare
happen	arriver	acontecer	acontecer	avvenire
hate	haïr	odiar	odiar	odiare
have (own, hold)	avoir	tener	ter	avere
hear	entendre	oir	ouvir	udire
				sentire
heat	chauffer	calentar	aquecer	riscaldare
help	aider	ayudar	ajudar	aiutare
hesitate	hésiter	vacilar	vacilar	esitare
hide	cacher	ocultar	esconder	nascondere
hide	se cacher	ocultarse	esconder-se	nascondersi
hinder	empêcher	impedir	impedir	impedire
hire	louer	arrendar	alugar	prender a nolo
hit (strike)	frapper	acertar	acertar	colpire
hold	tenir	tener	ter	tenere
hope	espérer	esperar	esperar	sperare
hunt	chasser	cazar	caçar	cacciare
hurry	se dépêcher	apresurarse	apressar-se	affrettarsi
hurt (injure)	blesser	herir	ferir	ferire
hurt (ache)	faire mal	doler	doer	far male
imagine (figure)	se figurer	figurarse	imaginar	figurarsi
imitate	imiter	imitar	imitar	imitare
increase	augmenter	aumentar	aumentar	aumentare
indicate	indiquer	indicar	indicar	indicare
infect	infecter	infectar	infectar	infettare
inflate	gonfler	inflar	encher	gonfiare
inform	informer	informar	informar	informare
inhabit	habiter	habitar	habitar	abitare
inherit	hériter	heredar	herdar	ereditare
inquire (ask about)	s'informer	informarse	informar-se	informarsi
insult	insulter	insultar	insultar	insultare
insure	assurer	asegurar	assegurar	assicurare
interest	intéresser	interesar	interessar	interessare
interfere with	se mêler de	meterse en	meter-se em	immischiarsi in
interrupt	interrompre	interrumpir	interromper	interrompere
introduce (person)	présenter	presentar	apresentar	presentare
invent	inventer	inventar	inventar	inventare
invite	inviter	invitar	convidar	invitare
irritate	irriter	irritar	irritar	irritare

ENGLISH	FRENCH	SPANISH	PORTU-GUESE	ITALIAN
join (put together)	joindre	juntar	juntar	giungère
joke (jest)	plaisanter	bromear	gracejar	scherzare
judge	juger	juzgar	julgar	giudicare
jump	sauter	saltar	saltar	saltare
keep (retain)	garder	guardar	guardar	guardare
keep (maintain)	maintenir	mantener	manter	mantenere
kick (of humans)	donner des coups de pied	dar puntapiés	dar pontapés	dar dei calci
kill	tuer	matar	matar	uccidere
kiss	embrasser	besar	beijar	baciare
kneel	s'agénouiller	arrodillarse	ajoelhar	inginocchiarsi
knock (at door)	frapper	llamar	tocar	toccare
know	connaître savoir	conocer saber	conhecer saber	conoscere sapere
last	durer	durar	durar	durare
laugh	rire	reír	rir	ridere
laugh at	se moquer de se rire de	mofarse de reirse de	mofar-se de rir-se de	burlarsi di rider di
lean (against)	s'appuyer (contre)	apoyarse (contra)	apoiar-se (em)	appoggiarsi (contro)
learn (to)	apprendre (à)	aprender (a)	aprender (a)	imparare (a)
leave (behind *or* in certain state, allow)	laisser	dejar	deixar	lasciare
lend	prêter	prestar	emprestar	prestare
let (house)	louer	alquilar	alugar	affittare
lie (tell untruth)	mentir	mentir	mentir	mentire
light (set fire to)	allumer	encender	acender	accendere
light (illuminate)	éclairer	alumbrar	iluminar	illuminare
like *or* love	aimer	gustar *	gostar de	piacere *
limp	boîter	cojear	coxear	zoppicare
listen	écouter	escuchar	escutar	ascoltare
live (be alive)	ʼvivre	vivir	viver	vivere
live (dwell)	demeurer habiter	morar habitar	morar habitar	abitare dimorare
load (put on vehicle, etc.)	charger	cargar	carregar	caricare
lock	fermer à clef	cerrar con llave	fechar à chave	serrare a chiave
look (appear)	avoir l'air	parecer	parecer	parere
look after (take care of)	s'occuper de	cuidar de	cuidar de	attendere

* With change of subject, e.g. Sp. *me gustan los pasteles* (I like pies).

ENGLISH	FRENCH	SPANISH	PORTU-GUESE	ITALIAN
look at	regarder	mirar	olhar para	guardare
look for	chercher	buscar	buscar	cercare
lose	perdre	perder	perder	perdere
love (person)	aimer	amar	amar	amare
		querer	querer bem	
lower	baisser	bajar	baixar	abbassare
make a mistake	se tromper	equivocarse	enganar-se	sbagliarsi
make sure (of)	s'assurer (de)	asegurarse (de)	assegurar-se (de)	accertarsi (di)
manage (direct)	diriger	dirigir	dirigir	dirigere
manufacture	fabriquer	fabricar	fabricar	fabbricare
marry (take in marriage)	épouser	casarse con	casar-se com	sposare
get married	se marier	casarse	casar-se	ammogliarsi (of man) maritarsi (of woman)
measure	mesurer	medir	medir	misurare
meet	rencontrer	encontrar	encontrar	incontrare
meet (assemble)	se réunir	reunirse	reünir-se	riunirsi
melt	fondre	derretir	derreter	fondere
melt	se fondre	derretirse	derreter-se	fondersi
mend	réparer	reparar	reparar	riparare
mention	mentionner	mencionar	mencionar	menzionare
mix	mêler	mezclar	misturar	mescolare
move (shift)	remuer	mover	mover	movere
move (budge)	bouger	moverse	mover-se	moversi
move (into new place)	déménager	mudarse de casa	mudar de casa	cambiar di casa
multiply	multiplier	multiplicar	multiplicar	moltiplicare
need	avoir besoin de	necesitar	necessitar	aver bisogno di abbisognare
neglect	négliger	descuidar	descuidar	trascurare
nurse (sick)	soigner	cuidar	cuidar	curare
obey	obéir à	obedecer a	obedecer a	ubbidire a
object (to)	s'opposer (à)	oponerse (a)	opôr-se (a)	opporsi (a)
observe (watch)	observer	observar	observar	osservare
obtain	obtenir	obtener	obter	ottenere
offend	offenser	ofender	ofender	offendere
offer	offrir	ofrecer	oferecer	offerire
omit	omettre	omitir	omitir	ommettere
open	ouvrir	abrir	abrir	aprire
oppose (with-stand)	résister (à)	resistir (a)	resistir (a)	resistere (a)
oppress	opprimer	oprimir	oprimir	opprimere

ENGLISH	FRENCH	SPANISH	PORTU-GUESE	ITALIAN
order (goods)	commander	pedir	ordenar	ordinare
owe	devoir	deber	dever	dovere
paint	peindre	pintar	pintar	dipingere
pardon	pardonner	perdonar	perdoar	perdonare
pass (close to)	passer (à côté de)	pasar (al lado de)	passar (ao lado de)	passar (davanti a)
pawn	engager	empeñar	empenhar	impegnare
pay	payer	pagar	pagar	pagare
perforate	perforer	perforar	perforar	perforare
permit	permettre	permitir	permitir	permettere
persecute	persécuter	perseguir	perseguir	perseguitare
pick up	ramasser	recoger	apanhar	raccogliere
plan	projeter	proyectar	projectar	progettare
plant	planter	plantar	plantar	piantare
play (game)	jouer (à)	jugar (a)	jogar (a)	giocare (a)
play (instrument)	jouer (de)	tocar	tocar	suonare
poison	empoisonner	envenenar	envenenar	avvelenare
possess	posséder	poseer	possuir	possedere
pour out	verser	derramar	derramar	versare
praise	louer	alabar	louvar	lodare
pray	prier	rezar	rezar	pregare
precede	précéder	preceder	preceder	precedere
prefer	préférer	preferir	preferir	preferire
prepare	préparer	preparar	preparar	preparare
press (hold tight)	serrer	apretar	apertar	serrare stringere
pretend (feign)	feindre	fingir	fingir	fingere
prevent (from)	empêcher (de)	impedir	impedir (de)	impedire (di)
print	imprimer	imprimir	imprimir	stampare
produce	produire	producir	produzir	produrre
profit (from)	profiter (de)	aprovecharse (de)	tirar proveito	approfittare (di)
promise	promettre	prometer	prometer	promettere
pronounce	prononcer	pronunciar	pronunciar	pronunziare
propose (suggest)	proposer	proponer	propôr	proporre
protect	protéger	proteger	proteger	proteggere
protest	protester	protestar	protestar	protestare
prove (give proof of)	prouver	probar	provar	provare
publish	publier	publicar	publicar	pubblicare
pull	tirer	tirar	puxar	tirare
pull out	arracher	arrancar	arrancar	strappare
pump (water, etc.)	pomper	dar a la bomba	dar à bomba	pompare

ENGLISH	FRENCH	SPANISH	PORTU-GUESE	ITALIAN
punish	punir	castigar	castigar	punire
pursue	poursuivre	perseguir	perseguir	perseguitare
push	pousser	empujar	empurrar	spingere
put (place)	mettre	poner	pôr	porre
	poser	colocar	colocar	mettere
quarrel	se quereller	disputar	disputar	altercare
	se disputer	reñir	renhir	bisticciarsi
be quiet (say nothing)	se taire	callarse	calar-se	tacere
quote	citer	citar	citar	citare
rain	pleuvoir	llover	chover	piovere
raise (lift)	lever	levantar	levantar	alzare
react	réagir	reaccionar	reagir	reagire
read	lire	leer	ler	leggere
receive	recevoir	recibir	receber	ricevere
recite	réciter	recitar	recitar	recitare
recognize	reconnaître	reconocer	reconhecer	riconoscere
recommend	recommander	recomendar	recomendar	raccomandare
reconcile (make it up)	se réconcilier	reconciliarse	reconciliar-se	riconciliarsi
recover (get better)	se remettre	recobrar	restabelecer-se	rimettersi
reduce	réduire	reducir	reduzir	ridurre
reflect (light)	réfléchir	reflejar	reflectir	riflettere
refuse (to)	refuser (de)	rehusar (+ infin.)	recusar (a)	rifiutare
regret (be sorry)	regretter	sentir	sentir	rincrescersi
rely upon	compter sur	confiar en	contar com	contare su
remain (be left over)	rester	restar	restar	restare rimanere
remember	se souvenir de	acordarse de	lembrar-se de	ricordarsi di
remind	rappeler	recordar	lembrar	ricordare
repeat	répéter	repetir	repetir	ripetere
replace (substitute)	remplacer	reemplazar	substituir	rimpiazzare
reply	répondre	contestar	responder	rispondere
represent (stand for)	représenter	representar	representar	rappresentare
reprimand	réprimander	reprobar	repreender	riprendere
repulse	repousser	repulsar	repulsar	respingere
resemble	ressembler (à)	parecerse (a)	parecer-se (com)	rassomigliare (a)
reserve (seat, etc.)	réserver	reservar	reservar	riservare
respect	respecter	respetar	respeitar	rispettare
rest (repose)	se reposer	descansar	descansar	riposarsi

ENGLISH	FRENCH	SPANISH	PORTU-GUESE	ITALIAN
restrict	restreindre	restringir	restringir	restringere
retain	retenir	retener	reter	ritenere
retire (with-draw)	se retirer	retirarse	retirar-se	ritirarsi
return (give back)	rendre	devolver	devolver	restituire
return (go back)	retourner	volver	voltar	ritornare rivedere
revise	réviser	revisar	revêr	
revive (restore to life)	ressusciter	resucitar	ressuscitar	risuscitare
revolve	tourner	girar	girar	girare
reward	récompenser	recompensar	recompensar	ricompensare
ring (bell)	sonner	tocar	tocar	suonare
rise	se lever	levantarse	levantar-se	alzarsi
risk	risquer	arriesgar	arriscar	arrischiare
roll } *roll*	rouler	rodar	rolar	rotolare
row	ramer	remar	remar	remare
rub	frotter	frotar	esfregar	fregare
ruin	ruiner	arruinar	arruinar	rovinare
run	courir	correr	correr	correre
save (from danger)	sauver	salvar	salvar	salvare
save up	épargner	ahorrar	poupar	risparmiare
say	dire	decir	dizer	dire
scatter	éparpiller	esparcir	espalhar	spargere
scrape	gratter	rascar	raspar	raschiare
scratch	égratigner	arañar	arranhar	graffiare
see	voir	ver	ver	vedere
seem	sembler paraître	parecer	parecer	parere
seize (grasp)	saisir	agarrar	agarrar	afferrare
sell	vendre	vender	vender	vendere
send	envoyer	enviar	enviar	mandare
send back	renvoyer	devolver	devolver	rinviare
separate (from)	séparer (de)	separar (de)	separar (de)	separare (di)
serve (meals *or* persons)	servir	servir	servir	servire
sew	coudre	coser	coser	cucire
shake (agitate)	secouer	sacudir	chocalhar	scuotere
share (hand part over)	partager	compartir	repartir	spartire
sharpen	aiguiser	afilar	afiar	affilare
shave	raser faire la barbe	afeitar	fazer a barba	far la barba

ENGLISH	FRENCH	SPANISH	PORTU-GUESE	ITALIAN
shave	se raser se faire la barbe	afeitarse	fazer a barba	farsi la barba
shine	briller luire	brillar lucir	brilhar luzir	brillare risplendere
shoot at	tirer sur	tirar a	atirar a	tirare a
shoot (execute)	fusiller	fusilar	fuzilar	frcilare
shout	crier	gritar	gritar	gridare
show	montrer	mostrar	mostrar	mostrare
shut in	enfermer	encerrar	encerrar	rinchiudere
side with	prendre le parti de	ponerse de parte de	tomar a parte de	prender le parti di
sigh	soupirer	suspirar	suspirar	sospirare
sign	signer	firmar	assinar	firmare
signify	signifier	significar	significar	significare
sing	chanter	cantar	cantar	cantare
sink in	s'enfoncer	hundirse	afundar-se	affondersi
sit (be sitting)	être assis	estar sentado	estar sentado	sedere
sit down	s'asseoir	sentarse	assentar-se	sedersi
sleep	dormir	dormir	dormir	dormire
slip	glisser	resbalar	escorregar	scivolare
smell	sentir	oler	cheirar	sentire
smell (of)	sentir	oler (a)	cheirar (a)	sentire
smile	sourir	sonreír	sorrir	sorridere
smoke (tobacco)	fumer	fumar	fumar	fumare
smoke	fumer	humear	deitar fumo	fumare
snore	ronfler	roncar	ressonar	russare
snow	neiger	nevar	nevar	nevicare
sob	sanglotter	sollozar	soluçar	singhiozzare
soil	souiller	manchar	manchar	sporcare
solve (problem, etc.)	résoudre	resolver	resolver	risolvere
sow	semer	sembrar	semear	seminare
speak	parler	hablar	falar	parlare
spell	épeler	deletrear	soletrar	compitare
spend (money)	dépenser	gastar	gastar	spendere
spend (time)	passer	pasar	passar	passare
spit	cracher	escupir	cuspir	sputare
split	fendre	hender	fender	fendere
stand (be on one's feet)	être debout	estar de pie	estar de pé	stare in piedi
stand on	se tenir sur	estar sobre	estar colocado sôbre	stare sù
stay (reside temporarily)	rester	quedarse	ficar	stare
steal	voler	robar	roubar	rubare
stimulate	stimuler	estimular	estimular	stimolare

ENGLISH	FRENCH	SPANISH	PORTU-GUESE	ITALIAN
sting	piquer	picar	picar	pungere
stop (cause to stop)	arrêter	parar	parar	fermare
stop	s'arrêter	pararse	parar	fermarsi
strike (go on strike)	se mettre en grève	declarse en huelga	declar-se em greve	far sciopero
struggle (with)	lutter (avec)	luchar (con)	lutar (com)	lottare (con)
study	étudier	estudiar	estudar	studiare
succeed (be successful)	réussir	tener éxito	ter êxito	riuscire
suck	sucer	chupar	chupar	succhiare
suffer (from)	souffrir (de)	sufrir (de)	sofrer (de)	soffrire (di)
suffice	suffir	bastar	bastar	bastare
suit (be fitting)	aller bien	sentar bien	assentar bem	star bene
support (prop up, back up)	soutenir	sostener	suportar	sostenere
suppose	supposer	suponer	supôr	supporre
surprise (take by surprise)	surprendre	sorprender	surpreender	sorprendere
surround (with)	entourer (de)	rodear (de)	rodear (com)	circondare (di)
suspect	soupçonner	sospechar	suspeitar	sospettare
swallow	avaler	tragar	engulir	inghiottire
swear (curse)	jurer	jurar	blasfemar	bestemmiare
swear (take oath)	prêter serment	tomar juramento	tomar juramento	giurare
sweat	suer transpirer	sudar transprar	suar transpirar	sudare traspirare
sweep (floor)	balayer	barrer	varrer	spazzare
swim	nager	nadar	nadar	nuotare
sympathize (with)	sympathiser (avec)	simpatizar (con)	simpatizar (com)	simpatizzare (con)
take	prendre	tomar	tomar	prendere
take away	enlever	quitar	retirar	ritirare
taste	goûter	probar	provar	gustare
teach	enseigner	enseñar	ensinar	insegnare
tear (rend)	déchirer	rasgar	rasgar	lacerare
tell (say)	dire	decir	dizer	dire
tell (relate)	raconter	contar	contar	raccontare
test	mettre à l'épreuve	probar	provar	provare
thank	remercier	agradecer	agradecer	ringraziare
think (about)	penser (à)	pensar (de)	pensar (de)	pensare (a)
threaten (with)	menacer (de)	amenazar (con)	ameaçar (com)	minacciare (di)
throw	jeter lancer	echar lanzar	deitar lançar	gettare lanciare

ENGLISH	FRENCH	SPANISH	PORTU-GUESE	ITALIAN
thunder	tonner	tronar	trovejar	tuonare
tie (bind to-together)	lier	liar	ligar	legare
tolerate	tolérer	tolerar	tolerar	tollerare
touch	toucher	tocar	tocar	toccare
translate	traduire	traducir	traduzir	tradurre
transport	transporter	transportar	transportar	trasportare
travel	voyager	viajar	viajar	viaggiare
treat	traiter	tratar	tratar	trattare
tremble	trembler	temblar	tremer	tremare
turn (twist)	tordre	torcer	torcer	torcere
type	taper (à la machine)	escribir a máquina	dactilografar	scriver a macchina
uncover	découvrir	descubrir	descobrir	scoprire
underline	souligner	subrayar	sublinhar	sottolineare
understand (comprehend)	comprendre	comprender	compreender	comprendere
undress	se déshabiller	desnudarse	despir-se	svestirsi
unfasten	détacher	desatar	desatar	staccare
upset	renverser	trastornar	transtornar	rovesciare
urinate	uriner	orinar	urinar	orinare
	pisser	mear	mijar	pisciare
use (employ)	employer	emplear	empregar	adoperare
	se servir de	servirse de	servir-se de	servirsi di
visit	visiter	visitar	visitar	visitare
vomit	vomir	vomitar	vomitar	vomitare
	rendre			
vote	voter	votar	votar	votare
wait for	attendre	esperar	esperar	aspettare
waken	éveiller	despertar	acordar	svegliare
wake up	s'éveiller	despertarse	acordar	svegliarsi
walk	marcher	andar	andar	camminare
walk (go for a walk)	se promener	pasearse	passear-se	far un giro
wander about	errer	errar	errar	errare
	vaguer	vagar	vaguear	vagare
want (wish)	vouloir	querer	querer	volere
	désirer	desear	desejar	desiderare
warn	avertir	avisar	avisar	avvertire
wash	laver	lavar	lavar	lavare
wash	se laver	lavarse	lavar-se	lavarsi
watch (keep an eye on)	surveiller	vigilar	vigiar	sorvegliare
wave (hat, etc.)	agiter	agitar	agitar	agitare
wear (clothes)	porter	llevar	usar	portare
weep	pleurer	llorar	chorar	piangere

ENGLISH	FRENCH	SPANISH	PORTU-GUESE	ITALIAN
weigh ⎱ weigh ⎰	peser	pesar	pesar	pesare
whisper	chuchoter	cuchichear	cochichar	sussurrare
whistle	siffler	silbar	assobiar	fischiare
win	gagner	ganar	ganhar	guadagnare
wind (coil)	enrouler	enrollar	enrolar	arrotolare
wind up (watch)	remonter	dar cuerda	dar corda	caricare
be wont to	avoir coutume de	soler	soer	solere
work	travailler	trabajar	trabalhar	lavorare
worship	adorer	adorar	adorar	adorare
be worth	valoir	valer	valer	valere
wrap up	envelopper	envolver	embrulhar	avvolgere
write	écrire	escribir	escrever	scrivere
yawn	bailler	bostezar	bocejar	sbadigliare
yield (to)	céder (à)	ceder (a)	ceder (a)	cedere (a)

6. ADVERBS

a) PLACE AND MOTION

above, upstairs	en haut	arriba	em cima	di sopra
abroad	à l'étranger	en el extranjero	no estrangeiro	all'estero
anywhere, wherever	n'importe où	donde quiera	onde quer	dovunque
around	autour	alrededor	à roda	intorno
backward	en arrière	atrás	para trás	indietro
before (in front)	devant	delante	diante	davanti
behind	derrière	detrás	atrás	dietro
below, downstairs	en bas	abajo	em baixo	giù abbasso
beyond	au-delà	más allá	além	oltre
downward	en bas	hacia abajo	abaixo	in giù
elsewhere	ailleurs autre part	en otra parte	noutra parte	altrove
everywhere	partout	en todas partes	em tôda a parte	dappertutto
far	loin	lejos	longe	lontano
forward	en avant	adelante	adiante	avanti
hence	d'ici	de aquí	daquí	da qui
here	ici	aquí	aquí	qui
here and there	ça et là	acá y allá	cá e lá	quà e là

ENGLISH	FRENCH	SPANISH	PORTU-GUESE	ITALIAN
hither	ici	aquí	aquí	qui
	par ici		qui	quà
home (home-ward)	à la maison	a casa	a casa	a casa
at home	à la maison	en casa	em casa	in casa
inside	en dedans	dentro	dentro	dentro
near	près	cerca	perto	vicino
nowhere	nulle part	en ninguna parte	em nemhuna parte	in nessun luogo
on the left	à gauche	a la izquierda	à esquerda	a sinistra
on the right	à droite	a la derecha	à direita	a destra
on top	dessus	encima	em cima	sopra
over there (yon)	là-bas	allí; allá	acolá	collà; laggiù
opposite (facing)	vis-à-vis	enfrente	defronte	dirimpetto
outside	dehors	fuera	fora	fuori
somewhere	quelque part	en alguna parte	em algum lugar	in qualche luogo
thence	de là	desde allí	dalí	di là
there	là	allí	alí	lì
	y	allá	acolá	là
		ahí	lá	
thither	là	allí	para alí	lì
	y	allá	para lá	là
through, across	à travers	a través	através	attraverso
underneath	dessous	debajo	debaixo	disotto
upward	en haut	hacia arriba	para cima	insù

b) TIME

after, after-ward	après	después	depois	dopo
	ensuite	luego	em seguida	in seguito
again	de nouveau	de nuevo	de novo	di nuovo
	encore	otra vez	outra vez	ancora
already	déjà	ya	já	già
always	toujours	siempre	sempre	sempre
as soon as possible	le plus tôt possible	cuanto antes lo más pronto	quanto antes o mais pronto	quanto prima il più presto possibile
at first	d'abord au commence-ment	al principio	ao princípio	dapprima
at last	enfin	por fin al fin	em fim por fim	finalmente alla fine
at once	tout de suite à l'instant	en seguida al instante	já no instante	subito immantinente

ENGLISH	FRENCH	SPANISH	PORTU-GUESE	ITALIAN
at present	à présent	al presente	presentemente	adesso
	maintenant	ahora	agora	ora
at the latest	au plus tard	a más tardar	o mais tardar	al più tardi
at the same	en même	en mismo	ao mesmo	allo stesso
time	temps	tiempo	tempo	tempo
at times	quelquefois	a veces	às vezes	qualche volta
	parfois			talvolta
before	avant	antes	antes	prima
				innanzi
daily .	tous les jours	diariamente	diàriamente	ogni giorno
	journellement			
early	tôt	temprano	cedo	di buon' ora
	de bonne heure			
ever (at all times)	toujours	siempre	sempre	sempre
ever (at any time)	jamais	jamás	jamais	mai
finally	finalement	finalmente	finalmente	finalmente
formerly	autrefois	antes	antigamente	altre volte
	jadis	antiguamente		
from time to time	de temps en temps	de cuando en cuando	de quando em quando	di quando in quando
	de temps à autre	de vez en vez		
from that time on	dès lors	desde entonces	desde então	sin d'allora
henceforth	désormais	en adelante	de hoje em diante	d'ora innanzi
hitherto	jusqu'ici	hasta ahora	até agora	finora
in future	à l'avenir	en lo venidero	para o futuro	per l'avvenire
in the evening	le soir	por la tarde	de tarde	di sera
in the morning	le matin	por la mañana	de manhã	di mattina
in time	à temps	a tiempo	a tempo	in tempo
last night	hier soir	anoche	a noite passada	ieri sera
last week	le semaine dernière	la semana pasada	a semana passada	la settimana passata
late	tard	tarde	tarde	tardi
lately	dernièrement	ultimamente	ultimamente	recentemente
meanwhile	en attendant	entretanto	entretanto	frattanto
monthly	par mois	mensualmente	mensalmente	al mese
	mensuellement			
never	jamais	nunca	nunca	mai
	ne . . . jamais	no . . . nunca	não . . . nunca	non . . . mai
no longer	ne . . . plus	ya no	já não	non . . . più
		no . . . más	não . . . mais	

ENGLISH	FRENCH	SPANISH	PORTU-GUESE	ITALIAN
next week	la semaine prochaine	la semana próxima	a semana pró-xima	la settimana ventura
not yet	pas encore	todavía no	ainda não	non ancora
now	maintenant	ahora	agora	ora adesso
nowadays	de nos jours	hoy día	hoje em dia	oggigiorno
now and then	parfois	de vez en cuando	de vez em quando	di quando in quando
often	souvent	a menudo	muitas vezes	spesso
per day	par jour	al día	por dia	al giorno
previously	auparavant	anterior-mente	antes	innanzi
recently	récemment	recientemente	recentemente	recentemente
repeatedly	plusieurs fois à plusieurs reprises	repetida-mente	repetidamente	a più volte
seldom	rarement	raramente	ràramente	raramente
since then	depuis lors	desde entonces	desde então	d'allora
soon (shortly)	bientôt	luego pronto	cedo logo	fra poco
soon after	peu de temps après	poco después	pouco depois	poco dopo
still, yet	encore toujours	aún todavía	ainda todavia	anche tuttora
then (after that)	ensuite	luego	logo	poi
then (at that time)	alors	después	depois	allora
the other day	l'autre jour	el otro día	o outro dia	l'altro giorno
this evening	ce soir	esta tarde	esta tarde	stasera
this morning	ce matin	esta mañana	esta manhã	stamattina
today	aujourd'hui	hoy	hoje	oggi
tomorrow	demain	mañana	amanhã	domani
tomorrow evening	demain soir	mañana por la tarde	amanhã de tarde	domani sera
tomorrow morning	demain matin	mañana por la mañana	amanhã de manhã	domattina
three weeks ago	il y a trois semaines	hace tres semanas	há tres se-manas	tre settimane fa
weekly	chaque se-maine hebdomadaire-ment	semanalmente hebdoma-dariamente	semanalmente	settimanal-mente
yearly	annuellement	anualmente	anualmente	annualmente
yesterday	hier	ayer	ontem	ieri
the day before yesterday	avant-hier	anteayer	ante-ontem	avantieri

ENGLISH	FRENCH	SPANISH	PORTU-GUESE	ITALIAN
the day after tomorrow	après-demain	pasado mañana	depois de amanhã	posdomani
a week from today	d'aujourd'hui en huit	de hoy en ocho días	de hoje a oito dias	oggi a otto
What is the time?	quelle heure est-il?	qué hora es?	que horas são?	che ora è?
it is one o'clock	il est une heure	es la una	é uma	è la una
it is five o'clock	il est cinq heures	son las cinco	são cinco	sono le cinque
half past five	cinq heures et demi	las cinco y media	cinco e meia	le cinque e mezzo
quarter to five	cinq heures moins un quart	las cinco menos cu-arto	cinco menos um quarto	le cinque meno un quarto
quarter past five	cinq heures un quart	las cinco y quarto	cinco e um quarto	le cinque e un quarto
twenty to five	cinq heures moins vingt	las cinco me-nos veinte	cinco menos vinte	venti minuti alle cinque
twenty past five	cinq heures vingt	las cinco y veinte	cinco e vinte	le cinque e venti

c) Manner, Quantity, Affirmation and Negation

about	environ à peu près	cerca	cêrca	circa verso
above all	surtout	sobre todo	sobretudo	sopratutto
actually	en fait en réalité	en realidad	na realidade	infatti
a little	un peu	un poco	um pouco	un poco
almost	prêsque	casi	quási	quasi
aloud	à haute voix	en alta voz	em voz alta	ad alta voce
also, too	aussi	también	também	anche
as (like)	comme	como	como	come
as it were	pour ainsi dire	por decirlo así	por assim dizer	per cosí dire
as much	autant	tanto	tanto	tanto
at least	au moins	a lo menos	pelo menos	almeno
at most	tout au plus	por lo más	ao mais	tutt' al più
badly	mal	mal	mal	male
besides (more-over)	d'ailleurs en outre	además	de mais	inoltre
by all means	à toute force	sin falta	a todo o custo	ad ogni modo
by no means	en aucune manière	de ningun modo	de nenhum modo	in nessun modo
by chance	par hasard	por suerte	por acaso	a caso
by heart	par cœur	de memoria	de cor	a memoria

ENGLISH	FRENCH	SPANISH	PORTU-GUESE	ITALIAN
by the way	en passant	de paso	a propósito	a volo
	à propos	a propósito		a proposito
certainly	certainement	ciertamente	certamente	certamente
chiefly	principale-ment	principal-mente	principalmente	principal-mente
completely	complètement	completa-mente	completa-mente	completa-mente
directly	directement	directamente	directamente	direttamente
enough	assez	bastante	bastante	assai
even	même	aun	ainda	perfino
evidently	évidemment	evidentemente	evidentemente	evidentemente
exactly (just so)	justement	justamente	justamente	giusto
extremely	extrêmement	extremamente	extremamente	estremamente
first (in the first place)	d'abord	primeramente	primeiro	prima
	en premier lieu	en primer lugar	em primeiro lugar	in primo luogo
for instance	par exemple	por ejemplo	por exemplo	per esempio
fortunately	heureusement	por fortuna	felizmente	per fortuna
hardly (scarcely)	à peine	apenas	apenas	appena
hastily	à la hâte	precipitada-mente	precipitada-mente	in fretta
indeed	vraiment	verdadera-mente	verdadeira-mente	davvero
	en vérité	de veras	de-veras	
in general	en général	generalmente	geralmente	generalmente
in vain	en vain	en vano	em vão	invano
less and less	de moins en moins	menos y menos	menos e menos	di meno in meno
little	peu	poco	pouco	poco
little by little	peu à peu	poco a poco	pouco a pouco	poco a poco
more and more	de plus en plus	más y más	mais e mais	di più in più
more or less	plus ou moins	más o menos	mais ou menos	più o meno
mostly	pour la plu-part	en su mayor parte	pela maior parte	per lo più
much	beaucoup	mucho	muito	molto
	bien			
	fort			
namely		(see viz., below)		
no	non	no	não	no
not	ne . . . pas	no	não	non
not at all	pas du tout	de ningún modo	de nenhum modo	niente affatto
not even	pas même	ni aun	nem mesmo	neanche
				neppure
of course	naturellement	naturalmente	naturalmente	naturalmente
	sans doute	sin duda	sem dúvida	si capisce

ENGLISH	FRENCH	SPANISH	PORTU-GUESE	ITALIAN
only	seulement ne ... que	solamente no ... más que	sómente não ... mais que	soltanto non ... che
on purpose	exprès	a propósito	de propósito	apposta
partly	en partie	en parte	em parte	in parte
perhaps	peut-être	talvez	talvez por ventura	forse
probably	probablement	probablemente	provàvelmente	probabilmente
quickly	vite	de prisa	depressa	presto
rather (prefer-ably)	plutôt	más bien	mais	piuttosto
slowly	lentement tout douce-ment	lentamente despacio	lentamente devagar	lentamente pian piano
so (so much)	tant tellement	tanto	tanto	tanto
so (thus)	ainsi	así	assim	così
somewhat	quelque peu	algo	algo	alquanto
suddenly	soudainement tout à coup	de repente de sopetón	subitamente de repente	improvvisa-mente d'un tratto
together	ensemble	juntamente	juntamente	insieme
too, too much	trop	demasiado	demais	troppo
unfortunately	malheureuse-ment	desgraciada-mente	desgraçada-mente	per sfortuna
very	très	muy	muito	molto
viz.	c'est à dire	a saber	a saber	cioè
well	bien	bien	bem	bene
willingly	volontiers	voluntaria-mente de buena gana	voluntària-mente de boa vontade	volentieri
yes	oui si	sí	sim	sì

7. SOCIAL USAGE

good morning good day	bonjour	buenos días	bom dia	buon giorno
good evening	bonsoir	buenas tardes	boa tarde	buona sera
good night	bonsoir bonne nuit	buenas noches	boa noite	buona notte
good-bye	adieu au revoir	adiós hasta luego	adeus até a vista	addio arrivederci

ENGLISH	FRENCH	SPANISH	PORTU-GUESE	ITALIAN
good speed	bon voyage	buena suerte	boa viagem	buon viaggio
your health	à votre santé	a su salud	à sua saúde	salute
many thanks	merci bien	muchas gracias	muito obrigado	tante grazie
thanks	merci *	gracias	obrigado	grazie
don't mention it	il n'y a pas de quoi	no hay de qué	não há de quê	non c'e di che prego
	ce n'est rien	de nada		
I beg your pardon	je vous demande pardon	perdone usted	perdoe-me	le domando scusa
excuse me	excusez-moi	dispénseme	desculpe	mi scusi
I am sorry	je suis désolé	lo siento	lamento muito	mi dispiace
please	s'il vous plaît	por favor	se faz favor	per piacere
with pleasure	avec plaisir	con mucho gusto	com muito gôsto	con piacere
good	bon	bueno	bom	buono
how are you	comment allez-vous	cómo está usted	como está	come sta
		qué tal	que tal está	
so so	comme ci, comme ça	así así	assim, assim	così così
come in	entrez	adelante	entre	avanti

* When accepting an offer say *s'il vous plaît*, or *avec plaisir*, or *volontiers*; when refusing say *merci* or *merci bien*.

APPENDIX III

Greek Roots in Common Use for Technical Words of International Currency

WHAT follows are Greek words with roots which survive in words of our own language and in scientific terms which are international. The latter include especially medical words and names of classes or genera of animals and plants, many of which will be familiar to the reader who has an interest in natural history. Greek abounded in compounds and words with derivative affixes. Loan words often come directly from a combination of elements indicated separately by the reference number of each item. The most important Greek affix which does not occur as a separate word is *a-* (without). Generic and class names listed below have an initial capital letter, as do proper names.

Use of a Greek dictionary in order to find the origin of a technical term involves knowledge of the conventions of Romanized spelling; and the order of the signs of the Greek alphabet: α, β, γ, δ, ε, ζ, η, θ, ι, κ, λ, μ, ν, ξ, ο, π, ρ, σ(ς), τ, υ, φ, χ, ψ, ω. The Greek aspirate is the transposed apostrophe ' written before an initial letter. Thus ʽα = *ha*, ʽρ = *rh*. Dictionaries do not separate words with aspirated from words with unaspirated initial vowel. The transcription of the peculiar Greek consonants is as follows: ψ = *ps*, χ = *ch*, ζ = *z*, φ = *ph*, ξ = *x*. If γ comes before a guttural (γ, ξ, χ) it is equivalent to *n*. Thus γγ = *ng*. The Latin transcription of κ is C, but some modern words render it as K. The equivalents of the simple vowels are ε = *e*, η = *e* or *a*, α = *a*, ι = *i*, ο or ω = *o* and υ = *y*. The conventions for the double vowels are ου = *u*, ει = *i*, αι = *ae*, and οι = *oe* or *e*. The final ια of many Greek substantives becomes *y* in English.

When the *stem* of other case forms of a noun or adjective is longer than, or different from, the nominative the following rule holds good. The nominative form occurs in a *final* syllable, elsewhere the stem. Thus from (232) ασπις (*aspis*—nominative) and ασπιδος (*aspidos*—genitive) we get the zoological names *Hemiaspis* and *Aspidocotyle*. From the nominative θριξ (*thrix*) and genitive τριχος (*trichos*) we get the genera *Ophiothrix* and *Trichina*. Where confusion might arise, the nominative and genitive forms of a noun appear below. An asterisk (*) marks the genitive, if given alone.

The number of verbs listed is small, because the root which turns up in technical words is more transparent in the corresponding abstract noun. Greek prepositions have widely different values depending on the case forms which go with them. The ones given are those which they usually have in technical terms.

Many Greek words transcribed in accordance with the foregoing conventions have come into use with little or no change. These include:

a) Mythical persons such as *Medusa, Hydra, Gorgon, Titan, Andromeda, Morpheus, Nemesis,* and *nectar* (the drink of the gods). The myths have furnished many technical terms for zoological or botanical genera, constellations, etc.

b) Medical terms of which the following are samples:

αρθριτις	*arthritis*	καθαρσις	*catharsis*
αποπληξια	*apoplexy*	καταρροος	*catarrhoos*
ασθμα	*asthma*	λεπρα	*lepra*
διαρροια	*diarrhoea*	μαρασμος	*marasmus*
δυσεντερια	*dysentery*	παραλυσις	*paralysis*
εμπλαστρον	*emplastron* (plaster)	προβοσκις	*proboscis*
επιληψις	*epilepsy*	ρευματισμος	*rheumatismos*
γαγγραινα	*gangreina*	φλεβοτομια	*phlebotomy* (blood letting)
θωραξ	*thorax*	ψωρα	*psora* (itch—psoriasis)

c) A few nontechnical words such as the following:

αινιγμα	*enigma* (riddle)	ιδεα	*idea*
ακμη	*acme* (top, pinnacle)	κριτηριον	(*criterion*)
ασβεστος	*asbestos* (unquenchable)	κυδος	*kudos* (glory)
βασις	*basis*	ὁριζων	*horizon*
δαιμων	*daemon*	πανακεια	*panacea*
διαβολος	*diabolos* (slanderer)	πραξις	*praxis*
δογμα	*dogma*	στιγμα	*stigma* (branding)
δραμα	*drama*	συνταξις	*syntax* (arrangement)
θεμα	*thema* (theme)	ὑφεν	*hyphen*
εικων	*ikon* (image)	φαντασια	*phantasia*
εμφασις	*emphasis*	χαρακτηρ	*character*
ηχω	*echo*	χαος	*chaos*

a) GENERAL NOUNS

1) αγων	(*agon*)	contest	— *protagonist*
2) αγωγη	(*agoge*)	training	— *pedagogue* (220), *galactogogue* (127)
3) αιτια	(*aetia*)	cause	— *aetiology* (36)
4) αισθησις	(*aesthesis*)	perception	— *anaesthesia, aesthetic*
5) αρχη	(*arche*)	beginning origin	— *archaic, archetype* (71), *archenteron* (301), *archegonium* (11), *Archaeopteryx* (348)
6) αυτος	(*autos*)	self	— *autolysis* (37), *autarchy* (202), *autonomy* (217)
7) βιος	(*bios*)	life	— *biology* (36), *symbiosis* (668)
8) βολη	(*bole*)	toss	— *hyperbole* (669), *anabolism* (653), *catabolism* (663)
9) γενεσις	(*genesis*)	origin	— *oogenesis* (387), *ectogenesis* (658), *epigenesis* (661)
10) γενος	(*genos*)	kind, race offspring	— *antigen* (654), *nitrogen* (193), *genealogy* (36), *photogenic* (119)
11) γονη	(*gone*)	generation, womb	— *gonad, opisthogoneate* (580)
12) γωνια	(*gonia*)	angle	— *polygon* (593), *trigonometry* (267, 629)
13) γυρος	(*gyros*)	ring, circle	— *gyrate, Gyrocotyle* (140)
14) γνωσις	(*gnosis*)	knowledge	— *agnostic, diagnostic* (656)
15) δοξα	(*doxa*)	opinion	— *orthodoxy* (582), *heterodoxy* (545)
16) δρομος	(*dromos*)	race, running	— *anadromous* (653), *katadromous* (663)
17) δυναμις	(*dynamis*)	power	— *dynamic, dynamo*
18) δωρον	(*doron*)	gift	— *Dorothea* (252)
19) ελεγος	(*elegos*)	lament	— *elegy, elegiac*
20) ελεημοσυνη	(*eleemosyne*)	pity	— *eleemosynary*
21) επιστημη	(*episteme*)	knowledge	— *epistemology* (36)
22) επος	(*epos*)	speech	— *epic*
23) εργον	(*ergon*)	work	— *erg, synergic* (668), *energy* (659)
24) ερως	(*eros*)	love	— *erotic, autoerotic* (6)
25) θανατος	(*thanatos*)	death	— *euthanasia* (546)
26) θαυμα	(*thauma*)	marvel	— *thaumasite, thaumaturgy* (23)
27) θεραπεια	(*therapia*)	attendance, care	— *therapy, therapeutic*
28) θεσις	(*thesis*)	arrangement order	— *antithesis* (654), *parenthesis* (665) (659)

29) θεωρια	(*theoria*)	reflection, contemplation	— *theory, theoretical*
30) ιστορια	(*historia*)	narrative, research	— *history, story*
31) κεντρον	(*centron*)	center, sting	— *egocentric* (εγω = *I*), *geocentric* (91)
32) κυβos	(*cubos*)	cube	— *cubical*
33) κυλινδρos	(*cylindros*)	cylinder	— *cylindrical*
34) κυκλοs	(*cyclos*)	circle	— *cyclic, tricycle* (267), *epicycle* (661), *Cyclostome* (363)
35) κωμos	(*komos*)	revel, comedy	— *comic*
36) λογοs	(*logos*)	discourse reasoning, word	— *logarithm* (264), *eulogy* (546), *analogy* (653), *apology* (655), *prologue* (667), *dialogue* (656)
37) λυσιs	(*lysis*)	release	— *haemolysis* (281), *analysis* (653), *catalysis* (663)
38) μαθημα	(*mathema*)	learning	— *mathematics*
39) μεθοδοs	(*methodos*)	process	— *method* (107), (664)
40) μεροs	(*meros*)	part	— *metamerism* (664), *meroblastic* (484), *pentamerous* (269)
41) μιμησιs	(*mimesis*)	imitation	— *mimetic, mimicry*
42) μιξιs	(*mixis*)	mixing	— *amphimixis* (526)
43) μισοs	(*misos*)	hatred	— *misogynist* (206), *misanthrope* (201)
44) μνησιs	(*mnesis*)	memory	— *amnesia, mnemonic*
45) μοναs	(*monas*)	a unit	— *monad, Ochromonas* (612), *Trichomonas* (370)
46) μουσικη	(*musice*)	art of the Muses	— *music, musician,* etc.
47) μορφη	(*morphe*)	form	— *morphology* (36), *amorphous, metamorphosis* (664), *Myomorpha* (425)
48) ονομα	(*onoma* or *onyma*)	name	— *onomatopoeia* (632), *anonymous*
49) οργια	(*orgia*)	secret rite	— *orgy*
50) παθοs	(*pathos*)	suffering, passion	— *sympathy* (668), *apathy*
51) πραγμα	(*pragma*)	deed, fact	— *pragmatic, pragmatism*
52) προβλημα	(*problema*)	proposition	— *problem, problematic*
53) πυραμιδοs *	(*pyramidos*)	pyramid	— *pyramidal*
54) ρυθμοs	(*rhythmos*)	rhythm	— *rhythmic, eurythmics* (546)
55) σαρκασμοs	(*sarcasmos*)	mockery	— *sarcasm, sarcastic*
56) σημα	(*sema*)	sign, symbol	— *semantics*
57) σθενοs	(*sthenos*)	strength	— *asthenic, neurasthenia* (325)

58) σκανδαλον	(*scandalon*)	offense	— *scandalous*
59) στασις	(*stasis*)	standing still, posture	— *epistatic* (661), *ecstasy* (657), *apostasy* (655), *statolith* (188), *statocyst* (315)
60) στιγμα	(*stigma*)	mark, puncture	— *stigmata*
61) στροφη	(*strophe*)	twist	— *apostrophe* (655), *Strophan-thus* (483)
62) σφαιρα	(*sphaera*)	sphere, globe	— *spherical, stratosphere*
63) σχημα	(*schema*)	plan	— *scheme, schematic*
64) σοφια	(*sophia*)	wisdom	— *philosophy* (648), *sophism*
65) τελος	(*telos*)	end, purpose	— *entelechy* (659), *teleology* (36), *telosynapsis* (668, 124)
66) τερας	(*teras*)	omen	— *amphoteric* (526)
67) τεχνη	(*techne*)	art	— *technical, pyrotechnic* (111)
68) τονος	(*tonos*)	stretching	— *tonus, tone, tonic*
69) τοπος	(*topos*)	place	— *topography* (619), *ectopic* (657), *topical*
70) τροπη	(*trope*)	direction turn	— *heliotropism* (95), *entropy* (659), *geotropism* (91)
71) τυπος	(*typos*)	model, impression	— *typical, typography* (619), *typewriter*
72) φοβος	(*phobos*)	fear	— *hydrophobia* (114), *xenopho-bia* (575)
73) φρασις	(*phrasis*)	phrase	— *periphrasis* (666), *paraphrase* (665)
74) φρην	(*phren*)	under-standing	— *oligophrenia* (577), *schizo-phrenia* (641)
75) φυσις	(*physis*)	nature	— *physical, physiography* (619)
76) φωνη	(*phone*)	sound, voice	— *phonetics, phonograph* (619), *gramophone* (249), *antiphony* (654), *cacophony* (555)
77) χρωμα	(*chroma*)	color	— *panchromatic* (584), *poly-chrome* (593), *chromosome* (367)
78) χρονος	(*chronos*)	time	— *chronometer* (629), *synchro-nize* (668), *chronology* (36)
79) ψυχη	(*psyche*)	mind	— *psychic, psychology* (36)
80) ωσμη	(*osme*)	thrust	— *osmosis*

b) NATURE—OUTDOOR THINGS

81) αγρος	(*agros*)	field	— *agronomy* (217), *agrophobia* (647)
82) αηρ	(*aer*)	air	— *aerial, aerobic* (7), *aeroplane, aerotropism* (70)

83) ακτις, ακτινος	(actis, actinos)	sunbeam	— actinic, Hexactinia (270), Actinozoa (399), actinomorphic (47)
84) αιθηρ	(aether)	sky	— ether, ethereal
85) ανεμος	(anemos)	wind	— anemophilous (648), anemometer (629)
86) αστηρ	(aster)	star	— astrology (36), astral, asteroid, Aster, Asteroidea
87) ατμος	(atmos)	vapor	— atmosphere (62)
88) αυλος	(aulos)	pipe	— hydraulic (114)
89) βοθρος	(bothros)	pit	— Stenobothrium (597), Bothriocephalus (310)
90) βροντη	(bronte)	thu.ider	— Brontosaurus (434)
91) γη	(ge)	earth	— geography (619), geology (36), geometry (629)
92) δροσος	(drosos)	dew	— Drosera, Drosophila (648)
93) ηως	(eos)	dawn	— Eohippus (401), Eoanthropus (201)
94) ζεφυρος	(zephyros)	west wind	— zephyr
95) ἡλιος	(helios)	sun	— helium, perihelion (666), heliograph (619), heliocentric (31)
96) ἡμερα	(hemera)	day	— ephemeral (661)
97) θαλασσα	(thalassa)	sea	— Thalassemma, Thalassoplancta
98) ιρις	(iris)	rainbow	— iridescent
99) κοσμος	(cosmos)	world	— cosmogony (11), cosmic
100) κρυσταλλος	(crystallos)	ice, crystal	— crystalline, crystallography (619)
101) κυμα	(cyma)	wave	— Cumacea, kymograph (619)
102) λιμνη	(limne)	lake	— limnology (36), Limnanthemum (483)
103) νεφελη	(nephele)	cloud	— nephelometer (629)
104) νησος	(nesos)	island	— Polynesia (593), Micronesia (569), Melanesia (610)
105) νυξ, νυκτος	(nux, nyctos)	night	— Nyctiphanes (646), nyctinasty, nyctotropism (70)
106) ουρανος	(uranos)	heaven	— uranium, uranian
107) ὁδος	(hodos)	way, journey	— period (666), anode (653), cathode (663)
108) πλανης	(planes)	wanderer	— planet
109) ποταμος	(potamos)	river	— hippopotamus (401), Potamogeton
110) πτυξ, πτυχος	(ptyx, ptychos)	cleft	— Ptychodera, Amphiptyches (526), Aptychus
111) πυρ	(pyr)	fire	— pyrex, pyrexa, empyrean (659), Pyronema (148)
112) σεληνη	(selene)	moon	— selenium, selenodont (328)

113)	σπινθηρ	(spinther)	spark	— spinthariscope (639)
114)	ύδωρ	(hydor)	water	— hydrogen (10), anhydrous, hydrant, hydrostatics (59)
115)	ύδατις	(hydatis)	drop	— hydatid
116)	φλοξ, φλογος	(phlox, phlogos)	flame	— phlogiston
117)	φραγμος	(phragmos)	fence	— Phragmatobia (7), Phragmites
118)	φρεαρ, φρεατος	(phrear, phreatos)	cistern	— Phreatokus
119)	φωτος *	(photos)	light	— photic, photograph (619), photon
120)	ψαμμος	(psammos)	sand	— Psammoclema, Psamma
121)	ωκεανος	(oceanos)	ocean ꭝ	— oceanic, oceanography (619)

c) DOMESTIC THINGS (Building, Clothes, Furniture, Tools)

122)	αγγειον	(angeion)	box, chest	— Angiosperm (511), Angiopteris (507)
123)	ασκος	(ascos)	bottle, bag	— Ascomycetes (504), Ascidian
124)	αψις	(apsis)	knot	— synapsis (668), parasynapsis (665)
125)	αξων	(axon)	axle, shaft	— axis, axial, triaxon (267)
126)	βουτυρον	(butyron)	butter	— butyric
127)	γαλα, γαλακτος	(gala, galactos)	milk	— galactic, galaxy
128)	δικτυων	(dictyon)	net	— Dictyota, Palaeodictyoptera (348, 583)
129)	δισκος	(discos)	dish, quoit	— disc, Cephalodiscus (310), Discoglossa (292)
130)	εκκλησια	(ecclesia)	church	— ecclesiastical
131)	ζυγον	(zygon)	yoke	— zygote, azygos, zygoma, zygomorphic (47), homozygote (579)
132)	ζωνη	(zone)	belt	— zone
133)	θαλαμος	(thalamus)	bedchamber	— thalamus, hypothalamus (670), thalamencephalon (297)
134)	θεατρον	(theatron)	theater	— theatrical
135)	θηκη	(theke)	box	— gonotheca (11), blastotheca (484), thecophore (649)
136)	ιστος	(histos)	web	— histology (36), histogenesis (9)
137)	κανων	(canon)	ruler, rod	— canonical
138)	καθεδρα	(cathedra)	chair	— cathedral
139)	κλινη	(cline)	bed	— clinic, clinical
140)	κοτυλη	(cotyle)	small cup (sucker)	— hypocotyl (670), Heterocotylea (545), Monocotyledon (570)

141) κρατηρ	(crater)	mixing vessel, bowl	— crater
142) κτενιον	(ctenion)	comb	— Ctenophora (649), ctenidium, ctenoid
143) κυτος	(cytos)	vessel (cell)	— amoebocyte, phygocyte (645)
144) λυρα	(lyra)	lyre	— lyrical
145) μαρσιπος	(marsipos)	bag	— Marsipobranchii (287)
146) μιτος	(mitos)	thread	— mitosis, mitochondria (384)
147) μιτρα	(mitra)	girdle	— mitre, Haplomitrium (528), Gyromitra (13)
148) νημα, νηματος	(nema, nematos)	thread	— Nematoda, nematocyst (315), Nemathelminthes (396)
149) οικος	(oecos)	house	— ecology (36), dioecious (266)
150) οψον	(opson)	food	— opsonin
151) οργανον	(organon)	tool, instrument	— organ, organic
152) πλασμα	(plasma)	figure, image	— protoplasm (265), cytoplasm (143)
153) πλινθος	(plinthos)	tile	— plinth
154) πυλη	(pyle)	gate	— micropyle (569), apopyle (655)
155) ραφις	(raphis)	needle	— raphide, Raphidae
156) πλαξ, πλακος	(plax, placos)	tombstone, slab	— placoid, Placophora (649), — Placodontea (328)
157) σαλπιγξ, σαλπιγγος	(salpinx, salpingos)	trumpet	— Salpingoeca (149)
158) σιφων	(siphon)	siphon	— Siphonophora (649), siphonoglyph (618), Siphonocladus (495)
159) σκυφος	(scyphos)	cup	— Scyphozoa (399), Scyphistoma (363)
160) σωλην	(solen)	pipe	— solenoid, solenocyte (143), Solenogaster (290)
161) στεγη	(stege)	roof, tent	— Stegocephali (310), Stegosaurus (434), Stegostoma (363)
162) στηλη	(stele)	pillar	— stelar, monostely (570), polystely (593)
163) στεφανος	(stephanos)	wreath	— Stephanoceros (309), Stephanops (338), Stephanotrochus (172)
164) συριγξ, συριγγος	(syrinx, syringos)	shepherd's pipe	— syringe, syrinx
165) στυλος	(stylos)	pillar	— endostyle (660), heterostyly (545)
166) σφην	(sphen)	wedge	— sphenoid, Sphenodon (328), zygasphene (131), Sphenopteris (507)

167)	σχολη	(schole)	school	— scholastic, scholar
168)	ταφος	(taphos)	grave	— epitaph (661)
169)	ταπης	(tapes)	carpet	— tapestry
170)	τραπεζα	(trapeza)	table	— trapezoid
171)	τροφη	(trophe)	food	— atrophy, autotrophic (6), trophoblast (484)
172)	τροχος	(trochos)	wheel	— trochophore (649), Trochhelminthes (396)
173)	τρυπανον	(trypanon)	gimlet	— Trypanosoma (367)
174)	τυρος	(tyros)	cheese	— Tyroglyphe (618)
175)	χιτων	(chiton)	tunic	— chiton, Chiton
176)	χλαμυς	(chlamys)	cloak	— Chlamydomonas (45), monochlamydeous (570)
177)	χορδη	(chorde)	cord	— Chordata, notochord (327), Hemichorda
178)	χυμος	(chymos)	juice	— parenchymatous (665, 659), mesenchyme (568, 659)

d) MATERIALS and SUBSTANCES

179)	ανθραξ	(anthrax)	coal	— anthracite
180)	αργυρος	(argyros)	silver	— Argyrodes
181)	ἀλς	(hals)	salt	— halogen (10), halometer (629), halophyte (518)
182)	ηλεκτρον	(electron)	amber	— electricity
183)	εριον	(erion)	wool	— Eriocaulon (494), Eriophyes (651), Eriobotrya (486)
184)	θειον	(thion)	sulphur	— thiosulphate, thiourea (335)
185)	κεραμος	(ceramos)	clay	— ceramics
186)	κινναβαρι	(cinnabari)	vermilion	— cinnabar
187)	κολλα	(colla)	glue	— colloid, collencyte (659, 143), collenchyma (659, 178)
188)	λιθος	(lithos)	stone	— monolith (570), eolith (93), lithograph (619)
189)	μαγνης	(magnes)	lodestone	— magnet
190)	μαργαριτης	(margarites)	pearl	— Margaret
191)	μεταλλον	(metallon)	mine	— metal, metallic
192)	μολυβδος	(molybdos)	lead	— molybdenum
193)	νιτρον	(nitron)	saltpeter	— nitric, nitrogen (10)
194)	πετρα	(petra)	rock	— petrology (36)
195)	πυριτης	(pyrites)	flint	— pyrites
196)	στεαρ	(stear)	tallow, fat	— stearate, stearic, stearin
197)	χρυσος	(chrysos)	gold	— Chrysopa, Chrysosmonas (45), Chrysochloris (614)
198)	ψηφος	(psephos)	pebble	— Psephurus (334)

e) HUMAN SOCIETY—LAW AND FAMILY, OCCUPATIONS

199)	αδελφος	(adelphos)	brother	— Philadelphia (648), monadelphous (570), polyadelphous (593)
200)	ανδρος *	(andros)	male	— polyandry (593), androgynous (206), androecium (149)
201)	ανθρωπος	(anthropos)	human being	— philanthropy (648), anthropocentric (31), Pithecanthropus (431), lycanthropy (422)
202)	αρχων	(archon)	ruler	— patriarch (222), heptarchy (271), monarch (570), oligarch (577)
203)	βουκολος	(bukolos)	herdsman	— bucolic
204)	γενετη	(genete)	birth	— genetics, eugenics (546)
205)	γεωργος	(georgos)	farmer	— georgic, George
206)	γυνη, γυναικος	(gyne, gynaecos)	woman	— gynaecology (36), epigynous (661), perigynous (666), polygyny (593), gynandromorph (200, 47)
207)	δημος	(demos)	people	— democracy (625), demography (619), endemic (659), epidemic (661)
208)	δεσμος	(desmos)	fetter	— Polydesmus (593), desmids, desmognathous (293)
209)	διακονος	(diaconos)	servant	— deacon, archdeacon (202)
210)	δυναστης	(dynastes)	ruler	— dynasty
211)	κλεπτης	(cleptes)	thief	— kleptomania (321)
212)	κριτης	(crites)	judge	— critic, criticism, hypercritical (669)
213)	λαος	(laos)	people	— lay, laity
214)	μαγος	(magos)	magician	— magic
215)	μητηρ	(meter)	mother	— matriarchy (202)
216)	ναυτης	(nautes)	sailor	— nautical, aeronautics (82)
217)	νομος	(nomos)	law, custom	— astronomy (86), autonomy (6), antinomian (654)
218)	νυμφη	(nymphe)	bride	— nymphomania (321)
219)	οικονομος	(oekonomos)	steward	— economical, economics (149, 217)
220)	παιδος *	(paidos)	child	— pederasty (24), pediatrics (551), orthopaedic (582)
221)	παρθενος	(parthenos)	virgin	— parthenogenesis (9)
222)	πατηρ	(pater)	father	— patriarchy (202)
223)	πλουτος	(plutos)	riches	— plutocracy (625)
224)	πολις	(polis)	city, state	— policy, cosmopolis (99)
225)	πολιτης	(polites)	citizen	— politics

226) πρεσβυς	(presbys)	an old man	— presbyopia (338), presbyterian
227) προφητης	(prophetes)	interpreter	— prophet
228) τεκτων	(teoton)	builder	— architect (202)
229) τυραννος	(tyrannos)	dictator	— tyrant, tyrannical
230) ὑποκριτης	(hypocrites)	actor	— hypocrite
231) φυλη	(phyle)	tribe, clan	— phylum, phyletic, phylogeny (10)

f) ARMY AND NAVY

232) ασπις, ασπιδος	(aspis, ·aspidos)	round shield	— Aspidocotyle (140), Hemiaspis, Pteraspis (348), Anaspidacea
233) ἡρυς	(heros)	demigod, warrior	— heroic, hero
234) θωραξ	(thorax)	breastplate	— thoracic, metathorax (664)
235) θυρεος	(thyreos)	shield	— thyroid, parathyroid (665)
236) κολεος	(coleos)	sheath	— Coleochaete (378), Coleoptera (348)
237) κορυς	(corys)	helmet	— Corymorpha (47), Corydendrium (488), Corylophidae (319)
238) κορυνη	(coryne)	club	— Syncoryne (668), Podocoryne (346)
239) κωπη	(cope)	oar	— Copepoda (346)
240) ξιφος	(xiphos)	sword	— Xiphosura (334), Xiphias
241) σκαφη	(scaphe)	boat	— scaphognathite (293), Scaphopoda (346)
242) στιχος	(stichos)	row, line, verse	— Polystichum (593), Stichopus (346), Stichaster (86)
243) πολεμος	(polemos)	war	— polemic
244) στρατηγος	(strategos)	commander	— strategy, strategic
245) ταξις	(taxis)	battle array, order	— phototaxis (119), rheotaxis (635), phyllotaxis (517)

g) LITERATURE AND RELIGION

246) αγγελος	(angelos)	messenger	— angel, evangelical
247) ασυλον	(asylon)	sanctuary	— asylum
248) βιβλος	(biblos)	book	— bibliophile (648), bibliography (619)
249) γραμμα	(gramma)	letter	— epigram (661), telegram (601), phonogram (76)
250) ειδωλον	(idolon)	image	— idol, idolize
251) επισκοπος	(episcopos)	bishop	— episcopal

252)	θεος	(theos)	god	— theosophy (64), polytheism (593), pantheism (584), theocracy (625)
253)	ιερευς	(hiereus)	priest	— hieratic, hierarchy
254)	λατρεια	(latria)	worship	— idolatry (250), mariolatry
255)	μυθος	(mythos)	fable	— mythical, mythology (36)
256)	μυστηριον	(mysterion)	secret, doctrine, sacrament	— mystery, mystic
257)	παπυρος	(papyros)	paper	—
258)	ῥητορικη	(rhetorice)	rhetoric	—
259)	συλλαβη	(syllabe)	syllable	—
260)	ὑμνος	(hymnos)	hymn	—
261)	χορος	(choros)	dance, chorus	— choric, chorus, terpsichorean
262)	χριστος	(christos)	anointed	— Christ, christian
263)	ψαλμος	(psalmos)	psalm, song	—

b) NUMBERS AND TIME

(Numbers given as they occur in derivatives)

264)	αριθμος	(arithmos)	number	— arithmetic
265)	πρωτος	(protos)	first	— Protozoa (399), Protista, Protococcus (501), protandrous (200), protogynous (206)
266)	δις	(dis)	twice	— Dibranchiata (287)
267)	τρια	(tria)	3	— trilogy (36), Triarthrus (284), trimerous (40)
268)	τετρα	(tetra)	4	— tetramerous (40)
269)	πεντε	(pente)	5	— pentadactyl (294)
270)	ἑξ	(hex)	6	— hexagon (12), Hexapoda (346)
271)	ἑπτα	(hepta)	7	— heptameter (629)
272)	οκτω	(octo)	8	— Octobothrium (89), octopus (346)
273)	δεκα	(deca)	10	— decalogue (36), Decapoda (346)
274)	δωδεκα	(dodeca)	12	— dodecahedron
275)	ἑκατον	(hecaton)	100	— hectogram, hectameter (629)
276)	χιλιοι	(chilioi)	1,000	— kilogram, kilometer (629), Chilopoda (346)
277)	ἑβδομας	(hebdomas)	week	— hebdomadal
278)	ἑσπερα	(hespera)	evening	— Hesperornis (427)
279)	ὡρα	(hora)	hour	— horoscope (639)

i) ANATOMICAL and MEDICAL TERMS

280)	αδην	(aden)	glandule	— adenoid, adenuma
281)	αιμα	(haema)	blood	— haemal, haemoglobin, haemocyanin (607)
282)	αλγος	(algos)	pain	— analgesic
283)	αορτη	(aorte)	aorta	— aortic
284)	αρθρον	(arthron)	joint	— Arthropoda (346), Xenarthra (575)
285)	αρτηρια	(arteria)	artery	— arterial
286)	βλεφαρον	(blepharon)	eyelid	— Monoblepharis (570), Polyblepharis (593), Blepharipoda (346)
287)	βραγχια	(branchia)	gills	— branchial, Branchiopoda (346), Branchiura (334)
288)	βραχιων	(brachion)	armpit	— brachial
289)	βρογχος	(bronchos)	throat	— bronchi, bronchitis
290)	γαστηρ	(gaster)	belly	— gastric, epigastric (661), Gasteromycetes (504)
291)	γαστροκνημη	(gastrocneme)	calf of leg	— gastrocnemius
292)	γλωσσα	(glossa)	tongue	— hypoglossal (670), epiglottis (661), glossopharyngeal (376), Ophioglossum (429)
293)	γναθος	(gnathos)	jaw	— gnathite, prognathous (667), Gnathobdella (392)
294)	δακτυλος	(dactylos)	finger	— hexadactyl (270), polydactyly (593), Pterodactyl (348), Syndactyly (668)
295)	δερμα	(derma)	skin	— epidermis (661), mesoderm (568), dermatitis
296)	διαιτα	(diaeta)	regimen	— diet, dietetics
297)	εγκεφαλος	(encephalos)	brain	— mesencephalon (568), encephalitis, anencephaly
298)	εκτομη	(ectome)	cutting out, castration	— thyreodectomy (235), hypophysectomy (651, 670)
299)	εμβρυον	(embryon)	embryo	— embryonic, polyembryony (593)
300)	εμετος	(emetos)	vomit	— emetic
301)	εντερον	(enteron)	gut	— enteritis, coelenterate (560), mesentery (568)
302)	ηπαρ, ηπατος	(hepar, hepatos)	liver	— hepatic
303)	θηλη	(thele)	teat	— thelin
304)	ισχιον	(ischion)	thigh	— ischial
305)	καρκινος	(carcinos)	crab	— carcinoma
306)	κανθος	(canthos)	corner of eye	— epicanthial

307)	καρδια	*(cardia)*	heart	— *cardiac*
308)	καρπος	*(carpos)*	wrist	— *carpal*
309)	κερας	*(ceras)*	horn	— *keratin, Rhinoceros* (355)
310)	κεφαλη	*(cephale)*	head	— *acephalic, Cephalopoda* (346)
311)	κονδυλος	*(condylos)*	knuckle	— *condyle, Condylarthra* (284)
312)	κορη	*(core)*	girl, pupil	— *corea* (of eye)
313)	κρεας	*(creas)*	flesh	— *creatine, creatinine, pancreas*
314)	κρανιον	*(cranion)*	skull	— *cranial, Craniata, chondro-cranium* (384)
315)	κυστις	*(cystis)*	bladder, bag	— *cystitis, nematocyst* (148)
316)	λεκιθος	*(lecithos)*	yolk	— *lecithin, alecithal*
317)	λαρυγξ, λαρυγγος	*(larynx, laryngos)*	gullet	— *laryngeal*
318)	λεπις, λεπιδος	*(lepis, lepidos)*	scale	— *Lepidoptera* (348), *Lepido-stei* (331), *Osteolepis* (331), *Lepidonotus* (327), *Lepido-dendron* (488)
319)	λοφος	*(lophos)*	comb, crest	— *lophodont* (328), *Lophopus* (346), *Lophogaster* (290)
320)	μυς, μυος	*(mys, myos)*	mouse, muscle	— *myomere* (40), *myotome*
321)	μανια	*(mania)*	frenzy	— *maniac, hypomania* (670) (643)
322)	μυξα	*(muxa)*	phlegm	— *Myxomycetes* (504), *Myxococcus* (501), *Myxosporidia* (512)
323)	ναρκη	*(narce)*	numbness	— *narcosis, narcotic*
324)	ναυσια	*(nausia)*	seasickness	— *nauseating*
325)	νευρον	*(neuron)*	nerve, tendon	— *neura, neurosis*
326)	νεφρος	*(nephros)*	kidney	— *nephridium, mesonephros* (568), *nephritis*
327)	νωτον	*(noton)*	back	— *notochord* (177), *notopodium* (346), *Notostraca* (332)
328)	οδους, οδοντος	*(odous, odontos)*	tooth	— *Odontophore* (649), *theco-dont* (135), *Odontoceti* (410)
329)	οισοφαγος	*(oesophagos)*	oesophagus	— *oesophageal*
330)	ορχις	*(orchis)*	testicle	— *cryptorchid* (626)
331)	οστεον	*(osteon)*	bone	— *osteology* (36), *periosteal* (666)
332)	οστρακον	*(ostracon)*	shell	— *Ostracoda, Conchostraca* (411), *Entomostraca* (398)
333)	ονυξ, ονυχος	*(onyx, onychos)*	nail, claw	— *Onychophora* (649), *Ony-chomonas* (45)
334)	ουρα	*(ura)*	tail	— *urostyle* (165), *Ophiura* (429), *Anura*
335)	ουρον	*(uron)*	urine	— *uric, urea, hippuric* (401)
336)	οφθαλμος	*(ophthalmos)*	eye	— *ophthalmic, ophthalmoscope* (639), *exophthalmos* (657)

337)	οφρυς	(ophrys)	eyebrow	— Actinophrys (83), Ophryo-cystis (315), Ophrytrocha (172)
338)	οψις	(opsis)	appearance, eyesight	— autopsy (6), Bryopsis (487), Sauropsida (434), Ichthyop-sida (402)
339)	παρεια	(pareia)	cheek	— pareital
340)	πελμα	(pelma)	sole	— Pelmatozoa (399)
341)	πεψις	(pepsis)	digestion	— pepsin, eupeptic (546)
342)	πιλος	(pilos)	wool	— Pilochrota (386), Pilocarpus (492), Pilobolus (8)
343)	πλευρα	(pleura)	side, rib	— pleural, pleurocentrum (31), pleurisy
344)	πνευμα	(pneuma)	lungs, breath	— pneumonia, pneumatic, pneumatophore (649), pneu-mococcus (501)
345)	πρωκτος	(proctos)	anus	— proctodeum, aproctous, Ec-toprocta (658)
346)	πους, ποδος	(pous, podos)	foot	— Amphipoda (526), Platypus (588), Isopoda (553), Che-nopodium (453), Lycopo-dium (422)
347)	πτερνα	(pterna)	heel	— Litopterna (λιτος = smooth)
348)	πτερον	(pteron)	wing	— Aptera, Hymenoptera (372), Neuroptera (325)
349)	πτερυγιον	(pterugion)	fin	— archipterygium (5), actinop-terygial (83)
350)	πτιλον	(ptilon)	feather	— coleoptile (236), Trichop-tilum (370)
351)	πυγη	(pyge)	buttocks	— pygostyle (165)
352)	πυρετος	(puretos)	fever	— antipyretic (654), pyrexia
353)	πυος	(pyos)	discharge	— pus, pyogenic (10)
354)	ραχις	(rachis)	backbone	— rachitis, rachitomous, and Rachitomi (643)
355)	ρις, ρινος	(rhis, rhinos)	nose	— rhinitis, Rhinoceros (309), Antirrhinum (654)
356)	ρυγχιον	(rhynchion)	snout	— Rhynchota, Rhynchocepha-lia (310), Rhynchobdellida (392)
357)	σαρξ, σαρκος	(sarx, sarcos)	flesh	— perisarc (666), sarcoma
358)	σπασμος	(spasmos)	spasm	— spasmodic
359)	σπλαγχνα	(splanchna)	bowels	— splanchnic, splanchnopleure (343)
360)	σπλην	(splen)	spleen	— splenetic
361)	σπονδυλος	(spondylos)	vertebra	— diplospondylous (540)
362)	στερνον	(sternon)	breast	— sternal

363) στομα   (stoma)   mouth   — stomata, Gnathostomata
                                                 (293), Bdellostoma (392)

364) στομαχος   (stomachos)   opening of   — stomach
                                 stomach

365) συμπτωμα   (symptoma)   symptom   — symptomatic
366) σφυγμος   (sphygmos)   pulse   — sphygmoid, sphygmomanom-
                                                 eter (566, 629)

367) σωμα   (soma)   body   — somatic, centrosome (31),
                                                 Pyrosoma (111), Sphaero-
                                                 soma (62)

368) τραχεια   (tracheia)   windpipe   — tracheal, tracheate, tracheide
369) τραυμα   (trauma)   wound   — trauma, traumanasty
370) θριξ,   (thrix,   hair   — Polytrichum (593), Trichina,
     τριχος   trichos)   Ophiothrix (429), Tricho-
                                                 mastix (628)

371) ὑγιεια   (hygiia)   health   — hygiene, hygienic
372) ὑμην   (hymen)   membrane   — Hymenoptera (348), Hy-
                                                 menomycetes (504), Hy-
                                                 menophyllaceae (517)

373) φαλαγξ   (phalanx)   joint of toe   — phalanges, phalangeal
                                 or finger

374) φαλλος   (phallos)   penis   — phallic
375) φαρμακον   (pharmakon)   drug   — pharmacist, pharmacology
                                                 (36)

376) φαρυγξ,   (pharynx,   throat   — glossopharyngeal (292),
     φαρυγγος   pharyngos)   Pharyngobranchii (287)

377) φλεψ,   (phleps,   vein   — phlebitis
     φλεβος   phlebos)

378) χαιτη   (chaite)   long hair,   — Polychaeta (593), Chaetog-
                                 mane   natha (293), Chaetocladium
                                                 (495)

379) χαλαζα   (chalaza)   tubercle,   — chalaza, chalazogamic (617)
                                 pimple

380) χηλη   (chele)   talon   — chela, chelate, chelicera (309)
381) χειλος   (chilos)   lips   — Chilognatha (293), Chilodon
                                                 (328)

382) χειρ   (chir)   hand   — Chiroptera, chiropodist (346)
383) χολη   (chole)   bile   — glycocholate (536), melan-
                                                 cholia (610)

384) χονδρος   (chondros)   cartilage   — Chondrial, Chondrostei
                                                 (331), Chondrichthyes (402)

385) χοριον   (chorion)   skin, leather   — chorion, chorionic, choroid
386) χρως,   (chros,   skin   — Chrotella
     χρωτος   chrotos)

387) ωον   (oon)   egg   — oogenesis (9), oogonium
                                                 (11), oospore (512)

388) ους, ωτος   (ous, otos)   ear   — periotic (666), otolith (188),
                                                 otocyst (315)

j) ANIMALS

389)	αραχνη	(arachne)	spider
390)	αρκτος	(arctos)	bear
391)	αστακος	(astacos)	lobster
391a)	βατραχος	(batrachos)	frog
392)	βδελλα	(bdella)	leech
393)	βομβυξ	(bombyx)	silkworm
394)	γλαυξ	(glaux)	owl
395)	ελεφας	(elephas)	elephant
396)	ἑλμις, ἑλμινθος	(helmis, helminthos)	worm
397)	εχινος	(echinos)	hedgehog
398)	εντομα	(entoma)	insect
399)	ζῳον	(zoon)	animal
400)	θηρ	(ther)	beast
401)	ἱππος	(hippos)	horse
402)	ιχθυς	(ichthys)	fish
403)	καμηλος	(camelos)	camel
404)	καμπη	(campe)	caterpillar
405)	καρκινος	(carcinos)	crab
406)	καρις, καριδος	(caris, caridos)	shrimp
407)	καστωρ	(castor)	beaver
408)	κανθαρος	(cantharos)	beetle
409)	κερκοπιθηκος	(cercopithecos)	monkey
410)	κητος	(cetos)	whale
411)	κογχος	(conchos)	shellfish
412)	κοκκυξ	(coccux)	cuckoo
413)	κοραξ	(corax)	crow
414)	κοχλιας	(cochlias)	snail
415)	κορις	(coris)	bug
416)	κροκοδειλος	(crocodeilos)	crocodile
417)	κυκνος	(cycnos)	swan
418)	κυων, κυνος	(cyon, cunos)	dog
419)	λαγως	(lagos)	hare
420)	λαμπουρος	(lampuros)	glowworm
421)	λεων	(leon)	lion
422)	λυκος	(lycos)	wolf
423)	μελισσα	(melissa)	bee
424)	μυρμηξ, μυρμηκος	(myrmex, myrmekos)	ant
425)	μυς	(mys)	mouse
426)	νυκτερις	(nykteris)	bat
427)	ορνις, ορνιθος	(ornis, ornithos)	bird

428)	οστρεον	(ostreon)	oyster
429)	οφις	(ophis)	snake
430)	περδιξ	(perdix)	partridge
431)	πιθηκος	(pithecos)	ape
432)	πολυπους	(polypos)	octopus
433)	σαλαμανδρα	(salamandra)	salamander
434)	σαυρα	(saura)	lizard
435)	σελαχος	(selachos)	shark
436)	σηπια	(sepia)	cuttlefish
437)	σκιουρος	(sciuros)	squirrel
438)	σκομβρος	(scombros)	mackerel
439)	σκορπιος	(scorpios)	scorpion
440)	σπογγια	(spongia)	sponge
441)	στρουθος	(struthos)	ostrich
442)	ταυρος	(tauros)	bull
443)	τερηδων	(teredon)	timberworm
444)	τιγρις	(tigris)	tiger
445)	τραγος	(tragos)	goat
446)	υστριξ	(hystrix)	porcupine
447)	φασιανος	(phasianos)	pheasant
448)	φρυνη	(phryne)	toad
449)	φωκαινα	(phocaena)	porpoise
450)	φωκη	(phoce)	seal
451)	χελωνη	(chelone)	tortoise
452)	χην	(chen)	goose
453)	ψιττακη	(psittace)	parrot
454)	ψυλλα	(psylla)	flea
455)	ψυχη	(psyche)	butterfly

k) PLANTS AND THEIR PARTS

456)	αγρωστις	(agrostis)	grass
457)	αμπελος	(ampelos)	vine
458)	ανεμωνη	(anemone)	anemone
459)	ασπαραγος	(asparagos)	asparagus
460)	ἑλλεβορος	(helleborus)	hellebore
461)	ερεικη	(ereice)	heather
462)	θυμος	(thymos)	thyme
463)	ιρις	(iris)	iris
464)	καρδαμον	(cardamon)	watercress
465)	κεδρος	(cedros)	cedar
466)	κιναρα	(cinara)	artichoke
467)	κραμβη	(crambe)	cabbage
468)	κροκος	(crocos)	saffron
469)	κυπαρισσος	(cuparissos)	cypress
470)	μινθα	(mintha)	mint
471)	μορεα	(morea)	mulberry

472)	ναρκισσος	(narcissos)	daffodil
473)	ορχις	(orchis)	orchid
474)	πεπερι	(peperi)	pepper
475)	πισος	(pisos)	pea
476)	πλατανος	(platanos)	plane tree
477)	ραφανις	(rhaphanis)	radish
478)	σινηπι	(sinepi)	mustard
479)	συκον	(sycon)	fig
480)	ὑακινθος	(hyacinthos)	hyacinth
481)	ὑσσωπος	(hyssopos)	hyssop
482)	ακανθα	(acantha)	spine — Acanthocephali (310), hexacanth (270)
483)	ανθος, ανθεμον	(anthos or anthemon)	flower — Helianthus (95), Anthozoa (399), perianth (666)
484)	βλαστη	(blaste)	bud — blastoderm (295), meroblastic (40), hypoblast (670), blastocoele (560), holoblastic (578), epiblast (661)
485)	βοτανη	(botane)	herb — botanical
486)	βοτρυς	(botrys)	bunch — Botryllus, Botrydium
487)	βρυωνη	(bryone)	moss — Bryophyta (518), Bryopsis (338), Dinobryon (539)
488)	δενδρον	(dendron)	tree, branch — dendrite, Dendrocoelium (560)
489)	ἑλιξ	(helix)	tendril, spiral — helicoid, helicopter (348)
490)	ζυμη	(zyme)	yeast — enzyme, zymotic, zymase
491)	καλαμος	(calamos)	reed — Calamoichthyes (402)
492)	καρπος	(carpos)	fruit — carpal, pericarp (666), zyncarpous (668)
493)	καρυων	(caryon)	nut — Caryophyllaceae (517), Caryopsis (338)
494)	καυλος	(caulos)	stalk — cauline
495)	κλαδος	(clados)	bough — Cladophora (649), phylloclade (517), Tricladida (267), Cladothrix (370)
496)	κλων	(clon)	shoot — clone
497)	κνιδη	(cnide)	nettle — cnidocil, cnidoblast (484)
498)	κρινον	(crinon)	lily — Crinoidea
499)	κωνειον	(coneion)	hemlock — coniine
500)	κωνος	(conos)	cone — conifer, Conidiospores (512)
501)	κοκκος	(coccos)	berry, grain — Pleurococcus (343), Diplococcus (540)
502)	κορυμβος	(corymbos)	cluster of flowers — corymb, Corymbocrinus
503)	λινον	(linon)	flax — linen, lineic
504)	μυκης, μυκητος	(myces)	mushroom — Oomycetes (387), mycetozoa (399)

505) ξυλον	(xylon)	wood	— xylem, xylonite, xylophone (76)
506) πεταλον	(petalon)	petal	— polypetalous (593), sympetalous (668)
507) πτερις	(pteris)	fern	— Pteridophyta (518), Pteris
508) ραβδος	(rhabdos)	stick	— rhabdite, Rhabdocoelida (560)
509) ριζα	(rhiza)	root	— rhizome, mycorhiza (504), Rhizopus and Rhizopoda (346)
510) ροδον	(rhodon)	rose	— rhododendron (488), Rhodites
511) σπερμα	(sperma)	seed	— Spermaphyta (518), spermatozoa (399), polyspermy (593), Batrachospermum (391a)
512) σπορος	(sporos)	seed	— sporocyst (315), Sporozoa (399), ascospore (123), zygospore (131)
513) σταφυλη	(staphyle)	bunch of grapes	— staphylococcus (501)
514) στρυχνος	(strychnos)	nightshade	— strychnine
515) ὑλη	(hyle)	timber	— Hyla
516) φυκος	(phykos)	seaweed	— Phycomycetes (504), Rhodophyceae (510), Chlorophyceae (614)
517) φυλλον	(phyllon)	leaf	— mesophyll (568), phyllode
518) φυτον	(phyton)	plant	— holophytic (578), phytology (36)

l) ADJECTIVES *

519) αγαθος	(agathos)	good	— Agatha
*520) ἁγιος	(hagios)	holy	— hagiolatry (254)
521) αγλαος	(aglaos)	bright	— Aglaophenia
522) ακουστος	(acoustos)	audible	— acoustic
523) ακρος	(acros)	high	— Akrogyne (206), acropetal (506), acromegaly (576), acrodont (328)
524) αλλος	(allos)	other	— allotropic (70), allogamy (617), allopathy (50), allergy (23)
525) αμβλυς	(amblyo)	blunt	— Amblypoda (346), Amblystoma (363)
526) αμφω	(ampho)	both	— Amphibia (7), Amphineura (325), Amphicoelous (560)

* Nominative singular masculine forms.

527)	ανθηρος	(antheros)	flowering
528)	ἁπλοος	(haploos)	simple

527) ανθηρος (antheros) flowering — antheridium, anther
528) ἁπλοος (haploos) simple — haploid, Haplosporidia (512), Haplodiscus (129)
529) αριστος (aristos) best — aristocracy (625)
530) αρτιος (artios) perfect — Artiodactyl (294)
531) αυστηρος (austeros) austere — austerity
532) βαθυς (bathys) deep — bathymetric (629), Bathycrinus, Bathynectes
533) βαρυς (barys) heavy — barometer (629), isobar (553)
534) βραχυς (brachys) short — brachydactyly (294), brachycephalic (310)
535) γιγαντικος (gigantikos) gigantic — Gigantosaurus (434), giant
536) γλυκυς (glycys) sweet — glycogen (10), glycolysis (37), glucose
537) γυμνος (gymnos) naked — gymnastics, Gymnoblastea (484), Gymnosperm (511)
538) δηλος (delos) manifest — Urodela (334)
539) δεινος (dinos) wonderful — Dinosaur (434), Dinornis (427), Dinopsis (338), Dinophyceae (516)
540) διπλοος (diploos) double — diplococcus (501), diploblastic (484)
541) δολιχος (dolichos) long — dolichocephalic (310), Dolichoglossus (292)
542) ελευθερος (eleutheros) free — Eleutheria, Eleutheroblastea (484)
543) εναντιος (enantios) opposite — enantiomorph (47)
544) εσχατος (eschatos) remote — eschatology (36)
545) ἑτερος (heteros) different — heterogeneous (10), heterodyne (17), heterozygote (131)
546) ευ (eu—adv.) well — eulogy (36), euphony (76)
547) ευρυς (eurys) broad — Euryale, Eurypterida (348), Eurylepta (563), Eurynotus (327)
548) ευθυς (euthys) straight — Euthyneura (325)
549) ἡδυς (hedys) sweet — hedonism
550) θερμος (thermos) hot — thermal, thermometer (629), isotherm (553)
551) ιατρικος (iatricos) medical — paediatrics (220)
552) ιδιος (idios) proper, private — idiosyncrasy (668), idiot
553) ισος (isos) equal — isosceles, isomerism (40), Isoptera (348)
554) ισχνος (ischnos) lean — Ischnochiton (175)
555) κακος (cacos) bad — cacodyl, cacophony (76), Cacops (338)

556) καθολικος (*catholicos*)   general   — *catholic*
557) καινος   (*cainos*)   new   — *cainozoic* (399), *Oligocene* (577), *Eocene* (93)
558) καλος   (*calos*)   beautiful — *callisthenics* (57)
559) καμπυλος   (*campylos*)   curved   — *campylotropous* (70)
559a) κενος   (*cenos*)   empty   — *Oligocene*, etc., *Kenocis*
560) κοιλος   (*coelos*)   hollow   — *acoelous, coeloni, Coelenterata* (301)
561) κοινος   (*coenos*)   common   — *coenocyte* (143), *Coenonympha* (218), *Coenurus* (334)
562) κομψος   (*compsos*)   elegant   — *Compsognathus* (293)
562a) κρυος   (*cryos*)   frozen, cold — *cryohydric* (114)
563) λεπτος   (*leptos*)   thin   — *Leptostraca* (322), *Leptocephalus* (310), *Leptothrix* (370)
564) μακρος   (*macros*)   long   — *macroscopic* (639), *Macrocystis* (315), *macronucleus*
565) μαλακος   (*malacos*)   soft   — *Malacostraca* (332), *Malacocotylea* (140)
566) μανος   (*manos*)   scanty   — *manometer* (629)
567) μεγας   (*megas*)   big   — *megalithic* (188), *megaphone* (76), *megaspore* (512), *Megatherium* (400)
568) μεσος   (*mesos*)   middle   — *Mesozoic* (399)
569) μικρος   (*micros*)   small   — *microscope* (639), *micrometer* (629)
570) μονος   (*monos*)   alone   — *monosyllable* (259), *monolith* (188), *Monocystis* (315)
571) μυριος   (*myrios*)   innumerable — *Myriapoda* (346), *Myriads*
572) μωρος   (*moros*)   foolish   — *moron*
573) νεκρος   (*necros*)   dead   — *necrotic, necromancy, necrophilia*
574) νεος   (*neos*)   new   — *neolithic* (188), *neologism* (36)
575) ξενος   (*xenos*)   foreign   — *xenophobia* (72), *Xenopus* (346)
576) ξηρος   (*xeros*)   dry   — *xerophilous* (648), *xerophyte* (518)
577) ολιγοι   (*oligoi*)   few   — *Oligocene, Oligochaete*
578) ολος   (*holos*)   whole   — *holoblastic* (484), *Holocephali* (310), *holozoic* (399)
579) ομος   (*homos*)   similar   — *homology* (36), *Homoptera* (348)
580) οπισθε   (*opisthe*)   hindmost   — *Opisthobranchiata* (287), *opisthosoma* (367), *Opisthocoelous* (560)
581) οξυς   (*oxys*)   sharp, acid — *oxygen* (10), *Amphioxus* (526), *Oxyurus* (334)

582)	ορθος	(orthos)	straight	— orthogenesis (9), orthodoxy (15), orthotropous (70), Orthoptera (348)
583)	παλαιος	(palaios)	old, aged	— palaeozoic (399), palaeography (619), palaeolithic (188)
584)	παν	(pan)	all	— pangenesis (9), panmixia (42)
585)	παχυς	(pachys)	thick	— pachydermatous (295), pachymeter (629)
586)	πλαγιος	(plagios)	crooked	— Plagiostomi (363)
587)	πλαστος	(plastos)	modeled	— plasticine, plastic, chloroplast (614), leucoplast (609)
588)	πλατυς	(platys)	flat	— amphiplatyan (526), Platyhelminthes (396)
589)	πλειστος	(pleistos)	most	— Pleistocene (559a)
590)	πλεος	(pleos)	full	— pleopod (346)
591)	πλησιος	(plesios)	near	— Plesiosauria (434), Plesianthus (483)
592)	ποικιλος	(poecilos)	various	— poecilothermic
593)	πολυς	(polys)	much	— polygon (12), polygamy (617)
594)	πυκνος	(pycnos)	compact	— pycnic, Pycnogonida (11), pycnidia
595)	σαπρος	(sapros)	putrid	— saprophyte (518), Saprolegnia
596)	σκληρος	(scleros)	hard	— sclerite, sclerosis, megasclere (567), Scleranthus (483), Scleroderma (295)
597)	στενος	(stenos)	narrow	— Stenodictya (128), stenography (619)
598)	στερεος	(stereos)	solid, stiff	— stereoscopic (639), stereoisomerism (553, 40)
599)	στρογγυλος	(strongylos)	round	— Strongylus, Strongylocentrotus (31)
600)	στρεπτος	(streptos)	twisted	— streptococcus (501), strepsiptera (348)
601)	τηλε	(tele—adv.)	afar	— telescope (639), telegram (249), telepathy (50)
602)	τραχυς	(trachys)	rough	— Trachymedusae, Trachysoma (367), Trachypterus (348)
603)	τυφλος	(typhlos)	blind	— typhlosole, Typhlops
604)	υγρος	(hygros)	wet	— hygroscopic (639), hygrometer (629)
605)	φανερος	(phaneros)	visible	— Phanerogam (617), Phanerocephala (310)

m) COLORS

606) ερυθρος	(*erythros*)	red	—*erythrocyte* (143), *erythema, erythrophore* (649)
607) κυανος	(*cyanos*)	azure	—*cyanosis, Cyanophyceae* (516)
608) ιοειδης	(*ioedes*)	violet	—*iodine, iodoform*
609) λευκος	(*leucos*)	white	—*leucocyte* (143), *Leucosolenia*
610) μελανος	(*melanos*)	black	—*melanic, melanophore* (649), *Melampyrum* (111)
611) ξανθος	(*xanthos*)	yellow	—*xanthia, xanthoderma* (295), *xanthophyll* (517)
612) ωχρος	(*ochros*)	sallow, pale	—*ochre, ochreous*
613) φαιος	(*phaeos*)	dusky, gray	—*Phaeophyceae* (516), *Phaeosporales* (512)
614) χλωρος	(*chloros*)	green	—*chlorine, chlorophyll* (517), *Chlorophyceae* (516)

n) VERBS *

615) βαλλω	(*ballo*)	throw	—*ballistics*
616) βαπτω	(*bapto*)	dip	—*baptism, baptize, Baptist*
617) γαμεω	(*gameo*)	marry	—*gamete, monogamy* (570)
618) γλυφω	(*glypho*)	tunnel	—*Tyroglyphe* (174), *siphonoglyph* (158)
619) γραφω	(*grapho*)	write	—*phonograph* (76), *photograph* (119)
620) δαιω	(*daeo*)	distribute	—*geodesy* (91)
621) καλυπτω	(*calypto*)	cover	—*Calyptoblastea* (484)
622) κινεω	(*cineo*)	move	—*kinesis, cinema, kinetic*
623) κλινω	(*clino*)	*bend*	—*klinostat* (59), *syncline* (668), *anticline* (654)
624) κοιμαω	(*coemao*)	sleep	—*cemetery*
625) κρατεω	(*crateo*)	govern	—*plutocratic* (223), *democratic* (207), *technocracy* (67)
626) κρυπτω	(*crypto*)	hide	—*cryptogram* (249), *cryptozoic* (399), *Cryptocephala* (310)
627) λαμπω	(*lampo*)	shine	—*lamp*
628) μαστιγοω	(*mastigoo*)	whip	—*Mastigophora* (649), *Mastigamoeba, Polymastiginae* (593)

* All forms given are first person singular, present indicative, unless otherwise stated.

629) μετρεω	(*metreo*)	measure	— *metric, meter*
630) νηχω	(*necho*)	swim	— *Notonecta* (327), *Necturus* (334), *nectocalyx*
631) ὁρμαω	(*hormao*)	rouse	— *hormone*
632) ποιεω	(*pœeo*)	create, compose	— *poetry, poem, pharmaco-poeia* (375)
633) πωλεω	(*poleo*)	sell	— *monopoly* (570)
634) πριω	(*prio*)	saw	— *prism, prismatic*
635) ῥεω	(*rheo*)	flow	— *rheostat* (59), *rheotropism* (70)
636) ῥηγνυμι	(*rhegnymi*)	burst	— *haemorrhage* (281)
637) ῥιπιζω	(*rhipizo*)	fan	— *Rhipidoglossa* (292), *Rhipid-ium*
638) σηψω *	(*sepso*)	putrefy	— *sepsis, antiseptic* (654)
639) σκοπεω	(*scopeo*)	look at	— *gyroscope* (13), *telescope* (601), *periscope* (666), *laryngoscope* (317)
640) στροβεω	(*strobeo*)	spin	— *stroboscope* (639)
641) σχιζω	(*schizo*)	split	— *schizocarpous* (492), *Schizo-mycetes* (504)
642) κεραννυμι	(*ceranymi*)	mix	— *idiosyncrasy* (552)
643) τεμνω	(*temno*)	cut	— *Temnocephali* (310), *anat-omy* (653), *atom*
644) τοξευω	(*toxeuo*)	to shoot arrows	— *toxic, toxaemea*
645) φαγειν †	(*phagein*)	devour	— *phagocyte* (143), *entomoph-agous* (398), *Myrmecoph-aga* (424)
646) φαινω	(*phaeno*)	show	— *phenotype* (71), *phenomenon*
647) φοβεω	(*phobeo*)	frighten	— *phobia, hydrophobia*
648) φιλεω	(*phileo*)	love	— *philology* (36), *philanderer, entomophilous* (398), *philo-progenitive* (667, 10)
649) φορεω	(*phoreo*)	wear, carry	— *chromatophore* (77), *xan-thophore* (611)
650) φυω	(*phyo*)	grow	— *symphysis* (668), *hypophysis* (670)
651) ψευδω	(*pseudo*)	deceive	— *pseudopodium* (346)

o) PARTICLES

652) αμφι	(*amphi*)	around	— *amphitheater* (134)
653) ανα	(*ana*)	(*a*) up (*b*) again	— (*a*) *anabolism* (8) (*b*) *anabaptist* (616)
654) αντι	(*anti*)	opposed to	— *antiseptic* (638)

* Future.
† Infinitive.

655)	απο	(apo)	away from	— apocarpous (492)
656)	δια	(dia)	among, through	— diapedesis (346)
657)	εκ, εξ	(ec or ex)	out of	— ecstasy (59), exogenous (19)
658)	εκτος	(ectos)	outside oppos. to entos = inside	— ectoplasm
659)	εν	(en)	in	— endemic (207)
660)	ενδον	(endon)	within	— endosperm (511), endogenous (10)
661)	επι	(epi)	on	— epiblast (484)
662)	εσω	(eso)	within	— esoteric
663)	κατα	(cata)	down, by	— catastrophe (61), catabolism (8)
664)	μετα	(meta)	after	— Metatheria (400)
665)	παρα	(para)	beside	— parabiosis (7)
666)	περι	(peri)	around	— perianth (483), perimeter (629)
667)	προ	(pro)	before	— prologue (36)
668)	συν	(syn)	together, with	— syndrome (16)
669)	ὑπερ	(hyper)	above, over and beyond	— hyperaesthesia (4)
670)	ὑπο	(hypo)	under	— hypogastric (290)

Index

o och.

'73